CITIZEN WELLES

'Well-written, fresh and sympathetic to its subject but neither blindly uncritical or overtly partial . . . a commendable and exhaustive account of a tangled, multifaceted, mercurial man, Brady's book should stand as the definitive account of Welles' countless professional endeavours'.

Scotland on Sunday

'Splendid'

Financial Times

'Affectionate, well-written and thoroughly researched'

Time Out

'This is a behemoth of a book, large of girth and weighty of matter, yet propelled by an unflagging energy, mischief and a zest for life. Very like the subject itself'

London Evening Standard

'Excellent'

Sunday Express

About the Author

Frank Brady teaches contemporary cinema at St John's University, New York. He is the author of previous biographies of Bobby Fischer, Aristotle Onassis and Barbra Streisand.

CITIZEN WELLES

A Biography of Orson Welles

Frank Brady

CORONET BOOKS
Hodder and Stoughton

Copyright © Frank Brady 1989

First published in Great Britain in 1990 by Hodder and Stoughton Ltd.

Coronet edition 1991

The right of Frank Brady to be identified as the author of this work has been asserted by him in accordance with the Copyright, Designs and Patents Act 1988.

This book is sold subject to the condition that it shall not, by way of trade or otherwise, be lent, re-sold, hired out or otherwise cir-culated without the publisher's prior consent in any form of bind-ing or cover other than that in which it is published and without a similar condition including this condition being imposed on the subsequent purchaser.

No part of this publication may be reproduced or transmitted in any form or by any means, electronic or mechanical, includ-ing photocopying, recording or any information storage or re-trieval system, without either the prior permission in writing from the publisher or a licence, per-mitting restricted copying. In the United Kingdom such licences are issued by the Copyright Licensing Agency, 33–34 Alfred Place, London WC1E 7DP.

British Library C.I.P.

Brady, Frank, *1934–*
   Citizen Welles: a biography of
   Orson Welles.
   1. Cinema films. Directing.
   Welles, Orson. Biography
   I. Title
   791.43'0233'0924

ISBN 340 54407 4

Printed and bound in Great Britain for Hodder and Stough-ton Paperbacks, a division of Hodder and Stoughton Ltd., Mill Road, Dunton Green, Sevenoaks, Kent TN13 2YA (Editorial Office: 47 Bedford Square, London WC1B 3DP) by Clays Ltd., St Ives plc.

To my daughter,
Erin Brady
1953-1985

PREFACE

I HAD TO quickly pull, almost drag, myself out of quite an elaborate dream—I can no longer remember its content—as the ringing abruptly awakened me in my hotel room in Hollywood several years ago at seven o'clock in the morning. It was a Sunday in July. "This is Orson Welles," said the polite voice at the other end of the telephone. That rich velvet sound could not have belonged to anyone else.

In an instant I was alert. Welles was responding to my letter. I had been given an assignment by *American Film* to write an article entitled "The Lost Film of Orson Welles" about the short motion picture that he had completed before he made his Hollywood debut with *Citizen Kane.* This earlier work was not a complete feature film. Welles had created it for inclusion in a play named *Too Much Johnson,* which he had directed for the Mercury Theatre in 1938, and it depicted some scenes that could not take place on stage. No one had seen the film in over forty years.

I was eager to do the piece and had already discussed the possibility of writing a biography of Orson Welles with my publisher. For that reason, our first telephone interview went beyond *Too Much Johnson* and became involved with other matters: the technical details of *Citizen Kane;* the correspondence he'd had with Sergei Eisenstein; his less-than-cordial relationship with John Houseman; his specific preferences in comedy film.

Welles was not particularly enthusiastic when I discussed the potential biography. "The idea of someone studying my life makes my teeth chatter," he said. Though I might have hoped for a more positive response, I wasn't really surprised. I remembered an interview I had read, conducted by the late Kenneth Tynan, in which Welles had stated: "I don't want *any* description of me to be accurate, I want it to be flattering. I don't think people who have to sing for their supper ever like to be described truthfully—not in print anyway."

That, of course, was the heart of the problem. Even if Welles agreed to cooperate with a biographer, there could never be any guarantee that such "facts" as he might supply would be accurate. He freely—even delightedly— admitted to having so embellished certain stories about himself that they seldom came out the same way twice. And many of the stories that other people told about him—about the dinner party he is supposed to have attended with Adolf Hitler, or his supposed brief affair with Marilyn Monroe, indeed, almost any of the tales relating to his prodigious childhood and early youth—sounded so fantastic that it was difficult to credit them. But by the same token, when the subject was Orson Welles, almost nothing could be dismissed *solely* on the grounds that it sounded incredible.

He liked to talk on the phone. He seemed to have the habit of talking for a long time and then, after hanging up, calling right back to clarify some point or to add something he had forgotten. It was both charming and disarming. He seemed to want to please.

When he pressed me as to *why* I wanted to write his biography, I told him that I believed that his life, more than that of just about any other person in this country, touched upon and revolved around the world of arts and entertainment, in all its phases: the theater, radio, the movies, television. In effect, I went on, the story of his life *is* the story of dramatic performance in twentieth-century America. "That makes me sound like an institution," he complained.

I tried to reassure him that I was a sympathetic and experienced biographer, and he seemed flattered and intrigued by the idea. "For sure, for sure," he said deeply. And then he added, "Let's have a meal together." But it never happened: I was leaving Hollywood. He was in Las Vegas one day, Rome or Paris the next.

It soon became abundantly clear to me that if I were to attempt to tell Orson Welles's story, I'd have to do it on my own. Obviously, it would be a daunting task. Just as obviously, it was an irresistible one.

Orson Welles had a remarkably complex life, filled with contrasts and extremes, and just getting down the bare facts of his various adventures and many careers over a half-century of relentless activity spanning several continents would prove to be a personal saga of my own, a mini-epic to which he could probably relate. It isn't only that he had, for example, acted in many, many films. It's more that he had spent his life changing disciplines, constantly switching back and forth from one career to another. Radio, theater, film: Welles mastered each of them, dominated them at one time or another, and through his innovations he profoundly influenced succeeding generations of artists in all three media.

A biographer must know intimately the coinage of his subject: Van Gogh's brushwork, Beethoven's chords, James Joyce's linguistic machinations. Fortunately, most of Welles's films, virtually all of his radio shows, and many of his television broadcasts proved extant and available for listening or viewing. Other details of his work were not so easily forthcoming. Recreating in writing some of his stage productions was a little like putting a jigsaw puzzle together with some of the pieces missing and others turned blank side up.

Like the reporter Thompson in *Citizen Kane,* I set out to discover by a sort of literary and biographical archeology something of what went into the making of Welles the actor and director. And, as in the life of Charles Foster Kane, wherever I went I found conflicts and disagreements in his story. My attempt, then, was to try to create a balance and make the reader "see" Welles's career in all of its parts.

PREFACE

Certainly, I would have preferred to have spent at least some time watching how Welles worked, but attempts to arrange such meetings always went awry. Orson's life-style made him, sometimes, as inaccessible as a Garbo, as unreachable as a head of state. But even if he had been available I don't suppose he would have felt comfortable having me roam through his psyche while he filmed or directed, despite the fact that the biography was, by definition, concerned more with a discussion of his extraordinary gifts than with his highly publicized excesses. I emphatically make no claim to have the final answer to the life of Orson Welles; his story has been one of great ambiguity and paradox.

I also wish that I had had more opportunity to have talked with him and to have shared that "meal" together that he had so warmly offered. It had always been my intention to send him the galleys of this book before it was published, so that he could comment upon his own life and correct any factual mistakes that I might have made. I was shocked and saddened at his death. After spending so many years studying his life, his films, and his career, I had Orson constantly in my thoughts. He often entered my dreams. I find his death all the more regrettable because he seemed, finally, to be so close to realizing some of the projects that he held so dear. When I see a Welles film now, I am overcome by a certain wistfulness, almost as if I were reading a letter found after the death of a close relative. The fact that one of his last offers for an acting part in a film was the role of St. Nick in *Santa Claus: The Movie*—Orson, the great director, turned into a jolly buffoon—strikes me as more sad and strange than I can express.

I make no excuses for the book's omissions other than to wish irrationally that Welles had not tried to accomplish so much in his life; it was simply impossible to record or comment on it all.

Welles's real biography lies in his work, and a careful study of his films and other pursuits will show what is most human in the man and what is most characteristic of that which motivated him throughout his uncommon life.

Frank Brady
New York, N.Y.

ACKNOWLEDGMENTS

I AM GRATEFUL to the friends and colleagues of Orson Welles who opened their cabinets of Wellesian curios. Actors and actresses who had been directed by Welles graciously invited me to Beverly Hills swimming pools or cramped West Side apartments. I visited once-marvelous old thespians at the Actors' Home in Englewood, New Jersey; I met people in their flats in Paris or in their dressing rooms in Broadway theaters, to discuss how Welles had affected their lives.

Micheál MacLiammoir, although ill, along with his lifelong friend Hilton Edwards, entertained me in his upstairs living room in Dublin with tumblers of gin and stories of the irascible but charming sixteen-year-old Orson in his first professional roles on the stage. Virginia Nicholson, Orson's first wife, had me to tea in London to discuss unabashedly her life and problems with Orson and then to ask me to send her love and regards to him; it had been some twenty years since they had seen each other. Robert Wise magnanimously interrupted his filming of the first *Star Trek* movie on the Paramount lot to trace his collaboration with Welles on *Citizen Kane* and *The Magnificent Ambersons,* both of which he edited. There were literally hundreds of other people who gave of their feelings and memories to help me to get to know the enigmatic Orson, through personal or telephone interviews and by correspondence. Film directors, sound technicians, costumers, lighting experts, press agents, and producers, all of whom knew or worked with Welles at some point in his career, gave me time, information, and their impressions. I am deeply and sincerely grateful to all.

Welles's personal papers—a lifetime of letters, scripts, proposals, and other miscellany ranging from crucial notes scrawled on the backs of envelopes to full-length scenarios never produced—housed in the handsome Lilly Library of the University of Indiana and kept by Saundra Taylor and Becky Williams proved to be an invaluable source of information, both original and confirmational.

The late John Hall, brilliant and witty archivist of RKO's numerous corporate files on Welles and his films, spent weeks patiently guiding me through the materials and records that were *de rigueur* reading to understand Orson's delicate and important relationship with that studio.

The librarians at New York's Lincoln Center Library of the Performing

Arts, especially Monty Arnold, were of great help over the years, as were the people who care for the Federal Theatre Collection at George Mason University in Fairfax, Virginia.

My former schoolmate, Rod Granger, jumped in when I needed him and gave me well-written and well-appreciated descriptions of a number of Orson's film fragments that have never been released.

Much-needed assistance was also given by the British Film Institute; the Academy of Motion Picture Arts and Sciences; the American Film Institute; the Museum of Broadcasting; and the Players Club.

The summer lectures of Dr. William Simon of New York University, on the style and techniques used in many of Welles's films, proved to be a catalyst to my own understanding.

I offer special thanks for the profound observations and meticulous research of film critic Jonathan Rosenbaum who seems to understand the modern Orson more than anyone else. His translation from the French of *Orson Welles: A Critical View* by André Bazin; his afterword in *The Big Brass Ring,* Orson's unproduced screenplay; and his articles in *Sight and Sound, Film Comment* and other periodicals over the years, have greatly helped me to grasp what Orson was trying to accomplish.

Richard France's *The Theater of Orson Welles* led me to all kinds of sources about Orson's early years in the theater, and without Dr. France's initial research, of which I am deeply in gratitude and I acknowledge with respect, I could not have completed mine.

Joseph McBride's two books—both called *Orson Welles*—were also invaluable as research tools, as keys to information and perception, and as contemporary glimpses of Orson.

Roger Hill's memoir, *One Man's Time & Chance,* combined with my interviews of him and his late wife Hortense, about the *very* young Orson, enabled me to connect other research that I had unearthed.

Other works by Peter Noble, Maurice Bessey, Peter Cowie, and John Houseman gave me specific and broadview insights into the life and career of Orson Welles.

Orson Welles was such a fascinating mortal, that he was the source of thousands of articles, monographs, interviews, books, news stories, features and sketches, all during his life and even afterward. I have read much of what has been written of him and I am deeply grateful to those journalists, critics, authors and writers who seemed to love Orson as much as I did and who tirelessly chronicled and commented upon his abundant work and unpredictable career.

In addition to those already mentioned, I give thanks to all those who directly helped me with the biography, including Keith Baxter, Lord Laurence Olivier, the late Arnold Weissberger, Augusta Weissberger Schenker, Joan Blair, the late Glen Anders, the late Hans Conreid, Joseph Cotten, Norman Corwin, the late George Coulouris, Ruth Ford, Arlene Francis, Roger and the late Hortense Hill, Christopher Welles, Rebecca Welles, John Houseman, Denis Johnston, Betty Chancellor, the late Karl

ACKNOWLEDGMENTS

Struss, Janet Leigh, Harold Kennedy, Henry Mancini, Ernest Nims, James McCann, Frank Mankiewicz, James Morcom, Dan O'Herlihy, the late Bill Morton, the late Mark Robson, the late George Schaefer, Howard Koch, Darrell Silvera, Aaron Stell, James G. Stewart (Orson's sound engineer on *Citizen Kane*), the late Samson Raphaelson, Ferdy Mayne, Ann Loughlin, Sam Leve, Albert Zugsmith, Richard Jewell, Vernon Walker, Richard Baer, the late Paul Stewart, Richard Wilson, Frank Readick, Michael Winner, Ira Wohl, Theodore Gottlieb, Jean Louis, Lodge Cunningham, John Stransky, Jr., Peggy Webber, Phil Bowles, Harry Keller, Dennis Weaver, Richard Rietty, Gary Graver, Norman Rodway, Michael Aldridge, Wolf Mankowitz, Andrew Faulds, Henry Sember, Paul Monash, Valentine de Vargas, Robert Carringer, Barry Sabath, the late Jay Leyda, Whitney Harris, Steven Handzo, Robert O'Malley, Frank McShane, Cary Glieberman, Maxine Brady, the late Herman G. Weinberg, Clark Goding, Susan Roth, Ellen O'Neil, Mary Ployart, Judith Pasternak, Hugh Paulk, Stewart Isacoff, William Johnson, Brian Egan, Wendy Goldman, and Quinn Sansevere.

CITIZEN WELLES

CHAPTER 1

WEARING A BLACK silk cravat, knotted bohemian-style around his neck and flowing voluminously over his ample chest, the lecturer confidently, almost brazenly, strode to the front of the Washington School auditorium in Madison, Wisconsin, to deliver his speech on the history of art. He spent a few minutes knowledgeably discussing the Paleolithic cave paintings of Altamira, the Great Pyramid of Giza, the Doric temples, the *Mournings* of Giotto. Then, abruptly, he launched into a violent attack on the school's system of teaching art, which, he felt, stifled creativity and self-expression by insisting that the students limit themselves to copying rather than inventing.

The year was 1925; the ground-breaking Armory Show had assaulted the sensibilities of New York art critics twelve years earlier. Nevertheless, art in the public schools was still an academic and dispiriting affair. The students cheered the exuberant speech; the onlooking faculty, especially one reproachful art teacher, was aghast at the presumptuousness of the lecturer and mumbled disapproval. The speaker, already an old hand at producing dramatic effects, paused, drew himself up to his full height, and brought down the house with the retort: "Criticism is the essence of creation. If the public school system needs criticizing, then *I* will criticize it." The quote made headlines in the local newspapers; later it was repeated in major cities from Chicago to New York.

The lecturer was George Orson Welles, already a well-known figure in Madison, as well as in his hometown, Kenosha. A writer, actor, poet, cartoonist, and magician, who mingled with the leaders of the local intellectual and artistic community, he had already been the subject of news features in various newspapers. The reason for his celebrity was not only his impressive array of talents: at this time the iconoclastic Welles was just ten years old.

His life tended toward the unusual even before his birth. One night in Rio de Janeiro, over a few drinks, his cosmopolitan parents, who had been married in 1903, christened their unborn child in honor of the two old friends who had joined them on their South American jaunt—the well-known playwright and humorist George Ade, and Chicago businessman Orson C. Wells. Actually, his great-grandfather's name was Orson, but the boy was first called George until his father became annoyed with it. "Hell, we had to call you 'Orson,'" he told his son who inquired one day about what his name

1

really was. "Every damned Pullman porter in the country is named 'George.'"
Years later, Orson told his friend Maurice Bessy that his name was bestowed upon him in honor of Italian ancestors named Orsini. No trace of such forebears has ever been found.

The child's actual birthplace, though, was less exotic than Rio: Kenosha, the county seat of the Wisconsin county of that same name. Orson Welles was born on May 6, 1915, the second son of Richard and Beatrice Welles. Their first child, his brother Richard, Jr., was born ten years earlier. Beatrice Ives Welles was a highly skilled concert pianist—although not a professional—and Richard Head Welles was an inventor, engineer, and businessman who owned factories and hotels. One of his plants was the Badger Brass Co. in Kenosha, which manufactured one of the earliest auto lights.

Beatrice was born in Springfield, Illinois, into the well-to-do Ives family that had made its fortune in the coal business. Abraham Lincoln had been a neighbor and longtime family friend of her grandparents. When Beatrice's father celebrated his first birthday, Lincoln presented him with a christening mug that eventually was handed down to Orson. Whether Gideon Welles, statesman and Lincoln's Secretary of the Navy, was Orson's great-grandfather has been disputed for years. Orson claimed it was so.

Beatrice, who was known in the concert world as Trixie Ives, was considered a brilliant and talented musician. She was the center of a wide circle of friends and followers. Many celebrities from the art and entertainment worlds enjoyed both her charm and her lavish hospitality. It was not unusual for a visitor to find her in the drawing room with Stravinsky, Ravel, or their like, having an animated conversation to which little Orson listened avidly.

A tall woman with chestnut brown hair, gently rounded features, and large, expressive green eyes, she was considered a great beauty. Well read, with a broad range of interests, she had an elegant speaking voice and great sensitivity to the spoken language. She was elected head of the Kenosha Board of Education and was an outspoken advocate for women's rights, and at least one account reports that she was jailed briefly in 1914 for disturbing the peace while speaking out at a pro-pacifist demonstration.

Beatrice frowned upon verbal sloppiness and impressed Orson with the importance of choosing his words with care. And she succeeded: he was speaking in polished sentences, with invisible commas and semicolons where they belonged, all syntactically precise, by the age of two. Occasionally, she allowed Orson to attend one of her many lectures to women's groups throughout the state, on subjects as diverse as the meaning of the basic doctrines of Buddhism or the results of the Spanish-American War. Orson would sit in the first row, atypically quiet, as her lilting tones would flow through the hall. She was an ardent debater.

Richard Welles, the son of a wagon manufacturer, had become a minor legend in his own time. A restaurant and a racehorse were named after him—and he had his own private cigar brand—facts that give a few clues to his character. A charmer of sorts, although somewhat self-absorbed, Richard Welles was a man of caprices. He once bought a hotel in Grand Detour,

Illinois, because he liked the service, then ordered all of the other guests out of it because they annoyed him. Located about five miles outside Dixon, Illinois, in the north central part of the state, the Sheffield Hotel was a historic landmark, famous for its excellent food. Orson remembered it as not a "welcoming hostelry." Guests were by invitation only: all friends or newly made acquaintances of his father.

Orson spent a few summers in Grand Detour. He recalled its ambience as a sleepy, Mark Twain-kind of Midwest town. He roomed at the hotel on rare evenings when his parents permitted it and at other times stayed at the lovely country home they bought on the outskirts of town.

Most people found Richard Welles to be an endearing, although flamboyant character, a chain smoker and given to drink. Orson remembered him as being sensitive, gentle, kind, tolerant, and generous, not necessarily in that order and not necessarily all the time. He had a great interest in the theater, attended constantly, and once took a small role in *Charley's Aunt* for five months, in a company that toured the Southwest. Richard Welles had earned his wealth by inventing a carbide bicycle lamp that replaced the old-fashioned kerosene lamps used until that time. Royalty checks from this invention and others enabled him to live relatively well. He used his money for travel, for pursuing women, and for sampling the best that the world could offer him in the way of food and drink. Sitting with friends exchanging tales, sipping an Armagnac or finishing a bottle of rye, and enjoying a rich panatela was to Richard Welles as joyful as watching a rainbow.

He also invented a collapsible picnic outfit and sold it in huge quantities to the government, which distributed it as a mess kit during World War I. His invention of an automobile seemed opportune, but he considered the gadget impractical; so he never bothered to patent it. Orson also recalled a couple of his father's less successful inventions: a mechanical dishwasher that dispatched dirty dishes by smashing them to pieces and a steam-powered airplane that flew behind the family auto, which pulled it along via ropes.

In addition to the other very personable members of his immediate family, Orson Welles's early years were enlivened by the sporadic presence of a prattle of highly individualistic aunts. His favorite one habitually bathed in ginger ale—because, she explained, it was cheaper than champagne. Another, presumably wealthier aunt, owned an old-fashioned limousine. A confirmed jogger before the sport was considered chic, she would attach herself to this car by means of a lengthy rope and instruct her chauffeur to set the pace by driving along ahead of her.

A third aunt wore a riding habit and a wig of flaming red. When meeting an acquaintance on the street, she would politely doff—her wig. Another aunt was a recluse who consoled herself by practicing card tricks after her magician husband abandoned her. Still another aunt, regrettably, remained a stranger to Orson. She disappeared while on a trip to China and was never heard from again.

As an adult, Orson claimed that his paternal grandmother, Mary Head Welles, had put a curse on the marriage of his parents. The ballroom on the top floor of the house she owned in Kenosha, Wisconsin, had been converted, first into a miniature golf course, complete with sand traps, hill, tunnels, barrels or other impediments through which to putt the ball, and later into a sort of darkened haunt where she practiced witchcraft.

Orson recalled sneaking up to the huge room and seeing dead birds strewn across the floor and a pentagrammed altar deeply stained with blood, where she apparently performed her sorcery. "A dwarfish, obese, and evil-smelling woman," as he remembered her.

As a child, Welles had a large circle of acquaintances, not only because both of his parents were attractive personalities but because, for most of the time as he was growing up, they maintained separate households, each with its own set of diverse and highly entertaining characters. The Welles marriage was not a compatible one. She detested the kind of fast life that her husband continued to live. He believed that her interest in the artistic life was pretentious, an attempt to climb socially. Beatrice and Richard spent increasingly longer intervals apart, the father mostly in hotels, the mother in the homes of various friends and relatives. They separated permanently when Orson was six.

As ebullient and attractive as Orson was as a child, his brother, Dickie, was just the opposite. The older boy stayed home most of the time, rarely venturing out of his room. At dinner, he spoke only when asked a question, and then he stammered to the point of embarrassment for all of those present. After a lifetime of near-catatonia, at the age of twenty-three he was committed as a schizophrenic to a state mental institution.

WHEN ORSON WAS TWO, he was introduced to a man who would become the most profoundly influential member of his parents' circles, or at least his mother's. Orson was staying with his mother and brother at the home of his grandmother, Mrs. Benjamin Ives. No stranger to eccentricity herself, she lived in a wooden, Victorian, castlelike house on the outskirts of Kenosha.

Once, when his grandmother was ill, a bone specialist was called in to attend her. The physician was Dr. Maurice Bernstein, an outstanding surgeon in his late twenties who specialized in diseases of the knee joint. Lean, impeccably dressed, he was a charming man who radiated warmth, intelligence, and humor. He was also an accomplished amateur cellist and composer, and he and Beatrice soon found that they had many friends in common among the great figures of the musical world. He was newly divorced. Drawn together by a shared love for music, Bernstein and Beatrice Welles soon developed a close, deeply caring relationship that eventually blossomed into an affair.

Bernstein was astounded by Orson's precocity. He began to advise and encourage the little boy, whom he nicknamed "Pookles." Orson responded by calling the doctor "Dadda" and effectively adopting the gentle man as his mentor and surrogate father, much to the ire of his real father.

Even as a very young child, Welles demonstrated artistic talent. Bernstein wondered whether Orson might also have inherited his mother's musical ability. When Orson was three, the doctor bought him a violin. Orson couldn't play it, however; his arms were too short. Eager to give the child a taste of the joys of music, Bernstein then bought him a conductor's baton and put together a makeshift podium. This attempt was a bit more successful. Orson waved his baton forcefully, keeping time with a gramophone recording of classical music while Bernstein, an audience of one, seated in the back of the room, applauded each correct movement.

As Beatrice's marriage deteriorated, with her husband's increasing alcoholism and dislike of many of the things that she held dear, she became absorbed with Bernstein and began relying on him more and more to assume the role of husband to her and father to her children. The closer Bernstein became to Beatrice and Orson, the more enmity Richard showed to the doctor. He grew to detest him.

Meanwhile, Orson met virtually every famous musician who visited Chicago. He continued to move his little baton while following musical scores and listening to the gramophone in the presence of such giants as Heifetz, Casals, Schnabel, Wallenstein, and Mischa Elman. That year, 1918, was an important one for the three-year-old Welles. While in the living rooms and kitchens throughout the nation news of the Armistice and the murder of the Russian royal family were the main topics of heated discussion, Welles had reached certain landmarks in his own short life: he received his first book, a copy of *A Midsummer Night's Dream,* and he made his stage debut.

Cleofante Campanini was then principal conductor of the Chicago Opera Company, and industrialist Samuel Insull was head of a group of businessmen that guaranteed $500,000 a year to support the company. A visiting soprano who was singing in *Madama Butterfly* asked if Orson could play the part of her illegitimate son, sometimes known as "Trouble." Beatrice agreed, and Orson became a professional actor at the age of three.

The opera was performed at the idyllic Ravinia Opera House on July 10, 1918, with Claudia Muzio singing the title role for the first time in America. Orson went on to play several child roles in the Chicago Opera Company until he became so heavy that the sopranos began complaining about lifting him. His opera career ended when tenor Giovanni Martinelli indignantly refused to hoist him in a performance of *Samson and Delilah.*

At an age when most children are still mastering the rudiments of language, Orson already spoke like a miniature Brahmin and could enter into discussions on most world topics. He made attempts, often successful, to sound like a "grown-up" and seemed unafraid to engage in verbal controversy. A beautiful child with a face expressing an uncanny wisdom far beyond his years, he was regarded by the adults around him with affection that was sometimes mingled with awe and occasionally with uneasiness. Phyllis Fergus, a Chicago composer, was so impressed with his intellectual force that she composed and dedicated a musical suite to him.

Even at four, Orson hated school—an aversion that was to last for several years. He feigned an attack of appendicitis to avoid going to kindergarten. When his illness was unmasked as the performance it really was, he complained that he didn't want to be confined with a bunch of kids whose only ambition was "to be Boy Scouts."

He was educated at home, learning the alphabet, then reading by a method he devised on his own. Beatrice felt that children had an intellectual capacity that was equal to adults and treated her sons accordingly. When Orson was two, she began reading Shakespeare to him. She started with Charles Lamb's *Tales from Shakespeare.* When Orson discovered that the versions were adaptations and often read to children, he demanded the originals. Beatrice also read aloud to him the work of Swinburne, Rossetti, Keats, Tennyson, and Whitman.

Believing that environment was a crucial factor in a child's education, as he grew a little older, she took Orson with her nearly everywhere she went. Each drawing room he entered became Orson's classroom; the artists and intellectuals he encountered there became his instructors. He learned by a process of cross-examination. When he received conflicting answers, he thought them through, then sought clarification asking further questions until he finally received the answers he was seeking.

Dr. Bernstein was fascinated by the stage. One of his earliest gifts to Orson was unquestionably the most significant: a puppet theater. The puppets included an old man and a mouse, both made of cardboard and operated by wires. One of Orson's first productions opened with the old man drowsing over a book he had been reading by candlelight. His sleep is interrupted by a mouse who runs out from the wings and tips over the candle so that the wax drips on the old man's beard. The old man wakens to find his beard stuck to the book. The rest of the play is about the old man's efforts to separate beard from book. Orson spent hours playing with his puppet theater. He actually wrote, designed, and produced original plays for it and presented them to his family and friends. By the time he reached the ripe old age of four, he was already a budding impresario.

Later, Dr. Bernstein helped Orson build a larger theater from a packing crate and a window shade. The theater was set up in an attic studio, which rapidly became so crowded with dramatic paraphernalia that the entire room came to resemble the backstage and wings of a little theater. Props, masks, fragments of costumes, and jars of makeup were strewn about the room. Here Orson carved and painted puppets, wrote dialogue, and afterward, as puppeteer, provided his actors with voices by "throwing" his own voice like a ventriloquist.

It was Dr. Bernstein who introduced Orson to another lifelong interest. He bought him a toy magic outfit and later, when the boy was five, gave him a professional magician's box of stage tricks. To further Orson's apprenticeship as a magician, Dr. Bernstein took him backstage at the theater where Houdini was performing so he could meet the master magician and escapologist. Impressed by the child's knowledge of the art of magic through the ages and his grasp of the technical aspects of the craft, Houdini taught the boy a simple but effective trick with a red handkerchief. Orson accompanied Houdini to his dressing room, and while the magician was changing, performed the trick for him. Houdini, not exactly bowled over by the youngster's legerdemain, counseled the boy sternly never to perform any trick until he had practiced it a thousand times.

Over the next few weeks Orson did practice the handkerchief trick close to a thousand times. The next time he paid a backstage visit to Houdini, he came with Richard Welles. They had not been there long when Carl Bremer, a manufacturer and artisan of magic tricks, arrived with a vanishing lamp trick that he had just perfected. Houdini accepted the lamp, and totally shocked Orson by adding, "Fine, Carl, I'll put it in the act tonight."

IN 1920, WHEN Orson was five, America was recovering from the First World War and everything looked promising. Orson was already sipping wine. In another three years he would be imbibing mixed drinks in a rather pathetic attempt to resemble the adult he thought he was and perhaps as an imitation of his father. So great, in fact, was his desire to appear adult that he hastened the process with makeup, drawing lines across his forehead and painting hollows in his cheeks. Occasionally, he would go out into the streets made-up, and people began talking about the oddball, Orson Welles. By nine he was roughening his voice in order to sound older; by ten he was smoking cigars.

Except for rare intervals when Orson's brother was home from school, his only companionship seemed to be with adults, primarily his mother. He lived mostly with her after his parents parted, and the two became almost inseparable. He spent time with his father, of course, and with Maurice Bernstein who seemed to be doing everything he could to "win" Orson *and* Beatrice from Richard. His mentor brought him to all the new plays that opened in Chicago and to the stars' dressing rooms afterward. Once they went to New York to hear a Stravinsky concert. Later, at the Waldorf, Orson discussed the music with a group of people who were sitting in the lounge. A young stage actress, just beginning her career, was most impressed by the child. Her name was Agnes Moorehead.

To round out the boy's education, Orson's father introduced him to his kind of Chicago friends, as opposed to Beatrice's. These included sportswriters, cartoonists, and other Chicago fast types. He met Bud Fisher and George McManus. The elder Welles encouraged Orson to try his hand at cartooning, a career that might prove lucrative for him. Orson complied, and showed real promise by the age of ten.

Reading and writing were passions of Welles from an early age. He has described himself as being marinated in poetry before he reached the age of seven. His first book was only the beginning of his library, for which he collected more Shakespeare, books on theater and cinema, philosophical works, and Greek drama. He asked his father to buy him a typewriter, and on it he typed short stories, plays, lectures, and drama theses. At eight he wrote a paper on "The Universal History of the Drama." By ten he had written a critique of Nietzsche's *Thus Spake Zarathustra.*

King Lear was perhaps Orson's favorite play at the time. In any case, he considered the role of the aged king to be his greatest performance as a child.

He knew all the speeches by heart when he was seven. At nine he presented his own abridged version of the play in his backyard. He played Lear, of course, and the King's purging of his rage and bitterness, "Pray do not mock me; I am a very foolish fond old man," may not have seemed all that inconsistent coming from the mouth of the nine-year-old Orson.

Never robust, even as a baby Welles was given to ill health. He suffered from chronic asthma and sinus headaches and had had bouts with diphtheria, measles, whooping cough, and even malaria. As he grew older, his ill health was exacerbated by the late hours he was allowed to keep, an early penchant for alcohol and tobacco, and the inordinate amount of time he spent in the attic closeted with his theater. He also suffered from back pain, almost from infancy. Dr. Bernstein insisted on some form of outdoor exercise. They settled on fishing as the least active and disagreeable, but only on the condition that Beatrice or somebody else would read to him while he, uninterested, dropped his line in the water.

JUST BEFORE ORSON was eight, his world changed. Suddenly, shockingly, his mother became ill with hepatitis. The last time he was allowed to visit her in her upstairs bedroom was when he was celebrating his eighth birthday. With great effort she forced herself to sit up in her darkened bedroom to receive him.

Orson remembered that she quoted some of his favorite lines of Shakespeare to entertain him and told him that he was to puff very hard to blow out the candles on his cake. "That stupid birthday cake is just another stupid cake," she said. "You'll have all the cakes you want. But the candles are a fairy ring. And you will never again in your whole life have just that number to blow out."

Orson puffed and blew out all of the candles but in his resolve to succeed, forgot to make a wish, something he still regretted as his deepest mistake sixty years later.

This was the last time he saw his mother alive. She was just barely forty.

Her death was a tremendous blow to Orson; nor was his brother around to share the loss—Dickie was away at school at the time. To soften the shock, it was decided that Orson should spend the summer with the wife and three daughters of Dudley Crafts Watson, a Chicago educator. The Watson family was staying at Hillside Farm, a summer colony in Syoming, New York, run by Lydia A. Ward. Watson has recalled that Orson was at first depressed over the loss of his mother but then quickly snapped out of it. He was lovable but incorrigible, Watson said, constantly getting himself and others into trouble. One of his minor but memorable infractions was keeping the Ward girls up half the night with his terrifying tales of supernatural characters he invented on the spot.

For a few months after that, Orson lived with both his father and Dr. Bernstein in a townhouse they shared in Chicago, which they had taken temporarily until they decided what to do with the boy. Richard retired from active business to devote himself to full-time parenthood. He began by taking

Orson with him on his travels, first to Jamaica and then to the Far East. Orson returned with a collection of books on magic that he had gathered during their journey, and the two settled down in the hotel in Grand Detour.

Later, when the hotel burned to the ground, the pair hit the road again, taking with them the only objects they had managed to save from the fire—two bottles of Holland gin. During the three years that Orson lived with his father, some observers wondered who took care of whom. After an on-board ship party outside of Hong Kong, Orson actually had to help his father on with his pants: they had somehow slipped to his father's ankles in the lounge.

Orson was a constant companion in his father's adventuring with wine, women, and song, even in his solitary moments. Richard Welles hated to be alone. And since he had never taught Orson the usual parental myth about early to bed and early to rise, Orson would sit up with him far into the night as Richard philosophized and told stories.

WHEN ORSON WAS ten he was—briefly—the subject of a psychological study. Maurice Bernstein had a friend named F. G. Mueller, who was a psychologist in Madison, Wisconsin. Mueller, aware that Bernstein considered Orson a prodigy, requested permission to include the boy in a study he was conducting of what he called "fate-marked" children, children who were so unusual that they seemed destined to lead extraordinary lives. The psychologist examined Orson, providing various stimuli so that Orson's responses could be measured and recorded. He or one of his associates would ask the child to free-associate with such words as "teddy bear" or "mother" and to respond with whatever first came to mind. Orson would invariably reply enigmatically. Once he responded with Oscar Wilde's epigram, "Children begin by loving their parents; as they grow older, they judge them; sometimes they forgive them." Another time he quoted an aphorism from Voltaire: "Who serves his country will have no need of ancestors." The scientists finally gave up; their "subject" seemed more inclined to provide his own creative stimuli to see how his observers would react.

At about that same time, Orson's father and Bernstein decided it might be a good idea to expose the boy to formal schooling, and the ten-year-old Orson was enrolled as a fourth-grader in a public school in Madison. Orson arrived at the school lugging his makeup box, and once after a bully had attacked him, Orson repaired to the school washroom where he applied makeup so his face would resemble a bloody pulp. The bully screamed and fled. After that he left Orson alone.

The other students either ignored him or tormented him. Orson was reading Sir Walter Scott at that time, and, after learning that Scott had achieved popularity through his conversational and storytelling abilities, Orson would gather the other children around him and tell them stories, drawing pictures to illustrate the action and plot. This worked for a while, but when the stories were over, his audience abandoned him to return to their games. Orson's sojourn in the fourth grade didn't last very long.

His next school experience, a far more happy and successful one, lasted until he was fifteen. The Todd School, in Woodstock, Illinois, was an expensive private school that Orson's brother, Richard, had attended for ten years until he was expelled as a troublemaker. The headmaster was Roger "Skipper" Hill, a lean white-haired man who had formerly been in advertising and who had the look and bearing for the job as though cast for a Hollywood movie. Skipper Hill had come to the school at the behest of *his* father, who owned Todd at the time. Although he was officially employed to teach English, Hill's real interest was drama, and he had quite a few theories of his own about drama training that he was eager to try out on the students. He soon became known throughout the Chicago area as a top-notch director of schoolboy productions.

Todd School seemed like an ideal place for Orson to be introduced to some disciplined academic study. Although educated far beyond his age level in some areas, in others he was surprisingly incompetent. At that point in his life, he was unable to even add or subtract. When it was pointed out to him that even geniuses ought to know how to do simple arithmetic, Orson shrugged airily that he would always have people around to do it for him, but eventually he did learn arithmetic.

Todd students were educated up to the tenth grade, then graduated with the necessary credentials for entering college. It was a school for talented children, most of them rich. There were boats, horses, and even a farm on the grounds. There were also a number of puppet theaters and a stage.

Hill had already heard of Orson's reputed genius and was eager to recruit him. His wife, Hortense, was at first charmed by the cute little round-faced boy who was introduced to her wearing a Sherlock Holmes outfit. Quite soon, however, she realized that she was going to have her hands full keeping such a self-willed and demanding student "a little bit under" as she told me over a half-century later. Orson protested his threatened loss of liberty and pronounced the theatrical equipment old-fashioned and the lighting inadequate. But the quick-witted Dr. Bernstein managed to head off the rebellion by reminding Orson that if the theater had been perfect there wouldn't be any room for him to improve it. That clinched it. Orson became a Todd student in the fall of 1926 and remained there the next four years, spending his shorter holidays with Bernstein, who at the time was living with music critic Edward Moore and his wife in Chicago. Longer holidays were spent traveling with his father.

A new rivalry was established among Bernstein, Hill, and Richard Welles, all vying for Orson's attention. Bernstein and the elder Welles had reason enough to hate each other: both men had been in love with the same woman, and each of them saw Orson, symbolically, as a representation of her. Hill's concern for Orson was more altruistic. He genuinely liked the boy and wanted to bring him along in the world of arts and letters. His fear of Richard's influence over Orson was shared by Bernstein. Both men felt, perhaps rightfully, that the drunken antics of Richard could only produce untoward results in the personality of the impressionable Orson. They did not encourage

Welles senior to visit. Hill often made excuses to keep Orson away from his father, a situation Richard deplored but felt, nevertheless, helpless to correct.

Before Orson became a full-time student, however, he managed one last fling—he eloped with Dudley Craft Watson's nine-year-old daughter, Marjorie. The Watsons were in Europe at the time, and the children were staying at the Sheffield Hotel under the supervision of a practical nurse. Orson assured Marjorie that they could support themselves from their earnings as traveling players, then launched their adventure in self-sufficiency by emptying his pockets and throwing all of his money into a nearby stream. With theatrical bravado, he informed Marjorie that thereafter they would have to live on their own talents—or starve to death.

Marjorie slept on pine boughs at night covered by Orson's coat. During the day, her hair cut short and wearing Orson's oversized garments so she would resemble a boy, she stood on street corners with him and acted out plays. The State Rural Police of Illinois looked for them for four days and finally spotted them in a small town where Marjorie gave the show away by pulling off her cap to reveal the evidence: the telltale ragged haircut that Orson had given her.

Orson's friendship with Marjorie was apparently one of the rare ones that he enjoyed with a child of his own age. When he was at the Todd School, he spent most of his time with teachers or with younger students. He would perform magic tricks for the little children and tell them stories until bedtime, when he got them to agree to go to bed by bribing them with a promise of more stories the following night. When "lights out" came, Orson disregarded the curfew and kept his usual night-owl hours.

Coach Roskey, who was the faculty member in charge of the dormitory when Orson lived there at the age of fourteen, has recalled some of the storytelling sessions:

"He watched their eyes and could tell when they wanted more, or when they wanted something else. He'd just make up the story according to what he saw in their faces. Orson was gifted like that. You could see the talent in him. It was like he'd do something and you'd say, 'Hey, that's nice,' and then he'd go one step further and turn it into something you never thought of. That's the way he did things, always just one step beyond what you'd expect." Orson was always reciting, talking, debating, or eating.

"Once," Roskey remembers, "I got him to open his mouth real wide and said, 'I want to take a picture of that mouth because some day it's going to be famous.'" Orson opened wide and then wider and slowly moved up to the camera. Roskey still cherishes the picture of an "extreme close-up" of Orson's mouth.

There are contradictory reports about Welles's athletic activities. Roskey, who ought to know, maintains that Orson was not much of an athlete. Orson even forged a note from his father once that stated he was too delicate to participate in gymnastic activities. Others maintain that he played football, swam, and even rode a horse. Hill claims that Orson escaped football and other sports by telling everyone he was a great swimmer. However, when Orson entered the school there was no swimming pool at Todd. When one was eventually built, he concocted a story about being a great mountain climber (in northern Illinois where even a high hill is difficult to find). Orson himself claims that he got most of his exercise strangling and dueling in Elizabethan dramas.

Athlete or not, his stature was impressive. Even at ten, Orson was much bigger than most of the boys his age, and he carried himself with adult assurance. Don Still, a fellow classmate, remembers some of the trips they made to town together.

"There was never a lot of contact between the school and the community. At most, the townsfolk would see the boys on weekends when they came in to buy a soda or something. Orson would always order his sodas in that big, booming voice of his, intimidating the hell out of the people around him. But he wasn't snotty. Just big, loud, and roustabout."

DRAMA, OF COURSE, was Orson's primary interest at Todd, and he was on stage almost immediately after he entered the school. At Halloween he gave a magic exhibition that firmly established him as an entertainer. At Christmas he played Mary, Mother of God, in a nativity play, then Christ in *The Servant in the House* and Judas Iscariot in *Dust of the Road*.

By spring, Orson was singing and dancing in a musical comedy. That settled the matter as far as Skipper Hill was concerned: he told Orson that he was destined for a great career in the theater. Orson already knew that, but he was pleased by Hill's comment because it gave him ammunition. Orson immediately capitalized on Hill's admiration and growing friendship by influencing school policy toward dramatic productions. Nativity plays and one-acts were strictly small-time, he argued. Todd was ready for full-scale productions of Shakespeare, Marlowe, and Jonson.

Orson became a member of the Todd Troupers, a company Roger Hill had organized to give his student actors road experience and exposure to outside audiences, who would be more critical than relatives and friends. The shows were presented in suburban movie houses and even at the prestigious Goodman Theatre in Chicago.

In addition to the tours, Orson's energies were also devoted to the weekly productions the Troupers presented at the school. For three years he was director of productions and mounted eight to ten plays a year. The job allowed him to display his many-faceted talents as producer, actor, designer, scenic artist, and composer. Some of his earlier directorial triumphs included Molière's *The Physician in Spite of Himself,* a version of *Dr. Faustus,* and an innovative *Everyman* staged with ladders and platforms.

Orson had somehow taught himself advanced elements of the craft, and his makeup for Richard III in *Winter of Discontent* was a sculpture of the grotesque, with carefully modeled features that a veteran many years his senior might well have been proud of.

The play was Welles's condensed and combined version of Shakespeare's *Henry IV* and *Richard III,* abridged so that both of them could be performed in forty-five minutes. Disregarding dramatic patterns and moral histories,

Orson concentrated on Richard's highly developed sense of evil, using Shakespeare's text as a bridge to link Richard's villainies.

By the time Welles was thirteen he was indisputably Todd's leading actor. He then directed and acted in a production of *Julius Caesar,* playing the parts of both Marc Antony and Cassius. The school entered the production in a high school drama competition sponsored by the Chicago Drama League. Numerous plays produced by the various high schools in the area were presented in Chicago's Goodman Memorial Theatre. There seemed to be no doubt in anybody's mind about the outcome of the competition.

At the end of the day, however, the judges announced that Senn High School had won the prize. The problem was that Orson looked and acted so much older than his years that the judges mistakenly thought the Todd School had improperly brought in *two* adult actors to play the parts of Cassius and Marc Antony. When the judges had been assured that both parts had been played by the same burly schoolboy, Whitford Kane, director of the Goodman Theatre, mounted the stage and announced in his broad and lyrical Irish brogue, that Welles had been awarded a special prize. There was a gasp from the audience, followed by a resounding cheer. Kane, who had been outraged by the original decision, took Orson aside after the play and told him, "You have a remarkable talent. I'm sure you'll go far in the theater . . . should you choose it as your profession." Kane and Orson became lifelong friends.

Kane was not the only influential Chicago drama figure who recognized Orson's talent. On November 11, 1930, Ashton Stevens, the dean of American drama critics at that time, upon seeing Orson play *Richard III,* wrote in his column in the *Chicago Herald American,* "I am going to put a clipping of this paragraph in my betting book. If Orson is not at least a leading man by the time it has yellowed, I will never make another prophecy."

ORSON WAS ALLOWED to experiment and explore to his heart's content. Not only the theater but the school's radio station was at his disposal. Although he didn't produce it, he wrote a radio adaptation based on the stories of Sherlock Holmes when he was about thirteen.

"He pretty much educated himself," Roger Hill observed years later to a New York reporter. "I don't take any credit for Welles at all." Even with Orson's mathematical incompetence, he had scored brilliantly on the school's IQ tests—146—which may be one reason why Hill allowed him free reign.

There was a period when Orson repeatedly locked horns with his instructor in ancient history, a follower of Professor James H. Brestead, the famous Egyptologist of the University of Chicago. Welles wrote paper after paper opposing Brestead, pointing out his contradictions and proving that Brestead misread inscriptions and did not understand the ancient world. In addition, Welles encouraged his fellow classmates to expose other authorities close to the heart of their teacher. The instructor complained to Hill, who did not respond with the expected sympathy. Instead, Hill exclaimed, "That's great! You're getting those boys to do ten times the research they would do ordinarily."

However, listening to history lectures was not a favorite pastime of Orson's. During one particularly boring class, he surreptitiously applied makeup to his face, then enraged his history teacher by posing at the back of the room with a handkerchief around his neck as if he were hanged. Again, Hill: "From the day Orson landed at my school, he was searching for some bizarre way to disturb people."

By the time Orson was fifteen, he had formed a close friendship with Skipper and Hortense Hill. That year a second tragedy occurred. His father died while staying at the Bismarck Hotel on State Street in Chicago during the Christmas holidays of 1930. Orson later once made reference to the fact that his father had committed suicide, and others have also remembered his demise by his own hand. Another account has Richard Welles having a case of whiskey delivered to his suite on Christmas Eve with the announced boast that he would consume the entire lot by New Year's. The death certificate, however, makes no mention of an intentional death: it lists the death to be from chronic myocarditis and nephritis. Orson claimed that his grandmother Mary performed Satanic rites at the funeral of her son.

Orson was left the largest portion of his father's estate, with the small remainder going to his brother. Although he wanted Skipper Hill to become his legal guardian, the headmaster declined, and the responsibility went to Maurice Bernstein, who was already administering Orson's mother's estate. A trust fund was established for Orson; he was to receive a yearly income and the balance of the principal when he reached the age of twenty-five.

He spent his school vacations with Bernstein at the home of the Edward Moores, but the adults who most influenced him during that period were the Hills.

Despite the fact that Orson had strong opinions and certainly a strong will, he apparently did not present the discipline problems that Hortense Hill had once anticipated, although she does recall one incident that involved a problem many parents encounter: Orson hated vegetables. His diet already excluded candy and pastries because of his hay fever and asthma, and now he announced that he was adding vegetables to the list of forbidden foods on the grounds that many doctors considered them harmful for children to eat. Hortense was skeptical and did some research that proved the contrary was true. When she confronted Orson with the evidence, he capitulated; intellectually defeated, he henceforth ate the horrid things without verbal complaint.

Orson was not, by any account, a docile child, but his misdemeanors showed a flash of imagination that made them almost endearing. His love of tall tales, for example, was sometimes unsettling. But the imperturbable Hill mostly took them in good humor.

One day Skipper and his protégé were at the Chicago Public Library waiting for the elevator to fill with passengers so they could ascend. Skipper, who hated to wait for anything, finally hopped into the cage with Orson and hijacked the elevator to their destination, leaving the astonished operator cursing them on the ground floor. After Orson had told the story a few times, the elevator was hovering between floors because the operator had called the police, while one of the passengers was delivered of a baby by Skipper, who acted as midwife. Skipper's wry comment on the embellishments was simply, "By the next time I hear the story it should be really good."

On another occasion the two got lost while driving to New York City. Skipper advised Orson to wet his finger and hold it to the wind so they could get their bearings. Orson obediently jumped out of the car and was standing beside the road waving his finger when a cop approached.

After listening to Orson babble about the wind for a while, the policeman declared, "You're drunk."

Orson insisted that he wasn't.

"Then you're crazy."

"I'm not," Orson told him, "but the white-haired guy at the wheel in the car is, and I'm just humoring him."

It took fifteen minutes to convince the cop that Orson was joking.

Sometimes, when it suited his needs, the tall tales included impersonation. Once when Orson was eleven, he had made plans to meet his father in Chicago. The hour arrived for the meeting, but Dick Welles didn't appear. Broke and hungry, Orson walked into the leading restaurant there and ordered a meal, afterward charging it to Ned Moore, his friend the music critic, cheerfully telling the waiter that he was Moore's son.

At another time when Orson was in Chicago he needed to get something from the hotel room that Skipper was staying in. But Skipper wasn't in the room at the moment, so Orson asked the desk clerk for the key. When the cautious man hesitated, Orson reassured him by claiming to be Skipper's son.

The desk clerk didn't think so; he'd seen the boy before and remembered his name. Thinking quickly, Orson acknowledged the accuracy of the desk clerk's memory—almost. His full name he said, was "Orson Welles Hill." The house detective was summoned, and both men looked in Orson's hat and found the initials O.W. inside. Undaunted, Orson maintained that the last initial had been dropped. A rather nasty scene ensued, at the end of which Orson admitted who he really was. The officials let him go. Orson turned to stride out of the lobby but found himself the focal point of a considerable crowd. Drawing himself up to his full height, he imperiously informed everyone in earshot that he would certainly not recommend this hotel to his friends!

When he was fourteen, one of Orson's less innocent deceptions nearly got him arrested. Passing himself off as a Greek scholar, Orson sold a translation of a Sophocles play to a theater group for $300. Later, the director discovered that Orson's version was not a true translation but a prose version that he had translated into iambic pentameter, a verse form he had learned from studying Elizabethan plays.

On his vacations from Todd, Orson continued to travel. Shortly before his father died, they took a second trip to China and the East. Orson spent hours wandering through the streets of Shanghai and Hong Kong. He rode along the

Great Wall of China, bought pictures and ornaments, and dined in restaurants where he ordered his meals in passable Chinese. He was particularly fascinated by the centuries-old Chinese theater and Chinese magic.

On the voyage to Shanghai, Orson unwittingly practiced another form of magic—he made his father's money disappear. By signing his name to the other passengers' bar chits, he discovered the secret of instant popularity. Nobody explained to the boy that his father would have to pay the bill, and Richard Welles knew nothing of the incurred expenses at the time. At the end of the voyage, when the pile of chits—and the resulting bill—had reached enormous proportions, Orson received a stern lecture on the value of money. It was the only lecture his father ever gave his son.

Not only did Orson have a careless disregard for money, he didn't care much for clothes, either. When he was fifteen and about to embark on his first solo journey—a bicycle tour through Europe—he packed his trunk with the things he considered the most essential for traveling: some books and painting gear. Bernstein came to see how the packing was coming along, looked in the trunk, and saw that Orson had omitted one important item: clothing. Orson insisted that he had all the clothes that he needed, those that he had on.

The doctor completed the job by putting in some socks, handkerchiefs, shirts, and suits, but Orson, as usual, got in the last word on the subject. Next morning when it was time for Bernstein to drive him to the train, Orson appeared coatless, hatless, and wearing a pair of shorts. When Bernstein objected, Orson explained the logic of his unconventional attire: if he had a hat he would probably lose it, and it was too hot for a tie or coat.

DESPITE UNANIMOUS PREDICTIONS that he was destined for a great stage career, Orson himself claimed that his own ambition was to be a painter when he graduated from Todd. He had filled several sketchbooks during his travels with his father (who had wanted him to go to Harvard) and had displayed a talent for painting scenery. A mural he painted in one of the Todd School's classrooms hung for years as one of the showpieces of the school.

Nevertheless, the stage still loomed large in his plans. Shortly before graduation he shrewdly inserted the following ad in *Billboard*:

> Orson Welles—Stock Characters, Heavies, Juveniles, or as cast. Also specialties, chalk talk or can handle stage. Young, excellent appearance, quick, sure study. Lots of pep, experience and ability. Close in Chicago early in June and want place in good stock company for remainder of the season. Salary according to late date of opening and business conditions. Address Orson Welles, Care H. L. Powers, Illinois Theatre. 65 East Jackson Blvd., Chicago, Ill.

Note the "Close in Chicago early in June." The veteran imposter was at work again—this time trying to pass himself off as a professional actor. The ad brought only one response—from a touring company that closed down a week later when it ran out of cash. His next advertisement, inserted a month later, brought a far more enthusiastic response:

Orson Welles is willing to invest moderate amount in cash and own services as Heavy, Character and Juvenile in good summer stock or repertory proposition. Reply to Orson Welles, Dramatic Coach, Todd Academy, Woodstock, Illinois.

Touring companies, traveling carnivals, showboats, and flea circuses hastened to respond to Orson's attractive proposal. Bernstein, however, quashed any ideas of investments. Surely, he explained, the future had greater things in store for the boy wonder than being a stooge at a flea circus or a barker at a sideshow.

Apparently, Orson thought so, too. One day, while riding in a New York City elevator with Hortense Hill, he pointed out another passenger and whispered, "That's so and so, the famous producer."

Mrs. Hill was properly impressed. Welles stood quietly, thinking about what he had just said. A moment later he confided, "Someday, people will point to me and say, 'That's Orson Welles, the famous *actor*-producer.'"

CHAPTER 2

IN THE SUMMER of a depressed 1931, when the sixteen-year-old Orson Welles arrived at the docks of Galway and stepped ashore from the SS *Baltic,* he was surrounded by hundreds of indigents. The Irish revolution and civil war, a scant decade old, had left poor Ireland even poorer and the signs of poverty were everywhere visible. If some of the other passengers found the vivid tableau to be intimidating, to the young Welles it only added instant charm to the beginning of his journey, ostensibly a sketching and painting tour of what was then known as the Irish Free State. Orson Welles was immense in stature and mock-confident in the ways that some teenagers are. His imposing six-foot, two-hundred-pound baby fat frame was matched evenly by his deep, dark, authoritative voice that was occasionally tempered by a youthful giggle. Even in childhood, and more so after the death of his father a year before, he had been obsessed with a compulsion to falsify his real age. Orson Welles, the teenager, considered his youth a terrible affliction, and he liked to think of himself as an adult, perhaps someone in his middle or late twenties. He played this chronological ruse so convincingly that almost everyone either believed or accepted it. To eradicate any skepticism and perhaps overcome his occasional inner lapses of self-assurance or the unguarded social errors that youth can rarely conceal, he often smoked, drank brandy, and would occasionally spout a vulgar word, a foreign phrase, a sophisticated observation, or a line from Shakespeare, and sometimes all of the above, sequentially and with great speed and authority, to inform the suspicious of his cosmopolitan and seasoned presence.

Upon his graduation from Todd, everyone close to him in Chicago had made plans for the talented, attractive, but unpredictable Orson. Roger "Skipper" Hill had arranged for his enrollment at a leading dramatic school in the Midwest; Maurice Bernstein wanted him to go to Cornell, and there was even talk of a scholarship being available at Harvard; the artist Boris Anisfield of the Art Institute of Chicago, with whom Orson had studied for a few weeks, urged him to continue the pursuit of painting. Orson was suffering from his annual bout with allergies that summer and used the illness as an excuse to insist that he be permitted to leave the United States and go to a country where the air might be clean and presumably pollen-free. He desperately wanted to travel, as he always had, and thought he could continue his

18

studies while touring. After all, journeys combined with education were considered the epitome of learning and were an integral part of the philosophy of the Todd School, and Orson used the tradition as one of his arguments.

There were many heated internecine battles over what might be the most beneficial action for him to take. In a letter written to Skipper Hill, and eventually published in Skipper's memoirs, *One Man's Time and Chance,* he confided:

> My head remained bloody but unbowed, and my nose, thanks to the thoughtful blooming of some neighboring clover (which I assured the enemy was ragweed!) began to sniffle hay-feverishly, and the household was illusioned into the realization that something had to be done.

Only the meek and thin of blood went to college, Orson argued, and besides, his school record was magnificently unimpressive: he had managed to graduate from Todd only because of careful prompting by fellow students and the compassion and beneficence of faculty. The confines of curriculum at a university seemed impossible, smothering, to him. School occupied no part of his personal program. A proven genius he was; a dedicated academician he was not. Stage or canvas, he pleaded.

Finally Dr. Bernstein agreed, "in the spirit of true martyrdom," as Orson wryly described it, that painting might not be as injurious to character or intellect as acting, and his consent for a six-month trip abroad was given. Bernstein wanted his ward to go to Paris, historically the most frequented academy-without-walls for aspiring painters; Orson, however, selected Ireland, partially as a statement of his independence and also because it was a country he had never visited. Four days after Orson's career conference, he was sniffle-free in New York, his handkerchiefs as dry as biscuits, waiting to set sail to the Emerald Isle. He had $500 and a one-way ticket in his pocket, and he was not due back in the United States until October. Further plans for his possible schooling were to be decided then.

Travel was in Orson's blood. In addition to a boyhood of wandering with his father, he had spent a previous summer touring and bicycling through Europe with fellow students. The painting trip, however, would be his first significant time away alone, and visions of late nights, submissive women, gargantuan feasts, and generally high adventure danced in his head. He expected to spend a few months walking through Ireland and Scotland, he told Bernstein, complete some paintings, and go to England; and then, in a complete turnaround, explained that if he found a school suited to his burgeoning creative, autocratic, and unconventional tastes, he *might* just enroll. Also, the thought that he would be able to attend the theater in London *constantly* was a delightful dream that he had every intention of turning into reality. He once stated, looking back at those times, that he definitely felt that his trip to Ireland was going to be the beginning of his career as a painter.

HIS WALKING TOUR was to be short-lived. He started toward Clifden, the capital of Connemara, but soon discovered that because of his somewhat flat feet and the rugged Irish roads, it would be difficult if not impossible to manage. For a few Irish pounds he secured an ass and a cart, a traditional method of transportation in Ireland at that time, especially among visitors. After some brief instructions on how to handle the harnessing and some tips on caravan lore ("Never stand behind the donkey" and "Never let her graze in an open field"), he was on his vagabondish way, a word of encouragement to the donkey named Sheelagh, his paints, brushes, and canvases atop the cart, and his bicycle, Ulysses, strapped to the back.

The few months that Orson spent growing to know Ireland, while traveling and sketching and sleeping under the cart in the open air, were of such personal educational and ontological consequence that the experience would remain with him for the rest of his life. "It was a grand summer," he has recalled, as he ambled along roads lined with breast-high boundary walls and explored the dozy towns of Connemara. The countryside was a desolate and enchanting wedding of mountains and crashing sea, offering a stark beauty matched by few other places in the world.

He fell in love with the Irish people, and they accepted him with warmth. Tall, broadly handsome, ingenuous, eloquent, filled with the blarney, Orson was as talented a yarn-spinner as any salt from the sea and had the gift of gab that seems to be the special heritage of the Irish. He could listen, too; his love of "story" was as quietly reverent as that of any schoolchild. There was hardly a singing pub that he could pass without stopping in, and even some of the lifetime inhabitants of the "snugs," those smallish semiprivate compartments that often line Irish bars, would welcome him to their hallowed sanctuaries as though he were family. The initial interest in him by the Irish, of course, was often due as much to his nationality as to his charm. Although Clifden was the nominal capital of Connemara, Boston was its heart. It seemed that almost every Irishman wanted to emigrate to the United States during those impoverished days; conversation with Americans about life across the Atlantic was always welcome fare, and Orson did his best to create a verbal mosaic of 1930s America as he drank and talked and listened. He was virtually overcome by the poetry and melody of the country. The sound of the Irish voice greatly affected him; the gentle urging of a phrase, the turn and resonance of a word, the rhythm of diction in ditty, dirge, and hymn. Being a natural mimic, he found it quite simple to adopt and master the accent so perfectly that it was difficult to discern that he wasn't born and bred of the soil.

It is quite possible that a knowledge of John Millington Synge's one-act drama *Riders to the Sea,* which Welles had read at Todd, and the hope of capturing the legendary Celtic twilight on canvas, was what propelled him to take the steamer *Dun Aengus* from Galway to the Aran Islands off Ireland's western coast, those small barren pieces of land constantly besieged by the sea. He may also have been influenced by Synge's description of the nobility of the islanders and his transformation of the catastrophe of the Arans into a universal theme; his art teacher's advice that the light and sky and sea there were unsurpassed for certain landscapes may have also affected Orson.

The Arans exemplified the poverty-stricken people left gaunt and guinea-less by the Great Famine. Fishermen struggling against the sea and the wind in order to survive still used the crude, hand-hewn boats, *carraghs,* to go down to the sea, and their lives were as difficult as those of villagers from medieval days. Their language, too, was an echo from the past; many of them still spoke Gaelic—or Irish, as they called it—as their native tongue. At night, groups gathered at the crossroads of the towns and, against the flickering light of huge bonfires, their *seanachaidh,* the old storytellers, told ghost stories and legends of the island's misty past.

Coincidentally, Robert Flaherty, maker of such documentary films as *Nanook of the North* and *Moana,* was on the smallest of the islands, Inisheer, when Welles was there. Flaherty was selecting locations and just beginning the production of his eventual *Man of Aran,* and although Welles had some curiosity as an observer, he appraised the whole project gingerly and with a lack of enthusiasm. "I was a bit of a motion picture snob at that time," Welles told me, "and I didn't think movies were all that important." It's entirely possible that Flaherty, somewhat of a god on Aran since he was the first person to honor the islanders on film (and it also didn't hurt that most of the population was named Flaherty), hardly noticed Welles. The motion picture crew was deeply involved in making a creatively challenging and physically dangerous film and had little time for a young American painter.

Orson did as many paintings as he could on Aran, but instead of landscapes he took to portraits. He found it an absorbing way to make friends and thought that the immediate commercial prospects—if he could learn to do them well enough—might be more promising. If nothing else, the works would serve as a visual diary of his trip. He wrote to Dr. Bernstein that he would carry away with him "perhaps a half dozen of them—simple sketches of men and women I have known here" and added with a refreshingly critical self-appraisal, "some of them will be bad pictures and some fair—most of them will be fair likenesses but as portraits of that undefinable Erin spirit they will all be dismal failures."

There is a story, perhaps apocryphal, that has often made its way into articles written about Welles over the years and that was neither confirmed nor denied by him. If true, it would explain why and how he left the Aran Islands sooner than he planned. According to the story, Orson was quite attracted to the young, wholesomely beautiful Irish girls, and several of them were more than friendly toward him. Some of the older islanders began to worry about the fates of their daughters and complained to the Catholic priest from the mainland who visited the islands every week. Finally, the priest met Orson and one day brought the matter to a head. Their conversation supposedly went something like this:

Priest: "I heard confession this morning, Orson."
Orson: "Did you, Father?"

Priest: (His voice taking on a sterner tone) "Yes, I did, Orson . . ."

Orson: (Acknowledging to the priest that he understood his point) "Yes, Father?"

Priest: "When are you leaving, Orson?"

Orson: "On the next boat, Father."

What is known is that despite his love for the islands, Orson wanted to get back to "civilization," and he was conspicuously low on funds. He wrote to Dr. Bernstein asking for additional money to be sent to Dublin; then he ferried back to the mainland, took a two-week barge trip up the Shannon from Limerick to the ancient city of Athlone and then a six-hour bus ride into Dublin. Sitting in the bus, Orson composed a letter to Roger Hill in which he told an amusing story of espying two young people making love in a trench outside Athlone, while their dowager chaperone pretended to be asleep nearby, although she opened her eyes and winked mischievously at Orson when he passed by. But the letter was not all drollery; Orson was reflective about what he had already learned on the trip: "A great deal happened here of which I have not written," he said mysteriously, perhaps a reference to his amorous adventures. "I am riding into Dublin with glad thoughts about Ireland." And as he entered that historic city, really a provincial town by habit and attempting to become a capital city through proclamation and self-esteem, it must have been with a sharp sense of buoyant anticipation for further happenings to come.

ORSON'S FIRST ORDER of business in Dublin was to visit the post office to retrieve the money that he thought would be waiting for him. It hadn't arrived. Depressed, he searched for a room and tried to become acquainted with the city by roaming through the streets, a somewhat difficult feat since in the days preceding his arrival, Dublin had experienced its greatest rainfall in a century. The Liffey was overflowing, parts of the downtown section were ankle-deep in water, many residents of the outskirts had been evacuated, bridges and roads were damaged, and some were closed. Mud was everywhere.

Sloshing through that first night in Dublin, Orson was almost over-whelmed. He had expected a quainter, quieter town but instead found a "very big city and one of the great beauties of the world." The moans of the lumbering double-decked buses played in concert with the cacophony of the trams clanking and clattering through the boulevards and narrow streets, illuminated by the lamps that writer Liam O'Flaherty once described as "sinister yellow moons." In tandem with the rains, Dublin was experiencing what the Irish call "St. Martin's summer," when the leaves grow thin but the weather is still warm and some plants and bushes persist in blossoming. Storks roosted on the eaves of the houses of Sackville Street, and everywhere people seemed to eat ice cream. Morris Minors were the new cars that were most frequently seen. Castles in the suburbs could still be bought for a few thousand dollars. The smell of coffee, which wasn't really coffee at all but the roasted malt and hops of the breweries, blended with the pungency of stout ferment-ing in the Guinness plant. The combined aromas drifted through the streets. Wandering through the city, sensing it with unabashed curiosity, Orson discovered that the Hollywood stereotype was wrong; the people of Dublin were not merely a collection of stage Irishmen—undertakers, priests, lovable drunks, and recruits for the New York City police department. Dublin, like Berlin at the time, had a sense of abandon and debauchery about it. The city was filled with attractive women dressed in velvet bridge coats and men in handwoven Donegal tweeds carrying blackthorn canes, some sporting a small white circle, embroidered on their labels, signifying their preference for speaking Gaelic. There were also men with riding breeches and girls with mud-stained long dresses, back from the morning ride to the Kildare hounds or grouse shooting, who could be seen entering the Shelbourne Hotel just in time for tea. In blurred contrast, however, there were also legions of pug-ugly urchins who roamed the streets begging for coins.

Part of Orson's dwindling funds that first night in Dublin was spent on something that always interested him: a good meal. For one penny he purchased a copy of the *Irish Press,* a new national newspaper that had its debut just days before he arrived in Dublin, and which he read while he dined. It offered the editorial promise to foster truth in news: "Independent in its comment, fearless in its assertion of national rights, scrupulously fair in its treatment of all sections, the *Irish Press* will cater for the whole people." Its entertainment columns advertised a variety of diversions on that evening, giving Orson a wide choice of possibilities to pass away the time in a strange city. At the movies, Charlie Chaplin's *City Lights* was being held over at the Metropole for the fourth straight week; Harold Lloyd was starring in *Feet First* at the Capitol; John Gilbert in *Gentlemen's Fate* and Marie Dressler in *Reducing* were in other downtown film palaces. On the stage, there was the prospect of seeing *The Student Prince* at the Gaiety Theatre; the famed Abbey was showing a four-act tragedy, *John Ferguson* by St. John Irvine; the Olympia Theatre had a vaudeville night with the comedians Pell and Curtis, billed as "the only two Scotch Jews in captivity"; and at the small but vital Gate Theater was a production of Gogol's satire, *The Inspector General.*

Orson had no idea how momentous a decision he was making by choosing how to amuse himself that first night in Dublin, or how it would affect his life. With virtually only a few cents in his pocket before financial relief arrived from Bernstein, he could have elected to purchase an aluminum disc at a cashier's box to allow him to enter a movie house and spend the evening in the smoke-filled blackness seeing a lively film and mouthing the words of the captions in unison with the rest of the audience. But movies were not very attractive to Orson at that time, certainly not enough to spend one's "last" money to watch. He elected to go to the theater that night because a good seat could be had at the Gate for less than twenty cents; because earlier that summer he had met a vacationing young actor, Cathral O'Callaigh, who had a small part in the company; and simply because he enjoyed the stage more than the movies. As a result of Orson Welles's subsequent involvement with the Gate Theatre and its principals, which became so integral to his professional theatrical career, a short profile of the history of the group is essential.

In 1927 two young actors, Micheál MacLiammoir and Hilton Edwards, met in an Irish touring company that was directed by Anew McMaster, one of Ireland's most colorful theatrical entrepreneurs. MacLiammoir, who was McMaster's brother-in-law, had studied with the famous Sir Herbert Beerbohm Tree and acted at His Majesty's Theatre in London when he was only twelve years old. His performances on the English stage were invariably hailed by critics, but MacLiammoir eventually returned to his beloved Ireland to try his hand at directing and producing the experimental plays of his fellow countryman and personal idol, William Butler Yeats. MacLiammoir would later proclaim Yeats as the chief force in forming his personality and, for good or ill, as MacLiammoir wrote, the shaper of his life.

Edwards, born in London, first acted in his teens in a small but fine Shakespearean company and by the time he was twenty-one had performed all of the Bard's plays, save two. He had a reputation as a fine young actor capable of virtually any role. Edwards shared MacLiammoir's interest in Yeats, and when the two men met in the McMaster company, they established an affinity that would remain for a lifetime: an irrepressible love and knowledge of the theater, an obsession to travel, blithe dispositions, and a sense of the outrageously naughty. Their creativity and fey grace made an impression on the Irish stage and Dublin society that lasted for over a half a century.

Although, or perhaps because, he was self-taught outside of the theater, MacLiammoir could read, write, and speak almost every European language and was an accomplished painter and set designer, as well as a witty and worldly author of prolific accomplishment. Welles once said of him that he looked like something Beardsley would have drawn if his pencil sharpener had been taken away, an overripe flower of a man: soft, warm, and brilliantly hued in speech and dress.

In addition to his prowess as an actor, Edwards's claims to exceptional talents consisted of being a raconteur, a connoisseur of fine wines and cigars, and a marvelous appraiser, producer, and director of theatrical talent. He was well known in the Dublin movie houses, but not from the screen. During the days when each feature film was accompanied by at least several acts of vaudeville, Edwards's classical baritone voice would enchant the Irish audiences. He looked quite like that lisping and unctuous English character actor, Eric Blore, the gentleman's gentleman.

In 1928, MacLiammoir and Edwards founded the Dublin Gate Theatre Studio. Drama critic Seamus Kelly described their beginnings:

> Their first productions were offered in the Peacock Theatre, a 101-seater experimental annex of the Abbey. Here, on a stage not much bigger than a Victorian dining table, they produced *Peer Gynt,* Wilde's *Salomé,* and a febrile symphonic surge of expressionistic brilliance called *The Old Lady Says 'No!'* by the most remarkable young Irish dramatist they discovered, Denis Johnston.

By the time Orson Welles visited the Gate Theatre that night in September of 1931, they had moved to larger quarters and had soundly established their reputation as being, if not the equal in theatrical status to the Abbey, then superior to it in their production of plays not often seen in Dublin. As theater historian Patricia Goldstone observed in *Sight and Sound*:

> The golden era of the Irish national theater was said to have ended when O'Casey exiled himself to London in fury at Yeats' rejection of *The Silver Tassie,* and young actors and playwrights found themselves stifled by its parochial naturalism and conservative Catholic morality. Edwards and MacLiammoir swept into Dublin bringing the traditions and innovations of the European mainstream. Their aim was to present to the Irish public a theater divorced from the national question, a theater limited only by the limits of the imagination.

Their repertory was close to amazing: full-scale productions were mounted in a matter of weeks by a closely twined family of followers of Michael and Hilton, ready to work around the clock for the sake of the two men and the play. Through the Gate Theatre, Dubliners were made familiar with some of the plays of O'Neill *(The Hairy Ape),* Tolstoy *(The Power of Darkness),* and Shakespeare *(The Merchant of Venice),* works not normally performed at the Abbey or anywhere in Ireland.

MacLiammoir's performance that autumn night in 1931, as the lead in *The Inspector General,* captured Orson's heart, and he went backstage at the instant of the play's end, ostensibly to visit his friend O'Callaigh. Attracted to the company, to the theater, and to the whole idea of possibly working with a professional group, Orson made a brash attempt to be accepted on his own terms, as a self-discovered and self-proclaimed star. And although he had every expectation that additional funds from Bernstein would be forthcoming, he was temporarily without any money and needed replenishment immediately. Since necessity has no law or conventions, he penned the following note to directors MacLiammoir and Edwards and had O'Callaigh deliver it to them: "Orson Welles, star of the New York Theater Guild, would consider appearing in one of your productions and hopes you will see him for an appointment." Orson not only looked a great deal older than his sixteen years, he also conducted himself as a fully mannered adult and was as arrogant as an exclamation point, "like the young man a suburban Gilbert and Sullivan society would cast as the Mikado," as Russell Maloney so aptly described him in his profile of Welles in *The New Yorker* some years later.

Both MacLiammoir and Edwards made no secret about their partiality to actors who were high of talent, fair of face, and splendid of body, and since Orson overtly possessed at least two of those characteristics, Edwards took a swift liking to the boy. He gave him a copy of *Jew Süss,* a future Gate production, and told him to return the following morning to talk. Perhaps an audition could be arranged. That night, a power failure caused by a storm plunged most of Dublin into blackness, but it is possible that Orson might not have seriously noticed the lack of light in the city or the dinginess of his room, so stimulated was he by the idea of the next morning's confrontation.

The following morning, MacLiammoir was painting the sets for *The Melians,* the next scheduled play, written by Lord Longford, when Welles arrived for his appointment. Edwards greeted him and then found MacLiammoir, who in his memoir, *All for Hecuba,* describes the meeting:

> Hilton walked into the scene dock one day and said, "Somebody strange has arrived from America; come and see what you think of it."
>
> "What," I asked, "is it?"
>
> "Tall, young, fat: says he's been with the Guild Theater in New York. Don't believe a word of it, but he's interesting. I want him to give me an audition. Says he's been in Connemara with a donkey, and I don't see what that's got to do with me. Come and have a look at him."
>
> We found, as he had hinted, a very tall young man with a chubby face, full, powerful lips, and disconcerting Chinese eyes. His hands were enormous and very beautifully shaped, like so many American hands; they were coloured like champagne and moved with a sort of controlled abandon never seen in a European. The voice, with its brazen transatlantic sonority, was already that of a preacher, a leader, a man of power; it bloomed and boomed its way through the dusty air of the scene dock as though it would crush the little Georgian walls and rip up the floor; he moved in a leisurely manner from foot to foot and surveyed us with magnificent patience as though here was our chance to do something beautiful at last—yes, sir—and were we going to take it? Well, just too bad for us if we let the moment slip. And all this did not come from mere youth, though the chubby tea-rose cheeks were as satin-like as though the razor had never known them—that was the big moment waiting for the razor—but from some ageless and superb inner confidence that no one could blow out. It was unquenchable. That was his secret. He knew that he was precisely what he himself would have chosen to be had God consulted him on the subject of his birth; he fully appreciated and approved what had been bestowed, and realized that he couldn't have done the job better himself, in fact he would not have changed a single item. Whether we and the world felt the same—well, that was for us to decide.

MacLiammoir, in his writings and interviews years later, could not recall exactly what at first Welles said to him. He thought he remembered Welles talking of acting in the Theater Guild, traveling through China, and some of his adventures, to date, in Ireland. He attempted to manipulate both men with a combination of bluster and lie into believing that he was something that he was not quite: a professional actor and a man of the world. Actually he was an actor in every sense; his experience at Todd, his short lifetime of personal inspection of the drama, and his natural talent for everything theatrical made him, even at sixteen, an actor of promise, but without the credits of the veteran. And the years of travel behind him, combined with the influence of his cosmopolitan parents and their wide range of artistic friends, certainly qualified him as something of if not a man, then at least a boy of the world.

"He didn't have to lie to us," Edwards recalled in an interview with the author years later. "We could tell he had the bump of the theater just from talking to him. And there was always room for one more on our boards."

Welles suggested that he read for them, anything from the surrealism of James Joyce to the ladled-on pathos and melodrama of Florence Barclay, but Edwards took the copy of *Jew Süss* and said, "Read the Duke. Come on." Welles knew that the Duke was not the star's role and on a gambit asked if he could audition for the part of the Jew instead. Edwards had already begun rehearsals to perform that part himself, however, and the only role that was left uncast was that of the Duke. They insisted Welles read the Duke, and he was left no alternative except to comply. MacLiammoir recalls, in colorful detail, what then occurred:

> There followed one of the strangest sights I have witnessed in my life. The young man looking larger, taller, softer and broader in the face than ever, bounded onto the stage with our poor little book in his hand. He confronted us with glazing eyes and seemed, as far as we could judge from our seats at the back of the two-and-fourpennies, in a towering rage. A chair was hurled through the air, and he struck an attitude suggestive of sated repose. Then he thought better of that and a small table followed the chair. A violent cloud of dust, like a miniature sand-storm and an accompanying desiccated rustle of paper and twigs informed me that some branches of plum blossom were sharing the same fate. A few books and a harmless necessary cushion or two concluded the holocaust, and after a brief prayer of gratitude that the valuable clock used in Act Three was in the prop room and that I myself was out of reach for the moment—my partner I was sure could take care of himself—I began to wonder what was to be left of our theater before it was ready for this young man to play in it.

After complaining that there was not enough light, Welles finally got into the reading. MacLiammoir continues:

> It was an astonishing performance, wrong from beginning to end but with all the qualities of fine acting tearing their way through a chaos of inexperience. His diction was practically perfect, his personality, in spite of his fantastic circus antics, was real and varied; his sense of passion, of evil, of drunkenness, of tyranny, of a sort of demoniac authority was arresting; a preposterous energy pulsated through everything he did. One wanted to say, "Now, now, really you know," but something stopped the words from coming. And that was because he was real to himself, because it was something more to him than a show, more than mere inflated exhibitionism one might have suspected from his previous talk, something much more.

Orson instinctively knew that he would get the part, so confident was he in his ability to act and establish a rapport with people. His self-appraisal of the reading was honest and astute, however, and he wrote to Hill, "There are two

27

big parts in *Jew Süss.* One is the George Arliss title role and the other half is the Emil Jannings, half-Douglas Fairbanks contrast to the Jew, Karl Alexander, the Duke. I read the play, decided I had no chance as Süss and though I scarcely dared dream of getting it, learned Karl Alexander. My first audition was a bitter failure. I read them a scene and being terribly nervous and anxious to impress I performed a kind of J. Worthington Ham with all the tricks and resonance I could conjure up."

Whatever Orson did in that first audition it was right for Messrs. Edwards and MacLiammoir. Aside from desperately needing a Duke for *Jew Süss,* they had another problem: one of their general *aides-de-camp,* Charles Margood, was leaving the company. Orson agreed to fill all the jobs that had been Margood's: actor, assistant scene-painter, and press agent. The salary offered—two pounds, ten shillings—was laughably low, but Edwards would not negotiate it. Orson accepted.

After moving into a service flat in the fashionable section of Fitzwilliam Square, within a few minutes' walk of the theater, Welles got down to the art and science of becoming a professional thespian and a man of Dublin. While MacLiammoir was acting in a run of Karel Capek's expressionistic *R.U.R.,* Welles, under Edwards's tutelage and directorship, rehearsed and studied for his part as the Duke. Orson soon discovered how fortuitous the casting had been: it was an almost perfect role for a beginner in that it contained a seduction scene, a murder scene, and a deathbed scene. Edwards urged and gentled him into the role so that he could determine just what his talents and limitations were. "Don't obey me blindly," Edwards told him, "but listen to me. More important still, listen to yourself. I can help you to learn how to play the part, but you must see and hear what's good about yourself and what's lousy." Edwards attempted to instill in the boy as much mastery of the craft as he had learned in his lifetime on the stage. He could see that Welles had a perfect and natural mimetic sense, and so he continually demonstrated, not told him, what was wanted in a role, making every attempt to help Welles retain the looseness of gesture he possessed while ridding him of a certain formal "elocutionary" style of delivery of his lines.

Orson's voice was a prodigious instrument, and Edwards attempted to get him to use it with rustic innocence rather than stagey sophistication. The "official" speech of the Gate was a cross between that of the educated Dubliner and that of the peasant folk, combined with a subtle influence of Gaelic sentence rhythm and word patterns. Though the attentive listener could still catch the nuances of Welles's midwestern inflections, which included pronouncing some words with a lively but tense, somewhat circular motion of the lower jaw that affected the sound of his "r" and his vowels, he soon took to duplicating the rolled "r" and additional beauties of the Irish language with what sounded like an authentic city brogue.

Welles rehearsed constantly and began to refine his speech, movements, and gestures. He knew, from his amateur experience, such basics of the dramatic skill as delivering dialogue directly to the audience, maintaining a straight line when moving in any direction across the stage, and executing turns toward, not away from, the footlights. The classic subtleties, however, were sometimes more difficult to master, either because of philosophical difference or because of his lack of physical deftness: while standing stage left or right, he had to remember to rest his weight on his downstage foot, or recall while in an embrace to keep his upstage arm above the woman's and his downstage arm, below. Eventually, it did all begin to flow.

MacLiammoir has recalled that Orson was filled with the unswerving energy of those who are born for the stage. With almost tireless eagerness he would paint the sets, clean the theater, attend a performance of Tretiakov's *Roar China* by a group of leftists reciting it in a gaslit garage, argue the merits of a fellow actor's role, and sit in the last row of the Abbey listening to Yeats's verse play, *The Land of Heart's Desire.* And all at once his aversion to school dissipated. He attempted to enroll in Trinity College, partly as a device to change his visitor status to that of a quasi-permanent Dubliner, but was not accepted, because of a lack of formal prerequisite courses.

In addition to being exposed to the social whirl surrounding MacLiammoir and Edwards, Orson was also quickly accepted by other members of the company, Lord Longford, Betty Chancellor, and Denis Johnston. Betty told me that she remembered him as being "highly immature in any kind of sexual discussion or even in playing a part that called for a romantic side" but noted that even then his knowledge of the theater and his self-assurance were "immense." MacLiammoir was impressed with his ability to memorize and theorized that he used some sort of mnemonic system.

Although the plays at the Gate were often received with enthusiasm, the company had not yet generated the affection it would receive and continue to receive later on. MacLiammoir's *R.U.R.* performance had been acclaimed, but most of the Gate audiences considered the play little more than a crude melodrama about a robot. Still, it was impossible to discourage a Dubliner from the theater.

THE FIRST-NIGHT PERFORMANCE of *Jew Süss*, October 13, 1931, in which Orson Welles had his professional debut and the Gate its first American actor, was a sell-out event for the 400-seat theater, despite the fact that the film *Morocco,* with Gary Cooper and Marlene Dietrich ("At last! The talking screen has found its voice of love!"), opened at the Capitol in downtown Dublin the same evening.

The audience for *Jew Süss* was, if not feral, at least traditionally Irish; first nights in Dublin theaters have sometimes ended in near riots. Like an Elizabethan audience at the Globe, theatergoers arrived early and ate, drank, smoked, and talked while waiting for the performance to begin and continued, usually, throughout the duration of the play. "Speak up!" was a favorite cry of Dublin theatergoers from time immemorial, and directors always warned their actors that no matter what they said, they must say it with force.

Welles claims that he had nothing resembling first-night nerves simply because he didn't know any better. Of course, he did know, only too well; he had given many performances in the past. The difference in his role in *Jew Süss* was that he was being paid for it, a factor that might cause, rather than diminish, stage fright. Whatever his emotional state, however, it is a fact that he underestimated the spunk of the Irish theatergoer. On a BBC telecast years later, he described his flash of recognition of the dynamic of that audience:

> My particular period of nightmare commenced in Act IV. I was supposed to be playing an old man but I aged a good deal under the greasepaint when a terrible truth suddenly dawned on me—that an audience was not so much a complement to an actor's ego as a challenge to its capacities. I should have known that I was going to receive my first challenge very soon. After all, this was Ireland, where audiences take a sort of professional pride in unpredictability.

Betty Chancellor, playing Naomi, had just left the stage and Welles, as the wicked old Duke, was to look after her lecherously. "A bride fit for Solomon," he recited. "*He* had a thousand wives, did he not?" Just then a voice cut through the smoke and the audience, coming from about the fifth row of the stalls: "That's a dirty black Protestant lie!" boomed the deeply Irish brogue. The theater went dead silent for a moment as Welles first looked astonished, then intimidated, and finally bewildered. Thirty years later Welles revealed that he was still brooding over the remark and had not thought of an adequate reply. Somehow, he mumbled through the next few lines, the curtain fell, and Welles crept backstage in preparation for Act V. But now he had experienced the baptism of the theater: fear. By the time he returned for the final act, he was so nervous that he began to transfer an otherwise credible performance into something of an unintentional comedy. As if in a Laurel and Hardy film, his sword actually got stuck in his scabbard. At his crucial death speech he was to say, "Ring the bells and fire all the cannons!" Instead, his voice, no longer the sound of a perfectly tuned oboe but now the shrill of a teenage girl's, blurted out: "Ring the cannons and fire all the bells!" Before anyone in the audience could audibly guffaw, Welles, "in a mood of suicide," as he recalled it, but in what developed into a *coup de théâtre,* instantly flung himself in a sort of backflip, head-first down a flight of stairs. "I didn't care whether it killed me or not," Welles has said, but the act of theatrical desperation brought the house down in applause. "In all the striving years since my debut, I have never received such an ovation."

Orson Welles was now a professional actor. He had lived, though barely, through his first first-night, and as he bowed with Hilton Edwards at the curtain call, it was with more than a sense of pride and triumph. Chris Kiely, the Gate's wardrobe mistress, remembered that night and Welles's reaction to his ovation: "Such a playboy! God, he looked twice as big as life. Upon me soul. Oh yes, indeed. Such gas! Standing there as bold as brass and them lads out there in the front roaring for him, and him as stiff as a bloody roebuck." (She meant "robot," as she had been the costumer for *R.U.R.*)

And MacLiammoir has perhaps the most poignant recollection of Orson's opening night reaction to the audience's applause:

Orson swelled visibly. I have heard of people swelling visibly before, but Orson is one of those who really do it. The chest expands, the head, thrown back upon the round, boyish neck, seems to broaden, the features swell and burn, the lips, curling back from the teeth like dark tropical plants, thicken into a smile. Then the hands extend, palms open to the crowd, the shoulders thrust upwards, the feet at last are satisfied: they remain a little apart, at peace, set firmly on the stage. Then he bows slowly, sedately; that they should realize him like this merits a bow, so slow and sedate the head goes down and quickly up again, up higher than ever, for maybe this is all a dream, and if the eyes are on the boots, blood rushing to the ears, who knows that sight and sound may not double-cross and vanish like a flame blown out, and Orson be back at school again, hungry, unsatisfied, not ready yet for the world? No, the people are still there, still applauding, more and more and more and back goes the head, and the laugh breaks out like fire in the jungle, a white lightning slits open across the sweating chubby cheeks, the brows knit in perplexity like a coolie's, the hands shoot widely out to either side, one to the right at Hilton, the other to the left at Betty, for you don't mean to say that all this racket is for Orson?

Although he was out late that night celebrating his debut, Orson managed to rise fairly early the next day to get over to O'Connell and Parnell streets for the daily papers. Despite the incoherence and clumsiness of the death speech, the reviews were fairly unanimous in their praise, or anticipation of better things to come. The *Irish Times* said of Orson's performance that he made "an excellent Karl Alexander" and further: "It will be necessary to see him in other parts before it can be said that he is the accomplished actor that he seemed last night in a part that might have been especially made for him." The *Irish Press* reported that the "Duke was played with notable success by Mr. Orson Welles. He held the audience tense." The *Irish Independent* also called his performance "notable" and went on to state that despite the unpleasantness of the character, Welles gave the role "a touch of humanity and simplicity in his [the Duke's] swinishness which in less expert hands might have been lost. It is this quality that makes him tolerable. Orson Welles captured it magnificently, for he played the part with supreme naturalness."

After the opening of *Jew Süss,* Orson settled into the day-to-night life of the Gate and of Dublin. He met most of the Irish intelligentsia and was a frequent and much coveted guest at parties. In addition to his attractive flamboyance and his adoption by MacLiammoir and Edwards as their certified protégé, Welles was also something of a novelty in Dublin simply because he was an American: the Depression had reduced American tourism to Ireland, as elsewhere, almost to a standstill. Everyone in Dublin talked about Orson Welles as he seemed to grow into and nurture his role as *enfant terrible* of the Gate. Insolent remarks, charming rapport with both men and women, bizarre conversation, and sometimes scandalous, often drunken antics, elevated his persona into something of a modern-day Celtic legend. It's apparent now, after almost fifty years, how much the "young Welles," as he came to be known, meant to MacLiammoir and Edwards. He was mentioned in and was often the focus of their writings and interviews, and they maintained a theatrical relationship and deep friendship that spanned the decades with all three rotating in the roles of actor, director, or producer in a variety of projects.

WHEN ORSON COULD be convinced to leave the Gate—sometimes he would have to be dragged out—he spent time in the other theaters and some of the movie houses of Dublin. Unfortunately, the Abbey players were on tour during most of the time that he was in the city, and so he had little chance to observe or appreciate that great theater company. He ate at Noonan's, frequented the pubs, occasionally went to one of the few nightclubs in the city, and argued away some time in the cafés.

On one particular late evening, when Orson and some new friends from the theater were sitting in a downtown bistro, the famed actor and playwright Noel Coward entered with several companions. He sat at a table within earshot of Welles who could overhear that Coward's conversation was about his stirring new play *Cavalcade,* which he had written and produced and which had just opened in London. Great Britain had recently come off the gold standard, its traditional symbol of security, and British patriotism was at an extremely low level: *Cavalcade* was virtually a call to arms to support the Empire. The play had become a national sensation; King George V and Queen Mary had attended a performance and were moved by it. Coward had given a rousing footlight speech—by demand—in which he stated: "In spite of the troubled times we are living in, it is pretty exciting to be English."

As Coward and his friends discussed both the play and the state of the Empire, Welles misheard the conversation and believed anti-English statements were being made. Welles invaded the issue. With both brashness and alcohol firing his temper, possibly combined with a desire to be noticed, he stood and in a fiercely Anglophilic polemic, began to berate the theatrical elder statesman. Coward, not to be verbally intimidated by any man, even if he agreed with him, and certainly not by a teenager, no matter how bombastic, also stood and shouted right back. "Neither of us said anything in the least brilliant," Welles remembered, but both men recalled the incident years later and laughed over it.

One night, MacLiammoir suggested that everyone in the company not engaged in that evening's performance should listen to a radio broadcast by Yeats. Although no one can now remember exactly who was present, Orson was probably one of those crowded round MacLiammoir's Heterogram cabinet radio listening to Yeats's cultured voice, aired from the Belfast studios, deliver a revolutionary lecture on his new translation of *Oedipus the King.* The radio performance of the play was broadcast throughout Ireland, so that everybody "would understand as easily as he understood a political speech or an article in the newspaper." Calling *Oedipus* ". . . the greatest dramatic masterpiece of antiquity," he asked the radio audience to suspend their disbelief and exercise their imaginations. "You should try to call up not the little Abbey Theater but the open-air Greek theater, with its high-pillared stage and yourselves all sitting tier above tier upon marble seats in some great amphitheater cut out of a hillside." For the next several hours, the nation was quietly and magically transported to another age. The impact of the broadcast, on Ireland and on the fledgling medium of radio, was enormous. The power of radio drama, not quite as advanced at that time in the United States, but beginning to flower in the British Isles, was given an important thrust forward with Yeats's *Oedipus.* If Welles didn't listen to the actual show, he could not have helped hear *of* it, and it's altogether possible that Welles's later attraction to both radio drama and the popularization of difficult plays had its roots, in part, in that one autumn evening.

Edwards introduced Welles to an appreciation of truly fine acting and confirmed his interest in good cigars. MacLiammoir taught him the value of stage lighting—how to place it, how to play to it—the importance of Wilde and Yeats, the dynamics of expressionistic sets, and a love for everything Irish and poetic. Mainly, however, Welles learned more about the theater during his Gate days by working, rather than listening.

Jew Süss closed after a few weeks, and then Welles played in a repertory of varied roles, each of which allowed him to learn more about the craft of acting: *The Archdupe* (as both a French general and a Mexican colonel); *The Dead Ride Fast* (as tycoon Ralph Bentley); *Mogu of the Desert* (as Chosroes, King of Persia); *Death Takes a Holiday* (as Duke Lamberto); and *Hamlet* (as the Ghost and Fortinbras). MacLiammoir thought Welles was "the best Ghost" he had ever seen in Hamlet. Edwards, the director, saw the young Orson's faults more clearly and gave him a brutally detailed, albeit helpful, critique of his acting ability, as described in MacLiammoir's memoir:

> You've been playing Shakespeare, of course, I don't know where you've learned it, but you have more tricks and subtleties, more versatilities of voice placement, than the average actor acquires in a lifetime. You've got something fine that you'll never lose. You're already at the point a matinee idol arrives at when it has got on in years and people are writing plays around his little tricks and capers. But that won't do here. We have nobody to write nonsense for you to show off in. You have a gorgeous stage voice and a stage presence in a million, and you're the first overactor I've seen in eons, but you couldn't come in and say, "Milord, the carriage waits," as well as Art, our stagehand. You could put more somersaults into *Hamlet* than John Barrymore, and handle theatrical, very theatrical restraint with more delicacy than Matheson Long, but you couldn't say "How do you do?" behind the footlights like a human being. You handle your voice like a singer and there isn't a note of sincerity in it.

Strangely proud of the critique, and deeply moved that Edwards cared enough to provide such personalized instruction, Welles sent a copy of it to his guardian, Dr. Bernstein. He also took the suggestions very much to heart, working hard to improve his acting ability.

By the end of the year, Welles not only was acting, creating publicity, and assisting MacLiammoir with the painting and decoration of the sets of the

Gate but was also put to work constructing and painting all the scenery for the Peacock, an art-theater group that came to life in the Abbey's absence and was managed by the directors of the Gate.

Welles's performances continued to be hailed as highly promising. His Ghost in *Hamlet,* according to one review, had "seldom been presented more convincingly," and in *Mogu in the Desert* one critic mentioned how Welles used "his fine physique and great voice to advantage." His reputation began to grow even in the United States when J. J. Hayes, the Dublin critic, gave him rave notices in the drama section of the Sunday *New York Times.* About his performance in *The Dead Ride Fast,* Hayes said, "I have never seen on any stage a more true-to-life portrait than that of the wealthy self-made millionaire who, away from his field of activity, gives himself up with complete abandon to the enjoyment of the hour. Played by Orson Welles, the young American actor, Ralph Bentley came to life in convincing fashion." And later: "The *Archdupe* has raised the Gate Theatre to a new level of achievement. At the premiere, Orson Welles, the young American actor, scored heavily. . . ."

In an Irish weekly tabloid devoted mostly to sports, society, and entertainment, regular columnist Knowles Noel Shane eloquently championed the art of Orson Welles week after week and gave the young actor some of the best notices and reviews he received. The same columns, however, sometimes strangely ignored the rest of the Gate company. Why was Shane so partial to Welles? Well, perhaps because he *was* Orson Welles. Since Orson could not use his own name in reviewing his performance when penning press releases for the Gate as its press agent, he adopted a pseudonym. Most newspapers traditionally print notices without the publicist's name as a by-line, but the drama criticism of Knowles Noel Shane became a permanent fixture of this paper's editorial fare. As a consequence, the mythology of Orson Welles in Dublin continued to flourish. All of this activity, wrote Welles to Roger Hill, kept him in a state of "sweaty bliss," but his Irish theatrical apprenticeship was about to come to an end.

As soon as Welles found out that the Gate was going to mount a production of *Othello* in the late spring of 1932, he wanted to play the lead role. He knew that the character offered the auspicious possibilities of exhibiting what he was now beginning to feel as his particular acting strength: the portrayal of natural human emotion in larger-than-life situations. Additionally, Othello was on the stage frequently throughout the play, an attractive idea to Welles, who undoubtedly could see himself swathed and turbanned in togas and djellabas, each night heavily blackened, tortured, and torn, creating broad dramatic strategies in what he hoped would be a classical and memorable exposition of one of the great tragic figures in the history of the drama.

The soul and role of Iago were attractive to MacLiammoir, and he could easily have played the part with Welles as Othello. But Edwards vetoed the idea. He himself had every intention of playing Iago to his partner's Othello. MacLiammoir and Edwards had a certain sentimental attachment to both roles, in part because Edwards had been Iago to MacLiammoir's Othello during their first acting job together in 1927.

But Edwards's decision wasn't made just because of nostalgia. He realized that Welles was not yet mature enough to successfully master the complexities of the Moor's character. The actor who plays Othello must be able to display not only doubt, agony, passion, and fire but also nobility and tenderness; and these last two dramatic facets, Edwards felt, were at that time beyond Welles's scope. That Welles could electrify there was no doubt; that he could convince was much in question. Edwards, by then totally familiar with his young ward's range of voice and explosive temperament, understood that Welles's acting style and ability were not suitable for the part of Othello. He refused Orson permission to play the role.

Welles had no recourse other than to accept the edict, but he decided that it was time for him to move on to seek other theatrical opportunities. He resigned from the Gate in March of 1932. The nine months he'd spent there had an enduring effect on his life and his career.

CHAPTER 3

ALTHOUGH SOMEWHAT DISAPPOINTED about not landing the role of Othello, Welles left Dublin for London in high spirits and with a bond of friendship that connected him with the Gate company. He knew he was an actor of talent, and his heart centered now on England, the land of Garrick and Shakespeare, of Stratford and the Old Vic, where the art of acting was considered next to godliness. It was the spring of 1932, and Orson Welles was nearing his seventeenth birthday.

London proved to be almost everything, and nothing, that Welles had expected but oh, to be in England now that April's there, as Browning said. Like Paris and New York it was by far the best month for a first or a fifty-first visit, and Orson never quite recovered from his love at first sight. It was an actor's paradise with more good theater than any other city in the world, playing at that time the greatest productions of Priestley, Sherwood, Van Druten, Ibsen, and Shakespeare. Yet there was no room on the stage for the young American actor. It wasn't that he was unknown in London. Reviews of his performances and feature articles about him and his work at the Gate had drifted across the Irish Sea and had appeared in a variety of London papers. This material, combined with the favorable reviews that had appeared in the Dublin press, comprised an impressive résumé for any young actor seeking work. As he made the rounds of the Criterion, St. Martin's, the Lyric, the Lyceum, and other working houses, he gained favorable responses to his readings and informal auditions but could not generate a commitment to play. The problem, as it became clear, was not with Orson's talent or credentials nor with the theaters that showed interest in him. The Welles embargo lay with the British Ministry of Labour, which would not or could not permit, by law, any foreigner to work at a job that might be filled by an Englishman. During lush times, the authorities were known to glance the other way on occasion and permit an alien to work in England, but in those Depression days, almost any vacant job was doled out to an able and willing Londoner within hours of its known existence.

After several disappointing weeks, Welles made plans to return to the United States, hoping, now that he was equipped with more confidence from his Irish stage experience, for a staff position as a teacher of drama at Todd. Before leaving, however, he squeezed in a quick trip to Paris where he dined, drank, and attended parties with exuberance. At one affair, he had a fortuitous meeting with Brahim, eldest son of Si Hadj T'hami El Glaoui, the pasha of Marrakesh, one of the great lords of the Atlas and all Morocco, and one of the richest men in Africa. Brahim, who lived in Paris and operated as his father's shadow ambassador, was, at the time Welles met him, attempting to aid his father in the suppression of the first edition of a controversial book, *Son Excellence,* a 275-page journalistic vituperation that painted a portrait of the Glaoui as, among other things, a sexual orgiast, sadist, homosexual, and ogre. Brahim and his outraged father bought every copy of the book that still remained in the publisher's warehouse and then burned them. They also scoured bookshops all over the continent and bought all the copies they could find; whenever one was discovered in private hands, Brahim would offer to buy it—at any price—and consequently virtually succeeded in eradicating every copy of the book extant. Although Welles was not particularly in favor of these tactics of censorship, he was sympathetic to Brahim's plight, and he and Brahim became close friends. They made indefinite plans to rendezvous sometime in the future.

BACK IN ENGLAND, Welles wanted to meet and pay homage to one of his personal idols, George Bernard Shaw, before returning to the United States. Shaw was then seventy-six and revered as the greatest British dramatist since Shakespeare, a world-renowned playwright who, one might think, would have little time for an aspiring teenaged actor, no matter how talented. But through Welles's enthusiasm and perseverance, combined with some letters of introduction, Shaw grudgingly agreed to a rare audience.

They met in the old man's famous revolving study in his garden at Ayot St. Lawrence in Hertfordshire and had a surprisingly friendly visit. Despite the sixty years that separated their ages, Shaw and Welles found they had a few things in common in addition to their knowledge and respect for the arts: both had abandoned their common name, George ("I hate to be 'Georged,'" said Shaw); both had given up their schooling, and both had a contempt for formal education. "As a schoolboy I was incorrigibly idle and worthless," Shaw said, "and I am proud of the fact."

Shaw thought of himself as a licensed cosmopolitan and saw no real necessity to love the country of one's birth. Hence, he and Welles had a number of laughs about what Shaw considered the notorious bad manners of the Irish. Also, the playwright had recently been embroiled in a tiff, if not a controversy, about his political extravaganza, *The Apple Cart,* staged by German director Max Reinhardt. Shaw claimed that in the Berlin production, Reinhardt had taken too many liberties and changed the platonic narrative of the threat of the abdication of the King of England into a real bedroom farce with acrobatics in and around the bed. He was further upset when Reinhardt, without permission or apparent reason or rationale, changed the name of the play to *The Emperor of America.*

Welles talked to British journalist Peter Noble years later about his visit to Shaw: "He had real simplicity. I recall the way in which he received me, listened to my ideas on the theater, gossiped about Dublin and shared a joke with all the enthusiasm of a schoolboy. I remember his walking me to the gate as if I were as grown as he. Shaw was a great man and like all great men, essentially kind and simple."

UPON HIS RETURN to the United States, it was undoubtedly with a joyous stride that Orson Welles first walked the pavements of Manhattan's theater district, attempting to secure a part. His fondness for his own country had been reinvigorated, as it always was after he had been away from it for a while, and he was optimistic about his theatrical career. To be denied the opportunity to act in London was, under the circumstances, understandable, but he felt that he surely would be accepted as a lead "at home."

Unfortunately, he soon discovered there was no worse time for an actor to make an assault upon the boards. In 1932, the cruelest year of the Depression, thousands of playhouses throughout the country were closed, and most stage actors (or *players* as they were still then called) were unemployed; many New York theaters were dark, and the regular acting population had taken to other pursuits. There were only six plays open on Broadway during the month of August. The disastrous economy was only partially responsible for the decline in theater attendance; the rapid rise of the talking picture was damaging legitimate box office receipts as theatergoers flocked to movie houses in droves. Over half the nation was going to a movie once a week as Hollywood "offered a great bargain sale of five and ten cent lusts and dreams"—as John Dos Passos described it—to see such modern-day fables as *The Public Enemy, Grand Hotel,* and *Horse Feathers.* Marie Dressler, Janet Gaynor, Joan Crawford, and Maurice Chevalier were national stars that guaranteed over-flowing theaters. The films of Chaplin and Jolson were making millions. Garbo was already a legend.

The 1931-32 theatrical season was the worst year that Broadway had seen in decades. Even burlesque theaters, courtesy of William Minsky, were beginning to creep into the Times Square area, and dire predictions about the future of the American theater infiltrated dramatic circles. Plays that everyone believed would be natural hits, such as *The Breadwinner* by W. Somerset Maugham and *Payment Deferred* starring Charles Laughton, both successes across the Atlantic, were dismal flops on Broadway. Although the plays of Elmer Rice *(The Left Bank* and *Counsellor at Law)* managed to be well-received and attended, and *Mourning Becomes Electra* was the unqualified *succès d'estime* of the season, few plays were making any kind of money at all. For every successful production that year, there were four or five disastrous failures.

Although Orson had his sheaf of impressive raves from his Gate Theatre performances, there was little he could do about the dispirited state of the Broadway stage. The one Irish play that had made it to New York that season, *The Moon in the Yellow River,* written by Orson's colleague at the Gate, Denis Johnston, failed quickly. Perhaps the New York impresarios connected Orson's name to the Johnston play. Whatever the explanation for his lack of success, the final defeat came when applying for work at the Shubert brothers office, specifically for a part in Lee Shubert's production of *The Silent House*. Orson failed even to get past the snips and sarcasms of the office boy. In a matter of days, Welles was back in Woodstock, Illinois, somewhat bowed but glad to be among friends. His adopted Irish brogue was so pronounced that people like Bernstein had, at first, trouble understanding him. Within a few weeks, however, he reverted to his normal quasi-Oxonian accent and was eager to do some serious work.

Welles had long talked with Roger Hill of a play he wanted to write, produce, and star in, about the legend of the American abolitionist, John Brown. The young Welles was displaying his first signs of professional opportunism combined with an appropriate sense of timing: the nation seemed recently to have rediscovered John Brown, and a current of poems, novels, and biographies about him was sweeping the country, perhaps as a delayed echo from five years earlier of Stephen Vincent Benét's highly successful, Pulitzer Prize winning novel-in-verse, *John Brown's Body*. The gallantry and martyrdom of Brown and his gentle and eloquent plea to the court were of great dramatic attraction to Welles. He went at it.

On the title page of the playscript, Welles had written, "A play of the exciting days just before the Civil War, concentrating chiefly on John Brown, prophet-warrior-zealot—the most dramatic, incredible figure in American history." Orson could see himself leading the insurrection and quietly and dramatically going to his death upon the scaffold as the audience wept and cheered, finally carrying him on their shoulders to the town square. Hill wrote a first draft of the first act, enough to get Orson started on the project, and together the two sketched out a rough scenario for the rest of the play. They called it *Marching Song*. Then, with a suitcase of history books about the incident at Harpers Ferry and related times, Orson was sent to a summer camp, actually an Indian reservation at Lac du Flambeau, Wisconsin, where he spent months working the play into finished form. He was as incongruous as a peacock in a barnyard as he slept and wrote in an actual wigwam constructed for him by the Ojibwa Indians.

What he returned with was a 45-character, 10-scene, historical extravaganza, a Cecil B. DeMille epic for the stage, complete with blazing torches, exhilarant speeches, and four hours of colorful, Breughelian detail. To establish the locale of the scenes and the tenor of the times, Welles planned to project, before each act, stereopticon slides on a plain, traverse curtain. These views would blend into each other, kaleidoscopically, and would depict newspaper headlines and photos of the immediate physical surroundings, ending, in each case, with the exterior scene about to be opened. In two instances, live action was planned to be played in front of the screen; in all cases, while the images were being projected, popular songs of the period would be played by the orchestra. Both he and Hill felt that the play was not only inspired but good enough for a legitimate production. That others thought less of it, though impressed with Orson's promise, was temporarily ignored. Hill sent a copy of the play to his old school friend, Samson

Raphaelson, prolific author of such Broadway smash hits as *Accent on Youth, Skylark,* and the first talking film, *The Jazz Singer.* Raphaelson wrote back to Hill from Hollywood: "Stick with this boy! I damn near ruined my eyes with your dim carbon copy but it was worth it. Any three pages of this script sing. But any twenty pages fall apart. Tell your star pupil to either turn this into a novel or teach him that stage plays are tight little miniatures."

Failing to accept the coin of Raphaelson's advice, Orson, Hill, and Hortense took five days to drive to New York in early fall and, with unaccustomed flamboyance, rented a suite at the Algonquin Hotel. They felt this was the right setting for the proper entertainment of producers, moguls, angels, and other theatrical types who they believed would be clamoring to invest in *Marching Song.*

Since childhood, Hill had known Dwight Deere Wiman, originally from Moline, Illinois, and by then one of Broadway's most prolific producers (in association with William A. Brady, Wiman did *The Road to Rome, By Jupiter, The Damsel Cheek,* and others), and therefore gave him the first opportunity to look at *Marching Song.* Wiman was also a budding motion picture producer, and his corporation, Film Guild, had already released two films, *The Second Fiddle,* starring Mary Astor, and *The Lap of Luxury,* starring Wiman himself. Hill's idea was that if Wiman wouldn't consider producing *Marching Song* as a play, he might accept it as a film; their personal contact and Wiman's reputation of never taking more than seven days to read, decide upon, and set all production details for all the properties in which he was interested made him a logical first choice to consider *Marching Song.* After holding the play a few days, however, Wiman managed some words of encouragement but then kindly turned it down.

A number of other possible producers were approached and they, too, were unable to generate enough excitement over the play. The Depression was still affecting the theater and New York was caught in a defaulted turmoil; soup lines stretched all over the city. Although it was easier in some ways to mount ambitious theater projects, since salaries, cost of costumes and sets, and other expenses were at an all-time low (and almost everyone was willing to work for small wages just in order to have work), producers argued that there were enough plays written by well-known playwrights that could be produced rather than wager a chance on an unknown.

Orson still had hopes, however. The Hills finally returned to Wisconsin; Orson abandoned the suite at the Algonquin and moved into an inexpensive room down the street and continued to circulate the play and talk to anyone he could about having it produced.

Welles approached Ben Boyar, general manager of the famed Max Gordon hits, *Three's a Crowd, The Band Wagon,* and others. Boyar was well known on Broadway for being encouraging to playwrights, friendly to actors, pacifying to directors, and creatively helpful to budgets. Even though Boyar was gentle in rejecting the play, Welles was beginning to grow somewhat bitter; it was painfully obvious that the play was just simply not going to be bought. He wrote a letter to Roger Hill that, despite its tone of depression, was surprisingly mature, and indicated a strong resiliency by launching a new project. Since *Marching Song* appeared to be, at least then, doomed, he was already thinking of future theatrical horizons:

> I am aware that disappointments, it matters not how many, should in no way affect my confidence, but they do. Today, for example, it was not a shock nor a sense of failure, just the realization of a fact, the cementing of a proud conviction. I refer to Ben Boyar's returning the manuscript. I wasn't even surprised. He said, "It's a swell show. It makes good reading. It would be a good book. I think maybe it's even a good play. But that doesn't matter. It won't make money. It isn't a commercial piece. At least that's what I think." He thanked me for letting him read it, nicely, I thought, repeated himself, and said goodbye. . . .
>
> I got an idea earlier this evening (it's now half after three) for a comedy-drama, let us say, on the subject of aphasia. That's the medical word, isn't it, for loss of memory?* The idea, like so many others on ice, is merely embryonic.

Although the play on memory-loss never materialized, he did work on and complete another upon his return to the Midwest, *Bright Lucifer,* a three-act drama about a demonic adolescent, Eldred Brand, who not so coincidentally resembled the young Orson Welles. If other roles were not particularly forthcoming, as he had bluntly discovered in London and New York, he concluded that he might as well write parts that were exclusively tailored for his type, age, and personality. If the play was accepted for production, he wanted the negotiation to include a major part for himself.

Like the teenaged Welles, Eldred is an orphan, suffers from hay fever, smokes cigars, and is generally considered educated and brilliant, often quoting the more esoteric and profound observations of Nietzsche. He is an evil character, but his style and intelligence elevate him into something almost likable, a theme of characterization of evil-as-possibly-not-so-evil that intrigued Welles then and later.

Literary scholar James Naremore in his study *The Magic World of Orson Welles* believes *Bright Lucifer* to be a revelation of Welles's personality and the title to be a self-deprecatory description of his whole career. Naremore's observation about the autobiographical essence of the play is astute, but such delineation of Welles's personality as a "bright Lucifer" could not be predicted about his life until he had lived more of it. Naremore goes on to say that "*Bright Lucifer* is a curious blend of philosophical argument and Gothic fantasy, loaded with playful and sometimes troubled autobiographical references; it indirectly summarizes Welles's childhood and adolescence, and it foreshadows much of his later work."

If a dramatist's job is to keep himself out of sight, as some have argued, and to let nothing appear but the character, then *Bright Lucifer* fails because Orson draws attention to his own opinions. The illusion is damaged. *Bright Lucifer* was never produced. *Marching Song,* however, had at least one

---

*He meant amnesia.

production at his alma mater, Todd; a condensed two-hour version. It was favorably reviewed.

Hill was aware that after the disappointment in failing to get *Marching Song* produced in New York, and since there were no immediate prospects for *Bright Lucifer,* Welles needed a new project "to satisfy that constant creative urge." The school had enough printing equipment to publish professional-looking books, and The Todd Press, though dormant, had a history of self-publication. Why not use Orson's writing and sketching talent, combined with his and Hill's love of the theater and Shakespeare, to produce a series of books that would attempt to popularize the Bard's plays and show how Shakespeare should be read and produced? Orson, who had come to truly love Shakespeare when still a child, had recognized with surprise and then dismay that most high-school and prep-school students became haters of the Bard when they were forced to study and memorize long soliloquies or to become involved not with the depth and vision of the works but only with the dreary rhetoric of a dry textbook. In an attempt to infuse some passion into study, he wrote a poetic rationale in an introduction to the planned works:

> Shakespeare said everything. Brain to belly; every mood and minute of a man's season. His language is starlight and fireflies and the sun and the moon. He wrote it with tears and blood and beer, and his words march like heart beats. He speaks to everyone and we all claim him but it's wise to remember, if we would really appreciate him, that he doesn't properly belong to us but to another world; a florid and entirely remarkable world that smelled assertively of columbine and gun powder and printer's ink, and was vigorously dominated by Elizabeth.

Welles and Hill would be coauthors. It was hoped that the plays would be distributed to schools throughout the country and would not only bring them critical acclaim but also realize a modest profit. (The works were really promptbooks, carefully edited versions of the plays with Welles's added production notes.)

The first sketches that Orson submitted to Hill were heartily accepted. "Do you really like them?" he asked eagerly, filled with coltish insecurity. When Hill convinced him that they were fine, then Orson requested that he be allowed to travel abroad again where he could work on the plays alone, with more speed and without the intervention of friends or the Todd School social life. Brahim El Glaoui had given him a *carte blanche* invitation to visit Morocco anytime and to remain as long as he would like to rest, write, or play. In addition to his many holdings, Glaoui was vice president of The Hygienic Drink Company of Casablanca (actually Coca-Cola), and the family owned a large house, a mini-palace of sorts, in that city, complete with courtyard and gardens, staffed with servants, in which Orson was invited to ensconce himself. Although his inheritance was beginning to run out, Orson was determined to finance the trip himself, and by the spring of 1933 he was in Morocco, with a suitcase of theatrical history books, working on his new Shakespeare promptbooks. He wrote an affectionate and uninhibited letter, together with a poem, to Hill from the freighter he crossed on, giving his mentor a progress report:

> You'll find grotesqueries in my stage directions, repetitions and misfirings. You'll have to do a clean-up job. I'll be relieved when I can get this off in the mails. The mere presence of Shakespeare's script worries me. What right have I to give credulous and believing innocents an inflection for his mighty lines? Who am I to say that this one is "tender" and this one is said "angrily" and this "with a smile"? There are as many interpretations for characters in CAESAR as there are in God's spacious firmament. What nerve I have to pick out one of them and cram it down any child's throat, coloring, perhaps permanently, his whole conception of the play? I wish to high heaven you were here to reassure me.
>
> Mainly I just wish you were here. You'd love it! Everyone from the captain down is a real character and I can't tell you how out-on-the-ocean it seems in a tiny freighter wallowing in the wild Atlantic. Here's a crossing that's rare fun chasing the plates and cups around the mess and trying to keep chair and self within the shifting scene of the table. I tried to put some of it into verse:
>
> > Days now numberless it seems to me
> > We've lolled and wallowed in a lusty sea.
> > Time is a thing that used to be.
> >
> > The order and ascent of days is nothing now
> > A March-blown ocean mauls our plunging prow,
> > An acreage hysterical for us to plow
> >
> > Crash in the galley. Crashes are constant now
> > Shiver the empty "Exermont" from screw to prow.
> > Time is a thing that used to be.
> > The order and ascent of days is nothing now.
>
> Today for the first time it is fairly calm. There is only one other passenger beside myself. The radio won't work which is another blessing. It's all very Eugene O'Neill and salty. Quite the crossing of my experience.

Orson remained in Morocco for only a few months, but it gave him enough time to become re-attracted to the Moorish architecture; the heavily draped and veiled women who have only their eyes with which to invite; the couscous; the smell of kif; and the fabled *oifas* or banquets where dancing Berber women would weave their magic for hours on end. For reasons unknown, but probably because travel had, in addition to broadening his horizons, flattened his wallet, Orson left Casablanca by bus to Tangier and then took the ferry to Spain, eventually ending up in Seville. He had written some pop detective fiction for a few American magazines, using Bernstein's return address in Chicago and was surprised to discover all the stories had been bought for a nominal fee.

The idea of staying on in Europe as a writer appealed to Orson's romanticism. He wrote a few more stories from Seville and took to the serious reading of Ernest Hemingway's classic treatise on the corrida, *Death in the Afternoon,* which had just been released in Europe. It made Welles an instant aficionado.

Orson went to every bullfight he could attend and then began to take lessons in bullfighting from a matador at a nearby ranch. Although he knew he wasn't adept, he wanted to try his hand in front of an audience and had himself booked into a small ring as "The American."

His attempts and gestures were weak and clumsy and were poorly received by the public and roundly condemned by the critics. In retaliation or as a gesture of face-saving, he signed on at another ring as a picador: heavily padded, atop a huge horse, ready to take on the bull while sitting down on the job. Even here he was undistinguished, receiving a deep injury to his thigh after being horned in one of his first attempts.

BY THE SUMMER of 1933, he was back in the United States. Hill helped him find a small studio apartment, equipped with little more than a bed and a drawing board, in Chicago's slightly bohemian Rush Street section. Here, within walking distance of the Newberry Library, where he could do whatever research was needed, he worked relentlessly on the illustrations and stage directions for the promptbooks, taking only occasional evenings off to visit the World's Fair on the city's South Side. There he could meet Shakespeare in the flesh, so to speak, as a full-scale reproduction of the Globe Theatre had been constructed at the Fair and a half-dozen Shakespearean plays were produced in highly abbreviated form.

"To keep him out of trouble," as Roger Hill described it to me some fifty years later, he also had Orson help design and codirect *Twelfth Night* for the Todd School production to be presented at the Chicago Drama Festival that year. They would use Orson's promptbook as the official script for the play.

Orson came up with the idea, with Hill's modification of a production by Kenneth MacGowan, of a set with a twelve-foot-high book and pages that would be turned as each new scene unfolded. The point was to enable the audience to sense that literature, or drama, could come alive from its own pages and to give some subliminal promotion to the forthcoming publication of *Everybody's Shakespeare.*

Hill lent the boy his motion picture camera and suggested to Orson that he experiment with filming the play. During the dress rehearsal, Orson flooded the stage with even brighter lights and filmed nearly the entire play.

The print that I saw of Orson's *Twelfth Night* in Roger Hill's living room in Miami, a half-century later, was still perfectly preserved with rich color and quite professionally focused but without any camera movement, or pronounced flourishes or angles. It was simply shot from one point of view, perhaps from the middle of the tenth row of the theater: an amateur recording of the play on film rather than a piece of cinema.

Orson narrated this film by making a phonograph record that was to be played in accompaniment whenever it was to be shown.

Over the course of the summer, Orson produced thousands of drawings for such plays as *The Merchant of Venice, Macbeth, Twelfth Night,* and *Julius*

Caesar. Some of the drawings were not up to his own rigid and self-imposed standards, and he ultimately destroyed many of these. Over twelve hundred survived, however; more than enough to lavishly illustrate the entire series.

The *Macbeth* book included bold sketches—some of them close to full-page—of the three witches on the heath, Macbeth's imagined dagger scene, the march of Birnam Wood, Macduff's triumphal speech from the castle wall, and many others. They were precise and professional but with a spontaneous, relaxed look that made them especially attractive. Welles also included in the finished books a well-written and provocative essay on staging Shakespeare and the physical evolution of the Elizabethan stage.

The blue-covered, gold-labeled books were marvelous introductions to understanding and producing Shakespeare. In addition to Welles's work, Hill included a biography of the Bard, an essay on the quartos and folios, and an introduction to the play. The editions offered specific stage directions where Shakespeare had given little or none, or judiciously edited the long-winded or unnecessary pieces of stage business or dialogues that the Bard sometimes wrote. Welles's illustrations showed, for example, how to cope with stage readings, costuming, bits of action between players and even an occasional close-up of what kind of facial expression an actor should assume. One of the most interesting and helpful aspects of the books (in understanding Shakespeare) was the inclusion, before many scenes, in small type, of the actual passages of Holinshed's *Chronicles of England and Scotland,* from which Shakespeare took much of his source material. This gave the reader an opportunity to look over the Bard's shoulder, in effect, as he penned his lines.

In the *Merchant of Venice* book, Welles also contributed a series of sketches of famous Shylocks throughout theatrical history: Sir Henry Irving, Walter Hampden, Williams Charles Macready, James W. Wallack, George Arliss, Edwin Forrest, E. T. Davenport, Richard Mansfield, and David Walter Hampden, William Charles Macready, James W. Wallack, George Arliss, Edwin Forrest, E. T. Davenport, Richard Mansfield, and David that he had not given nearly enough: "There are a thousand Shylocks: grim patriarchs, loving fathers, cunning orientals and even comics with big noses." And with this he gave the sage advice that readers should play the characters exactly as they wished, the sketches being presented as a stimulus for experiment. Further: "This is a book of ideas, and whenever it inspires other ideas it will have value. Your idea is as worth trying as anyone's. Remember that every single way of playing Shakespeare—as long as the way is effective—is right."

To justify his inserting more complete stage directions, Welles referred to Shakespeare's economical *Enter So-and-So* or *Exit So-and-So* or the occasional *Dies,* which give little help to the novice actor or beginning director and which are without the benefit of the vast tradition of the art of stage business that had been developed over the hundreds of years since the plays were written. Stage directions in the Welles-Hill editions, therefore, were explicit for almost every line. In Act II, Scene 2, of *The Merchant of Venice,* for example, a piece of action appeared like this:

BASSANIO

(Noticing them for the first time; amused)
Gramercy! Wouldst thou aught with me?

GOBBO

(Bowing and indicating the place where he thinks Launcelot is standing)
Here's my son, sir, a poor boy—
(He falters, and Launcelot, also bowing, speaks up promptly)

LAUNCELOT

Not a poor boy, sir, but the rich Jew's man that would, sir—
(He stops in embarrassment; quickly, giving the old man the floor)
as my father shall specify—

Eventually, the books were produced and sold by mail order and to bookstores directly by Todd. Later they were bought for distribution by one of the largest publishers in the world, now known as Harper and Row, and issued in one volume called *Everybody's Shakespeare*. Ultimately, well over 100,000 books were sold for two-dollars per copy and were considered a huge success by educators, drama teachers, and students, and especially by Hill and Welles. The *Chicago American* said of *Everybody's Shakespeare* that "Orson Welles in endeavoring to unschoolmaster the Bard went a good distance in canceling the curse of compulsory Shakespeare." The *New York Herald Tribune* in its review of the book proclaimed it to be "a lifeline to Shakespeare."

Despite the fact that Orson was more than deeply involved with the Shakespeare editions, he found himself for once in his life, as someone remarked, persecuted by inattention. Although Bernstein and the Hills always had enough time and affection for him, now that he was eighteen he expected full professional recognition as a man of the theater. It was hardly forthcoming at that moment.

The taste of the Gate was still sweet; his failure to be accepted in his own country as either actor or playwright continually grated. He was beginning to feel that the theater in America *was* too difficult to penetrate and that maybe he should concentrate on other forms of writing. Since he had completed a great amount of research on the life of John Brown for *Marching Song* and possessed a broad understanding of the dynamics of the events surrounding him, he began considering a definitive biography of the life and times of the man.

It was at this time that Roger and Hortense Hill were invited to a cocktail party in Chicago's Near North Side at the fashionable home of Hazel Buchbinder. To elevate Orson's spirits, and perhaps his career, the Hills took him along.

Hazel Buchbinder was an enthusiastic supporter of the Chicago art scene and a composer (under the name of Hazel Felman), whose apartment was known as a *salon* where literary, musical, and artistic celebrities such as Carl Sandburg, Ben Hecht, Sherwood Anderson, Sinclair Lewis, and Andres

Segovia would meet to trade quips that might ultimately find their way into the next day's society columns.

One of the people Orson met there was Lloyd Lewis, drama critic of the *Chicago Daily News.* Lloyd Lewis had collaborated with Sinclair Lewis on *Jayhawker,* a play based on the life of General William Tecumseh Sherman. He and Orson talked a long time about their mutual interest in the Civil War, the older man occasionally giving advice on how a biography of John Brown could be shaped and sharing his opinions of the abolitionist as a historical figure. As more and more partygoers streamed into the room, the two men found themselves standing behind the grand piano. Another man, somewhat shy, who had not yet introduced himself to Welles but who seemed to be known by Lewis and everyone else, joined the conversation, and soon all three were talking of John Brown and the Harpers Ferry revolt. Eventually Lewis drifted away, and Orson was left with the newcomer and an awkward silence. Finally, the stranger gestured to the piano and asked if Orson played. "Yes, I do," he answered, "but not on the piano." That broke the ice, and the two were off on a lively conversation that ultimately revolved about the theater and Ireland. Slowly, through the substance and style of the discussion, Orson realized that he was talking to Thornton Wilder, author of the Pulitzer Prize winner *The Bridge of San Luis Rey.* Welles told Wilder that he was a writer, too.

"Funny," Wilder said, "I could have sworn that you were Orson Welles."

"I *am* Orson Welles," he replied defensively.

"But you said you were a *writer,*" stated Wilder with amusement. "Orson Welles is an *actor.*"

That one of the country's foremost authors would know his name was more than astonishing to Orson. He was dumbfounded and immediately wanted to know how Wilder knew of him. Wilder explained that he had first heard of Welles through his sister, who was a friend of the Longfords of Dublin. Not only had they sent clippings containing favorable reviews of Orson's acting but in their letters they had also praised the young, precocious actor from Illinois who was then delighting Irish audiences. Wilder had also heard of Welles through the columns of J. J. Hayes, whose Dublin reports to *The New York Times,* unbeknownst to Orson, had repeatedly mentioned and praised the young prodigy. It was the first that Welles had learned of Hayes's kudos. Although he had never seen a photo of Welles, Wilder explained, he inferred who he was by some unexplainable "jump of association."

Wilder, although only in his mid-thirties, had the tweedy air of a man of letters, a highly educated elder statesman's interest in the literary scene. Finding and nurturing dramatic talent was to him an enduring passion. He had "discovered" actress-playwright Ruth Gordon, among others, and now saw a chance, perhaps, to repeat the experience. Wilder suggested that Orson should continue to seek work as an actor. After all, he had proven himself in one of Europe's great theaters, the Gate. With some assistance in meeting the right people at the right time, he could pursue a professional acting career. For instance, Wilder knew that the celebrated and distinguished first lady of the theater, Katharine Cornell, one of the few major American performers to form her own repertory company, was about to go on a nationwide tour. She needed an actor to play Marchbanks, the young visionary poet in Shaw's comedy *Candida.* Welles had actually been mentioned for the part, but no one had known where to find him. There were also two other plays that were going to be performed along with *Candida,* and it was probable, if Cornell liked him, that he might be given additional parts in those productions.

Welles listened with growing excitement. How, he wondered, could he get to meet Katharine Cornell, to audition for her? Wilder said that he had a friend named Alexander Woollcott, who might be able to help.

Woollcott was a literary legend; author, and contributor to *The New Yorker,* drama critic first of *The New York Times,* and then of the New York *World,* and one of the founders of the Algonquin Round Table. He was perhaps best known by the American public for his radio show, "The Town Crier," in which each week he offered his opinions on books, plays, and issues, and during which he shared a wealth of well-told tales on everything from the adventures of Coucard, his French poodle, to the woeful story of a penniless acting couple alone on Christmas Eve. Woollcott was irascible and curmudgeonly. He was also one of the most influential cultural and critical figures of the day, his "yea" so coveted and his "nay" so feared, for he easily could—and did—make or break a play, a book, or an actor's career with a few sentences. He was flamboyant and irreverent; his customary top hat, cape, and cane, combined with his corpulent frame, were often the subject of caricature. Like Wilder, Woollcott was interested in unearthing new talent. One word from Woollcott to Katharine Cornell would gain the young actor an instant audition. But Orson would have to leave for New York immediately.

"Get on the train tomorrow," Wilder told him. "I'll phone Alex you're coming."

By late afternoon the next day Orson was on the Broadway Limited, arriving in New York the day after and checking once again into the Algonquin.

WOOLLCOTT TOOK HIM to dinner the first night in New York and was as impressed with Welles as Wilder had been, referring to Orson's voice as one of "effortless magnificence." They discussed their mutual dislike of the brothers Shubert, Orson for being ignored or rebuffed and Alex for being "locked out" of all Shubert productions after having written an insulting, and ultimately devastating, review of one of their plays. Within a few days, near the end of August, Orson was granted a meeting with Katharine Cornell's husband, director Guthrie McClintic, at his midtown Manhattan office. Cornell was in Europe, but McClintic had full power to cast whomever he wished for the remaining parts in *Candida* as well as in the two other plays that were to be part of the forthcoming Cornell repertory: *The Barretts of*

Wimpole Street and *Romeo and Juliet.* Welles hoped for parts in all three productions.

Although Guthrie McClintic had been working in the theater when Orson Welles was in diapers, it is not difficult to understand why, at first meeting, he was affected, then attracted to him. The recommendations of Wilder and Woollcott alone might have been enough reason for McClintic to pay extra attention to the young man seeking employment. After all, it was Woollcott who had been instrumental in getting Katharine Cornell the part of Candida with the Theatre Guild almost ten years earlier. He had done many favors over the years, written about her constantly, and remained a dauntless fan and a loyal friend. However, the fact that Welles had played at the Gate, could recite long sections of Shakespeare from memory, and had just completed writing four new promptbooks that were about to be published also argued for a hearing. And when discussing Marchbanks, Welles didn't damage his chances by being able to say that he had recently met Shaw in England and by being able to quote the great man. Additionally, through reviews and accounts from friends, Orson's work in Ireland was already known by the McClintics. Combined with the advantages described was the shock of his physical demeanor: very tall, very handsome, outwardly self-assured, and with a voice that even in conversation flowed over McClintic's desk, filling every corner of the office, permeating everything that it touched, sounding like the deepest, most melodic chords of a cello but with the strength and grandeur of an organ.

McClintic described Orson, after that first meeting, as an "extraordinary-looking young man with a beautiful voice and speech." Welles was hired almost on sight, a contract drawn up and signed by all parties. Eugene Marchbanks was to be his, as was Mercutio in *Romeo and Juliet.* Welles preferred not to play the stuttering brother, Octavius Moulton-Barrett, in *The Barretts of Wimpole Street,* feeling it too minor and undistinguished a part, but he accepted it, nevertheless, as a condition of being given the other two roles. With these three highly disparate characters Orson Welles would make his American professional debut.

Although Katharine Cornell had been phenomenally successful in *Candida* and in *The Barretts* in the past—the plays hadn't been considered as important works until she starred in them—she had never played, nor had McClintic ever directed, Shakespeare. She had been urged for years to try Juliet; now, in 1933, at the age of thirty-five, she felt that if she didn't confront the part soon, it would be too late. Hence her venture—and despite her slightly graying hair without wig—into *Romeo and Juliet.* The distinguished British actor Basil Rathbone, who had previously performed in twenty-three Shakespearean productions playing thirty-five different roles, was cast as Romeo.

Welles's knowledge of Shakespeare might have been important in getting the role of Mercutio: although not openly admitted, both Cornell and McClintic had great insecurity in confronting the Bard for the first time and wanted to surround themselves with as much help as possible. Having an American

Shakespearean "scholar," however young, in the company, added to their self-assurance.

All of the best *Romeo and Juliet* promptbooks were secured—David Garrick's, Maude Adams's, Mary Anderson's—and these, along with a copy of Beerbohm Tree's *Staging of Shakespeare,* became standard reading for all the serious members of the cast. With the arresting sets of Jo Mielziner and much trial and error by the actors, McClintic shaped the production into an elegant, precise, and strict interpretation. It was the first professional American production that retained all twenty-three scenes of the play; in order to avoid overtime, it was completed within three hours.

McClintic was so convinced of Welles's talent that he didn't insist on a formal audition. He assigned Mrs. Robert Edmund Jones, wife of America's most distinguished costumer and set designer, as Welles's coach, and rehearsal began immediately. Welles was allowed to use John Barrymore's personal copy of *Romeo and Juliet,* acquired by Mrs. Jones when her husband had worked with Barrymore on his own production of the play.

He was also given voice lessons by Margaret Huston Carrington, Walter Huston's sister, in her sumptuous Park Avenue apartment. Margaret Carrington was a singer who had damaged her vocal cords at the peak of her career and had gone on to develop a method of enhancing voice projection by utilizing breath control along with otherwise unused muscles of the throat and chest. In addition to Orson, she had also trained such distinguished actors as Lillian Gish, Alfred Lunt, and John Barrymore. Orson's voice, which seemed fully mature despite his age, already displayed great control, but he nevertheless learned a great deal about ways of conserving vocal energy for lengthy monologues and long runs.

During his time in New York before the company went on the road, Welles was the occasional guest of Woollcott at a dinner at Le Voisin or a breakfast at Woollcott's apartment overlooking the East River, dubbed Wit's End by Dorothy Thompson. In addition to writing and broadcasting, that season Woollcott had a play, *The Dark Tower,* written with George S. Kaufman, run for seven weeks on Broadway.

Once Welles had the opportunity of a partial reciprocation of Woollcott's freely given *cadeaux.* A friend of his parents, Cornelia Gray Lunt (daughter of Orrington Lunt, one of the patron saints of Northwestern University), famous for entertaining Nobel Prize winners and the like in her palatial lakeside house in Evanston, Illinois, was coming to New York for a few weeks. She knew there was a connection between Woollcott and Welles—she had met both separately a number of times—and with Orson's heartiest approval, arranged a dinner for the trio in her large suite at the St. Regis Hotel.

She was ninety-one years old, still beautiful, still charming, had an all-comprehensive memory, and seemed to know everyone in the world of the arts, science, and government. Welles loved the old lady. While entertaining in her home, Cornelia Lunt had the habit of sitting on a small stool, literally at the feet of her most interesting guest of the moment, listening attentively whether he was the mayor of Chicago or a teenaged next-door neighbor.

When she talked, the same attention was to be paid; she would raise a little silver bell from her tea tray and ring for silence; invariably the room would fall into an obedient hush. Cornelia would have her say, the bell would be rung again, and conversation between guests would resume.

Orson cherished his visits with her. She could cite explicit eyewitness details of life in America during the Civil War: her coming-out party was celebrated the year Abraham Lincoln went to the White House; in Boston she had attended the stage debut of Edwin Booth; she talked warmly and vividly of her meeting with Ralph Waldo Emerson. A dinner party consisting of the opinions of the loquacious Alexander Woollcott and the chronicles of the garrulous Cornelia Lunt promised to be an evening to remember.

Welles arrived first at the St. Regis, looking extraordinarily large dressed in a raincoat, with galoshes afoot, and just had time to greet his hostess when Woollcott also appeared. The suite was in magnificent disarray with books, magazines, copies of *The New York Times,* and other refuse of a cultural visit to Manhattan strewn about. The three companions, each separated by a generation or more—"the old, the young, and the ageless," as Woollcott described them—had no trouble entertaining each other for the evening. In addition to Woollcott's reputation as a raconteur, Welles, even as a teenager, was becoming known as a master of galvanic parlor-room dialogue. However, neither man had much opportunity that evening to display his conversational skill. Cornelia Lunt dominated the moment and left the two normally voluble chatterboxes in a state of silent awe. Aside from her poignant and slightly acerbic observations on the state of the current Broadway theater, she opened her antique Pandora's box of recollection with a story that held both men spellbound.

When she was nineteen, she had an admirer much older than herself, Alfred H. Louis, a slightly mysterious English Jew, educated at Cambridge, who had recently arrived in Chicago. Louis constantly besieged and flattered her with beautifully written letters. He had worked for the *Spectator* in London and, after that, *The New York Times.* Although she thought she loved him, that he was older and of a different religion prevented her from introducing him to her family; eventually her sister prompted her to discourage any further advances from Louis. Cornelia went away for an entire summer and asked him not to write; when she returned he had left Chicago and given no forwarding address.

Over the decades, Cornelia often thought of Alfred Louis, regretting her rejection. Occasionally his name would appear: author of a sonnet published in *Harper's*; a reverent description of him in Algernon Blackwood's autobiography, *Episodes Before Thirty*; a prodigious poem by Edward Arlington Robinson, "Captain Craig," recognized to be a portrait of Louis. Miss Lunt not only captured Welles's and Woollcott's attention but also commanded their hearts: that she remained a spinster all of her life after rejecting the one man she had begun to love or might have married was a narrative miniature with genuinely tragic overtones.

Both men became intrigued with the story of Alfred Louis and wanted to know more about him, but because Woollcott was scheduled to do a radio broadcast for "The Town Crier" show around the corner on Fifty-second Street, the evening was forced to come to an end. He invited both Welles and Miss Lunt to accompany him so they could continue the evening of talk before and after the show. Welles readily accepted, and Miss Lunt, still talking, accompanied the two men into the hall to the elevator. Just as the doors were about to close, she finished her story of Alfred Louis. "I have always understood," she said with great sincerity, timing, and dramatic flair, "that he was the illegitimate son of Mr. Benjamin Disraeli."

THE COMPANY'S TOUR began in a snow-bedecked Buffalo, New York, on November 29, 1933. And what a tour it was! Eight months, 17,000 miles, and 225 performances from New York to San Francisco, crisscrossing the United States and ending at the Brooklyn Academy of Music on June 20, 1934. *The Barretts* and *Candida* invariably played to packed houses, but the public was reluctant at first, even for a performance by the great Katharine Cornell, to attend and endure her Juliet. It had been over a decade since Barrymore's *Hamlet* had captured the attention and heart of American audiences, and Katharine Cornell's production would have to grow in reputation before the public would be lured again to Shakespeare. Eventually, however, the critics did hail her Juliet as glowing, one of the seemingly youngest ever seen on stage, despite Cornell's real age.

Welles's performance as Mercutio was not particularly noted, but Cornell was more than satisfied. "Orson Welles was excellent as Mercutio," she remembered in her autobiography, *I Wanted to Be an Actress.* "We were all struck by his beautiful voice and speech and always provocative acting methods. It was obvious from the time that he gave his first performance with us that he was a tremendously talented boy."* As Marchbanks in *Candida* he was flamboyant, loud, and funny, and he was usually given a rousing ovation by the audience despite McClintic's sour appraisal of his interpretation as "leaving more than a little to be desired." Some of the reviews of his performances were also less than ecstatic; a Denver publication referred to him as "a sea cow whining in a basso profundo."

As Elizabeth Barrett's brother Octavius he played a convincing stutterer and managed to evoke the reality of living at 50 Wimpole Street in the London of 1845. He needed his hair curled before virtually every performance, a tedious and time-consuming chore with the traditional iron heated over a gas flame. His solution was a permanent wave, acquired in a beauty salon. That course too had its drawbacks; he tried to make appointments when customers were few, but even so he remembers that people gathered outside the shop to sneer, or at least observe. Eventually the styling sessions

---

*Welles himself felt that he was "not a very good Mercutio and I should have been." At a seminar held in the late 1970s, he said, "I was terribly mismatched with Basil Rathbone. We represented two rather distinct schools."

became unbearable, so Welles resolved the problem, radically but effectively. He had his hair cut short. Ironically, no one from the cast, crew, or audience seemed to notice it with the exception of Katharine Cornell.

Because his heart wasn't in the Octavius part, he was, according to stage manager Gertrude Macy, only "adequate, reading his lines intelligently, but sloppy and careless as a member of that well-disciplined, strictly-ordered family." No matter what the criticism he received for of any of his parts, however, his voice was invariably noted as something quite remarkable.

As he had done at the Gate, Orson continued to show an enormous capacity for absorbing the total theatrical experience. This practice, combined with sharp-sighted powers of observation, helped give him a sense and understanding not only of his own part but of the complete production: the play as universe and his and everyone else's status in the scheme of things. He was interested not merely in the delivery and timing of the energy and cleverness of Mercutio but in the smallest details of everybody's role and stage appearance, in addition to the foot-candle intensity of the spotlights, the exact placing of the dagger, the amount of alcohol needed to thin out the company's supply of spirit gum, the problem of exit and entry traffic in the wings, the relationship of costume color to stage lighting, the number of tickets sold at any given performance, and even the replenishment of the cache of cough drops backstage or the quality of the take-out coffee from the café down the block. His seeming interference with every area of the production occasionally caused wounded feelings or outright anger among certain members of the cast and crew, whose terrains, they felt, were being invaded by someone far less professional. He made it clear to everyone—sometimes a bit too pompously—that he was interested in both directing and producing, as well as acting, and had every intention of doing either or both as soon as possible.

Members of the company remember him, sitting cross-legged like a Buddha in an upper berth as the troupe train sped west, telling them his plans for a bare-staged production of a modern-dress *Julius Caesar*. Although the principals and directors of the company found his youthful brashness amusing, if not challenging, he was not particularly popular with some of the more insecure members of the troupe. In an interview he gave at that time to journalist Willella Waldorf of the *New York Post*, he promoted the idea of himself as dramatist and impresario, stating that *Marching Song* was going to be produced at the Gate Theatre in Dublin in November. In fact, although MacLiammoir and Edwards had read the play, they had made no commitment to produce it. As he would do often in his career, Orson's natural brazenness and his hope of interesting a New York producer simply led him to color the interview.

Despite the sedate quality of the play's Barretts and the McClintics themselves—or perhaps because of it—Welles became something of the Peck's Bad Boy of the company, once describing himself as "noisy and faltering out of the age of innocence." According to one fellow member of the troupe, Orson slept until noon every day, went carousing after every performance, and occasionally participated in barroom brawls. He was almost always late for rehearsals, and although he never missed a curtain call, he often made it to the dressing room before a performance with barely minutes to spare for makeup and costuming.

During the company's week in Kansas City, perhaps as a need to produce an escape and certainly for the money, he rented a room in the city's seedy downtown section and put up a sign offering "$2 readings." With borrowed makeup, wearing a turban and robe from the troupe's costume chest, he went to the room each day to tell fortunes. He began with cold readings, general observations that apply to almost everyone: "You have a scar on your knee," or "You went through a great emotional change between the ages of twelve and fourteen." Then one day a woman wearing a bright red dress entered, and Orson blurted, "You've just lost your husband." The woman burst into tears, as it was true, which shook him considerably. "I believe I saw and deduced things my conscious mind did not record," he said in an interview years later. After Kansas City, he gave no more readings.

In San Francisco he caused a petty scandal late one night at the Mark Hopkins Hotel. After the performance, on a lark, he and another young member of the cast entered a restaurant in the hotel dressed in long sweeping capes, black ties, and tails, and wearing false mustaches. They talked with heavy accents, trying to convince the maître d' that they were foreign diplomats. The two boulevardiers looked like fugitives from a silent comedy but insisted on maintaining the ruse. They didn't know that Katharine Cornell and Gertrude Macy were dining together in a corner of that restaurant, watching the entire spectacle. Rather than chastise them in public, Miss Cornell left the restaurant and had a note delivered to their table instructing them to return the costumes to the wardrobe department and go home to bed, *immediately.* The next night they were called to her dressing room and severely reprimanded for jeopardizing the image of the company.

Tad Mosel, in his biography of Katharine Cornell, *Leading Lady,* tells of another scolding by her of Welles for some bizarre incident, as a result of which Orson wrote the following *mea culpa*:

> About twice a year I wake up and find myself a sinner. Somebody slaps me in the face, and after the stars have cleared away and I've stopped blubbering, I am made aware of the discomforting realities. I see that my boots are rough-shod and that I have been assertive and brutal and irreverent, and that the sins of deliberate commission are as nothing to these. This of course is good for me . . . just as the discipline of this tour is good for me. . . .

Despite his frequent mischievous acts and careless pranks (he once missed a train in the Midwest and was forced to charter a plane to arrive at the next city's performance on time), Welles remained with the company, turning in credible and creditable performances, honing his craft, patiently waiting for the company's June return to New York for his Broadway debut. Then, in the spring, he learned that the group's plans had changed. *Romeo and Juliet* was not earning its way in the provinces so Miss Cornell was temporarily dropping the production for the southern tour. It would be reinstated when the company reached New York, along with the *Barretts* and another play, and Orson was assured of the parts of Mercutio and "Occi" for his Broadway debut in the fall. Until then his services were no longer needed.

CHAPTER 4

WITH MOST OF the summer free, Orson Welles immediately returned to Illinois to pursue a project that had been long simmering: the inauguration of a summer stock drama festival. Without too much persuasion on Orson's part, Roger Hill consented to invest a small amount of money in the venture in the hope that it would help promote the Todd School and the town of Woodstock. Orson, now nearing his nineteenth birthday, was about to become a theatrical entrepreneur.

In addition to producing, directing, and starring in some of the plays himself, Orson wanted to attract two kinds of theatrical talents to Woodstock that summer: young, aspiring actors, perhaps even some potential students for the school itself, and more professional types who might be lured by the promise of a showcase production. The former group was relatively easy to recruit, but the seasoned actors needed a more delicate touch.

Orson knew that neither Hilton Edwards nor Micheál MacLiammoir had ever been to the United States and that both had said many times that they had a strong urge to visit. He also knew that the Gate was closed for the summer and that the two men rarely ever took engagements during that time. This meant that they were probably free but also might be reluctant to work. A trip to America combined with theater, however, was a plan difficult to refuse. Summoning as much of his charm as was possible to convey in a cablegram, he asked them to join him for the summer season at Todd and offered the part of Hamlet to Micheál and Tsar Paul to Hilton. He went on to tempt them with the description of the Victorian charm of the theater and town and promised that the experience would be a kind of holiday for the two actors.

There was much amused vacillation in Ireland. "It *won't* be a kind of holiday," complained Edwards. They had planned to go to Spain, Portugal, and Morocco, as they had for years, then to spend a month in Paris and a few weeks in London before returning to Dublin to start preparations for the Gate's fall season. "It won't be New York," he warned MacLiammoir, "or Washington, or Boston; it'll mean playing some little Midwestern town with Orson and a horde of stage-struck students." Nevertheless, it was Edwards who decided to accept Orson's invitation for both of them. After a three-week trip to Paris, they sailed for New York.

Orson met the *President Harding* as it docked in lower Manhattan, and he was filled with plans and ideas for a week's tour of New York for his two Irish friends before they headed west to begin rehearsals. Although it was barely two years since they had seen each other, the two men noticed considerable changes in their former ward. Since they had said good-bye in Dublin, Orson had been to London, met Shaw, toured with Katharine Cornell, lived in Morocco, worked on the Shakespeare books, and written two plays. Although he was not yet a force, he was becoming known in American theater. MacLiammoir noticed it immediately and observed:

> Now he had added to the swelling a new habit of towering. It was not only the jungle that yawned and laughed; a looming tree, dark and elaborate as a monkey-puzzle, reared above your head, an important, imperturbable smile shot down on you from afar.

The trio checked into the Algonquin. MacLiammoir and Edwards were interviewed by the press and the newsreel companies and later over the radio. It was a whirlwind week before they left for Woodstock, and Orson insisted on filling every spare moment of it in a sincere but exhausting attempt to help his friends see and do everything that one should as first-time visitors to New York and the United States. He escorted them to parties, films, and plays and even nudged them in the direction of some of New York's tourist attractions such as the statue of Shakespeare in Central Park, the area of which seemed as large as Dublin itself; the recently built Empire State Building; and the surrealistic and vaudevillian Coney Island.

When at last they reached the Midwest, the preparations for the festival proceeded—but not without problems. Orson had been attempting to get Whitford Kane of Chicago's Goodman Theatre, and who also was director of that city's Irish theater, to direct the plays. Kane's star pupil and colleague, Hiram Sherman, was to act in some of the productions. Both had tentatively agreed, and their names had been highlighted in the prospectus, but in the meantime Hollywood beckoned. Kane and Sherman were forced to back out at the last moment. Welles and Hill feared that the project would die aborning and that the students who had registered for the course in drama and paid a whopping $500 tuition might cancel. To their amazement not one cancellation was received.

To augment the tuition fees, fund-raising dinners were held in such places as Chicago's luxurious Tavern Club with some of the richest people in the Chicago Lake Forest area as guests and with Welles, MacLiammoir, and Edwards in attendance. Each event added to the festival's coffers.

The venerable Woodstock Opera House, a turn-of-the-century museum piece in the center of the quaint town, was secured for the festival. It was steeped in history—Count Leo Tolstoy and Jane Addams, among others, had spoken from its stage—and beautifully designed, with stained glass windows, a classic horseshoe balcony, stenciled and molded ceilings, and velvet drapes. It even had its own ghost. An actress named Elvira, who had once played there, now supposedly haunted the theater. She even had her own seat,

DD113, from which she reviewed each production and, if dissatisfied, caused mysterious happenings to occur. The theater was housed in the same building as the city hall and the town jail, so with the ingenuity born of necessity, the company converted the jail cells into dressing rooms.

Three productions were scheduled: *Trilby, Hamlet,* and *Tsar Paul.* Orson appointed himself casting director, and after dinner one night, in between mouthfuls of pie à la mode, he announced the parts. In *Trilby,* he would be Svengali. MacLiammoir would assume a part that he had done many times, that of Little Billee, and Hilton Edwards would play Taffy.

"But look here, Orson, I can't," Edwards said. "Why, damn it all, I should be six feet four, and I'm five ten."

"Never mind that," Welles answered. "You're right for the part. You'll be swell!"

"But I say—look here, couldn't we juggle it around a bit? I'll even play Gecko. Let me play Gecko!"

"I think you'll be fine as Taffy."

"But God in Heaven, what shall I look like in Piccadilly weepers?"

"I dunno—what are they?" Welles said.

"Well if you don't know, I shan't wear them," Edwards responded petulantly.

"You'll play it beautifully," Welles soothed, "no matter what you wear." And the matter was closed.*

For the title role, Orson had secured the services of Louise Prussing, a Chicagoan who had spent four years on the London stage, had played the part of Kate in *Berkeley Square* on tour with Leslie Howard, and had been featured in the part of the wife opposite Paul Muni in the Broadway hit *Counsellor at Law.* She was a proven professional and was liked and admired by everyone in the company.

The part of Angele went to a ravishing, blond, blue-eyed teenager named Virginia Nicholson, daughter of Leo and Lilian Nicholson, a socially prominent couple in the Chicago suburb of Wheaton. She was gaminelike and pencil-slender; she was also exceptionally bright and outspoken and had become a Todd student that summer through the urging of Hill's daughters Joanne and Bette; all three girls were students at Miss Hare's University School in Chicago and were involved in the drama society there. When Orson was auditioning Virginia and other Todd students for the parts, he asked if they knew anything about Shakespeare. Virginia responded with an impromptu recitation of a long passage from *Henry IV,* which she had just been studying in high school. Impressed with her apparent knowledge and her obvious beauty, Orson took a special interest in her, gave her a substantial part, made her an assistant stage manager, and rarely took his eyes off her flashing legs for the remainder of the summer.

Although it seemed strange and even slightly intimidating to be directing

---

*Piccadilly weepers, as they were known on the British stage, were long side whiskers sweeping down to the level of the chin.

his two former employers, Orson took to his new art with intelligence and sensitivity, often underplaying his own importance, sensitive to the difficulties of all the actors, gently helpful in interpreting action and motivation and only occasionally bullying someone into accepting his point of view. Having been directed by Guthrie McClintic on the Cornell tour, and remembering the masterful direction he had received on the Irish stage, Orson saw his new role not just as a director of action, but as one of gently helping his actors interpret and motivate their characters. At his best, he led and shaped his cast, helping each actor to master his lines, not just by cue, but by meaning and mood and cadence as those lines related to the entire scheme of the play. At his worst, he pushed too hard, was undisciplined about his own attendance at rehearsals, and sometimes could not or would not understand that some of the fledglings were unable to memorize or empathize as well as he.

Because of the intense heat wave that blasted the Woodstock area that summer, most of the actors wore bathing suits during rehearsals, which may have accounted for the sexual energy that permeated each session. In any case, there was hardly an absence or a latecomer to any rehearsal—except for Orson himself. He was both tardy and missing from time to time, only to appear later, smiling, and arm in arm with Virginia. MacLiammoir and Edwards would often stand in for him during those times, which may have caused the former to comment that Orson's direction was vague and indefinite and that he was filled with restlessness and intoxication.

TRILBY OPENED ON Thursday, July 12, 1934, to a sympathetically packed house consisting of Woodstock locals, relatives, and personal friends of the cast, members of the press, and a substantial number of "patrons," prominent Chicago and North Shore socialites who had lent their names and some cash to help promote the festival.

Welles's direction was thought, by some other members of the cast, to be partial and calculated to emphasize his own strengths. Drama critics, however, were amused by his energy and his masterful use of makeup, the latter no doubt influenced by John Barrymore's screen performance of Svengali, released in 1931. Whenever Barrymore, with a long, disheveled beard and padding in his shoes to make him look taller, exerted his mesmeric power over Trilby, the irises would fade from his eyes to leave gaping white holes, a makeup and acting trick that terrified the audience. Welles attempted to capture the ambience and appearance of Barrymore's Svengali. Charles Collins of the *Chicago Tribune* wrote of Orson's "lank, oily whiskers and Semitic nose" that totally disguised his real appearance, and continued with the observation that Welles was a youth "with a strong promise of a brilliant future." Lloyd Lewis, of the *Chicago Daily News,* said that he looked like "a composite photograph of a hoot owl, Abe Lincoln, Ben Hecht and John Brown of Osawatomie" and that so convincing was his performance that Lewis could only "quail and shiver." Welles added a horrifying Dracularian touch of fanglike teeth and pallid skin to the role. The audience was moved by some of Welles's better moments such as his classic line, said in demonic manipulation of Trilby's headache: "I have a better cure than music" or Svengali's dismayed, "Hast thou found me out, oh mine enemy?"

MacLiammoir seemed untypically cruel when he wrote later of his appraisal of Orson's role: "He could know nothing of that period of love, of intimacy, of Paris; even his fakes were on a titanic scale, his Svengali lacked grace and humor, he was a lowly barbarian."

If Orson knew of the dissension in his ranks about *Trilby*, it probably bothered him little. He was pleasing both critics and audiences with his heavily masked and weird-of-mouth rendition of Svengali and was quite aware that he was adding to his vogue; many famous actors had found their place in the theater by playing the same role. Even if Welles's direction failed to do justice to the atmosphere and mystery of George du Maurier's novel, his personal characterization was thought to be gripping and memorable.

In general, the cast members enjoyed working for and with him, although there were a few capers and practical jokes during the run of the festival, performed at his expense. One such *bon mot* concerned his nose. Orson felt that his short, somewhat puglike nose was attractive enough to be acceptable for his off-the-stage appearance, but for the theater he thought his nose was far too undramatic and immature. Since the nose is the most prominent feature of the face, the ideal theatrical proboscis, in his opinion, was one that could be seen, in perfect outline, from the last seat in the balcony, a John Barrymore nose that compelled notice, produced admiration, perhaps even awe, and might on occasion even strike terror in the hearts of the audience. Orson also felt that a corrected nose provided him a mask of sorts, something that would protect him from the slings and arrows of an audience; keeping his nose unclean was, paradoxically, his way of keeping himself *out* of trouble. As André Bazin once noted, for Orson to act without a fake nose was a little like acting naked in front of the footlights.

Orson also believed that the nose influenced, sometimes dominated, the meaning of the part. For the role of Svengali, Orson wanted his nose much larger and sharper, and he went to great pains early in the day, hours before the curtain went up, in constructing, for each performance, what he felt was a magnificently appropriate nose for his character.

He used traditional putty, kneading it with his cold-creamed fingers, molding it to the desired shape, covering it with hot water to soften or chilling it with ice to harden, continually pressing it over his real nose, examining it in the mirror until everything was *sans reproche*: the large-boned bridge, the depth and flare of the nostrils, the breadth and length and perfection of the entire organ. Finally, after an hour or so of strenuous creativity, the melted greasepaint would be swabbed on with a brush to duplicate the exact darkish pigment of the color that he would ultimately apply to the rest of his face.

When finished, the nose would be stationed in all of its sharpened and phallic splendor upon his dressing table, a small electric fan blowing on it to keep it intact and unliquefied from the heat, until such time as he returned to the theater for costuming and makeup.

Heaven had no rage, nor hell fury, like Orson's anger when he discovered, just moments before a curtain call, that the fan had been disconnected and his marvelous sculpture was ruined, a drooling pool of putty and paint, indelicately oozing off the side of his dressing table.

"Who ruined my nose?" he thundered backstage, so loudly that early arrived theatergoers could hear him from out front. The culprit could not be found, cast and crew attempted to conceal their snickers, and the blame fell to Elvira, the ghost. An improvised, much-inferior nose was substituted, and the performance was only a few minutes late in getting started that night.

After the first reviews appeared, together with elaborate coverage in Chicago society columns of who attended the performances and what they wore, going to the Woodstock Drama Festival that summer became *de rigueur* for the upper crust of the surrounding cities. An open air buffet dinner was served after the performance; candle-lit tables were spread all over the lawns of Todd, and it was an event of charm, gentility, and grace to which audience and cast were happy to become accustomed.

Everyone in the company could see that Orson and Virginia Nicholson had fallen in love. She had promised her parents she wouldn't do so, but Orson threw himself at her with the force of a medicine ball and the charm of a June rose. She succumbed. Virginia's parents became vigilant about her activities and were, as a result, often in the audience and on the campus with one pair of eyes supervising her and the other appraising Orson. When Virginia announced that she was not going to cooperate in having her "coming-out" party that summer because she was too busy rehearsing, her parents were forced, with much disappointment and anger, to cancel the debut.

Hortense Hill knew that Virginia and Orson were spending all their time away from the theater "getting that way," as she explained it, and did everything she could do to keep them from drifting off alone and unsupervised. Orson now was somewhat of an experienced man of the world who made no secrets about his interest in and infatuation with women. Hortense had every intention of protecting Virginia's innocence and the honor of the school. Oddly, it was partially because of this solicitousness on Horty's part to avoid a Todd scandal that Orson came to make his first motion picture.

William Vance, a tall, good-looking college student from Freeport, Illinois, who was given principal parts in all three plays, had come to Todd that summer equipped with a 16-millimeter camera and much enthusiasm to film everything in sight—any happening, social or dramatic, that occurred on campus. Vance had shot several homemade feature films in the past, including a ten-minute version of *Dr. Jekyll and Mr. Hyde* in 1932; now as a spur-of-the-moment inspiration, he and Orson decided they wanted to do a short silent feature together. They chose a day when there were neither rehearsals nor a performance. Virginia was one of the performers, as was Orson, a young hopeful named Edgerton Paul, and Blackie O'Neal (the grandfather of screen actor Ryan O'Neal). There was even a small part for Vance, the cameraman, during which time Orson did the filming.

Permission to do some of the shooting inside the Hills' home was sought, with Hortense readily agreeing. She told me in fact, that she had encouraged the entire project but not for artistic reasons: it gave her more time to chaperone Orson and Virginia, and she could also act as referee whenever the onstage clinches of the two lovers became too frequent or prolonged. Hortense served as costumer, helped with the makeup and, with some admonition, loaned her treasured silver candelabrum, a family heirloom, to Orson to serve as one of the props.

The film was called *Hearts of Age.* There was no script, just a general plan as to what to do, often interrupted with an instant change of direction. "Hey, let's shoot . . ." Orson would then name one thing or another, and they would create a scene on the spot.

The two young filmmakers might have had some idea of a plot but it is difficult, looking at the film now, to see how one scene or piece of action connects with another, let alone to understand the film's nuances of substance.

The opening shot shows a Christmas tree ball and then a Father Time figure walking past. This is followed by a close-up of bells ringing and then a shot of an old lady (played by Virginia with grotesque makeup), rocking back and forth. Welles, bald-pated, leers and prances and looks Dickensian at some moments and like the mad physician in *The Cabinet of Dr. Caligari* at others. There are gravestones, lighted candles, an eerie piano scene with a coffinlike bench, skulls, and a black-faced bell ringer. It is all amateur and crude and funny, but film historian Joseph McBride sees many flourishes in *Hearts of Age* that point to Welles's later work in film. He mentions cinematic touches in it drawn from *Nosferatu, The Phantom of the Opera,* and *The Cabinet of Dr. Caligari.*

However, although the film is worth noting as one of Welles's first experiences with constructing a motion picture, it cannot be considered as an important example of his ultimate craft. "It was a Sunday afternoon home movie that we did between two and five in the afternoon," Orson said bemusedly years later in an interview for the BBC. "I don't know how it has entered the *oeuvre.*" Later in his life, Welles told Joseph McBride (who was responsible for unearthing the film*) that it was a parody of the avant-garde, surrealistic films of the day, especially Cocteau's *Blood of the Poet.* In its expressionistic lighting, unsubtle symbolism, and baroque camera angles, it does somewhat suggest films of that genre.

Tolstoy's entries in his diary at eighteen or Dylan Thomas's *Hymn of Despair and Hope* at nineteen, for example, show more pronounced commitments to their tasks at hand than does Welles's four-minute dalliance in cinema. It is, nevertheless, a delightful artifact providing a quick glance at the dreams of the adolescent father of the filmmaker to come.

Because of Orson's increasing involvement with Virginia Nicholson, he asked Hilton Edwards to both direct and produce Merejkowski's *Tsar Paul* and *Hamlet,* with himself playing Claudius in the latter play and Count Pahlen in the former. When actors of the old Shakespearean tradition play Claudius, often they rely heavily upon the one scene that shows the King as

---

*As a part of the Vance collection at the Greenwich, Connecticut, Public Library.

something less than a "mildewed ear, blasting his wholesome brother" or a "remorseless, treacherous, lecherous villain." When Claudius tames the mutinous Laertes during the time of imminent danger to his own life and delivers the line "there's such divinity doth hedge a king that treason can but peek to what it would," most Shakespeareans would play it to the gallery as their most crucial moment in the limelight. However, Welles took that same speech and molded it into something distinctly his own, making the King look even more like a manipulative scoundrel.

Charles Collins of the *Chicago Tribune* said of Welles's novel treatment: "Trembling inwardly, he pours out his only rhetoric and bluffs Laertes into submission. This is a new idea, cleverly carried out and it deserves a cheer." Drama critic Claudia Cassidy, of the *Chicago Journal of Commerce,* wrote: "Welles's King Claudius thumbed a flat nose at convention, achieving a make-up somewhere between an obscene old woman and the mask of lechery that visits Doctor Faustus at the Old Globe. Mr. Welles's rich voice, however, is his passport to stardom."

Only the society columnist of the *Chicago Sun Times,* Mrs. Henry Field, was indefinite about the performance: "Orson Welles departed from the orthodox King and we have not yet decided exactly what we think of his new departure."

During the course of the summer, Orson, together with MacLiammoir and Edwards, and sometimes accompanied by Virginia and others, often made the seventy-mile trip into Chicago to visit the World's Fair, dine at the Drake and some of the city's other fine restaurants, attend plays at the McVickers or the Studebaker Theater, and generally cavort with the Irish community and the city's theatrical society. For the remainder of his life, Chicago always remained as Orson's symbol of the really big city, as he once described it.

One hot night, July 22, became especially memorable as all three men sat in Chicago's Biograph Theater on Lincoln Avenue watching the film *Manhattan Melodrama.* Loud explosions from the street, sounding like firecrackers, could be heard but the three actors didn't know what had happened until they emerged almost two hours later. John Dillinger, America's Public Enemy No. 1, had been to see the same film, was "fingered" by his girlfriend, and was cornered by the FBI and shot down in the alley right next to the Biograph when he had left the theater and attempted to escape. MacLiammoir was still seemingly shaking with fear when he told me this story some five decades later.

Toward the end of the Woodstock summer theater festival, Orson, Virginia, and a few members of the company were passing the time of night talking in the Spring House, a gazebo in the town square that was a favorite gathering spot on summer evenings for the young people of the area. In full earshot, Orson proposed marriage. Virginia hesitatingly accepted. Although she needed her parents' legal approval since she was only eighteen (and Orson nineteen), she thought it would be forthcoming. Actually, their consent was only begrudgingly given, as the Nicholsons felt that an actor, no matter how talented or attractive, was not the kind of person they wanted their daughter to marry. "Don't put your daughter on the stage, Mrs. Worthington. Don't put your daughter on the stage!" warned Noel Coward in song, and the Nicholsons concurred, believing that the play was not necessarily the thing at all; their daughter was becoming far too interested in the theater, and they tried to discourage her. Marriage to Orson would never allow her to enter the society to which they felt she belonged. Their concern, however, was mixed with some pride when she appeared in *Trilby,* enough so that they organized a theater party of their friends and relatives to see her.

Before the festival ended, a quick production of the uproarious, tear-jerking *The Drunkard, or, The Fallen Saved,* was mounted, with Orson playing a small part. The play was done in virtual homage to MacLiammoir and Edwards, since they had been curious about it ever since Charlie Chaplin had once described it as the funniest play he had ever seen.

Written by William H. Smith and "another gentleman," *The Drunkard* had been an American favorite ever since its first production in the 1880s; its cast of loafers, bumpkins, maniacs, and spinsters touched upon the themes that a Victorian audience loved: villainy foiled and virtue rewarded. The Woodstock theatergoers got into the spirit with hissing, booing and applauding at appropriate scenes. Choruses of "Little Brown Jug" and other standbys were sung by cast and audience during scenes, and the evening was a miscellany of pure Gothic Americana.

The Woodstock version proved to be so hilarious and charming to MacLiammoir and Edwards that it found its way into their Gate repertory in Dublin the next season.

IN MID-OCTOBER, ORSON left Woodstock to rejoin the Katharine Cornell company in Detroit. The company had reduced its repertory to performances of *Romeo and Juliet* at that point, with the hope of styling it into perfection before arriving in New York. Their announced Broadway schedule was to include six weeks of *Romeo and Juliet,* six of *The Barretts of Wimpole Street,* six of *Candida,* and six of a new play by John Van Druten, *The Flowers of the Forest.*

Just before what was to be Orson's grand entry on the New York stage, he was greeted with what he considered to be devastating news. His part of Mercutio had been given to motion picture star Brian Aherne, who was eager to play the role and was between engagements. It wasn't that Welles was not a satisfactory Mercutio, he was assured, but that Cornell felt that she needed Aherne as Robert Browning in *The Barretts of Wimpole Street* since they had played the same parts in 1931 and were hailed a success. As a prerequisite to Aherne's negotiations in accepting the part of Browning, he had insisted that he be given a Shakespearean role; Mercutio was the only part that was contractually available. So eager was Aherne to play Shakespeare, that he accepted Orson's beginner's salary, an amount much less than the one to which he was accustomed.

On November 20, Orson's and Virginia's engagement was announced. Actually they had already been secretly married (although most close friends and relatives knew about it) and were to be publicly wed in New York soon after Orson opened on Broadway.

As recompense for losing the part of Mercutio, Welles was offered two parts in *Romeo and Juliet,* albeit smaller than the one he'd had: that of Lady Capulet's nephew, Tybalt, and the other as the Chorus. Although neither character was as important as Mercutio, he accepted the parts anyway. He was determined to act on Broadway and felt that if he refused the two smaller parts he would have simply been out of a job.

Orson was furious about having to accept these lesser roles, however. One of the conditions offered him when he joined the company was that he would make his Broadway debut in a fairly substantial part. Virginia told theater historian Richard France years later: "Orson thought Brian Aherne was a terrible actor and very much resented losing Mercutio to him. He made Tybalt outstanding, however, and the change of roles didn't hurt him at all."

Aherne, in his autobiography, *Act II,* shares different feelings. He remembered: "Orson seemed friendly and good-natured about losing Mercutio but secretly, I am sure, the actor in him could never forgive me. In the famous duel scene I often had the impression that he slashed at me with unnecessary venom and twice he broke my property sword off at the hilt, leaving me defenseless."

As both carrot and balm, McClintic promised that Orson's name would be printed twice in the program, first as Tybalt along with the rest of the cast and then separately at the bottom below the regular credits, as the Chorus. From that moment on, however, the names of Brian Aherne and Guthrie McClintic were rarely mentioned by Orson with any feeling of pleasantness or friendship. *Romeo and Juliet* opened at the ornate Martin Beck Theater in New York on December 20, 1934, and ran for its scheduled twenty-one performances.

McClintic felt that Welles's performances were strong and was quite poetic in describing the young actor in his memoir, *Me and Kit:* "Before our beautiful sage-green curtains with the crest of the Capulets embroidered on one side and the Montagues' on the other, Orson—resplendent, shielding his face with a gold Benda mask—came through and in his magnificent voice began the Prologue: 'Two households both alike in dignity. . . .' When he finished, his spot dimmed out, the curtains parted and there was the first scene exactly as I had wanted it to be. . . ."

Romeo and Juliet played to packed houses every night and might have been directly responsible for a resurgence of interest in Shakespeare in the American theater of the mid-1930s. There soon followed John Gielgud's *Hamlet* and Maurice Evans's *Richard II* and *Hamlet.* That Orson, as a strolling player, helped reincarnate the Bard for American audiences there is no doubt; the credit, however, fell elsewhere.

Although Orson's dual performance received some adequate notices, he was subordinated to the glowing publicity that saluted Katharine Cornell, Basil Rathbone, and Brian Aherne. *The New York Times* referred to the opening night production as being "a high place of modern magnificence—

another jewel on the cheek of the theater's night," but there was hardly a mention of Orson. John Mason Brown's review in the *New York Post* must have hurt: Orson's Tybalt was deemed merely "passable" while Aherne's Mercutio was the "best" that Brown had ever seen. The review in the *New York Sun* also praised Aherne's performance, stating that his dash and sprightliness helped to light up the stage; neither Orson's name nor a critique of his feline interpretation of Tybalt nor his mellifluous introduction appeared in the review.

However, at least one member of the first-night audience was electrified by Orson's performance. John Houseman, the patrician, well-spoken, thirty-two-year-old director who had gained notoriety for mounting Gertrude Stein and Virgil Thomson's avant-garde opera, *Four Saints in Three Acts,* was virtually mesmerized by the vision of Tybalt, which he believed elevated Welles to almost a reincarnation of Thespis, a modern dramatic deity. All the excellent performances of Katharine Cornell and the rest of her main characters were blotted out for Houseman,

> When the furious Tybalt appeared suddenly in that sunlit Verona square: death, in scarlet and black, in the form of a monstrous boy—flat-footed and graceless, yet swift and agile; soft as jelly one moment and uncoiled, the next, in a spring of such furious energy that, once released, it could be checked by no human intervention. What made this figure so obscene and terrible was the pale, shiny child's face under the unnatural growth of dark beard, from which there issued a voice of such clarity and power that it tore like a high wind through the genteel modulated voices of the well-trained professionals around him. "Peace! I hate the word as I hate Hell!" cried the sick boy, as he shuffled along, driven by some irresistible interior violence to kill and soon, himself, inevitably, to die. Orson Welles' initial impact—if one was sensitive or allergic to it—was overwhelming and unforgettable.

So believable was Orson's performance that he made the audience really hate him. "He was like a great spitting cat with his claws out," actor George Coulouris said of his performance. "His impact on the stage was quite terrifying."

Houseman was backstage after the performance to offer his congratulations to the principals and had an eye peeled for Welles for special commendation. But Orson had left the theater hurriedly that night. He was to join his bride-to-be and a group of friends and Virginia's relatives at a late evening celebration of both his opening night on Broadway and his impending marriage. The ceremony was the following day.

Despite, or because of, a love-hate relationship with Maurice Bernstein, Orson selected him as best man; Virginia's maid of honor was her youngest sister, Caryll. This second, public wedding had all the trappings of a society affair and was duly reported with properly formal photographs and punctilious description in the social columns of most of the New York and Chicago newspapers. It was held in Llewellyn Park, New Jersey, at the lovely suburban home of Virginia's godmother, Mrs. Herbert Gay, a lifelong friend of the Nicholsons. Virginia was dressed in traditional white satin, carrying orchids; Orson, garbed in morning coat, looked taller and handsomer than usual. All the people most important to Orson's life were there: in addition to Maurice Bernstein there were Roger and Hortense Hill, Thornton Wilder, Alexander Woollcott, Katharine Cornell, and, despite the feelings of enmity, Guthrie McClintic. Virginia's side was represented with a contingent of friends and relatives and by the day's end, the Nicholsons felt that their daughter had been properly delivered from their careful hands into the bonds of matrimony. The young couple seemed to be genuinely in love, and, although some people felt Virginia was a bit too fragile for Orson's oftentimes tempestuous behavior, it was still looked upon as a good match.

Mr. and Mrs. Orson Welles lived in a variety of places after their brief honeymoon at Blind Brook Lodge in Rye, New York. Their choice of homes was dictated by problems with sagging finances and the desire to be closer to the activities and atmosphere of the theater: a small house in New Rochelle; the Hotel Mansfield on West 44th Street; a one-room apartment on Riverside Drive.

ONE EVENING, AFTER being "slain" on stage, sitting half-garbed in his dressing room awaiting the curtain call and working on a new version of *Bright Lucifer,* Orson had a visit from John Houseman. It was their first meeting. Houseman was not yet a cult figure, but his name was not unknown to Welles or to the intelligentsia of the New York theater. *Four Saints in Three Acts,* which was really about fifteen saints in four acts, contained no story, no plot, no development, but it was, nevertheless, a work of art. The critical establishment clucked loudly; Welles had taken notice. When Burns Mantle, one of New York's grand men of drama criticism, panned it, a certain outré reputation resulted: "Colored cast against a cellophane setting representing visionary Spain. Libretto incomprehensible."

Houseman attempted to enlist Welles's interest in a new and different theatrical project. The distinguished poet and Pulitzer Prize winner Archibald MacLeish had written *Panic,* a verse play with a social message, and his partner, Nathan Zatkin, and Houseman were about to produce and direct it through their newly founded and insignificantly financed Phoenix Theater. It was to be a play of angry mobs, long shadows, blank faces, the poetry of heroic themes. The idea of *Panic* was to attempt to capture the tragedy of the stock market crash of 1929 and the ensuing Depression, not through the eyes of the poor and downtrodden, as Elmer Rice had done and Clifford Odets would do, but through the story of the men at the top of the industrial spectrum. *Panic* would be a play about a tycoon named McGafferty, the leading financier of his time, who, during the U.S. banking crisis of 1933, experiences the destruction of his personal world, which he has so successfully dominated. He desperately attempts to persuade his financial colleagues to pool their reserves in order to prevent the panic, but he is totally unsuccessful. McGafferty's confidence is also shattered by the death of Immelman, his assistant, and despite the love of his mistress, he eventually kills himself: in MacLeish's words, "with grandeur; with the demise of a noble loser."

MacLeish seemed to be the perfect artist to create such a play; an attorney with a Yale law degree and then an editor of *Fortune* magazine, he understood the corporate mentality. The problem with the play was with its casting; McGafferty, the lead, had to be larger than life, something of a J. P. Morgan, John D. Rockefeller, and Andrew Carnegie all rolled into one. Houseman and Zatkin had initial dreams of securing the likes of Edward G. Robinson, Paul Muni, or Alfred Lunt for the starring role; however, their impecunious treasury and the general unavailability of well-known names precluded the possibility of a big star, and they were forced to look elsewhere. Orson was immediately interested in the idea of the play and, after a few drinks with Houseman at a local bar where they got to know each other a little better, took the script home that night to read.

Barely twelve hours later, Orson was on the telephone to Houseman, announcing that he wanted to play McGafferty. The verse was, he felt, a superb coordination of rhythm and meaning, form encountering and affecting content; the sensuousness and beat of the poetry and the intellectuality or meaning of the play converging harmoniously to build and enhance one another. Despite the fact that McGafferty was in his late fifties, Welles knew he could not only play the role but dominate it and bring it alive. With proper makeup, as he had worn in *Jew Süss, The Dead Ride Fast,* and *Hamlet,* for example, he could easily be made to look like an older man. Aging gestures and mature stentorian tones were almost natural movements and effects to him. If necessary, he told Houseman, he could give two weeks' notice to the Cornell company. Houseman describes the audition:

> Twenty-four hours later I saw MacLeish's eyes narrow in exasperation as a tall nineteen-year-old boy in gray pants and a loose tweed jacket, followed by a delicious child with blond, reddish hair and ivory skin, entered our bare one-room office over the Burlesque house to read the role of the aging tycoon, McGafferty. I gave him the hardest part first: the last despairing phase when McGafferty, harried and weakened with fear, becomes convinced, through the suicide of his trusted associate, that his own end had come ... sitting stiffly in that small grimy office (with only two wooden chairs, so that Zatkin and I sat on the floor with our backs against the wall), hearing that voice for the first time in its full and astonishing range, MacLeish stared incredulously. It was an instrument of pathos and terror, of infinite delicacy and brutally devastating power ... the poet had heard his play—including the choruses—read as he would never hear it again.

Orson was, of course, given the part and rehearsals began soon after and Virginia was signed on as assistant stage manager. He was joined by a company of theatrical luminaries so bright that the combination of play, playwright, cast, and crew pointed to the possibility of one of New York's most exciting cultural events of the season. James Light of Provincetown

Playhouse fame was secured as director; Jo Mielziner, thought of as one of the theater's most able artists, designed the sets; Martha Graham, with her special, magical form of discipline was taken on to choreograph the group scenes; Virgil Thompson supplied the Satie-like music; the principal parts other than McGafferty went to experienced men and women of the stage, many from the Group Theater.

The almost antique Imperial Theater was secured for *Panic,* and only three performances were scheduled: a preview performance for subscribers; an opening night for critics and the general public; and a final, closed performance, a benefit, for the *New Theater* and *New Masses* magazines. Orson stayed with *Romeo and Juliet* until it closed—he had given notice to Cornell and McClintic that he would not be with them for *The Barretts of Wimpole Street*—and he then began rehearsing for the March 15 opening of *Panic.*

He had little trouble with the role. The blank verse was simple and enjoyable to him. He also found MacLeish's play somewhat easier to memorize than if it had been in prose form. Mastering the characterization of McGafferty—one of the richest men in America, who, speech after speech, had to perpetuate his own almost-mythic ambience, power, and tragic demise—seemed innate to him. Orson's spontaneity and intelligence impressed virtually everyone connected with the play.

MacLeish had attempted to create a story in a special language. He stated that "to make a stage-American use Shakespearean or Marlowe's blank verse is precisely comparable to clothing a stage-American in Walter Raleigh breeches and a billowy cloak," something he felt was an insult to modern drama.

The set for *Panic* was expressionistic, more intended to call attention to itself rather than to create or alter mood. Projections from below and above converged to form a wall of light, made all the more dramatic and opaque as a result of the dust floating around in the old theater.

Unfortunately, despite the fact that *Panic* occupies a special place in American drama, the public and most of the critical establishment of the day did not take to it. By 1935, after six years of the Depression, audiences were beginning to look for more upbeat and escapist fare and found *Panic*'s message too grim-visaged and depressing. Such plays as *Accent On Youth, The Petrified Forest,* and *Merrily We Roll Along,* offering fun, dreams, or vicarious thrills, were hits at the time, as were films like *The Lives of a Bengal Lancer,* all of the Charlie Chan series (three were issued that year) and *The Gold Diggers of 1935,* which, coincidentally, had its premiere the same night as the first performance of *Panic.*

Despite the failure of *Panic* to amuse or inspire, Orson's role of McGafferty, his spacious bravura, his immense voltage, was respected, if not cheered. The *New York American* proclaimed him as "one of the most promising artists of our day." Whitney Bolton, in his syndicated column in the *New York Telegraph,* thought that "Orson Welles was the triumph of the hour—he is bluff, defiant, bullock-like and brutal." And Brooks Atkinson's normally important critique in *The New York Times* stated that Welles was, "an excellent McGafferty; the scene between McGafferty and his mistress has a note of delicate lyrical rapture."

As it developed, the message of *Panic* reached a much greater audience than those who saw one of its three performances at the Imperial. It ultimately enabled Orson to make his debut on the radio, the medium over which he would rule as undisputed master for years to come. Houseman had arranged for a special abridged version—actually, just one elaborate scene of the play—to be broadcast.

The March of Time, produced by the editors of *Time,* was, at that point in radio history, the most popular news documentary show on the air. After its inception in 1931, the show became *de rigueur* listening for tens of millions of Americans every week. Its sketches (which its producers and directors referred to as "acts"), together with the familiar and doomsaying Voice of Time, became a regular Friday night tradition. *The March of Time* newsreels, similar in concept and execution, began in January 1931 and within a short time were showing in over five hundred movie theaters throughout the country.

The radio show's format was not that of normal news broadcasting but of news acting. Dramatic re-creation touched upon the most significant and often most hair-raising stories of the day. Such events as the eruption of Mt. Vesuvius and the assassination of Huey Long were performed by professional actors and accompanied by convincing sound effects and a full symphony orchestra. Originally the shows were given free to radio stations across the country in exchange for publicity for *Time* magazine. In 1935, however, the programs were sponsored, first by Remington Rand and then by Wrigley Chewing Gum.

The show had also established a tradition of broadcasting excerpts, often with original casts, of some of the better plays and films throughout the year, usually those with some controversial theme so that it could be covered as a news item. A segment from Luigi Pirandello's *Tonight We Improvise* was broadcast in 1934, celebrating the announcement of his Nobel Prize; Max Reinhardt's production of *A Midsummer Night's Dream* was done that year after its performance in the Hollywood Bowl; Houseman's *Four Saints in Three Acts* was aired on the show just after Christmas in 1934. On March 22, 1935, one week to the day after its opening performance at the Imperial, a scene from *Panic* was broadcast on *The March of Time* with Orson playing his stage role of McGafferty. Ticker tape sounds are heard in the background. McGafferty is facing Immelman and the bankers. He is asked what he is going to do. Orson Welles's voice was heard for the first time on intercontinental radio:

MCGAFFERTY

Do? What do you think I'll do? Pull the blinds on the bank and sail to Bermuda? THIS BANK WILL OPEN TOMORROW AT NINE.

On the same show that night, a report on the Dionne quintuplets was going to be broadcast. The controversial guardianship act being argued in Ontario's House of Parliament was to be recreated, together with actors imitating a visit of Mr. and Mrs. Dionne to the famed quintuplet's hospital where the children were ensconced, somewhat against their parents' will. The script in part read:

NURSE

Oh! Mr. and Mrs. Dionne. Could you come back later? The babies are all asleep and Dr. Dafoe is busy writing their charts.

MRS. DIONNE

(to her husband and the nurse):
Could I pick them up . . . just for a moment?

~~BABY JABBER~~

The words "Baby Jabber" were crossed out of the script, because, despite the fact that *The March of Time* had a "stable" of hundreds of doubles, "D-men," as they were called, all of whom could affect several accents, dialects, or personalities, the baby-voices expert was unavailable that night. When Orson received his advance copy of the script for *Panic,* it also contained the Dionne episode and he noted the deleted words.

"I can do baby voices," he told the director and after a short audition of gurgles, coos, and infant talk, he was hired to stand in. The fact that Orson on his network debut played the imperious McGafferty *ex cathedra* only moments before he lapsed into the gurgling utterances of Yvonne, Annette, Cécile, Marie, and Emilie is a study in classic irony. The acoustical joke of the huge, booming, cascading Orson transforming his voice and scaling himself down into, separately and then simultaneously, the coos and cries of five infants sent Virginia howling as she sat in the CBS control booth watching him goo-goo his way through the performance.

WELLES REMAINED IN New York for a few more months making enthusiastic attempts to get backing to mount a play with himself as director and Houseman as producer. The two men became close as they grew to appreciate each other's strengths and weaknesses. Houseman was courteous, diplomatic, and capable of making important contacts for financing. He had a keen business sense combined with a charming and easy acquaintance with art, letters, and many different kinds of people from the theater. Orson had the spark of theatrical genius; he added a flare of effervescence to his and everyone else's performance. He always had big ideas, grand plans, and seemed to have an innate capacity to capture the attention of the press in almost anything with which he became involved.

Houseman described a visit he made after the closing of *Panic* to Orson and Virginia at their Riverside Drive apartment:

I went over there to collect Orson for lunch. He said he had been working all night, and when I arrived he was still in his bath—a monstrous, medieval iron cistern which, when it was covered at night with a board and mattress, served them as a marriage bed. Orson was lying there, inert and covered with water, through which his dead-white body appeared swollen to gigantic proportions. When he got up, full of apologies, with a great splashing and cascading of waters, I discovered his bulk owed nothing to refraction—that he was, in reality, just as enormous outside the tub, which, after he had risen from it and started to dry himself, was seen to hold no more than a few inches of liquid lapping about his huge, pale feet.

CHAPTER 5

EVENTUALLY ORSON WELLES and John Houseman set up temporary offices—in office space lent to them by Zatkin—in the Sardi Building on West Forty-fourth Street, the abandoned headquarters of the Mendelssohn Society of America. Here they attempted to keep the Phoenix Theater alive, and talked, dreamed, and seriously planned future productions. Perhaps as a retaliation toward his slight by the Cornell company, Orson wanted to mount—and Houseman gave him full cooperation—an Elizabethan production that would contain so much blood and thunder that it would send audiences and critics blushing and gasping up the aisles and out the doors to tell others that they had to go in. They selected John Ford's *'Tis Pity She's a Whore,* began casting, received promises of backing, which ultimately evaporated, and eventually let the production slide. Within days and with virtually no money, Orson and Virginia were back in Woodstock, taking the refuge of the Todd School and the love and affection of Roger and Hortense Hill.

For the entire summer of 1935, Orson and Virginia lived in a small, rustic cabin at Lake Geneva, Wisconsin, just a few miles from Woodstock. Roger Hill gave the couple a small weekly stipend so that Orson could work on writing another play, with the understanding that Hill would receive a percentage of any profits for backing him financially. Hill also bought a jalopy for $25 and gave it to Virginia. Orson not only did not drive, he didn't have any desire to learn.

Although Orson wrote and revised and made a number of enthusiastic starts on the play, perhaps as a result of the indolence that often infects newlyweds, no finished work was forthcoming during that period. The young couple did work, however, on more of the Shakespeare editions that Harper's was going to publish in the early fall; they checked galleys, made corrections, and attended to other matters concerning publication.

IN EARLY SEPTEMBER, despite the fact that they were equipped with only meager funds and owned a hardly negotiable automobile, they left for New York again with the belief that Orson would find work in the theater. The trip from Woodstock took two weeks; their car's maximum speed was twenty-five miles an hour, and since only Virginia drove, she tired quickly, and they were continually forced to stop. Orson's contribution to the journey was as navigator, storyteller, and reader. As they snailed across Indiana, Ohio, and through the Alleghenies in low gear, Orson would read aloud to his young wife: play after play, poem after poem, scene after scene, to keep both her and himself amused and alert. They arrived at the newly opened Holland Tunnel on a Sunday afternoon and, because of the slowness of their auto, were ordered to travel in the lane for trucks.

At last in Manhattan, they worked their way up to midtown and abandoned the car almost immediately by parking it in a garage near the Waldorf Astoria and never going back to reclaim it. They checked their bags at the baggage counter of Grand Central Station and set about to find a place to live. Finding an apartment with virtually no money was not an easy task, but they eventually settled in a seven-dollar-a-week basement studio on West Fourteenth Street, between Eighth and Ninth Avenues, within mooing distance of the Washington Meat Market and a quick stroll to Greenwich Village.

Although unemployment was staggering in 1935, and times were so tough that even Hollywood had reported only sixty divorces for the entire previous year, and Orson had no job promises or commitments, he thought his prospects were quite good. He had his credits from the Gate Theatre, Katharine Cornell and Company, and *Panic,* plus a wealth of contacts through Alexander Woollcott, Thorton Wilder, and the other theatrical comets he knew or had been exposed to during the previous two or three years. A survey made at that time of favorite American recreations listed reading first; radio, second; and films, third. Orson, although still hopeful for legitimate stage work, began to think of acting in radio as an alternative.

Until such time as work could be found, however, the struggling pair were forced to eat unadorned patchwork meals at home or mainly at one of the dozens of New York's Automats, cafeterias where, without the interference of waiters or waitresses, they could concoct marvelously ingenious combinations of mustard-catsup soups and relish sandwiches, paying only for the bread and taking advantage of the free condiments provided. Living around the corner from The Old Homestead, New York's oldest—and one of its best—steakhouses, with the delicious tang of grilled sirloin wafting into their apartment, didn't help to placate the voracious appetite of the always-hungry Welles. Virginia was forced to pawn a matching fur scarf and muff and then, one by one, virtually all of her best dresses, simply to pay the rent.

Orson dutifully made the rounds, hoping for a part in such plays as the Alfred Lunt-Lynn Fontanne production of *The Taming of the Shrew,* Maxwell Anderson's *Winterset,* or Sidney Kingsley's *Dead End,* but all roles for the fall and winter season of that year had been filled weeks or months before he arrived in New York. Almost desperate for money, and remembering his successful, although brief, performance on *The March of Time,* Orson approached the show's producers to see if they had any additional work for him. At first he was hired as an extra just to keep yelling "walla-walla, walla-walla" over and over again with a group of other extras as part of a radio mob. He was paid $10. His timing was providential. The show was expanding its news coverage to five nights a week, and a call went out to get the ten best acting voices in the business for principal roles, in addition to many more character voices to play smaller parts. Professionals such as Agnes Moorehead, Nancy Kelly, Jeanette Nolan, Ted de Corsia, Art Carney, Ray Collins, and Paul Stewart had been hired, but Orson's experience as McGafferty and the Dionne quints assured him an audition.

The regulars of *The March of Time* seemed not to be able to impersonate successfully the eighty-six-year-old munitions king, Sir Basil Zaharoff. His voice was deep, resonant, and unidentifiably accented. He was born in Turkey, probably of Greek-Russian parents, and was ultimately educated in England. More than a dozen actors were auditioned for the part. None was accepted. Orson read for it and was able to capture Zaharoff's tone, mood, and accent in what sounded like an exact duplication of the man. He was hired immediately and within a short time also played King Victor Emmanuel, Charles Laughton, Horace Greeley, Paul Muni, Senator J. Hamilton Lewis, and dozens of extra voices.

Orson proved to be the ideal *March of Time* performer: he was a superb impersonator *and* excellent actor. Many performers had one of those talents but few had both, and the directors of the show began to rely on Orson's quick grasp and convincing rendition of a voice. Synthetic accents are quickly detected by natives of any given area or country, who are usually annoyed by people wrongly imitating their style of speech; Orson's inflections rarely sounded bogus. When he was offered a principal part, he would visit Hendrik Booraem, the program director, be given a 78-rpm record of the character's voice and cram his substantial frame into a small, soundproof chamber just large enough for himself and a phonograph. After carefully listening and studying the timbre, inflections, and accent a few times, he would then be ready to test his impersonation by making a trial transcription, then comparing it with the original voice. Booraem and others on the show would appraise and comment on each initial reading. This process would be repeated, time after time, if necessary, but most often Orson emerged from the booth in short order with a voice so like its owner's that it was difficult to distinguish it from the original.

If the voice to be imitated could not be found on a phonograph record, he would visit *The March of Time* newsreel library and study screened film footage of the subject. Occasionally, he would have to go to a commercial theater to listen to his subject speak in a rival newsreel. Failing to actually hear the voice of the person, Orson would study photographs from the *Time* and *Life* files to see if the facial expression or bone structure could possibly *suggest* the probable quality of the voice.

It was the right time to try to break into radio. Other shows were hiring hundreds of actors. "The Lux Radio Theater," with its mixture of adaptations of movies and Broadway plays, provided both publicity and handsome fees for stars and extras. "The Cavalcade of America," a show that dramatized incidents from American literature ("to combine authentic history with the appeal of the bestseller"), had its debut in 1935, and stage actors were being drawn to New York to work in front of its microphones. If one had the right voice with the ability to affect a number of dialects and characters, it wasn't particularly difficult in that time to secure employment. Radio was at the beginning of its golden age; over sixty million listeners tuned in to any number of shows on a regular basis. The "Amos 'n' Andy" radio series was so popular that people stopped going to the movies when the radio program was on. In self-defense, theater marquees across the country would announce not only their double-bill but also the fact that "Amos 'n' Andy" could be heard inside. At 7:00 P.M. the film was stopped, a large console radio placed on the stage in front of the screen, and for fifteen minutes the audience would be treated to the latest misadventures of the redoubtable duo and their involvement with the Kingfish and Madame Queen. This homage to radio by the movie house managers was given not merely because they wished to render a service but because they knew the power of the competing medium: no one would come to see a film unless the movie theaters made such accommodation. Public utilities reported that listeners didn't flush toilets or run water during "Amos 'n' Andy" time. Bus lines and taxis had virtually no passengers when the show was on the air. It seemed as though the whole nation listened to them. George Bernard Shaw's statement—"There are three things which I shall never forget about America—the Rocky Mountains, the Statue of Liberty, and 'Amos 'n' Andy,'"—was not merely glib; it reflected sentiments shared by millions of Americans.

Such programs as "The Kraft Music Show," "The Rudy Vallee Show," "Buck Rogers in the Twenty-fifth Century," "Burns and Allen," "Death Valley Days," and "Easy Aces" had millions of regular fans, while people such as Robert Ripley and Will Rogers were promoting their names and talents through a quick mastery of the medium. Maude Adams, the original Peter Pan, made a dramatic reemergence to play in a broadcast of Sir James M. Barrie's *The Little Minister,* and by 1935 it was an accepted fact that radio would encompass almost all the performing arts and most of show business—the movies, operas and concerts, the legitimate stage and vaudeville. Radio had become one of the most effective sales mediums and news reporting vehicles in the world; by the late 1930s it was obvious that entire peoples could be made to march or work, save or fight, by listening to radio.

The symbiotic evolution in the career of Orson Welles from stage to radio was entirely natural and highly practical. His voice had been resoundingly commended in virtually every stage performance in which he was involved over the years; his command of diction and tone could have been easily thought of as the essence of his *persona,* the quintessence of his distinction and style.

Aside from having a radio voice so unique and unexpected that it seemed to spring from the head of Zeus, Welles also learned a great deal of practical value in a short time. He quickly grasped how to improve his own performance by mastering such techniques as distance from the microphone, when or when not to overlap the dialogue of others, how to do group scenes, how long to pause, control of breathing, and attention to entrance and exit cues. His knowledge of the nuances of the elements of radio as a dramatic form was also greatly broadened as he became aware of the importance of sharp, simple, direct characterizations; singleness of theme; unity of dramatic effect; crisp dialogue; instant captivity of the audience; swift movement of the plot. These factors, combined with the exact timing of music and sound effects and strong acting performances, produced memorable radio dramas. Orson absorbed everything concerning radio. It became his own very special *métier*.

Although *The March of Time* was highly structured in each of its productions and required that all its actors be in attendance for at least two five-hour rehearsals prior to its broadcasts, compared to the hundreds or at least dozens of rehearsals needed for a stage performance, the pre-performance work on radio was negligible. This abbreviated labor week appealed to Orson; after he became established in radio, he often eliminated any rehearsing at all, appearing at the microphone just moments before the scheduled air cast and reading his part "cold." He got away with it because he knew the medium so well that he could sense, almost instinctively, the proper timing to allow for sound effects; and his stage training enabled his impromptu performances to sound polished, almost inspired.

There were additional, more important, reasons why Orson enjoyed his newly found career. For the first time in his life, he was collecting a handsome paycheck; the CBS wage enabled him to partially live the life to which he was eager to become accustomed. While at first he received no public acknowledgement for his involvement with *The March of Time* (the names of the actors were never announced), he quickly became known to insiders of the radio industry as one of its principal adepts, and this led to additional work and opportunities on the air. To Orson, working with *The March of Time* family was not unlike being in repertory with Katharine Cornell or at the Gate Theatre. Once hired, most of the program's actors stayed with it for years; virtually everyone knew everyone else, and there was a strong professional and social rapport established among cast and crew. But more than that, now Orson was one of the privileged few allowed into the private side of the public media where the control booth became the proscenium and the microphone the stage, and where the invisible audience was tens of thousands of times larger than any he had acted for, all sitting obediently in their front parlors, bedrooms, Ford sedans, and lonely diners in every city of the land, all listening to his splendid voice.

More than anything else, however, what attracted Orson to broadcasting was the power of imagination it evoked and relied upon. As the listening audience became involved, sometimes entranced, with the story being broadcast, the actors gained the special ability to move with absolute freedom in time and space, era and dimension. To be in a studio-created Ethiopia as Haile Selassie during a bombing one night and as a cabinet member attending a state dinner at the White House the next, to be requested to display a full range of emotions—anger, outrage, bemusement, frustration, jollity, pity, disgust, horror—night after night, was an intense stimulant.

As their reputations grew, many of the actors from *The March of Time* received offers to appear on other shows. Since they were not known as personalities—only memorable voices without names—on *The March of Time,* the producers had no objection to their taking additional assignments as long as it didn't interfere with their contracted work with the news show. CBS looked to its own and self-raided *The March of Time* when it became interested in recasting for its new treatment of "The Shadow." Until 1936, the eerie voice of "The Shadow" (Frank Readick's) was merely the introducer and narrator of a series of mystery programs. He did not occupy a place in the script as a character. When the ratings for the radio program had begun to diminish, experiments with different formulas were attempted. Eventually, the producers emerged with a format they believed would be successful: a series that would revolve around the Shadow as an actual character, a modern day Sherlock Holmes, who would attempt to solve any baffling mystery that the police were unable to unravel. The new Shadow would be Lamont Cranston, a sophisticated playboy and an amateur criminologist, who, because of a secret he had learned when living in the Orient, had the power to cloud men's minds—making himself invisible.

New talent was sought to recreate the program in this new direction, and auditions were held for the title role. Orson read for the part and was hired as the first Shadow in the new format. Agnes Moorehead, from *The March of Time,* would be the Shadow's loyal assistant, Margot Lane. Everett Sloane, Ted de Corsia, and other *March of Time* staffers also joined the cast.

For thirty minutes every Sunday evening at 5:00 P.M., Orson would weave the Shadow's special magic. Soon millions of Americans were tuning in each week. "The Shadow" became the most popular mystery show on the air; a blizzard of fan mail reached the studio each day; "Shadow" clubs sprang up around the country. Orson would occasionally appear at stores and at social functions, swathed in black hat, cape, and mask, for special promotions. The music, special effects, and the Shadow's personal credo at the opening of the show entered the American vernacular: "Who knows what evil lurks in the hearts of men? The Shadow knows." This statement, followed by the Shadow's menacing laugh in a spectral crescendo, was accompanied by a terrifying musical rendition of Saint-Saëns' *Omphale's Spinning Wheel,* all of which combined to give the show an unforgettable trademark. Curiously, Welles had difficulty in voicing the opening statement with its bloodcurdling laugh; although his cultured voice personified Lamont Cranston, with the Oxonian pronunciation of "ahduh" for "order," "sacrifiss" for "sacrifice" or "dissapeagh" for "disappear." When he was transmogrified into the Shadow, he used a microphone filter to give his lines a chilling, sinister reading and his voice as the "invisible" Shadow was perfect. His laugh, however, seemed more an adolescent giggle than a terrifying threat, so the old introduction, recorded by Frank Readick, was retained as the opening of the new "Shadow" series, and no one knew the difference.

ALTHOUGH ORSON HAD begun to enjoy a certain financial and emotional security as a radio actor, the mid-1930s were still economically devastating for most of America's theatrical community. It took "that man in the White

House," as Franklin D. Roosevelt was sometimes deprecatingly known, to rally the theater in this country and save it from irreparable damage. Under Roosevelt's New Deal, the Congress authorized the greatest single appropriation of its kind in history: the Emergency Relief Appropriation Act of 1935. Nearly five billion dollars was allotted for the grand and single purpose of helping the 3.5 million Americans who were out of work. Roosevelt appointed his most trusted aide, Harry Hopkins, as Works Progress Administrator, and within a short while, the money began to flow into the economy, taking employable people off the relief rolls and giving them back a sense of self-respect. As the country began to dig itself out of the Depression, a vast number of public projects were realized. New hospitals, railroads, schools, airports, zoos, and playgrounds were constructed, thereby creating hundreds of thousands of jobs. Over forty thousand artists of all kinds were given jobs. The Federal Writers' Project was incorporated and gave thousands of fledgling writers, such as John Cheever and Richard Wright, and such established authors as Conrad Aiken, an opportunity to be published. The Federal Music Project employed some fifteen thousand musicians, including the personnel of three symphony orchestras; and the Federal Arts Project nurtured many painters, some of whom would become known as this country's most respected: Jackson Pollock, Stuart Davis, Willem de Kooning and Ben Shahn.

It was at this juncture of national hope transposing into realized dreams that the Federal Theatre Project was born as a "free, adult, uncensored" experiment, as Harry Hopkins described and envisioned it.

Hallie Flanagan, the dynamic, redheaded director of the Experimental Theater at Vassar, editor of collections of Pirandello and Chekhov, and a specialist in the European avant-garde theater, was approached by Hopkins to be the director of the new theater project. As Flanagan relates in *Arena,* she received a call from Hopkins, an old friend and classmate, who said to her: "We've got a lot of actors on our hands, suppose you come to New York and talk it over?" Eva Le Gallienne and other theatrical luminaries were also considered as possible directors, but Flanagan accepted the invitation to meet Hopkins, and she eventually took the post.

Although it might be argued that the government's major *raison d'être* in establishing the Federal Theatre Project was totally pragmatic in supplying jobs for the needy, the feisty Hallie Flanagan saw the possibilities of a truly effective National Theater working toward an art "in which each region and eventually each state would have its unique, indigenous, dramatic expression, its company housed in a building reflecting its own land scene and regional manners, producing plays of its past and present in its own rhythms of speech and its native design, in an essentially American drama." Flanagan believed that the theater should be more than a private enterprise: it was a public interest that could have a great social and educative force if properly administered and fostered.

Flanagan drew up an ambitious but realistic plan in which she proposed not only to get theater people working again but to create a dramatic collective so dedicated to excellence and with such a defined and enthusiastic audience that it could continue even if and when federal funds were ultimately withdrawn. Her design was to create theatrical projects that would offer entertainment all over the country for little or no cost, to support traveling troupes, build city and state theaters, and to bring theater to the people. The government earmarked ten million dollars for the wages of actors, writers, designers, and other theater personnel, and by 1936, nine thousand show people were employed in twenty states, entertaining a national audience of over three hundred and fifty thousand each night of the week.

In New York City, forty-seven hundred theater people were eventually employed. Noted playwright Elmer Rice was chosen as the city's theater director, presiding over five units: The Living Newspaper, which introduced the new concept of documentary plays to Broadway, tackling such popular themes of the thirties as power trusts, monopolies, and the rise of socialism; the Popular Price Theatre, which succeeded in presenting new works by new playwrights; the Experimental Group, which mounted surrealistic and other avant-garde dramas; the Try-out Theatre, a farm team for budding professionals; and the Negro Theatre Project.

Enlisting the proper personnel to direct the various groups was not an easy task, particularly for the Negro Theatre Project, because of the sensitive racial issues that touched upon potential performances in the South and in many other parts of the country as well. Rosamond Gilder, the genteel editor of *Theater Arts* magazine, who seemed to know and befriend everybody in the world of the theater, was asked by Hallie Flanagan to recommend someone who might qualify as the director of the Negro Theatre Project. The person she felt was a strong possibility was John Houseman. Miss Gilder explained to Hallie Flanagan that Houseman was a competent, published writer and producer, had worked with Negro actors with great success (in *Four Saints in Three Acts*), and was highly liberal. Houseman was still floundering for his niche in the theater, so when he was offered the opportunity of meeting Hallie Flanagan to be interviewed for the job, he unhesitatingly accepted. Flanagan was impressed by his knowledge of the theater, his old-world courtesy, and his charm. Within days, he was deep into the process of hiring personnel, setting up offices, and thinking of first productions. He determined to produce a theater, part of which would be dedicated to the production of classical works whose actors would be chosen without reference to color. He chose his young friend Orson Welles to be the creative force that would fire that theater. Orson first refused Houseman's offer to become the director for the Federal Theatre, somewhat frightened that it would slice into his radio income and plunge Virginia and him into quasi-insolvency again. However, it was Virginia, knowing that he longed to do Shakespeare and that this would be such an opportunity, who gave him her approval to accept the position. "Orson, I *want* you to take this job," she said. "It's a chance of a lifetime. You *must!*" Both Houseman and Welles beamed.

John Houseman was sharing an apartment with Virgil Thomson at that time and, although Welles and Thomson had met, it wasn't until then that they had spent much time getting to know each other. Some of Thomson's friends and colleagues, such as stage director Joseph Losey, thought Welles was too overbearing for the New York left-wing group. Losey, Thomson, and Houseman often spoke French during candlelit dinners, discussed the philosophy of the avant-garde theater, and were thoroughly engaged in the life of nonobjective art. They believed Welles was not quite of the same cut. However, perhaps because of Houseman's insistence, Thomson and Welles did eventually grow fond enough of each other to consider a collaboration as director and composer.

Despite the fact that Welles was still in his early twenties and Houseman entering his mid-thirties, the older man had a genuine awe and respect for the younger. As Houseman recounted:

> In my working relationship with this astonishing boy whose theatrical experience was so much greater and richer than mine, it was I the pupil, he the teacher. In certain fields, I was his senior, possessed of painfully acquired knowledge that was wider and more comprehensive than his; but what amazed and awed me in Orson was his astounding and, apparently, innate dramatic instinct. Listening to him, day after day, with rising fascination, I had the sense of hearing a man initiated, at birth, into the most secret rites of a mystery—the theater—of which he felt himself, at all times, the rightful and undisputed master.

If instinct is the pivot to dramatic excellence, Orson Welles had the master key. But he also possessed a special ability, a discernment of his career potential without any real foundation based on experience. And although, or because, he marched to a different drummer, Houseman offered Welles the job as director of the Negro Theatre Project. It paid barely $50 a week, which was much less than he was receiving for a single broadcast, but he immediately accepted the opportunity. Although his experience with working with black actors was limited, his association with blacks had always been more than cordial, and one of his favorite nighttime frivolities was to visit Harlem's black jazz parlor, Dickie Wells's place, which originally attracted him because it bore the same name as his father.

Welles's first dream for the Negro Theatre Project was to direct a Shakespearean drama that would not only star black actors but also display his own yet-to-be-disclosed verve and talent as a director. Shakespeare speaks everybody's language, Welles contended, but "with an Elizabethan accent." How would black actors react toward performing in a classical repertory? Welles was aware that, although the employment of the black actor throughout theatrical history had been mainly limited to roles as minstrels and in amateur comedy, or to usually demeaning character parts in legitimate theater, there had been sporadic, and sometimes highly successful, attempts over the years to give blacks dignified and self-respecting parts on the stage.

As far back as the mid-1800s, the black actors Ira Aldridge and James Hewlett, respectively billed as "vocalist and Shakespeare's proud representative," played lead roles in Shakespearean plays, Hewlett's performance as Richard III being particularly hailed. In the 1920s, Raymond O'Neil, together with Mrs. Sherwood Anderson, brought the Ethiopian Art Theater from Chicago to Broadway, and adaptations with black actors of Oscar Wilde's *Salomé* and Shakespeare's *Comedy of Errors* were successfully offered.

But for every advance made in behalf of black acting, for each attempt at putting a black actor into the natural role of Othello, for example, there were many critical and skeptical snipes about the abilities of blacks to play Shakespeare or, for that matter, any serious stage role. When Charles Matthews, the distinguished British actor, first came to the United States, he attended a black performance of *Hamlet* and claimed that the actor playing the title role delivered the most famous speech from the play as follows: "To be or not to be, dat is him question, whether him nobler in de mind to suffer or lift up him arms against a sea or hubble bubble and by opossum end 'em."

This highly prejudiced exaggeration on Matthews's part typified the reaction that most theatergoers had to the reality of black dialect. It was this widespread attitude that Welles was going to have to confront—and overcome—if the Negro Theatre Project was to be a success.

Other problems also surfaced: if white actors donned blackface when playing the part of a black man, shouldn't blacks use whiteface when playing the traditionally white roles of most of Shakespeare's characters? While Orson was attempting to solve these theoretical but very real problems, the business of establishing the Negro Theatre Project proceeded.

IT WAS THE autumn of 1935, and Orson Welles was now twenty years old. The old Lafayette Theater in Harlem was leased, and painting, patching, and general refurbishing begun. Hundreds of actors and other theater personnel were hired at the then fairly decent salary of about twenty-three dollars per week, optimistic stories began to appear in local newspapers, and almost everyone connected with the project confessed to a feeling of being a part of something that was going to be, if not big, then at least significant.

About two o'clock one morning, Welles called Houseman on the telephone and announced that Virginia had had an inspiration: they would do *Macbeth* as their first production. However, instead of the traditional Scottish setting, the action would take place in Haiti. Such a suggestion was not as illogical as it may have appeared at first blush, and Houseman accepted the dictate without a quarrel.

Haitian culture had been enjoying a vogue in America ever since the U.S. Marines had left the island the year before, and *Voodoo Fire in Haiti,* a somewhat romanticized view of the island by Richard A. Loederer had been a near bestseller in the previous months of 1935. These factors might have been the spark that ignited Virginia's bright idea. Whatever the genesis of the new approach to the theme, however, the sustained tragic tension of *Macbeth*, combined with an approach that would illuminate the best lines and scenes in Shakespeare while simultaneously making a statement by and for the black community, had tremendous appeal to Welles. *Macbeth* had long been one of his favorite plays; he had seen it performed many times; it was one of the plays he would choose for his continuing promptbook series; he knew virtually every speech by heart and possessed an understanding of the deeper logic behind every scene. *Macbeth* in the essence of its drama is no more inherently Scottish than *The Merchant of Venice* is Venetian. The African nature gods worshiped by voodoo would make a close parallel to some of the ghostly themes found in *Macbeth.* And the parallels with black American and Haitian culture were also great with most of the black Haitian population descendant from African slaves.

Welles visualized this *Macbeth* with voodoo priestesses as the witches and scenes that would capture the frenzy and magic of the occult, combining the rhythms of beating drums, blood, and mayhem, an expressionistic combination of the shadows and violence and chantings of Haiti, Scotland, and Manhattan all rolled into one. The costumes would be suggestive of those worn by the Haitians in their struggle against France. As one critic would describe it, he would fill the stage, with "mad and gabbing throngs of evil worshipers, beat the jungle drums, raise the voices until the jungle echoes, stuff a gleaming naked witch doctor into the cauldron, hold up Negro masks in the baleful light. . . ." And so on.

Welles decided to base his version of *Macbeth* "on an island that could have been Haiti at the time of the Black emperor, Jean Christophe." Theater historian Richard France has pointed out that Welles was probably familiar with W. W. Harvey's *Sketches of Hayti,* published in 1927, since a great deal of the subsequent flavor of the play can be found in its pages. France quotes a passage from Harvey almost as if it were a stage description written for Welles's version of *Macbeth*: "All the officers of the Army . . . were fond of dress to an extravagant degree, and often rendered their appearance ridiculous. Their coats were bedecked with gold and lace . . . their shoulders were burdened with epaulets of an enormous size; their caps were adorned with feathers nearly equalling their own weight: and these articles . . . rendered their appearance supremely fantastical."

Welles wanted the play to combine its most tragic elements with the exotic mysticism of the jungle. He hoped that the voodoo chants, dramatic lighting, strong winds, and lightning and thunder would transform *Macbeth* into a Shakespearean spectacle that would evoke both fear and awe in the hearts of the audience as it led the characters to their inexorable fates.

Because of the strict Federal Theatre Project regulations about hiring, anyone who was even remotely qualified to walk onto a stage could be employed. According to Houseman, the company consisted of "an amazing mishmash of amateurs and professionals, church members and radicals, sophisticated and wild ones, adherents of Father Divine and bushmen from Darkest Africa." Music was to be supplied by Virgil Thomson, the costumes and settings were created by Nat Karson. The lighting was provided by Abe Feder. All these men were practiced creators. Only four experienced, professional actors, however, made their way into the Negro Theatre Project: Jack Carter as Macbeth, Canada Lee as Banquo, Edna Thomas as Lady Macbeth, and Eric Burroughs as Hecate. The beginning rehearsals, therefore, with this mismatch of inexperienced black actors and the temperamental white director, were a study in conflict.

Confronted by a barrage of different black dialects—West Indian, Southern, New York, Caribbean—Orson found it difficult to be the rhetorician he wanted or to give individual attention to establishing a standard accent for *Macbeth*: so, aside from correcting such mispronunciations, for example, as *except* for *accept* or *allude* for *elude,* he concentrated mostly upon meaning, delivery, and action. He demanded absolute pitch and breath control and allowed the naturally beautiful rhythms of black speech to connect and meld with the pungent tones of the Elizabethan. He made a conscious artistic effort to eliminate the poetic delivery of a typical Shakespearean performance in favor of, as Houseman has noted, "a return to a simpler, more direct and rapid delivery of dramatic verse."

In order to build up the sound of some of the actors' voices, he borrowed a technique that went back to Elizabethan days. He employed musical sound effects, such as thunder, wind, or lightning, coming in at the end of a line, to make the force of the delivery seem greater or more dramatic. He had Thomson score these effects with kettle drums, thunder sheets, and a wind machine. The composer also supplied orchestrations of Joseph Lanner waltzes, a few passages of pathos similar to the classical *Hearts and Flowers,* and some original trumpet fanfares.

Thomson was somewhat unenthusiastic about the musical possibilities of Shakespeare, however, stating: "One can get in a little weather music and, once the characters are dead, sometimes a funeral. Otherwise, it's mostly fanfares to get the actors on and off the stage." Despite the negative appraisal of his own work, Thomson ironically produced a score of such dramatic pungency for *Macbeth* that it immediately brought him commissions to do the music for the forthcoming Leslie Howard production of *Hamlet* and the Tallulah Bankhead *Antony and Cleopatra.*

Sitting in the first few rows of the theater, his legs often atop the seat in front, and sipping a chilled Chablis, Welles would comment upon the rehearsed action, while Virginia or his young secretary, Augusta Weissberger, would take careful notes. Later, all the principal actors would be given copies of this corrigendum for their own reference; if the faults were not corrected by the next rehearsal, Welles was more outspoken in his denunciation.

During each session, like a watchful aunt, he was aware of virtually every detail. Rarely did a movement, whether of hand or of eye, lisp, dropped syllable, or inflection of meaning escape his painfully microscopic notice, and for hour upon hour he would choreograph his actors as though they were puppets. From his notes:

> You're not acting as though you have blood on your hands. . . . Lady Macduff should look *after* Macduff. . . . Start the voodoo drums *very low* on the scream by the women's "liar and slave" line. . . . Jack's tone of questioning too high. . . . I can't hear the witches' "All hail, Macbeth, Thane of Cawdor." . . . JACK, FOR

GOD'S SAKE, LEARN YOUR LINES AND TAKE THE WEARINESS OUT OF YOUR BODY AS YOU GO UP THE STAIRS. . . . Tommy, take the emotion out of your voice. . . . Ellis, your "gentle lady" is too disinterested. . . . No one should exit left in "meet in hall together". . . . The choir stinks. . . . Jack isn't pleading a cause at all. . . . When are we going to start using the blood? . . . Get a cushion for the crown. . . . Canada is not to speak until after the second murderer gets to the wall . . . the witches laugh too soon and the laugh is bad. . . . Nixon, please get the hell upstage. . . . "Behold" lacks terror. . . . Lady Macduff, like this: POUNDING, POUNDING, (softer) pounding, pound. . . . This scene has no atmosphere *whatever*. . . . Canada's hiding his face behind Jack in "'oft times". . . . Make "come what may" brighter and "let us toward the King" more decisive. . . . JACK *PLEASE* LEARN YOUR LINES. . . . Hecate is pausing too much. . . . The gate must make more noise or none at all. . . . Cripples: cut your "ughs." . . . Look up at the tower at "I dare do all." . . . Edna's thinking what the audience thinks. . . . Pace, pace, pace, pace, pace. . . ."

Welles got involved in all areas of the play. He made a Plasticine model of the basic set and conferred with Nat Karson on costumes, making some rough sketches to illustrate his own ideas. Only one set—a castle laid in a jungle—was used for the entire play. Welles had the backdrop painted a stylized design of huge tropical leaves. He felt that the lighting was particularly critical: the problem was to transform the traditional fog-laden grays of the Scottish heath into the verdant greens of the Haitian jungle. Along with his rehearsal notes to actors, he would usually include some highly detailed lighting asides that were as astute as if he had been born to the trade: "Left cradle #2 should be focused a bit higher to hit castle wall. . . . Miniature shot hookup needs to be fixed—the whole miniature set up. . . . Make 23 a single rather than a double chocolate . . . put tin bottom on beams across back pit . . . miniature spot on top of platform too light."

Abe Feder was a master lighting technician—one of the best in the business—and followed, although not always agreeably, Welles's dictates of helping to blend together the form and color of the set, the arrangement of the props, and the position and costumes of the actors, through the distribution of the variety of lighting. The slightly smallish stage caused design problems in creating the illusion of distance and perspective, and these, too, could be solved with nuances of lighting. Finally, since only one set was to be used, it was with lighting that the real and mystical scenes of the play would have to be defined. At the beginning of the second act, where Macbeth plots the murders, all of the stage lighting was dimmed, except for one shaft of light that remained on in the epicenter of the stage. This became the frame for the murder of Banquo, creating a counterbalance of fantasy to the realism of the rest of the set.

Welles had constant tempo tantrums. He would explain over and over again the operatic quality of the play and how timing and pace, not only from one scene to another but from speech to speech and in between lines as well, was one of the keys. "Don't ask for the meaning, ask for the use," the philosopher Ludwig Wittgenstein would often say, and Orson applied that reasoning to the theater. It was always the *what* of a moment of action that prevailed, rarely the *why*. Edna Thomas recalled to Richard France that once, while she was standing on the steps leading to the castle, Orson kept the actors downstage going over a piece of business again and again because they could not satisfactorily coordinate with the proper beat of movement. Finally, he said to her: "Darling, come down here. I'm not going to have you standing there all this time while these dumbbells aren't catching on." Orson seemed to be totally unaware that the actors took his jibe not just as a directorial remark but as a racial slur, and Edna privately explained that if he continued with that line of insult, not only would he have an insurrection on his hands—and no play—but, she feared, he might suffer bodily harm.

The tense and unpleasant moments, however, were often interspersed with enjoyable and exciting ones. At his most charming, Orson was capable of cajoling and encouraging everyone to stay up for thirty-six to forty-eight hours without sleep, inviting half the cast out for drinks after a rehearsal, and regaling everyone with long stretches of verse and stories of the theater and a general feeling of bonhomie. One cast member remembered Orson spontaneously quoting Diderot to an actor who had made a disparaging remark about the lack of sensitivity of the audience: "The citizen who presents himself at the door of a theater leaves his vices there, and only takes them up again as he goes out. . . . There he is just, impartial, a good friend, a lover of virtue. . . ." Everyone fell silent and was proud to be in the same building with the romantically lettered Orson.

Feeling that many classical plays, and *Macbeth* was one of them, could not be relied upon to reach an audience, Welles made sweeping changes—aside from the switch of locale—in the play as it was written by Shakespeare. Modern audiences, he contended, were unaccustomed to sitting through Elizabethan plays in their entirety, mainly because the language had changed. Certain passages, therefore, were rendered meaningless. Along with another man of the theater, Sir Herbert Beerbohm Tree, who was famous for his Shakespearean excisions, Welles believed that a play as written was like a block of marble to be carved and shaped into something of beauty by the director. Using his own *Macbeth* promptbook as a source, which already represented a streamlined version of the play, he further reduced the length of *Macbeth* by employing what he described as "a discreet and scholarly blue pencil." Speeches by characters in the same scene would often be abridged and combined, as was Banquo's in the initial moments of the play. The first and second acts were rearranged and made into one; many of the long speeches throughout the play were condensed. Donalbain was cut in total; Hecate's role was changed to that of a man and greatly enlarged as he accompanies Macbeth, Mephistopheles-like, through his tribulations. The character represents both chorus and director, orchestrating, commanding the three witches, sadistically using a bullwhip for a baton.

As Welles continued the rehearsals throughout the winter of 1935 and spring of 1936, rumors of strange happenings began to circulate. They were so strong that newspaper reporters began to explore the Lafayette Theater to see what they could find. To add to the mystery, most of the rehearsals were held after midnight because, during the days, another production, *Conjur Man Dies,* was in the process of being mounted. Bosley Crowther of *The New York Times,* who paid a nighttime visit to the theater, did not discover the source of the strangeness but reported:

> The scout, upon arrival, discovered a good-sized crowd of Negroes milling around at the back of the theater . . . These were the Shakespearean thespians themselves waiting to begin rehearsal. Not to them, however, but to John Houseman and Orson Welles, supervisor and director, respectively, of the Negro *Macbeth* it was that the scout went for information. Why, he wanted to know, had they mustered the audacity to take *Macbeth* for a ride? What sort of Thane of Cawdor would find himself in Haiti? Whither would Malcolm and Donalbain flee—to Jamaica and possibly Nassau? . . .
>
> Both Mr. Houseman and Mr. Welles . . . were pleased to talk, brightly and intelligently, about their unusual creation. But they were also quite serious about it. . . . "We were very anxious to do one of Shakespeare's dramas in the Negro Theatre," said [Mr. Welles], "and *Macbeth* seemed, in all respects, the most adaptable." . . . The stormy . . . career of . . . Christophe, who became "The Negro King of Haiti" . . . and ended by killing himself when his cruelty led to a revolt, forms a striking parallel to the [history] of *Macbeth.* . . . The costumes and sets of the production are therefore . . . in this period of Haiti's grimmest turbulence. Place names have been altered . . . with particular care to retain the rhythm of Shakespeare's lines.
>
> As to the company itself, they seemed as alert and enthusiastic . . . as the day—or night—they started. The New Deal, not only in the theater but in Shakespeare, was meat and drink for them. And any actor who will rehearse from midnight until dawn . . . must be interested in something more than a pay check.

The strange rumblings began on the first day of rehearsals. A troupe of dancers from the west coast of Africa, headed by a genuine witch doctor—a dwarf named Abdul, with gold and diamond teeth—but choreographed by Asodata Dafora Horton* had been hired by Welles to perform a voodoo ritual "with the greatest authenticity." On the day of the first rehearsal, the dwarf went to Welles and requested twelve live goats. Humorously perplexed, Welles asked why the animals were needed. "Goats, black goats, for make devil drums," the small man replied. "I suppose that in the entire history of Shakespeare in the theater," Welles has recalled, "there has never been a request, on the first day of rehearsals, for twelve live goats as part of the cast." Eventually, the goats were secured. (Welles remembers filling out the federal request form in triplicate for the goats and wondering how the bureaucrats in

---

*Horton was a Congolese who had experience producing dance spectacles with authentic African instruments.

Washington would respond.) They were slaughtered and their hides stretched and made into the "devil drums." A legend began to grow backstage that if anyone touched the drums, he would die. This story began to spread all over Harlem, and some of the local papers began making reference to the occult practices taking place in the Lafayette. When a stagehand did move a drum and shortly afterward fell from the scaffolding, breaking his neck, the rumors transposed into genuine fear.

The working relationship between Welles and Houseman was amicable, with the latter always operating as the responsible producer and usually having the final power in matters of money, operation, or promotion. Conversely, Welles's efficacious control of the staging and creative force of the production was rarely challenged by Houseman. Indeed, he was "barred" from all the initial rehearsals so that there could be no confusion or conflict about where the responsibility began or ended and also, claimed Orson, to prevent any inhibition that might occur if he had to demonstrate his directorial magic in front of a peer.

Despite the fact that Orson made close friends with some of the cast, such as Jack Carter, it was to the quiet, polite Houseman that the allegiance of most of the theater company was devoted, and it was Houseman who was often responsible for assuaging temperaments and preventing large-scale revolts. In her observation of how the two men functioned, Hallie Flanagan remarked of Houseman: "He worked marvellously with our Negro company, and while they were always, in the stress of production, threatening to murder Orson in spite of their admiration of him, they were devoted to Jack."

And although Orson had some very real problems with Abe Feder's lighting ("That red is typical Feder," he once said. "Pink.") and the fact that Jack Carter was drinking heavily, a problem for which Orson might have been partially responsible, the first-night date was finally set for April 4, 1936.

At opening night, ten thousand people clogged the streets outside the theater, the scarlet and gold bedecked marching band of the Negro Elks stormed by with banners proclaiming: "*Macbeth* by William Shakespeare." The police were needed to hold back the crowds, and the whole scene was recorded by newsreel cameramen and radio announcers. It was one of Harlem's proudest evenings.

Hallie Flanagan was thrilled with what Welles and Houseman had created. She described that night:

> African jungles beat, Lady Macbeth walked on the edge of a jungle throbbing with sinister life, Hecate with his bullwhip lashed out at the witches, Macbeth pierced by a bullet, took his terrific headlong plunge from the balustrade. Critics, even when occasionally impelled to lament a lapse in iambics, were stirred by the dark, sensual rhythms, the giant tropic fronds . . . architecture from the dreams of Toussaint l'Ouverture . . . costumes-Emperor Jones gone beautifully mad . . . sepia male witches stripped to the waist against the world's largest skeleton arch, a tragedy of black ambition in green jungle shot with such lights from both heaven and hell as no other stage has ever seen.

Although it's true that the critics were stirred by the spectacle and special effects of the production, many were condescending toward its interpretation of Shakespeare, or judgmental in a racial or political way. *Fortune's* critique was typical:

> When the U.S. Government produced William Shakespeare's *Macbeth* in Harlem, it stood them up, packed them in, and rolled them in the aisles. The opening was the blackest first night in New York history. The police roped off four city blocks and the sables from downtown and the high yallers from Harlem fought their way to their fifteen to fifty-five cent seats through the biggest crowd ever gathered on upper Seventh Avenue.... The play plus the price brought out white intellectuals as well as black enthusiasts.

Robert Garland in the *World-Telegram* treated the play as though it was a Negro minstrel, stating that it was "colorful, exciting, and a good colored show. It's like *Run Little Chillun* with intervals of familiar quotations." And Robert Littell, in an article entitled "Macbeth in Chocolate," disparagingly noticed that "the whites came in droves to spread their chilly fingers before the reviving fires of a warmer, happier, simpler race. In watching them, we capture briefly what once we were, long centuries ago before our ancestors suffered the blights of thought, worry, and the printed word."

There were a number of critics who condemned the production for what they considered the failure of the Negro actors to speak Shakespearean verse with a sense of poetry. Percy Hammond wrote in the *New York Herald Tribune*: "What surprised me last night at the Lafayette was the inability of so melodious a race to sing the music of Shakespeare." Burns Mantle, who left the theater before Lady Macbeth's famous sleepwalking scene, stated left-handedly: "Here is *Macbeth* in fancy dress, the Shakespearean lines falling awkwardly but with a certain defiant naturalness from the lips of the Negro actors unaccustomed to reading verse and quite satisfied not to try an imitation of their white brothers."

Edward R. Murrow reviewed the play for *Stage* and condemned it for its "blackface attitude," expressing his desire to see Negro Theatre that "would show the passion, beauty, cruelty, suffering, aspiration, frustration, humor, and yes, the victories of a deeply emotional race. . . ." The two most important reviewers—John Mason Brown of the *New York Post* and Brooks Atkinson of *The New York Times*—reviewed it oppositely although both felt it was too orthodox. Brown thought that "the pity is that this *Macbeth*, which should have been so interesting, wastes not only an exciting idea but murders an exciting play," whereas Atkinson, although he had some reservations, proclaimed the play as "logical and stunning and a triumph of theater art."

The poet and filmmaker Jean Cocteau, in New York for a short stop en route around the world in eighty days for a Paris newspaper, visited the production as a guest of Virgil Thomson. He gasped when the curtain went up. "Why this Wagnerian lighting?" he whispered to Thomson. Later, after the performance, which he hailed as exquisite, he answered the question himself, thinking of how the lighting contributed to the ambience of violence: "Well, I think for a jungle setting it's a perfectly good idea."

Despite the mixed reactions of the critics, *Macbeth* played for twelve weeks in Manhattan. It also went on the road to Bridgeport, Hartford, Dallas, Indianapolis, Chicago, Detroit, Cleveland, and Brooklyn, for a total of 144 performances. Some 117,244 theatergoers saw the play, and as a result, many blacks became acquainted with Shakespeare for the first time. Although the production, with its lush Haitian setting and voodoo witch doctors was no more typical of American blacks than of Elizabethan Shakespeare, Welles's *Macbeth* added to the self-esteem of the black community for, at that time, it was the only black production in American theatrical history that white people ever stood in lines to attend. The fact that Jack Carter, who played Macbeth, was a palefaced mulatto (a problem that had much relevance at that time) and that Macduff looked remarkably like Haile Selassie added certain political and social undertones to the production.

Some critics, such as the eminent Percy Hammond of the *Herald Tribune,* saw political relevance in the play, but of a negative kind. He wrote: "The Negro Theatre, an off-shoot of the Federal Government and one of Uncle Sam's experimental philanthropies, gave us, last night, an exhibition of deluxe boondoggling." Hammond went on to say, in effect, that blacks should be confined to play only black subjects in the theater and lamented what he considered "the inability of so noble a race to sing the music of Shakespeare."

Although Welles and Houseman were disturbed by the attack, some of the members of the cast and crew were devastated. Welles remembers that he was approached by Abdul the following night and engaged in a dialogue, "reminiscent of a Tarzan film." The story has become a part of theater legend and went something like this:

> Abdul: "This critic, bad man?"
> Welles: "Yes, he is a bad man."
> Abdul: "You want we make beri-beri on this bad man?"
> Welles: "Yes, go right ahead and make all the beri-beri you want to."
> Abdul: "We start drums now."
> Welles: "You go ahead and start the drums. Just be ready for the show tonight."
> Abdul: "Drums begin now. Bad man dies twenty-three hours from now."

After the performance, as Welles left the theater, he noticed that the drumming by the witch doctors continued, and there were later reports throughout Harlem that it went on all through the night. Hammond did not die twenty-three hours later; however, he did contract pneumonia. Within forty-eight hours, as predicted by the men of magic, he was dead. Welles has said that on reflection the story is "hard to believe, but it is circumstantially true," and its accuracy has been corroborated by journalists and theater people many times over the years.

DESPITE OR PERHAPS because of their success with the Negro Theatre Project, Houseman convinced Hallie Flanagan that it was time that he and Orson moved on to other federally funded projects. In an opportunistic calculation, Houseman saw the possibilities of greater acclaim for himself and Welles, with the federal government as their "angel"—by establishing a theater that would principally perform revivals of the great dramatic classics. It was also argued by the two men that the blacks should have an opportunity to produce and direct on their own and would be denied such a chance if they stayed with the project. A formal request was made that the Federal Theatre Project establish a classical wing and that they be permitted to move into the Maxine Elliott Theater in midtown Manhattan, which the government had just leased from the Shuberts. It was located between Sixth Avenue and Broadway and was less in the theater district than in the garment center. Pushboys with long racks of the next season's dresses competed with loading and unloading trucks for the right of way. At the "Artists' and Writers'" restaurant, down the block from the Maxine Elliott, models lunched with cigar-smoking apparel buyers while reporters from the *Herald Tribune,* located across the street, enjoyed a free lunch at the bar. The theater's location seemed earthy and bracing to Orson and friends.

Hallie Flanagan agreed with the philosophy of giving more opportunities to blacks and was also interested in allowing the two men as many creative people as they wanted. She consented to their request, and offices were set up in the theater to begin new productions. Concerned that their efforts would be lost to a large segment of the population who might be reluctant to attend a theater that had the word "classical" attached to it, they simply took the bureaucratic number given to them by the government and named their new group, "Project 891."

CHAPTER 6

THE REASONS FOR Orson Welles selecting the century-old French farce *Un Chapeau de Paille d'Italie,* by Eugene Labiche and Marc Michel, as his first effort for the classically oriented Project 891 were not readily apparent to many of his observers, or even associates, at the time he announced it. It seemed that only Virgil Thomson, aware of the possibilities of a farcical lilting score, was impressed. Welles had always been attracted to the comedy and was especially taken with its possibilities after he saw the silent film version, *The Italian Straw Hat,* directed by René Clair and originally released in 1927. Clair's film was an exquisitely choreographed piece of action, and Welles attempted to emulate its fast-paced, comic suspense throughout. He also wanted to give to the public a little more sex than they had been recently accustomed to. Movies, influenced by the National League of Decency, which was established in 1934 and with which Hollywood cooperated, maintained a long list of taboos such as long kisses, suggestions of adultery, use of words like "hell" and "damn," and even the appearance on the screen of nude babies. Broadway plays, although not governed by the code, began to be tempered by it. Welles thought that the theatergoing public craved some racy humor in its entertainment and therefore included some daring, off-color dialogue and action in the script. Other stage producers were also becoming acutely aware of the competition from motion pictures. With such 1935 film box-office hits and instant classics as *Mutiny on the Bounty, Les Misérables, The Informer, A Tale of Two Cities,* and *The Story of Louis Pasteur,* stage plays had to give more for their money or else be forced out of business.

Other versions of *Un Chapeau* had been done in the past, W. S. Gilbert providing two attempts, *The Wedding March* and *Haste to the Wedding.* It was Welles's intention to try a new approach altogether, and he collaborated with the noted dancer, critic, and poet Edwin Denby in writing an entirely different treatment of the script from anything that had been mounted before. The mischievous and roguish Gilbertian dialogue that sounded so peculiar and pretentious to some 1930s audiences would be avoided, the play's heavily Gallic flavor would be transformed into an American work of 1908, and pure nonsense, for its own rollicking sake, would be incorporated into virtually every scene. Welles's version, then, would be a staged circus, of sorts.

The play deals with the disastrous results to a young man when his horse happens to eat the straw hat of an errant wife who is having an assignation with a cavalry officer. The comedy revolves around the hilarious search for an identical replacement, which must be found before the young man can get to his own wedding. Welles wanted to transform the farce into a Juvenalian satire while retaining a strong element of fantasy and have it evolve as a bitter glimpse of the small-mindedness of the middle class. He was relentless in his constant reworking of the script and often would go through all-night revising sessions with his collaborator, sometimes creating entirely new acts in the course of one sitting. According to Richard France, Denby would read aloud one of the parts and Welles would criticize it; the two men would then attempt to simplify the language. As the night grew thin, one of them would write as the other slept, and they would alternate until morning arrived and Welles would have to go off to one of his other commitments.

Welles knew that if he could direct a successful satire, often the mark of maturity in an artist, he might lessen some of the criticism he had received about his all-too-youthful approach to drama. The 1930s were a time of musical comedy experimentation, and such hits as *Strike Up the Band, Of Thee I Sing,* and *On Your Toes* all attempted to combine a social message with a light, musical approach. Welles wanted the same and encouraged Thomson to come up with some zany music that would match the insanity he was preparing for the stage. Paul Bowles, a young composer, adapted some of his works for the play, and Thomson orchestrated them into what would eventually be a surrealistic mélange of Satie and Offenbach, a pastiche of gypsy waltzes and turkey trots, bugle calls and piano rags.

The horse that eats the hat, a life-sized animal puppet constructed and choreographed by Bil Baird, made of what looked like an old, abandoned leopard skin coat and a few cast-off kitchen utensils sewn up by a drunken taxidermist, was peopled by Denby and actress Carol King.

Welles did not exclusively hire actors who were currently on the relief roles, as the government regulation insisted upon, but cast some of the parts with people who he felt had special qualifications or with whom he could easily work. For some it would mark their New York debuts; for the major part of Freddy, the bridegroom, he cast a tall, quiet young man with a slight Southern accent whom Welles had met while both were rehearsing a radio broadcast, Joseph Cotten; Edgerton Paul, a theatrical colleague from the Todd School, was signed on to operate the nickelodeon; Hiram Sherman, the man who had planned to be part of the Woodstock Festival, came to New York and made his Broadway debut in the part of Robbin; Arlene Francis, a beautiful young lady in her twenties, played Tillie, the milliner. Welles's wife, Virginia, acted as Myrtle Mugglethorpe, and Welles himself as her father.

Joseph Cotten, a 6-foot-2-inch, blond-haired aspiring actor, has recalled meeting Welles in the winter of 1935 in the office of the CBS dramatic director Knowles Entrikin, stating that Orson had made an impression on everyone that afternoon when he accidentally set Entrikin's wastebasket afire after emptying the contents of his pipe into it.

Later, when Cotten and Welles were rehearsing for a show in the jungle for a segment of radio's "School of the Air," several of the double-entendre lines struck the two young men as particularly blue and funny, especially the use of the word "pith," as in helmet. They broke into what Cotten called "choirboy giggles" everytime the word was spoken from the script, and they became friends as a result of their collective insurgency. Although never again cast on the same "School of the Air" show, they became dinner and drinking companions from that day on.

Welles changed the name of his play to *Horse Eats Hat* for two reasons: he didn't want the public to mistakenly think that all of his productions would have ethnic connotations, i.e., the Negro *Macbeth* and *The Italian Straw Hat,* and he also feared that some people who had seen the René Clair film or other previous stage productions might avoid the play, thinking that their attendance would be redundant. A new title implied a new, entirely different production.

Horse Eats Hat opened on Saturday, September 26, 1936, an evening with a nip in the air. The deep baritone of Orson Welles was heard to sing the play's only song, a bawdy lament and lyrical salute about Mugglethorpe's faithful rubber plant:

> Fond memories, girl, have graced it,
> For the very day of your birth,
> I took this slip and placed it
> In a pot of the very best earth,
> In a pot of asparagus earth.

> And when of an evening your mother
> Unbuttoned her blouse and began,
> She fed one and I fed the other
> With the aid of my watering can;
> I too was a nursing mother,
> By means of my watering can.

Lest the song and some of the dialogue offend the audience, who might have held the government responsible, Welles had a leaflet inserted into each program indicating that a federal viewpoint was not necessarily expressed therein. He called attention to the fact that the play from which the work was adapted had been first produced in Paris in 1851 and had since been "studied in schools and performed in theaters all over the world," implying innocence through academic and past professional association.

"It would be a monumental joke," one reporter observed, "if the police backed up their wagons and raided, on charges of obscenity, a government show." Senator Everett Dirksen officially condemned the work in the *Congressional Record* as "salacious tripe."

Welles tried everything short of mayhem, on and off the stage, to capture the audience. He had actors continually bursting in and out, jumping into the aisles, making speeches to the audience while props collapsed and the scenery fell (intentionally); there was a seven-door hide-and-seek set; a ballroom with a crystal chandelier; and a functioning fountain. Between the acts, a military band—featuring a fancy female trumpeter in hussar uniform, entertained. A nickelodeon in an upper box and various grand pianos spread about other boxes also added to the pandemonium, and the slapstick chases continued all evening. The consensus, however, of both critics and audience was that the play was indeed wacky but not quite wacky enough.

John Chapman of the *New York Daily News* claimed that in preparation for the play Welles and his staff must have said: "Let us be crazy. And while we are at it, let us be good and crazy," but that the stylized lunacy expressed an explosive disintegration of sorts "in which the effort not to make sense is too often a strain upon players and audiences."

The reviewer for *The New York Times*, "L.N.," described it as "though Gertrude Stein had dreamed a dream after a late supper of pickles and ice cream" and added that it was certainly "not good in the usually accepted sense of the theater." But he argued that despite its failures it was a "swell production."

Other appraisals ranged from calling *Horse Eats Hat* "the most deliberately vulgar theatrical outburst in several seasons," to "the most excruciating eruption of noises and death fumes in town," or simply a "dismal embarrassment." Some disagreed, and Marc Connelly, in *Voices Offstage*, described his own reaction:

I remember not only *Horse Eats Hat* itself, but an odd circumstance surrounding the performance. With a large attending audience one night at the Maxine Elliott Theater on Thirty-ninth Street, only two individuals audibly enjoyed its performance.

I had gone to see it alone. From the moment the curtain rose I found it hilarious. So did someone else seated some distance from me whom I couldn't see. We were volcanic islets of mirth in a sea of silence. Hearing another man laughing as much as I was kept me from being intimidated by the general apathy.

The last scene of the first act was a ballroom in a Paris mansion. It was crowded with guests waltzing to the music of an improbably large band of zymbalon players, augmenting the conventional orchestra in the pit. The dancers floated around a fountain in the center of the ballroom. (You must remember another object of the Federal Theatre was to provide jobs for technicians.)

The fugitive hero of the piece, played by the young Joseph Cotten, whom we had seen being chased by half the population of Paris, dashed onto the stage pursued by gendarmes. The dancers and the music stopped as the hero leaped like a gymnast to the branches of a chandelier. As it swung back and forth, pistols were whipped back and forth out from full-dress coats and décolleté gowns. Everyone began firing at the young man on the chandelier. Simultaneously, the fountain yet rose higher, drenching the fugitive until the chandelier, on an impulse of its own, rose like a balloon out of range. While the shooting kept up, ten liveried footmen made their way through the crowd. As the curtain began to fall they announced to the audience with unruffled dignity: "Supper is served." The moment the curtain shut off the scene, a lady cornetist in a hussar's uniform appeared in an upper box and offered a virtuoso demonstration of her skill.

As the audience and I moved into the lobby, I spotted a man wiping tears of pleasure from his eyes. It was my friend John Dos Passos. For our own security—in case the second act proved as funny as the first—we sat in adjacent vacant seats we found in a rear row. For the rest of the evening we screamed with laughter together.

It is possible that if Welles had been able to concentrate all his energies on *Horse Eats Hat,* the play might have been more critically accepted. Despite the negative reactions, it played to almost packed houses every night for three months. His attempt at the use of comedic methods such as prop and scenery manipulation, to say nothing of exaggerated mannerisms, overstated makeup, and distorted voices to achieve his farcical aims, were often successful. Many of the young actors, however, including himself were unable to execute their lines with the lively sense of projection and the delicate precision of timing that is necessary to achieve even low comedy. As Virgil Thomson said of it in his memoir, perhaps a bit too immoderately, "Welles as an actor, for all his fine bass speaking voice, never did quite get into a role; his mind was elsewhere."

In this case, in addition to pressure by his constant radio broadcasts, he also signed for a lead role in an upcoming Broadway production of Sidney Kingsley's *Ten Million Ghosts,* a drama that everyone thought might duplicate *Dead End,* the young playwright's biting story of the gangster-breeding slums on the East River, which had played exactly one year before. Samuel Goldwyn had broken something of a record at the time by paying $165,000 for the film rights of *Dead End,* and Welles knew that if *Ten Million Ghosts* was a success, he might very well end up with his first Hollywood feature film role and with a considerable amount of money in compensation.

Before the opening of *Horse Eats Hat,* as he rehearsed for the part of the bumptious Mugglethorp, he was simultaneously preparing for and rehearsing his role as André Pequot in *Ten Million Ghosts.* The idea of the play was a slashing attack on the international manufacture of munitions, a theme Welles knew something about, since he had studied the life of arms magnate Sir Basil Zaharoff, "the mystery man of Europe" as he was called, for his characterization on *The March of Time* series. He planned to continue as Mugglethorp until the Kingsley play opened, then take a leave-of-absence from the first to do the second.

When *Ten Million Ghosts* opened at the St. James Theater on October 23, 1936, Kingsley, who also staged and produced it, did not know that the moneyless public at that time, eager to escape, would care little for a story that involved condemning the rich and powerful in a somewhat pontifical tone. The play ran for only one performance and Welles returned as Mugglethorp in *Horse Eats Hat.*

Welles helped Kingsley create one piece of stage business in *Ten Million*

Ghosts, about which he was particularly proud. As an echo of the Shakespearean device of a play within a play, in the second act a group of munitions makers attend a screening in a private theater to see films of soldiers being slaughtered on the battlefield. A real motion picture projector was set up on stage. When it appears that many of the men are being needlessly killed in the film, the arms makers rise to defend themselves against the accusations of a newspaper reporter and an idealistic young Frenchman, played by Welles. Silhouetted against the flickering screen, with the images of dying men projected on their bodies, they say, "But this is our business!" as the curtain drops dramatically for the end of the act. That one scene was lauded by virtually every critic, despite a general unenthusiastic reaction to the play itself.

BY EARLY NOVEMBER, only days after the opening and rapid closing of *Ten Million Ghosts,* Welles began casting for the next production of Project 891, *Doctor Faustus* by Christopher Marlowe.

Naturally, Welles cast himself as the scholar who sells his soul to the devil. Some critics felt the move was symbolic typecasting, an unconscious personal statement by the young man of the theater, and which Houseman characterized as "uncomfortably close to the shape of Welles's own personal myth." Welles thought the play as good as anything Shakespeare did. He gathered around him actors who he felt he could trust—Hiram Sherman, Harry McKee, and Joseph Cotten, who because of a previous contractual arrangement was forced to play the part of the second scholar using the unimaginative pseudonymn of Joseph Wooll.

It seems especially fitting that the twenty-one-year-old Welles's first major New York appearance in both a starring showpiece role and directorial effort, should have as its vehicle a play by the precocious Elizabethan dramatist Christopher Marlowe, whose reputation rests on plays written in his twenties.

From the start it was clear that Welles had no intention of staging a revival whose only virtue would be a dry kind of authenticity. Rather than running the risk of producing a creaky relic, Welles, through *Faustus,* would set in motion virtually everything that he had learned up to that point about acting, stagecraft, direction, and the appetites of the 1930's public.

He went at the script. Marlowe's five-act tragedy became a play of one act and many scenes. The running time would be reduced to about eighty-five minutes, streamlined for modern audiences. The cutting was not an emasculation of the script. It was, rather, a tasteful and faithful adaptation for a twentieth-century legitimate theater audience that would still be willing to do a little work in order to appreciate an Elizabethan drama. Modernizing the language itself was out of the question, as was censorship of some of the randier aspects of the dialogue. Welles contented himself with judicious excisions here and there, dropping some minor characters and scenes, reordering other action for swifter pacing and calculated comic relief. The alterations seem justified in a play that is rather loosely bound anyway, with rapid transitions between short and sometimes inconsequential scenes. The essence of the drama had always been Marlowe's magniloquent language. That would remain.

Doctor Faustus certainly offered no end of possibilities for staging a story of infinite, diabolical powers. Faustus, the legendary sixteenth-century German scholar, yearned for powers beyond those granted to possessors of simple human knowledge. His pact with the devil, written in blood and negotiated by the demon-messenger Mephistopheles, allows Faustus to enjoy twenty-four years of superhuman powers before relinquishing his soul to the devil. During his tenure, Faustus travels around the globe with Mephistopheles, renders himself invisible at will, and is able to conjure up virtually anything he pleases. But the twenty-four years are over all too soon, and when his last hour comes, the great doctor is reduced to a cringing wretch who is finally led off by a demonic horde to make his midnight appointment with the Prince of Darkness.

Welles's experience with radio would help shape this play. He had honed his skills as a clever radio writer and adapter, working within the very close tolerances of broadcasting air time. Familiar with the elaborate, requisite cues for sound effects and musical interludes in radio presentations, he was expert at exploiting the medium that relied so much on the manipulation of the radio audience's imagination. Welles would take advantage of every opportunity to combine these techniques with his already broadening mastery of the stage. Paul Bowles would create an eerie, dissonant music, also reminiscent of radio drama, scored for oboe, saxophone, clarinet, trumpet, piccolo, trombone, and harp and played by an unseen orchestra. A radio speaker system was used to amplify the cries of the souls in hell, carrying the sound out into the front of the theater and permeating the other sections, as well. Radio experts who saw the play would invariably praise the sound effects, especially the tolling of the bell when it strikes midnight and Faustus is beckoned.

What the audience at the Maxine Elliott Theater saw on opening night, January 8, 1937, was definitely not a production calculated to please Elizabethan scholars alone. Welles, who could have easily reproduced an authentic stage set faithful to the sixteenth-century theater, chose instead to select only those details he thought he could carry over to his advantage. There were no sets per se—a concept true to the old theater—and indeed there was a walkway (an extension of the stage apron built three rows into the orchestra), the other Elizabethan convention. But instead of requiring the audience to rely entirely on its imagination with a bare set, Welles had created spaces and effects through the manipulation of sound and light. Again, Abe Feder was Welles's lighting mastermind.

The rising curtain revealed a totally black stage. From the darkness a chorus appeared, guided by a lantern. At their exit a minute later, Welles, as the brooding Faustus, was revealed, his study defined by a brilliant cone of light. The bearded Welles, decked out in robe, shoulder-length wig, and heavy, grotesque makeup, portrayed Faustus as the imposing, cocksure savant who is urged by his friends Valdes and Cornelius to dabble in the black arts. Soon Mephistopheles, played by the black actor Jack Carter with bald pate and baleful mien, made his entry by being pushed to the vicinity of Faustus in a cart controlled by stagehands.

As the play progressed, comings and goings were defined by the waxing and waning of three main areas of light. This gave the production something of the air of a magic show, or a study in a secret mystical rite, with actors making miraculous entrances, suddenly appearing out of nowhere, effects made possible by a system of three trapdoors, strategically-placed black curtains, and sudden bursts of light. In the swirling action, players gained access to the stage by the wings, by trapdoor, and from under the stage apron. This large-scale legerdemain was complemented with offstage voices filling the theater by the public address system and with chilling dissonances emanating from the orchestra pit.

Hallie Flanagan visited the theater during rehearsals one evening and, overwhelmed by the poetry of the moment, described the production:

> Going into the Maxine Elliott during rehearsals was like going into the pit of hell: total darkness punctuated by stabs of light, trapdoors opening and closing to reveal bewildered stagehands or actors going up, down, and around in circles; explosions; properties disappearing in a clap of thunder; and on stage Orson, muttering the mighty lines and interspersing them with fierce adjurations to the invisible but omnipresent Feder. The only point of equilibrium in these midnight seances was Jack Carter; quiet, slightly amused, probably the only actor who ever played Mephistopheles without raising his voice. More subtle than the red flares and necromancy was the emphasis on an element of tragedy more in keeping with our age than that of a man being snatched away by the devil—that is, the search to lay hold on reality. Faustus, emerging out of darkness on the platform thrust boldly out into the audience, drew us into his imaginings of living in voluptuousness, of resolving all ambiguities, of being on earth as Jove is in the sky. Tragedy lay in seeing the Seven Deadly Sins from which rapture was expected reduced to the stature of puppets, lewd and nauseating, flopping about in the theater box or at the feet of Faustus. Helen, in whose embrace Faustus hopes at last to get what he is paying for, is a distant masked figure.

Because of his many activities in addition to directing himself and the rest of the other actors, Welles had some problems memorizing the Latin lines spoken by Faustus. For example, during rehearsals, instead of reciting, *"Orientis princeps Beelzebub, inferni ardentis monarcha, et demorgorgon, propitiamus vos, ut appareat et surgat Mephistopheles,"* he would often simply say: "Latin, Latin, Latin: down to line 28." And then reverting to his role as director, invariably something like, "Where are the border lights?"

From time to time the horrific action was relieved by clowns and bawdy language. There was time for a trip with Mephistopheles to see the Pope and his retinue—a slapstick comedy routine in which the invisible Faustus swipes the Pope's food from under his nose and ends up with Faustus sending the Pontiff reeling with "a box on the ears."

In other entertainments, Welles-Faustus was distracted in melodramatic, morality-play fashion by an evil angel and a good angel who vied for his attention in his study. The Punch-and-Judy diversion in scene 7 that Flanagan mentions consisted of a Bil Baird puppet show of the Seven Deadly Sins, played out in the theater's upper left box, with all seven voices offered by Baird's wife, Cora.

And at the last, Faustus is given a glimpse of the eternal beauty of Helen of Troy, her evocation accompanied by music: from hence the most famous lines of the play: "Was this the face that launched a thousand ships/And burnt the topless towers of Ilium?" It was remarked by John Mason Brown of the *Post* that one of the few shortcomings of the play was that the actress portraying Helen, Paula Laurence, didn't live up to the demanding standard of transcendent beauty—but then, who could? Perhaps that is the reason, observed by audience and critics alike, that Welles did not look at her face when he spoke the famous lines. But the fact that she played the part with a frozen mask to emphasize her aloofness seems to have been overlooked by everybody.

And so Faustus is damned, Mephistopheles and his unholy crew (showing their true colors at last) appearing out of "fire," another Welles illusion, to claim their due. Faustus's last hour is marked by the chimes of the clock resounding through the theater, midnight bringing on lightning and thunder, with Welles swept away ("Ah, Mephistopheles" his last agonized cry) as hell literally breaks loose. And then the chorus's epilogue, easing the piece to a close: "Cut is the branch that might have grown full straight, And burned is Apollo's laurel bough. . . ."

The curtain had come down on a major triumph of the New York stage. In other hands, the play could have been ludicrous; somehow, though, no one saw a young man barely out of his teens performing elaborate parlor magic. Welles had taken great risks—admittedly hedging his bets with the most expert of assistance—and had won. The reviews were excellent, praising him both for his innovations and for his ability to bring Marlowe's words to a modern audience without damage to either.

The New York Times theater critic Brooks Atkinson was fairly typical of the response, citing *Doctor Faustus* for being, on the one hand, "imaginatively alive" and "nimble," and, on the other, "frank and sensible theater" that was, for all its fidelity to Marlowe, "easy to understand." That Welles was able to fashion a truly popular piece of drama out of an Elizabethan play more revered than performed was a remarkable achievement. Atkinson went on to say:

> Modern stagecraft is represented in the wizardry lighting; the actors are isolated in eerie columns of light, which are particularly well suited to the diabolical theme of *Doctor Faustus*. On the Elizabethan stage the lighting was supplied from heaven; the plays were for the most part played in the afternoon under the open sky. Beguiling as that must have been for pastorals and gentle poetics, electric lighting is more dramatic because it can be controlled.
>
> The modern switchboard is so incredibly ingenious that stage lighting has become an art in its own right. The pools and shafts of light and crepuscular

effects communicate the unearthly atmosphere of *Doctor Faustus* without diminishing the primary importance of the acting. And when the cupbearers of Beelzebub climb up out of hell, the furnace flares of purgatory flood up through a trapdoor in an awful blaze of light, incidentally giving the actors a sinister majesty.

There was, it should be admitted, one dissident voice among the first-night reviewers of *Doctor Faustus.* The *Daily News*'s Burns Mantle was lukewarm and grudging in his praise. Mantle was very much concerned that this was a play put on under the auspices of the Works Progress Administration. "It seems to me," he wrote, "that the actors of the people's theater would be better employed, considering the greatest good for the greatest number, in producing plays of timely significance." Houseman felt it necessary to reply three weeks later, remarking that men both common and uncommon had *Doctor Faustus* playing to ninety percent capacity. Nevertheless in the *News* of January 29, 1937, Mantle insisted that it was nothing but a "curio."

By all accounts, the most striking feature of *Doctor Faustus* had been the unusual use of lighting. Here Welles outlined to Feder his theory of lighting, a reversal of Elizabethan stagecraft where the dialogue and the actor dominated totally. Obviously, Welles relied to a great extent on the talents of Feder. As Feder saw it, the key to the play was the extensive use of very powerful light sources and a careful coordination between them and the stage action, music, and special effects. Feder used a formidable array of lamps: eighty-three spotlights, including over two dozen 1,000-watt spots, plus thirty-one 1,000-watt beam projectors. To orchestrate all this, Feder had positioned his electricians at three separate switching stations, and like musicians at keyboards, they were directed by an assistant stage manager who, with a script before him on a music stand, gave the lighting cues as required. This fluid, adaptive system could follow the tempo of the play regardless of variation in time between cues for any particular night. The beauty of the system was its flexibility, and among the potpourri of technicians adopted by Welles, Feder's lighting was crucial.

Almost immediately, the Federal Theatre was playing to SRO audiences several days of the week. Welles could not have dictated better notices, nor could he have predicted the extent of his popular success. He later confided to a journalist that he and Houseman, although determined from the very first to avoid producing a museum piece, suspected that they might have enjoyed a five- or six-week run based mainly on the appeal to literature classes in schools and colleges. No one was prepared, it seems, for a run of several months.

Despite the success of the play, it was a costly production and the fifty-cent "top" seat did little to pay for the ongoing expenses. Although everything was federally funded, it would sometimes take weeks, even months, after requisitions had been made, to receive money for a particular prop or disbursement. Welles would short-circuit the bureaucracy by simply using his own money on many occasions, whenever something was needed in a hurry. In the end, he spent thousands of dollars of his own personal savings that were never reimbursed. "I was probably the only person in American history who ever personally subsidized a government agency," he recalled, somewhat ruefully, years later.

WHY DID WELLES approach the production in the way he did? In an interview he gave at that time he said that his aim was "to create on modern spectators an effect corresponding to the effect in 1589 when the play was new. We want to rouse the same magical feeling, but we use modern methods," he said. "I think Marlowe would be delighted." He went on to say that "every production of our classics should make its own impact in its own way."

In keeping with the deviltry on stage, Welles could be mystifying both in and out of costume. During this same interview, when the play was clearly recognized as a hit, he claimed that in fact the "greatest novelty" of the production came in rehearsals when he introduced "the radio method of directing." He elaborated: "Whenever I wanted anything or anybody, I spoke into a microphone, and my voice reached the remotest parts of the building. People came running as if they had heard Gabriel blow his trumpet." Radio was still a magic word. Orson had created in the Latin sense of the word his own *auditorium.*

Be that as it may, the light was the thing. As one writer pointed out two weeks after the opening, the effects were cinematic: as an actor moves downstage from under a shaft of light, his apparent size is seen to change most dramatically; in effect, the stage director is able to get move "shots" at distance and in close-up. When a sense of vastness was needed, the stage was more brightly lit; when compactness was necessary, it was dimmed. In all cases, the lighting followed the tempo of the play. To an audience brought up on evenly lighted rooms behind proscenium arches, the result was startling, and strains of bizarre music of the damned, produced a novel audience reaction. Simply watching Welles move around the stage gave spectators a kind of perspective dislocation that registered as a set of small shocks. Most reviewers fell, predictably, upon the same phrase: through Orson Welles, the devil had received his due.

So much did he live the part, Orson seemed somewhat filled with the dread of his own character, complaining to Houseman and others during the run of *Faustus* that he was having surrealistic nightmares almost every night about death, skulls, men donned in black, and other spatial disorientations. This feeling became more pronounced when Orson's brother, Richard, appeared on the scene tattered and incoherent, somehow having had himself released after ten years in a mental institution.

The two men barely got on, Orson feeling that his brother, at best an intrusion, was not to be trusted. Richard was confused as to wanting to become involved in the circle of his now famous younger brother, while simultaneously wanting to asperse, out of jealousy, that same reputation. In a matter of days, Richard left New York, but Orson still complained of darkened dreams and feelings of guilt and doom.

CHAPTER 7

BY THE BEGINNING of 1937, radio was firmly entrenched as one of the principal forms of entertainment in America. It was the period when Orson Welles enjoyed some of his most active and prolific experiences with the medium. He was now twenty-two years old and, in addition to his role on "The Shadow" and his frequent anonymous impersonations for *The March of Time,* he was appearing in *Doctor Faustus*; reading poetry over the air; making guest appearances on the Federal Theatre Radio Division's series of classical plays; voicing the commercials for My-T-Fine Chocolate Pudding; reading poems, soliloquies, and passages from the Bible on a CBS program called "Musical Reveries"; narrating and playing the great McCoy for the "Wonder Show" series; and appearing in "Roses and Drums," an NBC weekly series about the Civil War—sometimes costumed in a Union or Confederate uniform for the sake of the studio audience. He also flew to Chicago and back every Sunday to do a broadcast there. This was during the height of the Depression, and he was rarely making less than one thousand dollars a week; a virtual king's ransom by today's standards.

In late spring, CBS announced plans to air a summertime festival of some of Shakespeare's greatest plays, starring renowned actors of stage and screen. Welles was given the commission to construct the radio adaptation of *Hamlet* and was signed on to act in at least one of the other productions. He was delighted to be able to combine his knowledge of Shakespeare with his growing mastery of radio, so at a small country place he and Virginia had rented in Sneden's Landing, only a short drive from Manhattan, he worked on the script. He discovered that Shakespeare's use of description, subtly implanted in expository dialogue rather than in narrative asides, was perfect for radio, as were the Bard's compact scenes, his method of introducing a character expositionally, and his use of the rhymed couplet—which on radio could easily be translated into the familiar musical bridge, or flourish, to indicate a lapse of time.

While CBS was still arranging details of the weekly series, its rivals at NBC secured the great John Barrymore for their own Shakespearean series, which made it to the air on June 21, three weeks before the CBS show's premiere. Barrymore did special forty-five minute adaptations, consisting of a synopsis written by him and then the acting of key scenes of such plays as *Hamlet, Richard III, Macbeth, King Lear,* and *Richard II.* When CBS's first program of the Shakespeare cycle finally aired on July 12, it was scheduled on the same night—Monday—as the Barrymore show but, in order to compete, thirty minutes earlier.

Some of the same plays were to be offered with an impressive legion of stars, with a few of these performers making their first major radio appearances. Leslie Howard and Rosalind Russell acted in the comedy *Much Ado About Nothing*; Claude Rains played the imperious title role in *Julius Caesar* with Walter Abel, Thomas Mitchell, Reginald Denny, and a cast of sixty; *The Taming of the Shrew,* adapted by renowned critic Gilbert Seldes, starred Edward G. Robinson as a not-so-improbable Petruchio; Archibald MacLeish did an adaptation of *King Lear,* with Thomas Mitchell and Margo as the principals; Frank Morgan, Dennis King, and Gail Patrick starred in a version of the always popular *As You Like It,* proving that all the world—even the radio—is a stage. Even Humphrey Bogart, stepping out of his Broadway role as the terrifying Duke Mantee in *The Petrified Forest,* played the warrior Hotspur in *Henry IV, Part I.*

The show on which Welles appeared, the last of the seven-part series, was Shakespeare's fantasy *Twelfth Night,* starring Tallulah Bankhead as the lovable Viola, Sir Cedric Hardwicke as the affectatious Malvolio, and Orson as the sentimental and noble Duke Orsino. Ray Collins played Antonio. According to Lee Israel, one of Tallulah Bankhead's biographers, Tallulah agreed to the role as a warm-up for her impending stage production of *Antony and Cleopatra,* but her "classical acting was wanting." Welles, on the other hand, was strong as the handsome and sympathetic Orsino, his voice, with its special tone and depth creating a presence of character that dominated the broadcast. While many of the performers seemed as though they were doing nothing more than acting in front of a microphone, Welles sounded like a real person in the realm of Ilyria who just happened to drop into the listener's living room through the benefit of a strange electrical device.

The story of his hiring an ambulance with its sirens wailing and its red lights flashing to better dodge the impossible Manhattan traffic as he attempted to go from broadcast to broadcast and make it by airtime is not apocryphal. In those days before the advent of quality tape recording, virtually all radio shows were performed "live," often with a studio audience, and Welles's popularity as a radio voice was so great that he was kept busy hour after hour, almost seven days a week, traveling from studio to studio. Equally true is the story of an elevator in an office building containing a studio atop being kept waiting especially for him, so that after alighting from his vehicle to the sound of screeching brakes, he could soar to the upper floors in seconds and in a dramatic entrance make airtime in one of the studios with perhaps a second to spare.

Paul D. Zimmerman, a *Newsweek* critic, said that Welles's voice was sonorous, "full of elegance and easy virility," and other listeners readily agreed. Radio producers and directors kept Welles working for years because of the astonishing range he was able to produce. Standing before the microphone as though it were a mirror, he would seemingly be able to gesture with sound and move himself in space, creating illusions of intimacy or distance by employing only certain voice changes: an audible pantomime. He could play Iago as well as Hamlet, Othello no less than Prospero; a newsboy or a tyrant, a child or a patriarch. Somehow, his Ciceronian tones—he would say "actorrrr" for "actor," for example—were pleasurable and seemed unpretentious, and he knew how to give his performance just enough light and shade to prevent monotony or sameness, when to switch from quietness to tenseness, or from softness to shouting. One critic did feel that he went a bit too far in promoting certain products during commercials: "It's a shock to hear a plug for prune juice by someone who sounds like the Archbishop of Canterbury."

Each studio's acoustical balance—the presence of the room, the quality of the microphone and the equipment, and the expertise of the engineer—was different. Because Welles played in almost every radio station in New York City and had opportunities to experiment, he became familiar with whatever special demands were called for in a particular room or studio, and knew how best his voice would register most effectively in relationship to specific environments.

He would often appear at the radio studios in his makeup for *Faustus,* including his beard, but wearing a tuxedo. After delivering his last speech on the air, just a few minutes before nine, he would jump into his ambulance, or a waiting taxi, and speed to the Maxine Elliott Theater. As the chorus recited its passage in the opening scene, he would climb into his costume and make his entry on the stage with barely an instant before his cue. Somehow, perhaps because of the mystical aid of Mephistopheles, he never missed, nor was he late for, a performance.

By 1937, it seemed as if everyone owned a radio. Some ten million were being sold annually, and the new sets were designed to improve reception on an international scale. The reportage of world events over the radio propelled the medium into even greater heights of popularity. The marriage of the Duke of Windsor and his American "queen," Mrs. Wallis Simpson; the destruction of the *Hindenburg*; the Braddock-Louis fight for the heavyweight championship of the world; the funeral of John D. Rockefeller; Franklin D. Roosevelt's second inaugural; and the great flood of the Mississippi Valley, all within the first half of that year, were followed on the radio by millions who normally might not have been so informed. And these same millions were listening to radio not only as a source of news or public interest events but as the principal outlet of entertainment in their lives. Through radio, a wooden puppet named Charlie McCarthy, and his ventriloquist, Edgar Bergen, were becoming a part of the national consciousness; as were Major Bowes and his amateur hour; and the antics of stage and screen comic W. C. Fields.

The radio networks believed that there was an audience for more thoughtful entertainment in addition to the Shakespearean experiment and began to establish other dramatic programming of meaningful variety. A spokesman for CBS promised that the network's offerings for the year would be dedicated to "the introduction of serious dramatic efforts by well-known authors," and other stations also announced plans for similarly dramatic broadcasts.

It was CBS that first decided to start a regularly scheduled dramatic series to be aired each week. A young radio engineer, Irving Reis, suggested one called "The Columbia Workshop," where different kinds of dramatic experiments, technical and creative, could be performed. The series that followed, a "sustaining" show without commercial sponsorship, became radio history. After a few months of off-air experimentation, Reis received and accepted for broadcast a thirty-minute play entitled *The Fall of the City,* by Archibald MacLeish. Similar in structure to *Panic,* the new work was also a play in verse form, but with one important difference: it was written directly for the radio, to be performed over the air, not on the stage.

The Fall of the City was more than just the first American verse play written for radio; it was a polemic, a clarion call to the public that warned them against totalitarianism and told them to take heed against the false orators of fascism. It portrayed a mythical city but one that could be real: the similarities of a city about to topple in the radio play to one that might really fall under the growing and menacing boot of a Hitler or a Mussolini, who had just formed the Rome-Berlin axis, were clear. No time frame is mentioned in *The Fall of the City.* The message was for all times. The play made it clear that fascism could be overcome only with active resistance; freedom, if it was to be maintained, would have to be fought for.

Because MacLeish had been so pleased with Welles's performance of McGafferty in *Panic,* the poet suggested him for one of the principal voices, that of the all-important radio announcer or narrator, posted high above the city square, sharing everything he sees, and Welles accepted the role at a much lower fee than he was usually paid for radio work. Another young actor, Burgess Meredith, who had recently received $1,500 for his title role in *Hamlet* on radio, accepted twenty dollars to play in *The Fall of the City.* He, too, recognized its importance and wanted to contribute to what appeared to be a new art form in the making.

Irving Reis wanted an acoustical atmosphere that projected a huge city square, and arrangements were made to broadcast the program from the Seventh Regiment Armory on Park Avenue at Sixty-seventh Street in New York City. His theory was that the ear, though not quite as sensitive as the eye, could nevertheless judge the distance of sound, could discern its direction, and could discriminate between sounds, selecting those that were most important and ignoring others that were less so. He hired a group of about two hundred college drama students to play the crowd—the largest cast ever assembled for a radio show—and through a special technique made the throngs sound like a mass of ten thousand. After the show, Reis explained to an interviewer from the *Herald Tribune* how it was done:

At a given cue in the script, the crowd would be given a signal to cheer. When the persons around the microphone stopped cheering, the recordings of their own voices were brought in. These sounds took about three seconds to reach the microphone. With careful timing of both on-stage sounds and off-stage recordings, the resulting aural effect, as interpreted by the listeners, sounded exactly like the cheers of a great crowd, echoing in the distance.

Welles's function was to give to the listener an eyewitness view of the proceedings in the square. During rehearsals Reis had determined that the crowds drowned out even Welles's thunderous voice, so he constructed a small studio—actually an isolation booth—in the center of the Armory. Welles sat inside with a microphone and when Reis cued his turn to speak, the sounds of Welles's voice and the crowd were mixed for better clarity. It worked perfectly during the actual broadcast. Critic Gilbert Seldes noted, in *Scribner's* magazine, that the technique created a symphonic effect, "as the selection of contrasting voices and the balancing of sound when the narrator spoke over and under the crowd voices."

Welles's voice, its tones as round as pumpkins, began the first description:

We are here on the central plaza.
We are well off to the eastward edge.
There is a kind of terrace over the crowd here.
It is precisely four minutes to twelve.

The crowd is enormous; there might be ten thousand;
There might be more; the whole square is faces.

That voice, and those words, sent a spark through the listening audience that many have felt signaled a new renaissance of radio drama. More people heard the message of a single poet and a single poem that night than at any other time in history. As Eric Barnouw observed in his monumental text, *History of Broadcasting*: "They heard something that, by the very texture of its sound, gripped the attention and chilled the marrow. Orson Welles, its principal voice, established himself as one of the great performers of radio."

It is possible that no one connected with the production imagined the visual and emotional impact they were having on the imaginations of their audience. Welles, as narrator, said:

I wish you could all see this as we do.
The whole plaza full of these people:
Their colorful garments, the harsh sunlight.
The watersellers swinging enormous gourds.
The orator there on the stone platform.
The temple behind him.
The high pyramid.
The hawks overhead in the sky
Teetering slow to the Windward
Swift to the downwind.
The houses blind with the blank sun on them.

All who were listening *could* see the square in their minds, and the memory would prove to be indelible. Merril Dannison, writing in *Theater Arts* magazine, concurred: "Recalling the broadcast months afterwards, I find that it is not the words that I remember but the visual images they created. So rare were they, that I can still see the Conqueror's advance across the square, the crowd's tragic acceptance of defeat, the announcer's horrified amazement when he realized that there was nothing inside the armor, that no man, but an idea, had become the victor."

The story revolves about a people who anticipate the subjugation of an approaching conqueror, and horrifyingly welcome it despite the admonitions of wise men and priests. A dead woman comes from her tomb and warns them:

> The city of masterless men
> Will take a master.
> There will be shouting then:
> Blood after!

When the conqueror does come, an armor-clad figure, clanking with metal, the people prostrate themselves before him. When he opens the visor of his helmet the people cannot, or will not, see what is inside.* Only the announcer, Welles, is able to see:

> There is no one.
> No one at all.
> No one.
> The helmet is hollow.
> The metal is empty.
> The armor is empty.
> I tell you there is no
> One at all there.

Despite the fact that the program was aired at 7:00 P.M. on a Sunday night—competing opposite the extremely popular "Jack Benny Show," its audience was enormous; as if by instinct, millions tuned in.

The success of the drama did more than just elevate the reputations of MacLeish and Welles: it inspired poets and playwrights to use the medium for their message. Within weeks after its airing, W. H. Auden, Alfred Kreymborg, Irwin Shaw, and Stephen Vincent Benét wrote plays directly for radio, and CBS commissioned Sherwood Anderson to do an original radio script while NBC hired Maxwell Anderson to create one. Later came the works of Edna St. Vincent Millay, Norman Rosten, William Saroyan, Dorothy Parker, Lord Dunsany, and others. John Gassner wrote, in the introduction to his *Twenty Best Plays of the Modern Theater*: "For the future, the greater significance of

---

*In medieval times when a knight opened his visor, it was traditionally thought of as a gesture of peaceful intentions.

The Fall of the City lies in the fact that with it a real poet and an intelligent dramatist invaded the broadcasting studios. Thanks largely to Archibald MacLeish, the airways are no longer completely monopolized by Pollyanna and her laxative-sponsored cousins."

WELLES'S POPULARITY AS the preeminent broadcasting personality of the day grew even larger after *The Fall of the City,* which was easily the most famous radio show in history to that time. Now that he was given on-air credit, fan letters began arriving for him; even his friend and mentor, Alexander Woollcott, who had heard him on "Musical Reveries," was prompted to pen: "Imagine me writing a letter to a radio performer. I heard you by the wildest mischance. . . . Someone had tuned in to your station and I heard you read. I think you do it magnificently."

Now Orson was forced to turn down offers because of his hectic and overcrowded schedule. He had the rare opportunity to select only those vehicles he found appealing, so when the Mutual Network, eager to compete with CBS and NBC, approached him with the idea of doing a short series that he would not only adapt and write but also have complete creative control over and star in, he accepted. He chose Victor Hugo's long novel *Les Misérables*; it had substantial sections of dialogue. Welles adapted it to be broadcast in seven parts, making it an ideal radio piece.

Les Misérables was considered Hugo's masterpiece. Welles described his method of treating the work for radio as "a projection," an entirely new method to capture the essential character of the book, but not really a dramatization or adaptation. The most important narrative and descriptive passages were to be read; all dialogue was Hugo's own. Novels had been read on the radio before, in a condensed or dramatized form, but Welles's loyalty to the book, combined with carefully prepared sound effects and music, produced an effort that was not quite like anything previously heard on the air.

If a reader becomes confused or loses attention while reading a sentence in a book, he always has the opportunity of going back over what he has just read. However, a character in radio is in the listener's mind as long as he has words to speak. Conversation, rather than soliloquy, was the method Orson employed to keep a character alive. Welles aimed for clarity, shortening Hugo's sentences whenever he could, searching for onomatopoeic sounds having sensory meanings—like "grunt" or "splash." He managed to retain the flavor and identity of Hugo's intentions. In all, he tried to be simple but elegant:

> To the outcast all things are hostile and all things are suspicious. He distrusts the day because it helps to discover him . . . and the night because it helps to surprise him.

In his version, Welles developed the character of Jean Valjean more fully than it had been in the novel. He also voiced the part of the narrator. He played the part of Valjean with a deep, robust French accent one moment, and gave the narrator, which he also played, a clipped young tone the next. For most of the cast, Welles hired the actors who played on "The Shadow": Frank Readick, his predecessor as the Shadow's voice, took the part of the Bishop; William Johnstone, who would ultimately replace Welles on "The Shadow," was the young revolutionary Marius; Agnes Moorehead, Welles's Margot Lane in "The Shadow," played several parts. Welles's wife, Virginia, was cast in the part of Valjean's ward, Cosette; Martin Gabel played Javert; Hiram Sherman and Ray Collins did a number of roles. Some of Welles's Project 891 actors were also given parts.

So everyone would feel at home, the eerie strains of "The Shadow's" theme, *Omphale's Spinning Wheel*, by Saint-Saëns, would filter into many of the segments. Welles would open each program with the famous Hugo lines: "As long as these problems are not solved, so long as ignorance and poverty remain on the earth, these words cannot be useless." The listeners agreed; the series captured a large and appreciative audience and was hailed as a *succès d'estime.*

AARON COPLAND ONCE pointed out in his thesis *Our New Music* that no country's musical life appears to be entirely mature until its composers succeed in creating an indigenous operatic theater. It is mainly for this reason that Welles was attracted to a highly inventive operatic work offered to him for production, Marc Blitzstein's *The Cradle Will Rock*. Welles saw the possibility of adding another unique theatrical effort to his fast-growing credits of dramatic invention, one that might contribute to the definition of what American opera could be all about.

Blitzstein was an accomplished pianist and former soloist with the Philadelphia Orchestra. He had studied music with Arnold Schoenberg and Nadia Boulanger and later became a friend of Virgil Thomson and Paul Bowles. And like Orson he had also been a child prodigy, a musical *wunderkind* who performed publicly at the age of three. His sociological light opera (although he called it "a play with music"), *The Cradle Will Rock*, written in five weeks during September and October of 1936, could find no Broadway producer until Thomson convinced Welles to listen to Blitzstein perform it himself in a one-man audition.

Written after the death of Blitzstein's wife, *The Cradle Will Rock* was all at once a satirical, tender, bitter, and pessimistic cry that condemned big industry corruption and championed the gallantry of struggling labor unions. One of the lead characters, Mr. Mister, is a financial royalist who virtually owns, and certainly controls, Steeltown. He corrupts the press, swindles the church, and plots the assassination of a labor organizer. Labor conquers, however, and Mister is overwhelmed.

The style of musical presentation was similar to the works of Hanns Eisler or Kurt Weill; it contained not continuous melodies, but a succession of songs, and the message was decidedly Left. It was a musical version of what Clifford Odets's taxicab-strike play, *Waiting for Lefty*, was for American audiences in

1935: filled with energy, life, and conviction. Blitzstein dedicated it to Bertolt Brecht; *Cradle* contained a number of respectful echoes of political expressionism as could be found in Brecht's *Die Dreigroschenoper.*

At a dinner party attended by Welles, Howard Da Silva, Houseman, Virgil Thomson, and Hallie Flanagan for purposes of appraisal, Blitzstein performed *The Cradle Will Rock,* and, as Flanagan described that moment:

> Marc Blitzstein sat down at the piano and played, sang and acted with the hard, hypnotic drive which came to be familiar to audiences, his new opera. It took no wizardry to see that this was not just a play set to music, not music illustrated by actors, but music and play equalling something new and better than either.

Da Silva was being considered for a part in the play, and eventually he began to sing along with Blitzstein, giving everyone a sampling of his voice. It was perfect for the part: deep and a bit cynical, with a touch of gravel.

Welles fell in love with this "opera of labor" and was already convinced that *The Cradle Will Rock* should be his next directorial effort. He made Blitzstein promise that no matter what happened and who ultimately produced it, that he, Welles, would be named as director. After that evening, all the others involved agreed that it was an exceptional work and that the Federal Theatre should be the producing body. Da Silva had to resign his post as director of the Federal Theatre Radio Division when he was given the major part of Larry Foreman. Actor Will Geer, who had played in such hits as *Let Freedom Ring* and *Bury the Dead* on Broadway, and whose political sentiments were particularly radical after his two trips to Russia to play with the Moscow Art Theater, would assume the character of the opera's protagonist, the villainous Mr. Mister. Arrangements were made, details negotiated, and Welles began to cast and put together the next production for Project 891. The scheduled opening date was June 16, 1937.

Although it is true that Welles saw *Cradle* as sinewy entertainment, he was also deeply interested in its political message, its cry in behalf of the union struggle in this country. He said at that time that he had been "waiting for a good worker's play; *The Cradle Will Rock* is just that, offering a tale that is ideologically sound and a perfect fusion of music and drama."

As with all of his creations, Welles had ambitious plans for the production: a twenty-eight-piece orchestra; a professional chorus; dancers; glass scenery of his own ingenious design, upon which the cast would stand and which could be moved back and forth across the stage to create the illusion of courtroom, union hall, street corner. *Cradle* would not be all *Sturm und Drang,* however; it would be the first large-scale proletarian musical that would employ such Broadway staples as hit songs and straight comedy. Unfortunately, the government had other ideas.

Almost as Welles began, rumors were circulating in the theater world that the administration had plans to prevent the opening because of *Cradle's* anticapitalist stance. The unfair labor tactics of a combine called Little Steel was all over the newspapers at that time and, it was being whispered,

Washington was afraid of what *Cradle* might produce in adverse reaction from the manufacturing interests in the United States. Perhaps Welles had an instinctive feeling that the play was heading for trouble, for in spite of his initial enthusiasm, in the first few weeks he spent little time in rehearsals. Lehman Engel, the musical director of the play, remembered that a sunny day would send Orson out of the theater for a long lunch; an interesting group of friends were sufficient excuse for canceling the evening schedule.

"Dangerous" was the one word that was most often applied to the impending production. Houseman insisted that someone from Washington view the rehearsals to make a judgment of acceptability, so one of the administrators of the WPA, Lawrence Morris, came to New York, watched the action for an entire day and urged the men to continue with the production. "It's magnificent," he proclaimed.

There were certain obvious economic realities that bound the Federal Theatre Project to the WPA. When the Depression began to abate, the government had to reduce expenditures made to various programs. Cuts of 25 to 30 percent were expected in the white collar division alone—hundreds of thousands of jobs would be lost. It appeared that all of the arts projects might have to be entirely cut. In anticipation, a new form of strike was being conducted to protest the projected cuts: they were called "sit-ins" and consisted of audience, cast, and crew, all members or sympathizers of the WPA, refusing to vacate a theater until such time as the press would appear to hear—and report—their grievances.

On May 19, The Nora Bayes Theater on Manhattan's Forty-fourth Street and Eighth Avenue was seized by WPA members and surrounded by pickets as a demonstration against the projected slashes. A week later, seven thousand WPA workers went on strike (although some newspapers claimed the strikers numbered more than thirty thousand). All the Federal Theatres across the country went "dark" that night. In front of the Maxine Elliott Theater, Blitzstein, Will Geer, Da Silva, and others from Project 891 and *The Cradle Will Rock* cast handed out leaflets protesting the government's imminent action to crowds waiting to get refunds for that night's performance.

Blitzstein urged and then challenged Da Silva, "Do the leaflet scene. Do Larry," he pleaded. Da Silva, standing with his back against one of the theater's billboards, recognized the dramatic possibilities of the moment, and—much to the surprise, then the delight of those waiting—broke into song, "I'm Loaded, Armed-to the Teeth with Leaflets," at first softly and then with growing confidence, in his deep natural bass.

Rehearsals for *Cradle* went on for close to three months, all the while in the shadow of uncertainty as to its future opening. Over 14,000 tickets had been sold for various performances, and as the opening date grew closer, it appeared as though the government would probably not interfere. Then on June 12, four days before the first scheduled preview, Hallie Flanagan received an official memorandum from Harry Hopkins that the *Cradle* would not be permitted to rock at all: "Because of cuts and re-organization, any new production scheduled to open before July 1, 1937, must be postponed." Privately, Flanagan charged censorship but publicly she did everything she could, working with the bureaucrats to have them make an exception to the rule, citing the enormous expense already incurred for salaries, set design, and manufacture. She also talked of the general quality and importance of the opera itself and attempted to explain the historical moment of the production. Government officialdom was adamant: there would be no exceptions.

Welles, accompanied by the respectable and impressive attorney, poet, and friend of the play, Archibald MacLeish, flew to Washington the next day in an attempt to meet with Hopkins, who was unfortunately not available. David Niles, one of Hopkins's assistants, received the two men, who eloquently pleaded their case. Welles provided the specifics of the difficulties that had been met in mounting the play and the unconscionable waste of talent—after three months of work—that would be incurred if the play failed to open. MacLeish tried to reason with Niles from a legal and philosophical point of view, quoting a Supreme Court decision one moment and the words of Socrates the next.

The WPA simply could not authorize the exception, Niles insisted. If one play was permitted to open, he continued, other companies would also claim special circumstances and the budget could not tolerate it. Growing impatient, Welles threatened: "If the play cannot open as advertised under Government auspices, then Houseman and I will put it on ourselves!" Niles seemed totally unperturbed and perhaps grateful for the rationale of a rupture: "In that case, we would be no longer interested in the property."

Over fifteen hundred employees of the WPA Federal Arts Project were dismissed at that time, and Orson signed a petition protesting the government's action. He also urged and convinced other theater personalities to protest: Franchot Tone, Sylvia Sidney, Robert Benchley, Fredric March, Lionel Stander, and Rockwell Kent.

Meanwhile, a dress rehearsal for *Cradle* was held. In spirit it was an actual first performance, although no money was charged. Several hundred theater people, critics, and political, cultural, and amicable sympathizers attended, and the inflamed and indignant consensus was that *The Cradle Will Rock* was all and maybe more than everybody said it would be: a savage and ingenious work, totally conscious, but not offensively, of its own special corner of the theater, a theme of literal prostitution through the personification of the moll . . . and a prostitution of another kind, that of selling out one's professional dignity and talent to big business.

On the day of the announced first official performance, the front doors of the Maxine Elliott were padlocked and federal guards placed outside to protect its property and make sure that nothing was removed from the theater. Although no one of the cast or audience was permitted to enter the theater, through a guarded side door, Orson, Houseman, MacLeish, Lehman Engel, Augusta Weissberger, and a few others entered and met inside to determine what to do. Like a group of bomb-throwing anarchists at a secret meeting, they offered each other plotlike solutions to their dilemma. In between whispers at regular intervals would be heard, "The play *will* go on," from a booming Orson.

Someone suggested that if the play could not be performed at the Maxine Elliott, perhaps another theater could be secured for the evening. While some of the conspirators were attempting to find a suitable—or any available— Broadway theater that would accommodate a sell-out, first-night crowd, others continued trying to work with the WPA. A call was placed to Hopkins, who was still unavailable. Lehman Engel spoke to another Hopkins assistant, Ellen Woodward, and naively told her that he believed a great error was being made by the government. "The house is sold out," he told her. "Think of the scandal if the audience arrives and is not admitted. The WPA approved the show months ago. It has rehearsed for months. Much money has been spent." When she began to respond negatively, Lehman handed the phone to MacLeish who, in turn attempted to reason with her. The government could not and would not rescind its order to keep the play from opening, he was coldly informed. There was a rumor that surfaced later, which was never confirmed, that so potentially explosive was the Project 891 situation that FDR was approached by someone in the WPA to give his own personal ruling about *The Cradle Will Rock*. His decision, so goes the tale, was to follow Hopkins's policy of no new productions.

Meanwhile, the search for another theater went on, and all the houses that did not have a play on their boards were contacted. The Empire was empty but totally in mothballs, dirty and incapable of being put ready in a few hours. The Guild was being refurbished and more than half of its seats had been ripped out. The National proved too expensive. Another theater, whose name is now forgotten by those who were involved, seemed ideal but the arrangement failed when it was determined that it was being picketed, hardly the symbolic atmosphere for a play that strongly advocated labor unions.

In the final hours, the Venice Theater, on Seventh Avenue and Fifty-ninth Street, was secured for the yeoman sum of $100. The rental was arranged by the intervention of a small man whom Welles had been avoiding all day, "because he had the air of a process server." It turned out that the man was an agent for distressed theaters, knew of Welles's plight, and was attempting to give him exactly what he needed.

Welles immediately sketched out the mechanics of how an abbreviated version of the play could be performed. The orchestra could not be used, because the union scale would be prohibitive (now that the government wasn't paying for it), and the union problems with the cast would have to be worked out. A piano was rented for ten dollars and a truck en route to the Lincoln Tunnel, virtually commandeered for five dollars, transported it uptown.

Frank Fillmore, head of Actors' Equity, was telephoned for permission to allow the cast to appear at another theater. Fillmore, although a union man who believed in the play's message, could not give consent because actors appearing on the commercial stage while employed by the WPA might risk losing their relief status, an important source of income for most of the cast. It was Houseman who brilliantly solved this dilemma. "I am the producer of the show at the Venice," he announced to the waiting cast. "No one can prevent you from sitting in the audience and at the appropriate time standing at your seat to sing your part."

Nineteen of the forty cast members eventually made their way up to the Venice, the others feeling the risk of dismissal from the WPA was too great. The hundreds of people waiting outside the Maxine Elliott were told by Orson, standing on a box in front of the theater, that the performance would be at 9:00 P.M., at the Venice, twenty blocks north . . . and they should please bring their friends: the theater was huge and there would be no charge. He was beaming. The crowd was cheering.

Contrary to legend, there was no organized parade up Sixth Avenue that night led by Orson carrying a placard, illuminated by torchlight. But to those of the cast, crew, and audience, augmented by curiosity seekers, who made their way north by subway, car, trolley, taxi, or foot it was not just a little like a defiant march to the town square. Large groups, on the sidewalks, did stick together, talking with some of the cast and each other, as they walked. The sense of being part of a communal action, righteously defiant against unseen oppressions, was heady. The original audience of slightly less than one thousand had doubled by the time they reached the Venice.

Welles and Houseman, the now renegade director and producer of Project 891, ambled out onto the stage together. It was the older man who spoke first and, ever the diplomat, stressed that the forthcoming event was not to be considered a political protest, but an artistic one. He gently thanked Hallie Flanagan and the WPA for the opportunities that had been given them and then introduced Welles.

Orson also sidestepped the political ramifications of the project and immediately thanked the audience for "making the arduous journey to the northern reaches of the city." He explained to the audience what the play meant to him and what kind of performance the audience might have seen had not the WPA interfered. He talked of the scenery, the costumes, the special effects.

Da Silva, sitting in one of the boxes, at the ready for his performance as Larry Foreman, learned only then, listening to Orson, how the play was to be presented in the original performance. "We had no idea that at the finale the whole stage was to rock. Blinding lights were to shoot at us from below, the steelworkers' trumpets, fifes and drums were to blare at us from the loudspeakers located most unexpectedly all through the house." All of that pageant was gone, of course, replaced by a lone, battered, upright piano, on a bare stage, illuminated by a single spotlight. The back was pulled off, exposing the instrument's innards, to increase the volume. Welles briefly explained the narrative meaning of the play and noted that he could see some, but certainly not all of the cast, spread throughout the theater. Since cast was now audience, he went on, in a manifesto for living theater, that audience could become cast if they wanted: "If you have the urge to act, just get up and do so."

Although the audience was already experiencing a sense of anticipation of stage history in the making, it wasn't until Orson finished his speech that they were sure that they were in for a memorable evening. "We have the honor to present—with the composer at the piano—*The Cradle Will Rock!*" Blitzstein introduced the play: "A street corner—Steeltown, U.S.A." and thought he would have to play virtually all the parts himself. However, when he began to sing the moll's song, in his raspy voice, Olive Stanton, who played that role, courageously stood in one of the boxes and contributed her part, taking the words from Blitzstein's mouth:

> I'm checking home now, call it a night.
> Getting up to my room, turn on the light—
> Jesus, turn off the light!

For the rest of the evening, the audience was enthralled as each actor would pick up his cue. Blitzstein, in his shirt sleeves, belted out tune after tune and the actors dutifully stood and performed their parts, the chorus answering from the first few rows. People in the balcony often left their seats and raced to one side or another of the theater in order to get a better view of the performer at hand. Others moved their heads back and forth as if attending a theatrical tennis match.

Orson sat a few feet away from Blitzstein and would occasionally explain to the audience the changes in scenes, the fact that a telephone just rang or that an explosion had occurred, or stage business or sound effects that, under the circumstances, could not be produced visually or aurally.

It is possible that Welles, after studying the play in progress and its irresistible impact on the audience, without the pomp and spectacle he had intended to attach to it, became a sadder but wiser man. He learned a lesson in form versus content that he would apply, although not exclusively, to some of his future productions. All styles in dramatic design and production are possible, but it is the theatrical genius who can discern which will best enhance the harmony and message of the play. In his overpowering and, perhaps, overly youthful desire to be original, Welles had originally failed to truly understand the genre and personality of *The Cradle Will Rock*; had his conception been realized, the meaning of the play that night would have continually had to struggle against the dazzling interference of his props, scenery, and effects. The conditions under which the play was performed that night might have appeared stark and brutal; that humble, almost sordid, ambience was part of the play's message, however, and its informal charm made it work brilliantly.

Ruth Sedgwick, reviewing the play for *Stage* magazine, captured the experience of exaltation that everyone felt in her description of the theater, "At its angriest and best—at that high moment with the excitement mounting, mounting, a great art became a living crusade." And Archibald MacLeish was no less dramatic when he called it, "The most exciting evening of theater this New York generation has seen."

During the last part of the play, where Mr. Mister's strength is seen collapsing, and as Ella Hammer sings a lament for a dead worker's sister, Larry Foreman explains what unions really mean to the workers. It was a rousing and unforgettable finale. Everyone in the audience was on his feet. Flashbulbs popped. Welles, Blitzstein, Houseman, and MacLeish stood on the stage. Orson raised his hands and asked for quiet. "We will all now sit down," he said, "and the only one left standing will be Archibald MacLeish." The poet then went on to explain how this performance of *Cradle* comprised one of the most curious and spectacular evenings in American theater.

By the next morning, stories of the rousing and unconventional opening of *The Cradle Will Rock* appeared in newspapers all over the country. One New York daily accurately captured the feeling of most of the cast in its headlines: "WPA Opera Cast Fears Spanking." As it developed, the cast, despite its apprehension, took a two-week leave of absence from Project 891; the show was continued at the Venice, with bare stage and Blitzstein accompaniment, and, as legend has it, in his pocket a membership card of The Dramatists' Guild as librettist and composer; a membership card in the American Federation of Musicians as pianist; and a membership card in Actors' Equity to enable him to speak the lines.

SHORTLY AFTER THIS, a producer by the name of Arthur Hopkins agreed to back Orson in a production of *King Lear*.* Orson unhesitatingly accepted. He began making plans but abandoned the project when Hopkins continued to stall him in giving him even the first payment as stipulated in their contract.

---

*Hopkins had some fair success on Broadway producing and popularizing such Shakespearean offerings as *Richard III, Macbeth* and *Hamlet,* but his biggest success was with the decidedly non-Shakespearean *Burlesque,* which he co-wrote.

CHAPTER 8

WELLES WAS THEN earning approximately $150 to $200 for each radio broadcast and sometimes doing ten or more shows a week, making him one of the most highly paid voices in the medium. But being away from the legitimate theater would be, to him, like being out of work. The urge for many in the theater to go west was strong. Hollywood studio scouts were scouring Broadway for new faces and new talents, and Welles was approached on more than one occasion to consider a script or succumb to a screen test. If there was ever a time to get involved in motion pictures, it was then. New highs in payments from Hollywood for stage plays were being made, stars were becoming millionaires. Hollywood writers were amassing fortunes; Ben Hecht, a fugitive from the legitimate stage, earned $260,000 from Goldwyn as his year's writing income for 1937.

Although it received two Academy Awards, Warner Brothers was unhappy about their box-office experience with 1935's *A Midsummer Night's Dream,* directed by Max Reinhardt, with Jimmy Cagney and Mickey Rooney. The studio still believed, however, in the possibility of turning classic plays and novels into films that could be made profitable. Three scripts were sent to Welles as an enticement to join the Warner Bros. "stable." One had a part for him in *The Adventures of Robin Hood,* possibly that of Friar Tuck or King Richard, but it seemed uninteresting to him. The failure of Warner's to come up with what he considered enough money made him, after three weeks of considering, reject the offer.

When David O. Selznick was in New York in 1937 to promote *A Star Is Born,* with Janet Gaynor and Fredric March, he had invited Welles to the "21" for a drink, after seeing him in *Doctor Faustus,* and had attempted to persuade him to come to Hollywood. Selznick's offer was direct: he wanted Welles to become an executive of his motion picture corporation and to primarily head his story department. Welles would be given the power (although not unlimited) to select new properties and to adapt, or assign adaptations of, novels, short stories, and plays. The idea of Welles becoming one of Selznick's directors or actors was not entirely ruled out for sometime in the future, but it was implicit that Selznick's interest in Welles was literary and editorial: he saw him neither behind nor in front of a camera, but in an office, making deals, securing rights, and transforming classical stories into money-making films.

After thinking it over for a few weeks, Welles responded to Selznick in a letter on May 19, 1937, that, although he was both "intrigued and flattered" by the offer and convinced he could fill such a position "satisfactorily," and although it was true that he did a great deal of work on scripts and adaptations, he would not feel it justified his getting involved with anything that did not directly "represent a step toward my ultimate aim: my profession of actor-director." He made mention of his continued interest in theater. In a long conclusion to his letter, Welles wrote a glowing account of the career and abilities of his associate John Houseman and suggested that Selznick might be interested in considering him, rather than Welles, for the job.

If Welles's decision to reject his Hollywood offers seemed to be a youthful folly built on overconfidence and, perhaps, misdirection, it must be remembered that he had been on the stage since he was a child and was a willing victim of that dream called the theater. Although he was highly attracted to the magic of the screen and had become a fan of movies over the years, the very permanence of films, their character to endure without the possibility of change from night to night or scene to scene, was what he feared. On the stage, no Welles portrayal was ever the same; it varied in nuance and shade and tone in any given performance, dependent on the mood of the audience, the other actors, the temperature of the theater, Welles himself, and perhaps the position of the planets. As a director, Welles felt himself the master chess player, and each night was a different game. He continually annotated his actors' performances: always changing, attempting perfection. To be frozen in the same performance on celluloid, with what might be hideous mistakes, seemed anathema to him.

As Welles made his comparison of film and theater, time and again, he would stress that motion pictures released the theater of certain obligations; that it was impossible to have great acting unless one came to terms with the audience, and that confrontation, even if it was contemptuous, of which he admitted to being sometimes guilty, nevertheless shaped the performance. The playgoer must feel that the actor is acting for *him.* Disregarding the theory of the suspension of disbelief, where the filmgoer makes himself forget that the actor he is watching is not in front of a camera in a Hollywood studio and what he is watching is a piece of celluloid, Welles thought that the filmgoer *did* know. The magic of the theatrical moment was, to Welles, not so much that the acting was live, but that the stage performance was now, unique, never quite the same again, that the actor was capable of all things, great and small, that would never be repeated. The theater was an experience, like making love. Films were imitations, like reading about making love.

The height of Welles's dramatic ambition in 1937 was to establish in repertory, as he had started to do with the Federal Theatre, a classical theater with an occasional musical or comedy thrown in—where he would be able to write, act, design, cavort, plot, produce, and direct—and change what he wanted to change. Although the possibility of making huge amounts of money in Hollywood greatly attracted him, he was still totally, hopelessly, insanely in love with the theater, and it is there that he had every intention of remaining to make his mark. He was a bit saddened, however, when the Theater Union produced its last play that season, a propagandist, pro-labor production called *Marching Song*; although it had no connection with his John Brown play, he hated losing the title.

It is logical, therefore, that when the government funds were withdrawn, Welles would attempt to propel the theater momentum he had initiated with Project 891 and, with Houseman, continue on his own entrepreneurial ways. Without capitalization, without a physical stage, without properties of any kind, the two men agreed to carry on from where the government had left them and begin a new, privately owned theater company. A magazine called the *American Mercury,* found lying on a table in Welles's Sneden's Landing retreat, was the inspiration for the name they gave their new company. The magazine was founded by H. L. Mencken and George Jean Nathan and was a delight to the social rebels of the day, an inconoclastic journal against, as someone once described it, organized religion, organized politics, and organized anything else. The name and the philosophy of the new Welles theater—Mercury Theatre*—seemed apropos.

The idea of doing *Julius Caesar* as the first Mercury production was primarily Orson's, although at that time he received a letter dated February 9, 1937, from Sidney Howard, the Pulitzer Prize winning playwright who had just completed most of the script for the film *Gone with the Wind.* Howard had been to a performance of *Doctor Faustus* and wrote that "I could wish that you turn your attention to *Julius Caesar* in modern dress (have such fine ideas on that if you want them).... I have always believed that the best way to stimulate good modern plays is to keep the classics a part of what goes on." Houseman once again agreed to serve as the selfless producer and attempted to give Orson whatever help was needed in getting the production off the ground. A few thousand dollars was received from investors, Welles and Houseman retained 70 percent of the stock in the Mercury, the old Comedy Theater was secured, and work began.

Orson was filled with nostalgia and self-assurance for *Julius Caesar.* He had played Cassius and Marc Antony for the Todd School production; it was one of the three plays he had included in his promptbook *Everybody's Shakespeare,* and he appeared to understand it on many levels. The genesis of his idea of playing it on a bare stage in modern dress so that it could be seen as a contemporary allegory of the rise of fascism is unclear. The success of the bare-staged rendition of *The Cradle Will Rock* may have been the catalyst; there were also serious budgetary concerns that plagued the Mercury from its

---

*Not to be confused with the Mercury Theatre of London, founded in 1933 and dedicated to "non-commercial" productions; it was there that *Murder in the Cathedral* was first seen in England.

very beginning, and the necessity of frugality may have led to the creation. The stage would indeed be bare of props and scenery but would contain an elaborate system of platforms, traps, and ramps.

Sam Leve, who had just graduated from the Yale drama school at that time, was given the opportunity to design the set but with the impossible condition "not to spend any money." Welles had been impressed with a photograph he had seen of lights shooting into the air at Hitler's famous Nuremberg rally and talked with Leve about possibly using a similar technique. Leve did sketches and models, incorporated Welles's ideas and his own, and began to paint the entire back wall of the stage a blood red. Welles wanted the bricks of the wall to show, as a modern symbol, an urban milieu of the twentieth century instead of the usual scenery of stones connected with ancient Rome. And mixed with the deep, violent, and primitive red was just a small touch of blue. He also had Leve install lights and construct a series of starkly bleak platforms.

"I want to give the audience a *hint* of a scene," he told Leve. "No more than that. Give them too much and they won't contribute anything themselves. Give them just a suggestion and you get them working with you. That's what gives the theater meaning: when it becomes a social act."

The costumes were provided, at a discount, by the Brookes Costume Company. They consisted of the khaki-brown, high-necked uniforms of the style worn by the doughboys in World War I, which were left over from the 1924 Maxwell Anderson-Lawrence Stalling production of *What Price Glory?*

Orson had the costumes dyed black and had the dull black buttons replaced by inexpensive, shiny gold ones. The result was striking and altogether fascistic in appearance. The "masses" were dressed in gangsterlike costumes: dark, somewhat crumpled suits, black shirts, white ties, and light, broad-brimmed fedoras.

Welles had written in his *Everybody's Shakespeare* that it was inevitable that "Shakespeare would dramatize the assassination of the foremost man in the world," and, as Welles worked on the script, shaping the play to a more modern version, he saw clear parallels of the character of Caesar and one of the world's foremost dictators, the bald-pated Benito Mussolini. Caesarean Rome would, from Welles's pen, become Fascist Italy. He intended to infuse into *Julius Caesar* much of the speed and violence it had on the Elizabethan stage. Shakespeare knew little of the speech of the Romans and so *Julius Caesar* sounds like the Elizabethan London of his day. Orson wanted the play to sound like the New York of his.

As he did with *Doctor Faustus,* he made *Julius Caesar* into a ninety-minute, non-intermissioned play, cutting out the part of Octavius altogether, deleting the scene with Caesar's ghost, and virtually eliminating the last two acts with the suicides and the battlefield confrontation, feeling that "there was never a production of Caesar with actual armies in synthetic combat that was less than a little silly." It was his belief that, with the recitation of Antony's line, "Mischief, thou art afoot, Take thou what course thou wilt," Antony was then the victor of the struggle, and to every extent the play was really ended. With this thematic definition, he continued to trespass through the stanzas and syntax of Shakespeare and reduced and deleted major portions of the play, diminishing Antony's part and emphasizing that of Brutus as the focus of action.

Other events were transposed, such as the garden scene where Brutus reads the note thrown through his window and where Portia interrupts him. Some new dialogue was added. "If Welles needed a line to get somebody off stage or to end a scene," Martin Gabel told theater historian Richard France, "and it was not supplied by *Julius Caesar,* he'd say, 'Wait a minute! There's a line in . . .' and put it into the script." Speeches from *Coriolanus* and a few other Shakespearean vehicles (enough to make the Bard revolve in his grave, some suggested) made their way into Welles's *Julius Caesar.* A close study of the script might reveal more. So many deletions, additions, cross-outs, doodles, red, blue, and black pencil marks, scribbles and lines eventually permeated Welles's working script that the dog-eared pages seemed to take on a life of their own. Some of the nonliterary addenda to his script tells a story in itself:

> Clothes cleaned:
> 11-22-37
> 12-6-37
> Average gross, 11-20-
> $5628.90
> Conspirators in orchard—9½ minutes
> Betty—LA 4-6891
> Anderson's lute—see that it's tuned

His rehearsals were long and arduous, and pieces of action and lines of dialogue were practiced almost like acrobatic feats or balletic movements, over and over again, until they were perfect. The crowds and mobs were not permitted to mumble their words, as is customary on the stage, but each member had a specific line written for him that he had to memorize and speak. Since individual members of these crowds had no fictitious Shakespearean names, their real names are noted in the script:

> SCHNABEL
> There's not a nobler man than Brutus
> ALLAND
> That's much truth indeed
> MOWRY
> Indeed, we must consider rightly
> REID
> There's much in what he says
> COTTEN
> We must consider rightly of what he says

Using only the actors, the lights, the apron, the music and sound effects, and the profundity of Shakespeare's lines, Welles reduced—or elevated—the production to a truly Elizabethan, even Greek, presentation. On November 11, 1937, only days after the Anti-Comintern Pact was signed, completing the pattern of military alliance between Italy, Germany, and Japan, the so-called modern-dress version of *Julius Caesar* was scheduled to open.

Just moments before the play began, with the theater grayly lit, Welles gave the order to extinguish the red lights of the EXIT signs posted all throughout. Someone mentioned, perhaps tactlessly, the burning of the Brooklyn Theater in the 1800s, the tragedy that made necessary the constantly illuminated EXIT signs in theaters a part of the New York Civil Code. "It was a dread and fearful night, as through the flames and smoke they frantic fled," went the words of the popular song that lamented this catastrophe. "Mr. Welles," said one of the stagehands with genuine concern about the extinguished lights, "that's against the law." Welles was unmoved: "We'll turn them back on immediately. I want *complete darkness*. Don't worry. I'll take total responsibility." The red lights were somehow dutifully turned out.

Then the fixture lamps at the sides and back of the theater were slowly dimmed to blackness and everything was plunged into a frightening, dark void, a Stygian hue that all at once created the mood of death and fear and bewilderment. It seemed longer in time than it actually was for most of the audience, sitting there like silent and obedient souls in a darkened tunnel, unable to see even their hands before their faces. Finally, a lone, ghostly, ancient voice coming from somewhere in the darkness cried out: *"Caesar!"*

As the lights then came up, one could easily imagine the shock and drama and poetry of hearing that scream. That one word was among the most memorable moments ever experienced in a Broadway production of a Shake-spearean play. It both electrified and marked the audience to such a degree that, when they found the character of Julius Caesar, dressed in a fascist uniform, standing on the bare stage, exclaiming, *Bid every noise be still!*, they had no difficulty imagining him in the Roman Forum or accepting that this dictator with jutting chin and head thrown back in characteristic arrogance, searching for the voice of his doomsayer, was, in fact, Benito Mussolini or Adolf Hitler or any other tyrant of the unfree world. The audience sat absorbed as they witnessed events that had taken place almost two thousand years previously, written nearly four hundred years before that night in 1937, but that had assumed a modern reality about which they could have read in a newspaper purchased outside the theater twenty minutes before they entered.

Despite the modern implications and the clear parallels to modern fascism read into the play, Welles denied that a specific leader was being portrayed, a stand made all the more confusing because the play was subtitled *Death of a Dictator*. In the program, he affirmed that no attempt had been made to "caricature any existing dictator, would-be dictator, or dictatorships. We have employed the device of modern costumes and military uniforms for the very simple reason that we believe a play about the collapse of democracy under Caesarism and the tragedy of an effort to restore it by a short-sighted political assassination is more immediately interesting in the absence of a toga." The ritual of reenactment and Shakespeare's prescience is confirmed however by the following lines:

CASSIUS

... How many ages hence
Shall this our lofty scene be acted over
In states unborn and accents yet unknown!

BRUTUS

How many times shall Caesar bleed in sport,
That now on Pompey's basis lies along
No worthier than the dust!

CASSIUS

So oft as that shall be,
So often shall the knot of us be call'd
The men that gave their country liberty.

Welles, as Brutus, wearing tight, black leather gloves, dressed in a conservative blue serge suit and a green greatcoat, gave one of the most convincing performances of his career. Walking out of Brutus's orchard on the fateful March morning, he appears as a man of principle, a good man, committed to the demands of his conscience but somewhat bewildered. He was not altogether the Brutus of action that great actors have played in the past. But Welles saw him as more, or less, than that. Describing his characterization to an interviewer at that time, he said: "He's the classical picture of the eternal, impotent, ineffectual, fumbling liberal, the reformer who wants to do something about things but doesn't know how, and gets it in the neck in the end. He's dead right all the time—and dead at the final curtain. He's Shakespeare's favorite hero—the fellow who thinks the times are out of joint, but who's really out of joint with his time." James P. Cunningham, reviewing the play in *Commonweal* summed up much of the critical reaction to Welles's playing of Brutus, when he wrote of his "quiet but beautiful reading of the lines."

Marc Blitzstein's musical score was especially poignant: trumpets, horns, percussion, and Hammond organ all added to the believability of the action: sounds of bugles from distant camps, crowds marching, the fanfares for the dictator. When Caesar enters the Forum at the very beginning of the play, his processional music sounded not unlike German—or Nazi—band music and greatly helped to set the scene for the entire play.

One of the most powerful scenes in the play, specially choreographed by Welles and rehearsed almost endlessly, involved the character of Gaius Cinna, the poet, who is mistaken by Antony's vigilantes for Cornelius Cinna, one of Caesar's assassins. The role of the assassin was played by William Alland and that of the poet acted poignantly by Norman Lloyd.

The innocent poet comes to view from the back wall and begins to cross the ramp whistling a carefree tune, wandering freely. He delivers a short soliloquy about a dream that he had: "I dreamt tonight that I did feast with Caesar; and things unluckily charge my fantasy: I have no will to wander forth of doors. Yet something leads me forth." All at once he becomes aware that figures begin to appear very quietly from out of the shadows. They circle him and he attempts to ingratiate himself, not knowing that they represent a mob, that they are about to do him harm. Assuming that they think he is the poet, he tries to sell or give them some of his poems, written on pink paper, a gentler contrast to the blood red violence of the wall. Questions are asked. "But I am Cinna, the poet," he says mildly and continues to repeat the line, "Cinna, the poet," over and over again, gaining in crescendo. For several moments, he is not physically touched, but as he starts to move away, another group of men comes out of the darkness and blocks his way. He turns, and a new group is there to stop him. All of this action takes place in a forward, constantly circling movement as poet and mob make their way to the center of the stage, the crowd around the poet ever-tightening. They tear up his poems and throw them in his face. He pleads for mercy, for recognition, for sanity.

Then in one moment of mayhem and horror, with mean, little daggers flashing, the jaws of the mob come together and Cinna is swallowed up and disappears, screaming hauntingly, a man who sees the smoldering fumes of Hell: "THE POET!!"

In many ways, the sinister attack on Cinna had more immediacy than any other scene in the play. At that time in history, innocent Jews were being taken from the streets of Europe, charged with crimes they knew not of, and hideously murdered, their bodies disappearing, as did Cinna's on stage, never to be seen again. The terrorism and brutality of the mob as created by Welles was never shown more ruthlessly in Shakespeare than in *Julius Caesar,* and the scene became if not the actual, then at least the emotional, finale to the play.

Despite Welles's initial reluctance to publicly read antifascist sentiments into the play, three weeks after the opening he did admit to reporter Michael Mok of the *New York Post* that the Cinna the Poet scene represented, "the hoodlum element you find in any big city after a war, a mob that is without the stuff that makes them intelligently alive, a lynching mob, the kind of a mob that gives you a Hitler or Mussolini." One critic pointed out that a few lines had been interpolated from *Coriolanus*—"The other side of the city has risen. . . . Why stay we here?"—to add impact.

John Mason Brown, also in the *New York Post,* gave the play an imprimatur of an historical theatrical event: "Something deathless and dangerous in the world sweeps past you down the darkened aisles at the Mercury and takes possession of the proud, gaunt stage. It is something fearful and turbulent which distends the drama to include the life of nations as well as men. To an extent no other director in our day and country has equalled, Mr. Welles proves in his production that Shakespeare was indeed not of an age but for all time."

"Move over and make room for the Mercury Theatre," insisted Brooks Atkinson in his review in *The New York Times,* observing that the acting talent in *Julius Caesar* was "original" and that Welles's Brutus was one of "remarkable cogency"; that the play itself, "with nothing but men and lights for materials, creates scenes that are almost tongue-tied with stealth and terror, crowd scenes that overflow with savagery."

Richard Watts of the *Herald Tribune* proclaimed that Welles's *Julius Caesar* was "a production so exciting, so completely fascinating in all of its phases, that there is nothing to do but let ourselves go and applaud it unreservedly."

Stark Young of the *New Republic* had some reservations about the play, mainly that he considered it to be a cavalier attitude toward the "basic form and glow of the lines," but still managed to deem it "a capital event," admiring its "energy, lively attack, sincerity and bold theater intelligence."

The aptness of the message of *Julius Caesar,* the bravura performances, and the beautifully simple production were compared favorably to another Shakespearean play on Broadway that opened the night before: *Antony and Cleopatra,* with Tallulah Bankhead in a lavish production. It cost well over $100,000 to mount, an extravaganza of sphinxes, jewels, spectacular costumes, a multiplicity of scenes, and consistently poor acting. Comparisons with *Julius Caesar* were inevitable. Joseph Wood Krutch, whose review of *Antony and Cleopatra* appeared in the *Nation* after the play had closed, wrote that the best way to forget "the whole unfortunate business" was to consider instead the performance of Orson Welles in *Julius Caesar,* which he found as "absorbing as any seen in New York for many a year."

Variety, in its colorful code, headlined the difference as "Shakespeare B'way's In-'n'-Outa' 'Caesar' Clicks, 'Cleo,' 'Like' Fold," which translated into English meant that neither *As You Like It* nor *Antony and Cleopatra* was successful but that *Julius Caesar* was sensational.

When Tallulah visited Welles backstage she asked what the production of *Caesar* had cost. When told that it was $6,000, she was said to have exclaimed: "Six thousand dollars?! That's less than one of my fucking breastplates!" How much Welles's production was helped in audience attendance by the critical reaction to the rise and fall of *Antony and Cleopatra* is difficult to say, but *Julius Caesar* received almost unanimous raves.

A PLAY OF such high energy cannot run flawlessly every performance, and naturally there were some incidents, amusing and not so, connected with *Julius Caesar* during its run. At one of the dress rehearsals, in the assassination scene, there were not enough rubber knives for Caesar's murderers and so Welles as Brutus, temporarily wielded a real knife. As Caesar dies, after the famous line, *Et tu, Brute?* Welles dropped his knife and, quite accidentally, the point stuck into the stage floor and quivered for a few seconds, an eloquent and dramatic testimony to the foul deed just completed. He saw this as a valuable piece of stage business and made arrangements, when the play opened, to have a special spotlight focus on the trembling knife as a punctuation to the murder. He assured Joseph Holland, as Caesar, that he would be careful with the real knife. Unfortunately, the piece of action was more difficult than expected and more often than not, the knife did not stick in the floor but ignominiously fell flat to the stage, along with its bogus companions.

Performance after performance Welles continued trying to have it penetrate the wood. One evening, as he was doing the mock stabbing, either he or Holland, or both of them, lost their balance and the knife plunged into Holland's chest, severing an artery near the heart. As Caesar fell, he whispered to one of the actors, "Christ, I've been stabbed." As the ovation began, Holland, always the professional actor, now the dead Caesar, and in fact, virtually bleeding to death, maniacally refused to leave the stage until the curtain rang down. Towels were surreptitiously thrown out into the crowd on stage and used to stop the blood. There was also an attempt to clean it up as the other actors began to slip in the blood that was running all over the stage. Finally, at the conclusion of the scene, Holland was rushed by ambulance to Roosevelt Hospital. He was so seriously hurt that he was unable to act for two months.

The volume of Welles's diction, usually that of a grand organ, seemed to lose power as the weeks of *Julius Caesar* progressed. It is possible that because of all his radio work and his stage acting, he was straining himself, with the result that his intonations were gradually becoming softer. "Louder!" someone once cried from the audience, which Welles probably considered the ultimate insult of his career. He did not comply but simply continued at the same level, now fuming and scowling into the audience, his eyes hopelessly searching the sea of faces to determine the identity of the heckling culprit. After the performance, he fell into a genuine despair. "Stay with me," he was said to have told Joseph Cotten. "This is awful! Did you hear him? He shouted 'louder!' I'll never get over this."

At another performance shortly after that incident (with his voice back to normal), while giving the "... but I love Rome more" speech, Welles became even more disturbed when he thought the audience was hissing him. Suddenly, water began to stream down on him in an active cascade. It was all quite innocent, but destructive: the theater's sprinkler system went haywire as a result of a prank perpetrated by young Arthur Anderson, the boy who played Lucius, and the entire stage area together with the lighting control board was drenched with water, causing sparks and forcing a temporary halt of that performance.

WELLES PROVED WITH *Julius Caesar* that he was capable of mounting a classical work with a modern, relevant message and having it succeed on all levels. By not ritualizing Shakespeare and by stripping some of the play's Victorian shackles, he succeeded in presenting *Julius Caesar* with the same sense of newness as it must have had on the night of its first performance in the reign of Queen Elizabeth. He gave his actors lines that were to be *spoken,* not recited like poetry, and the audiences felt that they came away from the experience understanding Shakespeare, perhaps for the first time. Traditional Shakespearean diction sounded pompous to most audiences, Welles felt, and his experiment proved astute.

The play's impact on schoolchildren was enormous. They were given special rates, busloads from all over the New York area arrived for every performance, and somehow after the ninety-minute show Shakespeare seemed not to be as much of a chore. One grammar-school teacher wrote Welles after taking his class to see the show, "For the love of mercy, man, a little respite! No spectacle has ever left me so utterly flabbergasted! I beseech you, sir, a moment's release of tension, a pause for breath, a curtain, a curtain for even a split second, please. My solar plexus is still tied in a knot. I've seen them all, for the past thirty years. I should be able to endure more easily; but never, never Shakespeare like this! God bless you and spare you long to give us things like this, in such a world."

The WPA people were delighted about the educational impact that the play was having. A survey they had recently made indicated that only one high school student in thirty had seen a real live play. Welles's thriving theater had begun to reverse those statistics.

Welles also, as perhaps never before, proved himself an actor. As Brutus, he gave the public a reading they were not so soon to forget: the noble Roman became the man sitting in the third row of the balcony, a paradigm of fear and unknowing in a time of war and unrest. Alfred Kazin in his memoir, *Starting Out in the Thirties,* was aware of Welles's impact as Brutus in *Julius Caesar,* when he wrote that he

> ... was so masterful that his face swelled and brooded over the empty stage like an inflated goblin's. . . . He was more the actor than anyone else we had ever seen, he was the fat, vaguely crybaby face that was yet the ultimate in stage Svengalis. . . . Brutus was the nervous threat of the action, he was the conspirator, the assassin, the genocide, the suicide, whose movements incarnated the disturbance of our time. In *Julius Caesar* the disturbance was brilliantly brought home; the quick, alarmed movements of the conspirators back and forth, suddenly became a vision of the public anxiety in our minds.

So genuinely popular did *Julius Caesar* become that Columbia Records approached Welles to arrange for the Mercury to be the first professional theater company in American history to record a complete performance of a play. In the past, parts of plays had been recorded by other companies, but they usually consisted of the set speeches by just one or two of the principals. For the Columbia recording, everything audible in *Julius Caesar* was included—music, offstage noises, the cries of the mob, and the conversations of minor characters, as well as the traditional pieces of the play.

Even before *Julius Caesar* premiered, Welles and Houseman conducted lengthy, and sometimes catch-as-catch-can, discussions about what other plays should be produced by their new group. *The Silent Woman,* a farce by Ben Jonson, was considered a possibility by Welles, eager to act the character of Morose, the man who could not tolerate noise.

They seriously considered *The Duchess of Malfi,* John Webster's Italian-ate seventeenth-century horror play, about which Welles once exclaimed: "My favorite play!" Pavel Tchelitchew, the Russian émigré painter, began doing sketches on speculation for the sets and costumes of *The Duchess of Malfi*. Welles was unsure, however, whether the music should be composed by Marc Blitzstein or Virgil Thomson, believing the former's political sound might be more appropriate than Thomson's more luxurious, less stentorian one. Thomson was eager, however, to do *The Duchess of Malfi* and shrewdly surmised that the way to Orson's heart and mind was through his stomach. He describes what happened in his memoir, *Virgil Thomson*:

> I won by taking Orson and his wife to a blowout at Sardi's, with oysters and champagne, red meat and burgundy, dessert and brandy, before he pulled himself into his canvas corset for playing Brutus. "You win," he said. "The dinner did it. And it's lucky I'm playing tragedy tonight, which needs no timing. Comedy would be difficult."

THE CHRISTMAS CARD that Welles sent that year to all of his friends and relatives contained a sketch drawn by him, showing himself in grandiose proportions, along with a very-pregnant Virginia and their cocker spaniel, Bridget, crossing Times Square.

EVEN AS PRELIMINARY work began on *The Duchess of Malfi*, Welles and Houseman considered other plays to add to their repertory. Welles seriously thought of producing Ferenc Molnár's *Liliom* as an all-black musical. Then there was *Heartbreak House* by George Bernard Shaw, one of the most significant and impressive of all his works: a deep inquiry into the human character of Captain Shotover, an autobiographical model of Shaw himself— and a role Welles wanted to play. A light farce by William Gillette, *Too Much Johnson,* was temporarily slated, mainly because of some new production ideas Welles had for it.

After a few casual readings, *The Silent Woman* proved to be too complicated, and it was thought that even with generous pruning it would probably remain incomprehensible to most audiences. So Welles and Houseman decided that their first production of 1938, in complete contrast to their highly successful *Julius Caesar,* would be a bawdy and madcap comedy, *The Shoemaker's Holiday,* by Thomas Dekker. They felt it could be important to the radical image of the Mercury because it celebrated the ascendancy of the new class of merchants, traders, and craftsmen in medieval England who had risen rapidly to the level of the blooded nobility.

In the midst of running a Broadway hit, preparing for a second theatrical production, and maintaining the "Mercury Theatre on the Air," Orson strangely began showing signs of an interest in motion pictures, even though he was not quite ready to succumb to Hollywood. Although he was still more committed to theater, he said that he was beginning to become attracted to the versatility of film, the way it could transform scenes and moods, its capacity for elevating minutiae to importance, its startling effects, its ability to establish swift and powerful contrasts. These were elements that he now hoped somehow to integrate into his stage productions. In a lecture before a theater group at the time, he expressed his views on the parallels of stage and screen acting: "The actor is the exact equivalent of the moving picture projector. He is the source of an image. You believe in Lear but you believe in it the way the image is projected from the camera: he is projecting an image which says, 'I am King Lear.' It happens that this image he is projecting is thrown right in front of himself. What you are looking at is an idea, except that the dimensions of his body and his own face are the screen."

While some of America's film community may have noted Welles's directorial interest in motion pictures, it was his acting that first drew an actual job offer in the medium of cinema. Director William Wyler invited Welles to Hollywood late in 1937 to take a screen test. Wyler was about to begin shooting *Wuthering Heights* for Metro-Goldwyn-Mayer and offered Welles the part of the dipsomaniacal Hindley Earnshaw. Orson thought of himself more as a Heathcliff, a role already assigned to Laurence Olivier. "I'd like to make a movie for the experience," Welles told Wyler, turning down the specific offer but trying to keep the possibilities open. "I have some production ideas of my own, which someday I want to try out."

It wasn't only Hollywood that realized Orson's box office potential. Several of the directors of the Theatre Guild had come to the conclusion that, because of sagging subscriptions and the many lackluster reviews it had recently received, youth was needed to bolster the group's spirit and reputation. One member of the board of directors suggested that if Orson Welles could be persuaded to work with the Guild, he might be able to rejuvenate it. Alexander Woollcott, who had played in a Guild production, continually championed the name of the young prodigy, and this gave the idea a certain imprimatur. When approached, Welles was immediately enthusiastic. Doing one or more plays as joint ventures with the Theatre Guild would add to the prestige of the fledgling Mercury Theatre and relieve some of the ever-present financial stress from both companies by enabling them to pool their resources.

Welles suggested that they collaborate on a play to be called *The Five Kings*, a composite of scenes from several Shakespearean plays. *The Five Kings* would be presented by the Theatre Guild but produced by the Mercury. It was agreed that the Mercury would provide $5,000 in cash toward an estimated budget of $40,000 and Welles and Houseman would donate $5,000 worth of their services as, respectively, director and producer. The remaining $30,000 was to be supplied by the Theatre Guild; also, Welles would have complete artistic control of the production but would expect, and professed that he wanted, advice from the Guild's more experienced directors and crew members. Lawrence Langer, the founder of the Guild, revealed in his memoir, *The Magic Curtain,* that after the initial conversation with Welles and the agreement on details was made, with certain strong qualms on the subject, he let himself "be beguiled into the belief that I would, in some mysterious manner, recover my zest for the theater which at the moment had been dulled to some extent by a long series of failures."

With his long-standing love of Shakespeare, Orson was ecstatic at the opportunity to create his own version of the Bard. And it was indeed to be

Orson's restatement of Shakespeare's version of sixteenth-century England, for he assigned himself the massive task of interconnecting and adapting the separate plays into his spectacle of history.

He began the arduous development of the lengthy script, working on it intermittently as he continued to write or adapt, direct, and often act in the weekly radio broadcasts of "The Mercury Theatre on the Air." As it was evident that *The Five Kings* would not even be ready to go into production until late in 1938, at the earliest, Welles simultaneously worked on preparations to stage *The Shoemaker's Holiday,* which was slated to be the Mercury Theatre's first play of the new year.

Welles rescued *The Shoemaker's Holiday* and its author from near oblivion, opening it on New Year's night 1938—exactly the 338th anniversary of its first appearance. He was playing a hunch since the play had enjoyed nothing more than two obscure twentieth-century revivals in 1911 and 1913. Although Welles cut *Shoemaker* nearly in half, critics soon agreed that he had captured the rollicking spirit of the ribald Elizabethan world of the play.

A good complement to the Shakespeare tragedy, *Shoemaker* was a light, racy comedy chronicling the rise of Simon Eyre, a shoemaker, to the post of Lord Mayor of London and including the romancing of the fair Rose, a nobleman's daughter. Most important, though, it gave free rein to the madcap antics of the shoemaker's apprentices.

The Mercury Theatre company already had a reputation for dispensing with sets, but Welles changed course a little in this one, again employing Sam Leve as designer, in evoking the flavor of Elizabethan times. They erected slapdash planking resembling old shop fronts, thereby roughly sketching in a London street. Three canvas curtains hung from unfinished wood beams; at the proper time the curtains could be drawn back to reveal interior scenes such as the apprentices at work in Simon Eyre's shop.

Dekker's comedy was equipped with the standard elements of farce: the endless complications, mistaken identities, jokes about cuckolded husbands, and the liberal application of broad-beamed, lusty women. For Welles as well as Dekker, it was a tribute to the common working man and the exuberant life of sixteenth-century London. Such life is not without its naughtier aspects, but only a few playgoers objected to the bawdy language and anal sounds. It's also likely that some of the double entendres went over the heads of the audience as did the similarity of the name of the character "Firk" to another four-letter word, and Welles's unexpurgated script caused just the slightest flurry of protest in the New York papers.

Welles, still performing as Brutus in *Julius Caesar* and appearing on his all-pervasive radio broadcasts, worked solely as director in *Shoemaker.* Joseph Cotten was cast as Rowland Lacy, the son of a nobleman, who for the love of Rose disguises himself as a shoemaker's apprentice and competes for her attentions with Master Hammon, a rather effete and money-conscious young gentleman played by Vincent Price.

Led by the animated performance of Hiram Sherman, who played Simon Eyre's clowning, blue-humored assistant Firk, the characters came off larger than reality. Welles had turned the play into a one-act without intermission, or, as one critic put it, showed it as the "one-reeler it really is." Another called it "a comic strip." Thus Welles had remained true to Dekker's preamble: "Take all in good worth that is well intentioned, for nothing is purposed but mirth." In an unusual measure of its "honest merriment," Brooks Atkinson compared it to the blockbuster *You Can't Take It with You.*

After a look at *Shoemaker,* Richard Watts, Jr., confirmed that the Mercury Theatre was "the great comfort of the theatrical season." He also noted that "everything they do seems to come out successfully." And one reviewer quipped, "If Orson Welles can get this much enjoyment out of the stuff of Dekker, we can expect a thrilling revival of the telephone book any day now." The turnaway crowds for both *Caesar* and *Shoemaker* had the Mercury making plans to move into the more spacious National Theater.

LATE ONE NIGHT, following a performance of *Shoemaker,* Welles and Houseman called together a pickup cast to do an initial reading of *The Duchess of Malfi.* The session convinced both men that the spirit and mood of the play was too difficult for the average modern-day actor to capture, no matter how well directed or carefully trained. Further rehearsals for the play were canceled, and *Malfi* was taken off the roster of future Mercury Theatre plays.

With *Shoemaker* running and *Malfi* no longer being considered, Welles pushed himself to lock in the next play. He wanted it to be Shaw's *Heartbreak House,* but the playwright had not yet given his permission.

As negotiations began, Welles started preliminary rehearsals of *The Five Kings.* Although it had not yet been given a scheduled opening date, and in fact the script was not yet completed, Welles knew that the complex play would need a great deal of preparation.

Rehearsals ran into a delay that had nothing to do with the usual theatrical problems. On March 4, the newspapers announced that rehearsals of *The Five Kings* were being held up as Welles awaited the birth of his first child. Actually, Welles continued rehearsals and was in the midst of one when, on March 27, he received a telephone call that Virginia was being taken to the hospital to give birth. He raced—via taxicab—to the Presbyterian Hospital in upper Manhattan to be on hand when Virginia came out of the delivery room. As the taxi sped north, Welles was—sort of—doing business as usual; he conducted a publicity conference with his aide, Henry Sember.

The Welles's child was given the name Christopher. It was a lovely little girl. Some news stories speculated that Orson gave her a boy's name because of his great reverence for Christopher Marlowe. Another story that circulated at the time was that Welles named her after Marc Blitzstein's nephew, Christopher Davis. Actually, the *name* Christopher—the sound of it, both alone and in conjunction with "Welles"—was attractive to Orson; it had no further significance to him beyond its melody.

On April 23, at a luncheon at the Hotel Astor commemorating Shakespeare's birthday, Welles announced that the Mercury Theatre was preparing a marathon performance in conjunction with the Theatre Guild, for which it would adapt no less than seven of Shakespeare's history plays. *Five Kings** would be the story of the end of the Hundred Years War and the Wars of the Roses, the end of chivalry, through the history of the Tudors, presented in two evening-long segments. The gigantic undertaking seemed to owe something to O'Neill as well as the Bard. Around that time, Welles and his associates realized that the play could not possibly be ready to perform that spring. They promised a fall opening.

BY NOW, THE pattern of using plays that he had worked with before was becoming an integral part of Welles's style. Since he had done the adaptation and starred in *Twelfth Night* on radio, he considered presenting it on the stage, also with a modern message, as in *Julius Caesar*: Illyria would be transposed to the English seaside resort of Brighton, and Elizabethan costumes and scenery replaced with 1930s seaside attire and set. But the idea was dropped in favour of producing Shaw's *Heartbreak House*, which deals with the attitudes and emotions of both individuals and society in prewar England. It was a play about which Welles and Houseman were enthusiastic.

Negotiations with Shaw for the permission to produce *Heartbreak House* started by cable. After sending several wires to Shaw with no reply, Welles finally received a letter from Shaw's secretary, Blanche Patch, stating the reason for the delay. She suggested that the Mercury should place "New York" somewhere on their letterhead, since all Shaw had noticed was the word Pennsylvania (the theater's phone number was Pennsylvania 6-2530) and thought that the communication was coming not from Broadway but from the Keystone State. As a result the envelope with Shaw's reply had been returned marked "Unknown."

The first personal reply that Welles received from Shaw was a cable that asked who the proposed star would be for Captain Shotover and ended, "Who are you?" Welles called Shaw at his London flat and reminded him of their meeting when Welles was sixteen. The transatlantic telephone was an unusual way to conduct business in 1938, a three-minute call costing considerably more than it does today. After Welles had stated the purpose of the call, Shaw said, "You're a darn fool, and it's absolutely indecent." Welles replied, "You mean it's indecent for me to produce your play, Mr. Shaw?" Shaw replied, "No, I mean it's indecent for you to conduct business by transatlantic telephone." Eventually Shaw said that his terms would not be too "unreasonable."

Once permission was granted, Welles set about preparing his production while Houseman continued royalty negotiations with Shaw and his agent. *Heartbreak House* opened without a set royalty agreement. After the play opened, Shaw sent Welles a memorandum of agreement outlining his terms

---

*Orson had first planned an amalgamation of *Henry IV, Henvy V,* and *Henry VI,* calling it *Three Kings,* but his ambitions grew greater as to the eventual scope of the production.

and conditions. They were stiff: based on weekly receipts, Shaw was to receive 15 percent for everything over $1,500; 10 percent from $500 to $1,500; 7½ percent from $250 to $500; and 5 percent for under $250. Although Houseman sent Shaw a letter pleading for more equitable terms the old playwright was firm. The play lost money.

The play had been produced in the United States once before, in 1920, by the Theatre Guild. It was unsuccessful since it came after the end of the war, and most people did not think that the same conditions that led to the war could be repeated. During the play's first production, the Guild suggested cutting it, to which Shaw was violently opposed. The Mercury made no such suggestion, for, in Welles's opinion, "The play's not good enough to cut." But then in the same breath, "It's the greatest play of the last hundred years."

Heartbreak House opened on April 29, 1938, to favorable reviews. It ran for forty-eight performances. With the production of *Heartbreak House* taking up the Mercury, *Julius Caesar* moved to the National Theater, on Forty-first Street between Seventh and Eighth Avenues. In addition to that move, thirty-seven-year-old Tom Powers and twenty-two-year-old Edmond O'Brien headed up a touring *Julius Caesar* company, replacing Welles and George Coulouris in their roles of Brutus and Marc Antony.

Taking place in the shiplike home of Captain Shotover, an eighty-eight-year-old retired sea captain, *Heartbreak House* consists of three acts, each approximately an hour in length. Using more dialogue than action, Shaw shows that England, a country of people mostly concerned with the present and the past, and not at all with the future, was in great danger. Shaw's gloomy prophecies applied to all of civilization and were an explication of contemporary affairs.

Shaw had intended the play to take place in the Captain's house in Sussex, which was designed somewhat like the living quarters of an oceangoing sailing ship, and Welles further depleted the already small budget of the Mercury, incurring heavy expenses for large beams, cane used for the walls, and the bare wooden floor, hoping that the scenery would add some thematic rationale to the production, instead of being just the setting for action. Although the Mercury could have rightfully updated the play to 1938, the dress of 1915 was kept intact. Orson's gamble paid off, for most of the reviewers felt that without the scenery the long play would have been too much. Audiences sat enraptured. One reviewer, Sidney B. Whipple of the *New York World-Telegram* wrote: "In this instance the settings by John Koenig are decidedly an aid to the project. Even the Mercury could not do without scenery in this play."

Most actors who play Captain Shotover try to make themselves look like Shaw himself, but Welles dominated the production with his rather large frame stuffed into a baggy white suit, wearing a shaggy wig and beard, and quite heavy makeup that made him resemble a living version of Michelangelo's *Moses*. He looked a thoroughly believable octogenarian. His performances, however, were inconsistent. Said Richard Wilson, a long-time associate and a member of the cast: "Welles as Shotover was good . . . about every third performance." The Captain liked nipping from the bottle, and thus he tended to raise his voice whenever he was feeling the effect of the drink. With Welles's great range and projection on his stronger nights, he could stir the most lethargic in the furthest reaches of the balcony. The Captain is Shaw's voice in the play, and one of the points that he makes through the Captain comes in this speech:

> The captain is in his bunk drinking bottled ditch-water and the crew is gambling in the forecastle. She will strike and sink and split. Do you think the laws of God will be suspended in favor of England because you were born in it?

Mady Christians played Captain Shotover's daughter, Hesione Hushabye; Hector, her romantic husband, was portrayed by Vincent Price; and Geraldine Fitzgerald, who came to Welles as a young actress from Dublin, sent by MacLiammoir and Edwards, was allowed to make her American debut as Ellie Dunn.

In the play, the war has already begun. The eighty-eight-year-old Captain Shotover, who lives in his country home, Heartbreak House, putters around inventing instruments of death. The plot involves the young Ellie Dunn's romance with a rich and old businessman, Boss Mangan (played by George Coulouris) and her attempt to decide whether to marry him or not. She is given advice by Mrs. Hushabye, the Captain's daughter, who feels that the match would be a mistake. Mangan is invited to Heartbreak House in order that Hushabye might expose him. A typically Shavian creation is that of a burglar who breaks into the house, is caught, and passes his hat around for money while telling the sad story of his life. At the end of the play, *deus ex machina,* the burglar and Mangan are killed when the house is bombed. The others escape. Shaw refused to explain the play's meaning. "I am only the author," he said cryptically.

BY 1938, RADIO was in a state of change and experimentation. Some of the more successful shows continued exactly as they had, especially those with a dramatic format, such as "The Lux Radio Theater," broadcast from Hollywood, where it had an almost unlimited access to famous movie stars; and "The Cavalcade of America," based on historical subject matter, simplified and enlivened to be more acceptable to a mass audience. Other perennials such as "The Bob Hope Show," "Chase and Sanborn Hour" with Edgar Bergen and Charlie McCarthy, "The Rudy Vallee Show," "Amos 'n' Andy," and several other comedy-based skits were enjoying strength, but many of the networks were beginning to look to other formats in an attempt to bolster their ratings and entice advertisers.

As with motion pictures, radio directors found it difficult to get new comedy or dramatic material of quality week after week, and so they explored shows that could write themselves or they relied on material in the public domain that could easily be adapted. The action of major league baseball games was dramatized; entirely new formats were attempted, reduced to about an hour, and broadcast, without some of the radio listeners aware that they were not hearing a live event.

Radio station WOR in New York City recreated every Sunday morning, in living sound, some of the metropolitan area's most terrible auto accidents, complete with blaring horns, screeching brakes, collision noises, ambulance bells, and cries of mangled passengers. Toscanini was one of the most popular radio entertainers; he was getting $4,000 a performance to conduct the NBC Symphony Orchestra; Paderewski became his competition on another network. A new quiz show, "Information Please!," which cost little to produce, was spawning dozens of imitations.

Then, in the early spring, the Federal Theatre's Radio Division perplexed the commercial stations by announcing a new schedule of unsponsored dramatic broadcasts, which would include such classics and contemporary hits as *Winterset, Cyrano de Bergerac, Of Mice and Men, King Lear, Dead End, Journey's End, The Barretts of Wimpole Street,* and *What Price Glory?* Only weeks later, the NBC network also began a well-intentioned and, at first, unsponsored series, "Great Plays Through the Ages," on which they not only broadcast the works of such distinguished dramatists as Marlowe, Molière, and Synge but did so in the framework of the typical theater in which such a play would have been originally presented. Listeners, therefore, were treated to a description of such sacred theaters as the Globe, the Abbey, and the Drury Lane. Study materials were distributed to schools, and students were invited to submit compositions on what they heard and how they liked each play so that an evaluation by the network could be made. The show's first offering, *The Birds* by Aristophanes, was broadcast from an aural recreation of the Theater of Dionysos in Athens. "Great Plays" received polite but unenthusiastic reviews, the major criticism being that they had not been streamlined enough for radio and at times were too difficult to follow. Conversely, the Federal Theatre Radio dramatic programs were well-reviewed by critics, but did not produce a mass audience.

New methods of performing radio drama were also being attempted. One theory, quickly relinquished, was that it was impossible to act and read at the same time; that radio speech became blurred when the dual process took place over the air. In doing Maxwell Anderson's *Second Overture,* for example, one group of radio actors abandoned the customary scripts and spoke their lines from memory, as they would have on the stage. The result was poor because the voice was the only element being appraised by the listener: a slightly mumbled line or mistimed cue, forgivable or overlooked on stage, became impossibly annoying and flagrant over the air.

It was at this juncture of dramatic experimentation in broadcasting that executives at CBS, in a spirit of competition, decided that they needed a prestige series of radio plays of classical or distinguished contemporary works. The idea was to begin a new dramatic series for national radio on a sustaining, noncommercial basis, and if and when it proved to be creatively successful and captured a fair portion of the listening audience during its scheduled time, to then sell the show to an advertiser for sponsorship.

As standard operating procedure, the actors and creative talent for most dramatic radio shows were cast from the regulars used by that specific station or studio. However, CBS wanted to do something entirely different, to engage an already existing theatrical group and have them perform, in repertory, on the air every week. The choice of possible acting ensembles was somewhat limited. Requisites for the group that was needed were that it be somewhat nationally famous; its actors had to have some radio experience; and they had to be based in New York since the show would originate from there.

For months, CBS had been considering Welles as the possible host, director, and star, together with his ensemble, for their new series. "In a single year," said a spokesman for the network, "the first in the life of the Mercury Theatre, Orson Welles has come to be known as the most famous name of our time in the American drama." In order to make Welles an offer, CBS studied not just his New York reviews of the Mercury plays but national coverage that he had received. *Collier's* reported, "Twenty-three-year-old Orson Welles threw a bombshell into Broadway." United Press International, in thousands of newspapers all over the country, declared: "The meteoric rise of Orson Welles' Mercury Theatre continues unabated." Syndicated writers, such as Walter Winchell and Robert Benchley, seemed to mention him continually in their columns.

Then, on May 9, 1938, the made-up and bearded face of Orson Welles, as Captain Shotover of *Heartbreak House,* appeared on the cover of *Time* magazine. Inside was a long profile of the actor-director whom the editors deemed a "marvelous boy." Discussing both his life and his work, the *Time* profile pointed out that although he was a true innovator on the stage, radio was his "mainstay," as he played "The Shadow," appeared on *The March of Time,* and acted in other roles. Emphasizing his importance in American entertainment and what seemed to be his boundless enthusiasm and energy, the article concluded: "The brightest moon that has risen over Broadway in years, Welles should feel at home in the sky, for the sky is the only limit his ambitions recognize."

Officials at CBS were on the phone to Welles within a short time after the *Time* profile arrived at the newsstands. Would he consider doing an hour-long weekly series of dramatic broadcasts with himself as writer, director, producer, narrator, and star? Naturally, complete creative control and content selection would be his.

Welles accepted with alacrity. He had just received another flattering offer, as he put it, to go to Hollywood, but he had turned it down in favor of the radio series that, to him, allowed for greater flexibility. Welles's show would be a summer replacement for Cecil B. DeMille's "Lux Presents Hollywood." If the quality of the Mercury broadcasts could equal, or surpass, the Lux broadcasts, there was hope that most of the listeners committed to hearing a drama on Monday at 9:00 P.M. would continue to tune in. Commercial sponsorship would probably be available in the fall, and the show would become an institution.

Within days, working with Houseman as executive producer, Welles began to make arrangements for the first broadcast, only weeks away, scheduled for July 11, 1938. The format of the show was developed both by the network and by Welles: it would consist of Orson narrating each show in the first person and also playing, if not the starring role, a major part. Davidson Taylor, distinguished executive for the network, would operate as the on-line producer—although Welles was producer in name and fact—and as the liaison officer and production supervisor with CBS.

Welles believed that there was nothing as artificial as the announcer saying: "The curtain is now going up on a presentation of . . ." and then to have him set the stage and introduce the characters. The listener knew that the curtain wasn't rising, and the setting of locale and action was to Welles a clumsy and impersonal way to establish a rapport with the listening audience. Having a narrator, a man who leans back in his chair and says, "Now this is the way it happened . . ." was to him the most confidential and personal way to make contact with the listener, bringing him into a one-to-one relationship almost as though he were having a telephone conversation. In this way, the intimacy of Welles's own voice would be the key to his show. Sound effects, dramatic pause, and music would be combined to instantly produce in the listener's mind a new scene, a shift from past to future, from earth to the planets.

The show's title would be "First Person Singular." A press conference was called to announce the plans. Welles stated: "I think it is time that radio came to realize the fact that, no matter how wonderful a play may be for the stage, it cannot be as wonderful for the air. The Mercury Theatre has no intention of producing its stage repertoire in these broadcasts. Instead, we plan to bring to radio the experimental techniques so successful in another medium, and so treat radio itself with the intelligence such a beautiful and powerful medium deserves."

Since there was a limited time to create not only the first broadcast but the second and the third also, Welles moved to establish the criteria for selection. The stories would have to have a broad appeal, with either romantic, adventure, or mystery plots; their titles had to be popularly recognizable; they should be written in the first person so that the transition to that tense for the purposes of narration would be faster and easier; if possible, they should not have been dramatized on radio before. Three titles immediately came to mind: *Alice's Adventures in Wonderland, Treasure Island,* and *Dracula.*

In adapting the novels to radio scripts, Welles insisted that certain techniques be employed. The first five minutes of the show were vital; it was imperative that the listener be captured, seduced, and entertained immediately and that special effort be employed to make each script's opening moments pungent and dramatic. Obvious and dull exposition would be avoided. Since radio audiences can "see" a character only by the sound of his voice and cannot be expected to remember him if he comes into a scene infrequently, such characters would have to be subtly reintroduced. In order to avoid confusion for the listener, no more than three characters would talk in any one scene. On stage, some great effects can be accomplished through silence, but on the radio, silence only becomes a dead spot. Such silent intervals would be shunned. Sound effects, an essential part of radio drama, would be used sparingly, intelligently, but with as much realism as possible, in order not to clutter the action or the dialogue.

Concerned that the public might consider the show only for children if it began with the Lewis Carroll tale, the creators of "First Person Singular" quickly abandoned that story. The schedule, therefore, was to have *Treasure Island* run as the first show and *Dracula* as the second; after a short period, this was reversed for roughly the same reason as the deletion of *Alice's Adventures in Wonderland*. *Treasure Island* was originally written as a story for children—for over fifty years it had been the most popular boys' book, although it also appealed to adults. Welles and CBS wanted to be sure that for its first, all-important show, "First Person Singular" listeners would be certain that the programming would be adult fare.

Dracula contained all the elements that comprised gripping radio drama: romance, action, suspense, and mystery. Using Bram Stoker's 1897 novel as the basis for his radio script, Welles stayed as faithful to the original story line as possible. As a horror story, *Dracula* ranks among the greatest ever written, and Stoker told the tale of vampires and the living dead by means of contemporary diaries, letters, and newspaper accounts. In the transition from book to air, Welles wanted to retain the diary approach and to play two roles: Jonathan Harker, the narrator, and the king of vampires, Count Dracula.

The story of the Transylvanian count who lived only at night had had a record-breaking run on Broadway in 1927 and had appeared on the screen twice, as *Nosferatu* in 1923 and as *Dracula* in 1931 with Bela Lugosi in the title role, repeating his stage triumph. The popularity of the theme and plot was unquestioned. Whether Welles could make such a powerfully visual assault on the emotions into a phonic one was a mammoth creative challenge.

And difficult it proved—Houseman recalls working on one complete script of *Dracula* with Welles, scrapping it, and then suffering with him all night at Reuben's famous restaurant on a second. Their script retained the unearthly quality of Stoker's story, incorporating its terror. As in the novel, the narrator, through Dr. Seward's diary, gives the radio play a greater cohesive force than it had on the stage or in film. In the Lugosi film, audiences often laughed at Dracula's refusal of a goblet: "I don't drink . . . wine." An equivalent line on the radio produced no such levity, only genuine fear.

Listeners tuned in to an evening of radio on the night of July 11, 1938, would have heard several hours of fairly light entertainment on the CBS network. In the hour just preceding the "First Person Singular" debut, "The Monday Night Show" featured black comedian Eddie Green, sports expert Ted Husing, and singer Connie Boswell; the comedy team "Pick and Pat" appeared for a half-hour, starting at 8:30. Then, at 9:00 P.M., the Welles show began with the voice of Dan Seymour. "The first production of a unique new summer series by the 'Mercury Theatre on the Air,'" followed by what would become the show's weekly musical theme, Tchaikovsky's *Piano Concerto No. 1 in B-flat minor.* The seriousness of the announcer and the eloquence of the music indicated that what was to be broadcast for the next sixty minutes was important. After several minutes of accolades for the Mercury Theatre, the announcer pointed out that with its many hits, the Mercury could have closed its doors for the summer after a season unparalleled in theatrical history. But, he continued, Welles instead was interested in directing his creative talents toward all "the Broadways of America."

Welles, as Welles, then talked of the importance of Stoker's novel and shared his opinion that *Dracula* was the best story of its kind ever written, reminding the audience that it could be found in every representative library of classic English narrative. By implication, he thanked the network for giving the Mercury Theatre the opportunity and challenge to present in a new way a variety of classic works. He promised that in future weeks many different kinds of stories would be presented: tales of romance, adventure, biography (pronouncing it in his normal Oxonian as "*bee*-ography"), mystery, and human emotion by such authors as Robert Louis Stevenson, Emile Zola, Fyodor Dostoyevski, Edgar Allan Poe, and P. G. Wodehouse.

After a few chimes of sinister music, the gripping story of *Dracula* began, plunging the listeners into the eerie regions of Transylvania. At first, the show had difficulties. The sound of the coach and the horses that transport Jonathan Harker through the Borgo Pass to Castle Dracula drowned out the narration; the sound effects consisting of gusts of wind, thunder, and tavern crowds were too loud and enthusiastic. Within minutes however, Welles, functioning as director and standing on a podium and wearing a set of headphones, managed to calm the efforts of his effects man so as not to sacrifice the dialogue. Harmony was established, and both narrative and crashings could each be heard with clarity.

All of the performances were beautifully and realistically underplayed. Each actor added to the visual details of the tombs, produced action on the ship, changed the locale to Dr. Seward's living room, shifted to the stark terror of a confrontation with Dracula, all with the salutary exercise and control of his voice.

Welles as Jonathan Harker was convincing. As Count Dracula, however, he was masterful. Using a deep and frightening Romanian accent, he captured the very essence of Dracula: on the surface, a hospitable and civilized man but actually the personification of evil, capable of any ghoulish atrocity and personal, unspeakable depravity. As he is about to sink his teeth into Mina's neck, he whispers to his new bride of death, "Flesh of my flesh, blood of my blood, blood of my *blood.*" Mina, now a demoness herself, sighs deeply, contentedly, infused with similar thoughts of darkness and evil.

When Dr. Van Helsing informs his colleagues of the horrifying, perhaps unspeakable, risks they will be taking in attempting to find and destroy Count

Dracula, the lines, spoken ominously and effectively, also took on special significance, which some listeners inevitably applied to more universal, contemporary problems:

> My friends, it is a terrible task that we undertake. To fail here is not mere life or death. If we fail, *we* become as him, foul things of the night, as *him.*

At the end of the show, Welles was lavish in his praise for all the Mercury Players: George Coulouris as Dr. Seward; Martin Gabel as Van Helsing; Ray Collins as the Russian captain; Karl Swenson as the mate; Elizabeth Farrell as Lucy; and Mina superbly played by Agnes Moorehead. Welles talked briefly of the next broadcast, *Treasure Island,* asked for letters listing stories that the listeners would like to hear, and then ended with a routine that was geared to amuse, perplex, and frighten his listeners, while elevating him to the role of the nation's bogeyman:

> *(In his own voice:)*
> Until then, just in case Count Dracula has left you a little apprehensive, one word of comfort; when you go to bed tonight, don't worry. Put out the lights and go to sleep.
> *(Sound of wolf howling)*
> That's all right, you can rest peacefully. That's just the sound effects.
> *(Continuing, in a frightened stage voice:)*
> There! Over there in the shadows! See? It's nothing. Nothing at all.
> *(Hesitatingly:)*
> Noth . . . ing. I . . . think . . . it's . . . nothing.
> *(And then in his Dracula voice:)*
> But always remember, ladies and gentlemen: There *are* wolves, there *are* vampires!
> *(And back to his own voice:)*
> Such things do exist.

The first show of the new series was an unqualified success. Fan mail poured into the studio and critical comment emanating from the print medium was positive: "Adventurous," said *Newsweek.* "Realistically broadcast: the characters living electrically," proclaimed *The New York Times,* and CBS executives were pleased and hopeful.

Treasure Island, the second offering, was even more widely hailed, with Welles playing both the adult Jim Hawkins and Long John Silver. Robert Louis Stevenson's adventure classic, read by every schoolboy, had been made into a film twice before Welles's broadcast. The prose of the novel is simple, clear, and rhythmical, making it easier than *Dracula* to adapt to radio. This time, right from the beginning, the sound effects were in complete coordination with the rest of the production and contained just enough shading of gusting winds, bounding waves, belligerent parrots, and pirate swordplay to make the show firmly believable. The microphone seemed to be held to the lips of marooned pirate Ben Gunn as he was interviewed like a head of state or star athlete. He, and the other actors, *talked* to the audience.

In addition to many of his regular Mercury players, Welles included fourteen-year-old Arthur Anderson (repentant from his *Julius Caesar* prank) as Jim Hawkins, Jr., Eustace Wyatt, Alfred Shirley, Steven Fox, William Alland, and Richard Wilson.

As the weeks went on, a routine of production was established. Story selections would come from suggestions of listeners, people at the studio, Houseman and other members of the Mercury, and, of course, Welles himself. Orson's reading was voracious and his book bills at Brentano's grew enormous.

Although the show was officially called "First Person Singular" and was so designated in newspaper program listings, its more-often-used unofficial title was "The Mercury Theatre on the Air."

The Mercury brought the entire French Revolution and the clicking of Madame de Farge's knitting needles to the air with a faithful interpretation of Charles Dickens's *A Tale of Two Cities.* Welles played both Dr. Alexander Manette and Sydney Carton. His regular repertory of players included Erskine Sanford as the President, Edgar Barrier as Charles Darnay, Frank Readick as Defarge, Kenneth Dalman as the Counselor for the Defense, and Betty Gard as Madame Defarge.

A story of spies and intrigue during the weeks immediately before World War I was broadcast. Welles had been impressed by Alfred Hitchcock's 1935 macabre and romantic film version of the novel *The Thirty-nine Steps* by John Buchan, the distinguished statesman-novelist Lord Tweedsmuir and the Governor-General of the Dominion of Canada. However, he believed it bore little resemblance to its original; his radio show would attempt realism.

Welles again played two roles: the American suspect Richard Hannay and the Scotsman Marmaduke Jopley, with an accent not unlike to the Yorkshire inflections of James Mason. He concluded the show by talking of his fidelity to Buchan's book as opposed to the Hitchcock film: "Ladies and Gentlemen, if you missed Madeleine Carroll in our 'stage' version of *The 39 Steps,* the young lady in the movie, in common with almost anything else in that movie, was the child of its director's own unparalleled and unpredictable fancy. If you missed anything you must blame Mr. Alfred Hitchcock."

In a play that evoked an echo of Welles's childhood, and based on a Sherwood Anderson short story of lovesickness, Welles played the part of Joe, a young midwesterner in *I'm a Fool.* In another short story, *My Little Boy* by Carl Ewald (a moral fable that was astonishing because it dealt with anti-Semitism—a subject rarely heard over the radio at that time), Welles played the vocal and sometimes all too-foolish father who suffers as many, if not more, growing pains as his son.

As a promotional device, Welles wanted to quote Alexander Woollcott's opinion of the story since Woollcott had originally suggested it to Welles as a possibility for "First Person Singular." He telephoned Woollcott's apartment to get the required permission to use a quote over national radio but discovered that Woollcott was on vacation. A cable to Woollcott was answered with great dispatch, and with typical Woollcott frivolity and cynicism:

TO: ORSON WELLES
   CBS RADIO
   NEW YORK, NY

YOU MAY QUOTE ME IN SAYING ANYTHING ON ANY SUBJECT AT ALL TIMES.

ALEXANDER WOOLLCOTT

On August 15, 1938, ninety minutes before Franklin Delano Roosevelt addressed the nation, the Mercury Theatre, using the same network facilities, offered a radio version of John Drinkwater's chronicle play *Abraham Lincoln*, covering his life during the Civil War years, with Welles playing the title role, stating that "Lincoln's words are still entirely alive and his person preserved in a fine and very famous play." Unfortunately, Drinkwater's ingenious method of introducing each of his six scenes with rhymed prologues spoken by two chroniclers was abandoned so as to give the play a more modern, prose-like sound. Welles added additional biographical material of Lincoln, and also included excerpts from letters, speeches, debates, proclamations, and from the written record of Lincoln's own private conversations. "Much of this you will recognize," intoned Welles, "and much of it is news . . . as if it were happening in the White House tonight." Drinkwater, an Englishman, made no attempt to stress Lincoln's Americanism but emphasized the universal quality of his humanity. Welles maintained that approach.

The large, forceful, seemingly secure Orson Welles could not comfortably fit his personality into the gaunt and tortured Abraham Lincoln, however, and of all of the initial Mercury broadcasts, *Abraham Lincoln* was the least captivating.

Arthur Schnitzler's sophisticated tragicomedy of the highly cultivated social life of Vienna, *The Affairs of Anatol*, done anew by the Mercury radio theater, was a delightfully witty adaptation of the original dialogues—seven of them, each with a different lady—with Welles playing the story's Anatol and expressing the playwright's philosophy: "We all play parts. Happy is he who knows it."

Then, one night, Welles announced over the air with bravura: "I am the Count of Monte Cristo and the master of the world!" The mysterious Corsican made his debut in a Mercury broadcast of the memorable Dumas tale. The story had been made even more famous by four motion pictures of the same name: two in 1912; another in 1923 starring John Gilbert; and a 1934 "talkie" with Robert Donat. Written originally as a newspaper serial, the plot was gloriously complex, and converting it into a convincing radio drama sorely tried the ingenuity of the scriptwriters. Welles pointed out that Dumas must have been serviced by a legion of ghostwriters—it was no shame, he added—since no man could have written all the books for which Dumas received credit. Perhaps thinking of his own relationship with the "ghosts" he employed to work his scripts, Welles imperiously continued: "It is not expected of Pharaoh that he build with his own hands, his own pyramids."

The last offering for the first experimental season of "First Person Singular" was G. K. Chesterton's most famous novel, *The Man Who Was Thursday,* a fantastic spy story, filled with rich imagery and poetic prose, and written in the nihilistic bomb-throwing days of 1908. It dealt with religion, integrity, anarchism, and politics. Welles had a great affinity for the works of Chesterton and decided to write the adaptation himself, allowing no assistance. Chesterton's liberties with history appealed to Welles, as did his philosophy of a neo-medievalism of crafts, a reincarnation of Merrie Olde England. Welles respected G.K.C.'s unique brand of commonsense enthusiasm, his singular gift of paradox, and his deep reverence and high wit, but most of all he was a Chesterton fan because of his "free and shamelessly beautiful English prose." Perhaps Welles, already beginning to assume a stocky countenance, also admired Chesterton's girth: he was one of the most famous fat men in the world.

The Man Who Was Thursday is filled with surreal, sometimes Proustian, language and contains an amorphous, difficult to understand, plot. "All of the time there was a smell of lilac around me," says Gabriel Sime, otherwise known as "Thursday" and played by Welles, "and once I heard, very faintly, in some distant street, a barrel organ begin to play and it seemed to me that my heroic words were moving to a tiny tune from under or beyond the world." Somehow, through Welles's splendid adaptation and feeling for the theme, he was able to create one of the finest shows of the series. He knew, before the end of the program, that the Mercury would be renewed, but the official announcement to the nation made by a spokesman for CBS in the last few minutes of *Thursday,* gave him great pleasure.

IN THE LATE spring of 1938, Welles withdrew *Shoemaker's Holiday* from the repertory and closed the Mercury's season with alternating performances of *Heartbreak House* and *Julius Caesar.* He briefly toyed with the notion of taking *Five Kings* on the road for a national tour that summer, but the logistics were too complicated to overcome and the finances too precarious to risk. Welles also considered mounting a production of *The Importance of Being Earnest,* Oscar Wilde's "trivial comedy for serious people," in a summer stock theater on Cape Cod, as a trial run to determine whether the Mercury should bring the play to New York the following season. But that, also, foundered on complications.

To better handle all of his activities, and to attempt to defeat the unusually high amount of pollen in the air that summer of 1938, the twenty-three-year-old Orson, who was a chronic sufferer of hay fever and asthma, had temporarily moved from his house at Sneden's Landing to the relatively pollen-free and air-conditioned safety of Manhattan's St. Regis Hotel. Virginia, much to her regret, stayed at Sneden's Landing with the baby and complained bitterly that she thought Orson didn't want her with him because he was becoming interested in other women. Although Orson did have professional and health reasons for being in the city, Virginia's instinct was correct.

The St. Regis became Welles's base for several months. It was an incredibly hectic moment in his career, and he would sit cross-legged on his bed, issuing directives like an Oriental potentate. Food deliveries from the hotel's kitchen or from either of his two favorite restaurants, Reuben's or Jack and Charlie's (better known as "21" by the *innocenti*) arrived in a round-the-clock attempt to appease his insatiable hunger. Phone calls seeking money were made with great alacrity; incoming calls were received with tension. Statements of intentions were promised, often issued, sometimes retracted; threats occasionally flew, insults were frequently inflicted. Standing by were mini-legions of breathless messengers, note-scribbling assistants, and overly inquisitive reporters. Orson Welles was about to make his first film.

In the late 1970s, I conducted several lengthy interviews with Welles, specifically to discuss how he went about directing *Too Much Johnson.* He said he had an idea that, although not entirely new, would be an elaboration of something that had never been totally successful on stage. Welles planned to interweave a forty-minute silent film into the body of the next Mercury stage production, a revival of W. S. Gillette's comedy, *Too Much Johnson.* The film within the play would actually be a twenty-minute prologue, explaining the offstage action of the play, as well as two ten-minute introductions to the second and third acts.* The film would consist mainly of a madcap chase, done in true Mack Sennett style, complete with speeding cars, pratfalls, and frantic leaps, and Orson expected that it would greatly add to the play's hilarity. Although there were money problems, John Houseman, as producer, gathered about $10,000 from a group of friendly investors to launch the production. As soon as that was accomplished, Welles began to simultaneously conduct stage rehearsals and shoot the film.

Welles wrote at that time: "The first production of *Too Much Johnson,* at the turn of the century, revolutionized American comedy because of its fast-paced performance, its irreverence, and its absolutely delightful zaniness."

The plot of *Too Much Johnson,* in the manner of many farces, was somewhat complicated, involving romance, mistaken identities, hiding and switching of documents, and rapidly changing allegiances. It consisted of two love stories, one of the amorous adventures of the very married Augustus Billings (played by Joseph Cotten), a stockbroker, using the *nom de flirtation* of Johnson, who has an affair with a passionate Frenchwoman (Arlene Francis), is discovered by her husband, a wine merchant, Leon Dathis (Edgar Barrier), and is forced to flee to Cuba to save his life; and the other, the story of gentle, sad-faced ingenue Lenore Faddish (Virginia Welles), whose cruel father (Eustace Wyatt) sends her to Cuba as a mail-order bride, while her

---

*In an interview in 1978, Welles told me that his original intention was to make the prologue about thirty-five minutes long: "in effect, the whole first act."

suitor, Henry MacIntoch (Guy Kingsley), tries to prevent her from leaving and ultimately follows her aboard. Billings's wife and mother-in-law sail on the boat, also, and in a masterpiece of subterfuge he convinces them he has a plantation in Cuba. He borrows a ranch in Santiago from a certain Joseph Johnson (the husband-to-be of Lenore Faddish). How the too many Johnsons cope with all the subplots is how the play and film absurdly and hilariously advance.

Welles wrote the script, paring it down to its barest essentials—about an hour of stage time—and planned to use the film partly as the expository device to explain the narrative. Most of the film consisted of exaggerated movements: the cuckold chasing the roué, the father dragging his daughter away from her suitor, all interspersed with chases and slapstick comedy routines like slow burns and double takes in the old silent movie tradition.

Although the film was in black and white, the actors wore colorful Gay Nineties clothing rented from the Brookes Costume Company, which coincidentally had supplied the costumes for the original Gillette productions in 1894. Virginia Welles was variously dressed in a pink shantung gown trimmed with lace, a two-piece white suit, and a yellow linen dress. Joseph Cotten, for the most part, wore a gray three-piece suit and a straw hat, which he clutched wildly to his head as he ran, climbed, or leaped about.

The men's faces were covered with clown-white greasepaint, powdered profusely, and adorned with a dark red lipstick that appeared startlingly black on the screen. As part of the cast, Welles even included a corps of twelve bungling Keystone Kops dressed in long, blue, Edwardian topcoats and sugar-loaf helmets. In some of the scenes, for added atmosphere, there was an organ-grinder standing on the side.

Paul Dunbar, a young newsreel cameraman for Pathé news and a friend of Virgil Thomson and Paul Bowles, the Mercury staff composers, was signed on as the cameraman. Unable to convince his employers to allow him to use his regular 35-millimeter newsreel camera, Dunbar used a hand-cranked, key-operated, Bell and Howell Filmo Automatic 16-millimeter. Since Welles wanted the film to have the antic appearance of old silent movie action, he instructed Dunbar to under-crank the camera so that the chases would appear exaggerated and jerky when projected at normal speed.

Though Welles had become a constant moviegoer, his experience with filmmaking was limited to casual visits to the set of *Man of Aran,* directed by Robert Flaherty, when Welles was in Ireland in 1932; the narration of the filmed excerpt from *Twelfth Night* done for the Chicago Drama Festival Competition shortly after that; and the amateurish four-minute *Hearts of Age,* made when he was nineteen. Welles also told me that he had had a working knowledge of V. I. Pudovkin's volume *Film Acting,* which had been released in an English-language edition in 1937.

To learn how to make a comedy, Welles viewed as many great films of that genre as he could. In a screening room in midtown Manhattan, he and his all-around assistant Richard Wilson; Walter Ash, his production stage manager; and Jean Rosenthal, his lighting expert, screened a large number of

Mack Sennett shorts, including *Love, Honor and Behave* and *The Lion and the Girl*. (Although always popular, Sennett had received a special Academy Award in 1937 and his films were enjoying a revival.) They studied Chaplin's *The Kid* and *The Rink*. Harold Lloyd's comedy *Professor Beware* had just opened at the Paramount, and most of Welles's film personnel saw and discussed it.

Welles loved the spontaneity of slapstick and, like Sennett, decided not to use his scenario: natural sequences of events would be filmed until the chase began, and the comic scenes would then evolve on their own. Welles later recalled to me that Harold Lloyd's *Safety Last* had a direct influence on him and *Too Much Johnson*. "I loved that film and think it was one of the greatest, simplest ever made."

As a new film director, Welles immediately developed a highly personal style on the set. He constantly used his own acting talents to show his actors what he wanted. During many of the action scenes, however, he would bellow his instructions—no megaphone needed for him—from camera to set, urging his actors in the chase scenes through New York streets to more daring attempts. At one moment Welles was behind the camera establishing a shot, and the next he was gathering his extras together and placing them where he wanted them. He also was marvelously patient with the actors, gentling and then cajoling them into a style that would look spontaneous.

Welles was invariably amused by the overly serious ex-vaudeville actor Howard Smith. "Howard, I'd like you to sit in that chair as we roll the camera," he would tell him. "Certainly, Mr. Welles," Smith said, practically bowing, "but would you prefer the Fast Sit or the Slow Sit?"

In addition to his regular Mercury players, Welles gave bit parts to composer Marc Blitzstein, who played an extra (Welles told him to think of himself as a "French barber") and *New York Herald Tribune* drama critic Herbert Drake, who played a Kop. Others were pressed into service as extras. Richard Wilson played a cabin boy, and Houseman fought a duel—photographed as a long shot—on the edge of the Palisades, overlooking the Hudson. An attractive teenage actress, Judith Tuvim, who was interested in breaking into comedy, was also cast as an extra. Later she changed her name to Judy Holliday. Even Welles stood in as a Kop during a short scene.

One of the most difficult problems Welles had to confront, from the very beginning of the production, was caused by his own over-involvement in so many projects and his procrastination. Typically, he had allowed himself only a month to plan, shoot, edit, and process the film. The preview showing of the play and film were scheduled at a summer theater in Stony Creek, Connecticut, for the two weeks starting August 16, 1938. Welles had to film in mid-July almost simultaneously with the debut of radio's "First Person Singular." During those four incredibly hectic weeks, he also continued to produce and direct the radio programs.

The first scene in the film opens with Joseph Cotten en route to his assignation with Arlene Francis, which is rudely interrupted by the entrance of her husband (Edgar Barrier). This precipitates the first chase scene, as

Barrier pursues Cotten down a fire escape, across the rooftops, and through the streets of New York to the pier, where Cotten leaps aboard the boat. Barrier barely makes the jump, catches the railing with his hands, and is hanging out the side of the ship as it leaves New York and steams away toward Cuba. As he jumps to the deck (on the screen), he lands, in reality, on the stage of the theater. The film stops, and the play begins.

For the opening of the next scene, which had a special effects sequence and again employed film, Welles had had a model set constructed on the stage of the Mercury Theatre. It sat on a table about ten feet by four feet, and most of it represented the plantation that Billings secures from Johnson on his arrival in Cuba. A *papier mâché* volcano loomed in the background, surrounded by "jungle flora" (plants purchased at a local florist). The house itself was a model constructed by James Morcom, who also designed the sets for the play. Details of the outside of this house were kept consistent with the stage set of the interior, so the audience could easily make the transition from the filmed exterior shots to the interior scenes, which would be acted out on stage. The model was swathed in fog (from smoke bombs) to lend mystery to the scene and to disguise how clearly bogus it was.

In front of the diminutive plantation was a large plate of glass, painted black, and on the other side of the glass was a tank of water, in which floated a miniature steamship, a replica of the SS *Munificence* on which the characters traveled to Cuba. The first image on the screen was of the boat sailing the Caribbean. There was then a dissolve as the hand-held camera moved around the black glass to the coast of the island where, from the boat's perspective, one could see the jungle. The camera continued moving slowly along the coast until it reached the edge of the model, then turned right and then right again, up a roadway, until from a distance, through mist, appeared an imposing Georgian plantation house. The film stopped, stage lights came up to reveal the interior of the house, and the live scene began.

All of the other so-called studio scenes for the film of *Too Much Johnson* were shot in an empty lot in Yonkers, not far from the Bronx River Parkway. Sets, furniture, and props were borrowed from the Sherwood Little Theater, and a bedroom, complete with three walls, several windows, and a large brass bed but with no ceiling, was constructed. Local residents formed a bemused audience for much of the filmmaking activity until, to their shock, Arlene Francis appeared in a lacy black corset, flirting provocatively with Joseph Cotten, who seemed to be about to remove his pants.

There was one scene in which Arlene Francis clutches a photograph of Cotten to her bosom and hides it there when her husband arrives home unexpectedly. After a few takes Welles had secured what he wanted, with one exception. He felt that Arlene, then only in her early twenties, should have a more ample bosom as befitted the matronly character she was playing. Since Welles wanted to shoot a close-up of the photograph being hidden in her cleavage, and padding that normally would have been used on stage would easily be detected, an insert shot of another bosom had to be arranged.

A frantic, unique talent hunt ensued, and finally Welles's secretary, Augusta Weissberger, was prevailed upon to stand in. Although she was scarcely older than Arlene Francis and actually a rather small woman, the somewhat rounder, more abundant top half of her body fit the specific needs of the scene. Weissberger cheerfully complied and, amidst the catcalls of the cast and crew, gained her once-in-a-lifetime opportunity to be, at least in part, in a motion picture. Close-ups of her bosom, ensconced in the same black corset and heaving emotionally on cue, were photographed one afternoon on the roof of the Mercury Theatre.

One of the Cuban scenes was filmed in an abandoned rock quarry in Haverstraw, New York, north of the Welles home at Sneden's Landing. To add to the tropical ambience, rented palm trees were planted or propped up around the area; sometimes a tree was just held up by a crewman who was instructed to hold it steadily and keep his hand out of the camera's sight. Black "natives" in straw hats and bandanas milled about. Pith helmets were plentiful. Joseph Cotten was filmed riding a white horse, rented specially for the occasion—it was the white horse used for virtually all New York theatrical ventures—and also being chased through the "jungle." At one point he complained about having to wade through a ditch of brackish water to evade his pursuer.

Most of the scenes of the husband chasing Cotten were done on location in New York City, in either Battery Park or Central Park; some were shot in and around the old Washington Market. Other New York scenes were set in historic locales to capture the feeling of "little old New York." During one scene near the old aquarium, while the principals were to ride in three rented horse-drawn Victorian cabs, a huge downpour began. Welles welcomed it, believing it would add dimension and excitement to the chase, and insisted that the filming continue during the rain. The hackmen refused to move their horses, however, and shooting for that day was canceled. As it happened, it was the beginning of a hurricane and the rain continued for days.

Welles was frequently late for the day's shootings and would greatly annoy both cast and crew whenever he did arrive with a long, involved, and usually preposterous excuse for not showing up on time. Once he never got farther than the front steps of his hotel. One morning, just before noon, he left the St. Regis expecting to hail a cab to the location of the film. The entire area of Fifty-fifth Street and Fifth Avenue, and all the streets and sidewalks surrounding it, were jammed with people. A young man, twenty-six-year-old John Warde, sat on a ledge of the seventeenth floor of the Gotham Hotel, located across the street, threatening to jump. People from nearby offices and businesses began to gather. Reports were made on the radio and workers on their lunch breaks immediately went to the scene. Soon, over ten thousand people were crowded into the area, traffic was totally stopped, and Welles saw that he was going to be late again. Back in his room, he telephoned one of the crew. "You're not going to believe this," he said, "but I'm trapped in my hotel." It wasn't until the next day when the accounts appeared in the papers that

Welles *was* believed. Warde had sat there for eleven hours, keeping three hundred policeman at bay, and finally jumped to his death after saying to a nearby policeman, "I can't disappoint all these people."

Shortly after that, during one particularly sweltering day, Welles directed a scene on top of a five-story building on Albany Street, between Greenwich and Washington, in which Barrier rushed in blazing pursuit of Cotten. Cotten was to "jump" from the roof. A crowd gathered below, and someone thought another potential suicide was in progress and called the police. "Don't jump," people yelled. Squad cars, fire engines, and newspapermen fled to the scene. Filming stopped and Welles climbed down from the top of the building where he had been directing the action. Drenched in perspiration, he explained, "All we're trying to do is make a movie." Filming resumed, and Cotten jumped to a ledge six feet below the top of the roof. Barrier followed. The camera stopped for another setup, then Cotten jumped from a second-floor window into a moving horse-drawn wagon of cabbages, again followed by Barrier, making it appear that they had both jumped from the top of the roof into the wagon. No stuntmen were used. The next day a headline blared: ORSON WELLES CASHES IN ON LEDGE LEAP SUICIDES.

Welles wanted to shoot one scene in which Cotten would leap from a roof onto the top of a moving Ninth Avenue El train; at one point, as it made a sharp turn, the train was only inches away from the buildings near it. The Interboro Rapid Transit authorities were contacted, but approval to do the stunt never arrived in time and the idea was scrapped.

One of the funniest scenes showed both Barrier and Cotten stuck in a parade of suffragettes, both marching to time, with Barrier slowly inching up rank by rank on the advancing Cotten. Both men stopped to salute the American flag and then resumed their chase.

In order to film the scene on the SS *Munificence,* Welles borrowed a Hudson River Day Line excursion boat while it was docked at the Battery taking on passengers for its trip to Bear Mountain. Much to the delight of the vacationers, he spent an hour or so filming Cotten, Barrier, Virginia Welles, and Eustace Wyatt chasing each other around various parts of the boat.

After ten days of shooting, there were approximately twenty-five thousand feet of unedited film, and the play was only days away from opening. The budget had been almost totally depleted, and no further money was on the horizon. Welles had a Moviola and splicing and cutting equipment moved into his suite at the St. Regis and began editing the film himself. He rarely left the room except for one final rehearsal before each broadcast of "First Person Singular" or to take occasional trips to Stony Creek to conduct rehearsals of the play there. Bits and pieces of film were spread all over the room and as Houseman has recalled, Welles's assistants had to "wade knee-deep through a crackling sea of inflammable film." A large tip was pressed upon the maid with strict instructions that nothing, *absolutely nothing,* was to be taken from the room.

In addition to the very real practical problems Welles had in editing all the footage down to a sensible length and doing it in time for the opening, other annoyances and impending tragedies began to plague him. An attorney formally notified Welles that Paramount Studios owned the film rights to *Too Much Johnson*—Welles had leased the legitimate stage rights from Samuel French but had overlooked motion picture legalities—and that if the play reached Broadway with the film in it, payment, perhaps substantial, would have to be made.

·Many in the cast had not been paid in a month. In settling up their back pay, Welles tried to conserve what little money was left, so he attempted to treat any acting in the film as a rehearsal, to be paid for at the lower rehearsal rates. Several actors complained to Equity, and it was finally decreed that a film is a performance even if it's part of a play, so the cast and crew had to be paid full union rates.

Finally, the laboratory that was processing the film would not deliver the last reels until total payment was made, and there was no money to ransom it. There was also the problem of adding piano music to the film behind the screen although Blitzstein offered to play "live," and the intertitles* had to be printed and processed, all added expenses for which no funds could be found. Welles was convinced that with just a little more time and money he could edit what he had shot into a film that would be funny and memorable, but time and money had run out.

A few days before the opening of the play, some members of the crew brought a 16-millimeter projector up to Stony Creek and attempted a pre-screening of whatever footage was complete. Without the missing footage still to be delivered by the processor, nothing tied together. To add to the woes, the auditorium itself, with its low ceiling, was unsuited to project the film properly. If the film had been complete, the play might have been moved to another theater for the two-week tryout. As it was, this newest problem became the last straw, and the film portion of the project was abandoned.

Too Much Johnson opened on August 16, 1938, but without the film. Welles remained in his hotel suite, despondent, filled with guilt and self-recrimination. Two weeks later, the play closed without ever reaching Broadway.**

*Intertitles are the white-on-black printed dialogue or expositional commentary that often appeared within silent films.

**The last known print of *Too Much Johnson* was accidentally burned in a fire in Welles's villa in Spain in the 1970s while the late Robert Shaw was a guest there.

CHAPTER 9

IN THE FALL of 1938, Welles inaugurated the Mercury Theatre's second repertory season, with *Danton's Death,* a play by Georg Büchner.

Büchner, son of a former surgeon in one of Napoleon's armies who had settled in Germany, was born in 1813. The young poet and dramatist was also a part of the revolutionary, antiroyalist activity that was sweeping Europe and the German state in the 1830s. An activist who organized a "League of the Rights of Man," he was betrayed by a double agent in the group. In hiding, and awaiting his imminent arrest at the hands of the police who were already patrolling his house, Büchner wrote his commentary on revolutionary politics, *Danton's Death.* He hoped to sell the play and finance an escape.

Büchner was able to send the play to a friend with publishing connections in Frankfurt; while awaiting a reply, he was arrested. He did manage to escape to Strasbourg and then died at the tragically early age of twenty-four in Zurich in 1837. *Danton's Death* was never performed during his brief lifetime, but it did see publication in a censored 1835 edition subtitled "Dramatic Pictures from the Reign of Terror."

Danton's Death focuses on a brief but pivotal episode of the French Revolution, the spring of 1794. The king has been guillotined, and the political and social upheaval of the Revolution is in full swing. The world, shocked by the terrible bloodletting of the 1792 September massacres in which thousands of royalists and suspected traitors met their death, is now recoiling in horror at new atrocities. October 1793 sees Marie Antoinette lose her head. Members of the conservative Girondist party are being stamped out by the hundreds, and Paris streets are filled with jeering mobs. The tumbrils, two-wheeled carts that carry new victims to the guillotine, are seen everywhere. It is truly the Reign of Terror.

Büchner now charts the transfer of power in the Revolution. Georges-Jacques Danton, who along with Robespierre and Marat had voted for the death of Louis XVI, has had enough of bloodshed and is satisfied that the Revolution has accomplished its ends. The cruel and grotesquely misnamed Committee for Public Safety, the main agitating force once led by Danton, is now in the hands of Robespierre, the "Incorruptible." Former radicals are now seen as conservatives; the fanatical Robespierre calls for the purging of all undesirable elements, including Danton. Robespierre's views carry weight;

Hébert, another extremist fallen out of favor, has already been executed in March. Danton's time has come, and the irony of the situation is not lost on him. The juggernaut of revolution that he took such pains to put in motion is now about to crush him. In the end, vilified by the self-serving, puritanical Robespierre and his accomplice Saint-Just, he accepts his fate—and even laughs. He has not come this far without knowing that the Revolution is too much a force now for anyone to stop and that it will not be long before his accusers become the accused. Robespierre, Büchner seems to imply, is signing his own death warrant just as surely as he is signing Danton's.

A 1927 Max Reinhardt version of the play had been conceived on a grand scale, with the action played out against the background of real "mobs" of actors. Welles was limited by the diminutive size of the Mercury Theatre and decided to develop the play along different lines. Working from an English-language script by Geoffrey Dunlop, he pared down and modified the text, emphasizing the ideas of the play. It became a drama about the motivations behind a revolution, not the story of a mob.

Working through suggestion and clever stagecraft, Welles developed a richly textured drama composed of a series of crisply realized scenes, tableaux that could be described as terse and cinematic. Some were to say or imply that Welles did this solely to accommodate Büchner to the confines of the Mercury; however, it can be argued that Welles's version is truer to the spirit of Büchner than was Reinhardt's. In the long perspective of literary history, Büchner's *Danton* is seen as the forerunner of much modern theater, perhaps the first expressionist drama. Alexander Woollcott's review of the Reinhardt stage production from the *New York World* of December 1927 puts it succinctly: *"Danton's Death* was not produced until sixty years after his death and it was not until even more recently that young Büchner's ailment as a dramatist was diagnosed by the theater of our time. It was merely that he had been almost a century ahead of his."

In a sense, John Mason Brown's opinion, found in his *New York Post* review, that "like Reinhardt before him, Mr. Welles seems to have been interested in Büchner's script primarily because of the challenges with which it presents him as a director" seems probable yet incomplete. In truth, Welles was being cleverly opportunistic, hoping that Warner Bros. would offer a film directorship to him after they saw his stage version, when they would probably agree that this examination of demagoguery in intimate close-up was right in tune with the times.

Welles's modifications brought the play to a running time of about an hour and a half, one scene upon another in carefully crafted tableaux. As many critics pointed out, Welles's techniques in light, sound, and special effects were developing along the lines marked out by his productions of *Doctor Faustus* and *Julius Caesar*.

Danton's stage became a honeycomb of trapdoors by which actors' entrances and exits (one viewer would quip that it looked as though all the action took place in a belfry) would have them virtually appear or disappear out of thin air. The trapdoors were supplemented with an elaborate system of ladders and platforms. A portion of the stage could rise, allowing Welles to make full use of all three dimensions. If Reinhardt's production was magnificent and sprawling, this one was mounted with the concentration and intensity of a coiled spring.

The most striking feature of the setting, however, was the work of the designer Stephen Jan Tichacek. Physically embracing the rear portion of the stage was Tichacek's cyclorama, a curved backdrop composed of row upon row of masks, some fourteen hundred of them in all. Depending on the hue and intensity of the light playing over them, the masks suggested, in a vivid, hallucinatory way, revolutionary mobs or tribunals—or hundreds of grinning skulls, the silent but hideous presence of the Revolution's victims. Soaring several stories high, the curtain of masks was a brilliant device that created a terrifying sense of masses of grinning heads.

Lighting was crucial. It was now the hallmark of a Welles production, and he did not stint this time. The lights were coordinated with the aid of Jean Rosenthal. A press release gives a marvelously detailed account of her preparations by journalist and Mercury publicist Henry Sember:

> From the depths of the stage, crisscrossed with platforms like the top of a mince pie, a husky voice asked, "How's that, Mother?" "You're wrong," the girl replied gently but firmly. "After 22 you bring in 5 KW. Bring it up . . . bring it up five counts . . . no no no no—that's all wrong! Five KW is coming in too quickly. Listen, Joe, 5 KW is an actress, not an actor." An almost imperceptible glow of light was seen against the cyclorama of masks which formed the background of the setting. "How's that, Mother?" came the husky voice again.

Sember goes on to say that "Joe and his pals" did finally manage to bring in "5 KW" with the recommended finesse: "Like a swishy actress." Sember asked her how many lights *Danton* required:

> "Not very many," Miss Rosenthal answered. "About 14 on the front balcony, 6 over the boxes, 6 on the ceiling, 22 on the first pipe behind the proscenium, 14 on the second, 13 on the one which matches the contour of the cyclorama, 2 in the cellar, 18 in the tormentor, 4 on the pit tormentor, 4 behind the cyclorama. We know them all by their first names, practically. Joe said that we'd better watch out or we'll have to take out Equity cards for them."

Duly impressed, Sember got an impromptu lecture on the various purposes of lighting in a dramatic production, not the least of which, according to Miss Rosenthal, was the sense of continuity lent by the lights, analogous to musical transitions in radio. But probably the most revealing thing to be learned about the lighting in *Danton's Death* is not the intricacy and precision of the art but the incalculable strokes that show creativity at its best. Did it all take a lot of planning?

"Yes," Miss Rosenthal admitted, "but the irony of it all is that some of our best effects are just plain accidents, I think. One of our best effects in the show is one which suggests the shadows of marching men. We arrived at that just because someone forgot to turn up the light in the cellar."

If serendipity made life easier for Welles and his associates in the technical realm, coincidence apparently ruled when the cast began rehearsals. For instance, it was noted with some surprise that a movie covering the same period of history was playing at the Astor—*Marie Antoinette,* starring Norma Shearer. But strangest of all, an old, pre-Hitler vintage movie, *Danton,* directed by Hans Behrendt and starring Fritz Kortner, showed up at the Cameo. Thinking they might pick up a few tips from the German film, most of the cast went to see it. Billed now as "the first film banned by Hitler," it had been highly received at its Berlin premiere in 1931 because of its characterization of Danton as a chauvinistic fanatic. Back at rehearsals, Welles gave instructions to begin Act II, scene 1. Sitting in the seventh row he was eating his dinner, but as the actors began to speak he looked up and laughed—they were speaking in German dialect as a funny but not-so-practical joke on Orson.

Marc Blitzstein again was a key part of the Welles creative team for *Danton.* He did extensive research for the music and even made a musicological discovery in the process. In his search for authentic material, Blitzstein discovered the original version of the revolutionary hymn and French national anthem, the "Marseillaise," hidden away and forgotten, just two blocks away in the New York Public Library. It was an original manuscript score by composer Claude Joseph Rouget de Lisle, with the full title *La Chanson des Guerriers Marseillois.* * Blitzstein maintained that his find helped to shed a great deal of light on the true character of the piece, saying that the original was scored for a different kind of accompaniment and differed in its melodic transitions. In later times the "Marseillaise" had been "brassed up," the version everyone knows is generally similar but the old one "also had a Mozartian quality which has been lost through the years."

Blitzstein said that he wanted to do two things with the music—give a feeling of the flavor of the French Revolution's period but also, and perhaps more importantly, capture something of the mood of Büchner's dialogue. Two songs and one theme stand as examples. "Ode to Reason," sung by Adelyn Colla-Negri, was written in the manner of revolutionary hymns of the period denouncing the reign of kings. The song "Christine," sung by Joseph Cotten and Mary Wickes, was Blitzstein's tribute to Büchner, having been inspired by a reference to a certain "Christina" in the original text. A lively number about a soldier and his lover, Christine, the song blended motifs of old love lyrics with some elements of modern popular songs. And finally, Blitzstein produced the "Carmagnole," very close to the genre of song and dance performed in the streets in celebration of the cartloads of royalists going to their deaths at the guillotine—music for a carnival of the macabre.

*"Song of the Marseilles Warriors."

Welles cast Martin Gabel as the world-weary, womanizing Danton. Arlene Francis was Marion, his mistress. Recreating his role of Robespierre from the 1927 Vienna and New York Reinhardt productions was Vladimir Sokoloff, fresh from a film part in *The Life of Emile Zola.* Welles himself, after some indecision, took on the role of Saint-Just, Robespierre's right-hand man and the prosecutor of the tribunal that sentences Danton to his death.

Danton opened, after some delay, at the beginning of November 1938. Expectations for this first presentation of the Mercury's new season ran high, and it is possible that the theater was full the first few nights primarily because of Welles's canonization as a household name after the *War of the Worlds* broadcast of October 30. Mixed with the genuine excitement of people eager to see the latest from Welles, was a more cynical sentiment. Who would be the first to detect a falling-off and witness the inevitable burnout of the prodigy? Talent or luck, it simply couldn't hold out.

They saw Welles's expressionistic theater and came away with no consensus. Welles's tableaux moved some and left others with a nagging feeling that they had missed the meaning somewhere: Danton's dalliances with Marion; open sensuality suggested only by a divan; Robespierre, alone, addressing the convention with the leering masks behind him; Saint-Just, black-robed pseudo-prophet declaiming on the necessity of death. Throwing up his pencil, *World-Telegram* critic Sidney B. Whipple claimed, "It needs a student of the French Revolution to decipher it."

The settings were either a brilliant stroke or "a burlesque on Mr. Welles's favorite theories of staging," in the words of Richard Watts, Jr., of the *Tribune.* He added, "For the Mercury Theatre, the honeymoon is over." Welles had proved that you can't please everybody. A glowing review by Brooks Atkinson made some of the others easier to take.

A scene singled out for universal praise was the one in which Robespierre whispers, "I am alone," and the cyclorama is bathed in a green light to reveal the masks as death's heads.

All too many critics seemed to be preoccupied about the trapdoors, claiming to be on the edge of their seats in fear of someone's taking a wrong step and breaking his neck; or they mentioned that the toylike quality of some of the platforms reduced the pathos of the actors. Similarly, some cavils about Sokoloff's accented English did not seem to attempt to reach the logic of the matter.

Arthur Pollock of the *Brooklyn Daily Eagle,* author of one of the favorable reviews, took time two days later to register a complaint about the spirit in which the play had been approached. He spoke about the plight of bright young men:

> If they begin with work that is superlative where can they go from there? They must either repeat themselves or face the prospect of long years getting better all the time.
>
> At 23 a man's future must appall him if he has begun where others, at their peak, left off. Is he good enough to get better throughout two-thirds of a lifetime?

... If *Danton's Death* does not seem very important it is, after all, simply because Orson Welles did it. He suffers by comparison with himself. Done by anyone else this *Danton's Death* would have looked like an American miracle. Done by anyone else it would not seem quite so precious.

Requests for press and radio interviews were coming to Welles by the dozens every day but, unfortunately, they had little to do with *Danton's Death*. Newspapermen and radio broadcasters wanted further ink or air for their respective machines, but only if it concerned *The War of the Worlds*. Before he could do anything else, Welles had to express what he felt about *Danton's Death*. He took a day off, staying incommunicado at the St. Regis, and parodying Sidney Skolsky's column opener, "Don't get me wrong, I love Hollywood," wrote the following letter:

November 13, 1938

Dear Richard Watts, Jr.:

Don't get us wrong, the Mercury Theatre loves Richard Watts, Jr. When some of the reviewers don't like your show, it is fairly customary for us Broadway producers to launch a bitter tirade against the critics as an institution.

But we love the critics, no fooling. Yes, I know that some of the boys took us for a Louisiana hayride on the occasion of the opening of our first production of the current season, *Danton's Death,* but to date not one of the Mercury staff has made application for a hunting license.

We're all too well aware that it was the approval of the same critics, last season, that helped make the Mercury. Nor have we ever made a secret of the fact that it was the discreet suggestions of one critic who caught a preview that helped us make *Julius Caesar* the success that it was—all the critics didn't like that play, either.

It was John Hutchens, now an eminent Boston critic, who once pointed out that the prevailing system of play-reviewing, evincing as it occasionally does drastically different opinions on the part of the individual critics, is all in all, a healthy sign of democracy among the drama-appraisers. In brief, it proves that the boys didn't get together on the sidewalk during intermission to decide what they're going to say about a play. They can't at the Mercury where we seldom have any intermissions.

Mr. Hutchens may have been right as far as he went but he did not take into consideration the fact that some producers might look to the critics for guidance. What conclusion can a producer draw when the critics disagree as much as they did on *Danton's Death*?

For instance, Mr. Watts, you said that "it seems very sad to find the Mercury Theatre falling down around us." While you were penning that very line, a few blocks to the north Mr. Brooks Atkinson was writing: ".... overwhelming... it endows the Mercury Theatre with the same vitality it had last season. A worthy successor to *Caesar*."

Also, Mr. Watts, he found that "there has been no attempt to point any possible parallels with more modern revolutions." Simultaneously when Mr. Atkinson was writing that "like all vivid drama the expressionistic chiaroscuro of *Danton's Death* crackles with contemporary significance." And Mr. Lockridge informed his readers that we had "burned into the consciousness of the playgoers the strange and rather terrifying scenes of Georg Büchner's *Danton's Death,* a play, which, written more than a hundred years ago, still has a vivid immediacy." Also, Mr. Watts, you found the play "cloudy in its presentation." Burns Mantle declared that it "achieves a definite dramatic eloquence . . . not to be classified with the ordinary dramatic entertainment of the theater. It is a distinctive and different type of show."

John Mason Brown found that "what happens on the stage is often exciting to the eyes, but what it does to your emotions as a member of the audience is almost less than nothing at all." Almost as if in reply, Mr. Lockridge said: "The challenge of the whole is more to the emotions than to the mind and pictures rather than describes the souls of men in revolution and the text is lighted and extended by the ingenuity of unashamed theatricalism."

Walter Winchell found the play to be "fake art." In refutation, John Anderson said that "Mr. Welles lifts the whole beyond revolutionary melodrama to a different level, by the sheer visual effect of the staging," and Mr. Lockridge said that: "Throughout, imagination of a higher order is combined with theatrical ingenuity to produce effects which are at once amazing and curiously stirring."

Yes, this divergence of opinion may be very healthy for the theater-at-large, but, I repeat, it is quite confusing to the individual producer. Right now, I am more puzzled than when I first learned that a large number of people had taken our Martian invasion seriously.

Sincerely,

The Mercury Theatre
Orson Welles, Director

Danton's Death ran only twenty-one performances.

IT HAD BEEN announced on the last summer show of "First Person Singular" that there would be a new time slot for the series and that the story of Vincent Van Gogh, revealed through letters to his brother Theo, would be its first offering. Welles was to play the great painter, reading many of the sensitive letters that reveal his deep sense of and passion for beauty and his desire to serve his fellow man. Although the letters proved to be gripping to read, they were too difficult to adapt to radio and certainly not within the week's time that Welles had so injudiciously left for the preparation of his next broadcasting effort.

Another drama was needed—quickly—to start off the new fall 1938 season. Also, it had to be one that might have a chance to capture at least a portion of the audience during that highly competitive Sunday night hour of eight to nine. The series was now up against radio's most successful program,

"The Chase and Sanborn Hour" with Edgar Bergen and his dummy, Charlie McCarthy.

Like the purloined letter, Welles's stage version of *Julius Caesar* was so close in sight that at first it never occurred to him that it would be ideal for radio. The play had been trimmed of most of its fat, no scenery was needed, and although its lighting was a marvelous addition, a broadcast version could be sustained without it. *Julius Caesar* had received national publicity; if the original cast could be assembled, which wasn't a problem, people all over the country would have the opportunity of being exposed to one of the most dynamic productions of Shakespeare ever mounted. With just a bit of careful editing, thirty-three minutes was excised from the stage version and an innovation added.

Remembering the favorable reaction to the person who played the announcer in *The Fall of the City* (Welles himself), Welles thought that a similar actor should be introduced into the radio version of *Julius Caesar*. Both plays were concerned with how the populace reacts toward dictatorship, and both contained a moral that was directly applicable to the world situation. An omniscient announcer, who could develop the narrative action and who could comment on motivation would give the listener more insight and information than he would receive directly from the dialogue of the play. It would be as effective in *Julius Caesar* as it was in *The Fall of the City*.

At first, Welles thought of playing both the narrator *and* Brutus, but there was just too much dialogue for one person to handle. As it developed, the man who possessed the most recognizable and most mimicked voice on American radio, the dean of commentators, H. V. Kaltenborn, was available to play the narrator. As a CBS broadcaster, all he had to do was leave his Studio Nine and go downstairs to Welles's Studio One. He readily accepted the assignment. For the new narration to be added to *Julius Caesar,* Welles extracted sections of Sir Thomas North's translation of Plutarch's *Lives of the Noble Grecians and Romans,* which was Shakespeare's main source and inspiration for the play.

It might well have been Kaltenborn's imposing presence, and his reputation as one of the greatest commentators in the world, that slightly intimidated Welles during the rehearsal for *Julius Caesar.* Or it might have also been the many pressures he was facing with *Danton's Death* and the other inherent disorders of the Mercury Theatre. At any rate, at first he was on edge, his breathing became deeper, disrupting his usually smooth flow of phrases; his tone quality suffered and some words and phrases became breathy and muffled. "QUIET IN THE STUDIO!" he boomed on several occasions attempting to maintain his concentration. He became impatient when cues were not responded to immediately. "Oh, Christ!" he kept saying each time there was a second's silence or a miscue of any kind. But by the end of the rehearsal he began to relax when it appeared the show was coming together as a cohesive whole.

In addition to Welles as Brutus, all of the original cast of the stage version participated: Martin Gabel as Cassius, George Coulouris as Antony, and Joseph Holland as Caesar. Blitzstein's memorable score of military marches and parades was used in its entirety. Unfortunately, because of its powerful visual elements, the Cinna assassination scene could not be successfully adapted to the air, and that part of the play was deleted.

The Kaltenborn addition was a master stroke and the actual airing of *Julius Caesar* was one of the strongest shows ever broadcast by the Mercury players. When Kaltenborn began to paint the picture of the action in his precise tones, listeners were immediately intrigued: "This is the history of a political assassination, the killing of a man who tried to make himself king. It is an account of how the murder was prepared, how it was carried out, and what happened later to the men who took part in it." And when Cassius comes to Brutus, the most noble man in Rome, and asks, "Can you see your face?" all of the tension was out of Welles's voice. In his first line of the broadcast he answered with an expressive quality that delineated his usual, deep resonance: "No, Cassius, for the eye sees not itself but by reflection, by some other thing." Welles maintained the gentility of his voice as his characterization of Brutus, for the remainder of the broadcast, to his famous last line: "Caesar, now be still. I killed not thee with half so good a will."

The Mercury broadcasts that followed *Julius Caesar* were individual creative islands, each different from its predecessor. Many were ingeniously chosen, some marvelously adapted, a few poorly rehearsed, none badly acted, and all produced with what was easily becoming discernible as a Wellesian style of sound, consisting of a robust vitality and an authenticity bridged by the sonorousness and vehemence of Orson's voice.

In the weeks that followed, he played the gloomy Edward Rochester in Charlotte Brontë's *Jane Eyre,* booming over the haunted heath. He traveled to the North Pole as the sea-worn Captain Melville in the true-life and tragic adventure of the De Long expedition there, as recounted in *Hell On Ice,* by Edward Elsberg. He was William Sylvanus Baxter, the suffering adolescent who falls in love with Lola Pratt of the calf-like eyes, in Booth Tarkington's *Seventeen*, and the cold-blooded, globe-trotting Phileas Fogg in *Around the World in Eighty Days* by Jules Verne. One of his more popular portrayals was that of the most famous resident of Baker Street, "a gentleman who never lived and who will never die" as Welles described Sherlock Holmes. Welles went back via the airways to that unlikely London of the nineteenth century, where high adventure awaited all that would seek it, a world of hansom cabs, gas lamps and Inverness capes in damp, fog-laden, sinister streets.

Welles thought of Sherlock Holmes as one of the few permanent profiles, "ever-lasting silhouettes on the edge of the world" immediately recognizable in virtually every country, along with Punch; the two Charlies—Chaplin and McCarthy; Don Quixote; and Falstaff. He was attracted to all.

As a child, Welles had seen the famous stage version of Sherlock Holmes written by and starring William Gillette (also the author of *Too Much Johnson*). Gillette was celebrated for what might be called his introduction of underacting. He had died in 1937, and Welles used the radio broadcast of the play a year later as an unofficial homage to the great actor-playwright. Gillette's drama was as much a part of the Holmes literature as any of Arthur Conan Doyle's romances, and in the public's mind the image of Gillette, with his aquiline face, hawk's nose, underslung pipe, and deerstalker hat—fore and aft—was the actual embodiment of Holmes himself. (This was before the public was introduced to the Basil Rathbone portrayal.) Welles attempted to capture some of the Gillette mystique over the air. When he said, "Elementary, my dear Watson," it was with a perfectly clipped British accent, filled with pompous intelligence. "Elementary: a mere child's play of deduction," he chuckled. The transformation was complete.

Although Welles was a constant and enthusiastic reader of fiction, it is not to be implied that he had a thorough recall or reading knowledge of all the stories he considered for adaptation for the "Mercury Theatre on the Air." As ideas for stories came to him from listeners, friends, and associates, he or an assistant haunted bookstores and libraries for the suggested works to read for consideration. As a matter of course in his search for radio material, he continually searched through anthologies such as *Transatlantic Stories* and *Short Stories from The New Yorker,* and he was a consistent reader of magazines such as *Harper's, The Saturday Evening Post,* and *The Atlantic* or any periodical that might contain a wide mine of stories.

Many stories that were started in script never made their way on the air. In some cases, rights were impossible to secure for those works that were not in the public domain. Then, some stories appeared relatively dull on reading after the transformation from book-page prose to radio drama; others seemed adequate upon reading but after a trial rehearsal were abandoned.

Welles often used the word "tale" in describing the stories he sought for broadcasting. He wanted a story of a particular kind, a simple one that demands from the reader a certain acceptance of strange and extraordinary events, that he could transmit over the air the way an old *vaquero* of Mexico or *auta kara* of Africa might enthrall the villagers of remote towns night after night with tales of adventure and mystery.

Many of the stories chosen by Welles were originally written for children or young people, but they possessed a quality that also appealed to adults. Through the weekly spinning of these yarns, Welles seemed to be reliving—or living for the first time—reflected childhood.

Some of his favorites never were done, such as "Blow Up with the Brig," from Wilkie Collins's sea story *After Dark*; Conrad Aiken's "Silent Snow, Secret Snow"; Isak Dinesen's "The Sailor Boy's Tale"; W. W. Jacobs's "The Monkey's Paw"; and many of the short stories of Booth Tarkington.

AFTER SEVERAL WEEKS of broadcasting in the new format, an adaptation of *Lorna Doone* by R. D. Blackmore, one of the most successful nineteenth-century novels, was nearly ready in script form. The story had a swashbuckling ambience that appealed to Welles, and he was to play John Ridd, the narrator and the man who fights for and wins the lovely Lorna.

However, as the script neared finishing, Welles began to have doubts about its impact; it now seemed dull, dated, and slow-moving. Further work and revision were needed, but the time for the next show was growing thin, and it began to appear doubtful whether an acceptable script for *Lorna Doone* could be prepared in time. There was only one other available story for which the rights had been secured by the Mercury and placed in their inventory: *War of the Worlds,* based on the H. G. Wells novel originally published in 1897.

Up until then, radio had given little attention to the genre of science fiction other than "Buck Rogers in the Twenty-Fifth Century," and that show was considered an appropriate vehicle only for children. But science fiction was a particular favorite of Welles. In 1936, a pulp magazine called *The Witch's Tales* had appeared on the newsstands. It contained uncredited reprints of Victorian science fiction from the old *Pearson's Magazine.* It was in that collection of reprints that Welles first read *The War of the Worlds.* Two years later, searching for material to use on "The Mercury Theatre on the Air," he conceived the idea of adapting the novel as adult fare.

At that time, Welles also considered adapting two other science fiction stories from the Victorian era. One was M. P. Schiel's "The Purple Cloud," an end-of-the-world plot in which the last man on earth spends twenty years roaming the continents until he discovers a young girl alive in Constantinople. Welles also thought of using Arthur Conan Doyle's "The Lost World," an engrossing story in which the central character leads an expedition to discover dinosaurs who still survive on a volcanic plateau deep in the Amazon jungle; it had been made into a silent film in 1925, noted for its animation techniques in creating the "lost dinosaurs." Both stories, however, were overruled in favor of *The War of the Worlds.*

The Mercury purchased radio rights to the story early in 1938 for a small amount of money, and an initial scripting had been done. After studying the first script, Welles feared that the story might be too old-fashioned and too remote to sustain his audience's interest. The original H. G. Wells story told about an invasion of Martians who land in England around the turn of the century, and the initial version of the radio adaptation had retained those details. Welles believed that the story should be modernized, both in language and in time frame, and the action moved to locations in the United States. Such an extensive reworking would take time. Welles decided that if *The War of the Worlds* could be made ready to his liking, and a script prepared in time for the next broadcast—October 30, 1938—he would use it for that night's show. If it wasn't ready, *Lorna Doone* would be used.

The next week's selection had to be announced at the conclusion of the October 23 show, which was *Around the World in 80 Days.* Welles took a chance that the script would be acceptable and signed off that night by stating that the next offering would be *The War of the Worlds.*

IT'S IMPORTANT TO know how Welles constructed his radio scripts since some doubt about his contribution to them has been raised by critics, past and present. Welles maintained complete control and authority, creatively and legally, over the content of all his shows. He alone selected, sometimes after consultation with Houseman and others, the story to be dramatized. Often he had clear ideas of what approach was to be taken, what scenes were to be developed or deleted, which characters should be highlighted or excised. This was conveyed, usually by direct discussion, sometimes by memorandum, to whoever was responsible for putting the first, rough-draft script together. With some stories, such as *Julius Caesar* or *The Man Who Was Thursday,* Welles worked entirely alone in doing the first script and then all subsequent drafts. At other times, Houseman, more than anyone, worked on the week's effort, or if prior commitments or overwork prevented Welles doing the first draft, Orson assigned or approved the assignment of the script to another writer.

Once the first draft was written, Welles went over it to see how well the story flowed and to see how it *sounded.* What may read well as narration is often confusing or verbose when spoken. The best way to test the effectiveness of dialogue is to read it aloud, and often Welles gathered his actors around him, passed around copies of a new script, and they did just that: they read it aloud, changing lines as they went, revising and refining the words until the dialogue sounded like real dialogue, not prosy or mechanical transfers from published page to radio script. Above all, it had to flow smoothly.

Everyone made suggestions, and the group shouted down the poor lines and acclaimed those that worked. "We'll live under ground," was one of the lines in the first draft of *The War of the Worlds,* and "I've been thinking about the drains." One of the actors pointed out the fact that Americans think of drains as small strainers at the bottom of their kitchen sinks, so the word was changed to convey the sense of its intended meaning. The line became: "I've been thinking about the sewers."

In developing each show for the Mercury Theatre, after the first run-through, a second script was prepared, and Welles would work on it, still changing dialogue, shifting scenes, and adding action as he deemed it necessary. It was at this point that he would begin conferring with Paul Deitz, the sound engineer, using the script as a guide. What sounds or effects would be needed? Were there any too difficult to duplicate? Did some drown out the dialogue? Could other sounds be used to add drama or impact to a scene? As the sound cues were added to the script, sometimes necessitating further extensive revisions, Welles would either make these changes himself or have them made by one of the writers.

Musical bridges and cues had to be added; the CBS legal department had to check each script to see if there were any objectionable, possibly libelous, passages. Davidson Taylor, the network's executive producer, often made suggestions for last-minute changes that were creatively or practically helpful.

A preliminary "dress" rehearsal was then held, sometimes with Welles voicing his own part but often not. This rehearsal was meticulously timed, and further paring and honing of the script was done to make it fit into the scheduled time, approximately sixty pages for an hour-long show. After the final rehearsal, always with Welles in attendance as director and actor, he would continue his jottings, deletions, and additions to the script, frequently up to the last few seconds before air time.

NEITHER WELLES NOR Houseman had time to do the initial re-scripting of *The War of the Worlds,* so the assignment was given to Howard Koch, a young, lanky lawyer-turned-playwright, who had done the first drafts of *Hell on Ice* and *Seventeen.* Koch initially learned of the assignment on the night Welles announced that the Mercury Theatre was going to perform the H. G. Wells story, one week before it was broadcast. The official assignment was made to Koch the next day. Welles gave specific instructions to modernize the language and dialogue, to localize the action, and to dramatize the story in the form of radio news bulletins. Koch complained to Houseman that such massive revisions would result in very nearly an entirely original play, something he felt he could not accomplish in only six days. Houseman relayed Koch's concerns to Welles, with the suggestions that a substitution be considered, a story that could more easily be adapted in so short a time. However, Welles insisted that Koch proceed as directed. The usual system of draft-revision-draft-revision ensued, and Koch has recalled that sleep became a longed-for luxury. He worked "from early morning until late at night."

Why was Welles so adamantly determined to use a play concocted on such a tight schedule? If he had used a substitution for that week, he certainly could have broadcast *The War of the Worlds* at a later date. Moreover, he owned the radio rights and had the privilege of broadcasting the story at any time he so chose. A more considered adaptation, done at a more leisurely pace, also implied a better script. Apparently, a combination of forces was responsible for the sense of urgency that suffused Welles and caused him to insist on using *The War of the Worlds* on that precise evening. Despite historical protestations to the contrary, Welles clearly was attempting to make a statement with his broadcast of October 30, 1938. In a television interview years later he admitted, "Radio in those days, before the tube and the transistor, wasn't just a noise in somebody's pocket—it was a voice of authority. Too much so. At least, I thought so." He went on to say that he felt that "it was time for someone to take the starch . . . out of some of that authority: hence my broadcast." The scheduled evening of the broadcast, Halloween Eve, would be the perfect time to spoof, not just the public, but radio itself.

For the entire month prior to *The War of the Worlds,* radio had kept the American public alert to the ominous happenings throughout the world. The Munich crisis was at its height. Adolf Hitler, in his address to the annual Nazi party congress at Nuremberg in September, called for the autonomy of the Sudetenland, an area on the Czech border regions populated by three million Sudeten Germans, as they were called. Hitler ranted and lied over German radio, and for those Americans who could not understand German, the familiar voice of H. V. Kaltenborn provided a translation: "I say that if these tortured souls cannot obtain rights and help themselves, they can obtain them from us." For the first time in history, the public could tune into their radios every night and hear, boot by boot, accusation by accusation, threat by threat, the rumblings that seemed inevitably leading to a world war. Japanese power in the Far East was a genuine menace. On October 3, Hitler made a triumphal drive into the town of Asch, and within a week Nazi troops had completely occupied the Sudetenland.

Just days before the broadcast of *The War of the Worlds,* German filmmaker Leni Riefenstahl arrived in New York City to handle the promotion and distribution of her classic film of the 1936 Olympics. She captured headlines in the American press. No, she was emphatically *not* Jewish, she insisted. She also coyly denied that she was Hitler's mistress: "I get film orders from Hitler, that's all." The public was cynical, suspicious, and resentful that the film was being given critical acceptance. During the Riefenstahl visit came the news that Rome's fascist newspaper, *Il Tevere,* ordered all Italians to boycott the films of Charlie Chaplin and the brothers Marx and Ritz. The sourpuss reason? Their humor was not Aryan.

The involvement of the United States in helping its allies in the European crisis seemed certain, and radio listenership statistics released for September and October of 1938 indicated a massive and concerned audience. Broadcasts were being continually interrupted with the latest news bulletins of one major world emergency after another. The English people were issued gas masks as Germany marched into Austria and occupied the Sudetenland. The shadow of war was constantly in and on the air. People were on edge. Disaster loomed. The voice of H. V. Kaltenborn during the three tempestuous weeks of the Czech crisis in September clearly spelled out the feeling of perpetual uncertainty.

On Thursday, October 27, four days before *The War of the Worlds* was broadcast, at 10:00 P.M., Welles listened to *Air Raid,* a verse play by Archibald MacLeish that was aired on the "Columbia Workshop." The play opens with the announcer on top of a tenement roof in a European border town. Welles permitted Ray Collins, one of his Mercury regulars, to serve as the narrator. He can see everything around him; his microphone picks up the sounds and voices of women chattering and children playing. It is early in the morning of the day when the next war breaks out. More description of the town—a microcosm of the European condition—continues, and the play gives an unforgettable picture of the war at its inception and the confused psychology of modern warfare. A woman sings a scale that is parodied by a warning siren. The whine of raiding planes can be heard. The populace is noisy and in confusion, running for shelter. Machine guns sputter, antiaircraft guns fire explosively. Finally, a boy's voice is transposed into an agonizing scream as bombs begin to fall. The play ends. It is a broadcast that, even though written in verse, sounds almost cruelly real, as if it is actually happening, a live, on-the-spot news pickup.

You who fish the feathers of the night
With poles on roof-tops and long loops of wire
Those of you who driving from some visit
Fingering the button on the dashboard dial . . .
You have one thought tonight and only one:
Will there be a war? Has war come?
Is Europe burning from the Tiber to the Somme?

If Welles still had any reservations at all about doing *The War of the Worlds* broadcast, they were eliminated after he heard *Air Raid.* The use of the announcer to tell the story, which had been done in the radio broadcasts of *The Fall of the City* and *Julius Caesar,* was even more effective in *Air Raid.* The show had a wide audience, and its impact had been great. *Time* devoted a full page to a highly favorable review of *Air Raid,* and other periodicals had enthusiastic, virtually awed, responses. Welles too, was much impressed, and he incorporated many of MacLeish's most dramatic techniques into the script for *The War of the Worlds.* One of the differences was that MacLeish had taken *seven months* to create his broadcast; Orson was doing it in barely seven *days.*

We cannot be certain whether Welles was really aware, even partially aware, of the devastating impact that *The War of the Worlds* might have on the listening public. He did make the statement, in retrospect, that he was attempting to "diminish the authority of radio," which might indicate that in making use of a pseudo-announcer on a wholly fictitious show, he was deliberately trying to undermine radio's power and influence. Who would ever believe a newscaster after this? But he could not possibly have anticipated the degree to which listeners would accept the program as an actual news broadcast. Houseman claims that it is possible that neither he nor Welles was very familiar with the story but that situation would have been corrected after they both worked on the revision. Before air time, Augusta Weissberger, Welles's secretary, agreed with Howard Koch that the play was not particularly believable: "It's all too silly," she told Orson. "We are going to make absolute fools of ourselves." Skipper Hill was in New York at that time, and he also warned Orson not to use the Wells story.

On Thursday, Paul Stewart conducted a reading of the script while Welles was deep in a theater rehearsal of *Danton's Death.* After the *Air Raid* broadcast, that same night, when Welles returned to his suite at the St. Regis, Stewart played him a recording of the *War of the Worlds* rehearsal, without sound effects, and Welles felt that the reading was dull. One of the sound engineers also mentioned to Orson that he felt the show was weak; commentator Ben Gross, in his memoir, *I Looked and Listened,* remembers that one of the actors from the Mercury cast told him a few days before the *War of the Worlds* broadcast that he thought the projected show was, if anything, "lousy."

Welles continued to emphasize the importance of inserting into the script a sense of immediacy with news bulletins and eyewitness accounts, devices that he argued could be used with success.* Koch and Houseman attempted to make the play more realistic by inserting the names of real places and people wherever possible; they also increased the number of "flash" bulletins in the script. By Friday afternoon, the script was sent to Davidson Taylor of CBS for his usual pre-broadcast reading, and he, in turn, gave it to the legal department of the network for its approval. The response of both Taylor and the CBS attorneys was a total surprise to Welles and his associates: they contended that the script was *too* believable and that its realism would have to be diminished before the show could go on the air. They were also worried that the use of actual institutions' names could be legally actionable, that the American Museum of Natural History, for example, could sue for libel if they believed that the name of their institution was being improperly used in a fictional radio play. The network insisted upon some twenty-eight changes.

Protesting loudly, Welles, Koch, and the others systematically began to make the script *less* believable. The place names therefore were made less official- and real-sounding, and in some cases, were fictionalized, the very thing that they had originally set out to avoid. Here are just a few of the phrase changes made:

Working Script	Changed to	Censored Script
"The United States Weather Bureau in Washington, D.C."		"The Government Weather Bureau"
"Princeton University Observatory"		"Princeton Observatory"
"Magill University"		"Macmillan University"
"New Jersey National Guard"		"State Militia"
"United States Signal Corps"		"Signal Corps"
"Langley Field"		"Langham Field"
"St. Patrick's Cathedral"		"the cathedral"

Other changes continued right up until air time. The H. G. Wells story had been situated in "the last years of the nineteenth century," the actual period in which he wrote the story. In Koch's early draft of the script, the time frame had been set for "the thirty-ninth year of the twentieth century." Welles had changed the story to reflect the contemporary world; the attorneys for CBS somehow allowed "the twentieth century" to remain in the script. "They're starving in heaps... bolting... trampling on each other" was excised because it was thought to be an especially graphic scene of man's inhumanity to his fellow man. The cries of the advancing Martians, *"Ulia, Ulia, Ulia,"* were also deleted because CBS thought they sounded too terrifying.

Those listening to the radio on October 30, 1938, were not particularly

---

*During his broadcast of *Sherlock Holmes* on September 25, 1938, a news bulletin on the Munich crisis had been aired. Orson wanted to use this technique as a dramatic device to add tension to *The War of the Worlds.*

overwhelmed with scintillating programming. At 7:00 P.M., Secretary of Agriculture Henry Wallace, with General Hugh Johnson and Professor Lyman Bryson, discussed what this country should do with its farm surpluses. The radio public for the most part planned to listen to Edgar Bergen and Charlie McCarthy from 8 to 9 P.M. and then, at 10 P.M., tune in to a blow-by-blow description of the Welterweight Championship of the World between titleholder Henry Armstrong and his contender, Cerefino Garcia, direct from Madison Square Garden.

People who chose to attend a movie that night might have gone to see *Too Hot to Handle* with Clark Gable and Myrna Loy or *Young Dr. Kildare* with Lew Ayres and Lionel Barrymore or even *Boys Town* with Mickey Rooney and Spencer Tracy, all of which were in national release that week. New Yorkers had the opportunity of going to any of a few dozen fine Broadway plays. *Knickerbocker Holiday* with Walter Huston; the Pulitzer Prize winning *Our Town*; Robert Morley in *Oscar Wilde*; and Olson and Johnson in *Hellzapoppin* were playing to packed theaters every night.

At 7:58 that Sunday, after eight hours of rehearsals, Welles finally mounted a large, platformlike podium in the center of the studio, gulped down an entire bottle of pineapple juice, cleared his throat, made some rubbery gestures with his mouth, clamped on a set of headphones, loosened his tie, and gave announcer Dan Seymour a signal to start the show, precisely as the clock's second hand indicated 8 P.M. "The Columbia Broadcasting System and its affiliated stations presents Orson Welles and 'The Mercury Theatre on the Air' in *The War of the Worlds* by H. G. Wells," said Seymour in his perfectly modulated and estimably robust voice. Then Bernard Herrmann's orchestra played an introductory twenty seconds of the show's theme music, Tchaikovsky's Piano Concerto No. 1 in B-flat minor, followed by Seymour's introduction of "the Director of the Mercury Theatre and star of these broadcasts, Mr. Orson Welles." Welles slowly, somberly delivered the prologue, similar to H. G. Wells's, except for a few word and phrase changes. His voice was deep and scholarly, the tone expressing the fear of impending invasion:

> We know now that in the early years of the twentieth century this world was being watched closely by intelligences greater than man's and yet as mortal as his own.

After Welles's last words to the prologue drifted off, an announcer's voice came on with a routine weather report.

After a few moments of music, a "news" bulletin interrupted the music to announce that a Professor Farrell of Mount Jennings Observatory in Chicago had noted a series of gas explosions from the planet Mars. A remote pickup was then broadcast from the Princeton Observatory where a Professor Pierson (played by Welles) described the activity on Mars that he was witnessing through his telescope. While discussing with the interviewer details of the possibility of life on Mars, Pierson was suddenly handed a message: a nearby seismograph had registered a shock "of almost earthquake intensity" within a radius of twenty miles of Princeton. Pierson assumes that the reaction is from the crash of a meteorite of unusual size, but that it probably has no connection with the disturbance on Mars. Within a few minutes, the object's location has been identified as Grover's Mill, New Jersey, twenty-two miles from Trenton, and eyewitnesses report it to have been a "huge, flaming object." A special mobile unit is dispatched to the scene, and further reports are promised. In the meantime, the program is switched to "the Hotel Martinet in Brooklyn, where Bobby Millette and his orchestra are offering a program of dance music."

At this point, eleven minutes and ten seconds had elapsed from the beginning of the show. Although the broadcast was highly realistic, with its constant switching back and forth to dance music and the interruption of news bulletins, it seemed highly unlikely that any listeners would believe that what they were hearing was real. An announcement had been made at the beginning of the show that it was a performance of the Mercury Theatre, and a quick check of the program listings of any Sunday newspaper would reveal that the CBS offering at that time was a broadcast of *The War of the Worlds.* *The New York Times,* for example, listed the show in its regular program table and again, in a special radio section titled "Leading Events of the Week," included in fairly large type a further mention of the show: "TONIGHT— PLAY: H. G. WELLS' 'WAR OF THE WORLDS.'" On another page of the *Times* that day was a large photo of Welles, Agnes Moorehead, and other Mercury players, with a caption that stated "Tonight's Show is H. G. Wells' 'War of the Worlds.'"

Many people, however, must have missed the announcement in the newspaper, and the initial announcement of the Mercury broadcast was fleeting: the first bogus bulletin and weather report occurred within two minutes of the show's inception, and it is highly probable that many people turning their dials from station to station might have missed the initial qualifications. Had they begun listening to *The War of the Worlds* right after the first two minutes, there would not have been any way, other than their own critical ability, to tell if what was happening was real, since the next disclaimer, during a brief intermission, did not occur until after forty minutes: "You are listening to a CBS presentation of Orson Welles and the 'Mercury Theatre on the Air' in an original dramatization of *War of the Worlds* by H. G. Wells."

As a result of a weekly survey by the Hooper rating company, it was estimated that the Charlie McCarthy show normally commanded 34.7 percent of the total radio audience as opposed to 3.6 for the "Mercury Theatre on the Air." At exactly 8:12 P.M., Bergen and McCarthy had finished their first act with their usual comedic banter. This was followed by a light opera piece sung by Nelson Eddy.

Although Nelson Eddy was an enormously popular star of both radio and films, and his pleasant songs usually demanded little effort on the part of the listeners, apparently a large segment of the radio audience that night did not care to wait until he finished his rendition of "Neapolitan Love Song." It was a normal practice, especially in those early days of push-button or "airplane" dial turning, to switch from station to station when a predictable and unwanted sequence would come on the air; the listener would wait out the song or sketch he wanted to avoid and then in a few minutes tune back into the show he was tuned into originally—unless of course, the temporary, substitute show caught and held his attention. After Eddy's song, Madeleine Carroll was scheduled to do a dramatic interpretation and later in the program Dorothy Lamour was going to sing several popular songs.

As the Charlie McCarthy listeners switched their dials looking for something more entertaining until the Nelson Eddy song concluded, they found very little programming of a light nature on the air at that exact moment. In the New York metropolitan area, the dial-turner might have paused in tuning, momentarily, at WOR, where a Bach cantata was being offered; on WMCA there was a symposium on judiciary amendments; the Calvary Baptist Church's Choir was singing gospel hymns on WHN; on WEVD and WJZ, symphonic orchestral pieces were being offered; Professor Ralph Linton of Columbia University was lecturing on "How Civilizations Grow" on WQXR. Hooper later concluded that some 12 percent of the Charlie McCarthy audience—about four million people—stopped at the CBS network's offering of the Martian broadcast at that very moment. They would have heard, amidst crowd noises and police sirens, the concerned and authentic-sounding voice of a "newscaster," direct from Wilmuth Farm in Grovers Mill, New Jersey, painting a word picture of the strange scene of the projectile half-buried in a huge hole.

As the purported pickup continued from Grovers Mill, the announcer began describing the object more carefully, including a curious humming sound that seemed to be coming from inside of it. Suddenly, the top of the object began to unscrew and something emerged, a creature that sent out rays that could instantly cause automobiles, barns, and people to burst into flames. The reporter, with great dramatic sincerity, continued to describe what he saw then, his voice rising in terror as he screamed into the microphone that the whole field had burst into fire. Then, mysteriously the eyewitness description suddenly stopped, "due to circumstances beyond our control."

At this moment in the broadcast, with as many as six million people listening, a real story more bizarre than the science fiction tale being aired was beginning. The control room of the CBS studio received a telephone call from the local police precinct asking what was happening. The station house had started to receive phone calls from concerned citizens trying to determine whether the broadcast was real or just a dramatization. "Of course it isn't real," said someone in the control booth who then had to hang up quickly to continue with the business of the show. The calls kept flooding the police station switchboard, however, and finally a squad car with two officers was dispatched to the CBS building. One of the policeman kept peering through a window that gave him a view of Welles and the other members of the cast; he attempted to enter the studio to get more information. He was pushed away by an actor.

By now the CBS switchboard was receiving more calls than it could handle, and they were coming from all over the country. Davidson Taylor was informed of the problem, and he gestured to announcer Dan Seymour to come out of the studio. Once he heard what was going on, Seymour made the announcement—forty-two minutes after the show began—that what was being broadcast was in fact, a dramatization. It was a bit too late.

Already, thousands of people, believing that Martian poison gas was spreading death and destruction over the East Coast, began to leave their houses to speed to what they believed might be safety. Many fled to churches to pray; people gathered together in groups; some began to arm themselves to fight the invading Martians, described over the broadcast as having tentacles and a body as large as a bear; it glistened like wet leather, eyes black and gleaming like a serpent, a V-shaped mouth with saliva dripping from rimless lips that quivered and pulsated.

People all over the country were calling newspapers, sheriff's offices, radio stations explaining that the invasion was not real: "Note to Editors: Queries to newspapers from radio listeners throughout the United States tonight, regarding a reported meteor fall which killed a number of New Jerseyites, are the result of a studio dramatization. The A.P., 8:48 P.M."

In the Trenton area where people believed it would only be a few moments before the Martians arrived at their houses, the panic was the worst. The highways became clogged as cars raced toward Philadelphia or New York hoping to evade the pursuers from outer space. Some people dug out old gas masks that they had been keeping since World War I. Others wrapped their heads and covered their faces with wet towels as a possible aid against the poisonous gas.

The East Orange, New Jersey, police headquarters received more than two hundred calls from persons who wanted to know what to do to escape the gas. More than one hundred calls were received at the Maplewood, New Jersey, headquarters; two families from Manhattan also came to the station to inquire how they were to get back home now that the Pulaski Skyway had been blown up.

Other outbreaks of panic occurred in different parts of the country. In Indianapolis, a lady ran into a church where a service was being held and screamed that the world was coming to an end: she had heard it on the radio. Hundreds of parishioners fled.

In New York City, two women who had heard the program called a movie theater and demanded that their husbands be paged. This spread the news to the other people in the audience, and within minutes the entire theater was empty. Also in New York, a woman walked into the Forty-seventh Street police station dragging two children, all carrying extra clothes. She said she was ready to leave the city. The police convinced her to stay. According to a Rhode Island daily paper, "weeping and hysterical women swamped the switchboard of the *Providence Journal* for details of the massacre and destruction at New York, and officials of the electric company received scores of calls urging them to turn off all lights so that the city would be safe from the enemy."

A number of students at Brevard College in North Carolina were so gripped by the panic that fighting occurred when they attempted to use the few telephones available on campus to ask their parents to come and get them. From Pittsburgh came the story that a man who returned home in the midst of the broadcast found his wife in the bathroom with a bottle of poison in her hand, screaming: "I'd rather die this way than like that." In a small town named Concrete, in the state of Washington, a sudden power failure convinced the populace that the Martians were near at hand. The hysteria became so pronounced that many people, especially those who lived within sight of the Hudson River, where the Martians were supposedly crossing, reported that they actually had seen the invading hordes. And a woman as far away as Boston declared that she could "see the fire." Terror-ridden responses did not only come from the gullible. The usually sophisticated and worldly photographers at the *New York Herald Tribune* began donning gas masks in preparation for going into the streets to snap pictures of the advancing legions of Martians.

More policemen began to arrive at the CBS studios, and before the show ended, Welles was aware that he had created a sensation, although he had no idea just how emotionally shattering the program had been. As the show ended, Welles read a prepared statement:

> This is Orson Welles, ladies and gentlemen, out of character to assure you that *The War of the Worlds* has no further significance than as the holiday offering it was intended to be. The Mercury Theatre's own radio version of dressing up in a sheet and jumping out of a bush and saying Boo! Starting now, we couldn't soap all your windows and steal all your garden gates, by tomorrow night . . . so we did the next best thing. We annihilated the world before your very ears, and utterly destroyed the CBS. You will be relieved, I hope, to learn that we didn't mean it, and that both institutions are still open for business. So good-bye everybody, and remember, please, for the next day or so, the terrible lesson you learned tonight. That grinning, glowing, globular invader of your living room is an inhabitant of the pumpkin patch, and if your doorbell rings and nobody's there, that was no Martian . . . it's Halloween.

At the conclusion of the broadcast, with telephones still ringing, policemen standing in the halls, and newspaper reporters and photographers milling about, Welles left the studio together with most of the cast. Because of the crowd, he was forced to leave by the back entrance. He went to the Mercury Theatre to continue a previously scheduled all-night rehearsal of *Danton's Death*. He was aware of the apparent sensation he had caused with *The War of the Worlds* but at that point not quite clear of its extent.

At 9:00 P.M., Walter Winchell's highly popular commentary show came on the air on another network, and he announced with excitement in his voice to several million listeners: "Mr. and Mrs. America, there's no cause for alarm. America has *not* fallen; I repeat; America has *not* fallen." Although this announcement did not fan the flames of the panic, it did incite additional concern and curiosity in millions of listeners who might not have heard anything about the broadcast.

Shortly after midnight, after several hours of rehearsing *Danton's Death,* somebody in the cast who had arrived late told Welles that news of the program was being flashed in the lighted bulletin that circled the *Times* building in nearby Times Square. Welles and a few others immediately left the theater and walked to the southeast corner of Broadway and Forty-second Street to see if the story was true. It was: "ORSON WELLES CAUSES PANIC," the lights read.

Back at the theater, Welles continued the rehearsal, finally breaking shortly after dawn, and returned to his suite at the St. Regis for some sleep. When he awoke three hours later, he was an international celebrity. Virtually every morning newspaper, not only in this country but abroad as well, told of the bogus invasion from Mars, the panic that resulted, and the man who caused it. "I had no idea that I had suddenly become a national event," said Welles in retrospect. Right in the middle of the front page of *The New York Times* a headline proclaimed: "RADIO LISTENERS IN PANIC, TAKING WAR DRAMA AS FACT," and the *New York Daily News* covered half of its front page with bold black headlines that stated: "FAKE RADIO 'WAR' STIRS TERROR THROUGH U.S." The *New York Herald Tribune* blared on its front page: "Not since the Spanish 'fleet' sailed to bombard the New England coast in 1898, has so much hysteria, panic and sudden conversion to religion been reported to the press of the United States as when radio listeners heard about an invasion from Mars."

Welles was called to CBS to give a press conference. He walked into the interview room unshaven, his eyes somewhat red from insufficient sleep, and read the following statement, which appeared in papers all over the country:

Despite my deep regret over any misapprehension which our broadcast last night created among some listeners, I am even the more bewildered over this misunderstanding in the light of an analysis of the broadcast itself.

It seems to me that there are four factors which should have in any event maintained the illusion of fiction in the broadcast.

The first was that the broadcast was performed as if occurring in the future and as if it were then related by a survivor of a past occurrence. The date of the fanciful invasion of this planet by Martians was clearly given as 1939 and was so announced at the outset of the broadcast.

The second element was the fact that the broadcast took place at our regular weekly Mercury Theatre period and had been so announced in all the papers. For seventeen consecutive weeks we have been broadcasting radio drama. Sixteen of these seventeen broadcasts have been fiction and have been presented as such. Only one in the series was a true story, the broadcast of "Hell on Ice" by

Commander Elsberg, and was identified as a true story within the framework of radio drama.

The third element was the fact that at the very outset of the broadcast and twice during its enactment listeners were told that this was a play, that it was an adaptation of an old novel by H. G. Wells. Furthermore, at the conclusion a detailed statement to this effect was made.

The fourth factor seems to me to have been the most pertinent of all. That is the familiarity of the fable, within the American idiom of Mars and Martians.

For many decades "The Man from Mars" has been almost a synonym for fantasy ... this fantasy, as such, has been used in radio programs many times. In these broadcasts, conflict between citizens of Mars and other planets has been a familiarly accepted fairy-tale. The same make-believe is familiar to newspaper readers through a comic strip that uses the same device.

Questions from the assembled newsmen followed immediately and Welles, "looking like an early Christian saint," as he described his attempt to appear innocent, answered them as clearly as he could:

QUESTION: Were you aware of the terror such a broadcast would stir up?

WELLES: Definitely not. The technique I used was not original with me. It was not even new. I anticipated nothing unusual.

QUESTION: Would you do the show over again?

WELLES: I won't say that I won't follow this technique again, as it is a legitimate dramatic form.

QUESTION: When were you first aware of the trouble caused?

WELLES: Immediately after the broadcast was finished when people told me of the large number of phone calls received.

QUESTION: Should you have toned down the language of the drama?

WELLES: No, you don't play murder in soft words.

QUESTION: Why was the story changed to put in names of American cities and government officers?

WELLES: H. G. Wells used real cities in Europe, and to make the play more acceptable to American listeners we used real cities in America. Of course, I'm terribly sorry now.

During further questioning, Welles said that at 8:38, Davidson Taylor had asked him to direct himself and the other actors less facetiously; Welles and everyone else, therefore read their lines with more vigor from then on. It was at the point in the show that the Martians and their poisonous gas had begun to spread eastward over the island of Manhattan and a radio announcer, supposedly broadcasting from atop a tall New York City skyscraper, fatalistically and with great somberness, reported what he saw in one of the most gripping scenes from the play: "Now the first Martian reaches the shore. He stands watching, looking over the city. His steel, cowlish head is even with the skyscrapers. He waits for the others. They rise like a line of new towers on the city's west side.... Now they're lifting their metal hands. This is the end now.

Smoke comes out . . . black smoke, drifting over the city. People in the streets see it now. They're running towards the East River . . . thousands of them, dropping in like rats."

Welles went on to say that he was "deeply shocked and deeply regretful" about the results of the broadcast. It seemed that the twenty-three-year-old hoaxer was genuinely concerned over the consequences that might accrue from the havoc he had wrought. There were immediate rumors of criminal charges; Welles might have also feared being barred from radio forever. In 1978, however, on the fortieth anniversary of the broadcast when Welles was asked on the "Today" show, "Did you get a laugh out of it, Orson?" he admitted, "Huge, huge, yes, a huge laugh. I never thought it was anything but funny."

However, the Columbia Broadcasting System and other interested parties or victims did not think it was humorous. In a press release CBS issued its own apology to the nation: "Naturally, it was neither Columbia's nor the Mercury Theatre's intention to mislead anyone, and when it became evident that a part of the audience had been disturbed by the performance, five announcements were read over the network in the evening to reassure those listeners. In order that this may not happen again, the program department hereafter will not use the technique of a simulated news broadcast within a dramatization when the circumstances of the broadcast could cause immediate alarm to numbers of listeners."

The Federal Communications Commission requested a copy of the script and a recording of the broadcast to study, and Frank McNinch, chairman of the commission, called the program "regrettable." No official action was taken against CBS or Welles, however, because, according to the FCC, "steps sufficient to protect the public interest" had been taken.

The venerable H. G. Wells, then in his seventies, was outraged that his material was changed and demanded a retraction from CBS. After conferring with Wells by telephone, Jacques Chambrun, his spokesman in New York, stated: "In the name of Mr. H. G. Wells, I granted the Columbia Broadcasting System the right to dramatize Mr. H. G. Wells's novel *The War of the Worlds* for one performance over the radio. It was not explained to me that this dramatization would be made with a liberty that amounts to a complete rewriting of *The War of the Worlds* and renders it into an entirely different story. Mr. Wells and I consider that by so doing the Columbia Broadcasting System should make a full retraction. Mr. H. G. Wells personally is deeply concerned that any work of his should be used in a way, and with a totally unwarranted liberty, to cause deep distress and alarm throughout the United States." When Chambrun's statement was given to Welles, Orson expressed his admiration for the Wells classic and said that he doubted that there could be a ban or any action brought against CBS or him, since the program "constituted a legitimate dramatization of a published work." The matter was quietly dropped.

Damage suits against Welles and CBS to the amount of $750,000 were filed by listeners who claimed to have suffered injuries—falling down stairs, breaking bones, and the like—as a result of believing in the broadcast. Fortunately for Welles, his attorney, L. Arnold Weissberger, had removed an indemnification clause from his contract with CBS that stated that Welles would pay for *any* legal action against CBS and instead had amended the clause to make Welles responsible only for libel and plagiarism. Therefore, CBS had to deal with each case, none of which ever went to court. Several thousand dollars in out-of-court settlements were eventually made, however, as CBS concluded that it would be less costly and time consuming to settle rather than to fight each case.

There were some critics of the broadcast who believed that H. G. Wells was actually instrumental in having his *War of the Worlds* modernized purposely to create a scandal for publicity. October 27, the day before the broadcast, was the publication date of his latest novel, *Apropos of Dolores,* and bookstores all over the country were displaying it for the first time. Charles Scribner's Sons, the publisher, denied that there was any connection between the new book and the broadcast and affirmed that they were not even aware that *The War of the Worlds* was scheduled to be broadcast. Orson Welles in an interview with a reporter from *The New York Times,* also subsequently denied that he had planned the panic to promote his forthcoming production of *Danton's Death,* scheduled to open on Tuesday, November 1, two days after *The War of the Worlds* broadcast.

For weeks, editorials across the country raged about the terror that Welles had perpetrated on the listening audience, calling for more self-regulation or even possible further governmental restrictions. Unfortunately, not all of the outrage was altruistic. Newspapers were growing more resentful of the broadcasting industry's successful attempt to capture additional advertising revenue. Total advertising revenue on radio had increased steadily since 1935, whereas newspaper advertising revenue was declining. Newspaper publishers eyed radio as a source of financial trouble and were delighted that *The War of the Worlds* gave them something to complain to advertisers about.

The *Washington Post*, in addition to an editorial suggestion of censorship of the airwaves, capitalized on the effectiveness—or lack of it—of radio by publishing a full-page ad on November 15, 1938, in which they pointed out that although several announcements explaining the fictive basis of the story were made during *The War of the Worlds'* broadcast, the public apparently failed to listen to them. "Who listened to him?" they asked rhetorically. "Who listens to what your announcer tells them about your product?"

There were some people, however, who believed Welles had performed a great service to the country, as Dorothy Thompson stated in her influential column in the *New York Herald Tribune.*

After a few weeks had passed, the story began to fade from the newspapers until Princeton University announced that with government funding, it was embarking on a study of the psychology of panic and mass hysteria and was connecting the study with its ongoing inquiry into radio's influence on the lives of the listeners. The study, headed by psychologist Hadley Cantril, would be confined to the educational aspects of the situation, leading to "first, a determination of the general extent and nature of the public reactions to the broadcast; second, the social-psychological reasons for this reaction in various types of individuals."

Cantril's report proved to be fascinating and related such things as: the lower the education of those who were listening, the more likely they were to believe that the show was real; people from southern states, by and large, became more frightened than those from New England; and approximately two million people believed that the broadcast was a true and realistic description of an invasion from Mars. It was eventually issued in book form under the title *The Invasion from Mars,* published by the Princeton University Press. The book also included *The War of the Worlds* script, referring to Howard Koch as the author of the dramatization in its table of contents.

When Welles saw the galley proofs of the book and was asked to write a statement that could be used on the back jacket for publicity purposes, he became furious that Koch was named as author. Welles's arrangement with Koch was that as compensation for working on the script for a nominal fee (about seventy-five dollars), Koch was to receive copyright *ownership* of the scripts upon which he put his hand, although he was emphatically not, in Welles's opinion, the actual author. The case in point could be further clarified by examining Cantril's own book, *The Invasion from Mars.* The Princeton University Press did, and still does, hold and own the copyright of that book; Cantril, however, is the author.

Welles wrote to Cantril claiming the book contained "an error, so grave and so detrimental" to his reputation that he could not, in all fairness "speak well of it." Welles pointed out the inclusion of Koch's name as "author" of *The War of the Worlds* script, and took issue with it, saying: "Now it's perfectly true that Mr. Koch worked on *The War of the Worlds* since he was at that time a regular member of my writing staff. To credit the broadcast version to him, with the implication that its conception as well as its execution was his, is a gross mistake." Welles mentioned Houseman and the others under him in the writing department, including Paul Stewart, one of the actors, "who did a great deal of writing on *War of the Worlds,*" and who made, according to Welles, considerable contributions to the actual text. He also paid credit to John Dietz, the engineer who worked out a great deal of the detail and color; Davidson Taylor, who devised the scenes of news dispatches, mobile unit pickup and special interviews, and Bernard Herrmann, whose musical input directly affected and changed the script. As with all Orson Welles's broadcasts, the radio dramatization of *The War of the Worlds* was a collaborative effort, with Welles the chief architect who had the power and authority to employ as many draftsmen, designers, and workers as needed to construct the building.

"The idea for *The War of the Worlds* broadcast and the major portion of its execution was mine," wrote Welles. "Howard Koch was very helpful in the second portion of the script and did some work on the first, most of which it was necessary to revise."

Welles made certain that Cantril understood that he was not asking for more widespread use of his name in the book as author—although rightfully he believed such credit was his—but he insisted that if Koch's name was to be included at all, the others who worked on the script should be given full credit too. Reference to *The War of the Worlds* as "the Howard Koch dramatization" was, Welles said, "something worse than merely untrue." He explained to Cantril that although he often worked with a fairly large complement of writers on his broadcast, the initial emphasis and attack on a story, as well as its ultimate revised form, had been his in almost every instance.

Welles was willing to remain anonymous as to his more-than-editorial or advisory role in creating *The War of the Worlds* script except for the persistent use of Koch's name as author in Cantril's study. It was also Welles's contention that several of the actors "did quite as much of the writing by the time we were done with our rehearsals as the writers themselves." Why then, he complained, did Cantril persist in using only Koch's name as author?

Finally, Welles suggested that if the book had already been printed, an errata slip be inserted into every copy before distribution to eradicate the "slur" on his position as the creator and responsible artist of his broadcast. Cantril sympathized with Welles's argument but felt that an errata sheet placed in his book would create an unfavorable impression and perhaps discredit the study's integrity. Cantril's response was to suggest that the table of contents read:

Script idea and development by
    Orson Welles, assisted by John Houseman and Mercury Theatre staff.
Written by
    Howard Koch, under the direction of Mr. Welles.

This solution was not at all satisfactory to Welles who complained that the suggested revision was far too elaborate and "incorrect." He believed that his reputation would suffer greatly if the public was led to disbelieve that *The War of the Worlds* was not only his conception but also, properly and exactly speaking, his creation. In a telegram to Cantril, Welles erupted:

ONCE AGAIN, FINALLY, AND I PROMISE FOR THE LAST TIME, HOWARD KOCH DID NOT WRITE THE WAR OF THE WORLDS. ANY STATEMENT TO THIS EFFECT IS UNTRUE AND IMMEASURABLY DETRIMENTAL TO ME. I FAIL TO SEE HOW I CAN PUT THIS MORE STRONGLY.

ORSON WELLES.

To add to the confusion, Koch furnished a statement to Cantril, in addition to several affidavits from typists, that he *was* the sole author of the script and that contributions made by others such as Stewart and Houseman, were minimal. Welles was steadfast and threatened to produce his own affidavits, indicating that Koch was not the solitary author.

The Invasion From Mars was finally published, without an errata, and with reference on the title page to "the complete script of the famous Orson Welles Broadcast," but with Koch noted in several places, including the table of contents, as the author of the script. Despite his anguish and fury, Welles decided not to carry the dispute any further, preferring the unfair peace to the self-righteous war. As more stories appeared about his famous show, elevating it to a modern-day legend, they almost invariably referred to it as the "Orson Welles Broadcast" and this continued notoriety probably was effective in calming Welles's rage. As it developed over the years, Koch took some cash and some credit: he wrote the story of how he created the adaptation, with a copy of his script being made into a paperback book enjoying large printings and an album of the broadcast selling over 500,000 copies, part of the income also going to him as copyright owner.

Orson's outrage eventually diminished and he continued on to other areas.

AS A RESULT of his Martian broadcast, and combined with his personality profile in *The New Yorker,* and the prestigious *Time* cover story, Orson Welles had become an international celebrity at the age of twenty-three, his future a possible fairyland of theatrical triumphs. He was fearful, however, that the scandal of *The War of the Worlds* would force CBS to cancel "The Mercury Theatre on the Air." Instead, the Campbell's Soup people, who had had their ears cocked toward the show for some time, decided in two days to become the show's sponsor.

During the week following *The War of the Worlds,* Campbell invited Welles and Houseman to their plant in Camden, New Jersey. Together with officials of the company and Ward Wheelock, the head of the Philadelphia advertising agency that handled Campbell, they worked out a slightly new format for the show. "The Mercury Theatre on the Air" would become the "Campbell Playhouse"; the time slot would be changed to the less competitive one of Friday, from 9 to 10 P.M.; "name" stars, in addition to Welles, would appear for each broadcast; and although classic stories would continue to be used from time to time, attempts would be made to secure the radio rights for current best-selling novels, movies, and plays. Welles would receive a weekly salary of approximately $1,500, depending on other fees and expenses incurred.

Sitting in the Campbell conference room, discussing the kind of show that the sponsor and he wanted, Welles was at his most charming despite the fact that he was tempted to begin humming "Who put the overalls in Mrs. Murphy's chowder?" "This is a great big chance for me and a great big challenge," he said to the soup men. "With my faith in radio and your display of confidence in me by becoming the sponsor we can possibly create something important. Let's hope nobody's mistaken." Welles elaborated on his philosophy of radio: "Everybody loves a good story and radio is just about the best storyteller there is."

It was agreed that in order to surpass "Lux Presents Hollywood" in gaining an audience interested in quality adaptations, new story properties and stars would have to be secured. Welles agreed that most of the stories in the new series should be contemporary but stressed that whatever story was broadcast it would have to be chosen for its adaptability to radio, not necessarily for its public acclaim. Someone made mention of a radio script being a "play." Welles disagreed: "It's not a play. It's a story. Radio broadcasting is different from motion pictures and the theater and I'd like to keep it that way. The Campbell broadcasts will not be done in a theater but in a studio. The only illusion I'd like to create is the illusion of the story."

Inevitably, *The War of the Worlds* was discussed, with the Campbell people acknowledging the overwhelming publicity that the show had received but asking for assurances from Welles that there would be no such controversial programs under their sponsorship. Welles, expressing his regret over the scandal, dutifully assured everyone present that no similar infamy would ever again occur.

Having accepted Welles and his company as their new voice, Campbell began making plans to cancel another program that it sponsored, "Hollywood Hotel," hosted by gossip columnist Louella Parsons. "Hollywood Hotel," a mix of variety and drama, had a questionable history, mainly because big-name stars felt compelled to appear on it—and were paid no fees—simply to avoid the wrath of Louella's far-reaching power and influence. In turn, the show gave free publicity to new films and, as radio historian John Durning says in his monumental *Tune in Yesterday,* it became "a mutual backscratching vehicle, publicizing the stars' movies, promoting their names, and keeping Miss Parsons at the top of radio row." Because of commercial contracts, it would take five weeks before "Hollywood Hotel" could get off the air. In the interim, Welles continued with the unsponsored "Mercury Theatre on the Air," doing many of the radio adaptations that he had previously planned. These consisted mainly of those that he felt would not be acceptable to the new sponsors because of their content or classical appeal.

IN THE WEEK following *The War of the Worlds,* before opening *Danton's Death,* Welles atypically did two half-hour stories on the same night on "The Mercury Theatre on the Air": *Life with Father* by Clarence Day and *Heart of Darkness* by Joseph Conrad. The *Life with Father* radio adaptation consisted of a selection from the series of tales based on *The New Yorker* reminiscences that Clarence Day, Jr., wrote about his socially prominent and often irascible father. Day's writing was picked up with virtually no changes made in the script except, of course, to include sound effects. Welles played both the narrator and the father, and Arthur Anderson was young Clarence. Welles's description of the gaslight civilization of New York's fashionable Madison Avenue with elegant brownstones and strolling upper-middle-class residents, and his recounting of the smells and sights of turn-of-the-century America, made the era come alive.

Perhaps as an unconscious plug for his future sponsor, Welles included a scene from Day that concerned soup: "So we sat down, frightened, at table: Mother, my brother George, and I. But the soup was a lifesaver. It was more like a stew, really, with milk, oyster juice and big oysters. I put lots of small, hard crackers into mine and a slice of french toast. The hot toast soaked in the soup was delicious, only there wasn't much of it and as father particularly liked it, we had to leave it for him. Father came down in the middle of it, still offended, but he ate his full share." The waltzing and lilting music provided by Bernard Hermann was also an important ingredient to the story's lighthearted feeling. Buoyed, perhaps, by the Campbell contract, Welles was especially funny and unbuttoned during *Life with Father,* and it is probable that he was also associating the narrative of the play with the content of his life with his own father, Richard Welles. Orson even broke a self-imposed rule never to sing in public, although he merely untunefully bungled and blustered through the scales: "Do, re, mi, fa, so, la, ti, do-umph, umph!"

The second half of the show presented listeners with a program that went in an entirely different direction. Welles served as narrator and played the strange and evil Kurtz in *Heart of Darkness,* a story that first appeared as a serial in the British magazine *Blackwood's,* in 1899. Welles said on the air that *Heart of Darkness* could be described as a "deliberate masterpiece or a downright incantation; a fine piece of prose work at the least, its best aspects are an artful compound of sympathy for humankind and a high tragical disgust. Its successful contrivance of mood hides its craft as an octopus hides in its own ink and almost we are persuaded, there is something essential awaiting for all of us in the dark alleys of the world, aboriginally loathsome, immeasurable, and certainly nameless."

The special effects used in *Heart of Darkness* added much to the mystery: wailing, almost lamenting, foghorns; the boat slowly chug-chugging up the river; the beating of tom-toms; and native chants supplied, coincidentally, by Asodata Dafora Horton, of Welles's voodoo *Macbeth* days. Somehow, Welles managed in a half-hour to capture the greed and sickness and degeneration of Conrad's tale; and when, as Kurtz, he finally meets Marlow, Welles's voice was that of a man shrunken in his last tropical illness, obsessed with his own potency and its decline. Welles played the part with subtle credence. Ray Collins was Marlow; Alfred Shirley was the accountant; George Coulouris was the assistant manager; the second manager was played by Edgar Barrier and the agent by William Alland; Virginia Welles played Kurtz's intended bride, Anna Stafford. So involved did Welles become with the personality of Kurtz that at the end of the show, when he announced that in four weeks Campbell's Soups would become the sponsor, he did not speak in his own character, as was his custom, but continued in the mysterious and degraded tones of Kurtz.

For his next broadcast, Welles wanted to use an adaptation of the modern novel *One Light Burning* by R. C. Hutchinson, a story of a man who lost his great love and could have no peace and no sleep until he found her again. Unfortunately, Welles could not secure the rights in time and substituted *A Passenger to Bali,* a short story that had originally appeared in *Story* magazine. It was written by a young, somewhat obscure author, Ellis St. Joseph, based on his adventures on a tramp freighter in the Pacific. Welles, in one of the deepest voices of his career, played the Reverend Dr. Ralph Walkes, a corrupt and crafty Dutch missionary en route to the islands to distribute Bibles. The entire action of the story takes place aboard the freighter, on the ocean or docked in such exotic ports as Shanghai and Bangkok. Welles was intrigued by the theme, one that mixed fantasy and realism; the vessel serves as the micro-universe for Walkes and the master of the ship, Captain English, with whom he is in conflict. It is a battle between civilization and brute force, good and evil, and the broadcast was a poignant and faithful dramatization.

During the next three weeks, while arranging for the first Campbell broadcast, Welles presented three first-class works, beginning with Dickens's *Pickwick Papers.* He followed with *Clarence,* based on the 1919 hit of the same name by Booth Tarkington and played the young entomologist characterized on the stage so successfully by Alfred Lunt. And for Orson's last unsponsored show, as homage to the man who was responsible for getting him started in the theater, Welles did Thornton Wilder's brilliant Pulitzer Prize winning novel, *The Bridge of San Luis Rey.*

ONE OF THE most popular novels of 1938, an enormously successful bestseller, was Daphne du Maurier's story of passion and mystery, *Rebecca.* Together with *The Yearling, The Citadel,* and *My Son, My Son!* it sold more copies than almost any other book published that year, and motion picture rights were immediately purchased by David O. Selznick for eventual release as a film. Welles, with the backing of CBS and his new sponsor, was able to secure the rights to *Rebecca* for radio dramatization. He had a certain affection for the du Maurier family ever since playing in *Trilby,* which was written by Daphne's grandfather, George du Maurier. The young, ethereally voiced actress Margaret Sullavan was contracted to play the nameless new wife of Max de Winter, to be portrayed by Welles. Sullavan, a star of both stage and screen, had a special whimsical and innocent quality that made her performances memorable, and in 1933 she became known with her first film role, *Only Yesterday.* The role of de Winter's second wife was a highly coveted one, even for a radio broadcast. Actresses believed a critically successful characterization on the air could lead to an offer to do the prospective film. Sullavan needed no persuasion to accept the part. Agnes Moorehead would play the ominous housekeeper, Mrs. Danvers, loyal only to Rebecca, her dead mistress.

Campbell was extravagant in its praise of Welles on that first show. The announcer welcomed him as the "white hope of the American stage" and spoke of how Welles wrote and directed his own scripts, "making them live and breathe with the warmth of his genius," adding that his life combined the best features of "Baron Munchausen and *Alice in Wonderland.*" His radio productions, the homage went almost embarrassingly on, were known to attract "universal attention." Referring to *The War of the Worlds* as radio history and a national sensation, the introduction pointed out that Welles greatly regretted the unexpected result. "Orson Welles is a master of realism," the voice intoned, "over the air, on radio. He is unique, exciting. He shocks you and sends cold shivers racing up your spine. But that is not the thing he does best or best likes to do. He *loves* to tell a story, a great human story welling up from the heart, brimming with deep and sincere emotions and lively with comedy. Such are the stories, thrilling, delightful, amusing, he will bring to the 'Campbell Playhouse.'"

Welles played the part of the guilt-ridden de Winter with elegance, and Margaret Sullavan's portrayal of his shy, frightened wife was highly believable. Perhaps it was an unconscious apology to the millions of listeners that night for his *War of the Worlds* incident or maybe even a symbolic gesture of his docile submissiveness to his sponsors and the executives of CBS, when, upon introducing *Rebecca,* he used for the first time on radio a phrase that would be connected with him for the rest of his life: "So ladies and gentlemen, and Miss du Maurier, the 'Campbell Playhouse' is *obediently yours.*"

Daphne du Maurier listened to the show via shortwave from London. At the story's conclusion and while still on the air, Welles engaged in some flirtatious and humorous banter with Margaret Sullavan. This was a ploy previously unused by the Mercury but one that had worked very successfully with Cecil B. DeMille and *his* stars on the "Lux Playhouse." "You're going to be out of my life in six-and-a-half minutes," Welles said to her. "As the director of a theater, the Mercury Theatre, I'd like to know you better. What are you doing next year?" Sullavan asked if he was referring to a part in a forthcoming play. "I'll bring the script to you tomorrow," Welles said hurriedly, just as a transatlantic telephone call, placed earlier to Daphne du Maurier, came through as the show was ending. In a highly dignified British accent, Miss du Maurier delivered what seemed to be a prepared statement: "Good evening, Mr. Welles. It's nearly three o'clock here in London. It's not often that an author has the chance to hear the voices of her own characters speaking to her from across the Atlantic Ocean. I've enjoyed it enormously." Margaret Sullavan asked du Maurier two questions: Is there really a Manderley and what is Mrs. de Winter's first name? To the former, du Maurier answered, "When you next come to London, Miss Sullavan, get into a train at Paddington Station and travel West. When you've been 250 miles, get out of that train and walk southeast for half an hour. You'll come to some iron gates, and a large, narrow twisting drive. If you ever find your way to the end of that drive you *may* discover Manderley."* As to the latter question, the major literary mystery of 1938, Miss du Maurier simply thanked Sullavan and Welles for their performances and avoided the answer entirely, hanging up abruptly. Later, a cryptic cable from London was received by Welles from du Maurier: "The name of the heroine of *Rebecca* is Mrs. Max de Winter."

Changing pace from the gothic splendor of *Rebecca,* the next week's radio offering by Welles was *Call It a Day,* based on the three-act farce by British playwright Dodie Smith. It contained narrative elements similar to Joyce's

*Manderley was actually styled after Miss du Maurier's own mansion, Menabilly, in Cornwall, where she lived and presided as Lady Browning.

Ulysses in its depiction of the adventures of a middle-class English family—and their inner lives—during the course of sixteen waking hours of a single day. Welles played Roger Hilton, the father in the book.

Charles Dickens's *A Christmas Carol,* one of the greatest short stories ever written, was first dramatized on the air on Christmas Day in 1934 when Lionel Barrymore played the miserly Ebenezer Scrooge and Alexander Woollcott served as narrator. Although he was deprived of playing the part on film because of crippling arthritis, for years afterward Barrymore played Scrooge on the air and the broadcast became a Christmas tradition for millions of listeners. Campbell's Soup, the regular sponsor of the annual program, arranged to have Barrymore play the part again in 1938, but shortly before the broadcast he became ill, and it was necessary therefore to either cancel the show or find a replacement. Representatives of the sponsor and CBS approached Welles about using *A Christmas Carol* as a part of his "Campbell Playhouse" broadcast. Always nostalgic and sentimental about Christmas, Welles cheerfully accepted the idea and played both narrator and Scrooge on his show of December 23, 1938.

Lionel Barrymore heard the show from his sickbed and wrote to Ward Wheelock asking him to convey to Orson Welles his admiration for his performance, stating that it was "quite too good" and adding other superlatives.

THE EXPERIENCE OF producing, directing, and starring in the "Campbell Playhouse" did more for Welles than just enhance his reputation. It continued his apprenticeship in appraising stories to be dramatized. The reaction from both listeners and sponsors by mail and through personal comments was immediate, and he knew what had succeeded and sometimes, painfully, what had failed. His ability as an adapter continued to grow, and questions about how much of an original story was to be retained and how much was to be deleted were solved by him easily and with relative speed. He expanded, reduced, and even invented new scenes to add to the understanding of the story. But a literary grave robber he was not: he refused to allow his own sentiments to change, or tamper with the prejudices of the author. He interpreted authors' intentions while also attempting to protect them.

As this weekly confrontation with some of the greatest books and plays of the day went on and there was money available to secure the rights of valuable properties, Welles was also acting with some of the most popular and practiced actors in the business. Welles did a dramatization of *Beau Geste,* playing the title role, and Laurence Olivier, who was fresh from Hollywood and the filming of *Wuthering Heights* and in New York to star with Katharine Cornell in *No Time for Comedy,* agreed to act as John Geste. Noah Beery recreated his brilliant 1926 silent film role in playing the sadistic and tyrannical Sergeant Lejeune. Superb acting and the ambience of the desert, complete with bugle calls, battle charges, and the sound of horses racing in the wind, created a memorable hour.

Katharine Hepburn acted with Welles in the first radio dramatization of *A*

Farewell to Arms; Gertrude Berg left her persona as Molly Goldberg in her own daily radio series for the first time, to do another broadcast, and acted as Welles's mother in Elmer Rice's *Counsellor at Law.* The Hecht and MacArthur play *Twentieth Century* had Welles, Austrian-Italian star Elissa Landi, and Sam Levene soon after his bright performance in the film *Golden Boy.* Ida Lupino was the great love of Pancho Lopez, played by Welles in *The Bad Man.*

He did George du Maurier's *Peter Ibbetson,* with Helen Hayes, and played both the piratical tycoon and the matinee idol in Kaufman's *Dinner at Eight* with Lucille Ball, Marjorie Rambeau, and Hedda Hopper; he acted with Fay Bainter as the retired and quite typical American in a broadcast based on Sidney Howard's three-act adaptation of Sinclair Lewis's *Dodsworth,* the book that was probably more responsible than any other in gaining the first ever Nobel Prize for an American writer.

Wilder's three-act drama *Our Town,* which won a Pulitzer for 1937-38, was adapted by Welles for radio and the sceneryless play proved to be perfect for the air in allowing the listening audience to create its own mental sets as Broadway theatergoers had done while examining the humdrum lives of the humble citizens of Grover's Corners.

During Orson Welles's six-month relationship with Campbell, he avoided trouble. The only problem that emerged temporarily had to do with his Memorial Day program, called *The Things We Have,* a kaleidoscope of speeches, sketches, slogans, and other patriotic offerings. The CBS censors considered one passage too inflammatory and radical and made efforts to excise it: "This country, with its institutions, belongs to the people who inhabit it. Whenever they shall grow weary of the existing government, they can exercise their constitutional right to dismember or overthrow it." The passage remained, however, when Welles revealed who had said it: Abraham Lincoln.

All of this distinguished acting activity did not go unrecognized. In a nationwide newspaper poll conducted by Scripps-Howard, Welles was chosen as the nation's favorite broadcast personality of 1938 and was designated "Outstanding New Radio Star of the Year." Lest this honor go to his head, Elsa Maxwell, heading a jury of "glamour experts," which included beauty authorities, photographers, and artists, picked Orson as one of their Glamour Kings of 1938. The reason? "His clean-cut ugliness has created a new standard of masculine attractiveness."

CHAPTER 10

FIVE KINGS, THE joint project of the Mercury Theatre and the Theatre Guild, was Welles's most ambitious project; many would say it was overly, unrealistically, ambitious, and considering its ultimate failure, perhaps they're right.

The original plan, dubbed by Welles as "a cavalcade of the fifteenth century," was to run together the last scene of *Richard II,* the play in which Henry Bolingbroke becomes Henry IV, with *Parts I* and *II* of *Henry IV* and *Henry V* in a single night; then they would tackle the three parts of the lesser-known *Henry VI* and *Richard III* on the following night. The fifth king of Welles's title was Henry VII, who assumes the throne at the conclusion of *Richard III.*

Production on *Five Kings* really erupted in January 1939, right in the midst of Welles's most active period with the "Campbell Playhouse." The *New York Herald Tribune* reported on the fifteenth of that month that the play was ready for rehearsals and that Welles had at least the core of the cast. Burgess Meredith, at a salary of $1,000 a week, was to play Prince Hal. John Emery, husband of Tallulah Bankhead, was to be Hotspur. Robert Speaight, the distinguished British actor, would embody the chorus. Welles himself would play Shakespeare's most engaging comic character, Sir John Falstaff. Rehearsals began in the last week of January with Welles absent on Friday evenings while he performed on the air.

As usual, Orson had a hand in everything. He had decided on a completely different conception of Shakespearean drama from that presented in his somewhat formal, bare-stage, modern-dress *Julius Caesar.* For the blustery tavern world of *Five Kings,* with its scene upon scene of battles, bedchambers, and revels in the Boar's Head, Welles wanted a kind of realism obtainable only in cinema. He would attempt to come as close as possible to transcending the limits of stage drama.

The most important aspect of this assault on the traditional stage in *Five Kings* was a twenty-eight-foot revolving platform, powered by electric motors, to contain the sets. The idea of a revolving stage was not a new one; others had seen it as the answer to rapid scene shifts: one set could be mounted as another was being played on in view of the audience. What made Welles's approach original was that rather than showing the revolution of the platform as a distracting necessity for scene switching, he would work the motion of the stage into the action of the play and even allow the motion to create action.

The sets themselves were designed by James Morcom who had worked with Welles on the ill-fated *Too Much Johnson*. A 180-degree turn would present either a "London" set or a "battlefield" set. But since the scenery was all of wood slats painted a nondescript bluish gray, all angles of view could be used. With this arrangement Welles sacrificed something in naturalistic detail but gained tremendous impressionistic flexibility. He was also able to suggest mood and even detail through lighting techniques. An impressive score composed by Aaron Copland added to the tone of the play.

As described by visitors, the scene during the practice drills—for they were not really rehearsals in the formal sense—was complete mayhem. Connected to the revolving platforms were a ganglia of electric cables; Welles stood in front of four microphones located in the center of the theater, barking and bellowing through them, sometimes employing a megaphone but more often using his own voice. "I WANT THAT CUE! WHAT IS THE MATTER WITH THAT CUE? DON'T YOU KNOW THAT I GAVE THAT CUE? HOW MANY TIMES DO I HAVE TO SET A CUE?" According to one report, he was seen running from the microphones and leaping onto the stage: "WILL THE SEVEN STAGE MANAGERS AND THEIR ASSISTANTS PLEASE COME OUT HERE?" he thundered. As it developed, every one of the stage managers and their assistants believed someone else was attending to the elusive cue about which Welles was so upset. It took some time before everything was straightened out and Welles could continue with the action.

Welles's conception of *Five Kings* was one of a unified, continuous flow of action. Nor is this untrue in any way to Shakespeare, since Welles's *Part I* (Shakespeare's two *Henry IV*'s and *Henry V*) charts the progression of Prince Hal from pub-crawling prankster to the triumphant monarch Henry V, just as Shakespeare's three plays do.

Because a sense of continuity was such a key feature, Robert Speaight's role as Chorus was vital. Shakespeare had used a number of prologues in the plays, so these were combined for Speaight. And since Shakespeare had relied so heavily on Holinshed's *Chronicles* for his history plays, excerpts were included in the role. Speaight became the full-time commentator, a Shakespearean master of ceremonies, compensating for any loss resulting from Welles's editing of the original text and, just as important, acting as explicator in plays that presume a great deal of knowledge about the genealogies of English kings.

In February, the play's itinerary was announced. *Five Kings* would open in Boston for two weeks, Washington for one, then Philadelphia for two more with the hope of a New York premiere after that. The curtain went up in Boston's Colonial Theater at about a quarter past eight on the night of February 27, 1939, without Welles ever completing an entire rehearsal all the way to the end. The play went on through thirty-two scenes and two intermissions, finishing up at twelve-thirty. Several Boston papers reported the next day that keeping all those homebody Bostonians in their seats until that hour of the night was a minor triumph in itself. But as they had come to pray at the feet of Shakespeare, many of them went home to scoff at the expense of Welles.

Through the early part of *Five Kings,* or the territory of *Henry IV, Part I,* the London set, with its "castle," "street," and "tavern," was employed for the comings and goings of Prince Hal and his drinking companion, Falstaff. As Hal, Burgess Meredith was able to leave his friends at the tavern and walk to another part of the set to join his father, while remaining in view, by virtue of the revolving platform. Later, in the battle scenes where Hal defeats Hotspur at Shrewsbury (*Henry IV, Part I,* conclusion) and mauls the French at Harfleur and Agincourt (*Henry V*), the stage revolved faster to underscore the violent action. Bands of men representing armies marched along with scenery passing by.

But the Boston opening had its problems. There was just too much to do, too much drama in action at once, too much history to encapsule—1377 to 1485—even for the prodigious Welles. Some of the flaws in the production can be ascribed to inadequate rehearsals. Others point to the inadvisability of opening out of town with a new piece of machinery and complicated lighting cues. What is more, there seems to have been some miscalculation about choosing the Colonial Theater, for the platform that seemed adequate in New York was seen by one Boston reviewer as being too small for the theater.

There were some of Welles's associates, Houseman among them, who believed that Orson's excessive life-style was the major factor in the failure of *Five Kings,* stressing stories about intemperate drinking, late hours, bombastic parties, and other social disruptions. They fail, however, to explain how this supposed behavior could have also accommodated the success of his acquisition, adaptation, and production over the radio on the "Campbell Playhouse" week after week. It is certain that Welles was attempting too much at one time. In the very midst of what seemed to be hopeless confusion with *Five Kings,* he intermittently worked on modernizing the humor in the script of *The Importance of Being Earnest* with the idea of producing it as his next play; and then he announced to the press that he was planning to produce a Shakespearean repertory at the New York World's Fair, consisting of capsule versions of the better plays, six to eight performances a day, and charge forty cents admission. The British beat him to it, however, with a replica of the Globe Theatre and their own encapsulated chapters of the Bard.

It is possible that the emotional complications that he was experiencing at that time also contributed to his inability to exert enough energy to propel *Five Kings* into the success he knew it could be. Welles had moved into an enormous, stained-glass-windowed Manhattan apartment on East Fifty-seventh Street, a short walk from the East River. His living room contained a balcony, perfect to use as a dramatic device while talking down to the people gathered below in his living room in front of a huge, stone fireplace. It was in this baronial setting that Orson announced to Virginia, during the run of *Five Kings,* that he wanted a divorce. He seems to have been in love with two women—two other women—at the same time, Virginia recalled years later, "and they were both dancers, Vera Zorina and Tilly Losch." Because of his —and their—marriages, and as a result of the complicated love affair, Welles kept the facts of his personal life hidden from even his closest associates.

Tilly was an Austrian exotic dancer, fourteen years Orson's senior, who had just come to the United States and made two films in Hollywood, *The Garden of Allah* and *The Good Earth,* and was beginning to get Broadway stage roles. She was as enamored of Orson's brilliance as he was with her beauty but she had no interest in breaking up his marriage. He was the one who attempted to advance the relationship, often without success.

Vera Zorina was a tiny and lovely ballet dancer who had joined the Ballet Russe de Monte Carlo in London when she was only seventeen. She had spent time in the United States on tour with the company all during the mid-1930s and finally went to Hollywood in 1937 to make *The Goldwyn Follies,* choreographed by George Balanchine. Although Zorina (she eventually dropped her first name) loved Balanchine, she was not *in love*, as she described her feelings for him, even after he proposed. It was at that time that she developed a "tremendous crush" on Orson Welles. In her autobiography, *Zorina,* she wrote of him as somewhat Byronic, precocious and brilliant, with "a dynamic presence and a beautiful and vibrant voice. . . . He was tall and handsome, with unusually wide-set eyes and a full sensuous mouth."

Orson had a deep physical attraction for the willowy and lithe Zorina; she had a dancer's walk, striding on the balls of her feet, but in a slightly sideways fashion.

Gossip columnists began to follow the pair as they wined and dined their way through many of the New York clubs and restaurants, most often after Orson's performances with the Mercury Theatre. The coverage given by the columnists, Walter Winchell, Ed Sullivan, and Jimmy Fiddler, greatly annoyed Zorina, jealously enraged Balanchine (but he eventually married her), and caused Orson and Virginia to have constant battles over what she thought was his infidelity. Zorina still claims to this day that despite her deep affection for him, her relationship with Welles was entirely platonic. After months of bedazzlement, they decided to take leave of each other before the incipient affair became all too real and all too difficult to end.

Virginia finally divorced him on the grounds of mental cruelty (although after the decree was final, she said Orson wasn't cruel at all—just that matrimony and his career didn't mix) in Reno in February of 1940.

No one could deny the boldness of the *Five Kings* conception, but coordination of all the varied elements in the production was lacking. The opening show had the earmarks of a dress rehearsal; it was daring, breathtaking, spectacular—and marred by the kind of mishaps one expects in high school plays. In one of the worst moments, a lighting mixup left Speaight groping for a way off the stage in the darkness, and he often had to chase his spotlight— inexplicably often in motion—to read his commentary.

Burgess Meredith complained that each platform whirled continuously while he was on stage, sometimes in opposite directions, setting up a centrifugal force competing against a centripetal one that dizzied and confused him and forced him to speak his lines on the run. He swore that the machinery threatened to hurl him into the orchestra pit or pin him against the proscenium arch. Someone once asked him what role he was playing in *Five Kings*. "I'm Henry V," Meredith said, "and it's too bad I didn't perish at Agincourt."

During one performance in Boston, Welles almost went down in theatrical history for reasons other than his innovative techniques. He came close to assassinating the audience. At the moment of the great charge—"I see you stand like greyhounds at the slips"—he had devised a plan where forty of his soldiers—drama students from Harvard—wielding real bows and arrows, would fire into a huge cork target off in the wings. At the moment when Welles was saying, "Cry God for Harry, England and St. George," the cue line for the soldiers to shoot, the turntable revolved too soon, and the soldiers faced the audience instead of stage left. Welles has recalled that in a flash of panic he thought to himself: "Well, they're university fellows. They know better. They're just not going to shoot into the audience." But then, suddenly, there was a tremendous roar coming from the other side of the footlights as the members of the audience began to dodge, and fend off, the arrows, all forty of them being shot directly at them. No one, miraculously, was hurt.

Because of the difficulties that plagued the production, Welles made changes from performance to performance: shifting or transposing scenes, deleting action, revising dialogue, modifying relationships, as he attempted to make the whole production glide with ease. Before every performance each actor received a revised scene agenda, neatly typed, indicating what costumes, cues, and personnel were to be used at any given moment. On one occasion, a particular scene was typographically dropped from the agenda, although the costume and actor list remained. No one in the cast noticed the mistake. Actors therefore, who were dressed in armor for the battlefield scene, entered the Boar's Head tavern where they were supposed to be casually dressed; and later when the battle commenced, the actors dressed as revelers—not armor-clad soldiers—entered the battlefield.

The Boston reviews were mixed. Welles was, without exception, hailed as an ideal Falstaff. Meredith received both high praise and backhanded dismissals. Despite the mishaps, Speaight was recognized for an outstanding performance. The *Boston Daily Record*'s E. F. Harkins referred to *Five Kings* as nothing more than a "dramatic curiosity."

Some of the scenes, however, received special commendation by reviewers such as the St. Crispin's Day speech in *Henry V,* Hotspur's violent tirade, and the King's admonition to Hal in *Henry IV.* To add lustiness to his character, Welles introduced a water closet on stage to which the cacophonously anal Falstaff would repair. The famous banishment scene, "I know thee not, old man," also had a special power, owing to a magical Wellesian effort. Falstaff, now alone on stage after being humiliated by his friend, turns front to the audience, his eyes filled with tears but his pride still intact. "Well, he's just saying that *now,*" Falstaff says, in an all-too-human attempt of face-saving. Martin Gabel, who was no longer in the Mercury company, but who saw the performance, recalled: "Not Henry Irving, not Beerbohm Tree, not anybody could have done this scene as effectively as Welles did it."

In the most negative of the Boston reviews, John K. Hutchens of the

Evening Transcript complained of "lights and curtains that were on vague terms with one another" and "backstage noises which occasionally suggested an unscheduled battle scene taking place somewhere back there."

The bemused Boston critics weren't the only ones to see the production flaws. *Five Kings* continued to be plagued with difficulties, many resulting from poor advance planning. In Philadelphia, for example, the crew discovered too late that they couldn't get the proper electrical hookup for the platform's motors, so stagehands had to push it around, thus keeping the audience waiting a full two hours before the curtain rang up.

But for all its faults, *Five Kings* still impressed audiences and reviewers on several counts. The pageantry of this fifteenth-century chronicle, including the two scenes using conventional backdrops to represent palace rooms, was commended. The battle scenes, performed on an elaborate construction of platforms and ramps, received particular notice: the battles in France even included cannon fire flashing in the direction of the audience.

More than anything else, though, Welles's Falstaff was the show, and it is probable that one of the major factors in his cementing all the plays together was so that he could play the fat man, with all his corpulent pluck, throughout. In Shakespeare's conception, the rollicking, irreverent Falstaff must be cleared away for the new, regal Hal who subjugates France, proves himself a superlative leader of his men, and lends dignity and a sense of greatness to English history. But in the Welles version, you simply could not forget Falstaff. As the *Christian Science Monitor* put it, *Five Kings* had two stars—Falstaff and the revolving stage.

If Burgess Meredith fell short, it was understandable. He had been granted the unprecedented opportunity to play the whole career of Henry V in one evening. But he was competing with those two costars. Nor did the length of the production work in his favor. Several people pointed out that by 11:20 the audience had seen so much that they were ready for the conclusion, when in fact the entire *Henry V* was slated to begin. The audience could not get over the Welles acting performance, which in the *Boston Evening American* reviewer's words was "magnificently lusty and splendidly vulgar" and finally "robustly comic." *Five Kings* stands as a daring, perhaps overly ambitious project that succeeded in its broad outlines, failed in many details, and brought the theater the best Welles acting performance it had ever seen. It also served as the continuation of Welles's experimentation in motion pictures, which had begun with *Too Much Johnson,* despite the fact that *Five Kings* used no actual film. The words of the interlocutor, Robert Speaight, could be thought of as intertitle cards such as could be found in silent film, and the tableaux without dialogue reminded both audience and critics of old-time silent movies. Nelson B. Bell said in the *Washington Post* that Welles had been using, in his own words, "fadeouts, pan shots, dissolves and all the other tricks of the cinema written in with deliberate intent." The mobility of settings and characters blended together in continuous action. The play had the pacing of a motion picture, and its revolutionary dramatic technique had no parallel in theatrical history.

Because of large overtime bills and other extravagances, Welles's relations with the Guild had begun to erode even before the Boston opening. By now the disenchantment was complete. After its two weeks in Philadelphia, with an audience that dwindled nightly, *Five Kings* closed and the Theatre Guild refused to back its New York opening. As *Five Kings* eased into the shadows, another Theatre Guild production opened in New York, *The Philadelphia Story,* with Katharine Hepburn and a Mercury staff actor in his first big smash hit, Joseph Cotten.

Orson frantically searched for backing to open in New York before his cast would have to disband. He and John Emery met with Tallulah Bankhead in her suite at the Hotel Elysée, to see if she could help through some of her affluent contacts. After all, she had a vested interest of sorts: Emery was her husband, and Orson was her friend. But it was the eleventh hour: unless down payments could be made immediately on costume rentals, and newspaper advertising begun the next day, the theater space would be gone. The money had to be raised by nine the next morning. All $25,000 of it.

Tallulah called playwright Marc Connelly, who lived in the same hotel, and Connelly suggested Sherman Billingsley, the owner of the Stork Club. It was well past midnight, but Billingsley was at his club when Tallulah called and agreed to meet with them at the hotel. From the time Billingsley arrived until dawn broke over Manhattan, the three coaxed and wheedled and cajoled, but even Orson's promise to turn over his inheritance from his father failed to convince Billingsley to invest in Shakespeare. With no money in hand, the play had to be abandoned.

IN 1939, THE sacred rites of vaudeville were being performed for the last time, a victim of radio and motion pictures. One attempt to enliven it was called "Vaude-vision." Dispensing with sets, scenery, and live music, a screen was mounted on stage, and images, with a musical soundtrack, were projected from the rear. Performers would then dance and sing, synchronizing their action to the activity on the screen behind them. "Vaude-vision" lasted only a few weeks, however, being criticized and condemned by everyone: musicians, stagehands, film operators, and their unions . . . and the public.

Welles had another idea that was closely allied to "Vaude-vision" but did not replace any artists or workers and therefore was more likely to succeed if only because the concept was not controversial. As he wanted to do with *Too Much Johnson,* Welles began to make plans to project a short film on the stage that would explain the opening narrative of a play and then continue, intermedia, with live actors and minimal scenery with the remainder of the drama.

There were some extremely successful and creative motion pictures in 1939, such as *Goodbye, Mr. Chips, Mr. Smith Goes to Washington, The Wizard of Oz,* and, later in the year, *Gone with the Wind.* There were also weaker efforts, *Conspiracy, Sorority House,* and *The Rookie Cop,* among others, which were very temporarily driving people away from the movie theaters. Vaudeville entrepreneurs made a hasty attempt to exploit what they were hoping would become a mass disillusionment with films by presenting highly popular radio personalities, such as Jack Benny and Major Bowes, and their acts on what was left of the vaudeville circuit. Tabloid versions of hit musicals and other successful plays, boiled down to about thirty minutes each, were also attempted in this revival. Rudy Vallee was somewhat successful in a vaudeville tour of a half-hour version of *A Connecticut Yankee in King Arthur's Court.* When Welles received an offer to go on the road as a vaudeville entertainer, at what was reported to be a huge sum, he accepted. It was, he believed, an opportunity not only to experiment with his idea of combining film and play but also, if he could last the projected twelve-week, six-a-day schedule, to return to New York with enough money to mount *Five Kings* on Broadway.

The first idea considered for his act, however, was not his nor was it to his liking. He was asked to present an onstage performance of *The War of the Worlds,* condensed to less than thirty minutes, without costumes and scenery and using microphones and scripts, as though it was an actual radio broadcast. Already afraid of being typed for life as "the man from Mars"—people had been calling him that for months—Welles categorically refused to consider a stage version of *The War of the Worlds.* However, he felt that *The Green Goddess,* a broadcast he had done earlier in the year, was perfectly adaptable to the concept of a compact vaudeville rendition. Written in 1921 by William Archer, the biting Scottish dramatic critic and friend of George Bernard Shaw, it was an improbable but immensely popular melodrama that had enjoyed many stage revivals.

It is a play that attempts nothing more nor less than to be a thriller. Into an inaccessible kingdom of the Himalayas a plane crashes, aboard which are two British officers and the wife of one of them. The plot revolves around the reigning Rajah's attempts to seduce the wife and keep her in his kingdom, and how the prisoners try to get help from across the mountains while also attempting to steal the sacred emerald. In the radio version, Welles had played the Rajah, and Madeleine Carroll was the object of his affections.

Eventually Welles was booked to produce a twenty-minute vaudeville version of *The Green Goddess* and to present it in theaters throughout the Midwest and in Chicago and Pittsburgh.

Using stock footage from a New York film house that had a library of scenes and situations that could easily be spliced into any motion picture, and shooting just a few insert shots himself, Welles created a four-minute introduction for *The Green Goddess.* The film opens with a map of India. Slowly, the camera moves up toward the country of Nepal, then to the city of Katmandu, and finally closes in on the area of Mount Everest. Next, the film cuts to an airplane, flying at night, lights ablaze in its windows, in the midst of a terrible lightning storm, and being deluged with torrential rains. The plane is in desperate trouble as it is buffeted and shaken by the storm, but somehow it continues to fly through the night. A mountain range looms in the distance. It is obvious that the visibility of the plane is zero: the inevitable crash occurs. There was no soundtrack incorporated into the film, but a recording of an airplane motor accompanied by thunder, wind, rain, and then the boom of the airplane crash was to be synchronized with the film and played on the public address system.

On June 21, 1939, billed as "the man who scared the world, then charmed it," Welles opened at the Stanley Theater in Pittsburgh. It was a typical evening of vaudeville. The first act consisted of a musical-comedy dance trio, Jack Lanny and the platinum-haired Statler Twins; this was followed by Jack Talley, ostensibly a serious baritone who was interrupted by the repetitious iddy-biddy-kiddy comic routine of Terry Howard. The Coon Creek Girls, a foursome of hillbilly singers who had gained national fame by entertaining the King and Queen of England at the White House, ended the musical portion of the show. Welles's production of *The Green Goddess* was the last act—and the one prestige item—on the bill.

A voice was heard over the public address system: "Good evening. This is Orson Welles and the Mercury Theatre in a presentation of *The Green Goddess.*" There was polite applause. The screen was lowered in front of the curtain and the projector started. Suddenly, the audience began to howl. Welles, in the wings, could not tell at first what was causing the uproar. Then one of his assistants who went into the theater to find out came rushing back. "The film's backwards!" he blurted. After its last viewing, the film had not been rewound, and so the plane appeared to revive itself from the explosion and then flew backward into the map of India. The sound was also much too loud and, of course, not synchronized with the backward motion.

But on with the show. The screen was raised, the curtain went up, and Orson, as the Rajah, with an enormous turban and very thick, black Pan-Cake makeup, stood in the middle of the stage. The three survivors of the crash are brought to him and the dialogue begins: "Welcome to my kingdom," the Rajah says. Again, there were problems. Somehow, the sound system continued with the loud plane noises blasting the ears of the audience so that no one could be heard from the stage. Welles, now out of character as the Rajah, glared annoyingly into the wings: *"Will you please shut that thing off?"* he boomed. Then, turning to the audience, he said: "Ladies and gentlemen, I apologize for this. If any of you feel that you are not seeing the performance that you should, please go to the box office and ask for your money back and you will be reimbursed. I will personally guarantee it. However, those of you who wish to stay may do so as we will now begin again." No one left and the performance continued as planned.

Unfortunately, Welles's flirtation with vaudeville proved disastrous. The audiences seemed bored and although the mechanical mishap never occurred again, the lilt of the playlet never worked smoothly. In an attempt to save it, Welles decided to do impersonations, that is, to play the role of the Rajah in different voices. First, he did Charles Laughton, in a sort of portly, matronlike voice; he followed this by trying the bombastic ham of John Barrymore; then a well-modulated Alfred Lunt; and finally a rapid-talking and debonair Herbert Marshall. This all was as logical, one reviewer pointed out, as Welles playing Falstaff by imitating Raymond Massey, Jimmy Durante, or Victor

Moore. The effort did little to heighten the interest in the performance.

Instead of continuing on the eleven-and-a-half-week schedule that was originally planned, *The Green Goddess* was abruptly canceled, and Welles's first and only vaudeville experience came to an end, "turning the whole thing," as *Variety* condemned it, "into the worst fiasco ever to leaden the heart of an agonized actor."

AS EARLY AS 1937, during his production of *Julius Caesar,* Welles's progress was observed and noted by executives of RKO Radio Pictures. Lillie Messenger, the studio's cleverly aggressive East Coast story editor, was overwhelmed both by the production and by Welles's performance as Marcus Brutus. Although RKO was undergoing arduous financial strains at the time, she wrote to Leo Spitz, the head of the studio in Hollywood, urging him to see the play during his next scheduled visit to New York. It is "brilliantly directed," wrote Messinger, and Welles is "such a brilliant talent that he cannot be ignored." Somewhere at RKO there had to be a script for Welles to act in or direct.

It took well over a year before RKO made an attempt to bring Welles to Hollywood. The studio's new president, George J. Schaefer, who had come to RKO from a distinguished career as General Manager for Paramount and United Artists, was appointed on October 21, 1938. Nine days later, he, too, was listening to CBS at 8:00 P.M., when Welles made his infamous broadcast. Welles's seemingly innate ability to generate publicity was reason enough to want him aboard; the fact that he was also a highly talented actor and an innovative director clinched it.

The studio was famous for its many Fred Astaire-Ginger Rogers musicals, all of the early Katharine Hepburn films, and such 1930s financial blockbusters as *Cimarron* (1931), *King Kong* (1933), *Of Human Bondage* (1934), and *The Informer* (1935). Schaefer also wanted to revive the system of independent production units introduced by David O. Selznick, and thought that the Mercury group was a possible candidate for RKO to take aboard. Admittedly, RKO wasn't the biggest studio in Hollywood, but Schaefer argued that to someone like Welles, size was less important than opportunity. Although he respected Welles's directorial skills, Schaefer was certain that he would be immensely important as a film actor, and he began pursuing him on that level, in competition with most of the other large film companies, which also were trying to persuade Welles to come with them.

A few possible roles were mentioned, but the first serious offer was that of the part of Quasimodo in a two-million-dollar extravaganza of Victor Hugo's *Notre Dame de Paris,* usually known by its subtitle, *The Hunchback of Notre Dame.* Schaefer and many of his colleagues at RKO believed that *The Hunchback of Notre Dame* would be the studio's biggest film of the following year, similar to its *Gunga Din* of 1939. The version made in 1923 with Lon Chaney had been a rousing success, and the first talking edition, they were convinced, would prove to be even more popular. Welles was both tempted and flattered by the possibility of starring, for his first part in a major motion picture, in a film that a top studio was going to consider its biggest and finest release of the year.

Several important directors were being pursued to take charge of the production: Alfred Hitchcock, Julien Duvivier, James Whale, and William Dieterle were all mentioned as possibilities. The music of Alfred Newman was to be used; a beautiful leading lady, yet to be chosen, was to play the gypsy girl La Esmeralda, friend—and finally love—of the hunchback.

Welles's decision about whether to accept the role was a difficult one. He had no problem with the story: Victor Hugo's melodramatic tale of adventure and suspense was gripping and intriguing. The part itself was one that many actors dream of doing once in their lifetimes. But there were other considerations. The leading figure of the film, Quasimodo was a character part, and Hollywood and the public were quick to typecast performers; Would not only other character parts follow? Wouldn't Welles be cast to play more monster types, especially since the public already related him to Martian monsters? He was afraid that once he played the part of an ogre, he would inevitably be doomed to such grotesques for the remainder of his film career. Although he was the first to admit that he could never be a matinee idol in the sense that Rudolph Valentino and Douglas Fairbanks were, he had no desire to become a Boris Karloff or a Bela Lugosi.

His directorial ambitions were also to be considered. If and when he finally succumbed to Hollywood, as he had previously informed David Selznick, he wanted to go on his own terms. He wanted to duplicate the centrality of style that he had created for himself on the radio and in the theater: actor, director, producer, writer, and Pooh Bah. Besides, he was still committed to the "Campbell Playhouse" and to bringing his *Five Kings* to Broadway.

Shortly after his rejection of the role, it was offered to Charles Laughton, who eventually played a memorable Quasimodo. William Dieterle directed. Although winning no prizes, *The Hunchback of Notre Dame* remains one of the highlights of Charles Laughton's career, and it was a needed money-maker for RKO.

Other offers, or at least overtures, were made to Welles by Samuel Goldwyn and Warner Brothers, the latter suggesting that Welles star in a remake of *Napoleon,* a remarkable notion considering Welles's six-foot-two-inch height and more than two-hundred-pound weight. The tiny but powerful Adolph Zukor and his lieutenants at Paramount Pictures were also interested in Welles and conducted several high-level conferences to discuss making him an offer. But they were really looking for a new lighthearted, money-spinning series and never became convinced that Welles was the one who could develop it. MGM had the Hardy family; all that Welles had was his Shakespearean-inclined Mercury actors. Ultimately, Paramount's desire was fulfilled without Welles and with their 1939 production of *What a Life,* followed by a number of other adventures in the life of Henry Aldrich.

Sinclair Lewis's controversial and best-selling novel, *It Can't Happen Here,* was another film possibility. The motion picture rights were purchased by Metro-Goldwyn-Mayer studios, and a screen adaptation was prepared by Sidney Howard. The story was about "Buzz" Windrip, a politician who is more street thug than statesman but who nevertheless is eventually elected as the president of the United States, and who then moves to establish a full-scale dictatorship. The plot revolves around a small-town editor, who first supports Windrip and later joins the underground in an attempt to overthrow his fascist state when Windrip engages his crack elitist guard, the Corpos, in acts of brutality and violence. The Hitlerian comparison was sharp and obvious, and the book was a timely statement on how totalitarianism can govern if people fail to recognize it for what it really is.

Attempts to produce *It Can't Happen Here* seemed blocked at every juncture. A story circulated in the film industry that Will Hays, overseer of the Motion Picture Production Code, was banning it because of fear of international complications and also because he did not want to displease the Republican Party. Hays denied any ban. A spokesman for MGM complained that they had two problems with it: costs and casting. The script lay dormant in the MGM story files until early in 1939 when a young producer who had worked for Paramount, William Selwyn, approached MGM with the idea of getting Orson Welles involved.

In 1936, Welles had been greatly impressed with a Federal Theatre Project stage version of *It Can't Happen Here,* which caused much controversy and enjoyed considerable critical success. Some people thought the play was designed to elect Franklin Delano Roosevelt; others saw it as a plan to defeat him. It was called sympathetic to communism, fascism, and the New Deal, almost all in the same breath. The people at MGM bristled when reviews of the play offered judgments such as: "Where the motion pictures fear to tread, the Federal Theatre, tomorrow night, goes boldly into the limelight of controversial issues. . . ."

Selwyn suggested to the MGM hierarchy that Welles be given the Howard script in an attempt to pare it down in production expense, but not in value, and to make it economically feasible to produce. As for the long-standing difficulty with casting, who would be better to play "Buzz" Windrip, the tyrannical oppressor, than the loud, forceful, and overbearing Orson Welles? King Vidor, who was then directing *Northwest Passage,* was given the existing script to study for his possible involvement, and the name of Orson Welles began to appear in memoranda and in meetings held throughout MGM. Yes, the influence of his pen on the script might be exactly what it needed, and yes, he would make a perfect Windrip. His relative inexperience, they felt, ruled out offering him the director's job, but there they could offer other temptations: top billing and the leading role in the film; a writer assigned to him for as long as he needed, to help on the script revision; the right to work with a director who would promise to listen to Welles's directorial suggestions "in getting the best out of every situation"; the privilege of importing to Hollywood with him the acting and producing personnel from his Mercury Theatre company, "if they would be any value to this particular script"; and cancellation of the usual option clause, which forced an actor, if the studio so designated, to make more than one film with them.

The conditions were attractive to Welles, and he might have even relinquished his directorial demand had the project developed any further. But before additional talks with Welles could take place, quietly and without explanation, the film was abandoned. No open reason has ever been given for its cancellation, but one possibility was offered by playwright Sidney Howard, who claimed that he had seen a long memorandum from Joseph I. Breen, director of the Production Code Administration, listing objectionable sections and pointing out the "dangerous" material in the film. Also, the lack of the usual international market for *It Can't Happen Here* in Germany and Italy, and in those countries sympathetic to them, could undoubtedly have been an important economic factor in giving it up.

George Schaefer of RKO still pursued Welles to accept a film role. His studio wanted to do a remake of the Robert Louis Stevenson thriller, *Dr. Jekyll and Mr. Hyde.* The last time it had been made, in 1932, Fredric March won an Academy Award for his performance, and the story was perfect for an actor who wanted to play the two parts, not only of Hyde's personality but of his own; that of character actor *and* that of leading man. Welles was offered the role and despite his admiration for the Stevenson tale and its setting of the London of the 1880s, he turned it down for almost the exact reasons that he had refused the part of Quasimodo: he could not address the material, he felt, without trapping himself. Spencer Tracy ultimately developed the role into a stunning characterization.

It soon became clear to Schaefer that there was only one way he was going to seduce Welles into the RKO empire. He had to make a deal where Welles would be accommodated to express whatever it was that was making him a presence in the first place. He would be permitted to both act and direct and also be allowed to exert his influence on choosing whatever film he was to make under his own name.

All during the time that Welles was attempting to stage *Five Kings,* and through the spring and early summer's 1939 "Campbell Playhouse" presentations, he talked and negotiated with Schaefer and occasionally other RKO officials about going to Hollywood to make a film, or films, for them. On his behalf, Albert Schneider, who had served for a while as his booking agent for radio shows and other theatrical events and had then become his manager, attempted to work together with Arnold Weissberger on a favorable situation for Welles with RKO. Welles still had hopes that *Five Kings* would be a success, and his prospective jaunt on the vaudeville circuit, it was thought, could continue for months. As late as May 15, 1939, Schneider sent a telegram to George Schaefer, stating in part: "NEW DEVELOPMENTS REGARDING WELLES MAKE IT IMPOSSIBLE HE CONSIDER FILMS THIS TIME. WILL INFORM YOU AS I PROMISED OUR LAST MEETING SHOULD THIS SITUATION CHANGE."

In a matter of weeks, the situation did change—and drastically—with the crushing defeat of *The Green Goddess.* Welles was now more willing to consider an exodus to Hollywood, and serious contractual negotiations began between his representatives and RKO. He still planned a New York production of *Five Kings,* and Hollywood became another possible means of earning enough money to realize that end. Years later, in a television interview, Welles said, "You know, when you don't really want to go to Hollywood—at least this was true in the old days, the golden days of Hollywood—when you didn't honestly want to go, then the deals got better and better. In my case I didn't want money; I wanted authority. So I asked for the impossible, hoping to be left alone; and at the end of a year's negotiations, I got what I wanted."

THOUSANDS OF WORDS were written about the famous Welles contract with RKO at the time it was signed, and critics and film historians have continued to make mention of it. The stories usually went, and continue to go, something like this: Welles was given the most lavishly attractive and unrestrictive contract in motion picture history. He was to do one picture a year, for which he was to receive $100,000 (in some stories this figure jumped to $150,000) to serve as writer, producer, director, and actor. He had the right to hire whom he wanted as cast and crew and had only certain very loose budgetary limitations. He could choose whatever film he wanted to make, had complete artistic control over it, and had the right to refuse to show it to anyone from the studio until it was finished. *The New York Times* of August 20, 1939, reported that he was to be paid $100,000 a picture and that "it is understood that the studio will exercise no supervision over the picture, merely footing the bill." The *Hollywood Tribune* of that same week stated that he had complete autonomy and that he had been "granted *carte blanche.*" *Life* reported that Welles resented authority and that "in his RKO contract he made careful provision that none would be imposed upon him." In later years, such distinguished critics as André Bazin would refer to Welles's "unprecedented contract of total freedom," and Pauline Kael would talk about the fact that Welles had held out "until Schaefer offered him complete control" over his productions.

The myth still continues to this day. Two recent works on the life of Welles perpetuate the story, one referring to his "creative *carte blanche"* and the other talking of his "unique autonomy." A close reading of the actual contract tells more.

In some ways the contract *was* epoch-making. It is true that RKO hired a twenty-four-year-old man who had never made a large-budget feature film before, although his experience with the making of the abbreviated film for *Too Much Johnson* was real enough. In fact, *Too Much Johnson* was screened by Schaefer and other RKO people before they signed the contract, just to see what Welles could do. They were impressed. And it is equally true that virtually no one in motion picture history, with the exception of Charlie Chaplin and possibly one or two others, ever had the opportunity to write, produce, direct, and star in his own film. However, the offer of "total freedom," supposedly given to Welles, was grossly exaggerated by both him and RKO, perhaps for publicity purposes in an attempt to promulgate his image as a boy wonder and creative insurgent, unfettered and unpredictable. Consequently, the "complete license" story emerged as the official one in the press.

Actually, there were many restrictions in the two-film contract signed on July 22, 1939. It stated that RKO, among many other things, had the right of story *refusal.* That means that after Welles submitted an idea for a film, *before the first camera began to roll,* the studio had the right to reject it.

According to the provisions of the contract, Welles had the right to submit six such ideas for a "Class A" motion picture (and ideas that might possibly exceed an agreed-upon amount were not acceptable). The studio promised to exercise "utmost good faith" in appraising Welles's concepts for films, but it was stated in the contract that those ideas could not be "political or controversial." If none of Welles's six ideas could be agreed upon, RKO would then submit six of its own to Welles for *his* approval. If no agreeable film concept emerged after this twelve-film appraisal, the contract would be annulled.

If and when a subject was agreed upon, Welles would receive for the first film the sum of $35,000 as producer and $30,000 as actor, in addition to 20 percent of the net profits of the film, if any. For the second film he was to receive a slightly smaller cash payment—$35,000 as actor and $25,000 as producer—but more of the net profits: 25 percent after expenses.

The definition of a story "idea" in the context of the contract was one that could be described in a detailed outline, not necessarily a completed script. Once RKO approved the story for the film and a script was prepared, Welles was then legally bound not to "substantially depart from the basic story finally approved" by RKO.

The first film, still to be chosen, was to be completed by January 1, 1940, which gave him barely five months from the date of the contract; the second film was to be finished within the calendar year of 1940. All copyright ownership and all rights of ownership of every kind would belong to RKO. Welles agreed to be available for acting six days a week; the other day he was permitted to take off to appear on his radio broadcast. No employee or actor could be hired by Welles, even those of his Mercury Theatre staff, unless first approved by RKO. Welles agreed to confer with RKO on the title of the film, and RKO reserved the legal right to change it as often as it wished. Welles agreed not to work on any other film or screenplay as either director, writer, star, or producer until the two RKO films were completed.

Finally and most important, *Welles agreed to show RKO rushes of the film and to confer with studio executives on the final cutting and editing of it before the film was to be considered complete and finished.* At the same time, RKO reserved the right to edit, cut, dub, and change the film in any way that it wanted for censorship purposes, in accordance with the Production Code of the Motion Picture Producers and Distributors of America, and also for any foreign or international release.

On the set, Welles was to have the "complete freedom" that was discussed so frequently by the press. This kind of directorial independence was not so uncommon in the Hollywood and European system of filmmaking. However, it did *not* allow him to disregard schedules, to hire or even fire indiscriminantly, or to use other studio personnel or property for his own purpose without authorization.

Welles's agreement with RKO was large enough in scope, however, to match his swelling ideas. Schaefer was brilliant. By giving Welles as much liberty as the studio could afford, he was hoping to enlarge Welles's cinematic faculties without allowing the possibility of plunging the studio into ruin owing to possible youthful excesses and inexperience. Despite the restrictions of the contract, it enabled Orson to be the kind of film professional he wanted to be: bold, broad-stroked, totally in charge on the set, involved with infinitesimal details, the father of his acting family, using all of the experience he had gained from radio and theater.

Only days after he signed the RKO contract, in late July, Welles flew to Los Angeles with John Houseman and Richard Baer, who had been with him in *Five Kings.* He checked into a suite at the baronial Chateau Marmont on Sunset Boulevard, a hotel that was touted as discreet, casual, and accommodating to the original or the eccentric. He then made contact with his new employers. Eventually he planned to have almost all of his other Mercury players come to Hollywood, too, but the initial order of business was to come to terms with the studio on a suitable first film.

Before formal talks began or memoranda were exchanged, Welles discussed a number of film ideas with Schaefer and his colleagues. There were several decision-makers at RKO who believed that Welles's first picture should be a film version of *The War of the Worlds,* pointing out that the world situation, along with the previous publicity, could stimulate much activity at the box office. Although he was not against *ever* doing a film version of the Martian invasion—in fact, he thought it was a sound idea—Welles was adamant about not producing it as his *first* picture.

And Schaefer, having had similar talks about *The Hunchback of Notre Dame* and *Dr. Jekyll and Mr. Hyde,* now backed him up. In a memorandum to one of his executives who was enthusiastically pushing what he called *The Man from Mars* script, Schaefer told him to desist with his talks to Welles on the subject and said: "The only way I was able to secure Orson originally was because of my sympathy with his viewpoint that he did not want to go out, and be tagged and catalogued, as the 'horror' man by appearing in a picture such as *The Hunchback of Notre Dame* or immediately going into the production of a picture such as *The Man from Mars.* He was anxious to do something first, *before* Hollywood typed him."

A film Welles was quite eager to do, and suggested as his first picture to fulfill the contract, was *Cyrano de Bergerac,* based on the play about the real Cyrano by Edmond Rostand. One of the great romantic and swashbuckling comedies in dramatic literature, it had been since its first appearance on the stage in 1897 also one of the most popular and successful plays ever produced, enjoying revivals again and again in virtually every country in the world and in almost every modern language. Cyrano, the brilliant and gallant Gascon poet and novelist with the enormous nose and marvelous talent for dueling, was to Welles one of the most engaging roles in the theater, as it was to many actors. Errol Flynn desperately wanted to play it, with Olivia de Havilland as Roxane. Laurence Olivier announced his willingness to accept the role with Vivien Leigh as the leading lady. Garson Kanin, among others, wanted to direct it. When Ben Hecht completed a screenplay, a number of stars attempted to interest various studios in buying it. Welles was among those interested in having RKO buy it for him. He even offered to put up some of his own money if RKO's bid for the script was lower than competing offers.

Welles could see himself spending hours, days, weeks, in applying makeup to create that rock—that crag, that cape, that peninsula!—of a proboscis, and in his most fluent and fluid voice, with cape flourishing, sword flashing, and nose shining, reciting those lines that kill:

> So may the turn of a hand forestall
> Life with its honey, death with its gall;
> So may the turn of my fancy roam
> Free, for a time, till the rimes recall,
> Then, as I end the refrain, thrust home!

Money was not the main problem that RKO had concerning whether or not to produce *Cyrano*, however. The fact that the play was known by virtually every high school and college student in the country, and that a translation of it appeared in the great anthology *The Treasury of the Theater*, actually militated against it. The studio was afraid the story had a textbook ambience about it, that people would think of it as just another dull classic. Welles's protestation of its immense popularity over the years notwithstanding, Schaefer and his associates were not convinced that it could make money. To test their theory, and to disprove Orson's, they had George H. Gallup of the American Institute of Public Opinion conduct a scientific poll of a cross section of typical moviegoers.

The accuracy of Gallup's results had been considered authentic ever since, through samplings, he had in 1936 predicted Roosevelt's reelection, missing the actual popular vote by only 6½ percent. Later refinements in his procedures had reduced the margin of error in a national poll to about 3 percent. Many of the Hollywood studios were subscribers to his service, or to his many competitors, and if Gallup's tests indicated that a film was going to be unpopular, it usually meant instant shredding of the script.

Without Welles's knowledge, *all* of the ideas that had been under discussion as the possible first film were sent to Gallup for testing among the public. They included *Cyrano de Bergerac* and *The Man from Mars*; six titles for which RKO already had scripts or treatments, *Vigil in the Night, Nellie Bly, Kitty Foyle, American Way, My Favorite Wife,* and *Brave New World*; and two additional film ideas suggested by Welles, Conrad's *Heart of Darkness* and

The Smiler with the Knife. (The last, by C. Day Lewis, using the pseudonym Nicholas Blake, was about a sinister plot to establish a dictatorship in England.)

Gallup found that audience acceptance of *Cyrano de Bergerac* was about equal to *Vigil in the Night* but was weaker than all of the other RKO suggestions. Only one moviegoer in five had ever heard of Cyrano, claimed Gallup. *The Man from Mars* drew more interest from the public than *Cyrano*. Other tests indicated *Cyrano* to be approximately equal to *Heart of Darkness* and *The Smiler with the Knife,* but all three were substantially lower than *The Man from Mars.* Further sampling indicated that if *Cyrano* were cast with a romantic team such as Laurence Olivier and Vivien Leigh, rather than Orson Welles and perhaps an unknown female co-lead, the interest in the film would be greater, but it would still remain lower than *Favorite Wife.*

Gallup also constructed a poll for RKO in which moviegoers were asked, "Here are four stories that are being made into movies. Which one do you think would make the best movie?"

The results:

> *Northwest Passage*—44 percent
> *Rebecca*—28 percent
> *The Grapes of Wrath*—25 percent
> *Cyrano de Bergerac*—3 percent

Eventually Welles was informed of the outcome of the Gallup poll. He reluctantly agreed to postpone his nasal camouflage and *Cyrano de Bergerac* if RKO would do the same for *The Man from Mars,* but he believed in *Heart of Darkness* and continued to campaign for it among studio executives and especially with Schaefer. The radio version barely nine months before had left him thinking of the story's film possibilities. As he had done with his stage version of *Julius Caesar,* he wanted to modify *Heart of Darkness* so that it would emerge not only as a story of the corruption that results from total power but also as a modern political parable, a portrait of Kurtz as a contemporary victim/perpetrator of the totalitarian state. He also immediately had cinematic innovations in mind, chiefly having the camera *become* the character of Marlow. The other actors would play to him, relate to him, speak to him, and the audience would see what the camera/character sees and possibly, he hoped, experience some of the same emotions, adventures, and visual stimuli. In this way, Welles contended, people would not merely *see* the film, they would be participants in it. The film would *happen* to them. It was an idea filled with spark and ginger, but it seemed to many at RKO overly ambitious as a first directorial effort. Schaefer countered: "This is what was said about all of Welles's productions, and look what happened with the voodoo *Macbeth* and *War of the Worlds.*"

His and Orson's arguments were convincing, and despite the apathetic results of the Gallup survey and an attempt at an executive blockade, RKO finally gave Welles the formal signal to proceed with *Heart of Darkness.* The film rights were secured from Conrad's widow, Jessie, for $4,500, and $4,000 was paid for a waiver of an option owned by an entrepreneur, R. L. Griffin.

Houseman was offered a fee of $15,000 to write the first draft script, under Welles's supervision, but he had problems with the project from the very beginning. As he unabashedly relates in *Run-Through*: "I was an editor and an adapter rather than a writer. On our radio show, over the past year, I had *taken* finished texts of varying qualities, condensed and translated them successfully into another medium: it had been one of my virtues as an adapter that I managed to retain much of the quality and texture of the original works—including *Heart of Darkness*. But in this new venture I was a failure. Frightened by the necessities of an unfamiliar medium, worried by the ambivalence of my own feelings for Orson and in my anxiety to give him what he wanted, I found myself unable to give him anything at all."

Finally, Houseman flew back to New York to work on the forthcoming fall season of the "Campbell Playhouse," and Welles took over the creation of the *Heart of Darkness* script. He ensconced himself in a large house that he had rented in the Brentwood section of Los Angeles, and within a week he had a working draft. It was the first screenplay he had ever written.

Unlike Conrad, he attempted to delineate the fine line of Marlow's personality, having him emerge as someone who can be more easily identified. He was careful, however, not to introduce characteristics to which a member of the audience would find difficulty relating. Marlow was to be the camera-viewer. If he did things or engaged in activities that were too unfamiliar, the viewer would cease to believe that it was happening to him.

Welles constructed a carefully reasoned profile of the filmic Marlow: he was fifteen years older than Kurtz, a gentleman, poet, and adventurer of no outstanding identity beyond the important rationale of his persona-as-character—a man who cannot tolerate a lie.

In Welles's view, Conrad's prose, filled with dazzling imagery, and deep, sometimes purple reflections, was somewhat inconsistent with Marlow's personality. He made Marlow capable of speaking Conrad's language but purposely attempted to reduce or weaken some of the vitality and pigment of his dialogue, again to make him appear less defined. Welles's Marlow would not be permitted, as he is in the book, to say such lines of Conrad's as the following:

> Watching a coast as it slips by the ship is like thinking about an enigma. There it is before you—smiling, frowning, inviting, grand, mean, insipid, or savage, and always mute with an air of whispering, Come and find out. This one was almost featureless, as if still in the making, with an aspect of monotonous grimness. The edge of a colossal jungle, so dark-green as to be almost black, fringed with white surf, ran straight, like a ruled line, far, far, along a blue sea whose glitter was blurred by a creeping mist.

Marlow, to Welles, was to be completely disassociated not only from any specific class of people but also from any part of the country. Although

American, he was not to be a type, such as a southerner, westerner, and the like. "The Marlows of the world always are unclassifiable," wrote Welles in a brilliant description of the character. "They have a charm and it might almost be said that the charm is a consequence of their lack of roots. They are easy to talk to and this quality is the result of their lack of identification." Marlow, therefore, was never a portrait to Welles but a figure and a face in a larger canvas. He is literate and educated but he is not literary as he is in Conrad. Above all as he is in the film, he emerges as a man in love and a man of honor. As Welles's sketch continued: "I have met him many times. He is willing to tell you how he murdered his wife but seldom volunteers his name. Being lonely, he protects himself from the spirit of loneliness, by candor. You are immediately in his confidence but he never gives you intimacy."

The script was duly delivered to the estimating and budget department of RKO, who in turn, in the same day, sent it to the two leading banks with which the studio did business. Hollywood banks, even then, had their own rule-of-thumb estimators who, after decades of lending money to studios for films that had both succeeded and failed, had developed a fairly sophisticated sixth sense based on basics. Does the film have a leading motion picture star? Well, no, but Orson Welles *is* a personality. Is the story based on a recent best-selling novel or play? No, but Conrad *is* a great author. Does it have a happy ending? No, but the point of the story *is* meaningful. Has the director made money for the studio, or any studio, before? No again, but Welles *has* had theatrical hits. The bank's cautious recommendation: $400,000.

Noting the bank's reluctance, RKO set the same amount as the budget for the film. In effect, the studio was saying to Welles that it would help him produce *Heart of Darkness,* but it wasn't ready, just yet, to invest its *own* money in the project. It was mid-August 1939.

Then the great beard controversy began. Welles had arrived in a clean-shaven Hollywood wearing the beard he had grown for *Five Kings.* Now that it appeared that he would be playing Kurtz in *Heart of Darkness,* he continued to grow his facial hair, much to the consternation of the film colony. It seemed that people in the film business were more concerned with Welles's hirsute appearance than with his creative ability. *The New York Times* actually did a fairly serious story entitled "Bearded Bogeyman Goes Hollywood," in which it said he had been "looked upon on his arrival with open suspicion because of his beard."

The fact that Paul Muni had recently let his beard grow for eight weeks before starting to act in *The Woman I Love* and then kept it on for *The Life of Emile Zola,* over six months in all, seemed not to bother anyone. Muni was an already established actor of distinction and a renowned film personality. Welles, to many, was still just a boy, yet to prove himself: the beard, it was argued, seemed pretentious. It was also a symbol of disrespect to those in the film business who were already resentful that a newcomer had been given such an attractive opportunity to work in motion pictures.

Officials at RKO were also upset about his beard, so much so that Lillie Messenger sent a fretful memo to George Schaefer predicting dire consequences should Welles insist on maintaining it: neither the critics nor the public would take him seriously, warned Messenger. Schaefer began to receive so much criticism from other RKO officials that he secretly had George Gallup conduct a poll to determine the public's general attitude toward Orson and specifically toward his beard. Twenty-six cities and small towns were canvassed and people were asked, "What do you think of Orson Welles?" The answers ranged from "He's a genius" to "I think he stinks." Violent reactions were the rule rather than the exception. Finally, 36 percent of the replies could have been said to be definitely favorable; 14 percent were noncommittal; 17 percent had no opinion; and 9 percent volunteered that they had never heard of Orson Welles. On the most critical issue to RKO, the beard: 2 percent of the American public took offense at it. Such comments were given as: "I enjoy his radio program but I feel he carries his acting too much into real life, that is, his beard, cut of hair, etc. I can't say whether his genius is real or not." Or, "He never shaves." Or, "He doesn't look like much of an actor with a beard." Or, "I think he's swell. I like him as an actor but I don't like his beard."

Schaefer was appalled, not at the 9 percent who had never heard of Welles, but at the 2 percent who disapproved of the beard. In similar polls conducted at that time, 13 percent of the public had never heard of Kay Kyser; 29 percent had never heard of David Selznick; 39 percent had never heard of Frank Capra; and 43 percent had never heard of Maureen O'Hara. They were probably not moviegoers. But if 2 percent of the public took issue with Orson's beard, Schaefer feared, it might mean a financial loss on any film with which Welles was involved. Schaefer and his RKO colleagues actually conducted a formal executive meeting to discuss the meaning of the Gallup poll and Orson's beard, which they could not force him, legally, to shave off. It was determined that Welles, if officially asked to remove it, might keep his beard as a symbol of individuality or rebellion. Finally, all agreed that subtle influence might have a better effect than a direct order. Meanwhile, the beard silently grew.

Then, when it appeared that the whole whiskers tempest was about to calm down, F. Scott Fitzgerald had a short story published in *Esquire* that used Orson—and his beard—as the subject. A familiar Fitzgerald fictional character, Pat Hobby, an unemployed screenwriter, begins to resent Orson's presence in Hollywood and thinks that because Orson sports a beard, he belongs back in New York with "the rest of the snobs." Hobby feels that Welles is edging him out of his film-world position:

> There is an old Chaplin picture about a crowded street car where the entrance of one man at the rear forces another out in front. A similar image came into Pat's mind in the ensuing days whenever he thought of Orson Welles. Welles was in; Hobby was out.

A series of pranks confronted the real-life Welles. Someone sent him a bearded ham; newspapers caricatured him as a wild boar and as a hairy caterpillar; a firm of Beverly Hills interior decorators had a black, crocheted, chenille snood delivered to his home; his tie was cut off in Chasen's restaurant; and on more than one occasion someone grabbed his facial hair and gave it a yank. As bosom jokes at that time always mentioned Mae West, all funny stories with bearded characters invariably were named Orson. Gene Lockhart, the actor and writer, composed a poem dedicated to "Little Orson Annie," which criticized the twenty-four-year-old's new involvement in film and mentioned his beard. The doggerel was published and the nickname stuck. Orson just kept on with the beard; he would shave it off when *he* was ready to do so.

Welles made a few attempts at the very beginning of his life in Hollywood to ingratiate himself, but when many prominent members of the movie colony invited to his first party failed to show up, he settled down to creating his own circle of friends among his Mercury staffers and the new people he was meeting at RKO. An article in *Vogue* sarcastically reported the inaugural party incident:

> He invited everyone who was anyone to partake of his hospitality. The lawn was full of butlers and food, music and lights—but nobody who was anybody came to Orson's party. In fact, nobody who was nobody. In short, nobody.

Despite the social sabotage, Welles and the technicians and executives at RKO started making preparations for *Heart of Darkness*. He was formally scheduled for day-long visits to all the studio's departments, one by one, to learn how their operations functioned and how a major studio assembled a feature film.

He spent time with the electrical people learning about the specific intensity of arcs and the effectiveness of back lighting; he talked with the art directors and heard about the science of perspective and ornamentation and architecture, and *trompe l'oeil* and fantasy backdrops. The special effects people explained the mysteries of matte and glass work, rear projection, and split screens. He learned that a gaffer was the chief electrician and that a grip was an assistant to the cameraman, on hand to move equipment. The editors discussed wipes and how rough cuts were assembled. The cameramen showed him how to accomplish tracking and panning and bridging shots with massive cameras and taught him what depth of focus was all about. From the optical department he learned of lap dissolves, and he had a marvelous time in the sound department, sitting at a console, watching and listening to the engineers mix a half-dozen various sounds into a single track. He fell in love with the sound library, or bank as it was called then, that contained a catalogued cornucopia of sound effects greater than any radio studio he had ever been in. One could find everything from a clanging trolley, fight noises, gun shots, crowd roars, dishes breaking, thunderstorms and dogs barking, to soft-falling snow and twelve variations of kisses, all of which could be synchronized to the action in the cutting room after shooting on the film had been completed.

A young and dedicated RKO employee named Miriam Geiger constructed a personally edited textbook of sorts for Orson: it consisted of a glossary of dozens of terms, such as "swish pan" and "fade out" and "extreme closeup," and various camera angles, put together with studio stills and sketches from the art department as illustrated examples, and also with actual pieces of film pasted into a space cut out of the page so that it could be held up to the light to be studied. For example, in explaining a Long Shot, there was a strip of seven frames of a shot of Westminster Tower and Big Ben, with the following information appended:

Long Shot
the country—the sky—the place—where you might wish your film to begin. A long, wide view, preferably with a recognizable landmark: the U.S.A.—the Statue of Liberty; Paris—the Eiffel Tower; London—Big Ben; San Francisco—the Bridge with the Pacific Ocean beyond.

Orson used the book constantly, adding to it and modifying it with other shots and notes whenever he spotted an unfamiliar visual technique, optical effect, or dramatic flourish, such as a hidden cut or a split screen. He insisted on analyzing such techniques with studio craftsmen and technicians until he understood how they were accomplished.

He had discussions with people from publicity, promotion, distribution, scheduling, budget, and foreign rights. He was a fast learner and constantly asked questions. Some people resented having to share their areas of knowledge with him; others became his friends, or at least cooperating colleagues. He seemed to love every aspect of the moviemaking craft and its technical and financial concerns. It was at this point that he made his famous and since oft-quoted statement: "This is the biggest electric train set a boy ever had!"

As he was refining the *Heart of Darkness* script, Welles and his associates began to screen several films a day, studying them for a variety of reasons. He looked at films of jungle or island themes that might contain some actual footage he could buy. Most of what he intended to do with *Heart of Darkness* would have to be original shooting, but if he could save time and money by using an already existing shot of a crocodile crawling into the river, or a quick glimpse at a sunset, for example, he had no objection.

He was interested in footage of the jungles of Siam and the elephant charge from a 1927 silent film, *Chang,* and he actually purchased the rights to the magnificently photographed footage of the hippo stampede from the 1929 silent version of *Four Feathers.* The Malayan plantation scenes of *Red Dust,* made in 1932, were considered a possibility; some of the jungle background from *Trader Horn,* shot in Africa in 1930 (the first such expedition by a major studio), was also considered. *Stanley and Livingstone,* with Spencer Tracy and Cedric Hardwicke, was viewed. The 1935 English film *Sanders of the River,* directed by Zoltán Korda and starring Paul Robeson and Leslie Banks, had some outstanding footage he thought he could use. He also examined such documentaries as *Dark Rapture, Isle of Bali, Wings over Africa,* and *South Seas.*

Peter Noble, the English journalist, observed that in addition to the films noted, Welles also screened pictures of such filmmakers as Hitchcock, Lang, Clair, Vidor, and Capra, "some of the most brilliant pieces of filmmaking turned out by Hollywood during the talking-film era."

The point of Welles's screening sessions was more thematic than practical. He wanted to absorb the grammar of the film, learn its syntax, understand how the great directors accomplished their ends. Everything that John Ford directed he wanted to see and study. His specific screening requests were for *Arrowsmith, The Whole Town's Talking, The Informer,* and *Stagecoach,* legend having it that he studied the last named as many as forty times. Using what critic André Bazin has called, "invisible editing," Ford created poetic moments of mood and picture with his camera. This continuous and seemingly effortless flow from scene to scene, and within scenes, was what arrested Welles. But that wasn't all that Welles received from his inquiry into and examination of Ford. He began to see the development of a nostalgia, a sentimentality, a romantic vision of history, that seemed to permeate all of the man's films; they were beginnings of what film historian Andrew Sarris once called a cinema of memory, and Welles, perhaps unconsciously, wanted membership. Studying Ford's films, he learned the value of maintaining authenticity of sets and costumes in each scene. The use of deep shadows, sometimes placing characters in silhouette, was another lesson. John Wayne's delayed and electrifying entrance in *Stagecoach* was noted, as was the way Ford's medleys of music captured the spirit of the image, whether it be humor, action or tension. Saddled with what seemed to Orson an impossibly tight budget to produce *Heart of Darkness,* it also helped to know that Ford had created *The Lost Patrol* and *The Informer* on extremely low budgets, both also for RKO and under the same prevailing attitudes: in fact Ford had to coax the studio to allow him to make both films. This was exactly what Welles was doing with *Heart of Darkness.* In an interview years later, he referred to Ford as one of the "old masters" and admitted: "John Ford was my teacher. My own style has nothing to do with his, but *Stagecoach* was my textbook."

Welles also studied the films of Jean Renoir at that time, specifically the fascinating *Les Bas-Fonds (The Lower Depths),* done in 1935, and *La Grande Illusion,* which appeared the following year. He admired Renoir's great warmth and sympathy in developing character and his motile, intimate camera, but in *La Grande Illusion* something else also caught his eye: the sensuous actress Dita Parlo, who played the peasant German girl. After then viewing *Mademoiselle Docteur,* a 1936 French film directed by Edmond Greville in which Dita Parlo also starred, and seeing her in Jean Vigo's *L'Atalante,* he decided she had the dark, European eroticism that he wanted. Dita Parlo would be the actress to play the female lead, Elsa, in *Heart of Darkness.*

Without violating the essence of Conrad's tale, Welles began making substantial changes in the story. He planned a series of unusual introductory sequences in order to educate and ease the viewer into a new visual experience. After the regular RKO trademark, a transmitter atop the world (the "Beeping Tower," as it was called by studio insiders) surrounded by clouds and sending out radio waves, followed by the title of the Mercury Theatre, Welles planned to fade out to a completely black screen. Then only his voice would fill the theater:

> Ladies and Gentlemen, this is Orson Welles. Don't worry. There's just nothing to look at for a while. You can close your eyes, if you want to, but—please open them when I tell you to. . . . First of all, I am going to divide this audience into two parts—you and everybody else in the theater. Now, then, open your eyes.

The darkened screen then brightens, by iris,* to the interior of a bird cage as it would appear to a bird who was inside, looking out. The image fills the entire screen. A huge mouth can be seen outside the bars. Welles speaks again:

> The big hole in the middle there is my mouth. You play the part of a canary. I'm asking you to sing and you refuse. That's the plot. I offer you an olive.

Gargantuan fingers appear from below the cage and thrust a huge olive through the bars toward the camera.

WELLES

You don't want an olive. This enrages me.
(Welles's chin moves down and his nose and eyes are revealed. He is scowling fiercely.)

WELLES

Here is a bird's-eye view of me being enraged. I threaten you with a gun.
(Now the muzzle of a pistol is stuck between the bars of the cage. It looks like a Big Bertha.)

WELLES

That's the way a gun looks to a canary. I give you to the count of three to sing.
(Welles's head moves up, showing his mouth on the words, "one, two, three." His voice is heard over echo chambers and the narration is synchronized on the count with the movement of his lips.)

WELLES

One—*(on normal level)*. That's the way I sound to you. You canary *(on echo again)*. Two—three *(normal level, cheerfully)*. You still don't want to sing so I shoot you.

---

*An old technique often used in silent films in which the camera lens opens or closes and the screen goes from an expanding or contracting circle, like the iris of the human eye.

The gun goes off with a cloud of smoke, a large bang, and a shower of brightly colored sparks. As this fades out, Welles says: "That's the end of the picture."

As the screen once again retreats to black, Welles's voice continues as he makes clear that the picture the audience is going to see is *not* about canaries and revolvers. He explains: "But I do want you to understand that you're part of the story. In fact, you are the star. Of course, you're not going to see yourself on the screen, but everything you see on the screen is going to be seen through your eyes and you're somebody else."

The introduction of camera as character continued with other experimental tableaux: a prisoner-camera-character being led down death row and then suffering electrocution; a human eye, Magritte-like, with clouds reflected in it, filling the entire screen and then transposing into the view of a golfer who hits a ball; an interior of a motion picture theater seen from Welles's perspective on the screen, so that all the members of the audience are cameras.

In Welles's script, the heart of darkness is no longer the Belgian Congo but a land of nowhere on an unidentifiable continent, a place of mystery. The part of Elsa, who appears only in the end of the novel, was enlarged. Instead of learning about Kurtz's fate at the denouement, Welles had her accompany Marlow up the river to help find him. She is virginal, sexy, full-bosomed, unfulfilled, and Marlow is in love with her. She is in love with Kurtz, but spends only a few moments with him at the end of the film. Kurtz has taken up with a beautiful native girl, "a real black type," as Welles described her in the script. (He was hoping that he could somehow get around the censor's objections to showing an interracial couple in loving embraces on the screen.)

As the boat travels up the river, it goes from savanna and open plains to woods, from woods to forests, and from forests to jungle, and as each step closer to Kurtz is made into the heart of this universe of obscurity and gloom, the film becomes less civilized, the natives less subdued, and the people in the boat closer to hysteria. When they finally reach Kurtz's compound, there is a spectacular fire with stampeding natives and animals, and then one of the most violent storms ever to be created on the screen, the inspiration for which Welles took from Conrad's *Typhoon*:

> It was something formidable and swift, like the sudden smashing of a Vial of Wrath. It seemed to explode all round the ship with an overpowering concussion and a rush of great waters, as if an immense dam had been blown up to windward. In an instant the men lost touch of each other. This is the disintegrating power of a great wind: it isolates one from one's kind. An earthquake, a landslip, an avalanche, overtake a man incidentally, as it were—without passion. A furious gale attacks him like a personal enemy, tries to grasp his limbs, fastens upon his mind, seeks to rout his very spirit out of him.

Everything in the film, like Kurtz himself, would be a bit off normal, a little oblique.

Welles planned few close-ups and no intercutting or reverse angles. The camera would pan from one subject or object to another without cuts or smears (the blurring effect of quickly moving the camera from one time period to another), with some scenes lasting as long as twelve minutes without a cut. In order to maintain this continuity of action the actors would have to know their lines perfectly and be thoroughly rehearsed. They must even be prepared to ad lib if necessary.

To cope with the technique of camera-as-character, Welles began making arrangements to have a double "finder" attached to the camera so that he, as director, would see *exactly* what the cameraman was seeing at all times. In many cases, a gyroscopic camera would be used, so that the camera-character could, without the jerkiness of a hand-held camera, appear to walk, stand up or sit down, go through doors, and in some cases even run.

As for the thematic approach to the film, Welles saw the characters in *Heart of Darkness* as representing a fascist mentality and morality, vicious and unintelligent, similar to the kind of people who were at that moment attempting to gain control of the world. Kurtz, to Welles, was the symbol of dictatorship. "The picture is, frankly, an attack on the Nazi system," Welles told his assistant, Herbert Drake.

KURTZ

Yes, that wasn't anarchy—it was law.

MARLOW'S VOICE

Whose law?

KURTZ

My law. They were traitors to the state.

MARLOW'S VOICE

Your state?

KURTZ

You're a foreigner, Marlow. Understand that our nation has no borders. Humanity depends on our race. Outside, there are ten thousand savages. Until I came, the most primitive of mankind.

MARLOW'S VOICE

And now?

KURTZ

Now they are enlightened, the tribes unified in the service of their leader.

MARLOW'S VOICE

Who pretends to be God.

KURTZ

The leader, the strong voice of authority, is the highest expression of our culture. The fulfillment of a superior race. I tell you, God is made in the image of man.

For the most part, casting proved to be fortuitous, if not simple. Most of Welles's Mercury staffers would play the same roles that they had on radio:

RKO had contracts negotiated with Edgar Barrier, Everett Sloane, Hiram Sherman, George Coulouris, Ray Collins, John Emery, Norman Lloyd, Erskine Sanford, Gus Schilling, and Frank Readick, all of whom were brought to Hollywood.

Everett Sloane would play the character Ernest Stitzler, a crow of a man with a long beard, who grabs for everything he can reach, a complete opportunist who has probably never uttered a true word in his life. Ray Collins was cast as Beaver, the head of the company: bland, round-faced, clean-shaven, with little blue eyes peering through thick-lensed glasses, an adventurer with the morality of a pirate, whose most important talent was the ability to stay alive.

Welles also wrote into the script a larger part for the steersman, which he wanted played by Jack Carter, his former Macbeth and Mephistopheles. Carter would play a faceless ferryman, a modern-day Charon guiding Virgil and Dante through the marshes of a contemporary version of Styx. Called "the half-breed," Carter was to be as proud as a wild, great beast, never understanding why he is so miserable. A contract for the part was signed between Carter and the studio.

Although eager to play the leading lady, Dita Parlo had difficulty getting out of France because of her German citizenship. While her theatrical agents in the United States were doing all they could to help her emigration, the people at RKO suggested to Welles that other actresses be approached in case she couldn't take the part. They were interested in having a star to act with Welles. Carole Lombard was offered the costarring role but declined.

Swedish actress Ingrid Bergman, who had recently come to Hollywood and who was awaiting the release of her first English-language film, *Intermezzo,* was available for the part. From advanced screenings, it looked as though in a matter of months she would be propelled into stardom, but her representatives asked a flat fee of $75,000. When RKO pointed out that $75,000 was more than Welles was getting for each picture, Bergman's spokesman reduced their demand to $50,000. It was still too much for RKO for five weeks of shooting. Welles's actors were not known on the screen, but they were Broadway stars, and they were being paid nowhere near the money Bergman was demanding. For a projected five weeks, Everett Sloane was to receive $600 a week; Ray Collins $750; and George Coulouris $1,000.

Other problems were beginning to plague the project. Welles had hoped that he might use the bayous of Louisiana for location shooting of the jungle scenes, but a studio representative, after traveling there, insisted that the transportation and maintenance of camera equipment in the muddy and humid swamps would have been too difficult.

Welles conducted some preliminary shootings of the characters in costume and makeup, with himself marvelously disguised as Kurtz and Marlow. A scene consisting of the boat and wharf in miniature, combined with rear-screen projection, was rehearsed by Everett Sloane as Stitzler talking to the camera-as-Marlow, with Welles's voice answering him.

There were also actorless rehearsals involving only the moving vision of Marlow-camera, such as a pan shot across a process screen, registering the hill and settlement. Welles's written directions said, "Now the key is moving, bringing the hill and settlement toward us, getting over the fact that Marlow is walking up the hill." Welles proclaimed the results "a dud," calling for more precision on everyone's part: the camera operators, the miniature technicians, the actors, and himself.

All the departments of RKO were working steadily on Welles's picture, and his elaborate miniatures, special effects, and lavish sets were beginning to elevate the original estimated expense of the film. A budget meeting was conducted, and a revised figure of $1,057,761 emerged.

In the midst of a project they felt could not be stopped, RKO officials approved the new figure, but with the admonition that nothing higher would be tolerated; in fact, they asked for a rescheduling and another calculation to see if the amount could somehow be lowered.

One of the biggest expenses in the budget for *Heart of Darkness* was Welles's request for 3,000 "natives" as extras. It was also an enormous problem in logistics as well as somewhat of a problem in ethics. The offices of the Central Casting Bureau reported to RKO that in the just-completed Johnny Weissmuller film, *Tarzan Finds a Son,* they could only supply about 500 "natives" and there was no reason to assume that figure could be increased. Welles was unconvinced. He also wanted extras with "very black skin," a rarity in Hollywood at that time. Lighter-skinned black actors were much more available, but their employment caused an increased financial burden. Extras were paid $8.25 a day, but in order to achieve a realistic native look, the lighter extras had to spend additional time in the makeup department being covered with black greasepaint. As a result, they had to be paid $11.00 a day. Some producers, such as those for *Stanley and Livingstone,* in order to avoid this $11.00 fee, kept the lighter-skinned natives in the background, a solution that Welles could not or would not work out in his script.

Even if Welles could somehow locate his 3,000 extras, the sequences in which they were to be used would cost in excess of $150,000, a figure that the RKO financial office considered ridiculously excessive. Under pressure, Welles reduced the number of natives needed to 800, and eventually a revised estimated budget of $984,620 was released. A plea to Welles from everyone at RKO to cut out or shorten some scenes was greeted with a promise of cooperation.

The Motion Picture Production Code censorship group, known as the "Hays Office" after its chief administrator Will Hays, read the preliminary script and offered their feelings and opinions. Although stating that the basic story "seems to meet the requirements of the production code," they had a number of objections that they considered minor. The value judgments were so difficult to understand that Welles needed a combination Talmudic scholar, mathematician, and Supreme Court justice to decipher them. Some of the suggestions:

In the introductory scene, the gun could not be pointed and fired directly at the audience; the prisoner could not be shown in an electric chair that appeared to be realistic. Care had to be taken with the costumes of the natives. No bare breasts, of course, and no highly abbreviated clothing, as to show too much skin, could be used. All phrases such as "Thank God!", "My God!" and "For God's sake," had to be deleted. They recommended that a scene with a snake be reduced in length and impact, "because of the bad effect such scenes almost always have on mixed audiences." It was recommended that any direct references to Kurtz being "insane" should be deleted. Although the scene with human heads posted on poles dripping with blood was permitted, the censors warned Welles about not using "undo gruesomeness." Finally, in the scenes between Kurtz and the native girl, no intimation of miscegenation could be hinted.

All Welles could do was laugh, then groan, when he read the censorship memorandum; it was his abrupt initiation into how little freedom directors really had in Hollywood: in dealing with the censors, everything seemed so irremediably, if obscurely, wrong. (No attempt was made legally to force motion picture producers to comply with MPAA's production code but those that did defy it would find their films able to exhibit in only about 500 of the 18,000 theaters in the United States.) As Welles began to make the script changes that were demanded by Hays, more comments arrived from Schaefer. He had spent a weekend on his boat reading the script, and he thought it contained too much dialogue. The story, he said, was mystifying and unusual enough in itself without Welles's connecting it to the growing dictatorship in Europe. "When Kurtz begins to talk of dictators in Europe, you are tying in one world with another world," Schaefer wrote to Welles. "At that point it loses something."

Welles was the model of docility when he received Schaefer's comments. He felt that the picture was getting away from him; that the casting, censorship, and budgetary problems were pushing his producing capacities to the limit; but if the film did die aborning, he wanted it to be known that he had cooperated with the studio to the fullest. He wired Schaefer: "HONESTLY AGREE WITH ALL POINTS IN YOUR LETTER. URGE YOU TO BURN THAT SCRIPT, AND BELIEVE THAT REWRITES AND REVISIONS UNDERWAY WILL ACCOMPLISH EVERYTHING AND MORE THAN YOU ASKED FOR."

The death knell for *Heart of Darkness* began to sound as the world situation continued to worsen. RKO's foreign distribution had been energetic and successful in almost every European country, but by the fall of 1939, it began to decline considerably. Only 40 percent of the movie theaters in England remained open, and with a six o'clock curfew in the inner area of London and a ten o'clock curfew in the outlying districts, the number of scheduled film performances was drastically reduced. It was already impossible to get money out of France, and although theaters were open in Paris and some of the other larger cities, many of these were being used for mobilization and training purposes. When films were shown, attendance would invariably be sparse: people were afraid to congregate in groups for fear of a bombing. Some theaters advertised on their marquees, "Air Raid Shelter for Audience." Later, during the height of the war, despite the danger, Parisian movie theaters were usually crowded: it was one of the few places in which one could keep warm.

Schaefer informed Welles that, because of the shrinking market, he would have to maintain a $500,000 budget on *Heart of Darkness*. He told Welles, "RKO would have lost money on every important picture in the last five years if we eliminated the markets of Great Britain, France and Poland." Monetary restrictions had already occurred with New Zealand and Australia, and it appeared that such limitations would also be soon imposed in England. Schaefer made a personal plea in writing to Welles to "eliminate . . . every dollar, and for that matter, every nickel possible from the *Heart of Darkness* script and yet do everything to save the entertainment value."

Welles's response was respectful and optimistic. He immediately cut two sequences from the script, and in a communiqué to Schaefer he promised that "Every cent will be counted twice in *Heart of Darkness*: no single luxury will be indulged, only absolute essentials to effectiveness and potency of story." That the budget for such an inventive project could *not* be kept to a half million dollars while still maintaining the integrity of the concept was nobody's fault.

On request from Schaefer, a respected leader from the RKO story department, William Koenig, offered his opinion: "Conrad is not so much of a story-teller as he is a philosopher and the fact that he is called 'the artist-philosopher' is the clue to the success of his stories. They are beautiful as a painting is beautiful, because of his use of words. There is no use looking for a story, in the screen sense of the word, here. This is not one of Mr. Conrad's best stories. He is wholly concerned here with building up a philosophical and mystical picture of a man who is a mystery to the readers of the story even at the story's end . . ."

Schaefer's business sense began to overrule his promotional flair, and much to the disappointment and chagrin of Welles, who disagreed with Koenig's report and believed that such a story *could* be told on the screen, eventually *Heart of Darkness* was canceled.

BEFORE THE OFFICIAL rejection of the *Heart of Darkness* project occurred, Welles had convinced Schaefer, at a luncheon in New York, to allow him to proceed on *The Smiler with a Knife,* the story of a newlywed couple who stumble on a secret organization that intends to take over England. Welles changed the locale to the United States, and in an attempt to give what seemed to be a routine thriller some vitality, he added satire and sophisticated humor to the script. The major character, Chilton, who could be played by Welles, became a sort of antihero, like Nick Charles of the *Thin Man* series.

The theme was political and controversial, but not enough so that Schaefer was worried about it. Another character in the film is "W. N. Howells, the great newspaper publisher, also to be avoided in dark alleys," as Welles described him in his notes. He showed Schaefer about 65 percent of the completed script on which he alone had worked since coming to Hollywood, and offered a tentative budget of $359,000. The entire film could be shot in about thirty days, Welles contended. Orson suggested that the studio attempt to convince Carole Lombard to play the leading lady in *Smiler.* He included a salary of $75,000 for her in his budget, just in case. If she was adamant about not working with him, Welles thought either Rosalind Russell or Lucille Ball would be ideal substitutions.

One of the cinematic innovations Welles planned to use in *Smiler* was a newsreel sequence based on *The March of Time,* showing the decaying world situation; as the segment ends, the camera tracks back from a movie screen in the film to show the young couple seated in a smoky theater, after having just watched the movie.

As budget, banking, and scheduling meetings were begun for *Smiler,* Welles and the studio scouts continued to look for other film ideas or existing properties for his second film. Schaefer sent Welles a synopsis of Kaufman and Hart's play *The Man Who Came to Dinner,* for possible consideration. This phenomenal success on Broadway was a hilarious comedy about a cantankerous character named Sheridan Whiteside who was based on the real-life personality of Alexander Woollcott. Moss Hart had once promised that he would write a play in which Woollcott could star, but after reading some of the work in progress, Woollcott felt it more caricature than characterization and suggested the stage role be given to Robert Morley or Orson Welles, both of whom were unavailable at the time. It finally went to an ex-Yale professor, Monty Woolley.

The idea of a film based on *The Man Who Came to Dinner* attracted Welles, but the character wasn't as large in theme or in scale as he had wanted. Also, if he directed and starred in the *The Smiler with a Knife,* a relatively lighthearted film, for his Hollywood debut, he wanted to follow it up with something more impressive, perhaps even stately. And, too, he wanted a story in which he could try some of the film experiments he had planned for *Heart of Darkness.*

Two of Welles's most creatively successful and popular radio broadcasts had been *Jane Eyre* and *The Pickwick Papers.* Both had fine parts for Welles—Edward Rochester in *Jane Eyre* and Mr. Samuel Pickwick himself —but the film rights were not available.

Welles talked of creating a Renaissance spectacle by doing a life of Leonardo da Vinci, or perhaps Girolamo Savonarola. Orson also registered the title *The Life of Machiavelli* with the Motion Picture Producers Association as a possible film to direct and in which to star.

Welles wanted to recreate on the screen the era of the Italian Renaissance, the intrigue of the city-states, the days of the commercial princes and the anti-popes, the cultural revolution whose artists, scholars, poets, and craftsmen were encouraged and supported. All of the color, violence, romance, and explosive change of the times would help his immense filmic schemes, he believed.

Another title registered was *The Life of Alexandre Dumas*. Dumas's life had, according to Welles, "no reasonable explanation," and he was intrigued with this grandson of a marquis and a black woman, born to wealth as Napoleon became emperor, dying in poverty as the Germans marched into France, a wild romantic who maintained numerous sexual relationships well into his seventies.

Welles considered literally hundreds of other ideas, a virtual cafeteria of stories. He secured film rights, for example, to *The Fair God* by Lew Wallace (author of *Ben Hur*), the story of Cortez and his invasion of the Aztec empire, which he planned to rename *Cortez and the Conquest of Mexico*. The Borgias greatly interested him, and he thought of playing the dual roles of Cesare and his father, Pope Alexander VI, in a film to be named *The Borgias and Their Times*. But he seemed to be unable to get anything going.

DURING THE FALL and winter of 1939 and into the spring of 1940, Welles continued to make sincere attempts to relate to the movie industry socially, creatively, and economically. He arrived in Hollywood during the last year of its Golden Age, when one could still see long Rolls-Royces and Marmon touring cars, driven by chauffeurs with plum-colored livery, stopping at fruit juice and snack stands in the shape of huge cuckoo clocks, igloos, lighthouses, frogs, countless lemons and oranges, and an occasional banana.

The era of Hollywood opulence and ostentation was still alive: some men still wore handkerchiefs monogrammed in diamonds; there were neon lights atop stucco palaces and medieval castles only a few hundred yards from Sunset Boulevard; swimming pools were so large that, when one was being filled, the water pressure of the county of Los Angeles dropped; the film colony escaped to lush villas and *palazzi* in Malibu; writers were making tens of thousands of dollars a year without ever having a script produced; autographs of Garbo sold for $25 each, a week's salary for most of the nation; Gloria Swanson turned down a five-year contract for $22,500 a week; 255,000 people were employed in an industry that was spending some 125 million dollars a year in motion picture production.

Despite his attempts at being friendly, Welles began to criticize the glitz and glitter of the town as an institution and a way of life, a place where, as someone once said, the inhabitants knew only two words of English: "swell" and "lousy." He made friends with some of the European exiles who had just settled in California—Fritz Lang, Thomas Mann, Jean Renoir—but he considered the town hopelessly unsophisticated.

Soon after his arrival in Hollywood, he was invited to a party to celebrate Aldous Huxley's forty-fifth birthday and also the completion of Huxley's latest novel, *After Many a Summer Dies the Swan,* a book that was eagerly awaited by film people since it dealt with the movie colony. It was a fantasy, the story of a multimillionaire who owned studios and stars and yet retreated to his huge, moated Gothic castle with a special Louis XV boudoir for his child-mistress. The house in the novel became more than just a symbol of the man: it was *all* he was, all he wanted out of life, a Xanadu or a Shangri-la. As Huxley described it:

> About a half a mile from the foot of the mountains, like an island off a cliff-bound coast, a rocky hill rose abruptly, in places almost precipitously from the plain. On the summit of the bluff and as though growing out of it in a kind of efflorescence, stood a castle. But what a castle! The donjon was like a sky-scraper, the bastions plunged headlong with the effortless swoop of concrete dams. The thing was Gothic, medieval, baronial, doubly baronial, Gothic with a Gothicity raised, so to speak, to a higher power, more medieval than any building of the thirteenth century.

Everyone was talking about the book and whether it had any possibility of being made into a film. The consensus was that it didn't stand a chance: its lack of reverence for Hollywood was too obvious and it was also too close to a profile of newspaper magnate William Randolph Hearst and his fabled mansion, San Simeon, where, Orson noted, Huxley had been a guest.

Helen Hayes and Charles MacArthur, Christopher Isherwood, and Lillian Gish were also at the party, as was Charlie Chaplin who, like Huxley, was preparing a *roman à clef* about another famous man of power, Adolf Hitler. Chaplin talked of his forthcoming film, which would be his first in four years and was mysteriously referred to as Production #6 (later it became *The Great Dictator*) and which he intended to start filming the following week.

Chaplin's wife, Paulette Goddard, brought an eight-pound white cake inscribed *Mon Coeur,* and Charlie provided a case of exquisitely dry *Cordon Rouge,* a dozen bottles of Mumm's champagne. Later, he gave a sneak preview of a brilliantly funny dance—with a balloon version of a globe—he was going to do in *The Great Dictator.* Hitler, known as Hynkel in the film and played by Chaplin, loves his globe: "My vorld, my vorld," he says affectionately to it. The denouement occurs when the balloon world explodes.

Orson quietly observed all the attention given to the abuse of power as a creative theme.

HE HATED HOLLYWOOD. Flying to New York for his radio broadcast once each week (usually late on Thursday for a rehearsal the next day and then the broadcast on Friday night) gave Welles the feeling that he was a transient, and he would often claim in later years that he was actually living in New York during the time that his permanent and legal residence was in California. His distaste for Hollywood had less to do with his already growing difficulties with producing his first picture than with an aesthetic nostalgia for the East and aversion to the land of gauche and plenty. He once described his feelings about Los Angeles in an article in *Esquire:*

The metropolitan air is what one misses. Neither the theater nor its artists are at their best work in a suburb. Or a gigantic trailer camp. Whether we work before a camera or behind the footlights, actors are, by nature, city people. Hollywood is most precisely described as a colony. (Colonies are notoriously somewhat cut off from reality, insular, bitchy and cliquish, snobbish—a bit loose as to morals but very strict as to appearances.) One expects a colony to be an outpost of civilization (a word which means, after all "city culture") but it's also the heart of its own empire of the movies; a capital without city, yet among its colonies are numbered the great cities of the world. . . . Hollywood is a way station on a highway. Drive as far as you like in any direction: wherever you find yourself, it looks exactly like the road to an airport. Any road to any airport.

Welles's lament for seedy old Times Square with its circusy bars and restaurants seemed to have its roots in the Middle Ages. Somehow, one could always find a congenial tavern in the theater district of Manhattan that was evocative of Falstaff's Boar's Head. In Los Angeles, he felt, all you could find was another country club.

Toward the end of the year, Welles was asked if he would narrate the RKO film *The Swiss Family Robinson*. Technically it would be in violation of his contract to work on another film, but everybody ignored the legalities and he did it anyway. Since the studio was already paying him what they considered a fortune, he did the narration for the wages of an extra: $25 per day.

Spending a partially white Christmas in New York that year was a delight for him. But after doing his Christmas Eve show—*A Christmas Carol*—this time with Lionel Barrymore in his rightful role as Scrooge and Welles as narrator, he was forced to fly back immediately to the dazzling sunburst of a city where he was trying to ease *The Smiler with a Knife* into production. He found himself at a Christmas party, on a dreary afternoon at one of Hollywood's fantasy castles, standing under an all-pink Christmas tree and sipping champagne. It was there, feeling incongruous, lonely, and angry, that he met for the first time one of the most significant figures in the history of motion pictures, D. W. Griffith.

Griffith was back in Hollywood, after a long absence, acting as an adviser to the Hal Roach production of *One Million B.C.* Reports initially issued by Roach indicated that Griffith was to direct the film, his first in almost a decade, but the reality was that the producers only wanted to exploit his name. When he learned the truth, and since he never directed a scene of the film, he had his name removed and divorced himself from it entirely.

The irony in the meeting of these two men of different generations was overwhelming: one yet to make his first film, the other never to make one again; one whose potential work was being solicited and coveted and about to propel himself into a new era of filmmaking, the other who had become an image of Victorian sensibilities, *silenced* as the case may be, because of his silents; one who really knew nothing about films, and the other who knew everything; one who was thought to be too young to make films and the other who was thought to be too old. They were together only in their bitterness and antagonism toward the same industry: one for not allowing him to express the things he wanted to invent, the other for not understanding and accepting the things he did invent.

"We stared at each other across a hopeless abyss," Welles has remembered. He was a great admirer of the man and his films, but Griffith wanted an opportunity to direct again, not a chance to enlist a new disciple. In an attempt to reach him, Welles tried to express what the older man meant to him and the art of film. He wasn't just talking about the first intelligent and extended use of the close-up, the moving camera, or the other Griffith touches that enlightened the art of cinema. The attempt to communicate failed "dismally," as Welles described it. The older man was courteous, but obviously affronted. "There was no place for Griffith," Welles said. "He was an exile in his own town, a prophet without honor, a craftsman without tools, an artist without work. No wonder he hated me."

WELLES CONTINUED TO do innovative broadcasting for the "Campbell Playhouse" during the fall and winter of 1939 and the spring of 1940, but gone were the halcyon days when Campbell was his new employer and its representatives respectful of his reputation as the preeminent radio personality of the day. Now, after twenty shows, the sponsors began to exercise more authority on the details and philosophy of what they wanted for the program. Whenever the ratings sagged, there was a rise in the amount of sniping and criticism. A new account executive from the Ward Wheelock agency, Diana Bourbon, was appointed as liaison between Welles and the sponsor. She acted as producer-in-fact, and she was not afraid of offering Welles, "often somewhat undiplomatically," as he described them, whatever comments she felt like making. She was intelligent, well-read, aggressive, thoroughly self-assured, and possessed an uncanny knowledge of show business and theatrical matters of all kinds.

It was a difficult time for Welles. Campbell had complete control over story selection and content. Welles's suggestions for stories to be broadcast were always considered but often not accepted, usually with the excuse, sometimes valid, that the rights could not be secured. For example, he wanted to do radio dramatizations of *Country Lawyer, Days Before Lent, Ladies and Gentlemen, Rogue Male, April Was When It Began, Wuthering Heights, The Little Foxes,* and *Smilin' Through,* none of which could be arranged.

Campbell made it stringently clear to Welles from the beginning of the season, by way of a formal memorandum, that they were interested, for the most part, in lightweight stories that would take the listener's mind off all the talk of war. Most of the shows, therefore, were such amiable classics as *The Adventures of Huckleberry Finn, Vanity Fair, Lost Horizon, It Happened One Night, Mr. Deeds Goes to Town, Dodsworth,* and *Dinner at Eight.*

After flying to New York for a number of the shows, Welles found that, even though he enjoyed the weekly trip back East, the demands upon him at

RKO made the flight increasingly difficult to manage. However, when he began arrangements to have the show originate from Los Angeles, Campbell was incensed and threatened an injunction to make him continue the shows from New York. Their argument was that "The Lux Playhouse," their principal airtime competition, originated from Hollywood and reflected that image. The agency and sponsors for Campbell's Soups wanted the "Campbell Playhouse" to reflect the opposite: the sophistication of Broadway, with an image of theater, plays, and the Great White Way. Welles insisted that originating the show in Hollywood was not in violation of his contract and that most listeners would assume the show was coming from New York anyway. Finally Campbell relented, and the switch was made.

Welles desperately wanted to do a radio dramatization of a George Bernard Shaw play—any play of his would be acceptable—and the sponsors agreed to either *Pygmalion* or *The Doctor's Dilemma.* Shaw himself, however, refused permission for the former and demanded for the latter that, if broadcast, "not one word" was to be cut. Since the radio show ran only fifty-five minutes and the play ran twice that long, Welles was forced to abandon his Shavian plans.

He wanted to do an adaptation of *Algiers,* the highly successful film starring Charles Boyer and Hedy Lamarr. He had heard the "Woodbury Playhouse" adaptation of it in the fall of 1938, with Boyer playing his film role, and was convinced he could generate a more meaningful production. Although the sponsors were doubtful about the popularity of a remade radio show, the rights were secured, and Welles went on to produce his most ambitious broadcast to that date.

He requested the lovely Miss Lamarr to play her original part as the Parisian Gaby. Welles himself would play the astute and suave jewel thief, Pépé le Moko, known for uttering one of the most imitated lines in all of film history: "Come wiz me to zee Casbah." MGM, however, refused to permit Hedy Lamarr to appear on the radio, privately citing two reasons: first, they felt that her great appeal was as a beauty, but that she lacked acting ability. Secondly, many of MGM's exhibitors throughout the country were complaining that when movie stars appeared on the radio, there was a direct decrease in attendance at that star's films. Theater owners contended that if you heard Katharine Hepburn on the radio Sunday night, for example, you wouldn't go to see her in a film on Monday. Eventually, theater owners began to understand that radio could promote their films, and no such embargos on stars continued.

Welles requested and was given Paulette Goddard as a substitute. The evil character Shimane had been played by Joseph Calleia in the film, but he, too, was unavailable. The radio version was acted by Welles's old standby Ray Collins.

One of the more remarkable aspects of the film was its depiction of the crooked and winding streets of Algiers's Casbah and their insidious influence on Pépé, establishing a conflict within him between the Casbah, an intricate maze of evil that afforded him safety, and his beloved Paris.

Welles wanted to use his aural re-creation of the Casbah as he would a character; so the sound effects of the calls and cries of the streets and the exotic music were developed far beyond the norm for a radio drama. He also went through four full scripts, juggling and sharpening dialogue and reducing the ninety-minute film down to fifty-five minutes with, according to him, "only a few lines excised."

Although he was delighted with the resulting broadcast, the sponsors were not, calling it "overproduced" and complaining that the sound imagery of the Casbah was, as Diane Bourbon put it, "just too damn much." Welles disagreed, of course, and held that the Casbah scenes were a brilliant solution to a complicated plot. He also claimed that Walter Wanger, the producer of the film *Algiers,* told him that the radio version had been better in exposition and construction than his movie. Fan mail was up, and it was all positive, Welles reported; if the sponsors disliked *Algiers,* then they were virtually the only listeners in the country who did.

That wasn't all: in introducing Paulette Goddard, Welles had given her husband, Charlie Chaplin, a long plug for his forthcoming film, the lacerating fable then publicly known as *The Great Dictator.* "We're not in the business of giving away free commercials," complained one of the sponsor's representatives. Welles fired back a countermemorandum to the agency: "Please remember that whatever gives our format individuality beyond regular interest attaching itself to our guest is my own, extremely personal, rather particular, style which *must* needs express, authentically, my own enthusiasm and tastes."

For the eighth show of the season, no story had been secured, either because rights had been refused or because they were too expensive. The sponsors, therefore, wanted to do an adaptation of one story they knew they could get, Booth Tarkington's Pulitzer Prize winning novel, *The Magnificent Ambersons.* Welles had read and liked the book, which was about the era of American life that he loved the best: the Midwest at the turn of the century, a time and place he was just a shade too young to remember but very much wanted to understand. But there was another dramatic and sensitive story that intrigued him even more, the film *Of Human Hearts,* and he wanted that inserted into the existing radio slot. Released by MGM in 1938, *Of Human Hearts* starred Walter Huston, James Stewart, Beulah Bondi, and Charles Coburn. It was the story of a fanatical minister, played by Huston, who denies his son, James Stewart, permission to become a doctor. The boy secretly enters medical school but then leaves to enlist in the Union army. He fails to write home, and his mother sends a message to President Lincoln. Lincoln contacts the boy, ordering him to write home weekly, which he does thereafter, chastened. He returns after the war with the family horse, Pilgrim, whom he has doctored to health after finding him on the battlefield. His mother had sold the horse to pay for his education.

Welles wanted to play two parts in *Of Human Hearts*: that of the son *and* Abraham Lincoln. He telegrammed the agency stating his preferences, "THE MAGNIFICENT AMBERSONS IS EXCELLENT BUT OF HUMAN

HEARTS SUPERLATIVE." The response was somewhat disheartening: the sponsors had seen *Of Human Hearts* and didn't like it. *The Magnificent Ambersons* it would be.

Booth Tarkington's epic novel is about the decline of a wealthy midwestern family and the eventual "comeuppance" of its scion son. But it also deals with the price of technological progress and the contamination of a medium-sized city as a result of the influence of the automobile and other advances of the twentieth century.

Welles said he would do his best with the radio script for *The Magnificent Ambersons,* and he worked on it personally until he had what he wanted. Some of the deeper resonances of Welles's life come from the sweet, small-town, middle-American ethos, and he began to see similarities between the Tarkington story and his own life. The character of Eugene Morgan, a developer and inventor, who has a principal part in the story, was similar in many respects to that of Welles's father.* Walter Huston met with Orson at the Knickerbocker Hotel to discuss the part, and at the same time Welles quietly auditioned Huston's wife, Nan Sunderland, whom he contracted to play the part of the lovely Isabel Minafer.

There were severe aesthetic limitations imposed in reducing the 140,000-word novel down to less than an hour of airtime. In order to develop the part of Eugene Morgan and Isabel Minafer to the fullest, and to retain a substantial role for George Amberson Minafer (played by Welles) he deleted the covetous Aunt Fanny altogether. Marion Burns, one of the Mercury radio staffers, played Lucy and Ray Collins was Uncle Fred Amberson.

Somehow, even without Aunt Fanny, one of its most crucial characters, and Wilbur Minafer, the father, who is also nonexistent in the radio script, Welles still was able to develop the narrative of the story: Eugene Morgan's bass-viol incident; the ball at which George meets Lucy; the tableau in the country snow where the carriage overturns; Georgie's discovery that his mother has affection for Eugene; the rebuff of Eugene; and Isabel's death. The final scene in the hospital where Eugene comes to accept Georgie is an almost exact duplication of Tarkington's language: "For then, I knew I had been true to you at last, my true love. And that, through me, you had brought your boy under shelter again."

Since the show did not originate in New York, the musical services of Bernard Herrmann were not available. Nevertheless, working with a staff conductor, Welles made exceptional use of music in the broadcast of *The Magnificent Ambersons:* lovely, soft, slow-sweeping strings, evocative of a gentility long past; short, light piano and flute duets in scenes of intimacy; and for the horse-drawn buggy episode, a bright, circusy fanfare with trumpets blaring, symbolic of Georgie's brashness. In the novel the characters had sung "The Star Spangled Banner" and the "Blue Danube" when they were all together in Eugene's "machine," but Welles felt the moment was more

*Years later, Welles claimed that the Eugene Morgan character was actually based on his father; it is possible, since Booth Tarkington and Richard Welles did know each other.

expansive and joyful, so he changed the melody to "The Man Who Broke the Bank at Monte Carlo." Walter Huston played the part of Eugene Morgan with subtlety, gentleness, depth, and a voice that was barely above a whisper. George Amberson Minafer's age was close to Welles's own, but his characterization of the young boy, using a higher voice than his normal one, was not particularly convincing. *The Magnificent Ambersons* was not necessarily the most popular of Welles's Campbell radio shows, but its evocation of a faded, aristocratic life stirred him and it remained one of his personal favorites.

The sponsors continued to put pressure on Welles's creative approach to the broadcasts. He wanted fine actresses to work with, not necessarily movie stars, but when he suggested such people as Eva LeGallienne, Geraldine Fitzgerald, Miriam Hopkins, and Lynn Fontanne, the sponsors came back with names like Irene Dunne, Marie Wilson, Dorothy Lamour, and Carole Landis. He wanted to do *The Philadelphia Story* with Katharine Hepburn, but the idea was stymied by the sponsors for no offered reason. Often he was criticized for trying to get his friends parts on the broadcasts, and when, half in jest, he mentioned that his selection of beautiful actresses was not "disinterested," he unknowingly enraged both agency and sponsor. At that time he did a remake broadcast of *The Fall of the City* for the "Columbia Workshop," and even though he was contractually free to do so (he could make three non-Campbell appearances) the sponsors became angry, claiming he was doing "too much."

Diana Bourbon's weekly critiques were difficult for him to accept. Once she wrote to Ernest Chappel, the announcer of the "Campbell Playhouse" and the sponsor's representative in Hollywood, who had liked a show that Bourbon had hated, warning him to be careful of Welles. "Orson sings a siren song to anybody that will listen," she wrote to Chappel. "Don't be hypnotized by him. He's dangerous."

Welles heard about the memo and became incensed. As a point of honor he attempted to defend his affronted pride and Chappel's opinions: "I have not charmed him. I have not befuddled him with soft music and lotus," he wrote. Bourbon was unconvinced: "You hypnotize in spite of yourself," she snapped. "You can't help it." Welles was honest in his self-appraisal, denying any hypnotic suasion over anybody but admitting to other flaws: "My fault as a personality, as you must know, is that I'm somewhat arbitrarily inclined and often unreasonable."

By the time the contract for the Campbell broadcast was coming to an end in March 1940, Welles knew there was little chance that the sponsor would renew, despite the fact that they were selling more soup, as they announced on the air, than ever before. And even if Campbell had shown interest, Welles would not have signed for another season. "I'm sick of having the heart torn out of a script by radio censorship," he contended, feeling the restrictions of cast and story were too formidable for him to confront week after week.

Just a short time before the show ended, the question of what story to use as the final broadcast had still not been settled. After having done two Tarkington stories on radio, *Clarence* and *The Magnificent Ambersons,* and having enjoyed doing both of them, Welles suggested as a possibility to end the season by doing another, perhaps *Alice Adams,* a masterpiece of small-town Americana about a lonely girl who finally finds the man she loves. If it could be secured, then he wanted Ginger Rogers for the title part, since Katharine Hepburn, who had played the film role, was at that moment unavailable and Rogers was "the only top-ranking star capable of doing a good job" with the part, according to Welles. But he also offered another suggestion if the rights for *Alice Adams* could not be secured or interest in the property could not be generated: a repeat of *Jane Eyre.*

He felt more than comfortable in the role of Edward Rochester—he believed he virtually owned the part—and thought that Vivien Leigh would make a perfect Jane. He suggested that it would be nice if he were permitted to do a role that gave *him* something worthwhile for the last show, and perhaps as a terminal gesture of friendship, the sponsor agreed. *Jane Eyre* was a masterful finale, and Welles ended his sixty-one-week relationship with Campbell on an amicable note.

CLOSE TO A year had passed since Welles arrived in Hollywood, and he had yet to begin filming his first picture. The cancellation of *Heart of Darkness* left him still searching for a film subject. *The Smiler with a Knife* was beginning to bore him and disinterest Schaefer, not because it would not have been a successful film, but for more visceral reasons. A shooting date of December 1, 1939, had come and gone without a camera being cranked or a female lead established. Dr. Richard Jewell, in his dissertation on the history of RKO, offers a possible explanation of why *The Smiler with a Knife* was abandoned: "Since the story has strong political overtones, one might suspect that George Schaefer quashed it because of his disinclination to deal with anything of that nature. However, the truth is that Welles and Schaefer decided against production. The problem related to expectations—the expectations of the public, the industry, the critics regarding Welles' initial motion picture."

ALTHOUGH WELLES SEEMED no closer to his cinema debut, he was making moves in his private life.

He had been unfaithful to Virginia all throughout the period that they lived in Sneden's Landing and continued his infidelity from almost the first day he arrived in Hollywood. The starlets and stars and singers and sirens of tinseltown were all temptations to him, and he freely engaged in one extramarital affair or brief encounter after the other in rapid succession.

Virginia was hurt and furious about the shenanigans and when I interviewed her, I sensed that she still never quite forgave him after decades of parting. "I really *liked* Orson," Virginia told me. "But it was always another woman coming between us." They legally separated in December 1939, five years to the day that they were married. Christopher Welles was barely two years old.

Aside from Orson's dalliances, which were constantly being touted in the Hollywood gossip columns, and throughout the social set of the motion picture community, all of which made its way back to Virginia, she was most deeply hurt to discover that Orson had actually fallen in love with someone else, movie actress Dolores Del Rio.

Virginia had waited out and survived Orson's love affairs in New York, but she began to understand he was resolute to his devotion to Dolores Del Rio. In terms of the time that he was spending with Virginia and the baby, almost none, the marriage was over in any event. Virginia felt she could not endure any more private or public humiliation and demanded a formal separation. Lawyers for both sides were immediately introduced into the situation.

Orson welcomed the possibility of a divorce then and quickly agreed, at first, to child support that was quite generous in those days of the Depression. Among other things, he would pay all the expenses for the future divorce; half of Virginia's rent; and $1,200 a month alimony. To the press, Virginia offered a stiff upper lip: "I can't keep up with him," she said. "He's a genius and sometimes works around the clock without sleep. He has no time for marriage and a family."

By February of the next year, 1940, Virginia was in Reno, and after qualifying for residency requirements, she and Orson were divorced on the grounds of mental cruelty (although after the decree was final, she said Orson wasn't cruel at all—just that matrimony and his career didn't mix).

EVER SINCE HER BARE-BREASTED (except for a lei) photograph had appeared in color on a 1932 cover of the *Evening Graphic,* Dolores Del Rio had been on Orson's mind. She was publicized and thought of by many as "the most beautiful woman in the world." She was a diminutive brown-eyed Mexican debutante with an aristocratic background, and married to Cedric Gibbons.*

Dolores Del Rio arrived in Hollywood at the age of twenty, appeared in many silent films *(What Price Glory?, The Loves of Carmen, and High Stepper* are three), and then learned almost flawless English to make the transition to talking pictures. In many ways she was one of the belles of the golden Hollywood era, moving in the society of Rudolph Valentino and Pola Negri, Douglas Fairbanks and Mary Pickford.

Orson met her during his first weeks in Hollywood, at a dual birthday party for her and Jack Warner. Ann Warner introduced them and, although both Orson and Dolores were married, it was apparently a case of spontaneous combustion. Although ten years his senior, she seemed to possess most of the things Orson felt a woman should have: extreme beauty, intelligence, sophistication, a love of the arts, and independent wealth.

Sunday afternoons were spent picnicking in the Hollywood hills, Orson with an easel and canvas painting the surrounding countryside and recuperating from his hangovers. Dinners and evenings out were almost all formal affairs; she lived in one of Hollywood's most luxurious homes and entertained lavishly. ("She lives so graciously," Orson observed at that time. "Eating is a

---

*Codirector of one film, *Tarzan and His Mate,* and designer of the "Oscar" statue for the Academy Awards.

great ceremony with Dolores. She would make it important even if she were dining in a one-arm lunchroom.") But her home was far from a lunchroom decor. Its furnishings reflected the elegance, and the personality, of Del Rio. Hanging on a wall was a huge portrait of the actress that had been painted by her friend, renowned Mexican muralist Diego Rivera, which captured her dark, wide-eyed beauty.

Their quarrels were as frequent as their scenes of rapport, however. They disagreed on such things as ballet (she did not prefer the classical form); jazz (Orson, yes; Dolores, no); and alcohol (she was practically a teetotaler). And as an echo of his relationship with Virginia, they too, had more serious disputes about Orson's long hours spent at work and his occasional dates with other women. Despite these difficulties, after they both were divorced, they "unofficially" announced their engagement in the fall of 1940.

The press, for a year, had been openly skeptical about the cinematic potential of the "boy wonder," and when no announcement of his first film was forthcoming, newsmen started to turn savage. The *Hollywood Reporter* reminded its readers: "Do you remember way back when a chap from the Mercury Theatre named Orson Welles was going to make a picture?" The *Detroit News* stated: "Orson Welles, the boy wonder who was expected to revolutionize the whole movie-making map, is still around town and still waiting for the right story. With his retinue of actors, he's been attached to one studio for nearly a year, without even starting a movie."

Just at that time, with bandwagon mentality, the all-powerful syndicated columnists also began a fusillade of sarcastic remarks. Hedda Hopper: "Orson Welles confers with himself in a three-way mirror, as actor, director and producer. The actor wants something, producer says budget won't stand it, director sees it another way. So it goes with Little Orson Annie fighting himself." Jimmy Fiddler: "Ha! They're saying Orson Welles has increased his production schedule. Instead of *not* making three pics for RKO, he'll *not* make five!" Louella Parsons: "Well, the boy wonder needn't worry too much since he almost inherited RKO in salary checks without making a single picture there." Ed Sullivan: "Orson Welles was chic in a silver fox beard trimmed with old RKO scripts."

Although the studio's financial problems were not solved, and the fear of a drastically shrinking foreign market worried him, Schaefer still retained faith in RKO and in Welles. In addition to completing the screenplays for the aborted *Heart of Darkness* and *The Smiler with the Knife,* as well as reading and discussing hundreds of novels, stories, and plays for possible production, the time Welles spent on the sound stages and in the editing rooms was hardly wasted. He was learning the craft of filmmaking, defining his screenwriting talents, and sharpening his judgment of possible literary properties.

Schaefer kept discouraging Welles's idea of directing a costume spectacle as his first film, because of the expense and complications. A budget ceiling of $700,000 was established for all RKO films for that year, and it was virtually impossible to do a period costume drama for that amount at that time.

Schaefer also felt the enormous crowd scenes and extravagant sets might be too difficult for an inexperienced man to handle, no matter how talented.

The motion picture trade journals and the gossip columnists continued to mention some of the films that were being set for shooting that year, and the competition, although keen, did not seem overwhelming to Welles. He had no way of knowing that the films being shot were destined to become blockbusters and classics. They included a John Ford film, *How Green Was My Valley*; a new Marx Brothers comedy, *Go West*; two Humphrey Bogart pictures, *The Maltese Falcon* and *High Sierra*; a James Cagney, Rita Hayworth romance, *The Strawberry Blonde*; a war story starring Gary Cooper, *Sergeant York*; a fantasy called *Here Comes Mr. Jordan*; and an adaptation of Lillian Hellman's play *The Little Foxes*.

Welles continued to search.

CHAPTER 11

THE GENESIS OF Orson Welles's first Hollywood film is almost impossible to trace; it is fairly certain that even Welles himself did not precisely recall how or when the idea came into being. He did tell the highly talented director-critic Peter Bogdanovich, in 1969, that he'd been playing with the old notion—later used so effectively in *Rashomon*—of telling one story several times, from several different perspectives. As he became more intrigued with the concept, he began searching for a specific subject, a man around whom the film would center.* He wanted it to be an American, and he wanted the person to be important. A politician would be too recognizable. His first idea was Howard Hughes; after rejecting that, he moved to the concept of the press lords, those men whose hold over the nation's media gave them inordinate power.

Why Welles thought that press lords or industrial figures were fair game when politicians were not is unknown. What *is* known, or may be inferred, about the source of the film, follows. Roger "Skipper" Hill, Welles's headmaster from Todd School and his lifelong friend, has said in interviews that even as a boy Welles was interested in the lives of such controversial tycoons as public utilities financier Samuel Insull and the right-wing journalist Robert McCormick, publisher of the *Chicago Tribune*. He sensed, even then, the theatrical impact that could be gained in assaulting, and possibly toppling, giants. Since Welles only came to films somewhat reluctantly after his involvement with theater, we might assume that ever since he was a teenager, he wanted some day to either write or star in, or probably both, a play about McCormick or Insull. Welles has also indicated in interviews that newspaper magnate William Randolph Hearst was a friend of Richard Welles, Orson's father. They knew each other as "young swingers," according to Welles. It is altogether possible that the elder Welles told Orson stories about William Randolph Hearst that served as a demystification of his greatness and captured the boy's imagination.

Many of the films that Welles wanted to direct as his first Hollywood effort were about real people, men who could be said to be "larger than life," such as

*Welles also told Bogdanovich that at least one scene was based directly on *Last Stand,* an old play of his about the boss of a ranch, "who fights a losing battle with the twentieth century."

Leonardo da Vinci, Niccolò Machiavelli, or Alexandre Dumas. The parts he had acted and the plays he had directed on the stage such as McGafferty in *Panic,* Saint-Just in *Danton's Death,* Brutus in *Julius Caesar,* and the lead in *Dr. Faustus* further suggest an interest in the larger-than-life character.

In an interview that appeared in *Les Cahiers du Cinéma,* Welles once offered a reason for his selection of subjects: "As an actor, I always play a certain type of role: kings, great men, etc. This is not because I think them to be the only persons in the world who are worth the trouble. My physical aspect does not allow me to play other roles. No one would believe a defenseless, humble person played by me. But they take this to be a projection of my own personality."

Welles's search for a subject, therefore, had certain physical *and* character limitations. No crying Lennie in *Of Mice and Men* could he be, no naive *Mr. Smith Goes to Washington,* no cowardly Gypo Nolan in *The Informer,* no defeated and caged Tony Camonte in *Scarface.* The concept of doing a film about a great and infamous man kept surfacing as the most reasonable choice. Further, his greatest successes on stage and radio, despite the age or setting of the original source (*Julius Caesar* and *The War of the Worlds*) had been about *contemporary* themes. It followed, therefore, that his first film should also be about something or somebody that existed then, at that moment in time, the spring of 1940.

Welles thought of himself as a potentially powerful man in the realm of the arts, a sort of Einstein of the stage or a Beethoven of the proscenium, and envisioning himself as perfectly typecast to play the part of a superman character was not difficult. In that same interview in *Les Cahiers du Cinéma* he said:

> When one plays a part, one begins by being everything in the character that is not oneself, but one never puts into it something that doesn't exist. No actor can play anyone other than himself.

Also, since Welles had become famous for using highly creative techniques to tell a story, such as in *Five Kings,* he also wanted to use similar methods in whatever film he directed. He hoped his ideas would be innovative in their own right, approaches that would help define for him and perhaps redefine for other filmmakers how one could present narrative on film, heightening illusion to allusion in an expressive delineation.

How much Aldous Huxley's book *After Many a Summer Dies the Swan* influenced Welles in choosing a story based loosely on the life of William Randolph Hearst is open to speculation. A more personal coincidence, however, might have helped fuel the idea. Virginia Nicholson, Welles's ex-wife, had moved to Los Angeles shortly after their divorce. Virginia was ravishingly beautiful, intelligent, and in her mid-twenties, and had legions of hopeful suitors from all levels of the Hollywood community. One of these suitors was a young screenwriter, Charles Lederer, a member of the Hollywood literary circle that included Charles MacArthur, Dorothy Parker, Robert Benchley, and, peripherally, Ben Hecht and Alexander Woollcott. In some ways, Charles Lederer reminded Virginia of Orson. Like Welles, Lederer was also a child prodigy, but without any of what she felt was Welles's callousness —although he too was a past master of the art of the insult. Soon Lederer was courting Virginia, and eventually they married.

Lederer was also the favorite nephew of actress Marion Davies, the longtime intimate friend and protégée of William Randolph Hearst. He adored his aunt, and he and Virginia were often guests at various social functions in California at Hearst's castle at San Simeon, Hearst's "secret" house in Bel Air, and his beach house near Venice. Lederer, like Orson, had a rebellious streak. He would often appear at the most august occasions dressed in white duck trousers, a sweatshirt, and sneakers and if asked by an overly concerned host to "dress" for a dinner party, he would appear in white tie and tails. He once arrived on a movie set in his pajamas when called for an urgent rewrite. The Lederers were married at San Simeon, with Marion Davies and Hearst as witnesses.

Hearst's weekend parties at San Simeon were legend, not for their debauchery (only one drink, a dry sherry, was encouraged before dinner mainly because Marion Davies had a drinking problem) but for their diverting guests and gourmet food, and often for the startling and innovative costumes worn by guests. To be included in Hearst's social set was a prize sought by many, and for those so chosen, Hearst's friendship usually meant *carte blanche* hospitality at San Simeon, at his yacht, or at any of his many other homes. As one observer noted, there were two castes in Hollywood, one that was invited to San Simeon and the other, which was not. The former included most of the aristocracy of Hollywood, with some notable exceptions. Frequent guests included Irving Thalberg, King Vidor, Charlie Chaplin, Samuel Goldwyn, William Powell, Adolphe Menjou, Douglas Fairbanks, Louis B. Mayer, Louella Parsons, and Hedda Hopper. During the years of his reign, more movie business was discussed and conducted at Hearst's dinner table than probably any other single place in California.

In 1929, when Actors' Equity called one of the first strikes by film actors, the Hearst-owned *Los Angeles Examiner* campaigned vigorously against it in its editorials and news columns. It was mainly because of Hearst's crusade that the strike was broken.

For years Hearst was one of the principal stockholders in Metro-Goldwyn-Mayer, but he liquidated his holdings in 1934 when the studio refused to cast Marion Davies as the lead in *The Barretts of Wimpole Street.* Within a short time, he secured stock in Warner Brothers, and soon after Marion Davies came under contract with that studio. Although the lords and princes of the cinema industry were counted among his friends, many of the workers considered him an enemy.

For someone like Welles, attempting to find his status in the film colony, being invited to San Simeon would have been an important boost to his career. However, the fact that Lederer and Virginia were a part of that circle made it awkward for Hearst to invite Welles. Besides, there was Hearst's code of temperance. On many occasions, guests who drank to excess had been asked to leave San Simeon, and they were never invited back. Welles, who had come to Hollywood with the reputation of a gargantuan drinker and done nothing to dispel it, was just not Hearst's kind of person.

Further, Welles had befriended, and then employed Herman J. Mankiewicz, a Hearst exile. Mankiewicz was a screenwriter, a legend of acerbic wit, outrageous social behavior, and advanced alcoholism. Richard Merryman, a biographer of Mankiewicz, has pointed out that by 1936, three years before Welles came to Hollywood, "Mank" was no longer a part of Hearst's group of companions. "Because Hearst hated the habit in Marion, he would not tolerate heavy drinking around him and Herman became an increasingly hazardous guest." If there had been any doubt in Hearst's mind whether to make an overture of friendship toward Welles, as difficult as such a move would have been under the circumstances, it was eradicated when he discovered that Mankiewicz had been hired by Welles to work on some of the radio scripts for the "Campbell Playhouse."

Mankiewicz was a spirit with many levels. A graduate of Columbia University, first drama critic for *The New Yorker,* a foreign correspondent, and writer and critic for *The New York Times* and several other large metropolitan dailies, he was a man who was saturated with the theater. He was also marvelously charming, and notoriously self-indulgent and self-destructive, the kind of a person everyone wanted to have as a guest for dinner as long as he didn't take off his clothes or throw up on the table between courses. Ben Hecht once wrote of him: "Most of Manky's utterances, including his deepest philosophical ones, stirred laughter. Even his enemies laughed. He could puncture egos, draw blood from pretenses—and his victims, with skewered souls, still sat and laughed."

Mankiewicz came to Hollywood in 1926 to write his first film for Lon Chaney, a silent called *The Road to Mandalay.* He was supposed to return East when he finished the job, almost six weeks later, but he remained sixteen years, writing the title cards for thirty-three silent films and then, when talking pictures emerged, scripting and sometimes producing minor features. By 1939 he had been involved in another twenty-nine films, most of them worth no more than a mention in the history of motion pictures. Even such a fairly renowned film as *Dinner at Eight,* which he partially wrote, was criticized for its trite, flippant dialogue. Critic Richard Corliss best sums up Mank's reputation in his history of American screenwriting, *Talking Pictures.* He described Mankiewicz as a "happy hack whose career reveals at best, a dull consistency."

Perhaps because of his drinking and his years of creating shortened captions for subtitle cards, Mankiewicz's best writing for films occurred when he could insert the short pithy remark, the humorous "one-liner," sometimes at the expense of Hollywood itself. The art of developing scenes with extended dialogue eluded him, however. For example, in the 1930 talking film *The Royal Family of Broadway,* Fredric March plays a thinly disguised John

Barrymore, Ina Clare a disgruntled Ethel, and Henrietta Crosiman their mother. At one point, the mother looks at a movie poster of her son, bare-chested and grinning fatuously, advertising his latest film, and says to Ina Clare: "Oh dear—all action, all talking, all terrible." All Mankiewicz.

Welles and Mankiewicz had actually met in New York a year before their meeting in California. They had shared a meal together, an experience Houseman described in a letter to Mankiewicz's wife. He wrote, in part:

> I so well remember the day Orson came back to the theater from "21" telling me that he had met this amazingly civilized and charming man. I can just see them at lunch together—magicians and highbinders at work on each other, vying with each other in wit and savoir-faire and mutual appreciation. Both came away enchanted and convinced that between them, they were the two most dashing and gallantly intelligent gentlemen in the Western world. And they were not so far wrong!

Mankiewicz had worked for a number of film companies, but in 1939 he was fired by Louis B. Mayer at MGM for gambling in the studio commissary. Playing poker, betting the horses, and other forms of wagering constituted a lifelong habit for him. Time after time, Mayer had warned Mankiewicz about his gambling and finally could no longer tolerate it. Down on his luck, Mank made plans to drive to New York with a friend, but an auto accident in the desert hospitalized him with a severely broken leg. Trapped in Los Angeles without money, sustained by the love of his wife, Sara, and his many friends, he went out for an evening of carousing and rebroke the almost-healed leg when he fell, drunk, on the steps of Chasen's.

Welles always needed writing help with his scripts for the "Campbell Playhouse," and although Mankiewicz had never written for radio, Welles put him on the Mercury payroll, at $200 a week, to work from his bed on the weekly broadcasts. Mankiewicz signed the usual Mercury contract for those who worked on radio scripts, which stated, in part, that all rights belonged to the Mercury Theatre and that no credit was to be given. One of his first scripts, *Rip Van Winkle,* was unusable. The next, *The Murder of Roger Ackroyd,* was broadcast, with Welles as both the murderer and the man who captures him, master-sleuth Hercule Poirot. Mankiewicz also crafted the radio scripts for *The Garden of Allah, Dodsworth, Vanity Fair,* and *Huckleberry Finn,* working all the time with Houseman's editing and under Welles's overview and final judgment. Some of the scripts had major flaws, such as the omission of a crucial clue in *The Murder of Roger Ackroyd,* but Mank's dialogue was crisp, alliterative, and thoroughly lively, and Welles was greatly impressed with Mankiewicz's use of language and especially his ability to produce, almost on demand, a pungent, and often brilliant, line of dialogue. He began to talk to Mankiewicz about working together on an idea for a film.

It's not difficult to understand how Mankiewicz, banished from the graces of William Randolph Hearst, and Welles, who had never been admitted to them, could have arrived at the idea of doing a film about Hearst's life.

Welles's jealousy over his ex-wife's entry into the sacred bastion of San Simeon, his plan to introduce W. N. Howells, newspaper magnate, into *The Smiler with a Knife,* and his proclivity to "great men" roles all lead to a natural conclusion that Hearst, or someone like him, would be the subject of the first Orson Welles Hollywood film. And now, all at once, the pressure was on. The RKO executive board had strongly suggested, almost ordered, that Schaefer cut off all further salaries to Mercury employees until such time as Welles had submitted a script that would be approved and a first shooting date had been scheduled.

The story of the Welles meeting at Chasen's restaurant with Houseman and a few other Mercury staffers has become part of Hollywood mythology. According to Houseman, when it was determined that the Mercury bank account was virtually nonexistent and the actors could not be kept in Hollywood in order to make the first film, Welles, who "had absorbed more than his normal quantity of alcohol," turned on everyone, knocking over a serving cart and throwing a chafing dish and burning cans of Sterno, claiming that he, Houseman, had stolen the money.

Welles, while not denying the incident, had accused Houseman of a "slightly theatrical fury" in describing it in his book, *Run-Through.* Welles claimed, "The act itself didn't really amount to much," and he told me it had always been exaggerated in the retelling. When I mentioned Orson's diminution of the seriousness of the event, Houseman said in his most clipped Kingsfieldian accent: "Orson is full of *shit.*" But Orson's recollection may have been more accurate since, a few weeks later, Houseman, who had left California and dissolved their partnership after that night, was again working for Welles, helping on the new film script.

In a court proceeding years later, Mankiewicz gave his account of how the idea of the Welles film began, saying that it evolved out of a discussion of technique: a character would be shown in a *March of Time* sequence, and then the film would tell about the person. "We were going to do *The Life of Dumas,*" remembered Mankiewicz, "and then I told him about how I would be interested in doing a picture based on Hearst and Marion Davies. I just kept telling him everything I knew about them. I was interested in them and I went into all kinds of details. In an odd way it wasn't really *Citizen Kane* at all, because we were going to do a great love story, which you remember *Citizen Kane* didn't turn out to be. . . ."

Welles mulled over the idea of a film about a publisher and a young woman. At first he thought of trying to manipulate the film into a murder mystery based roughly on the mysterious death in 1924 of film producer Thomas Ince aboard Hearst's yacht, *Oneida,* with Charlie Chaplin and film director Harry d'Abbadie d'Arrast also aboard. The story filled the front pages of the Los Angeles papers, and the rumors continued for months, even years. Ince, it was implied, might have been making sexual advances toward Marion Davies, which were reciprocated or at least appreciated. Hearst found them together and shot Ince, people said. His physician, Dr. Daniel Carson Goodman, supposedly covered up the murder and issued a death certificate to the effect that Ince had died of a heart attack. Hearst's biographer, W. A. Swanberg, after years of investigation, termed the story "ridiculous" and offered a complete explanation of how Ince actually did die: of heart failure, two days *after* he left the *Oneida.*

Long discussions took place between Welles and Mankiewicz at the latter's home, though Welles had no thought at that time of having Mankiewicz actually write the script by himself. Welles believed that he himself could do it alone, with perhaps perfunctory assistance from others. At this point, Houseman was also involved in the story conferences, and everybody's ideas were discussed and carefully considered. The murder angle was abandoned somewhere along the way.

Before anything was on paper, Mankiewicz said he wanted to write some of the scenes of the script itself. Since a number of the good ideas were actually his, Welles felt that ethically he should allow Mankiewicz to work on it. However, Welles's contract with RKO specifically stated that the film was to be produced, directed, performed, and *written* by him, the implication being *solely* by him. There was no possibility, he thought, of amending the contract, nor did he want to. The studio wanted his name exclusively attached to all areas for the publicity value of his "boy genius" reputation, and he agreed. Would Mankiewicz therefore agree to work on the script, together with Welles and Houseman, without receiving credit? For that matter, could Mankiewicz be relied upon to abstain from liquor and come through with the required material?

Undoubtedly feeling embarrassed to raise these points but having to protect his own interests, Welles put the questions directly to Mankiewicz. Yes, was the answer to both: no credit was needed, and abstinence was promised. Mankiewicz had never been fastidious about credit in the past. On many of the screenplays he had written he had received coauthor credit or occasionally special billing, such as "associate producer," a catchall phrase that could mean just about anything. As for the promise of refraining from liquor, he really had no other choice. Alcohol would be kept unavailable wherever he worked; besides, he knew that if he drank, he would not receive the money he desperately needed. A contract between Mankiewicz and Welles was drawn up and signed. There were four major points:

- Mankiewicz was to be paid $1,000 a week.
- Welles had the right to cancel the contract at any time by notice to Mankiewicz.
- Mankiewicz was to be paid no salary if he was "incapacitated by illness or any other reasons" that prevented him from performing his duties.
- All material "composed, submitted, edited, and interpolated" by Mankiewicz on the screenplay became the sole property of Mercury Productions who, for the purpose of the work Mankiewicz agreed to do as the Mercury's employee, "shall be deemed author and creator."

Welles was represented by his attorney, L. Arnold Weissberger, and

Mankiewicz was advised by his Los Angeles agents, Columbia Management of California. Minutes before signing, the bargain was again summed up for Mankiewicz: there was to be no payment if he failed to deliver, and all property rights and all credit of the work he did on the script belonged to Welles and his Mercury Theatre as "author and creator." It was clear. He understood and agreed.

With contract in hand and his broken leg still in a cast, Mankiewicz left for Victorville, California, a lonely town of 1,800 people in the Mojave Desert about eighty-five miles from his house in Los Angeles. He was accompanied by Houseman, as editor and temperance-enforcer; a secretary; a German nurse; and a very rough script of the project written by Welles, entitled *John Citizen, U.S.A.,* a three-hundred-page version consisting mostly of dialogue and a few camera directions. They stayed at the Campbell Ranch, where alcohol was prohibited and where Mankiewicz could have peace, quiet, and sobriety to work on revising the Welles script.

During the twelve weeks that Mankiewicz and Houseman worked together in the desert, the latter traveled frequently to Los Angeles to confer with Welles. Welles occasionally visited the ranch to check on the progress and to offer criticism and suggestions concerning scenes, dialogue, and narrative progression. In twelve weeks' time, a script emerged, retitled *American.*

The basic plot of *American* is the story of a controversial American publishing tycoon told in retrospect after his death through a series of recollections of people who knew him well. The script opens to describe a vast gateway of wrought iron somewhere in Florida. Then, using the camera-as-character technique of *Heart of Darkness,* the camera moves toward the gate,

> In the middle of which is clearly seen a huge initial "K" stretching clear across the road. As the CAMERA MOVES toward it, the gate opens and the CAMERA PASSES through. A few feet farther on, the gate having closed behind it, the CAMERA REVEALS, either because it has reached the top of a small incline or because it has turned a bend (depending upon the topography to be selected),
>
> THE LITERALLY INCREDIBLE DOMAIN
>
> Of Charles Foster Kane. Its right flank resting for nearly forty miles on the Gulf Coast, it truly extends in all directions farther than the eye can see. Designed by nature to be almost completely bare and flat—it was, as will develop, practically all marsh-land when Kane acquired it and changed its face—it is now pleasantly uneven, with its fair share of rolling hills and one very good-sized mountain, all man-made. Almost all the land is improved, either through cultivation for farming purposes or through careful landscaping, in the shape of parks and lakes. The castle itself, an enormous pile, compounded of several genuine castles, of European origin, of varying architecture—dominates the scene, from the very peak of the mountain.
>
> DISSOLVE

The script goes on to describe the property: an overgrown golf course, the fairways wild with tropical weeds; six championship-sized tennis courts with sagging nets and obliterated baselines; a cage of chattering monkeys, all that remains of a zoo; a series of boarded-up cottages in the shadows of the castle; a drawbridge over a wide moat, stagnant and choked with weeds.

The camera makes its way through an untended but exotically beautiful garden, toward the entrance of the castle, through a heavy door, dissolving into a great baronial hallway, ". . . completely furnished but empty, silent, abandoned, unreal. . . ." Up a huge ceremonial staircase the camera goes into a long gallery filled with museum pieces, crystal chandeliers, sumptuous carpets and draperies. On the door is painted a country scene in Louis XVI style. The door suddenly opens as a nurse, visible only from the waist down, can be seen wheeling a white hospital table. The table moves out of view and the sound of a faint voice can be heard. It is shrill and choked. It is the voice of Kane.

"Rosebud!"

WELLES ACCEPTED, WITH certain minor reservations, this two-minute expositional beginning from the script, as mysterious as it was. He liked the very murkiness of it; the lonely grounds and castle, the single, unexplained word, "Rosebud." It would create on the screen, he hoped, a deep, ominous shadow, which could then be eradicated or at least diffused or commented upon as the film progressed.

Aside from the subject of the credit, which legally belonged to Welles and his Mercury Theatre, the question of who did what to create the script has long been open to debate and speculation. How much of Welles's ideas or visions are represented here and elsewhere, or whether a given touch was an original invention of Mankiewicz's or a refinement of Houseman's, is difficult to clarify. The search for the single catalyst or motivating agent for a creative process dominated by a group of highly talented men is usually troublesome when an attempt is made to identify the genesis of responsibility. Lapovers, melds, and segues of thought and language are bound to occur when several people are working on the same project. Conversation, discussion, and argument were essentials in the working relationship of Welles, Houseman, and Mankiewicz.

A cable sent to Mankiewicz by Houseman, after the latter returned to New York to begin to mount a production of *Native Son,* proves that all three men worked on the script:

> Dear Mank: Leaving tonight for Carolina to confer with Paul Green and Richard Wright. Will report in detail. Received your cut version and several new scenes of Orson's. Approve all cuts. Still don't like Rome scene and will try to work on it my humble self. After much careful reading I like all Orson's scenes including new montages and Chicago opera scenes with exception of Kane Emily sequence. Don't like scene on boat. Query any first meeting scene between them. However, do not feel there must be some intimacy between them

before oil scandal comes to shatter it STOP Simply don't understand sequence or sense of Orson's telescoped Kane Leland Emily assassination scenes. There again will try and make up my own version. Please keep me posted. Love to Sara.

In a legally sworn and written statement, "Literary Material, 1941," found in the RKO corporate archive, Richard Baer, Welles's assistant, claimed (in addition to the fact that "the idea of *Citizen Kane* was the original conception of Orson Welles . . .") that the script was crafted as follows:

> Mankiewicz and Houseman went to Victorville and stayed for a period of from six to eight weeks and between them wrote the original script for *Citizen Kane*, Mankiewicz doing most of the writing and Houseman acting primarily as critic. As portions of the script were finished, the finished portions were sent in relays to Mercury Productions at RKO where they were revised by Welles. Some of this original script which was periodically sent from Victorville is still in the files of Mercury Productions. The revisions made by Welles were not limited to mere general suggestions but included the actual re-writing of words, dialogue, changing of sequences, ideas and characterizations and also the addition or elimination of certain scenes.

What *is* known and agreed upon by all concerned is that Mankiewicz came up with the concept of "Rosebud," the enigmatic word uttered by the dying mogul, the verbal icon around which the film revolves. Reporters for a newsreel company covering Kane's death are assigned to track down the meaning of that last word, to determine its importance as a clue to the man's life. As the newsmen go to the character's friends and enemies in search of the significance of the word, the film unfolds, jigsaw puzzle piece by jigsaw puzzle piece, with the viewer left to put the sections together.

However, there were many other scenes, characterizations and filmic business from that first scripting that Welles did not approve. The following are a few examples that appeared in the initial scenario but were never filmed:

• During the newsreel scene of the depiction of Kane's life, there was to be a series of still photographs showing him as a boy at Northeastern Military Academy, then at Brookfield, Groton, and Princeton, and finally at Nuremberg University. He is shown to have been a maladjusted, unsuccessful student, whose relationship to each school was flashy but brief. A reconstructed dramatization of an incident from his life at Nuremberg was to be included in the newsreel. He is seen, wearing a German student cap, being excised from the university along with his young friend Leland. An elderly, pedantic professor rises and says:

> We have heard and duly weighed the evidence before us. For placing an unspeakable object *(he holds up a chamber pot)* on the spire of San Josef

Tower, you are hereby deprived of your academic privileges and dismissed from this university.

The newsreel also shows the mature Kane being burned in effigy, openly accused of bringing about the shooting of an American president after clippings of Kane editorials attacking the president's policies are found in the pocket of the would-be assassin. "The rage of the American people was instantaneous, instinctive, bitter . . . ," comments the doomsaying voice of the newsreel narrator.

Continuing, the newsreel reveals that Kane is actually defrauded at the polls, losing the only election in which he, in fact, polled the majority of the votes.

Another newsreel scene shows a moonlit rowboat in the East River from which three men, presumably working for Kane's opposition, throw a ballot box into the water; in others we see people being turned away from election booths or sitting in back rooms with ballots they've stolen.

• In another scene, the script indicates that Thatcher, the administrator of the Kane fortune, together with Jefferson Park, the American ambassador to Italy, visit Charles Foster Kane on the latter's twenty-fifth birthday. The point of the visit is to terminate Thatcher's guardianship, now that Kane has come of age. They find Kane living in the most elegant and expensive Renaissance palace in Rome. The interior is covered with classic tapestries, cluttered with valuable statuary, reeling under millions of dollars worth of art treasures including a magnificent ceiling done by Michelangelo. Thatcher hopes to impress on Kane that his responsibility, the care of one of the world's largest fortunes, should be considered virtually a sacred trust.

Thatcher and the ambassador are shocked to discover that, upon their arrival, there is a party taking place consisting of, according to the script, "pimps, Lesbians, dissipated army officers, homosexuals, nymphomaniacs and international society tramps—without exception." As Thatcher enters the grand ballroom, Kane, dressed in black velvet tails, can be seen talking to a lady, under five-feet tall and weighing over three hundred pounds, sixty-five years old and attempting to look twenty-five. It becomes apparent that Thatcher and Parker feel uncomfortable in the setting of this degradation and refuse to meet any of Kane's unsavory guests. The next day Thatcher hands over a large, beautifully bound book to Kane. It contains a meticulous accounting and description of all of his holdings, extensively cross-indexed. Kane rapidly riffles through it and juggles it with his hands, like a producer estimating the value of a script by its weight and number of pages.

KANE

What's this?
(casually)
New York Inquirer?

THATCHER

That's a newspaper—
   (pauses)

KANE

A newspaper, eh?

THATCHER

In a manner of speaking. A few years ago we were forced to take over the building—a very rickety, inadequate structure—in a foreclosure proceeding. Unfortunately, we were also required to take the paper over with it.

Thatcher explains that an offer of $100,000 has been made for the *Inquirer* and he is considering selling it. Kane tells him he doesn't care to dispose of it, despite Thatcher's protestations that the paper is worthless. "Maybe you're right, Mr. Thatcher, but well, I had no idea I owned a newspaper. I think it might be fun to run a newspaper." Thatcher becomes almost apoplectic over the idea, arguing that newspaper publishing is a highly intricate and specialized business, and that to run a newspaper successfully takes a lifetime of experience.

KANE

Oh, I don't intend to have a lifetime of experience—at publishing, or at any one thing.
   (smiles)
But for a while—I can just picture people saying, "There's Charles Foster Kane—you know, the publisher."

• There was a scene planned to take place in the office of the publisher of the *Chronicle*, F. W. Benton, Kane's chief competitor, after the first issue of the *Inquirer* is published under Kane's editorship. Benton confers with his assistant, Reilly, an efficiency-expert type, and predicts Kane's failure: "If the young man thinks he's going to get anywhere just by pouring money into that bottomless pit he'll find out his error." Eventually, the *Inquirer* surpasses the *Chronicle* in circulation and Reilly goes to work for Kane. He appears in many other scenes throughout the script as a diametric opposite, in his precision and coldness, to Kane's other assistant, Bernstein.

The character of Bernstein, Kane's assistant, to be played by Everett Sloane, looked quite a bit like Orson's Dr. Bernstein—slender, bespectacled, and with an aquiline nose—but the autobiographical resemblance ended with the physical. It has been said the personal allusion to the Bernstein character was more directly thought to be Solomon S. Carvalho, William Randolph Hearst's loyal treasurer and business manager. Walter P. Thatcher, Kane's guardian, was nothing like Orson's real-life mentor in his disdain for his ward. Dr. Bernstein truly admired and respected Orson.

• One of the difficulties with the initial script, which quickly became apparent to Welles, was that there were just too many scenes, some of them highly expensive and difficult to produce. The film, as originally written, would have taken well over three hours. There were elaborate montage scenes, for example, showing the growth of the *Inquirer* under Kane's personal drive. Kane is shown at his desk, signing checks; pointing to something he doesn't like in a cartoon; ready to speak on a raised convention platform; in the city room, working on headlines, tearing up one attempt after another; breaking through mobs crowded at the front entrance to the paper; dressed in full evening clothes on the edge of a big fire, with photographers, seizing a camera and rushing nearer to the flames in a position of obvious danger.

Another complicated montage was planned to show his bitter attacks on the president in connection with oil leases, with *Inquirer* headlines leading up to the matter; Kane reading ticker tape and dropping it into a basket; Emily, Kane's wife, and her father, purple with rage, screaming, pounding on the table; Emily and her father and mother—but without Kane—in an opera box; Kane writing at his desk at the newspaper; front-page headlines condemning the president.

• The original script also has Kane in the composing room showing his two-year-old son, Howard, how to press the keys of the linotype machine; in the *Chronicle* office; with Benton offering to buy the rapidly expanding *Inquirer* (Kane refuses to sell but offers to buy Benton's paper); in his office reading a history of journalism, to the effect that the daily newspaper, in one form or another, is as old as civilization itself; with Emily honeymooning at a tranquil lake in a rustic cabin but having dinner served, nevertheless, by a full-liveried butler; with her again when she tells him she has been aware of his affair with Susan for a long time; in the Lincoln Room at the White House talking to the president; at the theater, unexpectedly meeting his father.

This last, fully five pages of script, shows Kane senior as a dandy with a wig, a world traveler who appears to have done nothing but carouse over the years ever since receiving the fixed income of $50,000 a year when the bank took over as the manager of the Colorado Lode fortune. Kane senior is with Henriette La Salle, a young tart thirty or forty years his junior, whom he introduces as his wife. The scene, set in Jedediah Leland's lavish apartment, begins with Kane senior behaving fatuously and ends with Leland bursting into the room to pull Kane junior away before he chokes his father to death.

To introduce the action, Kane senior, lighting a cigarette, halts the procedure in midair. Miss La Salle beams happily.

KANE, SR.

What did I tell you, dear?
(He reaches for the glasses.)
Here, Charles. Let's make a toast. Henriette, I've got a feeling you and Charles *(he interrupts himself)* . . . Charles, you're going to get along fine with your new Ma. The three of us . . .

242

He gets no further before Charles grabs him on the shoulder with an iron grip and swings him toward himself.

KANE

Are you telling me you're married to this . . .

KANE, SR.

Let me go, Charles, you're hurting me. Let me go. Let me . . .

Without a word, Kane puts his two hands around his father's neck and starts to choke him. Henriette, not moving, screams.

MISS LA SALLE

Help! Help! Help!

Leland bursts into the room and separates father and son.

• There are other elaborate or extended tableaux that Welles chose not to film: Kane discovering Susan, his second wife, in a loving embrace with Jerry Martin, the manager of his stable, and his suggestion to Raymond, the butler, that Martin should be killed. The next day Martin *is* found dead, thrown by his favorite horse (despite the fact that he was an expert rider); an around-the-world trip on Kane's yacht, with Susan pleading to go home; his now-grown son killed when he and members of a "half-baked, idiot fascist movement" attempt to take over an armory in Washington; Bernstein reluctantly attending a Wild West costume party at Xanadu.

FOR MANY REASONS, Welles could not use a great deal of the script of *American,* errors of continuity, logic, and motivation being the most prominent. How could the father be introduced later in Kane's life without any previous reference (other than the boardinghouse scene) to the father being alive and the mother dead? Why would Kane actually try to murder his father for taking up with a young girl, a situation that is not uncommon in the lives of rich widowers? Why would Kane, living the life of a reprobate for years in Rome, suddenly switch personalities and decide to come back to America and work almost around the clock as a tireless newspaper editor and publisher?

Welles also believed that some scenes, as Mankiewicz wrote them, were too exaggerated. "In the original script, the bad guy was *really* bad," Orson told an interviewer on BBC years later, and "the comic scenes were *totally* comic." There were not the expositional shades of gray that he wanted. Mankiewicz held, oxymoronically, that if the idea was to make the subtlety evident, then color had to be added. Orson insisted that whatever subtlety be infused in the film, it should be rarefied, elusive, unobvious. Orson's concepts prevailed and he went about to sculpt the screenplay in a more ethereal way.

There were also potential legal problems, having to do with specific resemblances to William Randolph Hearst. Many of the incidents and some of the dialogue are taken directly from Hearstian fact or mythology, tales that had been circulated in newsrooms around the country and published in a number of books and articles over the years.

Hearst, in 1896, sent noted writer Richard Harding Davis and artist Frederic Remington to cover the "war" in Cuba. Remington supposedly cabled Hearst that there would be no war and that he was coming home, whereupon Hearst cabled back: "Remington, Havana. Please remain. You furnish the pictures and I'll furnish the war. W. R. Hearst." (This line, although it never was conclusively proved to have been authored by Hearst, remains thematically intact in the film.) Hearst's yellow journalism (the term was invented to apply to his papers) is depicted throughout the script as Kane's gossip mongering. The scandal of Hearst's longtime May-December relationship with actress Marion Davies—they lived together for many years but never married—is shown through Kane's sponsorship of Susan Alexander. The controversial story of McKinley's assassination, after virulent attacks upon him in all of Hearst's papers, had been recounted for years: the assassin, Leon Czolgosz, had clippings from the Hearst editorials on him when apprehended, and as a result, Hearst was burned in effigy throughout the nation. This episode is scripted into the *American*; the only effort to fictionalize was to make the action more closely resemble the unsuccessful assassination attempt on President Franklin D. Roosevelt in Florida.

The character of Kane was not clearly enough defined, Welles felt. He later told author Richard Merryman:

> In his hatred of Hearst, or whoever Kane was, Mank didn't have a clear enough image of who the man was. Mank saw him simply as an egomaniac monster with all these people around him. So I don't think a portrait of a man was ever present in any of Mank's scripts. Everybody assumes that because Mank was an old newspaperman, and because he wrote about Hearst, and because he was a serious reader on politics, then that is the whole explanation of what he had to do with Kane. I felt his knowledge was journalistic, not very close, the point of view of a newspaperman, writing about a newspaper boss he despised.

Welles was clearly warned by RKO's legal department that the script of the *American* was too close a portrait of Hearst and that, if produced as it was, the film would almost certainly be the cause of an expensive libel or invasion of privacy suit. For this as well as thematic reasons, a complete reworking of the script was undertaken. Welles, Mankiewicz, Houseman, and Joseph Cotten met almost daily and worked on every scene: honing, paring, revising, adding. After seven complete revisions, Welles finally had what he wanted. The story as given in the official plot line, and released by RKO, was to evolve as follows:

> In 1940, alone at his fantastically surrealistic and magnificently opulent estate known as Xanadu, located in Florida, Charles Foster Kane dies at the age of seventy-five. When he dies his last word is "Rosebud" and from his hand drops a glass ball—one of those novelties containing a miniature snow scene.

Just after his death, a newsreel, similar to the "March of Time" is made showing the highlights of his life. It portrays him as one of the greatest, wealthiest, most loved and most hated newspaper tycoons of all time. It tells of his humble beginning, his sudden acquisition of wealth, his education under the guidance of a Wall Street financier who, in later years, denounced Kane as a dangerous man, a man of life, in short, "a communist." It shows his two marriages—the first to a niece of a President, the second to a young and uncultivated shopgirl type, a singer who finally left him while his Xanadu, the great estate he was building for her, was only half finished. It shows his near greatness as a politician, his retirement, and the breakdown of his newspaper empire.

But not once does the news digest of Kane's life show any human angle which will bring it alive on the fictional newsreel screen. Rawlston, the newsreel producer sets his reporters on the task of tracking down "Rosebud," thinking it may be a clue or something important.

First, Thompson, one of the reporters, calls on Susan, Kane's second wife. She turns out to be a drunken night club entertainer living in Atlantic City who refuses to talk to him. He then calls at the great Thatcher Memorial Library and is permitted to read that portion of Thatcher's memoirs which deals with Charles F. Kane. From this he sees Kane's early life, his humble beginning in his mother's boardinghouse, the Kanes' sudden acquisition of wealth through a hitherto worthless gold mine, the Colorado Lode. At this time Kane was put under Thatcher's wing. The little boy, resenting this, hits Thatcher in the stomach with his little sled. This was the original cause of Thatcher's vindictiveness toward him throughout his life. The chief cause, however, came later, when Kane acquired a newspaper, the *Inquirer,* and proceeded to turn it into a typical vehicle for yellow journalism in order to build up its circulation.

From old Bernstein, now Chairman of the Board of Kane's fallen newspaper empire, Thompson learns the truth of Kane's start in the business and the way he built it up. He sees Kane as a queer combination of lovableness and hatefulness, of honesty and treachery, and Kane broke the heart of Leland, a dramatic critic and his best friend. And he learns the story of Kane's first marriage to Emily, niece of a President.

Later, from Leland, now an invalid in a hospital, Thompson learns more sidelights about Kane. He sees the breakdown of the marriage to Emily, and the beginning of the romance with Susan, who wanted to be a singer but couldn't, only to be forced into one heartbreaking operatic failure after another by Kane's pride and refusal to accept defeat. Leland tells about how Kane's one chance to be a great political figure was ruined by the threatened exposure of his affair with Susan. There followed his divorce by Emily and marriage to Susan. . . . Thompson calls on Susan again. This time she talks—about her marriage to Kane, and the way she left him because he didn't love her, only wanted her to love him. . . . Raymond, Kane's butler in the later stages of his life, is also interviewed but is unable to clarify the enigma. "Rosebud," it is determined at the end of the story, is the name of the sled with which Kane hit Thatcher and is a symbol of his lost and innocent childhood.

It was George Schaefer who originated the title, *Citizen Kane.* He was afraid that *American* might seem too cynical, since the character of Kane was not a particularly commendable one. Also, the fact that many of Hearst's publications, such as the *New York Journal-American* and the *American Weekly,* had the word "American" in their titles might also be considered too strong a Hearstian identification.

As the characters were being refined through script conferences and re-writes, Welles began his casting. Through an arranged date to attend the premiere of *Gone with the Wind,* Orson met an attractive actress, Linda Winters, whom he believed would make the perfect Susan Alexander, "frightened, whining, pathetic," as he described the character. Rumor had it that Miss Winters had been Charlie Chaplin's mistress. Supposedly Chaplin had discovered her while she was appearing at the Carmel Little Theater in California and had sung her praises so loudly that a studio signed her. Winters had played several minor roles in such films as *Campus Cinderella, Adventure in Sahara, Comet over Broadway,* and even *Mr. Smith Goes to Washington,* but she was hardly known as a personality to the moviegoing public. This suited Welles, who wanted to maintain the illusion that all the faces in *Citizen Kane,* including his own, were new to the screen; he wanted them to burst *en masse* into the public consciousness.

"Susan is probably the most important character in the picture," wrote Welles in his series of personal notes based on the first draft of the script. Like a Kane counterpart, Susan is also viewed through different eyes and sentiments: Emily sees her as a little blond tootsie who causes the dissolution of her marriage; Leland's Susan, the cause of the break between himself and Kane, is spoiled and vapid, a kept woman nervously doing jigsaw puzzles because she is too stupid to do anything else. She is, to Leland, a symbol of the repudiation of all that Kane stood for.

Welles took Linda Winters under his wing and began coaching her into the role. Like Kane himself, Welles had great ideas for his protégée, although unlike the character she was to play, she came from a socially prominent family and was highly intelligent and educated. Her father, David N. Comingore was the former collector of Internal Revenue and an intimate friend of Presidents Harrison and McKinley, and she had spent much time at social functions in the White House. Welles insisted she change her name back to Dorothy Comingore and he began to be seen at various Hollywood nightspots and public and private events with her. Later, when the filming began, he treated her discourteously and callously on the set, claiming that he wanted her to really hate him, just as Susan eventually grew to hate Kane.

Ruth Warrick was screen-tested for the part of Emily, Kane's first wife and the niece of the president. Welles had become aware of her by simply going through hundreds of glossy photographs, submitted by agents and Central Casting, of beautiful actresses who were seeking a part. Her face was familiar to Welles; they had once appeared together on a radio show in the late thirties. She had a look of dignity about her that seemed to capture the sure and refined quality of Emily's character. Even her voice, poised and well-modulated as a result of her education as a singer and her experience as an actress in radio, had a cultured intonation. "I'm not looking for an actress that can *play* a lady," he told her. "I want an actress who *is* a lady." After talking with her in his suite at the Waldorf Towers Hotel in New York—he was there for RKO's annual sales conference—he came to the conclusion that she was right for Emily. Within days she was in California to take several screen tests on the RKO sound stage, including one playing opposite Welles as he acted as Kane.

The test marked not only the first time for twenty-three-year-old Ruth Warrick ever to be in front of a Hollywood camera, but the first time for Welles, also. By the time the cameras began to roll, a fairly large complement of studio bystanders and officials had gathered to watch. Welles gave himself a short line to speak, to which Warrick was to respond: "That is typical of you, Mr. Kane." Perhaps nervous because of the crowd assembling to see what he could do as a film actor, Welles muffed his first attempt. Warrick, however, responded perfectly. Again and again they did it, each time Orson somehow spoiling the take with a flubbed line, transposed word, or mispitched sound. Finally, Welles said the line perfectly, with the exact pacing and resonance. "That is typical of you, Mr. Welles," Warrick blurted, ruining the ninth take.

As some sort of psychological safeguard, Orson also had Ruth Warrick tested for the part of Susan Alexander, but it was quite clear that she possessed more of the cosmopolitan veneer of an Emily. After Welles and his colleagues examined the rushes, he was even more convinced than before that she was perfect for the part, and a contract was immediately drawn.

Most of the other principal roles and some minor ones were filled by actors who had worked with Welles in either the stage or the radio companies of the Mercury Theatre. Joseph Cotten, his old friend from the New York radio days, after playing Barrère in the short-lived *Danton's Death,* had been discovered by Katharine Hepburn and had toured with her as C. K. Dexter-Haven in the highly successful *The Philadelphia Story.* Cotten, unlike the other Mercurians, had preceded Welles to Hollywood. He had been brought to California by Alexander Korda and signed for an unspecified film to be produced in the near future. When Welles began to cast *Citizen Kane,* Cotten was "loaned" by Korda to him for the part of Jedediah Leland, Kane's best friend. Everett Sloane, perhaps best known for his long-run role on the Goldberg's radio series, would play Bernstein, Kane's loyal assistant; William Alland was Thompson the reporter (and narrator of the newsreel); Agnes Moorehead, Orson's Margot Lane on *The Shadow,* made her film debut as Kane's mother, Mary; Erskine Sanford played the bumbling and perplexed editor of the *Inquirer,* Herbert Carter; Gus Schilling was the waiter at the Atlantic City nightclub; Richard Baer played Hillman, one of the reporters, and Richard Wilson was also one of the reporters. Mercurians all.

George Coulouris was an exception. While waiting in Hollywood for the start of the shooting of *Heart of Darkness* and *The Smiler with a Knife,* he became impatient and accepted a part in the Bette Davis film *All This and*

Heaven Too, and then in Rita Hayworth's *The Lady in Question,* both films to be released in 1940, before *Citizen Kane.* Although Welles was annoyed that one of his stock actors was no longer a new face, he still hired Coulouris for the part of Thatcher. He'd worn heavy makeup in the Davis and Hayworth films, so his face would not have grown familiar to the public.

The casting proved to be one of the simplest chores concerned with the production of *Citizen Kane.* Except for the two lead female parts, Welles knew what his actors were capable of achieving dramatically, with certain allowances to be made for the differences between stage and screen acting. He could and did alter the script to accommodate the strengths and eliminate the weaknesses of many individual members of his troupe. The fussy, old-aunt quality that Coulouris was so expertly able to project in other roles was highlighted in his portrayal of Thatcher; Sloane's feisty warmth was employed and developed in Bernstein; Paul Stewart's ability to produce a sinister persona influenced the rewriting of his part of Raymond the butler (originally to have been played by Mercurian Edgar Barrier); Erskine Sanford's drift toward befuddlement colored the revisions in the character of Carter, the bewildered, imminently departing editor.

Used to being on stage, literally in the spotlight, in front of a hushed and attentive audience, Orson now found himself in a sound studio surrounded by cables, wires, cameras, lights, catwalks, pulleys, cranes, and dozens of people seemingly looking after their own demands. It was necessary, therefore, to draw more from oneself, to become more observant and introspective. This became a problem when Orson as person listened to Orson as actor deliver his lines, while Orson as director judged the aptness of the performance.

Orson had to teach himself and his other Mercurians how to act without direct response from an audience. He always had the crew, of course, for reactive comments, but they were usually so busy with their own chores and responsibilities that they often would not discern the differences from a trashy or stellar take. Sometimes he would feel almost neglected by his crew, especially after they didn't seem to notice what he considered to be a memorable or highly creative scene.

He had no trouble with his own voice as he modulated and shaded it in tone and intensity from scene to scene to get from it what he wanted. It was somewhat amusing to him when he discovered that a moving camera tracking him or another actor, for example, might not arrive at the designated spot by the end of the spoken line. Therefore, in order to synchronize movement with speech, pauses in speech would have to be inserted, either naturally as the camera rolled or, later, in the script, before the next take commenced.

Whitford Kane, Welles's midwestern friend who had played in *The Shoemaker's Holiday,* was to have played Kane's father, without change of name and despite the fact that he had appeared in one film before *(Hide-out* in 1934). As it developed, he elected to take a role in Katharine Cornell's revival of Shaw's *The Doctor's Dilemma.* Welles then made another exception to the rule against actors with previous screen experience and selected Harry Shannon, a former musical comedy hoofer, to play the role of Kane senior. Shannon had appeared in nine films before *Citizen Kane,* usually as a sympathetic father or rustic character actor, but despite this exposure, Welles believed him to be perfectly typecast for the part.

Welles had less confidence in choosing and developing the technical, behind-the-scenes crew that would be responsible for giving *Citizen Kane* the look, sound, and sensibility he wanted.

Fortunately, on the very day that Welles was discussing and worrying with his associates about whom he might approach to be the cameraman on the film, he found Gregg Toland sitting in the waiting room of his office. Toland, one of Hollywood's most distinguished cameramen, responsible for such visually appealing and significant films as *Les Misérables, Dead End, Intermezzo, The Grapes of Wrath, The Long Voyage Home,* and *Wuthering Heights* (the last of which had earned him an Academy Award just four months before), was interested in collaborating with Welles on *Citizen Kane.* While working with John Ford, Toland had begun experimenting with the new technical and artistic possibilities offered by the development of coated lenses and super-fast film, and was considered by almost everyone in the industry to be a virtuoso of the camera.

Gregg Toland said that he felt miserable after working on many run-of-the-mill assignments and that he wanted to collaborate with Welles *because* of the young director's inexperience. "I want to work with someone who's never made a movie," he explained. "That's the only way to learn anything—from somebody who doesn't know anything."

The cameraman's eagerness was not merely altruistic. He admitted later that in previous films he had had a few opportunities to make cautious, tentative experiments with lower-proportioned and partially ceilinged sets, heightening the actuality of certain images. This, combined with the recent technological advances in film and lenses, inspired him to want to attempt more. The iconoclastic reputation of Welles promised the possibility of more large-scale experiments with the images of the film and, perhaps, of film itself.

Toland and Welles established instant rapport and agreement, both recognizing the other's dedication to producing something graphically fine and special. To sweeten the partnership, Welles also learned that Toland was another Hearst exile. Before being expelled, like Mankiewicz, for overly alcoholized behavior in the presence of Hearst, Toland had spent many weekends at the San Simeon castle. Experience with Hearst and the details of his surroundings would definitely add dimension to Toland's vision of the film. Permission from MGM, Toland's home studio, had to be secured for him to work on an RKO film; when this was granted, a contract was signed.

Welles was already certain about how *Citizen Kane* should look. As he had planned for *Heart of Darkness,* he wanted the audience to see the film as they would "reality" and not as though they were looking at a movie, a gathering of shadows from light projected through celluloid, sitting in a smoke-filled theater on a Saturday night. He wanted the viewer to enter the film, become a part of it, and remain there to its conclusion. Everything was more difficult than planned: how to enhance the resources and demands of the iconoclastic lighting, photographing, and special effects; and most important, how to achieve the realism and intense detail demanded by the probing, relentless camerawork within the practicalities of a limited studio budget.

Unlike some directors, who discuss the overall look of their films with their art personnel and then allow them to create what they will, Welles insisted on working closely with Perry Ferguson, the art director, and approving all the designs and sketches and the mounting and building of every set that was to be used in *Citizen Kane.* Ferguson was one of the most innovative young art directors at RKO, with such set pieces as *Winterset, Bringing Up Baby, The Story of Vernon and Irene Castle,* and *Gunga Din* to his credit.

As each scene was approved or rewritten, Welles would do a sketch detailing how he wanted it to look and then confer daily with Ferguson and Toland as to what should be done in creating an appropriate set for that segment.

Early in the spring of 1940, Welles made arrangements to present the script of *Citizen Kane* to Schaefer for RKO's legal approval. The two men met with Harry Eddington, the RKO corporate attorney, privately in Welles's office on the RKO lot, poured themselves drinks, and sat back for a late afternoon introduction to the script. Instead of letting them read it themselves, Welles, with all the acting and storytelling prowess he could summon, read each part, expanded on the narrative with his ideas for camera angles, sets, and necessary properties, and generally created the mood he wished to evoke from the camera's first movement into Kane's castle to its exit two hours later. He followed with a memo confirming all he had said.

Welles explained and elaborated on what he was attempting to do, theoretically with the film: The *March of Time* sequence, the name of which was ultimately changed to *News on the March,* would have the look of the original Henry Luce product but be deeper in scope and cover a wider range. "The function of *our* March of Time" Welles said, "will be a special one, that is, the preparation, anticipation, and clarification of this man's entire life and general exposition for the entire picture." The newsreel sequence would be divided, roughly, into five parts, he went on: "a) The introduction, showing the extent and nature of this man's activity; b) the genesis of this man's power and the opinion which men held of him as a result of his use of it; c) his personal life as revealed to the public, culminating in the construction of the Alhambra*—the visible symbol of his great *personal* wealth and power; d) his public activity as expressed in journalism and politics; and e) the continued rise and then the collapse of his empire and the merging of his declining public and private life in his final retreat to the Alhambra and his lonely end."

Welles touched upon the meaning in other scenes and narrative business: the fact, for instance, that in the projection room scene, the riddle of Kane is

*The original name of Kane's estate, later changed to Xanadu.

expressed in direct words. "What kind of man was he?" Welles asked. "Fascist, Communist, Patriot, Progressive, *Reactionary*? Was he generous or cruel and ruthless? Is it possible that in the dying word 'Rosebud' will be found a clue which may unlock the enigma of this man's real personality?"

The scene in the nightclub in Atlantic City where Susan is first introduced to viewers was, Welles contended, "of course, a false start." But it did better than almost any of the other interviews to illustrate the nature of the reporter's quest, his manner of conducting it, the complexity that "we may expect to find in a man whose wife (to whom he has been married for ten years) can a few years after leaving him have fallen quite as low as Susan has."

Welles believed that Thatcher's account was told "in an atmosphere of Edwardian marble," and that the life, career, personality, behavior, and viewpoint of Kane were repugnant to him.

To Bernstein, Welles contended, Kane was "a prince of a man to serve and admire," a man to be followed, indulged, and adored. The audience must assume, Welles hoped, that much of Kane's success is due to Bernstein: his handling of the business when Kane is touring Europe, his attempt to build circulation, his slavish devotion to both man and business. "Bernstein represents in Kane's life the newspaper, pure and simple—the period in Kane's life when he was functioning the most effectively and the least complexly."

Welles said that Leland, although he jokes about it, is haunted and terrified by his own infirmity. "It is also evident that before his illness declared itself he had for years been leading a pretty dissolute, not altogether pleasant life." Leland is probably Kane's only boyhood friend but he represents more: through him is revealed the dual story of Kane's personality, the tremendous vitality, gaiety and *joie de vivre,* combined with, Welles continued, "the vital idealism which expresses itself in such a document as the Manifesto.* The difference between Bernstein and Leland is that the latter is more analytical, less admiring, more cynical, a man who knows Kane more intimately than Bernstein."

In some ways, Welles explained, the confrontation scene in Susan's apartment with Emily and Boss Gettys, his arch rival for the governorship, was the most revealing delineation of Kane's character: "Kane's monomania finally exerts itself: His enraged conviction that no one exists but himself, his refusal to admit the existence of other people with whom one must compromise, whose feelings one should consider, whose ability to damage one he must take into account."

When Welles was finished reading and talking, he took a long drink of his brandy and looked up at Schaefer. As the light of the California dusk began to fill the office, Schaefer smiled. He was heartened by what he had heard. Even Eddington, who was still in favor of *The Man from Mars* project as Orson's trial run, was somewhat infected by the buoyancy of the other two men. Welles capped the moment with a toast and a promise to have a neatly typed

*Changed to the "Declaration of Principles" in the finished film.

251

and totally completed script on Schaefer's desk, ready to be estimated as to potential cost, in a matter of days.

WITH SCHAEFER'S TACIT indication that the rough script of *Citizen Kane* would probably be acceptable, barring any financial conflicts, Welles initiated certain tests, which he shot privately. Meanwhile, Schaefer sent a memorandum to other RKO officials that *Citizen Kane* would be Welles's first motion picture.

The studio in which Welles was working was closed to the indefatigable press and to any personnel, including RKO executives or employees, who were not directly connected with the film. *The New York Times* heard of the "closed" lot and ran a brief story stating that "Welles is conducting secret film tests of himself in a secret role in a secret picture."

The secret screen tests conducted by Welles, beginning on April 16, 1940, were indeed of himself, in various stages of makeup, as the young Kane. He dressed in a variety of costumes provided by the Western Costume Company and a few furnished by Welles himself from his own personal wardrobe. (Eventually, he would wear thirty-seven different costumes in the film.)

Since Toland was not yet contractually on staff for RKO, cinematographer Russell Metty, who had filmed such features as *Sylvia Scarlett* and *Bringing Up Baby,* conducted the tests. Welles dressed in a tuxedo one moment and went tieless with open shirt the next; he asked for close-ups and medium and long shots, with himself walking, standing, and sitting still with different backdrops and with different lighting motifs. They worked from 3:00 in the afternoon until 5:40 and then the test film was rushed to the laboratory for immediate processing.

Welles felt that the initial rushes were adequate, close to satisfactory, but he wanted to try more. Again working with Metty, he spent a day on May 1 doing additional tests of himself, this time attempting to capture the aging process that Kane ultimately experiences in the film: in his early fifties as he runs for governor, then marries Susan Alexander; at sixty-eight, when Susan leaves him and Xanadu; at seventy-five, reclusive, "aloof, seldom visited, never photographed . . . ," as he is described at that age in the script.

Since he was going to play Kane from his mid-twenties to his seventies, a fifty-year life span, Welles was deeply concerned about how believable his character would look as he went through all the stages of makeup needed to appear as different ages. Other characters, such as Leland, Susan, Thatcher, and Bernstein, also aged in the film. There were great technical problems of creating a real aged look for all of them rather than the typical Hollywood effect of simply graying the hair and wrinkling the skin cosmetically in an attempt at instant decrepitude.

Welles's interest in the technique of applying makeup and its effect on characterization had been with him all of his young life, but his experience with it had been almost exclusively for the stage. When he played old men, Welles would usually use a darker base paint on his cheeks to help elongate his roundish face, whiten his hair and eyebrows with powder, add very dark rouge, paint out his lips entirely, and wrinkle his face and forehead with a deep maroon or chestnut pencil, highlighted with white. He discovered that a mere *suggestion* of a facial characteristic was sufficient to evoke the quality he was seeking as long as it could be clearly applied. The result was startlingly realistic when seen by the theater audience. In films, however, because of the use of the close-up shot where the viewer could see even the pores of the skin, makeup had to be more subtly realistic, less naive. On the screen, the risk of delusory makeup theatrically applied was to ease into farce.

There was another problem Welles had to confront in making up himself and his actors and actresses: Hollywood audiences were accustomed to "types," and although in real life it was possible to have an angelic-faced youth who was a homicidal maniac or a brutal-looking man who was a kindly priest, in motion pictures such incongruous casting rarely worked. The benign countenance and sparkling eyes of an Edmund Gwenn, the Milquetoast gasp of a Donald Meek, and the fast-talking whiskey-soaked voice of a Thomas Mitchell all conveyed certain character prototypes to audiences: Because most of them had not yet appeared on the screen, Welles's actors did not yet possess the distinguishing mannerisms that would make them quickly, easily, and believably identifiable in their assigned roles. Ingeniously planned and executed makeup could surmount the difficulty.

Welles hired a non-union man, Maurice Seiderman, a twenty-five-year-old Russian immigrant and former art student who had done virtually all of the makeup and created the wigs for most of the actors in such films as *Winterset, Mary of Scotland, Gunga Din,* and *The Swiss Family Robinson.* After doing Raymond Massey's makeup in *Abe Lincoln in Illinois,* Seiderman had gained a reputation as one of the most inventive and creatively precise up-and-coming makeup men in Hollywood.

Film writer Norman Gambill, who interviewed Seiderman for *Film Comment* about the latter's techniques, has stated: "To make the actors' faces and bodies conform to the symbolic needs of the script, as he interpreted them, Seiderman studied the appearances of the Mercury Theatre actors, and sculpted make-up portraits for them that followed Hollywood genre types."

For the character of Kane, Welles gave Seiderman a photograph of billionaire Samuel Insull, the public utilities financier, and another of William Randolph Hearst. From Insull, Seiderman took his brush mustache, his baldness and the general contours of his head; from Hearst, he took his aquiline nose, the receding hairline, and many facial contours and expressions. Gambill explains that Seiderman made the middle-aged Kane, "after the marriage to Susan, close to images of Edward Arnold, though his ultimate source is the D. W. Griffith tycoons seen in *Intolerance* and *A Corner in Wheat.*" The younger Kane was typed after a strong, heroic cowboy, as seen in Hollywood Westerns. It is possible that Spencer Tracy and Clark Gable were also used as model types for the slightly older, but not yet aged, tycoonish Kane.

Seiderman made a series of sculptures that showed the characters aging. With Welles he would apply his sculpted plastic pieces over the nose, chin, and eye sockets. Then over his head, he would sew a flexible skull cover into place for the wig.

During Orson's first sitting, which took hours, Seiderman had William Alland read aloud *The Kingdom of Evil—A Continuation of the Journal of Fantazius Mallare* by Ben Hecht, because he thought Orson could better relate to the character that Seiderman was creating and see himself, or Kane, as the "gigantic man with a large head" who had an expressionless face. Orson loved and accepted the mimesis.

Red plastic compound was applied afterward to the face and then painted with a liquid greasepaint. Finally, the wig was set in place, false teeth put in his mouth, special contact lenses inserted to make the eyes less bright and sparkling. The mustache was constructed with individual tufts of hair. The result was a masterpiece. Orson was entirely believable as an aging and then aged man.

After several more days of makeup and costume screen tests of himself and the other principals of the cast, on Saturday June 29, 1940, Welles conducted one more shooting—an actual scene. He called it a "test" so as not to draw attention to it by the press or by studio executives. He wanted to work in relative seclusion, unbothered by inhibition or interference, and since this was the first official scene he directed of the film and the first of his Hollywood career, it was important, he felt, that he experience the freedom of expression that he desired without worrying about budgetary or publicity considerations.

Although the scene in which the *News on the March* is viewed called for several actor-extras, Welles wanted to maintain the security of a closed set and instead used most of his Mercurians. Working with his own company relaxed him, and since the scene would be shot in the darkness of a screening room, it would be difficult to recognize the actors who would later be playing other roles.

At 9:20 A.M., Welles crammed Richard Baer, Joseph Cotten, Gus Schilling, Erskine Sanford, William Alland, a then-unknown Alan Ladd, and others into a real projection room at RKO and went through several off-camera rehearsals. He had selected the scene not only because he didn't have to import extras but also because he wasn't in it himself; as director, he first wanted to see what he could do with other actors on film, rather than having to also worry about any vagaries of his own performance. Also, without using an official studio sound stage, with its union crews, he could work around, and possibly reduce, the original budget for that and other scenes, as long as he could shoot in privacy. If the first "tests" were unacceptable, then he would not have wasted much time or money. If they could be used as actual footage, then he would emerge as a highly clever and frugal director.

Since this was the first scene to be shot, and the actual newsreel of *News on the March* had not yet been photographed, the action began with the light of the projector machine going out and Philip Van Zandt playing Rawlston, the producer of *News on the March,* asking his reporters their reactions:

RAWLSTON

How do you like it boys?

MAN

Well, seventy years in a man's life . . .

MAN

That's a lot to try to get into a newsreel.*

There was one technical difficulty that immediately presented itself. Welles had wanted the projector to stop, not at the exact end of the newsreel but just a moment before, where a huge close-up of the mature Kane might be frozen, stop-framed in time, indicating that the story of Kane was not entirely finished. As Rawlston discussed the Kane enigma while standing in front of the room in direct line of the projector, Welles wanted him to be flooded and engulfed with Kane's large image dominating both him and the room. Obviously because the scenes of the older Kane had not yet been shot, this projection of the head of Kane could not be accomplished. There was discussion that it might be achieved optically, somehow superimposed later in the laboratory, but neither Toland nor Welles was confident that it could be done successfully.

The shooting continued with a white screen in the background, and Rawlston appearing in silhouette. Over and over again, Welles had the scene shot, rearranging his actors, asking for more overlapping of dialogue, making sure there was enough cigarette smoke filtering through the light emanating from the projection booth in the hole in the wall, getting Van Zandt to pause ever so briefly, but significantly, when he said:

See them all. Get in touch with everybody that ever worked for him— whoever loved him—whoever . . . hated his guts.

Welles attempted shots that had never been successfully used in a film before: having the camera shoot directly into blazing arcs. The technique produced shadow and brightness, light and dark, good and evil, and the total effect was to heighten the impact of the dialogue. A special lens coating had to be used on the camera to cut the glare of the lights shining into it.

The actors and small crew labored without breaks until 7:30 P.M., when Welles, believing he had worked them all beyond the limits of productive return, dismissed them for the day.

When the rushes returned on the following Monday afternoon and Welles and Toland viewed them, Orson felt the flush of esthetic success. The scene expressed—just as he wanted—the Kane conundrum. And it was also much more: it was the scene upon which the logic of the film evolved—it established the need for a biographical exploration.

The faceless reporters in the smoke-filled room, Rawlston's somewhat

*Spoken from the darkness by Joseph Cotten.

licentious tone, the barren screen, and the brazen shaft of light all worked together in sinister harmony to create what could be described as an acid comment by Welles on the flamboyance and possible deceit of journalism itself, perhaps a retaliation against the dissonant coverage he had received the previous year by the Hollywood press. Film historian James Naremore referred to the projection room in almost mythic terms when he described the scene as "one of the most self-reflective moments in the film, shot in an actual RKO screening room which has been made to look more like a region of the underworld." But aside from or because of its theoretical importance, the scene looked right. Although in its finally edited form, it would run for less than three minutes of screen time, it proved that Toland could interpret and execute Welles's ideas and that Orson, all at once, overwhelmingly, could direct with imagination, precision, and visual sensitivity.

Welles's and Toland's partnership became one of the most successful artistic relationships and warmest professional friendships ever experienced in Hollywood. William Alland, who played Thompson the reporter, has remembered: "They got along beautifully. No matter what Orson wanted, Gregg would try to get it for him. Gregg had a tremendous responsibility because Orson was in almost every scene but Gregg kept an eye on everything."

Confidence usually imparts a strong sense of inspiration to whomever is fortunate enough to be so imbued. Welles, at twenty-five, began to experience, with his first success behind the camera, a perfect amalgam of his brashness and talent. Although he had taken almost a year to begin shooting his first film, because of a combination of factors—fear of failure, sloth, the declining world economic condition, plus the desire to find or create the one absolutely flawless and ultimately publicizable screenplay—once his cameras began to roll, he proved to himself and to the studio community at large that he was capable, indeed, of preeminence over the craft of filmmaking.

Aside from some special effects and process shots, in less than four months from his first test, Welles managed to direct some 573 separate camera setups or scenes for *Citizen Kane*. He worked from early morning—sometimes having to be on the set at 5 A.M. because of the difficulty of applying the old Kane makeup—until late at night, and often his directorial schedule would last as much as fifty or sixty hours without a break.* Toland and he constantly planned and discussed how each camera shot could give them something new and interesting. They attempted, whenever possible, to avoid cuts, which were antithetical to the impression of reality that they wanted the film to exert. So they would pan the camera from one piece of action to another or dolly it from part of a set to the next, avoiding the visual interruption of jarring incisions found in most films. All this took stopwatch planning and exact coordination of actors, sets, cameras, microphones, and lights.

*This time changes depending on the publication cited. In an interview in the *New York Daily News,* Welles claimed he was at the studio from 2 A.M. to 9 P.M., and in *Friday,* he wrote that he was there from 4 A.M. to 10 P.M.

In order to reduce a certain artificiality of light and to further the realism, virtually every indoor set contained a complete ceiling, almost unheard of in Hollywood films at that time. *(Stagecoach,* Welles's acknowledged paragon, had ceilings on the sets but the technique was still unusual enough to be considered revolutionary.) Toland also used a process that he had worked on for several years before shooting *Citizen Kane,* that of pan focus. This permitted the camera to record objects at varying distances in the same shot, in sharp, clear focus, rather than deemphasizing background. By allowing several points of view or interest to occur simultaneously, this deep-focus photography encompassed the same range of vision as the human eye. It permitted the spectator, not the camera, to decide which character or piece of action to concentrate upon. Essentially, this form of cinematography provided the same kind of freedom that a playgoer has while watching a stage play, where the audience is not forced to look at a close-up or a single character, for example, as he must in a film, but can allow his eyes to take in anything—or everything—that is happening on stage. (It has been stressed by critic André Bazin that Welles may have used this technique to show how his characters can be influenced by their surroundings.) It was an innovative and daring technique, and Welles had Toland shoot as many scenes as possible using the vitality of deep focus.

In spite of all his brilliance, it took time for Welles to find his tempo and to recognize his weaknesses and strengths as a motion picture director. Much of what he attempted worked successfully, but until a new technique could be proven as a possible alternative, and this could mean several or many trial shootings and then the inevitable wait for rushes, the pace at the very beginning of the film went slowly. And, as in every film, there were occasional mishaps and snags that boggled, although never bowed, the production.

While shooting the confrontation scene, for example, with Gettys and Emily in Susan's apartment in New York, Orson (playing Kane) broke his ankle running after Gettys shaking his fist, screaming, "I'm going to send you to Sing Sing, Gettys. Sing Sing!" He was treated at Good Samaritan Hospital and released. Maurice Bernstein was flown in from Chicago especially to take care of his former ward. In an attempt to help his old friend and mentor, whose medical practice in the Chicago area had diminished over the years, Welles wanted to have him named as the official physician for RKO. Schaefer was cordial to the suggestion but graciously declined it for undisclosed reasons. Sometime later, Welles was successful in helping Bernstein move to Hollywood with the hope of becoming the "doctor to the stars."

With ankle attended to by Bernstein, Welles sat in a huge cane-backed wheelchair, determined not to miss a beat in the shooting of *Citizen Kane.* He was ahead of schedule by almost two weeks and he wanted to maintain that advantage. Since this first take of the scene in Susan's apartment would have to be redone when his ankle healed, Welles instead called for Joseph Cotten to do his role as the old Jedediah Leland. A new set had to be constructed for this scene, and one of the fastest and easiest to build would be the rooftop solarium of the hospital where Thompson, the reporter, visits Leland.

Cotten was hardly prepared to play the part of an old man in his seventies the first time he was ever before a Hollywood camera. It was also his biggest scene in the film, since he would be on camera by himself for the longest amount of time. When Cotten had read the script and studied the original shooting schedule, it was indicated that he was to play all the scenes of the young Leland first. "Orson, you promised to break me in gently," he complained. Protestation notwithstanding, wheelchair to wheelchair, Welles directed Cotten as the "disagreeable old man" he had become.

Although Cotten's makeup was believable, Welles felt his eyes were too youthful and bright. Contact lenses filled with milk were provided and as a result, Cotten was unable to see anything at all in the scene. Cue cards were of no use to him and he was forced to learn his lines perfectly, all within a matter of hours.

Because of the hasty preparation, Cotten's wig did not fit properly. It was a bit too small for his head, and as the scene progressed so did the wig, easing itself up as he acted line by line, until it was virtually popping off his head. A green eyeshade was provided to help keep the wig in place.

Despite these problems, the scene was turned out quickly, efficiently, and so believably that upon release, many viewers thought that Cotten was indeed an old man instead of his actual thirty-six years. "I'll probably go on playing old men's parts until I'm fifty," said Cotten at that time, "and then people will say, 'My, doesn't Cotten preserve himself remarkably well. He hasn't changed a bit in twenty years.'" Welles, upon seeing the rushes of the hospital roof scene, was said to have quipped, adapting Herman Melville, "There are some enterprises in which a careful disorderliness is the true method."

Welles delighted in the slavish industriousness of making *Citizen Kane*: directing, acting, filming, editing, were all fun to him and that is probably why he could devote as many hours as he did on and off the set working and thinking about the film. It is also why he could, without guilt, spend time away from the film when he so chose. Occasionally, he would simply disappear for a few days at a time. He could not be reached by phone and informed no one, certainly not the studio, not even his closest associates, where he was going or when he was coming back. The cast and crew would wait patiently until Orson reappeared a few days later, no questions would be asked, and shooting would resume. Mark Robson, one of the film's editors, called Orson's vanishing acts, "typical of his need for failure." But it always worked out favorably: whether he devoted this time to a woman, a bottle, or a book—or just needed to be by himself—seemed unimportant. When he returned, he would be refreshed and invariably attack the filming with even greater vigor and speed than before.

From time to time, radio would also temporarily pull him away from his duties on *Citizen Kane*. In August 1940, he took time out to speak to the nation on "This Is Radio," a memorable program featuring dozens of stars. The program originated from the New York World's Fair and was sponsored by the National Association of Broadcasters to commemorate the pleasures and benefits of the medium.

On that day, after rehearsing and then filming the scene where Kane, Leland, and Bernstein invade the *Inquirer's* office for the first time, an intermission was called so that some minor rewriting could be done. During this interval, Welles gave his live transcontinental radio address, and seemed to imply that he had not yet totally committed himself to film. He said in part:

> The oldest kind of show business is what we call the living theater. We all still love it and I guess we always will. We're learning now to love another great theater art: the motion picture. I am, I know, because I am speaking to you between takes on an RKO movie set in Hollywood. And since we are on the subject of radio which is today's subject—and the only important subject today—I'd like to say that that is the wonderful thing about radio: that you can take it anywhere and send it anywhere. I'm very privileged and very glad for the chance to say today that radio is, in my opinion, the last great frontier in America. I'm very privileged to be able to serve it. I'd like to continue in any capacity whatsoever, even as a rather lost "adlibber" on a movie set ... to thank it and serve it in any way, as long as it will have me, and to remain as always, obediently yours.

Another guest appearance on the air by Welles during the time that he was filming *Citizen Kane* was opposite John Barrymore on the popular "Rudy Vallee Show." Barrymore had begun the unfortunate era of his life when he squandered his talents in a constant caricaturization of his alcoholism and debauchery; Vallee presented him regularly on his show as one of the great comedic finds of 1940, a somewhat tragic combination of Shakespeare and slapstick. As a result, Vallee's ratings soared. The show billed Welles and Barrymore in a pseudo-rivalry as "The Two Greatest Shakespearean Actors in the World Today." It was a madcap session filled with energy, irreverence, and even some love. Before Welles is introduced, the Great Profile *umphs!* and *bahs!* and *zounds!* in his inimitable way at the very mention of the young man's name: "*Orson Welles?!* why he's an exhibitionist, a publicity-seeker, a headline hunter, a cheap sensationalist . . . why, he's another John Barrymore."

Orson started off slowly doing a somewhat ineffectual rendition of his character as the Shadow; a skit between the two at Barrymore's farm was hilarious; the two men even sang a duet, crooning "By the Light of the Silvery Moon" to the tempo of a nonchalant soft-shoe. The highlight of the show, however, was in its last minutes when Orson Welles and John Barrymore had their one and only opportunity to do Shakespeare together. Choosing the tent scene before the battle of Philippi from *Julius Caesar,* Welles maintained his familiar role of Brutus, while Barrymore played Cassius, both characters hard-pressed to keep their advantage over the invading forces. When Barrymore spoke the line, "Must I endure all this?" in a sound barely above a whisper, it was as if he were commenting on his own life situation, recognizing the reduction of his talent to that of buffoon having to play on a comedy show. Brutus's last line of the sketch also seemed to be an awareness of the veiled lament by Barrymore, when he takes Cassius's hand "and my heart, too." However brief, and somewhat inappropriately staged, it was one of the most poignant Shakespearean readings ever to be broadcast over radio.

Instead of disturbing his colleagues by extending himself with appearances on the air and away from *Citizen Kane,* Welles's visits to various shows were looked upon by many at RKO as a continuing promotion to a national audience of his prodigious mythology. The only difficulty that arose was when, for financial reasons, he went on a two-week, highly lucrative lecture tour through the Midwest, right at the end of filming. Even though he received much local publicity in the cities where he spoke and the thousands who listened to his lecture on "The New Actor" were impressed, he could not convince his not-so-patiently-waiting cast and crew, who were eager to be done with the project and get on with other films, that his primary purpose was not to fill his pockets with money but to promote the film.

WELLES HAD DIRECTED himself many times on the stage, but somehow the very permanence of film, the possibility of displaying one version of a role, was somewhat formidable to him. On the stage, he would—and did—change his approach to a part almost from night to night to better hone it into shape and to sense what an audience, a *particular* audience, needed or wanted from any given performance. Once the curtain went up, the performance's success or failure was the actor's own; he had no director to say "Cut!" if he was bungling his lines or losing his audience. This fluidity was impossible when working with the terminal, packaged quality of a finished motion picture. The camera never laughed, nor did it fall asleep. It was impossible for it to gauge one's performance.

Chaplin had been successful in directing himself on film, but there were two important differences between what he had accomplished and what Welles was attempting to do: until that time, Chaplin had worked exclusively with silent film, and all of his films were comedies. Although it is true that drama did not contain the demands of pacing found in comedy, the dimension of spoken dialogue could add enormous problems for someone appraising himself. Welles, however, was choreographing *Citizen Kane* with the unhesitating measure and continual rhythm of an up-tempo musical comedy or, as someone has since suggested, a grand opera.

So that he could see how he would ultimately move amid and through a particular set and piece of business, he always had on hand a "double," not in the traditional acting sense of someone who looked like him, but an actor who was as nearly exact in his height, weight, and general bodily structure as possible. Sometimes he had William Alland, although smaller and thinner, walk through his part for him. When the young and eager Kane bounced out of the horse-drawn carriage and into the building of the *New York Inquirer,* for instance, it was Welles's double who first went through the motion without benefit of camera, so that Welles the director could follow and readjust, if necessary, any movements that Welles the actor would ultimately make on the screen. That was the easy part. More difficult was going through the gestures himself, first in rehearsal, and then for the initial shootings. How is one to know that a slight trembling of the lips, or the blink of the eye, or an awkward movement of the shoulder will not be recorded by the camera? He found it difficult hitting his own chalk marks, the predetermined place where he was to stand so that Toland could better work his magic. On the stage he could accidentally, or by choice, be slightly more stage left or right, but with film, although he still had to maintain rhythm and endurance with body movements, it was imperative that he hit these marks accurately and with absolute precision every time.

It took only a few sessions of directing himself and others, followed by a careful examination of the rushes, to prove how intrinsically different stage and screen acting really were. The lesson of the whole history of the art of acting in films began to wash over him: the fact that some of Eisenstein's best actors had never seen the inside of a theater; that some of the greatest stage performers—Bernhardt and Duse and Beerbohm Tree among them—were disappointments on the screen.

And how could an actor, who *acted* only before a camera and no audience, for perhaps just a few minutes a day, stay in character when the continuity of action is constantly interrupted? New demands were made of Welles and his Mercurians. What was true on stage was false on screen: faint whispers, subtle glances, suggestions of movement, all of which could be invisible and hence never used in the theater, were a major technique of film acting. Presentation and demonstration, the very essence of stage acting became overly dramatic when one's face was twelve feet high. An actor's eyes, not his voice, became the crucial communicative and evocative statement.

Aside from an intuitive censorship or acceptance of any particular scene, Welles looked toward Toland, Cotten, Alland, and almost anyone else on the set to approve or reject the takes in which he acted. If he discerned smiles at the end of a scene, he sometimes would call a halt; if there were a sea of poker faces on those watching, he would invariably shoot it again. It was not unusual for him to do as many as one hundred takes of the same scene until he had what he thought he wanted; and a hundred more after seeing the rushes, if the result of what appeared on the film did not coincide with his ideal expectations. He began to be able to assure other actors that they were understanding and delivering the nuances of the roles that were demanded of them, and he was something of an inspirational catalyst in helping them feel the characters they were playing. He had no similar ability in giving himself such assistance and so he had to play his role of Charles Foster Kane intellectually, without very much emotional involvement, hoping that his characterization would, nevertheless, be believable.

There was one apparent exception to the way he handled his acting, and it led to fresh responses and a certain emotional realization. That was in the scene where Susan leaves him:

KANE

You mustn't go. You can't do this to me.

SUSAN

I see, it's you that this is being done to. It's not me at all. Not what it means to me. I can't do this to you? Oh, yes, I can.

Immediately after she's gone, Kane demolishes Susan's elaborate bedroom with his bare hands. Welles realized that because of the expense of the destruction and the necessity of rebuilding the set, and the physical demands on himself, he could not do many takes of the scene. It was planned, therefore, that he film only two. In both cases, he literally and emotionally threw himself into the part, reaching down as deeply as he could into himself so that he could allow the anger to take control in a sort of cumulative excitation. His whole temperament quickened as the passion of the moment overwhelmed him and heightened his imaginative sensibilities. "He was absolutely electric," remembered William Alland, who had watched Welles's performance from the sidelines. "You felt as if you were in the presence of a man coming apart." Welles staggered out of the set. His hands were bleeding, his clothes torn, his face flushed, his eyes misted. He almost fainted, Alland recalls. "I really felt it," Welles mumbled, wandering off in a daze. "I really felt it."

ALONG WITH ALL the thousands of details and problems of minutiae that Welles had to store and solve in his head while directing *Citizen Kane* was his relentless attempt at holding the film together visually and audibly and with as much creative verve as he could imagine, execute, and afford. The music that was to be used in *Citizen Kane* became a key ingredient in how Welles wished the film to be perceived and received.

Since the opera scene in which Susan Alexander Kane made her debut was planned for very early in the shooting schedule, it was imperative that a fully orchestrated sound track be recorded before shooting of that scene began. Bernard Herrmann, still with CBS in New York, had been contracted to provide the music and was supplied with a completed script. Welles asked him to read it carefully and then come up with both general and specific suggestions regarding themes, bridges, and other musical business but as his first order of work to concentrate on the composition of the opera. Herrmann's first suggestion was that he do a version of *Thaïs,* the opera by Massenet, based on the novel by Anatole France. The character of Thaïs is that of a courtesan, and Herrmann reasoned that he could create an aria for Susan that would make her sound as untalented as she is intended to be. For both practical and creative reasons, Welles believed that the subject of *Thaïs*—staged in a Cenobite monastery and the city of Alexandria—was impossible to use as the opera in *Citizen Kane.* He wanted the elaborateness of costumes and sets found in more lavishly melodramatic productions.

Welles also asked Herrmann to pattern the opera after "a parody on a typical Mary Garden* vehicle" and to create a first scene in which Susan begins a major aria as the curtain rises, a device never used in real opera as it is too difficult to affect even for the most accomplished coloraturas. Welles suggested the opera *Salammbô*, by Ernest Reyer, based on the novel by Flaubert. It contained the possibility of huge production scenes of ancient Rome and Carthage, for which he could costume Susan as a pretentious, neoclassic courtesan of the grand opera. He awaited Herrmann's ideas.**

A telegram sent to Orson from Bernard Herrmann on July 21, 1940, clearly indicates his agreement and elaboration on Welles's original concept:

THINK SALAMMBO IDEA THE BEST. GRAND OPPORTUNITY FOR MAGNIFICENT FRENCH-ORIENTAL OPERA ARIA. I FEEL HOW-EVER, WE MUST SUPPLY SOME SORT OF TEXT OR SITUATION FOR IT SUCH AS GRAND CARTHAGINIAN PALACE, SLAVES, ET CETERA, WITH GREAT STORM COMING UP AND HEROINE SING-ING WILD AMOROUS ARIA WHILE AWAITING LOVER. YOU BET-TER SUPPLY FINISHED TEXT. HOW LONG SHOULD OPERATIC SCENE BE? FEEL YOU SHOULD ALLOW ABOUT A MINUTE FOR TUMULTUOUS ORCHESTRAL PRELUDE.

Herrmann believed a composer's job was to get inside the drama. If he couldn't do that, he often said, he shouldn't be composing music. During further communications, Welles and Herrmann agreed that Susan's voice should not be patently bad. Instead, although it had to be amateurish and weak, it also had to arouse a sense of pity. The music would be intensely dramatic, and because of her limited talent, she would be seen, or heard, as unable to handle it. Houseman was set to the task of writing the libretto for this pseudo opera, which they called "Salaambo."

Since the film had many montages, some of them quite long, Herrmann

---

*Ironically, Mary Garden, one of the most glamorous prima donnas of the twentieth century and reigning queen of the Chicago Lyric Opera, was also one of the greatest Thaïses.

**The question of exactly who Welles was parodying with the character of Susan Alexander has been discussed for decades. A composite figure of several personalities is probably the clue. The parallel to Marion Davies was strong in the scenes of Susan's drinking, doing jigsaw puzzles, complaining of having no friends at the castle, and so on; however, for Susan Alexander Kane the singer, it is fairly certain whom Welles had in mind. He has said that he drew a great deal of the picture from the heir of the farm machinery family—*not* Robert McCormick, the newspaper magnate as is often mentioned—but from Harold McCormick and his days connected with the Chicago Civic Opera House. After his divorce from Edith Rockefeller, Harold McCormick had married a temperamental and rather mediocre soprano, Ganna Walska, whom he attempted to propel into operatic stardom, unsuccessfully as it developed. Possible proof that Walska's career as a singer was the prototype of Susan Alexander in *Citizen Kane* rests in the following reference to her in a telegram from Bernard Herrmann to Orson Welles, July 23, 1940, which in part, states: "FEEL THAT SUZIE SHOULD HAVE A SMALL BUT RATHER GOOD VOICE. THIS IS THE TICKLISH PART OF IT. EVEN 'G.W.' HAD SOMETHING OF A VOICE."

worked complete musical numbers into them, designed specifically to fit a designated length rather than short cues. He also composed short but complete dance numbers in the style of 1890s music to accompany the montages, and he included zestful galops, polkas, hornpipes, and schottisches.

Once the music was written and established for a scene, Welles would often cut the film footage to fit the music, rather than the usual other way around. In the famous breakfast scene, where Welles shows, in barely three minutes of screen time, the growth of alienation between Emily and Kane over a period of twenty years, Herrmann used the classical musical form of theme and variations. A gentle lilting waltz is heard at the beginning of this scene; as their marital discord erupts, the variations begin with each shot elaborating upon a separate variation until the waltz theme is heard, dissonantly, played harshly by violins.

Another musical schema that was worked into the film developed as a direct result of the radio experience of both Welles and Herrmann. Besides bridging scenes, music can suggest a mood, provide background, offer exposition, punctuate narration, and, in comedy or fantasy, actually take the place of sound effects. The most frequent use of music in radio, however, and it is virtually mandatory, is to provide the transition from scene to scene or situation to situation. Even a single note becomes important in telling the ear that the scene is shifting. In film, the eye usually supplies the transition as the scene is cut or dissolves into the next. Welles and Herrmann both believed that an opportunity to include transitional music, whether it be symbolic or illustrative, to weave parts of the film together or to set it in context, should not be overlooked.

As Welles worked on the script, and as he began to direct specific scenes, he could hear in his mind the suggestion of the music that should be inserted, just as he could hear the additional dialogue or the sound effects that would eventually be added. He sensed where a scene would be more effectively transferred with a musical bridge and where music would conflict with the dialogue. Pencilled notations began to fill his script indicating where music was needed. For instance, as Thompson reads Thatcher's diary and his eye travels over the parchment with old-fashioned handwriting, "I first encountered Mr. Kane in 1871 . . . ," Welles asked Herrmann for a fully melodic transition that would evoke all at once the frivolity and innocence of childhood in the snowbound winter of the Victorian era, and Herrmann responded with a piece of lyrical music that used delicate flutes leading to a blizzard of strings and harps that perfectly captured the guiltlessness and simplicity of a former age. The "snow picture" sequence as it grew to be called, became one of the most charmingly innovative transitions to a flashback ever seen or heard on film.

Herrmann created two musical *leitmotivs.* One is a symbol of Kane's power in the first two bars of music at the beginning of the film—a vigorous piece of ragtime, sometimes transformed into a hornpipe polka. The other is connected with the secret of Rosebud—it can be heard when the light is snuffed out at the beginning and precedes Kane's deathbed utterance of the word and personifies Kane's nostalgic return to his youth; it is featherlight and harmonic and stresses the more positive side of his personality.

AS THE SHOOTING of *Citizen Kane* progressed right on schedule, and with its set still closed to the press, Welles stepped up efforts to gain publicity for himself and ultimately for the film. The process of insuring strong press coverage for a film in the Hollywood of the early 1940s followed an almost routine pattern that always involved publicizing the film's stars. Since Welles was not only the star of *Citizen Kane* but also the producer, director, and coscreenwriter, he was guaranteed a certain body of press coverage without much effort on his part. Items began to appear in the gossip columns about him and the film; romantic stories, often involving Dolores Del Rio, emerged in the fan magazines; photo layouts of Orson working at the studio or at home were published in quality picture magazines. It was important to him, once the film emerged, that the publicity not only continue but also be favorable.

The possibility that he was making a film about the life of William Randolph Hearst began to be noised about. Hearst was one of the richest and most powerful men in America. He could easily block a film's success if he elected not to review it or carry its advertising in his papers around the country. Welles decided it was time to ingratiate himself with the press.

Although it has been denied by Welles, it is altogether possible that he had Herbert Drake, his press agent, trickle to the press by nuance, and perhaps a whisper to an attentive ear, the possibility that Charles Foster Kane was really a not-so-veiled duplicate of William Randolph Hearst. Welles had to be careful, should Hearst decide to sue and claim an invasion of privacy, that it could not be proven that Welles had deliberately made a film based on the actual life of William Randolph Hearst. The publicity possibilities of a mischievous controversy—Hearst threatening a suit—were enormous and Welles's experience in gathering such coverage in the past was great. Publicly, Drake also denied that he had been the original source of the rumor that Kane was Hearst, and in a letter to William Schneider, a New York publicist, written before the film was finished he said, in part:

> The RKO executives have been told I precipitated the Hearst thing by announcing generally that Kane is the life of Hearst. This is, of course, a dirty lie, a base canard, a vile accusation, a vicious flight into the realms of imagination.

A luncheon at The Brown Derby was arranged with Hedda Hopper, one of the most powerful columnists in the country, and Welles turned on all his charm, without, of course, revealing very much about the substance of the film. He cavalierly offered her the part of the *Inquirer's* society editor as a cameo role. She need only be on the set for a day, he reasoned, and, since she usually appeared in at least one film every year anyway, why couldn't it be *Citizen Kane*? In order to keep her distance from a project that seemed destined for public contention, if not litigation, Hopper graciously refused. A grand bouquet of flowers, with a note of thanks from Orson for sharing the lunch with him, was sent to her nevertheless.

Similar social overtures—without the offer of a part, however—were also made by Welles to Hedda Hopper's rival-in-ink, Louella Parsons. After one interview with him, Louella quoted what she considered to be an evasive and highly mysterious reply from Welles as to the subject of his forthcoming film: "It deals with a dead man. You know when a man dies there is a great difference of opinion about his character. I have everyone voice his side and no two descriptions are alike."

Despite his not directly revealing the true plot and although the film was unfinished and months away from being released, both women began to run an almost embarrassing amount of publicity about Orson in their respective columns, which reached thousands of newspapers and millions of readers. During the months of filming *Citizen Kane,* Orson was mentioned in Hedda Hopper's column at least twice as much as any other Hollywood figure, and in Louella Parson's column items appeared about him more than any other film performer. Louella often gushed over the "tall, dark, handsome leading man," who, she predicted, "the girls would sigh over" when the film was finally released, and Hedda's words and observations were equally effusive.

George Eels, in his dual biography, *Hedda and Louella,* claims that Welles's silken handling of Louella during the filming of *Citizen Kane* was at least underhanded, if not dishonest: "It is easy to believe he wooed her, led her on, used her and finally intentionally humiliated her." As it would develop, it appears now that that behavior is more an accurate description of Louella's.

Sensing a genuine news story, and not just an attempt at press-agent puffery, the national wire services also began to seek interviews of Orson about *Citizen Kane.* In a matter of weeks, some eighteen full-length feature stories appeared on the Associated Press and United Press International wires alone, covering everything from Orson's precocious childhood in Kenosha, Wisconsin, and Chicago, Illinois, to his eating, drinking, dressing, and shaving habits while filming. Stories about his broken ankle, a short fishing trip to Catalina Island, or a quick location search with his cameraman, Gregg Toland, in Tucson, Arizona, became, unbelievably, national news. Experienced publicists were astonished at the amount of coverage being published in newspapers in advance of *Citizen Kane.* Only three other films in history seemed to have engendered as much: *The Birth of a Nation; Gone with the Wind;* and *The Great Dictator.*

Stories were leaked out of the studio purposely, and others eased out naturally. Welles's intensity and slavishness to detail were a press agent's dream, a fantasy for lovers of trivia. Statistics and attempts at creating instant legends spewed forth: New photographic and shock sound techniques were promised; the fireplace at Xanadu was the largest ever constructed in Hollywood—25 feet wide and 18 feet deep—and consumed, not huge burning logs, but 2,240 cubic feet of gas per hour; Fortunio Bonanova, who played Susan's singing coach in the film, was actually a highly successful opera impresario and singer who had managed his own repertory company for years; to add further realism to the scenes that showed stories and headlines in various papers ("Galleons of Spain Off Jersey Coast!") a real newspaperman, Ed Blake, was hired to write them; fourteen 300-pound barrels of casting plaster and 75 gallons of liquid latex were needed for the makeup; 116 scene sets had to be constructed (as compared to the normal 65 in most films); properties consisted of everything from antique snuff boxes to pieces of a fifteenth-century Shinto shrine from Japan; some of the Xanadu garden shots were photographed at Busch Gardens in Florida; Welles used nine different sets of false teeth to change his appearance and structure of his face as he had Kane go through the aging process; no glass ball with miniature snowstorm could be found that also had a tiny house and a boy on a sled inside of it, as indicated in the script (scouring the shops of Los Angeles, the prop man, Darryl Silvera, returned with glass balls containing everything from snowmen to Christmas trees and Santa Clauses to Eskimos), so four such balls had to be specially glass blown and constructed in the RKO shop to Welles's exact specifications and filled with water and Epsom salts; 72 wooden packing cases and 72 assorted crates, collected from the junkyards and fruit stands of Southern California, were used for the scene at the end of the film when Kane's *objets d'art* are being moved; a whopping 796 extras were hired for the film, together with 19 dancing girls, 84 bit players, 28 stand-ins and 28 players of parts.

But for every superlative and intriguing fact about the production, there were stories that, for reasons of possible adverse publicity, Welles wanted to keep from the eagle-eyed Hollywood press corps:

His two leading ladies, Ruth Warrick and Dorothy Comingore, were pregnant; he was on fighting, often nonspeaking, terms with Bernard Herrmann; Joseph Cotten contracted an infection in his eyes because of the contact lenses he was forced to wear; a rumor reached Welles that Mankiewicz was going to violate his agreement and seek sole credit for writing the film; the RKO front office was complaining about the Mercury's liquor bills for entertaining the press; Joan Blair, who was to play Georgie, the madam, in the ultimately excised brothel scene, secretly flew to New York to spend time with the infamous madam Polly Adler, to soak up atmosphere before acting on camera; George Coulouris petitioned the Screen Actors' Guild that he be paid for sitting and posing for two hours for the statue of Thatcher that is used in the Memorial Library scene (he won the case); Welles had written a risqué song that he and Cotten were to sing at Georgie's place ("This Is Myrtle's Wedding Day"), over which the studio executives, when they heard it, were becoming concerned; the Hays Office was already nitpicking the script and suggesting all kinds of excisions and changes on the grounds of obscenity or bad taste, many of which the studio agreed should be made.

Schaefer was becoming deeply worried that the similarities of the life of Charles Foster Kane to William Randolph Hearst would not only result in an embargo of publicity or advertising in Hearst's papers but also activate massive legal action against the studio on the grounds of libel and invasion of privacy.*

The film itself, its appearance and its dramatic appeal, was thought to be exactly on target. When studio executives screened some 7,000 feet of rushes with Orson—about three-fourths of the finished film—on an early September evening, they sincerely proclaimed it a masterpiece, and J. J. Nolan, the head of RKO studio operations, called it "great." But what about the inevitable legal hassle it was certain to bring? Welles kept insisting to Schaefer that the film was *not* about Hearst, that elements of many of the rich press lords and financial tycoons of America could easily be found in the personality of Kane; he pointed out that one might also conclude that the film could have been based—but it wasn't—on the life of Jules Brulatour, the multimillionaire distributor of Eastman Kodak film, who promoted his wife, Hope Hampton, into an ill-fated operatic career with the same fervor and dim-sighted stubbornness as Kane.

But no matter how much Welles attempted to convince the skeptics, the evidence of similarity between the Kane character and Hearst was overwhelming: after an unsuccessful career at the university, Kane buys the *New York Inquirer* and tries to gain the confidence of his staff by giving lavish parties; Hearst, after being expelled from Harvard, took over the *San Francisco Examiner* and held parties for his staff as an act of ingratiation; Kane has chorus girls at his party, acts the part of a dandy, becomes enamored by and eventually marries a young woman of lesser social standing; Hearst, as a young man, often appeared in public with ladies of the chorus, fell in love with Millicent Willson—twenty years younger than he—one of the high-kicking "merry maidens" in *The Girl from Paris,* and married her; in the breakfast scene, the Kane table, although set formally, can be seen, incongruously, to have ketchup bottles on it; Hearst's eccentric dinner table settings at San Simeon were well known to the press: amidst the elegant crystal and silver could always be found the unceremonious bottles of steak sauce and ketchup, complete with their brand labels; Kane and Hearst each had one of the largest privately owned zoos in the United States; Charles Foster Kane unsuccessfully runs for governor of New York, his campaign surrounded by political

*In a letter to RKO (July 15, 1940) referring to the script, Joseph I. Breen, then the head of the Motion Picture Association of America, listed some of their complaints: "scenes 17, et. seq.; Here and elsewhere, it will be necessary that you hold to an *absolute minimum* all scenes of drinking and drunkenness, wherever these occur. Have in mind that such scenes are acceptable only when they are necessary for characterization or plot motivation.... page 83: There should be nothing about this scene which indicates that Georgie is a "madam," or that the girls brought into the party are prostitutes. This flavor should be very carefully guarded against.... page 119: Please eliminate the word "Lord" from Kane's speech, "the Lord only knows...." page 152: The action of the assistant "petting the fanny of the statue" should be eliminated (when Bernstein and Leland are discussing Kane in the *Inquirer's* office). All requested changes were eventually made by Welles.

hacks and phony labor endorsements; politicians wrecked William Randolph Hearst's probable gubernatorial victory in 1905 by defrauding him at the polls. The parallels were unmistakable, and the studio was concerned.

CHAPTER 12

BY THE TIME the shooting of *Citizen Kane* neared its end in September of 1940, Welles was spending most of his time working on his editing in an attempt to splice, trim, shorten, and reshape the film as he had shot it. The Hays Office objection to the brothel scene could not be overcome; there was no way it could be pruned the way they wanted it to be and still make cinematic sense. Welles scrapped the whole episode.

Welles was fascinated by the process of editing and, like many other filmmakers of the past, such as Griffith and Eisenstein, soon concluded that transforming the selection and rhythm of shots into a work of emotive power was one of the most crucially creative acts in the production of a film. He discovered that it was possible, aided by the precision of a razor blade, to alter meaning, change expression, influence allusion, and expand upon sense on the editing table. It was the last chance to bring to the celluloid some of the transformation of a performance that Welles knew so well from the stage. Visual juxtaposition could be made to shape the narrative; aural manipulation was available to explicate import or establish feeling. Much could be changed, rejuvenated, renewed, saved.

Welles wouldn't actually handle the film himself during the editing process—that was the province of the unionized editor—but he would sit in the screening room selecting which one of his many takes he preferred for any given shot and become totally involved in the mesh of detail, requesting a splice here, calling for an eventual dissolve there.

George Crone, a veteran RKO editor, worked with him at the beginning, but not to his satsifaction. Crone couldn't seem to understand the editing dynamics that Orson was attempting to infuse into the film. Kane was a complex personality; the editing of the film had to go beyond the conventional Hollywood technique of long shot–medium shot–close-up, in order to help capture that intricacy.* A young RKO editor who had just finished editing *My Favorite Wife,* Robert Wise, roughly Orson's age, was eventually brought in

---

*In an interview in *Les Cahiers du Cinéma,* June 1958, Welles made an attempt to describe his editing philosophy: "But as for my style, my vision of cinema, editing is not *an* aspect, it is *the* aspect. . . . The whole eloquence of cinema is created in the cutting room . . . it's there that the director is in the full measure of his artistry, for I believe that a film is good only to the degree that the director has been able to control his various methods."

to confront the film, and a rapport was developed. Wise quickly grew to understand what Orson meant in his approach to editing. When he asked for overlapping dialogue, for instance, Wise understood that it was not only desirable for realism but essential for continuity and pacing.*

Although the development of character and the intertwining perceptions of reality were what intrigued Welles, he rarely forgot to consider the elements, the particulars that could, through their precision, hold the film together. For most of the footage of the *News on the March* segment, for example, he wanted the film to have an old-time flickering look, and, as he had done with *Too Much Johnson,* he consequently had every other frame removed to make the sequence appear jerky, older than it was. Often, his editing wishes were discussed in detail with Wise, followed by a memorandum of reminder:

> Have the announcer talk later on the frame "...as legendary"...a new window shot has to be made...new shot needed to follow "...the loot of the world"...put in ahead of "Xanadu livestock" shot of four horses and giraffes...on "here this week" cut to funeral procession ... on "America's Kubla Khan: Charles Foster Kane" put in new group of newspapers...make a new grocery store shot ...fill in a shot of men stacking gold bullion ... title superimposed over Little Salem, to read, "Little Salem, 1871" ... switch insert of boy and mother ... on "William P. Thatcher, grand old man ..." give close-up of Thatcher ... in large shot of Kane in front of microphone in front of *St. Louis Chronicle* building over which will be tracked "and still another opinion" (Kane's own), cut to title "I am, have been and will only be one thing—an American" ... title that reads "1940" change to "1941" ... on "Kane's papers scooped the world on many a great news story," cut in shot of extra edition newspapers traveling up a conveyor ... on White House wedding dialogue, "twice married, twice divorced, first to a President's niece," don't let the announcer talk so soon on "first marriage" ... on "died 1918 in a motor accident with their son," cut in newspaper insert of Kane with wife and son ... on "conceived for Susan Alexander Kane," change zoom shot for iris-in. ...

IN THE SEPTEMBER 16, 1940, issue of *Newsweek,* which appeared on the newsstands during the same week that Welles was filming the brothel scene, the following item appeared in the "miscellany" section:

> The script of Orson Welles's first movie, "Citizen Kane," was sent to William Randolph Hearst for perusal after columnists had hinted it dealt with his life. Hearst approved it without comment.

Schaefer had not heard that Hearst had been sent a script, and he was

---

*In a talk with the author, Wise recalled: "I would put several sequences together from the rushes and then project them for him; he would ask for changes, suggest improvements, ask me to re-change and then change again. It was a constant process of molding and building. We both learned from each other, but he overwhelmed me with his radio background and his masterful use of sound, stretching the boundaries of how I thought sound could be used."

annoyed and concerned that it might have been done without his approval. Publicists from the RKO publicity office, however, denied either sending the script to Hearst or planting the story in *Newsweek*. Welles also denied that he or anyone from his staff had sent Hearst the script or knew anything about the item. The entertainment editor of *Newsweek* refused to identify his source.

Welles may have been prescient when he assumed that Mankiewicz, perversely, might have been responsible for getting the script to Hearst. Pauline Kael has explained the maneuver as an "idiotic indiscretion" on the part of Mankiewicz:

> He was so proud of his script that he lent a copy to Charles Lederer. In some crazily naive way, Mankiewicz seems to have imagined that Lederer would be pleased by how good it was. But Lederer, apparently, was deeply upset and took the script to his aunt and Hearst. It went from them to Hearst's lawyers (who marked various passages) before it was returned to Mankiewicz, and thus Hearst and his associates were alerted early to the content of the film.*

Although Kael's source isn't given, it has the ring of authenticity to it, but it doesn't explain how *Newsweek* got the information and why the item stated that Hearst had approved the script. As subsequent actions occurred, Hearst's reaction would be shown to be quite the opposite.

Schaefer began to feel pressure from various RKO studio executives and members of the board of directors. Floyd Odlum of the Atlas Corporation and David Sarnoff of RCA, both heavily invested in RKO stock, asked for a clarification from Schaefer as to his position on the film. Had his *wunderkind* gone insane? Could or should Hearst be appeased? Should the picture be drastically altered, perhaps even withdrawn? Was there still time to salvage what was beginning to look like an $800,000 investment?

To determine for himself how closely Kane's life still paralleled Hearst's from the initial script of *American,* where the similarity was quite clear, Schaefer had RKO's research department compile a rapid and secret study of the similarities. Bessie McGaffrey, head of the research department, gave Schaefer what he considered was bad news. After appraising just a few of the more important sources of biographical information on the life of Hearst, including the *Encyclopaedia Britannica* and the *Pageant of America* and *Our Times,* McGaffey wrote: "These [biographical sources] tell practically the story *Citizen Kane* does excepting his death and the women in his life."

Schaefer kept this information to himself, not even discussing it with Welles, and went ahead to announce that the film would be released in February of 1941. He was forced to gamble. To confess that he had erred in contracting the controversial Welles, and to have to cancel one of RKO's

---

*Years later, in an interview with director Peter Bogdanovich, Lederer admitted to reading the script but nothing else: "I gave it *back* to *him.* He [Mankiewicz] asked me if I thought Marion would be offended and I said I didn't think so."

major features of that season, would have meant his almost immediate removal as the president of the corporation. He also believed, as did Welles, that there could be heavy publicity for the movie if the Hearst controversy continued. However, he sent a memorandum to all the executives of RKO asking them to refrain from *any* comment to the press about the film; it was important to gain coverage, but crucial to avoid an actual lawsuit, since a suit could not only eradicate any possible profits but also plunge RKO into an even greater financial bind than it was already experiencing.

At first, Welles attempted to maintain a somewhat blasé posture toward the growing adversity. He thought that everyone at RKO was overreacting to the *possible* ire of Hearst: "Relax," he was said to have told studio people and members of his own staff. "You're all behaving like characters in a melodrama—a bad one."

The film was caught in another dilemma; it was still being edited and musically scored, and the deadline for publicity in major news magazines was drawing dangerously near. If the incomplete *Citizen Kane* was shown to their editors, Welles would be taking a chance that without music and other refinements, they would not like the film. However, if the film was withheld until it was edited perfectly, the possibility of publicity in the mass-market magazines could be lost. Welles opted for the former. "As long as they spell the title correctly," he said to Herbert Drake, "let's take a chance."

WELLES HELD HIS first screening of *Citizen Kane* on January 3, 1941; a private showing for the editors of *Life, Look,* and *Redbook* only, the three periodicals that had reached their outside deadlines for February publicity and represented tens of millions of readers. The other publications—that had more lead time because they were on monthly schedules—could wait until the music was added. Also invited, although he promised not to write about the film until it was released, was the West Coast entertainment editor of *The New York Times.* Covertly, Welles and Drake established the time and place of that first screening. Then, with cloak-and-dagger secrecy, they, the four editors, and a projectionist, and absolutely no one else—not even members of the RKO publicity department and top studio officials—saw the first virtually complete screening.

On that morning, the *Hollywood Reporter,* through a leak, broke the story. That they had discovered it shocked Welles, and it angered some of the RKO staff when the article stated that "Welles was showing the picture that evening." With what could be considered self-righteous anger at being preempted, Hedda Hopper called Welles's office and left a message to the effect that she was inviting herself to the screening. Welles, not knowing how to refuse an invitation to Hollywood's most powerful gabber, sent back a telegram saying that since the film was not completed he would prefer it if she would wait until it was closer to perfect, but that in any event, she would be welcome if she decided to come after all. She acknowledged his cordial reservations but went anyway.

As fitful as the sea; as nervous as a cat; as worried as a lamb before the slaughter are some of the clichés that could have been applied to Welles during the two-hour period when *Citizen Kane* was first being screened on that Friday night in January. The reaction by the motion picture editors of three of the most widely read magazines in the country, the most prestigious newspaper, and the response of one of the most powerful gossip columnists in the United States could easily make or break *Citizen Kane*. These writers could virtually elevate or demolish both the film and Welles's career by how they felt at the film's end. However, all five left the screening room without discussing their respective impressions. It was Drake, using the telephone the next day, who had to gather the results. This was an extremely difficult task since the confirmation of the editors' respective reactions to a new film was usually kept secret until publication day.

Relentlessly prodded by the nervous and insanely curious Welles, Drake finally received the preliminary value judgments, aware that a positive personal reaction was no guarantee that an unqualifiedly friendly story would be forthcoming. It looked good, however. James Francis Crow, of *Look,* said it was one of the "most unusual pictures" he had ever seen. Dick Pollard, of *Life,* was disconcertingly awed by what he had experienced and was enthusiastic. *Redbook*'s editor was dazzled. Douglas Churchill of *The New York Times* felt he had to think the movie through further; his normal cinematic rhetoric could not cope with the transcendental originality of *Citizen Kane.*

Only Hedda Hopper was negative. She hated it. "Not only is it a vicious and irresponsible attack on a great man," she told Drake to tell Welles, "but the photography is old-fashioned and the writing very corny."

Hedda and Marion Davies were fast and close friends. They had acted together (in *Zander the Great*) and she was a constant guest at San Simeon, despite the fact that she didn't work for a Hearst newspaper. She called Bill junior, Hearst's son, and told him what he and his father already knew, or at least had guessed: that *Citizen Kane* was, in her opinion, a muckraking crack at Hearst and a distortion of the romance between him and Marion. Within hours of seeing the film, Hedda Hopper started blasting Welles and the not-yet-completed *Citizen Kane* in her column, despite the traditional, unspoken understanding that the press rarely preempts the release date of a film if they've seen an advance screening. "Cockhimers I can take," she wrote. "Arrogance, I abhor."

Welles was furious at her remarks. He was afraid that she would unfavorably influence movie editors in the small towns where her column was syndicated. "It is not only a shame but it's shameful," he told Schaefer. He thought of "disciplining" her—whatever that meant—but Schaefer advised him to assume the air of a trampled and innocent flower in any future dealings with her.

RUMORS THAT *LIFE, Look,* and *Redbook* were completely bowled over by *Citizen Kane,* plus the unfriendly barbs of Hedda Hopper toward it, might have strengthened Mankiewicz's determination to gain sole credit for writing the film. Both as an act of revenge directed toward Hearst (to let him know that he, Mankiewicz, was also responsible for hurting him) and the desire to exploit the possibilities of favorable reviews in the national media could have been factors motivating him. Gossip columnists said that Mankiewicz was going to appeal to the Screen Writers Guild and demand that only one name be placed on the titles of *Citizen Kane* as screenwriter: his.

According to screenwriter Nunnally Johnson, Mankiewicz asked Ben Hecht at that time whether he should request additional money from Welles to keep his name off the credits. An offer of a bribe of $10,000 was mentioned as having actually been made by Welles. "Why not take the money and screw the bastard?" was Hecht's reply. But Mankiewicz didn't want his name off the screenplay. He *had* worked on it; words such as "eminent," "distinguished," and "important" were already being associated with *Citizen Kane* before it was even screened. When Mankiewicz saw some of the rushes of the film, he was astounded by what Welles had created. The honor and distinction of being known as the writer for what could become one of the greatest films ever to have come out of Hollywood was an overwhelming temptation.

Having Mankiewicz's name included as part of the writing team that created *Citizen Kane* really didn't bother Welles. However, he was concerned that RKO might initiate a breach of contract suit against *him* if someone's name other than that of Orson Welles appeared on the credits as the screenwriter. That is the reason that his contract with Mankiewicz made it understood by both parties that Mankiewicz was *not* to receive credit. Never discussed, but a factor of consideration, was the high probability that Mankiewicz would have originally been paid much less for his work had it been possible and agreed upon that he *was* to receive credit.

At a later time, Welles claimed that Mankiewicz's contribution to *Citizen Kane* was enormous, and, in an interview with two writers for *Les Cahiers du Cinéma* in 1961, he said, "I was very lucky to work with Mankiewicz; everything concerning Rosebud belonged to him." Welles has also stated that the "best thing" in the movie, Bernstein's parenthetical remembrance of an experience that took place a half-century before, a Proustian echo, was pure Mankiewicz:

You take me. One day, back in 1896, I was crossing over to Jersey on the ferry, and as we pulled out, there was another ferry pulling in, and on it there was a girl waiting to get off. A white dress she had on. She was carrying a white parasol. I only saw her for one second. She didn't see me at all, but I bet a month hasn't gone by since that I haven't thought of that girl.

Mankiewicz let it be known to Welles that not only did he want the honor of being credited as the screenwriter, but, in a display of vanity that indicated he would lose something if praise was accorded to someone else, he additionally demanded that *his* name only was to appear on the titles; Welles's name was to be off.

Welles had the legal, artistic, and moral right to be listed as one of the screenwriters: all the people who worked on the film have since confirmed that Welles did substantial writing and editing of the script; the RKO corporate ledgers also list Welles as having worked no less than 111 days on the script alone.

Welles wanted his *and* Mankiewicz's names to appear, and he wanted Houseman's name to be in the credits, also. Houseman modestly demurred claiming that he had only edited the script. As it developed, Schaefer stated that he would have no objection to allowing Mankiewicz's name to appear in the titles as a co-screenwriter. This saved Welles from any legal repercussions from RKO. Before Welles could relay this information to him, however, Mankiewicz had already formally petitioned the Screen Writers' Guild and asked for arbitration in the matter.

After representatives of the Screen Writers' Guild carefully examined Mankiewicz's contract with Mercury Productions, they claimed to have no authority in the matter. In the absence of a written agreement, they told him, there was an implied obligation to name the co-screenwriter, and, under those conditions, the custom of the industry was to give such credit. However, the Mercury contract clearly precluded all of Mankiewicz's credit rights for recognition. There was nothing that the Guild could or would do. He was told that he would have to work it out with Welles personally.

The next day, January 3, 1941, Morris E. Cohn and Robert Kenny, attorneys for the SWG, wrote the following joint letter to both Welles and Mankiewicz:

> Gentlemen: In view of the hearing last night, the Board of Directors of the Screen Writers' Guild have directed me to advise you that it does not consider the matter of screen credit for *Citizen Kane* to be under the jurisdiction of the Screen Writers' Guild.

Eventually, and for no reason other than because he thought Mankiewicz deserved it, Welles had Mankiewicz's name included as the co-screenwriter. But, he made clear, he was doing it in goodwill, as a matter of simple decency. He had no legal obligation to do so. Despite Pauline Kael's essay in *The Citizen Kane Book,* a virtual tome that attempted to elevate Mankiewicz's position as the principal screenwriter on the film, some people believe that it was Mankiewicz, not Welles, who acted as the disreputable one in this legendary controversy: the facts make it clear that Welles was the injured party. Mankiewicz had violated his word and his contract and had demanded something that was not justifiably or legally his.

When the script was finally typed and ready to be sent to the title department for art direction, Orson noticed that the legend read:

Original Screenplay
Orson Welles
Herman J. Mankiewicz

Welles thought a moment and, without saying anything, quickly circled Mankiewicz's name and penciled an arrow from it to indicate that it was to be placed on top of his own. Mankiewicz, happily, and without thanks, accepted the gift of first billing. He had been paid $22,833.35 for his work on the script.

DURING THE SAME week that the Mankiewicz problem erupted, additional fuel further inflamed the Hearst controversy. A new and subsequently short-lived publication, *Friday,* which deemed itself "The Magazine That Dared to Tell the Truth," published a two-page pictorial feature article on the film, claiming that it had had a "sneak preview" of *Citizen Kane.* Actually, no one from *Friday* had seen the film; Drake had sent the magazine—as he had to a number of other publications—a series of still photographs of scenes from *Citizen Kane* and a basic press release with pertinent details of the plot of the film and information about its stars. *Friday*'s editor, Dan Gillmor, published a story, taking each still photo and writing a caption for it that proved to his own satisfaction that the film was about William Randolph Hearst.* The article attempted to show similarities in the life of Kane as seen in the photos. It ended with the following:

> Louella Parsons, Hollywood correspondent for the Hearst newspaper chain, has been praising Welles lavishly, giving *Citizen Kane* a terrific advance build-up. When informed of these outbursts of praise, Welles said: "This is something I cannot understand. Wait until the woman finds out that the picture's about her boss."

When Welles received an advance copy of the article, he exploded. Privately, he welcomed the publicity that the controversy would generate; publicly, he could not go on record—and he was warned about this by Schaefer, the RKO attorneys, and Weissberger—with any kind of statement that indicated that the film was about Hearst.

Not only did Gillmor mastermind the magazine's sensational treatment of *Citizen Kane* but he continued discussing the film and its Hearstian implications on his thrice-weekly radio show, "Truth on the Air," heard during prime time on WHN in New York and syndicated to other cities. On his shows he talked about "the most important and world-shaking events of the day," as he modestly described them.

"Where the hell did you get that quote?" boomed Welles over long-distance telephone to Gillmor, demanding a retraction. Gillmor admitted that the source of the quote was fabricated by a *Friday* staff writer, and sheepishly agreed to publish an article written by Welles giving his side of the story, in the very next issue of *Friday.*

---

*Gillmor attempted to become a mini-Hearst himself; not only did he start *Friday* but he bought out or founded other periodicals, many of them of dubious or sensational nature, as well, such as *Popular Psychology Guide, Unbelievable,* and the whole spectrum of *Silver Streak* comic books.

Since the *Friday* article with the spurious quote had not, as yet, been distributed to the newsstands, Welles, in anticipation of a fight with Louella Parsons when she eventually read it—and an attempt at advance palliation—sent her a telegram stating that the forthcoming article was false and that his statement about her could not be attributed to him; he also said that he was already working on an article of retraction that would appear the following week in the same magazine.

Louella received the telegram on the evening of January 8, en route to one of her perpetual parties. She had hardly arrived and had her first drink of the evening when her secretary tracked her down by telephone to make sure she was there. Within minutes, another call came in to her from San Simeon. It was the high-pitched voice of Hearst. "Yes, chief; yes, chief; yes, chief," she was heard to have said, over and over again. Hearst also had an advance copy of *Friday,* and he had begun to receive reports from his editors on the *New York Journal-American,* who had heard on Gillmor's program that Welles was saying that the film was indeed about him. Hearst didn't tell Louella that Hedda Hopper had already seen the film and that she believed it was an analogue of his life. He asked Louella to screen the film to determine whether she thought it was as close a parallel to his life as was being rumored, and, if so, to see if she could prevent its release.

At midnight that night, Hearst issued a directive to all his newspapers throughout the country stating that until further notice, there was to be no publicity, articles, or mention of any kind of *any* RKO film. All such planned stories were to be canceled. Several Hearst papers, such as the *Detroit Times* and the *San Francisco Examiner,* had major features scheduled on the RKO romance that was to be nationally released at that time, *Kitty Foyle,* with Ginger Rogers and Dennis Morgan, and this publicity was to coincide with a serialization of the novel by Christopher Morley. Hearst canceled the articles and the serialization despite the fact that his newspapers had been promoting their imminent publication for weeks. Too late to catch, Hearst's *Los Angeles Examiner* already had a complimentary review of *Kitty Foyle* in its early edition; it was peremptorily yanked in all further editions.

The next morning, Louella called Welles's office and announced, like Hedda, that she was coming to the studio, without benefit of welcome or invitation, that afternoon to screen the film. Orson was there to greet her when she arrived with two attorneys: Oscar Lawler, a Hearst corporation official; and A. Laurence Mitchell, Hearst's counsel in Los Angeles. Louella's chauffeur, Louis Collins, also joined the screening party.

At the film's end, Louella bolted from the screening room without saying a word to Welles, the two lawyers following in similar haste. Only the chauffeur remained to see the titles appear on the screen. "That was a fine picture, Mr. Welles," he said courteously, before joining his employer in her limousine.

Back at her office, Louella conferred with the two attorneys. Obviously, the film was about Hearst, and she feared it would hurt him deeply. How does one tell one of the most powerful men in America—and one's boss—that an exposé of his life is going to appear on the screen? Perhaps as a result of concern and anger, or possibly as a dramatic gesture, Louella chose to inform Hearst by way of telegram: the film was "worse" than any of them had expected and would blacken his reputation. A call came back to her from San Simeon from one of Hearst's assistants: stop *Citizen Kane*.

There is reason to believe that there were two major causes why Hearst became so incensed over the film. The first had to do with his own sense of immortality and fear of death. At seventy-eight, he knew his star had begun to dim, but he would not confront nor admit to his possible geriatric deterioration or eventual demise. The word "death" was taboo in his presence; discussion of wills and testaments or the death of friends or even talk of sickness was shunned by him and, consequently, his colleagues. The fact that *Citizen Kane* was so inexorably intertwined from its beginning with the death of the Hearst-like figure made the film especially anathematic to him.

Hearst also was concerned about the portrayal of Susan Alexander as a vacuous shopgirl with no talent who leaves Kane because she hates him and eventually becomes an alcoholic. The implied schema or tableau of Hearst's relationship with Marion Davies was too close a parallel. Forty years Marion's senior, Hearst took to wearing green checked suits and painted ties to appear younger; he was insanely jealous of her and acutely, painfully aware of the age gap, always frightened that she would leave him. He was also totally captivated by Marion's acting talent, often sitting for hours, transfixed in front of the movie screen in his private projection room, watching her films, tears of laughter or sadness streaming down his cheeks. The fact that most critics felt that she was only remotely a "star," with ordinary talent, always disturbed him. Again, the parallel, not with his actual life, but of his inner spirit, was too painful. He would have to retaliate.

AT 5:40 THAT evening, Louella called George Schaefer at his RKO office. When she learned he was in a meeting and had left strict instructions with his secretary, Lee Claire, that he was not to be disturbed, she worked herself up into a frenzied rage. "How dare Mr. Schaefer ever do a thing like that?" she said. She told Claire that this was a "matter of life and death to RKO," and she would wait only five minutes for Schaefer to return her call or else the studio would be hit with one of "the most beautiful lawsuits in history." As Claire scribbled the notes of the telephone conversation as quickly as possible, Louella indicated that the repercussions would be felt even beyond RKO: "Mr. Hearst will bring an incredible amount of pressure on the motion picture industry," she said. After demanding Schaefer's home telephone number, she hung up. When he learned about the call, Schaefer first conferred with Welles and, later that evening, called Louella to reiterate that the film, in RKO's opinion, was not a biography of Hearst and that they still had every intention of releasing it as scheduled. Louella's insistence that the film be scrapped only seemed to irritate Schaefer, who maintained his position.

"Mr. Hearst told me to tell you," she said, "if you boys want private lives, he'll give you private lives." Parsons went on to ask, on behalf of Hearst, for at least a hold on releasing the film pending possible legal action. "The release date of February fourteenth is final," said Schaefer somewhat formally, "and I can give no serious consideration to his proposal to hold it up."

The next day, Welles received a call from short story writer and newspaperwoman Adela Rogers St. Johns—one of Hearst's favorites—stating that she had been given an assignment to do an article about him in Hearst's Sunday supplement, the *American Weekly,* to appear on January 26.* The theme of the story was Welles's private and romantic life, particularly in reference to the hours of twelve midnight and 3:00 A.M. When Welles refused the interview on those grounds, St. Johns condescendingly said that she would settle for some statements by him on Hollywood. He still refused. The article never ran.

Welles was not the only one threatened. Louella Parsons made it clear to everyone that if *Citizen Kane* was released, other Hollywood notables would be exposed in Hearst papers and Hearst would also wage a relentless campaign against the hiring of aliens in the motion picture industry.

Louella would make up in wrath what she failed to receive in consideration from Schaefer. The telephone became her weapon. Within hours and in the next few days she seemed to have called virtually everyone in Hollywood who might either be sympathetic to Hearst's case or easily threatened by him. Louis B. Mayer acted outraged over the idea of a film about Hearst and the possible repercussions to the industry and promised Louella he would lead a cause to stop it. Louella also called producers Joseph Schenck, Nicholas Schenck, Y. Frank Freeman, Darryl Zanuck, and David O. Selznick to enlist their aid and received, if not outright support, a certain sympathy from all of them. What could be so important about another picture by a Hollywood newcomer if it meant a Hearst retaliation that could hurt the entire motion picture industry, they reasoned. And a national newspaper campaign attacking the large number of European aliens and refugee talent then employed in Hollywood could prove embarrassing.

Since their studios were not involved in the film, nor their money, nor their reputations, they could afford to be affronted and distressed, Welles claimed, when he heard of their supposed outrage.

Louella was relentless. She then called, one by one, every member of the RKO board of directors and threatened them with fictional accounts of their lives in Hearst papers and magazines if *Citizen Kane* was released. David Sarnoff, president of RCA (which had a controlling interest in RKO) and chairman of the board of NBC and a former chairman of RKO, was also contacted by her to see if he would or could intervene. W. G. Van Schmus,

---

*St. Johns was one of the most aggressive reporters of her day, rarely failing to come back with her assigned stories (her interviews with Edward VIII and Wallis Simpson made her famous). Hearst chose her for the Kane story as a threatening device used to intimidate, albeit unsuccessfully, Welles.

manager of Radio City Music Hall in New York, was informed that he would incur the wrath of Hearst if he accepted the film for exhibition and that no Hearst paper would ever again accept advertising for, nor would it review *any* film that played in the Music Hall thereafter. Schmus promised her that the doors to the Music Hall would be closed to *Citizen Kane.*

Although never confirmed, it was rumored that Louella also contacted Nelson Rockefeller, who, through his holding corporation, owned a substantial amount of stock in RKO. It was Rockefeller who had helped Schaefer become president of RKO and who approved of, some say suggested, the initial hiring of Welles by Schaefer. Rockefeller, who owned stock in Radio City Music Hall, could have insisted that the film open there, but he somehow went along with Schmus's decision. She also asked Harry M. Warner, of Warner Brothers, to refuse to exhibit the film in any of his theaters.

Louella insisted that Will Hays, of the Motion Picture Association, stop the film on the grounds that, "Under the code you can't make a picture about a living person." To punctuate her conversation with him, she asked various Hollywood producers and others sympathetic to Hearst's cause to lodge complaints with Hays against the film. At the very time that Hays was receiving calls about *Citizen Kane,* he was discussing in his office a forthcoming project with the eminent French pianist Germaine Schnitzer, who was planning a series of musical shorts with Arturo Toscanini. Madame Schnitzer recalled that Hays attempted to mollify the complainers and sounded as though he was personally against the release of *Citizen Kane*: "Well, it's very probable that the picture will have to be withdrawn. It's a terrible scandal," she reported Hays to have said. "It won't be the first time a picture was shelved." Publicly, however, Hays made no move to obstruct *Citizen Kane.* One mitigating factor against a move by the MPA was that Joseph I. Breen, of the Hays Office, claimed that, in his opinion, after carefully reading the script, the film was not about Hearst. (Later, Breen would be hired as the president of RKO.)

Louella was in constant contact with Hearst and his lieutenants, informing them, step-by-step, as to her progress, if any. After her call to Schaefer, Hearst became even further incensed. It was decided by him to release the story of the controversy to the press and to begin his fight in the open.

The next day, January 14, 1941, *The New York Times* headlined the battle:

HEARST OBJECTS TO WELLES FILM
Mention of RKO in his Press Barred as the
Withdrawal of "Citizen Kane" is Demanded.

In the article, Welles is quoted as claiming no biographical similarity between his character of Charles Foster Kane and William Randolph Hearst, "or any one else," but he made a statement that proved an irritant to Hearst nevertheless: "Had Mr. Hearst and similar financial barons not lived during the period we discuss, *Citizen Kane* could not have been made."

Meanwhile, Orson's rebuttal article in *Friday*—an ill-tempered one, as he described it—was published. Noting that retractions were notoriously valueless, Orson nevertheless pointed out most of the fallacies of the original story. Talking about his supposed statement about Louella's naiveté, he wrote: "This is not a misquotation. *Friday*'s source invented it. *Citizen Kane* is not about Louella Parsons's boss. It is the portrait of a fictional newspaper tycoon, and I have never said or implied to anyone that it is anything else." After giving an outline of what the film was *really* about, in his opinion, and writing his own captions for the stills, Welles finished up his *j'accuse* against *Friday* with an interpretation and an attempt at self-protection:

> Kane, we are told, loved only his mother—only his newspaper—only his second wife—only himself. Maybe he loved all of these, or none. It is for the audience to judge. Kane was selfish and selfless, an idealist, a scoundrel, a very big man and a very little one. It depends on who is talking about him. He is never judged with the objectivity of an author, and the point of the picture is not so much the solution to the problem as its presentation. The easiest way to draw parallels between Kane and other famous publishers is *not* to see the picture. *Citizen Kane* is the portrait of a public man's private life. I have met some publishers but I know none of them well enough to make them possible as models. Constant references have been made to the career of William Randolph Hearst, drawing parallels to my film. This is unfair to Hearst and to Kane.

Weissberger was working overtime for Welles to determine whether Hearst had any legal grounds for either a libel action or an invasion of privacy action. It was also being rumored that Hearst might attempt to obtain an injunction against the film. Conferring with the attorneys of RKO and doing his own research, Weissberger, however, began to feel confident. He relayed his buoyancy to Welles.

If Hearst decided to bring a libel suit or an invasion of privacy suit for damages against Welles and the picture, Weissberger informed his client, he could do so, of course—and Hearst might easily lose in court—but Hearst could not use such an action to obtain an injunction under the laws of most states. Under the Civil Rights Act in New York State at that time, for example, an injunction against a film could be obtained if a portrait or picture of an individual was used for advertising purposes; since that was not the case, and in no advertising or publicity issued by Welles or the studio was Hearst's name mentioned as the source of the film, it was highly unlikely that any court would grant an injunction against *Citizen Kane* simply because its central character *resembled* Hearst. Weissberger told Welles that Hearst could, of course, *instigate* actions for misappropriation of his supposed likeness under the invasion of privacy laws, as a means both to harass and to intimidate potential exhibitors of the film in movie theaters across the country.

In order to verify his reading of the potential legal difficulties, Weissberger obtained an opinion on the matter from another eminent and well-known attorney, Morris Ernst. It was Ernst's judgment that if Hearst did instigate action, his own attorneys would never allow the case to come to trial; that although the life details were similar, there could be no proof that Charles Foster Kane was a duplicate of William Randolph Hearst. Ernst felt that the case, if it ever managed to be argued in court, would rest on the question of whether a man, a public figure, had the right to copyright the details of his own life. Ernst was certain that he did not and that the court would rule in favor of Welles and RKO.

To be absolutely certain that any possible consideration by the court in any future action would recognize that Welles was *not* attempting to manipulate the public into thinking that *Citizen Kane* was about the life of Hearst, Weissberger asked him, on January 14, to issue a statement to the press indicating the fictitious nature of the film. Although many newspapers paraphrased Orson's statement or quoted portions of it, it has never until now been published in full:

I wished to make a motion picture which was not a narrative of action so much as an examination of character. For this, I desired a man of many sides and many aspects. It was my idea to show that six or more people could have as many widely divergent opinions concerning the nature of a single personality. Clearly such a notion could not be worked out if it would apply to an ordinary American citizen.

I immediately decided that my character should be a public man—an extremely public man—an extremely important one. I then decided that I would like to convince my audience of the reality of this man by means of an apparently legitimate news digest short concerning his career. It was of the essence of my idea that the audience should be fully conversant with the outlines of the public career of this fictitious character before I proceeded to examine his private life. I did not wish to make a picture about his public life. I wished to make a picture about the backstairs aspect of it. The varying opinions concerning his character would throw light on important moments in his career. I wished him to be an American, since I wished to make him an American president. Deciding against this, I could find no other position in public life beside that of a newspaper publisher in which a man of enormous wealth exercises what might be called real power in a democracy. It is possible to show how a powerful industrialist is potent in certain phases of government. It is possible to show how he can be good and bad according to the viewpoint of whoever is discussing him, but no industrialist can ever achieve in a democratic government the kind of general and catholic power with which I wished to invest my particular character. The only solution seemed to place my man in charge of some important channel of communication—radio or newspaper. It was essential for the plot of the story that my character (Kane) live to a great age, but be dead at the commencement of the narrative. This immediately precluded radio. There was no other solution except to make Kane a newspaper publisher—the owner of a great chain of newspapers. It was needful that Kane himself represent new ideas in his field.

The history of the newspaper business obviously demanded that Kane be what is generally referred to as a yellow journalist.

There have been many motion pictures and novels rigorously obeying the formula of the "success story." I wished to do something quite different. I wished to make a picture which might be called a "failure story." I did not wish to portray a ruthless and gifted industrialist working his way up from a simple lumberman or street car conductor to a position of wealth and prominence. The interpretations of such a character by his intimates were too obvious for my purpose. I therefore invested my character with sixty million dollars at the age of eight so that there was no considerable or important gain in point of wealth possible from a dramatic point of view. My story was not, therefore, about how a man gets money, but what he does with his money—not when he gets old—but throughout his entire career. A man who has money and doesn't have to concern himself with making more, naturally wishes to use it for the exercise of power. There are many, of course, in "real life" who are exceptions to this, but the assumption of flair and vigor on the part of Kane as a personality made such an inclination obvious in his makeup. It was also much better for the purpose of my narrative since the facts about a philanthropist would not make as good a picture as a picture about a man interested in imposing his will upon the will of his fellow countrymen.

If I had determined to make a motion picture about the life of a great manufacturer of automobiles, I should have found not long after I started writing it that my invention occasionally paralleled history itself. The same is true in the case of my fictitious publisher. He was a yellow journalist. He was functioning as such in the great early days of the development of yellow journalism. Self-evidently, it was impossible for me to ignore American history. I declined to fabricate an impossible or psychologically untrue reaction to American historical events by an American yellow journalist. The reactions of American yellow journalists—indeed all possible publishers—to wars, social injustices, etc., etc., were for a great period of time in the history of these matters identical. Some have identified their names with certain events, but all are concerned with them. My character could not very well disregard them. My picture could not begin the career of such a man in 1890 and take it to 1940 without presenting the man with the same problems which presented themselves to his equivalents in real life. *His dealings with these events were determined by dramaturgical and psychological laws which I recognize to be absolute. They were not colored by the facts in history. The facts in history were actually determined by the same laws which I employed as a dramatist.*

The most basic of all ideas was that of a search for the true significance of the man's apparently meaningless dying words. Kane was raised without a family. He was snatched from his mother's arms in early childhood. His parents were a bank. From the point of view of the psychologist, my character had never made what is known as "transference" from his mother. Hence his failure with his wives. In making this clear during the course of the picture, it was my attempt to lead the thoughts of my audience closer and closer to the solution of the enigma of his dying words. These were "Rosebud." The device of the picture calls for a newspaperman (who didn't know Kane) to interview people who knew him very well. None had ever heard of "Rosebud." Actually, as it turns out, "Rosebud" is the trade name of a cheap little sled on which Kane was playing on the day he was taken away from his home and his mother. In his subconscious it represented the simplicity, the comfort, above all the lack of responsibility in his home, and also it stood for his mother's love which Kane never lost.

In his waking hours, Kane had certainly forgotten the sled and the name which was painted on it. Case books of psychiatrists are full of these stories. It was important for me in the picture to tell the audience as effectively as possible what this really meant. Clearly it would be undramatic and disappointing if an arbitrary character in the story popped up with the information. The best solution was the sled itself. Now, how could this sled still exist since it was built in 1880? It was necessary that my character be a collector—the kind of man who never throws anything away. I wished to use as a symbol—at the conclusion of the picture—a great expanse of objects—thousands and thousands of things—one of which is "Rosebud." This field of inanimate theatrical properties I wished to represent the very dustheap of a man's life. I wished the camera to show beautiful things, ugly things and useless things, too—indeed everything which could stand for a public career and a private life. I wished objects of art, objects of sentiment, and just plain objects. There was no way for me to do this except to make my character, as I have said, a collector, and to give him a great house in which to keep his collections. The house itself occurred to me as a literal translation in terms of drama of the expression "ivory tower." The protagonist of my "failure story" must retreat from a democracy which his money fails to buy and his power fails to control. —There are two retreats possible: *death* and the *womb*. The house was the womb. Here too was all the grandeur, all the despotism which my man had found lacking in the outside world. Such was his estate—such was the obvious repository for a collection large enough to include, without straining the credulity of the audience—a little toy from the dead past of a great man.

Even if Welles's statement was entirely subjective and a self-serving attempt to protect his interests, and it probably was, it was nevertheless a fascinating interpretation of the film's ideation, or at least how he wanted the public to perceive the way he had conceived it. Some reporters were skeptical of Orson's psychoanalytical interpretation. "I admit that it's 'dollar-book' Freud," he said, "but, nevertheless, it's how I analyze the film."

Schaefer was encouraged by Weissberger's opinion and those of his own legal staff, only to receive a temporary setback when Gordon Youngman, RKO's corporate counsel, screened the film and proclaimed that it was *obviously* the life of Hearst. "You're looking for Hearst because you've been advised he'd be there," countered the irritated Schaefer. Youngman denied any such influence.

Youngman reported to the RKO board of directors that it was possible that

Hearst might move to enjoin the film and/or bring the matter to the courts. When pressured by the board to explain what he predicted would happen, Youngman explained that, while he couldn't say definitely that Hearst would sue Welles and RKO, neither could he say he wouldn't. Youngman's ambivalence swayed the group. Overruling Schaefer, the board agreed to put a temporary hold on the release of the film until such time as they could discern what kind of action or coercion Hearst might use. The February 14 opening date was canceled.

Welles's reaction to the RKO restraining order was cavalier. On January 27, at a luncheon in Los Angeles at which he was the guest speaker, he laughingly intoned, "When I get *Citizen Kane* off my mind, I'm going to work on an idea for a great picture based on the life of William Randolph Hearst." He was not then aware that Hearst's pressure was beginning to work, at first surreptitiously and then in the open. Both the major wire services, AP and UPI, which might have lost a number of important clients if Hearst cut off using their services, stopped mentioning the film altogether and gave no coverage to the Hearst-Welles controversy itself because, as one of the bureau chiefs explained, they "didn't carry private fights between two gentlemen."

Many other newspaper editors throughout the country, even those who could be counted on as traditional Hearst-baiters and haters were more sympathetic to Hearst than to Welles as they considered whether *Citizen Kane* should be released; it was something akin to media chauvinism: when one of the herd is attacked, publishers, like many other groups, stick together. Although some did not go so far as to support Hearst in their columns, neither did most editorialize on Welles's behalf even if they agreed with his ethical and constitutional right to make such a film.

THERE HAS BEEN almost fifty years of speculation as to whether Hearst saw the film before it was released. Orson has told the story of confronting Hearst, by total accident, in an elevator in the Mark Hopkins Hotel in San Francisco and brashly offering him two tickets to a screening of *Kane.* Supposedly, Hearst refused to even look at Orson, let alone acknowledge him. But Hearst definitely *did* screen it at San Simeon in the early spring, after the original release date was canceled by RKO. Schaefer claims that he sent him a print, on the gamble that once Hearst saw "himself" on the screen he would be placated. Schaefer has been quoted as saying: "Hearst personally sent a message to me at the studio and asked me to see a print, and we let him have it. This was before it was opened. There was no response, no comment. Orson knew this."

However, in an interview with this writer in London, Virginia Nicholson was quite emphatic about the screening details.

> Charlie [Lederer] and I were guests once again at a typical weekend at San Simeon. Everyone in Hollywood was talking about *Citizen Kane,* and, of course, I was eager to see it, because of the connection with Orson and the

possible connection with Hearst. After dinner—it was a Saturday night—we went to the screening room, and without saying anything, Hearst had *Kane* projected. In addition to Hearst, Marion—Muggins, we called her—was there, Charlie, myself, and a few other guests. When the film ended and the lights came up, we all looked over in Hearst's direction. He had a slightly scampish smile but didn't say anything. We were all afraid to utter a word. Then, he and Marion simply got up and went upstairs, in his private elevator, to retire. Although I saw him many times after that, I never heard him mention a word about the film.

Despite the mischievous smile, Hearst was devastated by what had been done to Marion Davies, according to Fred Laurence Guiles, her biographer. "It had never mattered to Hearst what was said or written about him. He was used to vilification, and he said now that he just was not interested in whether he was Welles's model or not ... but seeing the movie had an entirely different impact on him. He was an old man trembling with indignation over the way they handled her in the film."

Forty years later, Orson admitted that his portrait of Susan Alexander Kane as a vacuous Marion Davies was a joke, "a dirty trick," played on Hearst to enrage him.

A STORY THAT made its way into the popular press in the late 1970s suggested another, even more personal reason why Hearst was upset over *Citizen Kane*. It was claimed that Hearst's pet name for Marion Davies's pudenda was "rosebud." How Orson (or Mankiewicz) could have ever discovered this most private utterance is unexplained and why it took over thirty-five years for such a suggestive rationale to emerge, although the origins of everything to do with *Citizen Kane* had continually been placed under literary and cinematic microscopes for decades, is also unknown. If this highly unlikely story is even partially true—it is possible that the word "rosebud" was used in general as an affectionate euphemism for a woman's genitalia—Hearst may have become upset at the implied connotation, although any such connection seems to have been innocent on Welles's part.*

In any event, this bizarre explanation for the origin of one of the most famous words ever spoken on the screen, has now made its way into serious studies of Welles and *Citizen Kane*. And it is altogether possible that Orson, in his later years, in some curious and revisionistic sleight-of-mind, began to believe the story himself.

IN A CALL to Louis B. Mayer, Hearst did not specifically threaten the movie industry, but he quietly claimed that in order to protect himself and other publishers from additional attacks from studios, he felt he would have to do something in retaliation. He pointed out to Mayer the many times he had

---

*Eric Partridge in his *Dictionary of Slang and Unconventional English*, offers the word "rose" as "the female pudenda; a maidenhead."

buried or canceled a scandalous story, for example, about a drunken studio executive and a starlet, and how on many occasions he would plug an ailing film or publish lavish picture stories about it and its stars when a film needed pushing at the box office. Hearst claimed that he had always helped the movie industry when it needed such assistance; now he wanted some reciprocal aid. Mayer was more than sympathetic; it has been reported that when he finally saw *Citizen Kane* he wept in empathy for his old friend.

Whether with Hearst's money backing him or a pool of cash pledged by a group of Hollywood producers, as it has often been surmised, or his own money, it is not known, but Mayer called Schaefer and offered to buy the negative and all the prints of the film so that it could be destroyed. The film's production cost was exactly $805,527.53. Mayer made a firm and legally binding offer for that amount if Schaefer would relinquish the film.

Schaefer refused the offer, stating that *Citizen Kane* was "an important film of which we are proud." His personal loyalty to Welles was a crucial factor in his refusal, but Schaefer also believed, because of the attendant publicity, that the film might easily make back its cost and a sizable profit in addition. It was rumored, but never proven, that when Henry Luce heard about the Mayer offer, he quickly submitted a bid to Schaefer of one million dollars to buy the film for Time, Inc. so as to *insure* the film's release, putting his old rival Hearst in his place. The report that Universal also offered one million dollars for the negative, to promote what they considered to be a positive winner, was subsequently denied by studio head Nate J. Blumberg: "Never discussed. In fact, never broached. Had it been, we would not have been interested. We have our own movies to distribute."

When Welles became aware of all the insurgent undercover skirmishes being planned by or for Hearst, and as he read occasional personally negative comments about himself in the newspapers saying that, "if trouble becomes more acute, his film career may be ended," as reported in *The New York Times,* his inner confidence was shaken. In public, he still attempted to appear self-assured. In a retaliatory statement to *The New York Times,* subtly accusing the paper of giving the controversy too much space in their columns, he quipped: "The rumors that have reached the Welles organization are of such quantity and detail that we have come to the conclusion that where there is so much smoke, a lot of type is cast."

Privately, Welles continued to confer with Weissberger. Did he have any legal recourse should the film be held up either permanently or for so long a time that interest in it might dissipate? If RKO refused to release the picture, he was advised he might be able to sue the studio for breach of contract, since he was not merely an employee but held a one-fourth interest in the profits of the film; and a suit against Hearst proving that he was an instrumental factor in shattering Welles's agreement with RKO could also be brought. Welles considered the possibility, should the film be stalled beyond a reasonable time, of enlisting the aid of the general stockholders in demanding that it be released.

WHILE WAITING FOR Schaefer's decision as to exactly when *Citizen Kane* would be released—Schaefer told Welles that it was always a question not of "if" but of "when"—and while putting the last details of the film in order, he became involved in a new radio series, "The Free Company."

James Boyd, an historical novelist and an outspoken proponent of free speech and human rights, was asked by officials of the Department of Justice to help fight a growing problem of great national concern. Hostile propaganda, so tragically demonstrated in various European countries, was seeping into American media with increasing quantity and depth. After a series of meetings, the Department of Justice issued a memorandum to Boyd encouraging him to use radio, the country's most effective medium, to initiate a cycle of programs without government intervention that would present in dramatic form the meaning of America. It was an awesome and noble undertaking, but Boyd accepted the challenge and "The Free Company" was born. "Not to exhort, still less to prescribe, but by their power of the word to remind, no more than that, our people of their possessions."

The theme of each program would be an attempt to combat foreign propaganda through an interpretation of the true meaning of the Bill of Rights. The format would follow the method of the Bible or Aesop's fables and broadcast a sequence of weekly plays, each dealing with one of the basic civil rights or with the whole subject of freedom and each written by a leading American writer. Stars of stage, screen, and radio were asked to take leading roles. No one would be paid. Boyd elaborated on the focus of "The Free Company": "We would be, in short, a group of Americans, unsponsored and uncontrolled, expressing as a voluntary act of faith our belief in our fundamental institutions."

Before long, CBS gave "The Free Company" network airtime, and such noted writers as Robert E. Sherwood, William Saroyan, Marc Connelly, Stephen Vincent Benét, Maxwell Anderson, Archibald MacLeish, Paul Green, Sherwood Anderson, and Boyd himself contributed original dramas. Welles was also asked to participate, and he wrote an original play, *His Honor, the Mayor,* and acted as its narrator. "The Free Company" represented a banner moment in the history of both radio and dramaturgy; it was hoped that it would be an effective assault on the propagandistic elements that were at that time paralyzing the human spirit. The plays did not escape a certain religious connotation as they were broadcast across the nation at 11 A.M. on Sundays.

Burgess Meredith was the host for each program, and such stars as John Garfield, Nancy Kelly, Edmund Gwenn, Franchot Tone, Gail Patrick, Betty Field, Elia Kazan, Canada Lee, and Paul Muni, among others, took part. George M. Cohan lent his name to the project, and Ernest Hemingway enthusiastically supported the idea but could not return from China in time to participate. Boyd, as producer, had the steadfast cooperation of the Hon. Francis Biddle, Solicitor General of the United States, and the U.S. Attorney General, in determining themes and areas of individual rights that, in their opinion, needed to be addressed. This information was passed on to the writers. The first program was aired during the end of February 1941.

The series proved somewhat controversial, but overall it was a success, and most of the programs were enjoyed by millions of listeners. "Remarkable," was how John K. Hutchens of *The New York Times* regarded the pungency and significance of the dramas, feeling that they "made a gallant and prophetic chapter in radio history." Stephen Vincent Benét denounced Negro slavery in his *Freedom's a Hard Bought Thing*; and Paul Green deplored the state of the black people in America at that moment in *A Start in Life*. In *The Miracle of the Danube,* Maxwell Anderson explored the controversial theme of the possibility of Christian principles existing in anyone, even a Nazi. Marc Connelly's *The Mole on Lincoln's Cheek* was a serious plea for the freedom to teach and an appeal for honest textbooks that would deal truthfully with history.

Welles's *His Honor, the Mayor,* which he wrote during the last days of editing *Citizen Kane,* was a story of a plucky city executive who champions the rights of his enemies—a group of "White Crusaders"—to free assembly. It was broadcast on April 6, 1941. Welles successfully attempted to explore his theme with both humor and common sense. In addition to himself as narrator, he secured almost the entire cast of principals from *Citizen Kane* to act in the leading roles: Ray Collins played Mayor Knaggs; his wife was Agnes Moorehead; Paul Stewart, Erskine Sanford, Richard Wilson, and Everett Sloane also appeared.

"Right here I want to say that this broadcast isn't intended to be uplifting or inspirational," Welles started off irreverently at the beginning of the show. "It hasn't any moral to the end of it, or any message. You can draw your own conclusions, and I hope you do. I'd like to know what you think of Mayor Knagg's problem, and if you think he solved it the right way."

As the first signs of the encroachment of civil rights begin to erupt in his small, Mexican-border town, the mayor upholds the privileges of the White Crusaders to express whatever opinions they want to and to congregate when they wish. Of no particular political persuasion, Mayor Knaggs is, nevertheless, a lover of the freedoms of the individual espoused by one of his idols, Abraham Lincoln. Many of the townspeople prove to be anti-Semites as well as fascists, but at the end, the mayor overcomes the ignorance and prejudices of the masses.

Perhaps as a subtle gesture of friendship or in an attempt to break the coolness that had developed, Welles includes the name of Mankiewicz in the play, the only Jewish family in the county, who, although despised by the White Crusaders because of their religion, are good people loved by everyone else.

Welles could hardly believe what he was hearing the morning after the show when Drake telephoned him. There was a vicious attack on *His Honor, the Mayor,* "The Free Company," and Welles, plastered over the front pages of Hearst papers throughout the country. Hearst claimed that the whole series was communistic and that the producers, writers, and actors were "attackers of the American way of life," guilty of the same subversive propaganda that the series was attempting to diminish. In the *New York Journal-American,* the story claimed that "The Free Company" "includes a number of assorted left-wing writers and actors." Quotes from leaders of the American Legion and the California Sons of the Revolution were used as a basis for the assertions made in the article. "The Welles broadcast," said the Legionnaires, "was one of the most offensive of all in the series because it was an outright appeal for the right of a subversive fifth-column group to hold anti-American meetings in the public hall of an American city."

Since the series was almost two months old before the attack occurred, it was quite obvious that it was timed with the appearance of Welles's *His Honor, the Mayor* in an attempt to smear *Citizen Kane* and its director as un-American and ultimately to keep people away from *Citizen Kane* when and if it was released. Although the accusation may have fooled some of the readers, it hardly convinced professional observers of the media. *Time* immediately saw through the attempt and stated that the attack was particularly geared against Orson Welles personally. It pointed out the coincidence of the Hearst assault with the imminent release of the Welles film and went on to state that Hearst was trying to have the film suppressed on the "grounds that it looked too much like an unflattering portrait of Citizen Hearst."

Afraid that the historian of the future might be misled by Hearst's attack, an editorial in *The New York Times* pointed out that such a chronicler might be "unaware that the campaign against Mr. Welles was more concerned with a motion picture than with radio."

To emphasize the radicalism of the radio group, the Hearst article had concluded by pointing out that Welles and twenty-one others had signed a petition attacking the government's proceedings to deport West Coast labor leader Harry Bridges on the grounds that he was a Communist; some of the others who signed were Melvyn Douglas, Artie Shaw, Burgess Meredith, Dudley Nichols, Garson Kanin, Dalton Trumbo, Carey McWilliams, Vincent Sheean, Donald Ogden Stewart, and Irwin Shaw.

Welles retaliated immediately and issued the following statement to the press. In most newspapers, it ran under the headline of "Orson Welles Answers Hearst" or something quite similar:

> William Randolph Hearst is conducting a series of brutal attacks on me in his newspapers. It seems he doesn't like my picture *Citizen Kane.* I understand he hasn't seen it. I am sure he hasn't. If he had, I think he would agree with me that those who have advised him that "Kane" is Hearst have done us both an injustice.
>
> I have stood by silently in the hope that this vicious attack against me would be spent in the passing of a few weeks. I had hoped that I would not continue to be the target of patriotic organizations who are accepting false statements and condemning me without knowing the facts.

But I can't remain silent any longer.

The Hearst papers have repeatedly described me as a Communist. I am not a Communist. I am grateful for our constitutional form of government, and I rejoice in our great American tradition of democracy. Needless to say, it is not necessarily unpatriotic to disagree with Mr. Hearst. On the contrary, it is a privilege guaranteed me as an American citizen by the Bill of Rights.

Hearst papers and others whose actions have been suggested by those papers have had much to say about my having signed a protest at the second trial of Harry Bridges. Many others signed that protest, but my name was singled out. Why? Because Mr. Hearst doesn't like *Citizen Kane*. In signing a protest against Harry Bridges' second trial, I believed that the Federal Government was trying him a second time for the same offense. I have been taught that in America no man should be placed twice in jeopardy for the same offense. I would just as quickly sign a similar protest if Mr. Hearst were the subject of such double jeopardy. The Hearst smear campaign has chiefly concerned itself with my part in the Free Company broadcasts. I quote from the following non-Hearst newspapers: "If Orson Welles is a Communist, which he isn't, then all of his associates are destroyers of Americanism. If Orson Welles is a Communist for preaching free speech, free radio, freedom of worship, then Paul Muni is a Communist for being one of his associates; then too, is George M. Cohan, a leader in the Free Company, a Communist." *Pittsburgh Press*, April 24, 1941. "These members and the members of the original Free Company were picked at the suggestion of the Solicitor General of the United States to design and to execute a program to counter hostile propaganda in this country. They contributed their services without pay and they have stuck to the letter of their assignment: to restate the faith of the nation in the right of its fundamental freedoms. If it weren't sad, it would be silly. William Randolph Hearst is piqued with Orson Welles. The rest is camouflage." *Chicago Sunday Times*, April 27, 1941. I want to say that I'm proud of my American citizenship. As a citizen I cherish my rights, and I'm not fearful of uncertainty. I only ask that I am judged by what I am and what I do.

Welles never knew that a number of Hearst sympathizers began reporting Orson's activities to the FBI as potentially dangerous to the national interest. Therein started an investigation and surveillance of his private and public life that lasted for years. The groups that he belonged to such as the Theater Arts Committee, the Motion Picture Artists Committee, and the Foster Parents' Plan for War Children were examined for possible communist links. The bookstores that he frequented were spied upon, attempts were made to determine what kind of political works he was reading. The people that he associated with, and respectively, the people *they* associated with, were checked out by the bureau to see if they had any leftist leanings.

In a report by a special FBI agent to J. Edgar Hoover, it was noted: "It should be pointed out that this office has never been able to establish that Welles is an actual member of the former Communist Party or the present

Communist Political Association; however, an examination of Welles's activities and his membership in various organizations reflects that he has consistently followed the Communist Party line and has been active in numerous 'front' organizations."

Nothing really came of Orson's FBI investigation. It is possible that they backed off when Orson sued a gossip columnist for calling him a Communist in print and won in Los Angeles Superior Court.

WHILE AWAITING WITH advanced labor pains the delayed birth of *Citizen Kane,* Welles was offered *Sister Carrie,* a property owned by RKO, for consideration as his next film project. The screenplay was based on a highly popular and acutely controversial turn-of-the-century novel by Theodore Dreiser. In some ways, *Sister Carrie* was the *Citizen Kane* of its day, considered so shocking that distribution was held up by the unofficial censorship that controlled sales in those days.

The story is about a young girl who comes from her rural home in Wisconsin to the drabness of Chicago; eventually, purely as an escape, she drifts into a relationship with a salesman, then is won over by George Hurstwood, the manager of a large saloon, who deserts his family for her, steals $10,000, flees the country, and ultimately commits suicide. Carrie has a successful stage career at the end but remains isolated and lonely.

For the right actor, the role of Hurstwood was a perfect opportunity to display a bravura performance. Welles was seriously tempted. His problem with the acceptance of both the role of Hurstwood and the direction of *Sister Carrie* was the phlegmatic quality inherent in Dreiser's work. Welles believed that he could infuse the story with a certain lilt or poetry, but if he transformed it into an expression of his own vision, it would not be a faithful or even credible adaptation of the Dreiser work. He also felt Hurstwood's commonness was a problem. He refused the project.

Exploring more ideas for his next film, Welles had the studio provide synopses of various scripts and stories to refresh his memory of those works he may have read but had forgotten. They included many of the great stories of the day or from literature of the past. Among the other film projects he considered were *Balzac,* by George Middleton; *To Have and Have Not,* by Ernest Hemingway; *Juno and the Paycock,* by Sean O'Casey; *The Brothers Karamazov,* by Dostoyevski; *Mario and the Magician,* by Thomas Mann; *Benjamin Franklin,* by Carl Van Doren; *The Walking Gentleman,* by Grace and Fulton Oursler; *Splendors and Miseries of Courtesans,* by Balzac; *Les Misérables,* by Victor Hugo; *Paul Bunyan,* by James Stevens; *The Fountain,* by Eugene O'Neill; *The Man Who Corrupted Hadleyburg,* by Mark Twain; *Maurice Guest,* by H. R. Richardson; *The Devil,* by Alfred Newman; *Martin Eden,* by Jack London; *A Moment of Importance,* by G. Roy Walling; *Louisiana Hayride,* by Harnett Kane; and *Starvation on Red River,* by Zoë Akins.

After agonizing over more than forty film ideas, Welles emerged with two, either of which he believed he could mold into successful projects. An attempt at raising *Cyrano de Bergerac* from the dead was a form of audacious perseverance on his part, especially after the highly negative reaction Schaefer had received from the Gallup poll two years previously. Alexander Korda had purchased the Ben Hecht script, and Charles Laughton had been testing for the role. Laughton had worked on the script himself, trying to shape it to his fashion, and was extremely eager to do the film. Somehow, however, an elongated nose on the corpulent Laughton made him look not like a grotesque though brilliant cavalier but more like an ineffectual and pitiful penguin.

Welles knew that Korda would part with the script if he was given a substantial increase over the amount he had originally paid. Welles offered to go into partnership with RKO for the purchase of the script, but Schaefer quickly and not-so-cordially declined.

Journey Into Fear, a war thriller set in the Near East, written by Eric Ambler, one of the greatest of spy novelists, had been optioned by RKO. It seemed to be the one possibility with the fewest problems and also the one that would be the easiest to rush through to completion. Schaefer believed *Journey Into Fear* could be produced economically. He also thought that the lead character of Colonel Haki, a man of ravenous, perhaps evil, tastes, could be excellently interpreted by Welles. So did Welles. Yes, he would agree to directing and starring in *Journey Into Fear,* but he wanted to consider it as the *third* film to fulfill his contract. He still searched for a story as the follow-up to *Citizen Kane.* He hoped for a scenario that would be both epigrammatic and arguable, unusual and obvious, challenging and easy, a film of delicacy and power all at once that could frame what he felt was becoming his own consistent métier of cinematic style.

THE UNEXPECTED PRESENCE of John Houseman in Hollywood in 1941 served as something of a diversion for the twenty-six-year-old Orson. Houseman had been brought to California to discuss the job of his running the David O. Selznick studios while Selznick took a long-needed rest after his successes of *Rebecca* and *Gone with the Wind.* Just before leaving California, Houseman contacted Welles—something he had sworn he would never do again—and almost on a whim, as he has described it, offered him the job as director of a Broadway production of *Native Son,* a play based on the novel by black author Richard Wright. Pulitzer Prize winner Paul Green had drafted the first version of the dramatization with Wright, and Houseman, who had also included some magical editorial touches of his own, had secured the rights to produce it. Welles, always poised for the theater, read the script and after two days accepted the challenge with gusto.

Because of Welles's immense publicity value, backing was easily secured to mount a quality production, which is perhaps what Houseman had in mind all along. Welles proudly gathered the gems of his Mercurians together for principal parts in the play. Since *Citizen Kane* had yet to be released, most of his company were still unknown on the screen; as to the stage, well, like

Welles, they were famous for that magical Broadway season that included *Julius Caesar, Doctor Faustus,* and *Heartbreak House.*

In many ways, *Native Son* represented a change of direction for the Mercury; the material was contemporary and controversial, if not explosive, and the novel was still fresh on everyone's mind. The question was, could one of the year's most talked about novels make a successful transition to the stage. Novel to film is not without hazards; novel to play often produces a palpable letdown.

Richard Wright's novel had grown out of a crisis of spirit that he had faced as a black writer in the 1930s. Tired of seeing American blacks depicted as long-suffering and docile spiritual descendants of Uncle Tom, although he had written in this vein himself in the past, he had decided to tell the story of Bigger Thomas, a black caught up in overwhelming rage and confusion in contemporary society. Bigger Thomas was a murderer, and what was worse, the murderer of a rich white girl, Mary Dalton. Wright wanted to explain the black dilemma, but more than that, he wanted his book to act as a catalyst; he was not interested in sympathy for his protagonist. And as an outspoken Marxist, Wright made it tellingly clear in the novel that the American system of that time, with its racism and repression, would go on condemning blacks to a life of futility until someone like a Bigger Thomas made them open their apparently blind eyes.

Welles seemed to know what Wright was trying to do, and it is interesting that he did not attempt to wrest Wright's ideas away from him and make the play his own. Wright's message was highly personal, and Welles acted as a superb facilitator.

Wright was in charge of the script and had established a close relationship with Houseman as to its demands. Even at rehearsal time, he continued to have a hand in the production, shaping the cast's attitudes primarily by having them read a pamphlet, "How Bigger Was Born," the preface to the later editions of the book.

Wright's essay shows quite clearly that the author had no trouble envisioning his book as a play. He continually uses dramatic terms, having conceived of the book as a series of powerful dramatic scenes; he strove, he said, "for a density and richness of effect," trying "to keep before the eyes of the reader at all times the forces and elements against which Bigger was striving." Furthermore, Wright stated, "I want the reader to feel that Bigger's story was happening *now,* like a play upon the stage or a movie unfolding on the screen"; and lastly he wanted the reader to feel that "the story was a special *premiere* given in his own private theater." Wright as novelist was collaborating with Welles as director before they had even met.

With a workable script in hand, much of it in the original words of the novel, Welles put together a cast. The *Citizen Kane* army stood muster for General Welles: Ray Collins, Everett Sloane, Erskine Sanford, Richard Wilson, Jack Berry, and Paul Stewart were enlisted.

The casting of the nineteen-year-old Bigger was crucial, but Welles knew exactly whom he wanted for the role: Canada Lee.

Lee, a former prizefighter, violinist, jockey, and at that time nightclub owner of the Chicken Coop, known as the Twenty-One of Harlem, was a natural for the role ("perfect" was the word used by one reviewer), but he did cause a snag in the rehearsals, one that no one could have anticipated.

The opening scene in the cold-water flat calls for Bigger to kill a rat with a frying pan and then dangle it in the face of his terrified little sister. Early rehearsals went off without a hitch until it came time to abandon make-believe and practice with something approaching the real thing. One day Welles walked into rehearsals, pulled something out from under his coat and threw it on the stage. It was an enormous wharf rat that Welles had ordered; someone had shot it and it was then stuffed. Lee wouldn't go near it, much less pick it up and do the scene. Rats signified dirt, squalor, evil to him. "You've got to pick it up, Canada—go ahead, it's stuffed," Welles said. "To hell with it," Lee replied, "I'll quit first."

For four days Lee wouldn't touch it. Richard Wright empathized with Lee's position and even asked Welles if some other dramatic device could be substituted for the rat. As Lee recalled, "Finally this little kid in the play touches it and squeezes it. I said, 'What the hell, I'm a dope.' I start fooling around with it with gloves on and finally I am able to take off the gloves." When Lee finally mastered his fear, Wright wanted to know where he had studied acting. "I never studied acting," said Canada Lee. "What could a black man study in acting school, anyway? 'How yuh boss, yas suh boss.'" The two men became lifelong friends.

After seven weeks of preparation, the play opened at New York's St. James Theater on March 24, 1941. Canada Lee was an instant success, and Welles seemed to have won over all the critics.

Some observers were surprised by the sets. They were accustomed to the now-famous Welles minimal set treatment; his *Julius Caesar* sets, designed by Sam Leve, were still being championed. For *Native Son,* James Morcom's work was elaborate and detailed. One striking feature was the framing of the scenes, the depersonalizing vise of a slum tenement and prison that circumscribes Bigger's life and eventually crushes him. To portray a feeling of meanness, deceit, madness, Orson selected the color that in its most sinister form best symbolized those characteristics. "I want this show to be surrounded by brick. Yellow brick," he said to Jean Rosenthal the lighting director. In keeping with the "density and richness of effect" that Wright had striven for, Welles developed a multitude of sound effects to complement the sets: airplanes, sirens, car horns, shouts of the street. Infused in the play were Negro spirituals—the solace of Bigger's mother—and the rhythms of the jukebox, the improper and, to some, improbable anthems of the black world of Chicago streets.

Bigger gets a job as chauffeur with the rich Dalton family. His first night on the job ends in horror, when, crazed with fear that he will be discovered in Mary Dalton's bedroom (he had helped her in; she had been drinking too much), he accidentally smothers her while trying to keep her silent. In an instinctive bid for survival, Bigger puts the body in a trunk, drags it down to the basement, and shoves it into the furnace. Newspapermen discover her bones in the ashes; Bigger is arrested, tried, and sentenced to be electrocuted. The play ends with Bigger in the death cell.

Bigger believes he is totally unable to function as a human being in any sphere outside the street corner and the poolroom. His fear and resentment of the white world produces a deadly panic; so much is the play's explanation for the origin of the crime. But the final scenes in the courtroom and the prison cell are the true message—the white captors who approach him as a sub-human and another example of black inferiority.

The opening scene, the tenement room, is Bigger's life; the ominous blast and roar of the furnace's automatic stoker is the *leitmotiv* for Bigger's crime; the running gun battle with the police (described by one reviewer as "terrifying") that Welles staged in the balcony of the theater is the vengeance taken by the outside world, Bigger's fate.

Welles's staging innovations included the setting for the murder scene. The scene was played in the dark, the room strangely foreshortened and obliquely tilted toward the audience, a tableau of expressionistic claustrophobia and madness, and was generally agreed to be the most frightening of all.

Besides the police chase, members of the audience were made uncomfortably aware of being implicated in the proceedings when they found themselves as unwitting actors in the courtroom audience—the traditional wooden barrier of the court was placed immediately before the front row. *Native Son* was brilliant and electrifying, and its message was not reassuring to those who saw it.

Asked to pick out the most satisfying parts of his performance, Lee told the reporter for a school newspaper in a public interview at the theater that from the point of view of an actor, the prison scene was the best, but for sheer fun, Lee got a kick out of "picking up and throwing" Anne Burr (who plays his victim) around in the murder sequence. The act had been so convincing, and people so wrapped up in the reality created by the play, that they had to be reminded in publicity and in the play program that Canada Lee and Anne Burr were the best of friends.

In another little side note to the production, Welles had injected a bit of humor into the play at the very outset, though the exact nature of the inside joke was never grasped. In the first scene, Bigger's tenement room, Welles had put the "Rosebud" sled in among Bigger's belongings. This was definitely not some critic's hallucination; the sled is quite clearly shown in a photograph appearing in *Life* magazine during the play's run.

The critical reaction was outstandingly favorable. *The New York Times* called it a "powerful drama" and went on: "Orson Welles has staged it with imagination and force. These are the first things to be said about the overwhelming play that opened at the St. James last evening, but they hardly convey the excitement of this first performance of a play that represents experience of life and conviction in thought and a production that represents a dynamic use of the stage." Other comments ranged from, "a deeply moving, highly exciting evening," to one comparing it to the other productions of the current season, which seemed dim and old fashioned. Only Hearst's *New York Journal-American* found it in its heart to criticize the play as "propaganda" nearer to Moscow than Harlem.

Wright was more than satisfied with Orson's production. He wrote a somewhat overly enthusiastic endorsement: "I cannot stress too highly my profound respect and admiration for Orson Welles, the director of this play. He is beyond doubt the most courageous, gallant, and talented director on the modern stage in the world today."

Native Son worked; that much is incontestable. But the production was enormously taxing on the cast and on Welles. He had been praised for getting down to business in a remarkably short time, five weeks of work leading directly into the preview performances, normally a six-month procedure by Broadway tradition. But such a schedule proved nerve-racking behind the scenes. At one point, Welles, the perfectionist, kept an exhausted troupe in the theater for a thirty-six-hour stretch. Often working on them from Sunday straight through until the first Monday night preview.

In the middle of this incredible work load, Welles made some guest appearances on radio, playing George Washington on one show. He also gave a lecture on the future of the theater at the New School for Social Research, and he began to allow an idea for his next film to wash over him. He would do an adaptation of the Booth Tarkington novel *The Magnificent Ambersons.*

Two weeks after opening night, with the play at the height of its popularity, still harassed and perplexed over the state of the release of *Citizen Kane,* Welles admitted to exhaustion: mental, physical, emotional, and spiritual. He had himself admitted to a private sanitorium, stayed for about two days, and then returned to California to work on the release of *Citizen Kane,* while simultaneously attempting to convince Schaefer and others at RKO that *The Magnificent Ambersons* should be his next project.

Still nominally the director of *Native Son,* Welles's last official act concerning the play before returning West was to attempt to have recording equipment installed in the pit of the St. James, hidden from the eyes of the cast. It was his idea to have some of the performance recorded at random, without the cast's knowledge, and to have the results shipped to him by air freight the next day. He could then listen to the performance, hear the audience's reaction, or lack of it, to certain lines and scenes and be able to offer a critique by telephone to certain of his actors. Actors' Equity, however, insisted that even though only Welles would hear the results and they would not be made public, each actor would have to be paid for an extra performance because it would be recorded. The extra cost was prohibitive, and Welles abandoned the idea.

After almost four months of virtually packed, then slightly dwindling, houses, *Native Son* closed on Broadway and toured the nation for the following year.

BEFORE ORSON RETURNED to California, George Schaefer organized the first official screening of *Citizen Kane*. Schaefer was eager to determine the true feelings of the Hollywood establishment without Orson's inhibiting presence. If Orson, star and director, was present at their initial viewing, people might be inclined to respond courteously toward him even if they believed, for instance, that the film was of little value. Schaefer needed an accurate estimate of the film's worth; if the consensus was positive, he would use that information as ammunition with RKO's board of directors in getting them to agree to release it. If the response was unqualifiedly admiring, it would elevate Schaefer's own confidence in *Citizen Kane*; although he truly believed that the film was artistically important and wanted it released, the tension that was straining the future between the RKO board and him had escalated. The screening was held on the evening of St. Valentine's Day, 1941, and someone inquired, "Is he expecting a massacre or a bouquet of flowers?" This screening date was originally to have been the release date of *Citizen Kane*.

Some of the great personalities in Hollywood at that time were invited to the screening. Schaefer wanted a tough audience, film artisans whose reputations were towering in their own right. Directors King Vidor, Jesse Lasky, William Dieterle, Robert Stevenson, and Garson Kanin came, along with producer Howard Hawks. Distinguished agents from MCA showed up; agent Leland Hayward sat in. Cedric Hardwicke was an honored guest. Other producers, actors, and film technicians were also in attendance. The atmosphere before the film began was somber; everyone who was there knew why he had been invited. In some ways, not only the fate of one picture was at stake that night, but it was easy to believe that Hollywood's future could have been hovering in a sort of existential balance.

Although there were still a few more sound track editing chores to be completed before *Citizen Kane* could be considered perfect, the print—all 10,734 feet of it—that was shown that night was close to finished, much more fully integrated than the copy that had been projected for the five editors a month before.

By the time the first thirty minutes of the film had elapsed, after the scene where Thatcher visits the *Inquirer* office and Kane tells him sardonically that he could keep the paper going for sixty years, Schaefer began to feel confident, the total silence and absorption of the screening group a testament to the film's eloquence. At the conclusion, his optimism was confirmed; the applause was long, sincere, enthusiastic. As the lights came up and people began to stream from their seats, each came to Schaefer smiling and offered congratulations. Schaefer basked as he heard such plaudits as, "One of the greatest motion pictures that ever came out of Hollywood," and, "It will have to win an Academy Award as best picture," and other such elaborately heady remarks.

"They were virtually speechless," Schaefer said in a wire to Welles, "and some came back a second or third time after the picture was concluded and told me how much they were impressed. In my own opinion," he continued to Welles, "it was about the toughest audience that was ever called to look at a picture and naturally their expectations were high, and, even so, they were all fulfilled." Never in Schaefer's experience in the motion picture business did he screen a film before such a potentially difficult audience and yet receive such wonderful reactions.

The next day, Schaefer called all the members of RKO's board of directors and related his experience.

Welles was jubilant at the screening reaction. "Words can't express how happy you've made me feel," he counter-wired Schaefer. Then he brought up again the question as to exactly when *Citizen Kane* would be released. "It's just a matter of a short time," Schaefer told him. "Don't worry. It'll probably be in about two weeks."

After three weeks, there was still no release date set and Welles was extremely nervous. The Hearst attacks seemed to have subsided, but, Welles conjectured, that might have been because Hearst had learned through his contacts that the film was never going to be released. Welles badgered Schaefer to give him, if not a final decision as to a probable date when the film would be shown in the theaters, then at least a time as to when the decision would be made to exhibit it. Perhaps afraid of a lawsuit from Welles, and also hedging for more time for the RKO board to make up its collective mind, Schaefer became increasingly evasive.

In an agonized telegram to Schaefer on March 7, 1941, Welles clarified his dilemma. He said, in part:

> I never questioned your wisdom and I don't now. I did ask you for your reasons and I never got them. . . . I do not and cannot question your good will but if you're trying to make things easier for me, let me assure you that the effect is quite the reverse. . . . When this trouble first descended upon us, we spoke almost twice daily by phone. Now I have to sit up until four o'clock in the morning trying to get in touch with you and failing to do so. When I finally reach you, the only satisfaction you give me is expressed in the merest of generalities. I cannot think that you are deliberately avoiding me. I can only suppose that you are pursuing some policy the nature of which must be kept secret.

Citing his devotion as a friend, Welles accused Schaefer of veiled hostility and said that he was under a great strain to maintain his faith in him. Because of Welles's position as director of *Native Son,* he was meeting with newsmen almost daily, granting interviews, making statements, and cooperating with feature writers. Invariably the question of whether *Citizen Kane* would ever be released would arise. Welles remained obdurately silent and resisted attempts to draw him out about the film, afraid to make a statement that would later compromise his legal position should the film's release continue to be delayed. He received letters from the public, accusing him of "selling out," erroneously believing that he had the power to release *Citizen Kane* himself. Because of his enforced silence concerning *Citizen Kane,* he believed his relationship with the press and with his fans was beginning to erode into a miasma of bad will. "The whole state of affairs is progressively unfeasible," he told Schaefer, implying that he would not allow it to continue as it had been.

"My nights are sleepless and my days are a torture," he complained. "This is no exaggeration."

When *Time* magazine appeared the following week, an unsigned article in its cinema section implied that the death of the film was a *fait accompli,* referring to it in the past tense: "As in some grotesque fable, it appeared last week that Hollywood was about to destroy its greatest creation. That creation was *Citizen Kane*. . . ." Welles had been tipped in advance about the content of the *Time* article. He had had enough. Drake called the press to Welles's suite at the Ambassador Hotel for an "important statement." The room was filled with some twenty reporters, half a dozen broadcasters, and several newsreel cameramen and photographers. The door was kept open as others spilled into the hall. Welles started off by simply announcing that, unless RKO gave him a release date for *Citizen Kane,* he would start legal proceedings to compel its release or demand a financial settlement of his interest, twenty-five percent of the film. Working himself up into what appeared to be genuine anger, he went on:

> And, I am considering suit against Hearst also. I may sue him for identifying himself as the character I play. There is a hell of a motion picture in the life of William Randolph Hearst. If I had intended to make a picture of the life of Hearst, I should have been an ass to have left out all the incidents and anecdotes in his career that are known to everyone. . . . I have made a serious picture and I am not interested in having introduced into an artistic venture a note of yellow journalism. It is my duty as an artist and a citizen to sue.

Welles, incensed, went on to say that the failure of RKO to release the film had caused him financial embarrassment and losses. "How can you copyright an enterprise, a profession?" he asked the assembled reporters rhetorically. "I must be free to film a story of a newspaper publisher. If I am restrained, then it will force us all to go back and take our characters, say, from Greek mythology. And even then I suppose somebody would contend he was Zeus."

When asked if he had any retaliatory plans, he was definite about what he would do, sounding a little bit like a character he might play in a future film: "If RKO is afraid that the theaters will not exhibit the film, they should turn over the distribution to me. I'll show the film anywhere I can, in tents, in Masonic auditoriums, anywhere a crowd can be assembled throughout America."

Schaefer eventually convinced the remonstrant Welles, over the telephone, that he should postpone legal proceedings; one by one, he told Orson, he was eroding the fear of RKO's board of directors and winning them over to the film's side.

Even the most resolute member, Floyd Odlum, was beginning to weaken. The great publicity that the film had already received, argued Schaefer to his colleagues, could make it a smash hit and balloon the studio's sagging finances. Hearst, by his fulminations, was serving *Citizen Kane* as unwitting press agent and making it a legend before its release. As to the legal ramifications, Schaefer subsequently had a virtual legion of attorneys put the film through a microscopic examination. Their consensus was that, in the unlikely event that Hearst could prove he was Kane, there was only one scene in the film that could be ticklish, if not dangerous. Near the film's end, when Thomson visits Xanadu and interviews Raymond, the butler, there are a few lines that imply senility in Kane. In the shooting script and in the then-current print of the film, the conversation proceeds:

RAYMOND

Rosebud? I'll tell you about Rosebud—how much is it worth to you? A thousand dollars?

THOMPSON

Okay.

RAYMOND

He was a little gone in the head sometimes, you know.

THOMSPON

No, I didn't.

RAYMOND

He did crazy things sometimes—I've been working for him eleven years now—the last years of his life and I ought to know.

It was believed that the line "a little gone in the head," combined with the revelation that Raymond was with him as an old man, the last eleven years of his life, might be looked upon by a judge or jury as a malicious intent to make Kane (or Hearst, if the analogue was proven) appear mentally infirm. Welles readily agreed to change it. Paul Stewart added the new dialogue, and Robert Wise arranged to have it inserted in the proper place on the track. The new lines, masterminded by the RKO lawyers, went:

RAYMOND

Rosebud? I'll tell you about Rosebud, Mr. Thompson. How much is it worth to you, a thousand dollars?

THOMPSON

Okay.

RAYMOND

Well, I'll tell you, Mr. Thompson . . . he acted kind of funny sometimes, you know.

THOMPSON

No, I didn't.

RAYMOND

I've been working for him eleven years now, in charge of the whole place, so I ought to know.

The theory was that anybody could act "kind of funny" sometimes without being senile; omitting the reference to the "last eleven years of his life," presumably the time of dotage for the old man, also served to legally soften the implication.

It was about this time that Schaefer asked Welles to prepare the film for a special viewing in New York. Schaefer had accepted the fact that it was going to be impossible to gain circuit bookings for *Citizen Kane* in most theaters; he wanted the tacit consent of all of the exhibitors and studio heads, however, so that he could release the film without further pressure, fanned by fear of Hearstian reprisals from them.

A large group of industry executives, along with their complex of lawyers, met late one afternoon in January of 1941 in the screening room of the Radio City Music Hall to see the controversial *Citizen Kane*. Robert Wise, who had been editing the film with Mark Robson in Hollywood, flew in with a near-perfect print. Everything was hushed and formal, as if meeting in the chambers of the Supreme Court to determine a First Amendment issue. Orson was there and as each of the corporation officials arrived, he greeted them with his utmost charm and friendliness, sweet as a sugarplum, in what Robert Wise has remembered as ". . . Orson's finest performance of his career." After everyone was assembled, Orson stood before the screen and began his polemic with, "I believe that the public is entitled to see *Citizen Kane* . . ." and went on to touch upon the rise of totalitarianism in the world at that time, the implication that banning *Citizen Kane* would be an impediment to free speech, and how artistic expression in a free society must be protected. He ended with an impassioned and sincere plea for support of the film. There was polite applause.

Not one person, at the film's conclusion, expressed the opinion that *Citizen Kane* would hurt the film industry. The case for its release was, if not assured, at least building.

Meanwhile, back in Hollywood, Schaefer continued to have *Citizen Kane* shown in other private screenings. His logic was quite astute. Almost everyone who had seen the film considered it, if not a masterpiece, at least a work of art.* If more Hollywood leaders continued to become fans and supporters of *Citizen Kane* and let their evaluations be heard, the entire RKO board would have to relent and Hearst would find it difficult if not impossible to reverse the sentiment of public opinion. A successful whispering campaign about its inherent excellence was the film's best defense.

Hardly a Wednesday passed on which Schaefer did not have a major private screening for about one hundred fifty Hollywood notables, and getting on one of the invitation lists became a bit of a status symbol. Often accompanied by their wives or a friend, actors such as Basil Rathbone, Charlie Chaplin, Burgess Meredith, Ray Milland, Douglas Fairbanks, Gary Cooper, Tyrone Power, Herbert Marshall, and Ronald Reagan screened *Citizen Kane* in the

---

*D. W. Griffith's reaction was understandably sardonic and an exception. He told writer Ezra Goodman: "I loved *Citizen Kane* and particularly loved the ideas he [Orson Welles] took from me."

last weeks of February and the beginning of March 1941. Producers and directors such as Alfred Hitchcock, David O. Selznick, Ernst Lubitsch, Frank Capra, Hal Wallis, and Cecil B. De Mille came for a viewing. Many seemed to be amazed, touched, and gratified by what they had seen. *Citizen Kane* emerged as a symbol for some that Hollywood was still capable of innovative excellence.

"There's nothing wrong with this industry that a good movie can't cure," someone said at the film's end one night. No one publicly disagreed. In a little over a month, some fifteen hundred people had seen the film privately, which had *Variety* quip, "*Citizen Kane* has had the longest projection room engagement of any picture to come out of Hollywood."

Without Welles's knowledge, Schaefer had inserted at the beginning of the film a disclaimer that had been composed by the RKO legal department:

> THIS IS NOT THE STORY OF ANY MAN BE HE LIVING OR DEAD. THIS IS THE STORY OF THE POWER AND STRENGTH WHICH IMPELS THE LIVES OF MANY GREAT MEN SEEN THROUGH THE EYES OF LITTLE MEN.

Welles was furious when he heard about the statement because of its content and especially because he had not personally written it. He told Schaefer that "its style in no way matches the picture and I do not believe it expresses my intentions."

Although hardly an improvement, he created a new statement and this was added to the beginning of the film in place of the RKO disclaimer:

> *CITIZEN KANE* IS AN EXAMINATION OF THE PERSONAL CHARACTER OF A PUBLIC MAN, A PORTRAIT ACCORDING TO THE TESTIMONY OF THE INTIMATES OF HIS LIFE. THESE, AND KANE HIMSELF, ARE WHOLLY FICTITIOUS.

Later, the statement was deleted altogether.

Welles received direct commendations from William Wyler, John Ford, and Sam Goldwyn, which were eminently gratifying to him. He requested a print of the film himself, so that he could organize his own private screenings, especially after meeting people whom he hardly knew who had already seen it. Schaefer refused, stating that it was expressly against company policy, but the real reason was that studio executives were afraid that once Orson had his hands on a print, he might claim it as contraband of a sort, or take title in an unofficial eminent domain and bootleg it into the theaters himself, hoping that public opinion would exonerate him for protecting what he considered his inviolate work of art.

"But I have a request from the White House," Welles countered. He told Schaefer that Eleanor Roosevelt, through one of her aides, had asked to see the film. Henry Luce had also contacted him for a private screening; also, no one in the film's cast had seen the completed version. Schaefer agreed to have special screenings arranged for Welles for these three exceptions, but he could not agree to giving him his own personal print.

In mid-March, John O'Hara, the journalist and novelist whose *Pal Joey* had just been published, was one of those who were given an advance screening. Supposedly he lost his job at pro-Hearst *Newsweek* after the following review/feature/editorial appeared under his name:

It is with exceeding regret that your faithful bystander reports that he has just seen a picture which he thinks must be the best picture he ever saw.

With no less regret he reports that he has just seen the best actor in the history of acting.

Name of picture: *Citizen Kane.*

Name of actor: Orson Welles.

Reason for regret: you, my dear, may never see the picture.

I saw *Citizen Kane* the other night. I am told that my name had been crossed off a list of persons who were invited to look at the picture, my name being crossed off because some big shot remembered that I was a newspaperman. So for the first time in my life, I indignantly denied I was a newspaperman. Nevertheless, I had to be snuck into the showing of *Citizen Kane* under a phony name. That's what's going on about this wonderful picture. Intrigue.

Why intrigue? Well, because. A few obsequious and/or bulbous middle-aged ladies think that the picture ought not to be shown, owing to the fact that the picture is rumored to have something to do with a certain publisher, who for the first time in his life, or maybe the second, shall be nameless. That the nameless publisher might be astute enough to realize that for the first time in his rowdy life he had been made a human being did not worry the loyal ladies. Sycophancy of that kind, like curtseying, is deliberate. The ladies merely wait for a chance to show they can still do it, even if it means cracking a femur. This time I think they may have cracked off more than they can chew. I hope.

O'Hara said that prior to *Citizen Kane,* he believed the best picture ever made was Fritz Lang's *M*; he also mentioned *The Big Parade, The Great Gatsby,* and *The Birth of a Nation* as among his favorites. But to him, *Citizen Kane* dominated all: "It lacks nothing."

He concluded his unabashed celebration by further eulogy:

It is traditional that if you are a great artist, no one gives a damn about you while you are still alive. Welles has plenty of that. He got a tag put to his name through the Mars thing, just as Scott Fitzgerald, who wrote better than any other man in our time, got a Jazz Age tag put to his name. I say, if you plan to have any grandchildren to see and to bore, see Orson Welles so that you can bore your grandchildren with some honesty. There has never been a better actor than Orson Welles, I just got finished saying there has never been a better actor than Orson Welles, and I don't want any of your lip.

Do yourself a favor. Go to your neighborhood exhibitor and ask him why he isn't showing *Citizen Kane. Then* sue me.

Dick Pollard, the movie editor of *Life*, who had been among the first to see the film, compiled a four-page feature on *Citizen Kane*, which appeared the same week as the *Newsweek* piece and showed pictorially what Welles was attempting to do in his depth-of-focus photography and other cinematic innovations.

The Pollard and O'Hara stories proved formidable opposition to those who still maintained that *Citizen Kane* must be delayed, if not permanently censored. As a result of the two articles, hundreds of letters—from that segment of the public who believed they were being cheated from what was rightfully theirs—began to filter to some of the RKO chiefs, to Welles, and to Hearst himself. Everyone who was involved in the control of the film began to realize that with moviegoers and media fighting its embargo, there promised to be a bigger battle if RKO did *not* release it.

All of the minor dubs and splices, odd details concerning the production quality of the negative or a bar of music or a scrap of sound effect had been perfected, and with the exception of the titles the master print was ready.

The cast was reintroduced at the end of the film, with a single flashback to one of their principal scenes, each character saying a characteristic line, such as Bernstein's, "Who's a busy man, me? I'm chairman of the board, I got nothing but time. What do you want to know?" and then Orson's voice over, "Everett Sloane."

The screenplay credit had been worked out months before and Mankiewicz's name would ride atop Welles's. As those credits dissolved into the next, Welles was beginning to think a little like Irving Thalberg, in that if you are in a position to give credit, you don't really need it. He decided to give Gregg Toland co-billing with himself, an unheard of bouquet for a cinematographer. The title card then read:

ORSON WELLES
Direction-Production

GREGG TOLAND, A.S.C.
Photography

There was only one member of the crew that Welles could not honor in the credits: Maurice Seiderman, the brilliant makeup man who was so instrumental in giving the actors the look of realism that Welles was so eager they possess. Because Seiderman was not a member of the union, he was legally prevented from being listed in the film. Welles discovered another way, however, to pay homage to the genius that was Seiderman's. He bought full-page ads in such motion-picture industry trade publications as *Variety*, *Hollywood Reporter*, and others, to wit:

THANKS TO
EVERYBODY WHO GETS SCREEN
CREDIT FOR *CITIZEN KANE*

AND TO ALL THOSE WHO DON'T

TO ALL THE ACTORS
THE CREW
THE OFFICE
THE MUSICIANS
EVERYBODY

AND PARTICULARLY TO MAURICE SEIDERMAN
THE BEST MAKE-UP MAN IN THE WORLD.

ORSON WELLES
MERCURY PRODUCTIONS

Ultimately, when it appeared that Hearst's swift sword might not be so sharp after all, everyone at RKO agreed to agree. A date was chosen for advanced press screenings—April 9—and the opening date to the public, in those theaters around the country that would consent to exhibit, would be in the first week of May 1941.

The Roxy in New York City was the logical choice to premiere *Citizen Kane* since it was one of the biggest theaters in the city, accustomed to first-run features, and the Radio City Music Hall was still unavailable. On inquiry, however, the Roxy proved to be too expensive, and the studio decided to open *Citizen Kane* at one of its own houses, the RKO Palace, a comfortable and largish theater on Broadway and Forty-seventh Street. On the West Coast, the old Pantages theater, El Capitan, would give the film its Hollywood opening. Although neither theater was the first choice of either Welles or RKO, under the circumstances, they were acceptable, wholly adequate sites.

At first, only short radio commercials were used to promote the forthcoming opening of the film, in the hope that Welles's loyal broadcasting fans would be immediately attracted to it and by word-of-mouth, news of the impending opening would spread.

> Welles's *Citizen Kane*!
> Dynamic drama! Thrilling photography!
> Opening soon at the El Capitan!

> or,

> It's terrific! Orson Welles's *Citizen Kane*!
> The most eagerly-awaited picture of all time!
> Watch for opening date at the El Capitan!

Later, close to opening date, full-page advertisements in magazines and newspapers not owned by Hearst began to tout the film's merits. The only problem Welles had with the promotion campaign of the film was when he accidentally discovered a large color photograph of the fifty-five-year-old Kane, complete with rubber double chin and wig, advertising the imminent release of the film in the lobby of the RKO Pantages theater. "This seems to be a pretty serious mistake by way of exploitation," he complained to Schaefer. Welles believed that if people were going to be seduced into the theaters to look at him, it would be through photos or artwork of the younger, more virile Kane. Schaefer agreed, and the photo was yanked from not only the Pantages but all the other RKO theaters throughout the country.

A FEW WEEKS prior to the anticipated opening of *Citizen Kane,* RKO released a "Coming Attractions" trailer to promote it. Since the film promised to be unlike any other ever made in Hollywood, Orson wanted the trailer also to be unlike any other. He spent weeks on scripting, shooting, and editing it and emerged with a punchy and intriguing look at the behind-the-scenes life of the film. It was a highly effective advertisement and stood out from all the other trailers coming from Hollywood, clarifying that *Citizen Kane* was going to be something special.

Shot as a documentary, the trailer was longer than the average—it ran five minutes—and followed none of the rules that most trailers adhered to: a brief synopsis, sensational copy, a glimpse at the most dramatic and action-packed scenes. Orson's trailer presented his acting company on the bare backstage of the set for *Citizen Kane,* uncostumed and unglamorous, in the midst of rehearsals. Orson never appears himself but is present by way of his disembodied voice coming from a lone microphone. Everything is informal and seemingly impromptu as Orson interrupts his actors at work: "Now smile for the folks, Joe," he says to Joseph Cotten. He catches Ruth Warrick with her hair up and introduces her; has Everett Sloane do a brief slapstick routine bumping into a mirror; calls Agnes Moorehead the best actress in the world; and introduces Erskine Sanford enigmatically seated with two parrots, one on his shoulder.

As the microphone continues to speak, the voice of Orson reveals the reason why he is introducing all of his major characters: because, he says, *Citizen Kane* is worth the viewer's attention as a modern American story about a man called Charles Foster Kane. Then there follows a series of close-ups of characters that eventually appear in the film—and some that don't—giving *their* appraisals of Kane as a man of mystery, from Ruth Warrick looking directly at the camera and saying that she is going to marry Kane at the White House next week; to another woman saying that she gave him $60,000,000; to Thatcher repeating his line from the movie: "Charles Foster Kane is nothing more or less than a communist."

Orson, still never appearing, sums up Kane for himself, calling him a hero, a scoundrel, a no-account, a swell guy, a great lover, a great American citizen, and a dirty dog. What's the real truth about Charles Foster Kane? Orson suggests that everyone should decide for himself when *Citizen Kane* "comes to this theater."

THE OPENING NIGHT of *Citizen Kane,* May 8, 1941, was a typical Hollywood premiere, complete with searchlights in front of the El Capitan, popping flashbulbs, dozens of stars and crowds of onlookers. Bleacher stands opposite the theater were constructed, and thousands of fans crammed them so that they could watch the entering glitterati. Welles escorted Dolores Del Rio. Among those sparkling ones in attendance were Marlene Dietrich, Janet Gaynor, Maureen O'Hara, Adolph Menjou, Gloria Swanson, Busby Berkeley, Lupe Velez, Charles Laughton, Olivia de Havilland, Mickey Rooney, John Barrymore, Ted Lewis, Sonja Henie, Judy Canova, Billie Burke, Geraldine Fitzgerald, Conrad Nagel, John Payne, and Dorothy Lamour. Despite the fact that they had already seen the film, people such as Charlie Chaplin, King Vidor, Leland Hayward, Cedric Hardwicke, Herbert Marshall, and Jesse Lasky came again to be part of the festivities. When Welles spotted Hedda Hopper getting out of her limousine, he could only shake his head and smirk.

It was Orson's moment, and he gave interviews to radio broadcasters and then triumphantly stepped in front of the newsreel cameras to make a brief statement:

"Some of our scenes are the most difficult ever filmed," he said. "We were told they couldn't be done, but they were. Other things we did find impossible—at least of accomplishment in less than two years. Ten years from now, I hope, two months will be enough."

It really wasn't a surprise to anyone that the film opened to strong reviews:

The New York Times: "'Citizen Kane' is far and away the most surprising and cinematically exciting motion picture to be seen here in many a month. As a matter of fact, it comes close to being the most sensational film ever made in Hollywood."—Bosley Crowther

New York Herald Tribune: "A young man named Orson Welles has shaken the medium wide-awake with his magnificent film, 'Citizen Kane.' ... Welles, after a fiery brief period of trial-and-error experimentation, has fully mastered the idiom of the photoplay."—Howard Barnes

New York World-Telegram: "What matters is that *Citizen Kane* is a cinema masterpiece, that here is a film so full of drama, pathos, humor, drive, variety, and courage and originality in its treatment that it is staggering and belongs at once among the great screen achievements."—William Boehnel

New York Post: "Not since Chaplin's 'A Woman of Paris' has an American film struck an art and an industry with comparable force. Orson Welles with this one film establishes himself as the most exciting director now working. Assiduously avoiding obvious dodges of the arty, he brings a clear, unfettered intelligence to the problems of the sound picture. Technically the result marks a new epoch."—Archer Winsten

New York Daily News: "It is one of the most interesting and technically superior films that has ever come out of a Hollywood studio."—Kate Cameron

The New Yorker: "For introduction, gates and formidable fencing, and this formal difference seems revolutionary enough to establish Mr. Welles' independence of the conventions. This independence, like fresh air, sweeps on and on throughout the movie, and in spite of bringing to mind, by elaborately fashioned decoration, a picture as old in movie history as *Caligari,* the irregularity of the opening sets a seal of original craftsmanship on what follows. Something new has come to the movie world at last."—John Mosher

Esquire: "And just for a bit of mockery, Welles has made exactly the kind of picture that half-a-dozen writers have been describing and predicting for years. Some of the writers went to work in Hollywood, too, and forgot to make their picture. Welles never, to my knowledge, said a word about the movies one way or the other. But he has made the movies young again, by filling them with life."—Gilbert Seldes

CITIZEN KANE HAD opened in three major cities within one week: in New York at the RKO Palace on May 1; in Chicago at the Woods and the Palace on May 6; and in Los Angeles at the El Capitan on May 8. It was reserved seating only at the Palace at the two shows daily. In the weeks immediately after that, *Citizen Kane* was also showing in Boston, San Francisco, Seattle, and Washington, D.C.

Although most critics felt that *Citizen Kane* was a "great" motion picture, and it had captured the coveted Best Picture award of 1941 from both the New York Film Critics and the National Board of Review, it was not immediately popular with the general public.

Bosley Crowther of *The New York Times* may have exemplified the public's reaction when he commented that, although grand in scope and proportion, *Kane* did everything but explain itself. And Eileen Creelman of the *New York Sun* might have reflected another facet of the public's reaction when she called *Kane* a "cold picture," with intellectual interest but with no emotional or dramatic value.

There were others, of course, who never got to see the film. The national chain of theaters owned by Spyros Skouras, for example, did not exhibit *Citizen Kane,* for fear of possible lawsuits and retribution by Hearst, and many other major motion picture theaters that normally booked first-run RKO features, simply refused to schedule it. Although Hearst could not actually stop the picture, his influence hurt it at the box office. The first week's receipts of *Citizen Kane* in New York, for example, were adequate (something over $28,000), but they had dropped so considerably in just over two months of exhibition that the film was eventually withdrawn.

During the summer of 1941, *Citizen Kane* was road-shown throughout the United States as part of RKO's block-booking policy. A number of theaters took the film, paid for it, but then refused to exhibit it, writing off their rental fees as a loss. All of the Fox theaters on the West Coast took it but dared not show it, citing fear of the Hearst corporation for their reluctance.

In those cities where a chain would not accept the film in any of its theaters, and where the RKO block-booking theaters also refused to show it, RKO rented it to competing houses. Still, the public, for the most part, shunned *Citizen Kane.* After several months, RKO's corporate ledgers indicated a sad smudge of red ink. The greatest motion picture of all time had lost $150,000.

At Academy Award time in February of 1942, Orson seemed to be revivified: *Citizen Kane* had received no less than nine nominations, including Best Picture, Best Direction, Best Actor, Best Screenplay, and Best Cinematography. But at the first mention of the title *Citizen Kane,* during the ceremonies, there were eddies of boos, chortles, and hisses throughout the auditorium, in conflict with some dilatory applause.

It was not to be *Kane*'s night. John Ford's *How Green Was My Valley,* a film of sensitivity and intelligence, garnered many of the principal awards, seven Oscars in all, including Best Picture. The only Oscar given to Orson or his film that evening was for Best Original Screenplay, ironically to be shared with Herman Mankiewicz. In a way, it was a direct humiliation of Welles for causing all the trouble. All Hollywood knew of the controversy and mystery surrounding both the legal credit and the creative accolades that were due both men. In many ways it was more a night of embarrassment for Orson than an evening to remember.

It is probably fortunate for him that Orson was out of the country at the time of the awards and could not be at the ceremony to witness what he ultimately considered a slap rather than a defeat, a deeply hurtful action in any event.

Some of the films that were also passed over for Best Picture of 1941 have gone on, like *Citizen Kane,* to become classics in their own right, and some have vanished from memory: *Blossoms in the Dust, Here Comes Mr. Jordan, Hold Back the Dawn, The Little Foxes, The Maltese Falcon, One Foot in Heaven, Sergeant York,* and *Suspicion.*

CHAPTER 13

ORSON WELLES'S SELECTION in 1941 of *The Magnificent Ambersons* as his next film was accepted by the RKO chieftains with a relatively small amount of persuasion on his part. Actually, he brazenly began working on three films almost simultaneously. Before shooting started on *The Magnificent Ambersons,* he had been working on the script of another new film, *Journey Into Fear.* While shooting *Journey,* he was going back and forth from the States to Mexico, where he was also filming the first part of a documentary, *It's All True.* And he edited *The Magnificent Ambersons* from Rio de Janeiro while shooting further segments of *It's All True,* which by then had State Department sponsorship as part of a goodwill trip to Latin America. He was also involved in California in a new weekly radio program sponsored by Lady Esther cosmetics.

THE MAGNIFICENT AMBERSONS story had many of the stock elements that professional film producers wanted to see in a film: a family epic with several impressive characters, a bittersweet love affair that goes awry, an unfulfilled relationship between two physically attractive young people, a depleted fortune and fall from grace, and a spiritual reconciliation at the end. In order to demonstrate how he would handle the making of the film, or at least how he would treat the narrative, Welles played a recording of his radio version of the Booth Tarkington novel for the studio heads. It had been broadcast barely two years before and some of the RKO people had heard and been captivated by it, but even those hearing it for the first time seemed to agree that since Orson had been able to capture the poignancy of the story on the air he could also do it on film.

James Naremore has rightly suggested that the "novel's portrait of a midland town passing into the twentieth century was surely reminiscent of Welles's experience in the quasi-Victorian atmosphere of Kenosha and Woodstock," and it is likely, in an attempt to recapture that time as completely as possible—he had done so partially in the early scenes of *Citizen Kane*—he was inspired to choose *Ambersons* as his next effort. Welles's instinct that he could create a meaningful film of the story also played a major role in his decision; the idea soon developed into a considered opinion and finally emerged as a confident assurance that *The Magnificent Ambersons* could be, in its own lyrical way, if not a greater film than *Citizen Kane,* then at least one of less distancing, a film to which audiences might find it easier to relate.

Tarkington's life, which spanned three-quarters of a century, had seen America emerge as a great nation. He grew up in Indiana in a day and place of buggies and bicycles, of old elms and walnut trees, of flags on holidays and summer evenings with families sitting on the front porch enjoying themselves. In his work, he tried to include the best of that era, the heart-tugs along with the laughter. Welles was dedicated to evoking that time on film.

The formal decision to accept the Tarkington story as Orson's follow-up film to *Citizen Kane* was particularly sweetened by the ease and relatively nominal cost with which RKO secured the motion picture rights from Warner Brothers. A silent version of the film, *Pampered Youth,* released by Vitaphone in 1924, only a few years after the publication of the novel, had proved unsuccessful at the box office, despite, or perhaps because of, its changed ending where George Minafer relents and gives his permission to Eugene Morgan to marry Minafer's mother. Warners bought the sound picture rights in 1929 and proceeded to have a talking script created by Julien Josephson, the scenarist of the silent adaptation of Sinclair Lewis's *Main Street.* Unimpressed with the filmic possibilities of Josephson's script, Warner's shelved the project for almost a decade, reviving it in 1938 for another adaptive trial by screenwriter Charles Linton Tedford. The Tedford attempt continued to be uninspiring to the brothers Warner because it failed to capture the somewhat complicated message of a land and a great people in transition: no film was made. When negotiations began to buy the rights for Welles's version, Warner's was so happy to be rid of what was becoming a burden, RKO was granted rights for a small amount of money and Warner's threw in the Josephson and Tedford scripts to boot.

When given tacit approval by George Schaefer to move ahead with *Ambersons,* Welles sequestered himself on King Vidor's private yacht and, away from the temptation of the carefree intemperance of Hollywood life, he emerged nine days later with a vibrant screenplay. Using Tedford and Josephson's previous work merely as background, and taking some patches of dialogue from his own radio version, Welles relied mainly on the Tarkington original in crafting the screenplay.

The novel is filled with dialogue, and most of the talk and language that appears in the script is a direct, unedited, or slightly changed transplant, with third-person narrative sometimes replaced by first-person speech. For example:

In the novel:

> After the arrival of coffee, the Major was rallying Eugene upon some rural automobile shops lately built in a suburb and already promising to flourish.
> "I suppose they'll either drive you out of the business," said the old

gentleman, "or else the two of you'll drive all the rest of us off the streets."

In the script:

> *At the table, in a medium shot:*
>
> JACK
>
> Gene, what's this I hear about someone else opening up a horseless carriage shop somewhere out in the suburbs?
> *Major talks amusedly to Eugene.*
>
> MAJOR
>
> Oh, I suppose they'll drive you out of the business, or else the two of you'll get together and drive all the rest of us off the streets.

The Welles adaptation of *The Magnificent Ambersons* could easily be considered a model for a faithful reconciliation of novel and script; it included virtually nothing that is not represented in the book and successfully preserved the flavor of the action. Orson contended that the film would be the first adaptation to reach the screen with such little variation from its original source. "If it is a good picture," he told a group of newspapermen in a speech before Sigma Delta Chi, "it will not be because of what I did to it, rather because of what I didn't." Many of the Wellesian scenes, as outlined in the script, follow almost exactly the action and intent of their equivalent in the novel.

In the novel:

> Shifting fashions of shape replaced aristocracy of texture; dressmakers, shoe-makers, hatmakers and tailors, increasing in cunning and in power, found new ways to make new clothes old. The long contagion of the "Derby" had arrived: one season the crown of this hat would be a bucket; the next it would be a spoon. Every house still kept its bootjack, but high-toed boots gave way to shoes and "congress gaiters" and these were played through fashions that shaped them now with toes like box-ends and now with toes like the prows of racing shells.

The cinematic parallel to the above scene shows a reflection of Eugene Morgan (played by Joseph Cotten) in a mirror, in his underwear, wearing a derby. Everything that follows is shown on the screen, with the narrator supplying the dialogue:

In the film:

> *Music is heard. Eugene in a medium shot, removes his hat and puts on another.*
>
> NARRATOR
>
> The derby had arrived; one season the crown of this hat would be a bucket; next it would be a spoon.
> *The scene then cuts to a medium close-up of Eugene's feet kicking and pulling off boots on a bootjack.*

NARRATOR

Every house still had its bootjack, but hightopped boots gave way ... *(Cut to a close-up of Eugene's hands putting shoes on his feet)* ... to shoes and "congress gaiters" and these were played through fashions that shaped them now with toes like box-ends and now with toes like racing shells.

Orson was happy with the script that he had created, and Schaefer concurred. It was official: *The Magnificent Ambersons* would be number two.

Orson's script went through many subsequent changes but stayed delicately within the realm of Tarkington's world. Welles's *Ambersons* would start with a blank, black screen: music could be heard playing. It is a medley of charm and nostalgia. The narrator's voice comes in:

The magnificence of the Ambersons began in 1873. Their splendor lasted all the years that saw their Midland town spread and darken into a city.... *There is a fade-in to a long-shot of a house in the background; women walking in front of the gate; carriages passing; a horse-drawn trolley car.*

NARRATOR

In that town in those days, all the women who wore silk or velvet knew all the other women who wore silk or velvet ... and everybody knew everybody else's family horse and carriage. The only public conveyance was the streetcar....

A woman leans out the window of the house, waves and calls—

WOMAN

Yoo hoo. ...

The driver stops the car and it goes off the track. Everyone gets off the car and the men lift it back on to the track. As the people start getting back on, the woman runs from the house to get on. The men begin to push the car and then get on it as it begins to pull away.

NARRATOR

A lady could whistle to it from an upstairs window and the car would halt at once and wait for her while she shut the window, put on her hat and coat, went downstairs, found an umbrella, told the "girl" what to have for dinner and came forth from the house. Too slow for us nowadays, because the faster we're carried, the less time we have to spare.

Assembling his cast and crew for *Ambersons* was not quite as easy as it had been for *Kane*. Because of the long gap between the end of shooting *Kane* and the decision to proceed with *Ambersons*—about nine months—some of Welles's Mercury actors had drifted off to other theatrical appointments: Everett Sloane had committed himself to a weekly radio show and could not break his contract; George Coulouris had begun a national tour in *Watch on the Rhine*; Paul Stewart had landed a part in *Johnny Eager* and was already filming; Gus Schilling was given a small role in *Dr. Kildare's Victory*. Although not Mercurians by original design, Ruth Warrick and Dorothy

Comingore were regarded as part of the company by Welles; both ladies, however, were busy raising their respective newly born babies and could not consider parts in *The Magnificent Ambersons.*

Although Agnes Moorehead had appeared on the screen for only a few moments in *Citizen Kane,* it had been obvious that she was born to the medium. Welles would use her in *Ambersons* as the neurotic Aunt Fanny, a part he had eliminated entirely in the radio version but planned to expand in the film, mainly because of the qualities he could envision her bringing to the role. Joseph Cotten seemed to be a natural for the gentle inventor Eugene Morgan, and Ray Collins and Erskine Sanford would be given principal parts.* But what of Welles himself? It was obvious that he could not play the part he had performed on radio, that of the teenage George, since his weight had increased by forty pounds, and, even if he could have reduced to look younger, the character was also inconsistent with the kind of imperiousness he was seeking in a film role. For a while he considered taking the role of Morgan and then, as a brief cameo appearance, that of Major Amberson. Finally, he decided to concentrate only on directing and took no part in the film except that of unseen narrator. It would be the first and last time in his career that he would ever be given the luxury of not appearing in one of his own completed films. In later years he claimed that his not taking a role in *Ambersons* had been a career blunder in that he should have continued to capitalize on his star status earned from *Kane.* Although he cemented his image as director, he felt that he had lost momentum in Hollywood's eyes as an actor.

Orson tried convincing the studio of the idea of casting Dolores Del Rio in the role of the beautiful Isabel Minafer, but even he realized that although she was aristocratic and exquisitely ravishing, Miss Del Rio's Latin origins could not conform with the Anglo-Saxon look of a middle-American heiress that was so necessary in the plot. As an alternative, he somehow persuaded the genteel Dolores Costello, wife of his friend John Barrymore, to abandon her self-imposed retirement and take the part.** Anne Baxter was cast in the role of Lucy.

At about this time a new member joined the Mercury staff. He would prove to be unexpectedly influential. A professional magician, Jack Moss had been hired to give Welles personal magic lessons and to act as his business manager as well as Mercury's general factotum. Welles claimed that he hired him because when studying contracts, "he *only* read the fine print." Huge of neck

---

*Tarkington once gave (in a 1917 issue of *Metropolitan* magazine) a physical description of his characters, much more so than he had outlined in the novel. Welles read that delineation to help visualize the principal characters and as an aid for casting: "The Ambersons are Du Maurier-like people: tall, graceful, beautifully dressed, distinguished and aristocratic. Major Amberson wears a moustache. The others are smooth-shaven. Mr. Minafer wears a nondescript moustache. Fanny Minafer is not ugly or foolish-looking; she has been quite pretty. She dresses well. Isabel is a beautiful and beautifully-dressed lady, young looking to the end. Eugene looks like John McCutcheon. Lucy is any pretty and young cutie from Vassar or Smith: nifty clothes and brains, too."

**She had last appeared in an uninspired effort in 1939, called *King of the Turf.*

and girth and short of stature, Moss was highly organized, intelligent, and diplomatic, and in many ways he took up where John Houseman had left off as a buffer against the slings and arrows of front office types.

Orson was invited to appear as a magician at the California State Fair that summer, and he spent four to six hours each day practicing with Moss in an attempt to hone his act.

Since Gregg Toland had gone into the army, the question of who could serve as Orson's cameraman became of paramount concern. Other cinematographers throughout the industry were also enlisting, so it was decided that Welles should employ the services of an RKO staff cameraman. As he began to have sets assembled, Welles reviewed films in search of his new Toland. One name, Stanley Cortez, kept surfacing. Cortez had been with Universal for several years and had been recently signed at RKO. He had spent his earlier years studying art and working as an assistant for portrait photographers, influences evident in his framing of a scene in film. Welles screened some of his films, such as *Danger on the Air* (1938) and *The Black Cat* (1941), along with some tests he had made for David O. Selznick. He was greatly impressed, and Moss informed Cortez, then shooting tests for George Cukor in New York, that Welles wanted him for *The Magnificent Ambersons.* Cortez agreed to the terms of a contract over the phone and left that Sunday for the West Coast, to meet with Welles for the first time on the set that Monday.

A major problem arose with the budget before shooting began. Because of the shrinking international market for films, RKO had set a maximum budget in Welles's contract of $600,000 for *The Magnificent Ambersons.* Also, according to the arrangement that RKO had made with its bank, no film from the studio was ever to exceed $750,000. A pre-budget estimate of *Ambersons* came close to one million dollars. Pared down to more details in its final form just before shooting, the film looked as if it would still cost in excess of $850,000. Schaefer talked with Welles about finding ways to bring the cost of the film down under the $750,000 figure, and Welles agreed he would do all he could to minimize expenses. Although skeptical, but remaining hopeful, Schaefer gave his permission to proceed with production.

Welles had always maintained that the fundamental aim of the actor on screen (and on stage) was to create a true image and that it was in this struggle for unity that the character evolved into a believable performance. In any given scene, a superlative performance could result. But, because of the necessity to shoot a film out of sequence, often without reaction characters, and as a result of the hours, days, and weeks of waiting on the set between one piece of action with another, a consistently unified and balanced interpretation could easily be destroyed. He hoped to solve, or at least confront, this inherent difficulty with screen acting. The performances of the actors in *Citizen Kane* had been, he contended, close to remarkable, but he sought improvement.

Six weeks before the shooting began on *The Magnificent Ambersons,* Welles began a formal routine of rehearsals of all the principals. All at once, he felt that he was back on Broadway, establishing long, sometimes languorous, sometimes vital sessions. These times were especially relaxed and enjoyable for him since he had no lines or business to learn himself. As his actors began to understand their characters, he allowed each of them to include some of himself, or what he could do best dramatically, in his respective part: Joseph Cotten's special brand of Southern courtesy; Agnes Moorehead's ability to create a hysterical agitation; Ray Collins's intelligence and warmth. No actor was on trial in those initial sessions, and much of the time was spent in general discussion of each character's life, background, position at any given moment in the film, and thought content. Welles was in his directorial glory as he briefed, stimulated, and then attempted to influence everyone into understanding the situation, style, and mood of the film, shaping the performances into fully realized parts. The rehearsals would invariably end with almost all of the cast flushed with emotion, heading off with Orson to a night of dining, drinking, and talk about the theater.

Contrary to common myth, sometimes cultivated by Orson, all or most of the scenes in *The Magnificent Ambersons* were *not* improvised by the actors. He endorsed deviation from the script, however, whenever creative or sensible alternatives presented themselves. Line or word changes were always welcome; for instance, Tim Holt suggested that his character of teenage Georgie was too stuffy and probably wouldn't use the word "bum" in the line, "Most girls of sixteen are bum dancers." He changed it, with Orson's approval, to "Most girls sixteen are pretty *bad* dancers."

As the many rehearsals added to each actor's sharpening of his role, Welles, in an attempt at a further pursuit of excellence, came up with another idea that had never been tried before in Hollywood. After discovering and becoming enamored of how looping—the process of having an actor restate a line into the sound track of the film for additional or changed emphasis or perhaps to add or delete a word—could be used to refine the sound of the dialogue, he arranged to have an entire sound track made before the film was shot. The actors could concentrate on their speeches in the sound studio and have them recorded; then, on the set, in front of the camera, all they would need to do was synchronize their lip movements and gestures with the dialogue, which would be played through large speakers located in various spots on the set.

Orson gathered his cast together and continued rehearsing during daytime. Then at Radio Recorders, a separate studio located not too far from the RKO lot, the group would repair in the evenings to create *The Magnificent Ambersons* sound track. The entire process took weeks, because of changes and mistakes having to be rerecorded. By the final session, however, Orson had what he wanted.

On October 28, 1941, shooting began. It was a virtual disaster. The scene chosen to be the initial effort was the dinner party where the impertinent Georgie insults Eugene Morgan: "Automobiles are a useless nuisance. . . ." The scene was selected as the inaugural effort because the studio set was relatively simple to construct and furnish and the cinematography planned was to be unaffected. This would give Cortez, his first day on the job, an opportunity to find his way into the look of the film. Also, and perhaps most important, the characters would be seated, and all that was needed for them to do was to mouth their lines being projected from the nearby speakers. When the actors began the process, they discovered, to Orson's horror, that the logistics of mastering the exact length of any particular line, its rhythm and its meaning (as of facial gestures), was close to impossible.

As each actor attempted to recite the lines booming from the speakers, the synchronicity usually went awry because they were distracted by the echoes and reverberations. Welles understood immediately that unless there could be perfect precision, the originally recorded track could not be successfully integrated into the matching lip-movements as they appeared on the screen. After a few heartsick hours of trying to coordinate the two, with no success, the idea was abandoned and they reverted to regular live recording while acting.

After that incident, Orson seemed to become less and less interested in perfecting the sound track, except that he tried his system once again with the horse-and-buggy snow scene. It, too, failed. Eventually, when doing an outdoor scene, for instance, he would be unconcerned if an actor's lines were ruined by an airplane overhead or the screeching of brakes from a nearby auto. "Keep going," he would say quickly, "we'll loop it later, we'll loop it later." The entire cotillion scene had to be looped because the large cranes that carried the cameras squeaked and creaked across the old wooden floors of the studio and these noises could be heard on the first sound track.

Cortez has remembered that he was nervous about the first day's rushes. Everyone in the scene met at the screening room; Orson was there, of course, people from the RKO executive office, and others of the cast and crew: "When we all assembled to see the first day's work, we were all on edge; me especially . . . to fly from New York and start straightaway—my God! Then we saw it and Orson was delighted. Immediately there was a *rapport*. From then on, to work with Orson was a fantastic experience."

What resulted from the creative relationship of Cortez and Welles was a masterful manipulation of light and shadow, a depth of somberness that perfectly portrayed the grays of the Victorian era, a feeling of baroque sadness and mystery, and a harmonious and elegant look that fights to surpass the visual perfection of *Citizen Kane*. The rapport that Cortez speaks of, however, was limited: Welles would often become annoyed and short-tempered, not with the fruit of Cortez's product, but with his pre-camera personal style in presenting his ideas. Using his vast knowledge of art, Cortez would say such things as, "Orson, I see Major Amberson as Rembrandt's *An Old Man Seated*," in trying to explain his suggestion on how a particular scene could be lighted; or, "Why don't we see if we can produce a Goyan 'black painting' in the scene with Aunt Fanny by the boiler?" Welles would invariably roll his eyes at such comments, not because he disagreed with them or failed to understand the references, but because he considered them a touch pretentious, being said, as he felt they invariably were, for all the cast and crew to hear. It is also possible that Welles reacted against what was developing into an intellectual competition with Cortez and considered the brilliance or erudition of the cameraman's remarks threatening.

But however distasteful their association became on occasion, their respective urges to try to go even beyond *Kane* prevailed at least temporarily. André Bazin, in his posthumously published critique of Orson, perhaps best summarizes the cinematic feeling produced by the collaboration:

> In *Ambersons* particularly, the lighting system set up by Cortez, the director of photography, serves, doubtless, on the one hand, to re-create the ambience of gas lighting and, on the other, lets Welles have his actors evolve in a heterogeneous luminous space: a space in which the ordering of contiguous zones of dark and light constitute—within the immobility of the sequence—a kind of editing and a dramatic rhythm. But frequently, and paradoxically, Welles will see to it that essential lines are spoken at the exact moment when the actor is least well lit. The most significant moments thus evade us at the very instant when our desire to seize them is strongest.

Despite Orson's somewhat creative cathexis of Cortez, he continued to be annoyed by his personal style, referring to him at one point as a "criminally slow cameraman." Cortez seemed to take hours, sometimes days, to light a set whereas Toland would have accomplished a similar effect in minutes.

It was a lively set. "You must have a mustache and more lines on your face!" Welles, mustachioed himself, boomed at Agnes Moorehead in her character as Aunt Fanny. "I love women with mustaches!" he said, as he grabbed a makeup pencil and began working her over. In between takes, as props were moved and scenery readjusted, Welles continued with his magic lessons from Jack Moss, and at least once a day, to the delight of the assembled cast and crew, he would, with all the flair of an ancient conjurer, extract a large and lovable white rabbit from what appeared to be an empty high hat.

In *The Magnificent Ambersons* as in *Kane,* Welles's proclivities for the extraordinary were resoundingly abundant. He had 125 turn-of-the-century automobiles bought, borrowed, or commandeered and put into working order; the car that is used for the ride in the country was a 1905 model exactly as pictured in the Sears catalog of that year; an icehouse in east Los Angeles— filled with frozen fish—was rented and the outdoor snow scenes shot there, mainly to be able to show breath steaming from the actors' mouths, but also to give the scenes more of a sense of reality; Welles was forced to direct that part of the film dressed in a knit cap, long underwear, and a fur-lined aviator suit used especially for high-altitude experiments—it was so cold that Ray Collins contracted pneumonia and had to be hospitalized, holding up the filming; the scene in which the horse-drawn sled overturns had to be done directly by actors Tim Holt and Anne Baxter and not stunt people because Orson insisted on a close-up of their faces as they roll right into the camera and on remaining focused on them from the moment the sleigh overturns.

(above) Opening night of Welles's black *Macbeth* at the Lafayette Theatre (April 14, 1936) was one of Harlem's proudest events, and Orson was hailed as a great hope for the American theater. Traffic was jammed in every direction around the theater as first-nighters and those who hoped to gain tickets crowded the area. Police estimated that some 10,000 people were in the neighbourhood. Because of the tumult, the performance was delayed for almost an hour. *(WPA Federal Theatre Photos)*

(left) Orson looks serious as he puffs on his pipe and listens to his partner, John Houseman, prior to a rehearsal of the Federal Theatre production of *Horse Eats Hat* in 1937. Although Orson was influenced by the older man, he was highly independent and individualistic and actually forbade Houseman to attend any of the rehearsals. They spent a lifetime feuding. *(WPA Federal Theatre Photos)*

(above left) Orson's first wife, Chicago socialite Virginia Nicholson, was an aspiring actress who often appeared in early Welles stage productions. Here she is, without costume, in 1938, walking through the pacing for *Too Much Johnson*. *(The Authors Group Archive)*

(above right) The twenty-three-year-old Orson animatedly directing his first film, *Too Much Johnson*, in 1938 on the banks of the Hudson River. The film was to be inserted in the play of the same name as an expositional device, but because of projection difficulties, was never shown. *(The University of Southern California Archive)*

(right) Orson, with full makeup, as the septuagenarian Charles Foster Kane, just prior to shooting initial screen tests for *Citizen Kane*. With plastic wrinkles, contact lenses, false mustache, a puttied nose, and bald pate, the process of transformation took over three hours each day to complete. *(RKO Pictures, Inc.)*

(right) A famous expressionistic shot from *Citizen Kane*. The camera shoots up at an oblique angle to emphasize the power of Welles as Charles Foster Kane at Madison Square Garden during what will turn out to be his unsuccessful campaign for governor. *(RKO Pictures, Inc.)*

(below) Here, Welles and his cameraman, Gregg Toland, wait for the basement set in Xanadu to be completed and prepared before they commence shooting on *Citizen Kane*. The collaboration of the two men made motion picture history in creating one of the most visually arresting films ever made in Hollywood. *(RKO Pictures, Inc.)*

KANE MEETS SUSAN - #1.   SEE OTHER CARD FOR PIANO

EXT. DRUG STORE & STREET - WEST SIDE - N.Y. & INT. SUSANS 1ST APARTMENT.

FADE IN ON SUSAN COMING OUT OF DRUG STORE HOLDING FACE BECAUSE OF TOOTH-ACHE (WET STREET- R.K.O RANCH) SHE STARTS TO

WALK TOWARD HER APARTMENT AND AS ARRIVES IN FRONT

KANE COMES FROM OPPOSITE DIRECTION - STEPPING ON

AS LOOSE BOARD PUT THERE TO BRIDGE A MUD PUDDLE IT

FLYS UP SPLATTERING HIM WITH MUD AND AT SAME TIME

THE SAME TIME BUMPING INTO SUSAN - SHE INVITES HIM IN TO GET CLEANED UP

AND THEY ENTER APARTMENT HOUSE

PICK THEM UP ABOUT TO GO INTO THEIR DOOR AND CUT TO

INSIDE APARTMENT AS THEY ENTER FOLLOW AS

KANE GOES TO BUREAU- EXAMINING THIS AND THAT - SUSAN IN BATHROOM IN BACK

SHE BRINGS HIM WATER IN BASIN AND THEY DO BUSINESS IN CLEANING UP - DISSOLVE TO

SHADOW OF DUCK ON WALL PULLING BACK SHOWING KANE DOING TRICKS

FOR SUSAN - FROM HERE GO TO PIANO SEQUENCE AS

SUSAN SINGS FOR KANE AS MA PERKINS ENTERS FROM REAR -

DIALOGUE BETWEEN THE THREE END WITH BEER ACTION - (CONTINUED)

(above) Welles had storyboards made up for virtually every scene of *Citizen Kane*, which were, in effect, blueprints for camera angles and distances, subject matter, and insert shots. The entire film was choreographed in this way; the result was a great saving in time and money when the shooting actually began. *(RKO Pictures, Inc.)*

(right) A still from the famous breakfast room scene, in which the deterioration of Kane's marriage over a period of years is shown with great editing finesse. Note the incongruous ketchup and steak sauce bottles on the table next to the elegant silver and china, an echo of a scene reminiscent of Hearst's San Simeon dining lore. *(RKO Pictures, Inc.)*

(above) On the set of *The Magnificent Ambersons*, in off moments, Welles often performed magic tricks for the amusement of cast and crew. Here, he pulls the proverbial rabbit from a hat while his stars Joseph Cotten and Dolores Costello look on *(RKO Pictures, Inc.)*

(below) As he did with *Citizen Kane*, Welles shot a large proportion of film for *It's All True* from low angles, as this photograph demonstrates. Dancers in the carnival were thus shown thrusting themselves above the crowds, standing out as symbols of grace and energy. *(RKO Pictures, Inc.)*

(above) On the set of *Journey Into Fear*, Orson cracks up his long-time friend and colleague Joseph Cotten. Although they would know each other for almost fifty years, they claimed never to have had an argument. *(RKO Pictures, Inc.)*

(right) Orson was a tireless campaigner in 1944 for Franklin D. Roosevelt's bid for the presidency. Here, he gives a rousing speech at the Waldorf-Astoria in New York. *(Photo by Leo Rosenthal; The Authors Group Archive)*

(above) A photograph of the famous dénouement of *The Lady from Shanghai*. In the actual film, however, Rita Hayworth wore a suit in this scene. Harry Cohn, the film's producer, ordered special still shots to be made that showed his star with a plunging neckline, bare shoulders and back, for publicity purposes. *(RKO Pictures, Inc.)*

(below left) One of Orson's most famous roles was that of the anti-hero Harry Lime, in *The Third Man*, a film he did not direct. Here, Lime is seen hiding in the sewers of Vienna at the film's end. *(The Authors Group Archive)*

(below right) In *Compulsion* (1959), Welles played the Clarence Darrow-like character Jonathan Wilk, who defends the Leopold-Loeb killers. His summation speech to the jury was hailed by critics worldwide. *(The Authors Group Archive)*

(right) Perhaps Orson's greatest acting role was as Falstaff in his film *Chimes at Midnight*; his rejection by Hal in the coronation scene, one of his best moments on the screen. *(The Authors Group Archive)*

(below) The Yugoslavian actress Oja Kodar, with Welles, in a scene from *F for Fake*. They were companions and colleagues for nearly twenty-five years. *(The Authors Group Archive)*

With *Heart of Darkness* in mind, Welles still wanted to do scenes with camera-as-character. In one scene, eventually cut from the film, he had Cortez strap a sixty-five-pound camera to one of his operator's chests and walk the man slowly, trailed by cables, in and out of the rooms and up the stairs of the vacant and lonely Amberson mansion to the closed door of Isabel's room. Slowly the door opens and the camera enters. When the rushes came back, the images had blurred, because of the vibrations of the operator's movements. On a second try, Cortez had the operator remove his shoes, the camera was more tightly harnessed and each of the man's steps and movements were choreographed as though he were a ballet dancer. The take ran four hundred feet, or four and a half minutes, and was successful.

Cortez claims that he wanted to do another shot, going through six or seven rooms, all in one take, with no cutting. He suggested this to Bob Wise. "Orson must have overheard me, because when we came to do the scene, he said, 'Can we do this whole scene in one?'" Cortez continues, "Orson, we can, if you're ready to gamble with me." They tried it, and every time the camera went through a room, four walls and a ceiling could be seen. Leading his grips and cameramen like children crossing a busy intersection, Orson directed, commanding the walls and furniture and mirrors to shift on cue while the lighting also changed and the camera continued in motion. "It was a symphony of movement," recalls Cortez.

Things proceeded, but not always smoothly. Philip K. Scheuer, a writer for the *Los Angeles Times,* remembers visiting the set of *Ambersons* while Stanley Cortez was filming a close-up of Tim Holt as he was in the midst of emoting a lengthy plea to his mother. "Cut!" boomed Welles, who seemed to appear out of nowhere. "That was bad," he told Holt. "It sounded like movies. Do it again—and don't act." As Holt adjusted himself for another take, Welles directed from the prone position, lying exhausted on Isabel's bed, just a few feet from Holt's face. Eventually, after many more takes, Welles had extracted from him the performance he was seeking.

Welles had personal difficulties with Anne Baxter as a result of an incident that occurred after his consumption of nine demolitionary martinis at a party given by Joseph Cotten. As she explained in her memoir, *Intermission,* Orson, while drunk, secretly sent his chauffeur home and pleaded to having no transport. Would she drive him?

> Gad, what a drive. I prayed for a policeman. Six feet four and 250 pounds, and what seemed like six hands in my shirt. All he kept saying was, "Oh, the beauty of it. Oh, the beauty of it." In tears of rage I finally shoved him out at Sunset Boulevard, threw my tattered bra in the gutter, and gunned up the hill to home and Mother. Poor Orson. I always wondered how long it took him to get a cab.

She forgave him, however, and despite the trauma, was able to say at the film's end that Orson was the best director she had ever worked with.

WITH THE PROBLEMS of *Citizen Kane* still fresh in mind, Gordon Youngman of the legal department began worrying that the saga of the Ambersons might be construed as a *roman à clef* about the families of Ford or Chrysler or Dodge and that legal action of the same temper threatened by Hearst for invasion of privacy could possibly occur. The fact that a film *(Pampered Youth)* had already been made of the Tarkington novel without legal repercussions helped to convince Youngman that *The Magnificent Ambersons* would escape attack; he insisted, however, that in all publicity and advertising, no mention of any real dynastic families be made. To further diminish any possibility of lawsuits, the telephone books of Fort Wayne and Indianapolis, going back for decades, were checked by the RKO research department to see whether there were any "Ambersons" or "Minafers" listed who might complain about the similarity. No such names were found.

Schaefer, in an attempt to dissolve any kind of controversy or problem that could conceivably hurt *The Magnificent Ambersons,* began to lose judgment about the real and fanciful. He formally and legally protested the registration of the title *The Magnificent Jerk,* by Twentieth Century-Fox, for a feature film on the grounds that it was too similar in name to *The Magnificent Ambersons* and would "detract from our forthcoming picture."

Darryl Zanuck failed to sympathize with Schaefer's complaint, pointing out that if the Twentieth Century title had been *The Magnificent Johnsons* or *The Magnificent Wilsons* there could *possibly* be confusion, but his title simply implied a straight "hokum" comedy that could not be mistaken for Welles's picture.* To cement his argument, Zanuck pointed out that when he had made *The Giant Swing,* Warner Brothers released *The Little Giant* with no adverse effects on his film and that he did not object when MGM released *Yank on the Burma Road* when his own *A Yank in the RAF* was still in the theaters. Schaefer, somewhat embarrassed, promptly dropped the whole matter.

The Hays Office again began to insert their own special brand of pressure into the making of *The Magnificent Ambersons.* The genitals of the horse that topples in the snow scene could not be shown on screen, of course. Pictures and lithographs on the walls of Georgie's club could not have any hint of salaciousness.** They objected to the young Georgie calling the character of Reverend Smith an "ole billygoat," because, according to their reasoning, the characterization of a pastor must be "dignified." They urgently requested a change be made, since such a line "would certainly give offense to ministers and churchgoers." Because Welles had already shot and was satisfied with Georgie's lines, he was forced to defrock the character of Reverend Smith, making him not a minister but just a townsman and renaming him "Bronson" in the process.

As to the scene where Uncle Jack Amberson is in the tub while talking to the irritated Georgie, the Hays Office wrote a detailed memo insisting that "there be no objectionable exposure of Jack in the tub . . . the camera

---

*When released, Zanuck had changed the title to *The Magnificent Dope.*
**Eventually, all the clubhouse scenes were excised by RKO to shorten the film.

angle should be held, as much as possible, to shoulder shots to avoid giving any offense; otherwise we would not approve of the scene in the finished picture."

TENS OF THOUSANDS of feet of unedited film from *The Magnificent Ambersons* were shipped periodically to Welles who was then in Rio shooting *It's All True*. Viewing it on a locally provided moviola, where with the aid of a foot pedal he could stop or start the film at will and play it backward or in slow or fast motion, he would spend hours creating an editing memorandum for Robert Wise in California for each assemblage of the cans of film that he received. With Shelley's ever-changing joyless eye "that finds no object worth its constancy," Welles, through the editorial process, tried to create the film as he knew it could look.

Like the Russian filmmaker and theorist Kuleshov, Orson believed that, as a painter has color, a musician has sounds, and a writer has words, a filmmaker has pieces of film as his primary materials. He theorized that the film art itself did not end when the actors performed a scene and it was shot. This was merely the preparation, the rough notes or unarranged words of filmmaking. The film was made when the director, through his editor, combined the shots and elements together in various combinations.

However, the large-scale shaping of *Ambersons* could not solely be accomplished on an editing machine or in the laboratory by shortening a scene here, eliminating a defect there, dissolving faster or more slowly from one shot to another. Total restructuring of certain scenes was needed or wanted, new dialogue, sound-track amendments, and hundreds of other modifications incorporated into the footage.

The difficulty of transmitting his editing ideas to Wise via letter, cable, and intercontinental telephone was immense. Long, complicated messages that told, rather than showed, what Welles wanted, often became garbled or their nuances misunderstood. Even his clearer memos were difficult, at long distance, to understand. Here is a partial extract from Welles to Wise, on his editorial requirements on a fragment of a scene, dated March 5, 1942:

> In bedroom scene fadeout quick after Tim's line "Mother, what are you going to do about it?" ... Screen should be black before Tim's lips start on line "What kind of answer are you going to make?" ... Just as fadeout completes dissolve in letter pushed under door ... Blow night version up or re-stage so envelope fills screen as letter stops moving ... Cut back to night insert original size for shadow for this ... Retreating footsteps hold as before on this but do half fadeout between night and day inserts ... Try alternates three quarter fadeout also dissolving from close envelope to present framing. ...

"I didn't know what the hell was going on half the time," Wise has recalled. "It's untrue that he once sent me a 67-page cable of changes, but I did receive a memorandum of 20 to 30 pages. We often tried for clarification by telephone, and the problems were enormous, just getting through. Then when we reached him, we usually could not hear him because of the connection. It was a nightmare."

The result of this long-distance editing and call for changes in *Ambersons* was a study in chaos. Wise often had to do his own directing, such as in the scene where Lucy and her father talk under the tree. He attempted to give the studio what it wanted—more expositional classification—and maintain a visual consistency, the poetry infused by Welles, with the rest of the film.

As Welles, the cat, was away, everyone played. Jack Moss directed some new scenes, as did Freddie Fleck, an assistant director, and even Vernon Walker, the special effects man, directed some takes.

Despite the clash of styles and the difficulties of continuity, with so many people trying to do Orson's bidding, Schaefer, at least at first, loved what he saw. He cabled Orson as follows:

PLEASE FORGIVE ME FOR NOT HAVING WIRED YOU IMME-DIATELY ON MY RETURN FROM THE COAST TO TELL YOU OF MY HAPPINESS AS A RESULT OF WHAT I HAVE SEEN OF YOUR CUR-RENT PICTURE. EVEN THOUGH I HAVE SEEN ONLY A PART OF IT, THERE IS EVERY INDICATION THAT IT IS CHOCK FULL OF HEART THROBS, HEARTACHES AND HUMAN INTEREST. FROM A TECH-NICAL STANDPOINT IT IS STARTLING AND I SHOULD NOT FORGET TO MENTION ESPECIALLY THAT AGNES MOOREHEAD DOES SOME OF THE FINEST PIECES OF WORK I HAVE EVER SEEN ON THE SCREEN. ALTHOUGH I SAW ONLY PART OF THE PICTURE HER WORK IN PARTICULAR MADE A TREMENDOUS IMPRESSION ON ME. AGAIN, I AM VERY HAPPY AND PROUD OF OUR ASSOCI-ATION. CONGRATULATIONS AND BEST WISHES.

GEORGE J. SCHAEFER

It is possible that if Welles had not received such an unqualified commen-dation from Schaefer on the unfinished *Ambersons,* he might have elected to proceed differently with the film. Although the United States was now at war, he was, nevertheless, attempting to get Wise to come down to Rio for direct editing sessions where he could have been more accurately understood. This could not be arranged. Perhaps a brief trip or two from Rio to Los Angeles was called for by Orson, but the studio optimism and his own self-confidence in editing by proxy, to say nothing of his involvement in *It's All True,* precluded the obvious.

Schaefer arranged the first preview screening of *The Magnificent Amber-sons* in a theater in Pomona, California. Welles could almost hear the uproar thousands of miles away in Rio. In an airmail, special delivery letter marked "PERSONAL-CONFIDENTIAL," so that its contents would remain only for Orson's eyes to see, Schaefer admitted he felt "miserable" in having to tell him the bad news:

Never in all my experience in the industry have I taken so much punishment or suffered as I did at the Pomona preview. In my 28 years in the business, I have never been present in a theater where the audience acted in such a manner. They laughed at the wrong places, talked at the picture, kidded it, and did everything that you can possibly imagine. I don't have to tell you how I suffered, especially in the realization that we have over $1,000,000 tied up. It was just like getting one sock in the jaw after another for over two hours.

Schaefer went on to share with Welles the reactions of that first preview audience, some given directly to Schaefer and others written on cards provided for comment. The consensus was that although it started off well, essentially the film was too slow and heavy, its somberness never capturing the interest or heart of the audience. Many of the people felt that an obvious attempt at being "arty" had been made; such comments as the film's direction being "camera crazy" were common.

The next evening, there was a second screening of *Ambersons,* this time in a theater in Pasadena, and although the audience was a bit older and somewhat more receptive or at least resigned, the adverse reactions were totally similar; it was also clear from both screenings that the audience had difficulty understanding the relationships of some of the characters and their connection with the narrative.

Schaefer, Moss, Wise, and Cotten conferred over what could be done to save the film while waiting for Orson's suggestions. It was now clear that RKO would "not make a dollar" on *Citizen Kane,* or even break even, as Schaefer described it to Welles, and both films added up to a $2 million investment. If *Ambersons* could not be shaped into a film that could make some money, both Schaefer and Welles were in serious trouble. In a letter to Orson in Rio, Schaefer agonized over the problem:

All of which again reminds me of only one thing—that we must have a "heart to heart" talk. Orson Welles has got to do something commercial. We have got to get away from "arty" pictures and get back to earth. Educating the people is expensive, and your next picture must be made for the box office. God knows you have all the talent and the ability for writing, producing, directing—everything in *Citizen Kane* and *Ambersons* confirms that. We should apply all that talent and effort in the right direction and make a picture on which we can get well.

Orson could read between the lines; it was clear that his position as the individual miracle of RKO was being eroded. True, *Citizen Kane* was already hailed as a contemporary masterpiece; true, he had brought great prestige and publicity to the ailing studio; true, his potential as one of Hollywood's most renowned filmmakers was virtually limitless; true, also, he was losing money for his partners and employers—millions—and he could not continue in that fashion much longer.

Directly following the Pomona and Pasadena previews, the power over, or control of, *The Magnificent Ambersons* began to sweep from Orson back to his associates at RKO. Schaefer wanted three scenes to be added to help explain the story of the film: the death of Major Amberson; a conversation between Eugene and Lucy in the garden; and the final scene in the hospital corridor.

Welles did not object so much to the suggested additions but he was furious about the scenes the studio wanted deleted. As it stood, the film ran some one hundred thirty minutes and everyone at RKO wanted it reduced to the average length of most films: about ninety minutes. Wise was placed in a difficult situation: Welles was telling him by phone and cable that he *must* retain certain scenes. Schaefer was telling him the opposite. The scissor prevailed.

Wholesale cutting was responsible for the loss of Georgie's visit to the clubhouse of the National Order of the Aces, which demonstrated his need to dominate and his manipulative abilities in getting himself reelected; a cotillion scene where a rivalry over Lucy is established between Georgie and another suitor; a splendid scene on the veranda on a summer evening with Georgie, Isabel, and Fanny, filmed almost in total blackness, which clarified their interrelationship; Georgie's discovery that Amberson Boulevard was turned into Tenth Street, which proves that his family name no longer means anything in the town; Eugene's visit to the boardinghouse that was once the Amberson mansion; quasi-documentary footage showing the growth of the town.

Orson insisted that the whole meaning of the film was to show the family in its decay and that the very scenes that were to be deleted were those that best displayed and examined the familial decomposition. It is important to note here that Orson, flush with his critical success with *Citizen Kane,* believed that the forthcoming *Ambersons* was stylistically more consistent and unified. Referring at one point to the "bric-a-brac" of *Kane,* the flashbacks within flashbacks of multiple points of view, as opposed to the tangibility of exposition of the Tarkington story and its filmic rhetoric, Welles seemed to be lamenting the process of "story" as it was told in *Kane.*

George Schaefer also wanted to excise the scene that takes place with Georgie and Fanny sitting at a table in the kitchen during a rainstorm. Observed by a virtually motionless camera, it is a classic cinematic set piece; Fanny is teased, first by Georgie and then by Uncle Jack, about her possible interest in Eugene Morgan. She is finally reduced to tears. Schaefer thought the scene too long and too static, without any camera movement, and noted that it was the scene that received the most snickers at the previews. He ordered it cut.

When Orson, still in Rio, was informed by Wise in California about the elimination of the kitchen scene, he bellowed his protests. Threatening to abandon *It's All True,* he implored with bleeding pen that the scene be retained. Jack Moss served as his intermediary and met with, called, cabled, and wrote Schaefer, actually *begging* him not to remove the kitchen scene. Since all of Schaefer's other wishes were followed, he finally relented on this last petition and permitted the scene to be retained. Its unorthodox manner of handling Aunt Fanny's anxiety in such an objective long take was subsequently to become a part of film history.

A FLASHBACK IS needed here, because months previously, in the midst of all the energy and activity being expended on *The Magnificent Ambersons,* Welles insanely had agreed to begin directing and starring in *Journey Into Fear,* working on the second film at night.

The story of how he finally became creatively involved with his first thriller began as early as January of 1941. Hollywood was then considering a film adaptation of Eric Ambler's best-selling espionage novel of 1940. *Journey Into Fear* was the hair-raising account of a timid British mathematician named Graham who, in his job with an armament firm, is sent to Istanbul to help the Turks install new guns and torpedo tubes on their warships. Graham's expertise marks him for death at the hands of a couple of particularly repulsive Nazi agents, and an unsuccessful attempt on his life in an Istanbul hotel is followed by an escape to Russia by boat. The Black Sea journey becomes a living nightmare when he realizes that his would-be assassin had come aboard in Athens under an assumed name, thus foiling Turkish agents who had guaranteed Graham safe passage. Graham finally masters his fear and manages to escape his tormentors; he eventually returns, presumably to his wife and his nondescript life in London.

Late in January, the Goldwyn studios were toying with the idea of casting Gary Cooper as Graham. A few weeks later, attention shifted to Charles Boyer. By early April, however, the embryonic project started gravitating toward Welles. Harry E. Eddington gave a copy of the novel to Welles on April 3. David Hempstead was to produce, and the ubiquitous Ben Hecht, who had bought the property, was working on the screenplay. Virtually overnight, Welles made up his mind to get involved, and this is when he made an unofficial deal with Schaefer to do *Journey Into Fear* if he was first allowed to do *The Magnificent Ambersons.* Accordingly, RKO bought the script from Hecht. Two days later, Hempstead wrote Orson a long, enthusiastic letter outlining the producer's plans to match Welles with French star Michele Morgan.

Journey would be a new *Thirty-nine Steps,* according to Hempstead; Hecht would even be able to tailor a part for Welles, if he'd only give the nod. Hempstead had a firm cast in mind, down to a part earmarked for Maria Ouspenskaya who had just finished what would become her most remembered role as the lycanthropically sage gypsy in *The Wolf Man.* With Robert Stevenson as director, production could go ahead in an instant and shooting could be completed by July.

Once Welles was immersed in the project, however, Hempstead's plans for a quick shooting faded and then disappeared entirely. The project became too important for Welles; he wanted it for a Mercury production.

On July 10, 1941, Welles delivered a progress report on *Journey Into Fear* to Joseph Breen (who had made the opportunistic and controversial job change from the Hays Office to RKO). Shooting, according to the original plan, should have been completed by then but in fact was far from even starting. After extensive talks with Hempstead and examination of Hecht's partial script and treatments, Welles had become convinced that he could create a more gripping and mysterious film. In fact, he wanted to start from scratch, except that he was willing to retain the casting of Michele Morgan. In all other respects, the film would be made anew.

Welles recommended stage-director-turned-actor Thomas Mitchell and a supporting cast of his own devising, including Joseph Cotten in the male lead and Ruth Warrick as his wife, a role Welles believed perfect for her. With the exception of Mitchell, who was Scarlett O'Hara's father in *Gone with the Wind* and who had won an Academy Award in 1939 for his Best Supporting Actor performance as Doc Boone in *Stagecoach,* Welles argued persuasively for what he defined as new-face casting and infusions of comedy and greater human interest; the thriller aspect, he believed, was "already in the bag." The appearance of Warrick and Cotten in *Kane* still had not, he believed, typecast them.

Welles decided to direct it himself; Thomas Mitchell dropped out of the plan and was given a part in *This Above All* with Tyrone Power. As much as Welles wanted her, Michele Morgan proved difficult to cast; she had by the time Welles was ready to proceed with *Journey Into Fear,* commitments to do *Joan of Paris.*

Welles jettisoned, or at least tried to ignore, all scripts and treatments after consultations with his own writers, and began to coauthor an entirely new script with Joseph Cotten. It is difficult to say how the distribution of labor went between the two men, but they had worked together on the script of *Citizen Kane* and knew each other's strengths and weaknesses and somehow developed a satisfactory collaborative arrangement. "There was a Mercury style of acting," Welles said later of *Journey Into Fear* "and both Joe Cotten and I worked together perfectly in establishing that look and feel." Inherent in the Mercury mode was a fast-paced approach to editing always combined with an ironic understatement.

Despite the reworking, they preserved some rudimentary features of the Hempstead-Hecht version. Graham would remain American (Cotten said it was to allow him to keep his Southern accent), and they would play down Josette, the shady lady love interest who occupies Graham's attentions while on board the ship.

In deference to the prudishness of Hollywood at the time, they also decided to defuse the adulterous overtones of the book by bringing Graham's wife into a prominent role. In Ambler's rendition, Graham is sorely tempted indeed; in the new script, Graham is portrayed as an inveterate homebody who sees Josette as nothing more than a confusing sort of pal.

So *Journey Into Fear* was linked directly to the agreement made about *Ambersons.* Welles was signed to play a part in *Journey* (the head of the Turkish Secret Police) without additional compensation over the two-picture budget ceiling. He was originally to receive, in effect, salaries totalling

$200,000 for both *Ambersons* and *Journey*—$2,000 a week. The script was finished in the first week of August 1941.

Casting *Journey* came next and Welles, who may have begun to have second thoughts about Michele Morgan even if she had been available, finally was able to cast his *inamorata,* Dolores Del Rio (who had gotten her divorce and now was engaged to Orson), as the dancer-seductress, Josette. The real surprise came in the new-face casting by which Welles peopled the movie with nonactors, members of his staff—Robert Meltzer,* Herb Drake and Bill Roberts in bit parts as stewards and, in what apparently was a last-minute choice, a bit for his personal secretary, Shifra Haran. And in a brilliant stroke that made the movie, business manager Jack Moss was cast as the Nazi assassin, the loathsome Petre Banat. Moss agreed to the role—his first and only in motion pictures—on one condition: he refused to speak even one line and wanted to remain silent throughout the film. Welles agreed to the demand and, as a result, Banat took on a more evil and ominous character than he might have if he had been forced to speak.

In an economy measure, preexisting RKO sets would be pressed into service—even some constructions from the abandoned *Heart of Darkness.* One of Hollywood's greatest cameramen, Academy Award winner Karl Struss, who filmed such silent classics as *Ben Hur* and *Sunrise* and such early talkies as *The Sign of the Cross* and *Dr. Jekyll and Mr. Hyde,* was signed on as cameraman. It proved to be another wise decision.

With shooting to begin at any moment, the studio censors and professional worriers decided that there were many features of *Journey* not to their liking. Welles had, in fact, remained quite faithful to Ambler's thriller in the basic plot line—even the dialogue was remarkably close. Graham was now an American, but the nationalities of the other principals remained—the most noteworthy being Turks, Greeks, French, and Spanish. With the outbreak of war, everyone was wondering which way the Turks would go. While claiming neutrality, they seemed to be favoring the Axis powers. An immediate problem developed in that Welles's role as the imposing and mysterious Haki, the secret policeman, might make the War Department edgy about the characterization of the Turks. Edgar Barrier's role as Kuvetli, a Turkish agent, was also seen as a potential insult. Both roles made Turks out to be, at least in the eyes of the censors, incompetent and comical on the one hand and sinister and untrustworthy on the other. If the supposedly touchy Turks had read the script, here's what they would have found:

The naive Howard Graham (Cotten) is sent by the Bainbridge Corporation to aid the Turkish navy. He and his wife (Ruth Warrick) meet Kopeikin (Everett Sloane), the company man in Turkey, who drags Graham off to the none-too-respectable *Le Jockey* cabaret, where the two meet Josette and José, a second-rate dance duo. While at the club, a magician (Hans Conreid, in a fine cameo) gets the reluctant Graham to volunteer for a trick in which the

---

*Meltzer was one of Chaplin's assistant directors on *The Great Dictator* when Welles met him.

two will obviously switch places. The transfer effected, the hapless magician is shot to death when the lights go down. Evidently a slow-witted killer has tried to shoot Graham. Police chief Haki (Welles in makeup and greatcoat, an image probably inspired by Joseph Stalin) finally convinces the incredulous Graham that someone is intent on eliminating him and packs him off on a steamer headed for the Russian port of Batum, where he will be reunited with his wife. Haki sees him off that night, reassuring him that the Turks will keep an eye on Nazi murderer-for-hire Petre Banat and his boss, Moeller.

Once aboard, Graham discovers that Josette has also booked passage, and together they acquaint themselves with a whole bevy of peculiar travelers—an elderly French couple (Agnes Moorehead and Frank Readick), a garrulous Turkish tobacco salesman named Kuvetli, and an old German archaeologist. Even the clean-thinking Graham, however, begins to suspect that the cramped staterooms, the indigestible food, and the boring company are not the only things amiss aboard; thus begins his journey into fear. José is loud and insulting, Josette is turning on her charms, and Kuvetli, it develops, works for a nonexistent company. And then, none other than Petre Banat, the fat, silent, Nazi psychopath comes aboard. When Graham goes to tell the purser and captain that someone is trying to kill him, they laugh in his face.

Soon the "archaeologist" reveals himself to be Moeller. Banat murders the tobacco salesman, who Graham now knows was one of Haki's men appointed to watch over him. Beside himself with fear, Graham is forced off the boat at Batum and is taken on an ominous ride by Banat and Moeller. He manages to escape, however, and arrives at the hotel where his wife is staying only to discover that Banat and Moeller have arrived before him.

In the climactic scene, Graham has tried to evade the killers by climbing out the window of the hotel room; and now, in a driving rain, Banat, gun drawn, inches his way toward Graham, who has reached the end of the narrow parapet. Banat misses his target repeatedly, then grabs onto an awning and swings himself toward Graham, hoping to kick him off his perch. The awning comes apart and Banat hurtles to his death. Haki and his men take care of Moeller, and the journey into fear draws to a close.

The studio's attorney, William Gordon, told Welles that the August script did not pass muster with the censorship office. There were the predictable and aggrandizingly magnified complaints about moral standards—if Joseph Cotten was filmed in a tub, for instance, as the script required in an early scene, Welles would have to be careful about the angles. Since Graham was a family man, Cotten's dialogue and certain scenes with Josette would have to leave no doubt that Cotten was not considering adultery. José, an apparently willing cuckold, was too decadent. References to "girlies" and "other places" more interesting than the seedy Le Jockey cabaret were also considered too suggestive.

Such changes, further demonstrating the omnipotence of the censorious Hays Office, were fatal to the Welles script and the whole theme of Ambler's novel: Journey plunged Graham, the innocent, into a world where life is cheap and moral standards are conspicuously lacking. In the book, virtually every gesture, every personal habit of the foreign characters, is suggestive of obscenity. Haki reads Krafft-Ebing and correctly describes Banat as a "pervert." It is this depraved world, as much as the threat of death, that bathes Graham in a perpetual cold sweat.

But the script was corrected, only to face a host of other objections. Not only were the Turks portrayed in a bad light; their hotels and nightclubs were too tawdry and were being slandered. And the Greeks could be offended—the Greek ship captain was unpleasant; the Greek help on the ship not polite enough. In fact, Gordon and RKO thought that *Journey* would upset Latin Americans, Spaniards, Russians, Chinese, and British (something about irreverence toward the Victoria Cross), not to speak of bankers and the U.S. War Department.

In addition to issues international and sexual, there were also niggling objections to the accuracy of a disquisition on archaeology made by the Nazi spy Moeller, on the grounds that Germans are very thorough and Moeller would have his facts straight while posing as an archaeologist. No matter that the speech is taken verbatim from Ambler's book—it went, too.

In Ambler's book, Josette's husband, José, is an opportunist interested in card-sharking and any other scheme to line his pockets, including the selling of his wife's favors for two thousand francs a week. Ambler went so far as to give him some punning French lines about sodomy that would have been unprintable in English. Welles toned José down in the script, but not thoroughly enough to satisfy RKO or Hays. José should not be Spanish; he must have another name; he must not even be allowed to speak a word of Spanish—perhaps he should be Hungarian or Romanian so as not to offend anyone who they believed counted. He and the other characters who say that war is useless, or is a bad thing, whether they be socialist, antisocialist, or somewhere in between, must have their dialogue purged of those sentiments.

A new script was prepared, dated January 2, 1942. José was now the indeterminate "Gobo." RKO again objected; the script still had him muttering in Spanish. "Please, please have Gobo speak French, or even possibly in the Basque dialect," Gordon memoed everyone on the film who he thought would take heed. The script went through another revision.

Journey had continuity problems worsened by the bland and sometimes cryptic dialogue resulting from the PCA-inspired deletions. With nationalities blurred beyond recognition, much of the point of the ship scenes is lost, as are the national enmities that motivated many of the characters in the first place. What's more, credulity is stretched to the limit; the audience might buy Dolores Del Rio as the French Josette Martel, but they also have to deal with a French couple who seem to be British, and a Gobo, now truly a man without a country, who may or may not be Josette's husband. The "Turks" all have different ideas about what constitutes an appropriate accent, and Ruth Warrick seems uncomfortable pronouncing the name "Kopeikin." In a scene in which Cotten is particularly wooden, the captain and purser guffaw and carry on like a Hollywood version of Mexican bandits or the Three Stooges.

What saves *Journey* is its ambience, evoked to a great extent by the low-key lighting effects of Struss, and the scenes worked out by Welles. It is a movie of atmospherics and visual detail, a frame too fragile to support the comedic side of the Cotten role and the implausible, incomplete characterizations. Oddly enough it is the ship's interiors and the performance of Jack Moss that make the movie.

Because Welles would have to leave after filming his scenes to fulfill his commitment to Washington to make a goodwill tour in Latin America and to work on his documentary, *It's All True,* Norman Foster was brought in to direct *Journey.* Foster had written radio scripts for Orson and had also done some preliminary work in Mexico on *It's All True,* and the two men had a strong professional relationship.

Unfortunately, when Foster began shooting *Journey,* on the sixth of January, he was not a happy man. He had not read the book (Welles had told him not to bother), and he found the double identities and hidden motives of many of the Ambler characters bewildering. With the constant alterations and deletions of dialogue and the changing of names and nationalities (another alteration made the French "Mathis" couple "Mathews"), Foster threw up his hands. "I often didn't know what the hell it was about," he later complained. Privately he revealed his belief that Welles was keeping certain changes and additions to himself in order to maintain control over the picture.

Two days into shooting, the Motion Picture Producers and Distributors office let Welles know that many more passages in *Journey* unacceptable to the Production Code had been unearthed, suggestive of adultery and pandering. He was also warned about some leering reactions indicated in the script. A scene with Graham's wife in a nightgown was condemned. A line describing the Welles character seemed "to point up Haki as a man of numerous sex affairs," an unacceptable characterization.

The piecemeal nature of the work and Welles's perfectionism made the shooting painfully slow. One can imagine that Foster was not very pleased to have casting still up in the air as shooting began and to have characters' names, accents, and lines changed in order to accommodate the Production Code. Somehow Welles managed to hold things together and complete his scenes to his satisfaction before he went off again to Mexico and South America to continue work on the documentary. Karl Struss, the cinematographer, seemed to flourish under the adverse conditions.

Jack Moss was an inspired choice for a killer. He enjoyed not speaking, and his only expression was a reptilian stare from behind thick, steel-rimmed glasses. The pudgy-fingered and rotund Moss was given an eastern European potato-sack suit and a deep-crowned hat pulled down practically to eye level until he was all double chins.

In the book, Banat's presence is signaled by the sickly sweet odor of attar of roses with which he douses himself. Welles and Foster had put their heads together about this and come up with the idea of using a musical *leitmotiv* for an analogous effect. They found an old 78 rpm record of a French cabaret song, and the scratchy, distorted recording, with the needle skipping irritatingly over the grooves, marks the opening of the film. (Banat is observed cocking his Luger in preparation for a night's work.) The song, emblematic of his subhuman single-mindedness, betrays his presence on board the ship; it is his murder music. The opening shot is reminiscent of Renoir's radio scene in *The Rules of the Game.*

"For the first five sequences," Welles later said, "I was on the set and decided angles; from then on, I often said where to put the camera, described the framings, made light tests. I *designed* the film but can't be called the director. It's Norman Foster's film."

Welles followed a grueling sixteen-hour-a-day schedule, directing *Ambersons* by day and acting in and consulting on *Journey* by night, with some additional precious time set aside every week for the Lady Esther radio show.* He exerted close control over Foster's direction, feeding him new pages of revised script and filming all the Colonel Haki scenes first, so he would be free to go to South America in early February.

THE CONCEPT FOR the documentary, *It's All True,* developed in fairly conventional fashion. It was to be an anthology picture, four stories with some all-encompassing theme to link them. One story agreed upon from the outset was "My Friend Bonito" (also known as "The Story of Bonito the Bull"), which was to be based on a short story by Robert Flaherty, the creator of *Nanook of the North* and *Man of Aran.* "Bonito" was the sentimental tale of a little boy who befriends a fighting bull and comes near to heartbreak when the bull is chosen for the *corrida.* But the boy finally rejoices when, improbably, the bull's life is spared because of his bravery in the ring. Flaherty's story is based on a Spanish folktale; an RKO treatment by Norman Foster and John Fante transferred the action to Mexico. Orson had the idea of working Dolores Del Rio into the script so that she could visit her home in Mexico, and so they would be able to combine business with pleasure as he directed her. An announcement by the studio that she would be the star of the film appeared in *The New York Times* and other journals. As it developed, the relationship between Welles and Del Rio deteriorated.

Beyond "Bonito," the original plan for *It's All True* now appears sketchy. RKO legal documents of the time speak of a story of an Italian fisherman in San Francisco, a story not yet decided upon, and a history of jazz.

It was the history of jazz segment that Welles was most enthusiastic about, and the opportunity to develop this part was the carrot on the baton that led him into the whole project. It would allow him to work with some of his musical heroes, including Louis Armstrong and Duke Ellington. He informally auditioned Billie Holiday to perform in the film, and invited her to

---

*The show was a mélange of variety, drama, eerie tales by writers such as Saki, comedy, and jazz music, in an almanac format that often would celebrate famous dates or historical birthdays (such as George Washington's birthday; Mexican Independence Day) with an attempt, not always successful, to weave all the elements together into a unifying theme. Mercury regulars such as Ray Collins, Paul Stewart, and Brenda Forbes and Welles himself were often joined by such guests as Ruth Gordon, Betty Field, and Dolores Del Rio. Bernard Herrmann conducted.

RKO so that she could watch him film. But the two never came to an agreement to work together on the project. Bullfighting, jazz, and something to do with fishing or sailing, then, formed the nucleus of the new film. These disparate elements seem to have no unifying theme.

Welles was obviously pushing for an extravagant jazz section for his own interests and perhaps also for authenticity's sake. Duke Ellington was hired for $1,000 a week, promised more money for band members' salaries, offered a role in the film, ownership of the music, and other rights. Ellington remembered that he wrote a horn solo, promptly lost it, and never heard much more about the jazz history, except for receiving checks totaling $12,500. Other jazz figures (Louis Armstrong and Hazel Scott, it is said) benefited from the RKO payroll, which came to $24,750 in all. But the jazz section was ultimately dropped.

With *It's All True* still in its formative stages, the studio went ahead with the Bonito segment, sending Norman Foster to Mexico along with Welles to supervise him. The idea was that, as Foster became attuned to what was wanted, Welles could then return to Hollywood to complete *Ambersons* and *Journey*.

Then known as "Welles Number Four," the project began auspiciously. Through contacts aided by RKO cutter and native-Mexican Joe Noriega, the film crew was able to enlist the aid of matador Chucho Solorzano, who suggested likely ranches for filming the testing of the bulls and the fight scenes themselves. The "Bonito" filming was something of an idyll; the child star Jesús Vasquez, nicknamed "Hamlet" by Welles, turned out to be a marvel; young fighting bulls were found in abundance; and filming proceeded at a number of the best ranches available: Tlazcala, Hacienda La Punta, Atenco. Welles returned to the States and then would fly down occasionally to supervise, but Foster proved equal to the task. By the end of that month, Welles, in California, had viewed some of the Foster film. He cabled to his new star director, "I love you." After seeing more of the rushes on October 18, Welles was ecstatic, telling Foster that "the film is absolutely marvelous . . . you are now official film codirector."

In the meanwhile, however, the overall plan for *It's All True* had taken a surprising turn. Nelson Rockefeller, a large RKO stockholder and Coordinator of Inter-American Affairs and admirer of Orson Welles, became involved in the rethinking of the movie. Talks between the CIAA Office and RKO were taking place, and by December 20 something was worked out. John Hay (Jock) Whitney, head of the CIAA motion picture division, sent Welles a telegram making *It's All True* an extension of President Roosevelt's Good Neighbor policy. Rockefeller and Whitney closed a deal with RKO for the Latinizing of *It's All True*; the U.S. government would supply up to $300,000 against a possible RKO loss at the box office. George Schaefer, hedging his bets for his financially troubled studio, jumped at what seemed a guaranteed break-even scheme. Actually, this would guarantee the end of Schaefer's career at RKO.

The conversion of *It's All True* to an epic of South America is slightly bizarre. Certainly the Mexican "Bonito" segment would fit in nicely with the south-of-the-border flavor of the picture, but the other story ideas would have to be radically recast or abandoned altogether. As the tale goes, a compromise was reached: it would include the story of four heroic Brazilian fishermen. What is strange is that parallel stories were sought in the first place. Since the original *It's All True* segments were strung together on only the slimmest of pretexts, Welles, RKO, and the CIAA were perpetuating the very same continuity problems that severely weakened the movie from its inception.

The only explanation for this unusual course of conduct—besides the fact that it involved bureaucracies from the government and the studio—is that someone was convinced that a well-developed script was on hand.

There was no script. The problems of finding ways of developing a unified film would eventually wreck the project and plague Welles for years to come, some think for the rest of his life. Before anyone from the RKO project had set foot in Brazil, the several minds who hatched the plan had their wires hopelessly entangled.

BY THE END of January 1942, with South America looming, all the principal shooting on *Ambersons* had been completed, and much of the work on *Journey Into Fear,* certainly Welles's scenes as Haki, were also finished. The editing of *Ambersons* hadn't begun, of course, but Welles assured everyone at the studio that it could be completed with speed and accuracy by sending reels to him in Brazil and by his returning comprehensive memos to his editors explaining what he wanted.

"Ladies and gentlemen," he said on his last broadcast from the United States, "next week at this same hour, same station, Lady Esther brings you the music of one of your favorites, Freddy Martin and his orchestra." He went on:

> The Mercury Theatre starts tomorrow night for South America. The reason, put more or less officially, is that I've been asked by the Office of the Coordinator of Inter-American Affairs to do a motion picture especially for Americans in all the Americas, a movie which, in its particular way, might strengthen the good relations now binding the continents of the Western Hemisphere. Put much less officially, the Mercury's going down there to get acquainted.

Welles believed he had a psychic connection with Rio de Janeiro. It was the city where the pregnant Beatrice Welles and her husband, Richard, had named their future son Orson; and it was one of his father's favorites, a place that Orson had always wanted to visit.

The strange combination of city and forest that works successfully in Rio intrigued and captivated Orson. There were palm trees and trams; snow-capped mountains visible from downtown; gardens of bougainvillea; formal luncheons with full orchestras; enormous ghettoes of extreme poverty; the Copacabana and Sugarloaf; something wild yet urban, earthy but chic.

Welles understood that he was going to Brazil as both a goodwill ambassador and a busy filmmaker, hurrying down in time to shoot the February pre-Lenten Carnival. He began immersing himself in Brazilian culture, taking some lessons in Portuguese, and, expecting a workout, getting his trainer, Mike Sasiano, to help him lose some weight.

Welles left the States on February 5, barely twelve hours after completing as much as he could of the productions of *Ambersons* and *Journey*. While being made up for his last tour as *Journey*'s Secret Police Chief Haki, Welles candidly told a reporter, "I've got no script, no actors, no preconceived ideas. I'm going down there with a camera, and I hope to record something that will be of interest to the people of all the Americas."

It was also a fabulous opportunity to expand his audience and have a good time in the process.

However, RKO had more modest aspirations. Schaefer wanted Welles to get a full-blown script in the works in the shortest possible time and create a respectable movie for about $500,000—one that, at the worst, wouldn't lose more than the CIAA-guaranteed $300,000.

The motives of Rockefeller and the CIAA are obscure. They were venturing out for the first time into a large-scale production and perhaps hoped for large-scale goodwill. It has been suggested that the CIAA was hoping to keep in the good graces of Latin America and keep Nazi spies out. It is also instructive to note that Rockefeller, with his RKO stock interests, was seeing to it that his company was being eased through a difficult time by virtue of the government monies he had at his disposal.

There was also the problem of Welles and the draft. The United States was now at war and George Schaefer had seen to it that the twenty-six-year-old Welles had received a 2-B deferment based on the fact that Welles's employment by RKO assured the seven-member Mercury team of an income. In January, an RKO request to Local Board 245 succeeded in getting Welles permission to leave the country for four months, or enough time, people thought, for him to complete *It's All True*. Articles and column items in Hearst papers continually implied that Welles was a draft dodger and that he was enjoying a privileged status through the ministrations of George Schaefer.

On January 20, 1942, Richard Wilson, Welles's right-hand man, had left for Rio with the first group of cameras and men. According to a diary of activities prepared by the Brazilian division of the CIAA, this "Group 1" arrived in Rio on January 27, followed within the week by a second contingent with no equipment. Wilson and Lynn Shores, an RKO studio man with a barbed-wire personality, who was the unit production manager for the film, immediately began some tests and preliminary shooting with W. Howard ("Duke") Greene and his Technicolor crew. Although they had both color and black-and-white cameras, they had limited film stock and were missing the most important equipment of all, the lights. The ship carrying the lights, absolutely necessary for night color shooting, was rumored to be delayed by U-boat scares. Shores began making arrangements to get the Brazilian army's antiaircraft searchlights jury-rigged for film use.

Although Shores was the most important company man on the trip, at the last minute Schaefer decided to have his vice president of foreign sales, Phil

Reisman, accompany Welles on the Pan American Clipper to Rio and the arrival on the very eve of Carnival.

Besides the missing equipment and lights, the first problem to crop up in Rio that February was the instant antipathy developed between Welles's assistant Richard Wilson and RKO's Lynn Shores. Reisman, an RKO man with a better understanding of Welles and his methods, acted as a buffer. In the early stages of the shooting, Shores kept his own counsel but vented his feelings in his periodic reports to RKO's Walter Daniels in the States. While Welles, Wilson, and the Brazilian CIAA office were voicing their enthusiasm and high hopes for the project, Shore's weekly letters got progressively more sarcastic about the work that had fallen to him and the allegedly irresponsible conduct of those around him. As early as February 24, Shores described the venture as "a horrible nightmare for me personally," adding a suggestion that Daniels should read between the lines. Shores, however, left little to the imagination referring to some of the personnel as "excess baggage" and sarcastically remarking, "I get along swell with Orson and Reisman and in their saner moments we sometimes have a business-like conversation lasting a minute or two."

More patience is shown in the CIAA diary (unpublished) covering the *Carnival* period:

> Feb. 14-17 Night and day coverage Carnival. Plane for air shots never materialized.
>
> Note: It was only possible to choose basic coverage during these days. No one had the knowledge, nor had we the equipment or personnel to do anything more than we really did. Welles chose the subjects to shoot according to the best advice, what would add up to the best story, all governed by the physical limitations of our lack of lighting equipment. The most important Carnival activities happen at night. For Technicolor night shooting we had six army searchlights manned by eighty Brazilian officers and soldiers supervised by our electricians. Mobility through the thousands of people who behave abnormally all during Carnival was a major problem, as well as the physical handling of the soldiers who had little knowledge of our needs. Because of the uncertainty of the lighting everything was covered with black and white film as a protective measure. This made the personnel problem additionally hard.

So the *Carnival* segment was shot from static positions with the makeshift lighting directed through interpreters, Welles not knowing exactly what he was getting, in that Technicolor could not be developed there. Later, the *Carnival* would have to be reconstructed piecemeal and music for a sound track discovered and recorded. The more Welles shot, the more he was convinced that the samba music culture would be the unifying element for *It's All True.*

Welles was more than somewhat insecure about shooting in color—it would be his first experiment with it—but the people from both RKO and the CIAA insisted upon his using it, claiming that most travel documentaries (although they admitted *It's All True* was to be more than that) were in color for scenic interest and, it was argued, *It's All True* would have to look the same for competitive purposes.

Orson loved the crispness of detail and the subtlety of shading that black and white offered and the pure, abstract quality of the image that it was possible to capture. He recognized, however, that the subtle tones of color in contrast to the vivid, saturated ones that could be used in playful contrast to capture the depth and energy of the carnival, suggested possibilities of stylistic expression that might go beyond black and white.

But he was particularly concerned over using color for the nightime scenes. In order to delineate all the mystery and drama inherent in the carnival, he wanted those scenes shot darkly. This being the case, he then wondered if the impact of color would be lost. What was the point of having brilliant hues and startling tones if they became highly subdued and couldn't be seen in the dark?

Further doubts plagued him. Since he would have little or no control over the processing to ensure a print of high quality, he would be at the mercy of the creative discernment of laboratory technicians thousands of miles away. He became even more concerned about the situation after someone pointed out to him that color films also have a tendency to deteriorate after just a few years, with the magenta tones intensifying and the primary colors (red, yellow, and blue) invariably fading.

Despite his misgivings, Orson continued to shoot with color, hoping that luck would increase the ratio of what he would get in fine footage to what he ruefully expected and that would be great enough to result in a strong and unifying image, a film of pictorial excellence.

After the actual *Carnival,* Welles began working out ideas for another episode, the "Four Men on a Raft" sequence.

The men of the title were poor fishermen of northern Brazil: Jacaré, their leader, and his companions, Tata, Manuel, and Jeronimo. In 1941 they had taken to sea in their *jangada,* a primitive raft of rough-hewn logs, and, sailing by the sun and the stars, traversed sixteen hundred miles of open water to Rio, where they were granted an audience with Brazil's president, Getulio Vargas. They petitioned him for improvements and social reforms in their out-of-the-way community. Their touching story and their evident bravery brought them much attention in Brazil, and Vargas acquiesced. Welles was intent on getting these national folk heroes into his picture. Taking some liberties with what had actually happened, Welles envisioned a story in which the four arrive in Rio just in time for *Carnival,* thus forging a link with the "Carnival-Samba" material.

By the end of February, Welles was talking about "Four Men" as if it were an integral part of "Carnival," implying that it would have to be shot in color, too. Lynn Shores, concerned about the cost, cabled the studio to let them know about this new development. In a telegram to Phil Reisman on March 4, Schaefer gave an emphatic "no" to this proposal.

Arguments about the burgeoning budget just added to a growing list of problems, not the least of which was the low morale among the technicians. According to Shores, the conditions were nearly mutinous. The crews had already suffered through sunburn and the inevitable diarrhea; now, waiting around for the overdue equipment, many had nothing to do. Welles's apparently haphazard shooting schedule and his many absences, during which times he was often arranging radio programs and personal appearances, did little to help the film units feel a sense of purpose. And, of course, he was still trying to edit *Ambersons.*

For Welles, at least, new life was injected into the project when, in the first week of March, he arranged to fly north to Fortaleza to check out locations and research "Four Men." To Shores's horror, Welles agreed to rent a plane for $6,000. Shores, in charge of the books, ended up having to sign the outrageous contract himself. Shores's sarcastic bickering now turned into an openly expressed disgust.

Welles liked what he saw at Fortaleza. He seems to have struck up a genuine friendship with Jacaré. Although a writing team headed by Wilson had put much work into possible scripts for "Four Men," Welles himself wrote a treatment, the rationale for making the story of Jacaré run into *Carnival.* Since what remains of *It's All True* has nothing but disconnected takes of this phase, the document is important for what it suggests about Welles's plan. It is dated March 11:

> This is the way I visualize—Beautiful shots Rio, and I start kind of travelogue, looks like going to be boring and I say a few words, rush expensive music, Copacabana crowds of bathing girls and suddenly close shot of couple girls under umbrella looking out at water.... Guys stand up and look.... Make cuts showing tiny sail out in bay, no explanation for all this. Few more cuts people noticing, kids, crowds beginning to form and look at what is apparently refugees or guys on raft caught in storm. Sail keeps coming in.
>
> Show Copacabana Palace Hotel. Crowds of people around front, don't see President, then jangadeiros come through crowd.
>
> Then I either appear on screen or speak and say, "This is what happened when we were in Rio and we didn't understand who these people were. We found out and it is the best story in South America."
>
> Dissolve into interior hotel room and there are a lot of Brazilian reporters and jangadeiros.... And I say as though I were right there, "I wish you could tell us something about these people." While busy talking in Portuguese one fellow turns to camera and tells what jangadeiros are but doesn't say why they came....
>
> Then I lead into the story and four fellows talking and being translated. As I start to talk, fade into jangada village.... Whole track is not my telling story but they telling story....
>
> I get to arrival in Rio and last shot should be from their point of view seeing bay and people coming towards them. Dissolve back to hotel room. ... I finally turn to Jacaré and he says he has been talking long enough because we

have been hearing music outside. "We want to see Carnival and excuse us."
We go to Carnival. . . .

Still, the crystallization of Welles's thoughts on "Four Men" didn't count much with RKO, which was now digesting the bad news from Shores: exorbitant plane fares, squandering of Technicolor negative, and, perhaps most damaging, the fact that little or nothing had been shot after the conclusion of *Carnival* back on the morning of February 18. What's more, Schaefer's frantic long distance phone calls to Welles went unanswered. The RKO president did receive a curious cable on March 16: "HASTEN ASSURE YOU MY ONLY DESIRE HERE IS TO MAKE THIS BEST POSSIBLE PICTURE AT LOWEST POSSIBLE COST STOP HOPE YOU BELIEVE I WISH NOTHING MORE THAN TO BE FULLY COOPERATIVE IN EVERY RESPECT AND TO MAKE YOU PROUD OF ME MUCH LOVE—ORSON WELLES."

Welles playing the repentant son to a wronged father carried more emotion than substance, but the role did manage to keep Schaefer at bay temporarily. When Welles did want to speak to someone at length, however, he found plenty to say since, by Shores's estimate, he was spending $1,000 a week for telephone calls and cables. Added to incidentals and money for radio projects, his expenses came close to $2,500 per week. Welles always maintained that the radio appearances were doubling as promotions for the movie, but RKO was not in the mood for fine distinctions.

Reviews of the footage that Welles had sent back to RKO led to some disturbing conclusions. By all reports, most of the Technicolor material was properly exposed, but the takes appeared terribly disjointed, repetitive, and unpromising. Shores wrote to Daniels: "I am sure that by the time you will have received this letter you will have seen the film that Welles shot on the carnival here—that's it. We can shoot for six months and they will still shake and sway, to what purpose I cannot imagine." Those who saw the footage agreed.

By mid-March, the equipment boat had come in after a week's delay in customs, but the film's progress was bogging down. The difficulty of finding space in a decent studio was blamed on the Brazilian manner of doing business—slow, confusing negotiations and broken promises. Moreover, the Department of Press and Propaganda did not seem to be able to do anything right. Resentments continued to grow because the only person benefiting from DPP contacts was Welles himself; there were no difficulties in setting up testimonial dinners, awards, ceremonies, and tours of the countryside. He was often driven around Rio in a white, open-topped limousine and accompanied by a motorcycle escort. Too much of Welles's research was taking place in nightclubs and boudoirs, and his increasingly frequent absences from the shooting locations, with Wilson or Shores subbing, were blamed on massive hangovers. The March rain obliterated plans for outdoor shooting. In this dismal atmosphere, Reisman, who had been strongly supportive of Welles, was recalled to the United States. Welles then had one less friend in Brazil.

WELLES WAS ALSO having problems with his personal life; he found the Brazilian women, the Cariocas, as the female inhabitants of Rio are known, extremely attractive. They seemed more spirited, and less restrictive than his fiancée, Dolores Del Rio, and some even matched her beauty. He began refusing her phone calls. They were to meet in Mexico City, but he never confirmed the plan. After not hearing from him for weeks and afraid of the impending embarrassment, she flew to her mother's house in Cuernavaca and, through her press agent and other sources, permitted the leak that she had broken off their engagement. To Orson, the great magnet for trouble, her backing out was providential.

WITH THE FOUR *jangadeiros* flown in and residing at the Copacabana Palace Hotel, Welles concentrated on reconstructing *Carnival* sequences and farmed out the "Four Men" arrival scenes to Shores, who was unable to make a go of it, since the boats and crowds required by the script never arrived—another letdown by the DPP.

Welles filmed the followers of the samba, the *sambistas,* as they marched, danced, and sprayed each other with perfume and ether from atomizers—a peculiar custom of which no one knew the origin. Welles even staged some elaborate street fights of the kind that break out between rival *sambistas.* Progress again was painfully slow. Wilson recalls that if they needed a particular costume, they would have to bring in a seamstress, point out the costume, say, "Make that," and then wait a week for the result, shooting around the scene or just biding their time.

The Urca Casino was to be the scene of the production numbers that would climax the *Carnival* sequence. These numbers were to be scored by Paul Misraki in the one departure from Welles's plan to use exclusively native talent. Once the Urca had been filmed and the fill-in sections of *Carnival* were complete, Welles was to go up to Fortaleza again, film the background to the "Four Men" story, and wrap up the picture. The original plan had everything concluded by May 15, but that now seemed impossible. Shores's report in late March to Daniels:

> My problem is for the past two weeks Welles has been concentrating entirely on his radio program . . . and has left the picture high and dry. I have no script on anything and only have a catch-as-can-catch outline as to shooting details. As you know Welles wants to shoot a few miles of film and let the cutter try and make a picture out of it.

AS WELLES CONTINUED with *It's All True,* April brought problems from an unexpected source—the censors. To capture the story of the samba, Welles had to trace its origins in the poor quarters and shanty villages (the *favelas* surrounding Rio clinging to the bare rock of the Morro do Salgueiro). Like American jazz, the samba was a fusion of New World spirit with the transplanted cultural traditions of African slaves. The masters of samba were not sunning themselves on the Copacabana beach; they were blacks and *mestizos* who lived on the decaying edges of town, and if they came to Rio at all outside of Carnival time, they hung out in places that the upper class avoided. For, like jazz, the bordello too was a finishing school for musicians. Welles wanted it all on film. He investigated the *escolas da Samba,* schools of samba, the informal meeting places of musicians and apprentices; he dabbled in the music himself, learning about the homemade instruments; he hob-nobbed with those for whom samba was a way of life.

Some said Welles's new line of research was offensive. The Brazilian Department of Press and Propaganda and the Tourism Office was appalled. This was not the Rio they wanted to promote. And detractors of Welles could now call him either a dilettante who liked slumming or a questionable person with an unhealthy interest in blacks. The former view is suggested in a *Life* photo spread that appeared in the spring of 1942: one picture, of Welles behind a rope barrier apparently trying to reconstruct a carnival scene, with *sambistas* in the middleground, is subtitled "Poor whites and blacks are too dazed to respond to Welles's direction," because one woman in plain view has downcast eyes; another photo is captioned "Welles (foreground) feels good at one of the low-class 'people's dances.'"

But such a patronizing attitude looks innocent in comparison with a letter from Lynn Shores. "Despite repeated conversations with Mr. Richard Wilson," the letter reads, "I still find myself unable to control the tendency of Mr. Welles to utilize our cameras in matters which I do not feel are in accord with the wishes of the Brazilian government and, I am sure, not in harmony with the feeling of our executives in Hollywood." It goes on to say that the unpleasantness is "the continued exploitation of the negro and the low-class element in and around Rio," which is all "in very bad taste." Shores added that he was prepared to earmark possibly offensive footage for impounding.

Lest Welles's actions in South America from here on suggest a kind of mounting paranoia, let it be said that we know now that he had every reason to be suspicious. He might very well have begun to suspect that he was shooting scenes that no one had any intention of developing. Hearing of Welles's forays into the *favelas,* William Gordon of RKO's censorship department began to collect information and backing from the Coordinator of Inter-American Affairs office to pressure Welles into stopping this important phase of the production. The CIAA's worry was that other Latin American countries such as Argentina would react even more vigorously in opposition to any film that gave an accurate and sympathetic rendering of blacks in Latin America. A report critical of Welles's project was prepared by the CIAA, citing "national susceptibilities" of Latin Americans in regard to racial matters. The people of these countries, the report maintained, were not ashamed of Indian and black blood in their ancestry, but they resented any outsider's pointing it out.

Gordon thoroughly agreed with the report's recommendation that "it is better to play safe and always avoid any reference to miscegenation and even omit picture sequences in which mulattoes or *mestizos* appear too conspicuously; they would be the central figures on the carnival motif." In fact, the two unifying elements of all but the "Bonito" section would be Jacaré with the other Indian fishermen and the black Brazilian musician-singer-actor, a dwarf, Grande Otelo (or "Othello"). Quite simply, neither RKO in Hollywood nor the CIAA wanted the film that was taking shape in Welles's mind.

Welles did not try to reason with anyone or seek a compromise. He simply ignored the objections (at least when he heard of them) and proceeded with his plans. Even as the crisis approached, he was off on other goodwill junkets, including lectures beginning in late April on "The Development of Art and Literature in America." He was finding new ways of thumbing his nose at those who would destroy his picture to save their jobs, and he would give the CIAA what they said they wanted—Pan-American cultural exchange at the highest levels.

Nor did Welles care much about quibbling over expenses. In April he announced that the Urca Casino numbers demanded remodeling of the Urca according to his specifications, to the dismaying tune of $25,000. Schaefer was furious. Repeated attempts by him to reach Welles proved futile. When the two finally exchanged cables, Welles was not in a mood to change his mind. If the remodeling cost less than $25,000, fine. But remodeled it would be.

Schaefer had had enough. After *Kane* and *Ambersons,* and now the *It's All True* mess, Schaefer said he felt "punch-drunk." He would stand for no more of what he considered abuse. His job as RKO's president was slipping away from him because of the multimillion-dollar losses perpetrated by Welles, and he decided to emasculate Orson's project. He dispatched Reisman as an emissary, arming him with a letter that made it clear: Reisman will stop everything if he sees fit.

Even before he had heard Reisman's report, Schaefer decided to stop production, although he left one escape clause.

> Under certain conditions I would be willing to let Welles continue, namely that he deliver to you immediately complete story outline covering material to date and his plans from this point on including shooting FOUR MEN RAFT delivering at same time schedule of shooting days and permitting him finish within maximum cost of $30,000.... Unless you satisfied he means business... you authorized call project off immediately.

Reisman let Welles continue.

Ironically, and tragically, more was at stake than money. On May 19, the day after Schaefer made his last offer, Jacaré, the star of "Four Men," was drowned while the crew was trying to film the *jangadeiros'* arrival in Rio. The tragedy occurred through a misunderstanding. A motor launch was to tow the *jangada* to Golfo Beach for the filming. When they arrived and discovered that the beach was fogged in and the crew on shore was signaling to them, Jacaré told the operator of the launch to go on to adjoining Linda Beach. In the approach to Linda—which was, in fact, the wrong place—the launch was caught by an enormous breaker. The launch shipped water but held on until a second wave snapped the tow cable and threw the four raftsmen overboard. By the time Tata and Manuel had located the foundering Jeronimo, Jacaré had been lost.

Responsibility for Jacaré's death came to rest with the outsiders. *Diario Da Noite* moralized: "Jacaré died at the edge of a beach, in an adventure without any largeness. . . . They should have stayed on their own sand dunes, in their small houses of Carnuba straw, without ever having seen the seductions of Babylon, without ever meeting the American movie men. They should have stayed there far away, without ever meeting Orson Welles."

With Brazilian sentiment souring on him, Welles had few people to turn to. Rumor had it that Welles and his close associates holed up in their apartments for a week, fearing for their lives, but Wilson denies this. Another story had someone actually trying to assassinate Orson, shooting at him through his hotel window. Reisman told Schaefer that Welles, the champion of procrastination, was now working through the night to complete the Rio phase of the picture, since the crews were due to leave on June 8. "He realizes that his future is at stake."

But as May blurred into June, Welles's actions became quirky and capricious as he called calling off shootings at the Urca at the last minute and assembled camera crews to await sunrise. He did this perhaps, Shores bitchily suggested, because he wanted company when he had insomnia.

On a hot day in mid-June, passersby on the Avenida Atlantica were greeted by a number of objects raining down from a sixth-floor balcony: plates, vases, bottles, and (according to some accounts) more formidable items such as chairs. Inexplicably, Welles was throwing a tantrum, or engaging in a prank incited by some mid-afternoon imbibing of spirits ("Chopp," the splendidly delicious beer, as it is called in Portuguese) with his friends José Sanz, Eriveldo Martins, and the then ambassador of Mexico, Alfonso Reyes. One story had it that Orson was explaining the scene in *Citizen Kane* in which he demolishes Susan Alexander Kane's bedroom, and then began to demonstrate how he did it. It is hard to gauge the impact of this incident on the Brazilians; newspaper accounts and the inevitable cartoons did not see it as another menace on the same level as the Jacaré tragedy. Rather, they dismissed it with some sardonic humor as an even-tempered host might express disapproval of a childish and unpredictable guest who had overstayed his welcome. Perhaps more serious was the effect the indulgence had on the Rio office of the CIAA. The supposedly true version attributed to Welles by RKO's Ray Josephs in Buenos Aires didn't help Welles's case:

The members of the staff of a Latin American embassy, which shall remain nameless [it was Mexico's], were frequent guests, and at 3 P.M. of an afternoon before his departure he and a diplomat from the embassy in question were looking at some crockery which Welles's landlady insisted should be paid for as damaged. Orson and the diplomat went out on the balcony to [look at] the porcelain and, according to Orson, discovered stamped on the back the words "Made in Japan," whereupon the piece in question was hurled over the railing on to the beach-front sidewalk below. Several other pieces of furniture and assorted dishware followed, while an increasing crowd of cariocas gathered around to cheer. That's all there was to it, Orson insists. . . .

Not a jolly episode, no matter how it's told. Nor was it a jolly time back in the States. Schaefer had just submitted his resignation. With N. Peter Rathvon and Charles Koerner in charge now, the filming of *It's All True* would continue for a while, but the possibility of its ever reaching the screen shrank almost to the vanishing point.

Charles Koerner (his motto of "showmanship instead of genius" well exemplified by the double bill of *Ambersons* as second feature to *Mexican Spitfire Sees a Ghost* when it was eventually released*) wanted to focus on guaranteed moneymaking projects and get Welles out of his hair and his studio, as soon as possible. Welles was permitted to go to Fortaleza with a small crew including Richard Wilson, cameraman George Fanto, and secretary Shifra Haran to finish the "Four Men" with scenes of Jacaré's homeland. Somewhat surprisingly, they were treated with great kindness and received excellent cooperation from the Indian families (RKO was going to make a settlement with Jacaré's widow above the workmen's compensation insurance). A stand-in was selected for the Jacaré role, and a new subplot was worked out around a grieving fisherman's widow, to echo the true state of events. Welles's June 22 script concludes with a dedicatory statement about Jacaré.

Welles was fortunate to have Fanto, for the Hungarian cameraman's expertise made up for the shortcomings of the limited equipment: when Welles discovered that they had not shipped his favorite deep-focus lens which, Wilson said, he did most of his work, Fanto adapted a 25mm with Eyemo lens to the big Mitchell camera and went on, hardly missing a beat.

While the June-July shooting in Fortaleza proceeded, general manager Koerner began to take steps against Welles. First of all, there was the matter of the $300 in damages for the balcony incident as well as the back rent that may have been the root cause of the affair. Instead of settling the business quietly with the $1,000 or so that was needed, a negligible amount in view of everything else that had gone on, Koerner was intent on pillorying Welles. He instructed Shores to keep a file of any derogatory information about Welles so that lawsuits might be deflected from RKO and placed at Welles's doorstep instead. A nightclub pageant with the working title of "Pan-American Night" was planned and choreographed by Welles in which singers, dancers, and entertainers from all over South America would participate in a flag-bedecked musical ensemble. When Koerner received the budget, before the actual shooting, of close to $150,000 for one sequence, he nearly fainted. Enough was too much, he said.

---

*The motto seemed to imply: "We will give you good pictures *without* Orson Welles."

Koerner immediately had RKO lawyers look over all contracts and agreements made with Welles. It was decided that RKO should terminate the basic contract even at the risk of what was estimated to be a possible Welles suit of $125,000, because the risk was "not so dangerous as another Welles production."

Then, ostensibly because of differences over the cutting and editing of *Journey Into Fear,* Koerner had Mercury Productions thrown off the RKO lot and all pay terminated on July 1. Jack Moss and Herb Drake issued a joint statement saying, "We are Leonardo da Vinci, evicted from a draughty garret." As their last act at RKO, they stole the brass fixture essential to the functioning of the studio's steambath. Welles, who had for a week been sending Reisman cablegrams about what he called Shores's deliberate sabotage on Koerner's behalf, managed to compose himself enough to quip to his Mercury friends in the States, "Don't worry, boys, we're just rounding a bad Koerner on our way to immortality."

When Welles returned to Rio from Fortaleza in the third week of July, he found that Koerner, through Shores, had put a notice—an *aviso*—in all the Rio newspapers that RKO Radio Pictures would assume no responsibility for any acts committed or debts incurred by Orson Welles while in Brazil. A week later, Welles left Brazil, arriving in Buenos Aires on the first leg of a circuitous route back home.

By the time the United States had Orson Welles again, RKO had much film and an estimated $1,200,000 in expenses for the *It's All True* venture. Koerner didn't want to part with another penny if he could help it. Looking for someone else to assist with the burden, while keeping the CIAA in the mood to help, he investigated the possibility of getting a distributor for the film. With the backing of Floyd Odlum and the Atlas Corporation, a supremely profit-oriented holding company that had controlling interest in RKO, Koerner spent the remainder of the year terminating unprofitable projects and looking for anyone on whom he could unload the *It's All True* material. Perhaps to confuse his life even more, Orson decided at that time to personally "adopt" a baby. Under the Foster Parents Plan for War Children, he began to financially support six-year-old Veronica Kate Fitzgibbon, whose father had lost his life as an air raid warden in London.

If a distributor could be found for *It's All True* and if it managed to recoup its investment, RKO would then be willing to pay Welles one half the compensation originally planned on; in other words, Welles still stood to make $62,500 if everything clicked to his advantage. But Koerner's worst suspicions were confirmed when he found no likely takers.

Since much of the film had evolved into an epic of Brazilian music, securing the rights to that music was a lingering problem. Welles had made vague but extravagant promises to songwriters and music publishers. Now the day of reckoning was approaching, and RKO, even with the best deals possible, stood to lose more money.

By October 19, Rathvon in New York had come to new agreements with Welles. He allowed Welles to rework *Journey Into Fear* for a miserly sum not to exceed $1,000. But he confided to Koerner that this unpleasant reunion was really a strategy to soften Welles up for a final settlement in the *It's All True* dealings. Welles and the new RKO president discussed ways of converting the film into something "less pretentious than planned"—that is, "Bonito" and "Carnival" worked up as a documentary second feature to a Disney film about Latin America.* This Pan-American plan would keep the CIAA funds in the offing—or so Rathvon thought. At this stage, Rathvon found Welles "completely docile—for the moment." But Rathvon's letter to Koerner reaffirmed that everything now being done had but one end in mind: "to get rid of this property and Orson Welles if there is any way to do it."

Koerner was angered that the RKO New York office had been sweet-talked once more by Welles. What had happened, he wondered, to the offers hinted at by Twentieth Century-Fox, by Spyros Skouras? What were Rockefeller and the CIAA going to do to help them? (No one forgot that despite everything, Welles was still on good terms with Rockefeller.) Rathvon didn't know. Everything seemed to be eroding. All he knew was that Welles would "go to great extremes to get the picture finished."

On November 30, with several producers and potential backers in attendance, Koerner held a screening of selections from twenty-three reels of *It's All True*: "Bonito" and some "Carnival," supplemented with such Brazilian hit songs as "Amelia," sung by Chucho Martinez. There were no takers. Welles sat uncomfortably tight. It was clear beyond a doubt that no one but he could put the film together. It was now 1943 and Welles and RKO were deadlocked.

On February 5 Welles's draft board classified him 1A, just one more complication. A March screening of about fifteen minutes worth of the footage was viewed by Francis Alstock, Whitney's replacement at the CIAA. RKO suspected that Alstock could get Welles a four-month deferment to complete the movie. Alstock thought Fox might get interested again.

In May of 1943 Welles approached Rathvon once more with a new offer, asking for $75,000 for "Bonito" and $25,000 for a bargain-basement "Carnival" using tank shots of a *jangada* raft model and some stock footage for the smoothing over of missing sequences. In the first week of the same month Koerner told Rathvon that a screening at Warners had interested Charles Feldman of the Blum-Feldman agency, who thought he could get Charles Boyer and Irene Dunne into the project. However, Koerner thought the whole scheme was too nebulous and feared that a Boyer love story would monopolize the film and force Brazil into the background, jeopardizing the CIAA guarantee. Koerner shouldn't have worried, for the worst news hadn't arrived yet.

On May 24, the board of directors of the Motion Picture Society for the Americas met. Sam Goldwyn asked Nelson Rockefeller about the status of *It's All True*. Rockefeller clarified the terms, explaining that the $300,000 underwriting was no longer operative: the agreement had stipulated that a

---

*Disney had just finished one called *Saludos Amigos*.

Class A picture had to be produced and released, and that he wouldn't waste the taxpayers' money on anything less. And David O. Selznick and William Goetz of Fox agreed that what they had seen simply did not add up to a feature film. Two months later Rockefeller made the withdrawal official before the House Appropriations Committee.

As far as RKO activity went, the project now came to a virtual halt. But Welles pressed on, obsessed. Alstock pointed out that "little" Jesús Vasquez now weighed 175 pounds as a burly fourteen-year-old, and refused to accept a stand-in. Koerner thought the CIAA was just looking for excuses. A full year had passed since the Fortaleza shooting: the "Bonito" sequence was not only ancient history. It was dead.

Welles didn't give up. Back in June of 1942 he had prepared a detailed treatment for the original "Carnival," which was more than anything else a series of excuses for not having a finished script. Now in a treatment/script dated September 1943, he attempted to give a final, complete version as a rationale for salvaging his film. In his script, Welles himself is often the center of interest as both narrator and actor. Arriving in Mexico, Welles as naive visitor listens to the tale of Bonito and Jesus, polishing up his Spanish only to find himself journeying on to Brazil and a new set of linguistic and cultural traditions. The unifying elements of *Carnival* become the brash, exuberant Grande Otelo and another Brazilian find, the four-year-old Pery Martins. Pery closes the sequence as he falls asleep in *Praca Onze,* or Plaza Eleven, the subject of the theme song "*Adeus Praca Onze*" ("Farewell, Plaza Eleven"). The full sweep of *Carnival* has taken the audience from the poor quarters and the schools of samba in the hills outside of Rio to the streets of the city, where the competing groups of samba dancers flaunt their variegated costumes and occasionally break into stylized fights in the *capoeira,* or judolike, manner. Pery is caught in a welter of tangled limbs during one of these fights, then wanders off to see the masquerade balls *(bailes)* and the big dances at the tennis clubs.

Welles, his cameraman Duke Greene, and his secretary Shifra are also woven into the tale, and the *jangadeiros* are caught sight of as they pass in a gigantic float. It is never clear, however, when we are reading the new Welles version whether the actions described are actually on the film Welles thought he had shot. Some of the script is unconvincing and stilted (Hotel clerk: "Ah, Mr. Welles, you found interesting our mountain villages?") and some is silly ("Marguerita demonstrates the proper manufacture and consumption of a taco"). Details are carelessly rendered (a shortwave radio broadcasts a World Series "doubleheader"). The 1943 script did not move anyone to pick up the property.

One year later Welles signed a promissory note for $197,000 and took possession of the film himself: all in all, 375,000 feet of Technicolor, 90,000 feet of black and white. Welles paid $17.50 per month storage fee for the vault in Salt Lake City where the cases of film were safeguarded. As late as January 1945, he approached Francis Alstock and tried one last time to convince the CIAA that a film—some film, anything they wanted, really—could be made.

Alstock declined. Improbably, July 1945 found Welles still working on scripts for *It's All True.*

A defeated Welles finally defaulted on the promissory note. In May of 1946 RKO sued him and repossessed the film. Some footage found its way into *The Falcon in Mexico* and *The Gilded Pheasant,* but no one at RKO really remembers if any of the stock made it into any other film. Examination of those films does show footage that might be described as "Wellesian." When the hoard of film passed on to Desilu Productions and then to Paramount, some of it was destroyed and some dumped, they say, into the Pacific. Richard Wilson believes that, ironically, some was dumped in the ocean at Santa Monica right near Wilson's house on the coast.*

THE PERSPECTIVE AFFORDED by four decades allows us to make a few definite judgments on the *It's All true* affair. Welles should not have gone to Rio without a script, and yes, he did abuse the freedom granted him by the vague, perhaps overly generous terms of his RKO contract. On the other hand, he was often stymied by matters beyond his control: he fought a losing battle with rigid and narrow-minded people who caved in all too easily to all the pressures. And probably RKO could not have stayed alive financially while trying to get a finished picture out of Welles.

But if we believe that there was a true picture, one whose conception never fully emerged from Welles's mind and is not really reflected in the later scripts and treatments made for mopping up a lost cause, then we may believe, if we see the curious but marvelous footage that remains, that we have unfortunately lost a masterpiece of cinema and perhaps one of the greatest feature documentaries never made.

ALTHOUGH THE SAGA of *It's All True* stretched out for years, Welles was not idle during its troubled times. *The Magnificent Ambersons* was released in mid-August 1942, then a bad time to introduce a new film since the moviegoing public is prone to be sunning away on vacation rather then spending hours locked inside darkened, non-airconditioned theaters. In the six months between the release of *King's Row,* another slice of morbid Americana, and *Ambersons,* war-oriented and patriotic films such as *Mrs. Miniver* and *Yankee Doodle Dandy* appeared to make the subject matter especially dated. Although the critical reception by the media was mixed, most members of the audience left with more enjoyment directed toward the other half of the double bill, *Mexican Spitfire Sees a Ghost* in which Leon Errol rescues Lupe Velez in a series of precarious, slapstick situations. Even the accompanying

---

*In 1985, Fred Chandler, director of technical services at Paramount, discovered 140,000 feet of lost footage of *It's All True* while looking for vault space for the studio's new negatives. A 22-minute short film entitled, *"It's All True: Four Men On a Raft"* was constructed out of the stock by Richard Wilson and was shown at the 1986 Venice Film Festival. The remaining stock is now stored at the UCLA Film and Television Archive. Welles refused to see the newly found footage, saying that the film was "cursed" and that it marked the downfall of his career in Hollywood.

March of Time short segments about life in Washington, D.C., during the war seemed to many audiences to have more life than *The Magnificent Ambersons.*

The film was, to many viewers, exhausting, not sufficiently explained, fragmentary, and virtually humorless. One is never certain about the characters' relationships. Who is Fanny, the aunt of George; is she the sister of Wilbur or of Isabel? Who, for that matter, is Uncle Jack? Welles, of course, blamed the film's faults on the impaired editorial erasures and excisions, but even if he had had his way entirely, it is difficult to see how audiences might have been more captivated.*

Even with its obvious flaws, James Agee, writing in *Time,* called *Ambersons* a "great motion picture," dubbing Welles as Hollywood's most important "cinemaestro" and going on to say: "Artistically, it is a textbook of advanced cinema technique." The reviewer in the *Los Angeles Times* called it "a splendid technical achievement" and pointed out that it was, despite any criticism to the adverse, a vital American document: "The philosophic comments it contains on the effect of the automobile on this country alone would almost entitle it to the description, epical."

Despite its difficulties, *The Magnificent Ambersons* received four Academy Award nominations for 1942, including Best Picture, Best Cinematography, Best Interior Decoration, and Best Supporting Actress to Agnes Moorehead. (*Mrs. Miniver* walked away with the prize for Best Picture that year, in addition to receiving five other Oscars.)

WELLES HAD RETURNED to the United States on August 22, 1942, had worried the footage of *It's All True* through U.S. customs, and in a matter of days was pleading the film's case with RKO officials—without success. With the studio's refusal to release *It's All True,* the Orson Welles financial ledgers began to creep up to $4 million on the expense side and virtually nothing to show for profit. Hedda Hopper, perhaps thinking of Orson, wrote at that time that Hollywood only worshiped success, "the bitch goddess whose smile hides a taste of blood." In spite of the artistic accolades calling *Citizen Kane* one of the most significant motion pictures ever made and acknowledging even *The Magnificent Ambersons* as important, the fact was that Orson Welles had not touched the public taste. He had not loosened the pocketbooks of the mass moviegoing audience, and this made him in the eyes of those controlling RKO, and other motion picture producers, an unfruitful risk for the future, a director of stillborn projects destined—if he was allowed to make more films—to be responsible for continually diminishing studio bank accounts.

Film audiences had never been so large. In 1942, some ninety million people went to the movies once each week, and the total gross box office

---

*The recutting seems to have been fairly successfully hushed up. One review mentioned rumors about problems in the editing, but most critics blamed Welles rather than RKO for the gaps in continuity.

income for the previous year was over one billion dollars. Naturally, RKO wanted entry into the gold mine. Orson, it appeared, was hardly their conduit. He wasn't quite abandoned by Hollywood, however. His memorable acting portrait of Charles Foster Kane guaranteed him as much work as he wished in *front* of the camera. Eventually, he would avail himself of this continued opportunity in motion pictures, but for the present he immediately returned to the arena of radio, the medium for which at that time he had hardly a creative equal, his personal haven of security and a guaranteed source of massive, periodic paychecks.

Within weeks of returning to the United States, Welles became involved in the inception of two new weekly radio network series to be broadcast on subsequent nights; for both he was to serve as producer, writer, director, occasional star, and perennial narrator. Each was devoted, in its own way, to helping the war effort. The first was a series sponsored by the Lockheed-Vega aircraft Corporation, which would glorify the entire aviation industry and give an in-depth and dramatized view of the bombers and fighters that were being used by the Allies; the other was a program called "Hello, Americans," a series of dramatizations that it was hoped would counteract German and Italian propaganda and win the adherence of other American republics in the Western Hemisphere. It was to be broadcast under the sponsorship of the Coordinator of Inter-American affairs. Yes, the CIAA still loved Orson Welles and felt, Brazilian fiasco aside, that if not their spokesman in film, he would be eminently successful as their on-the-air ambassador.

For the aircraft show, Lockheed-Vega set up a research bureau in Washington to generate story ideas and to dig true sky adventures out of the files of various government agencies. One of the principal writers attached to Welles was a young man, the future Pulitzer playwright Arthur Miller. The two men had much in common; they were the same age—twenty-seven—and like Welles, Miller was also a refugee from the Federal Theatre Project. Each man knew the other by reputation, and this established an easy working rapport.

Welles wanted the title of the Lockheed-Vega show to be "Ceiling Unlimited"—he thought it both romantic and evocative—but the sponsors disagreed. For weeks, in publicity releases and other references, the program was called simply "the new Orson Welles Show," and it wasn't until two days before the broadcast, when it appeared that Orson would not relent, that "Ceiling Unlimited" became official.

Welles asked Miller—who was flattered and surprised at the responsibility—to create a format for the show, beyond the obvious dedication to aviation. After musing it about for a while, Miller wrote to Orson concerning that format:

> I've been thinking about it today, however, and I feel sure about one thing. You don't want any. Your voice is a format. The only two things that must be heard at the beginning of the show every week are your voice and Lockheed-Vega. Those are the two things that must be the same every week but around those two

things the variety should be infinite. They alone and by themselves do everything any format can possibly attempt to do. Your voice, if I may say so, portends much.

To acquaint himself with the various airplanes that would be featured on the program, especially the B-17, the Flying Fortress, Welles visited and toured Lockheed-Vega's California plants. Sporting an employee's identification badge and wearing a silver-colored hard hat, he poked his nose into machinery, ate box lunches with executives, and talked to the workers on the assembly lines. He became enmeshed in the love of flight. To heighten his poetic sensibilities toward the subject of flying, he read stories by Antoine de Saint-Exupéry: *Wind, Sand and Stars, The Little Prince,* and *Flight to Arras.* He also surrounded himself with friends; Ray Collins, Joseph Cotten, Paul Stewart, and other Mercury actors would be given principal parts.

As a variant to the usual wartime broadcasts and stories about heroes, each show concentrated on individual airships, making them come as alive as the men who flew them. Welles would introduce his "stars" with, "This is the story of..." "Snoozy," or "Cactus Sal," or "Rose O'Day" or "Alexander the Swoose"* and then go on to narrate dramatizations of their stories of raids and adventures, which included fighting fog and fire from Messerschmitts and Zeroes over Rouen, Guam, Berlin, Amiens, Rotterdam.

Stories were told week after week about the Flying Fortresses: how, through high-altitude precision bombing, they demolished aircraft factories and railroad yards; how they carried MacArthur out of the Philippines; how they aided Colin Kelly's sinking of the *Aruno*; how they fared in the air battles of New Guinea and Midway and the Solomons. Heroes from the past and present would be portrayed on the show to talk about flying: Leonardo da Vinci once reminisced about his fifteenth-century plans and dreams about a machine that could fly. Wilbur and Orville Wright talked one night. Eddie Rickenbacker, Wiley Post, and Charles Lindbergh turned up to talk about the sky.

The Arthur Miller prose—dynamic, almost mythological in tone and cadence, tempered by the patriotic fervor that was part of the day—and the masterful drama of the Orson Welles voice created a naturally and nationally spirited poetry; if there was ever a question of Orson's contributions to the war effort, it was dispelled after that series: "We leave the ground! This huge monster of metal, heavier than a building, rising with the ease and liberty of birds. The plane quivers, breaks with the earth. These thousands of thundering horses gallop through the marvelous air and *we're free*! We defy the sun and earth's friction! The motors beat like a giant single heart. Man has learned to control the sky! Man is at the helm of his century. Man can make assassins out of angels so he may live in freedom. He is well-armed. He is lightning riding the air. He is the stroke of thunder!"

Orson Welles's "Hello, Americans" series was as well-received as his

*A cross between a swan and a goose as that particular B-17 was affectionately known.

"Ceiling Unlimited" effort although the shows were more formally structured in the familiar radio drama format. "The Andes" told of Simón Bolívar and the South American struggle for freedom; "The Islands" dramatized Toussaint L'Ouverture's battle against tyranny; "Mexico" traced the story of Montezuma and the Juarez resistance to invasion.

The success of two national shows a week was a psychic exhilarant for Orson. After the difficulties of *It's All True* and the discredit of *Ambersons,* compounded by the humiliation of being turned away by RKO, he began to regain his confidence with the positive radio reviews that appeared across the nation. The deluge of fan mail that reached him each week also added buoyancy.

Also in demand for speaking and lecture engagements, he now seemed to drift into professional celebrityhood, accepting all offers to appear anywhere at any time to speak about anything. Aside from his masterful voice, he established a reputation as being a provocative speaker. His material was filled with vivid feeling, logical thinking, and an awareness of the true meaning of what he was trying to communicate. He expressed *himself* and audiences clamored for more and more Orson.

Gravitating between both coasts, sometimes commuting back and forth in a single week, very unusual in those days, he made what seemed like countless guest appearances on radio shows—everything from "The Fred Allen Show" to the "Radio Reader's Digest," and from "The Kate Smith Show" to "Take It or Leave It" and was engaged constantly as a lecturer, toastmaster, and master of ceremonies. Sometimes his invitation to speak seemed inappropriate, as when he appeared at the Hotel Ambassador as featured speaker at the annual conference of the California Association for Adult Education and delivered a speech on "New Techniques in Mass Education." Admitting his knowledge of the subject to be "problematical," he tried and succeeded in delivering an amusing, offbeat speech.

When the estimable Mr. McGuffey's first Reader applied what was, for his day and time, a generous chocolate coating to the bitter pill of knowledge, the statement in the First Reader, "The boy has a ball," was supplemented by a picture of an obvious boy who had an obvious ball and the illustration took up a large portion of the book. Then as literate America became conditioned to printed knowledge such succeeding generations left out more and more of the illustrations until finally, school books were published *sans* illustrations except in matters that had to do with the hypotenuse of the triangle and other similar geometrical and mechanical phenomena. The point I am trying to make is that the mind of a student can be conditioned to accept and understand information in a highly concentrated form without request of various beguiling blandishments. The early efforts in education via radio all pretend to be the start of little Billy and his sister Mary and their trips to the beautiful islands of the West Indies, etc. They were invariably accompanied by a kind old uncle who when little Mary said, "Look at the beautiful palm trees growing here on the island of Cuba," instantly replied, "Yes, Mary, Cuba exports 18,942 tons of coconuts."

Welles admitted to playing the role of such "erudite uncles" in his early days of radio and showed his allegiance to eradicating such feeble forms of education through the media in the future.

Being educated by early motion pictures, claimed Welles, was not unlike looking into an old-fashioned, sugarcoated Easter egg "wherein a static and highly improbable Fujiyama undulated beneath a sky of bilious blue." He evoked the documentary film tradition established by Robert Flaherty and claimed it was possible to discover more about Eskimos in a few minutes by looking at *Nanook of the North,* than one could learn from a lifetime of reading. Asking filmmakers to live up to their responsibility to civilization, he ended with a predictive view—a decade before it actually happened—of one educational possibility of the use of film: medical students all over the world will be able to see the finest surgeon of the day perform the most intricate and delicate operation. They will see it clearer and better than they would have if they were standing by the operating table, for they will not only be able to see it in full color but they will see it magnified by many diameters. They will hear the voice of the master surgeon himself, explaining each step of the procedure. Then they will see a review of the operation with a further lecture by the surgeon. And with the magic of motion pictures, they will be able to see it in slow motion.

The educators were awed. At the conclusion he was given a standing ovation.

Traveling to the other side of the continent, a Friday night in New York, in mid-October, Welles presided at Carnegie Hall over a meeting of the Artists' Front to Win the War. The Collegiate Chorale performed patriotic songs. Charlie Chaplin spoke for twenty minutes. Sam Jaffe, Lillian Hellman, Joris Ivens, I. F. Stone, and Rockwell Kent also made statements. The event was fairly reported and enthusiastically editorialized in most of the media, although Welles was privately criticized as being self-serving in relationship to his draft status. Among other things, he said:

> As I understand it, democracy doesn't end with the vote. It begins with it. If we don't like the leaders we're electing or the men our leaders have appointed, we can say so. It's our civilian duty to say so. As it happens we approve of our leadership. We endorse it. We thank God for our leadership. This isn't a protest meeting. The protests are about this meeting. The President says we're going to have a second front, numerous second fronts, he said. We don't have to have military tacticians to say we have the right to say we're glad to hear it. All of us don't have to go around the world to say we agree with Wendell Wilkie. And as to wearing uniforms? Our government decides how we dress these days.

Aside from his growing political interests and his veneration of Roosevelt, as exemplified at his speeches in civic-minded and public-spirited meetings and rallies, Orson occasionally could be persuaded to talk seriously about filmmaking. Four days after the Carnegie Hall convocation, he went to New

York University and talked for hours with the students who were studying how to make motion pictures.

The chairman of the NYU Department of Motion Pictures, Robert Gessner, a poet and novelist and the first university professor in the United States to teach cinema as a liberal art, was a loyal adherent of the merits of *Citizen Kane,* referring to it as "a *masterpiece,* studded with the jewels of major images that embody major ideas." Because of Gessner's enthusiasm for the film, Welles agreed to make his first appearance before a group of film students. He loved it. After Gessner introduced him as "the most original, creative force in motion pictures since D. W. Griffith," Orson, feeling relaxed and respected, spoke extemporaneously and made some of the most revelatory, uninhibited, and introspective remarks about his relationship to film-making and Hollywood that he had ever offered to that time.

Thankful that he had an audience of serious film lovers, he charmed everyone by stating that people's interest in motion pictures is usually restricted to wanting to know whether Veronica Lake's hair is all her own.* "The confusion in the movies is regretful because certainly it is the great art form of our century," he established. "It is just too bad that it isn't taken more seriously because it is so very powerful and yet so very meaningless most of the time. When I tell that to people in Hollywood they get mad at me and they say, 'You're just arty.'"

Welles called *Citizen Kane* "an experiment" and lamented the fact that no money is spent in Hollywood on experimentation: "Only in Russia have they experimented with films and there they do not have the technologically advanced film equipment that we have."

Relating his calamitous rejection by RKO, he said incredulously and bitterly: "Hollywood expects you to experiment but on a film which must make money and if you don't make money, you're to blame. Your *job* is to make money."

Although he answered individual questions about the techniques in *Citizen Kane,* he stated that he felt he was ill-equipped to do so. "When Chaplin tries to explain what he does, he is a perfect idiot with no possible notion of what he is up to," Welles said, claiming that, unlike Chaplin, he was no genius and was therefore probably even less able to explain specific technical aspects of his films.

One of the most important things he could share with the group was that if he was moving forward at all, "haltingly," it was not far from the tradition of Griffith—the creation of film as story. "For that is what the [films] are. *Kane* is a new way of telling a story *on film.* I got the idea from the Bible, from the appearances of witnesses who come to testify about a man's character."

Welles spent some time comparing *Kane* and *Ambersons,* claiming that the latter was a better picture, "Although I didn't cut it and have not seen it in its present form," he confessed sadly. In its original state, he felt *Ambersons*

*"I don't see how it could be," he quipped.

"makes a great deal of sense" in that it depicted, realistically, a changing town in a changing world and was not just about a family of people. "The movies are the nearest thing to reality," he philosophized. "They make the sort of comment only a novel can make, an allusion to the world in which people live, the psychological and economical motivations, the influences of the period in which they lived."

Attempting to explain what he wanted to capture in making a film, he offered the word "intensity" as the basic quality he sought. He went on: "I tell a story by explaining—visualization as explanation—then add implication. The great stories are told through implication."

As the afternoon came to an end, he gave his definition of a creatively successful film: "The picture must be better to see the second or third time than it is the first time. There must be more in it to see at one time than any one person can grasp. It must be so 'meaty,' so full of implications, that everybody will get something out of it. We must not forget the audience. The audience votes by buying tickets. An audience is more intelligent than the individuals who create their entertainment. I can think of *nothing* that an audience won't understand. The only problem is to interest them. Once they are interested, they understand anything in the world. That must be in the feeling of the moviemaker."

During this period, when he engaged in a combination of radio appearances and lectures, Welles was making more money, relatively speaking, than he had made directing films. Radio performances rarely, if ever, netted him less than $1,000 each, and on some of his guest appearances on the higher-rated and more popular shows, such as the "Chase and Sanborn Hour" or "Suspense," he earned $3,000 or more each night. A few appearances of this kind each week elevated his income to one of the highest in show business and one that was certainly as lucrative as that of any radio performer.

"Cavalcade of America" was one of the high-paying shows at that time. Just a week after appearing at NYU, Welles did a thirty-minute broadcast on Columbus Day on "Cavalcade" entitled *Admiral of the Ocean Sea,* roughly based on the superb biography of Christopher Columbus by Samuel Eliot Morison. The program was aired all over the Western Hemisphere and attempted to clarify and celebrate the story of the discovery of America. The highlight of the program was Welles's stirring recitation of Walt Whitman's "Passage to India" and Joaquin Miller's "Columbus," which he wove into the story.

BEFORE THE YEAR was completed, Welles had two serious offers to act in major films. Noted producer and director Alexander Korda, who was knighted and became Sir Alexander Korda* in September 1942, and who had made such Hollywood hits as *The Thief of Baghdad* and *The Jungle Book,*

---

*Korda was the first producer to be so honored by the Crown and the first naturalized Hungarian to achieve knighthood since Sir Aurel Stein, the archaeologist.

was interested in working with Welles. It was love, or at least awe and respect, at first sight. Both were tall men who shared a passion for hard work, long cigars, and beautiful women and a hatred of small dogs, noisy children, and southern California.

Why no one in Hollywood had ever seriously considered doing an adaptation of Tolstoy's *War and Peace* until Korda arrived on the scene is not known, but it is likely that the scope, breadth, complexity, and awesome length of the work might have loomed as too aesthetically and technically intimidating for most studios and too expensive for all but the most foolhardy of financial institutions.

But to Korda, such a project was more than a challenge. "The idea has been following me all of my life," he said. "It is impossible to jump away from your shadow." To Orson, involvement in a film of the world's greatest novel, a cornerstone of literature, was seductively irresistible.

The amiable, bumbling Pierre Bezukov would be played by Welles and the role of the ravishing Natasha would be taken by Korda's wife, Merle Oberon. Welles was also to co-write the script, working with Lajos Brio, who had scripted such classics as *The Private Life of Henry VIII* and *The Scarlet Pimpernel,* among many others. Filming in London and Moscow would begin as soon as the war ended; it was thought at that time that might be by the end of 1943. Welles would then presumably be finished with the script and could come to England. MGM was named as the producing studio. In the interim, Korda wrote to Sergei Eisenstein asking him to view the 1915 silent version of *War and Peace* directed by the actors Vladimir Gardin and Yakov Protaganov. He wanted Eisenstein to respond, by cable, whether he thought the story had cinematic value and whether a talking, contemporary version could be made successfully.

Eisenstein's response was thoughtfully and politely positive and after a "thank you" cable from Korda mentioning that Welles had begun to script the story and would play in the film, the great Soviet director answered as follows:

> Alma Ata, USSR
> Kazahkstan
> 3-10-43

Dear Colleague Korda:

I'm very glad that Poudovkin's and my cursory observations on screening "War and Peace" were, to a certain extent, of use and interest to you.

Always glad to be of assistance whenever and wherever we can. I appreciate the excitement with which you approach the Tolstoy's great work.

It seems, that from the very start, you have insured your undertaking by engaging Orson Welles for the production and the role of Pierre Bezukov.

I think, that here, your brilliant intuition will bring excellent results.

Curiously enough, Orson Welles, seems to me as one of the most interesting and promising figures of the Western Cinema, although I know very little about him (almost nothing about him; two or three comments about *Citizen Kane*; two or three stories about radio activity and I believe, a photo of him with a beard sitting at a table in "Brown Derby").

I would like to learn more of him in order to check up on my own intuition.

Anyhow, please extend to him and accept yourself my warmest greetings and heartiest wishes of success.

Personally, I am up to my neck in very difficult and serious work—I'm filming two series on the life of Ivan the Terrible.

You can imagine how fascinating and interesting the combination may be of the situational melodramatism of biography of the figure and the new treatment of that man as the greatest progressive statesman of the 16th century who foresaw the possibility of the revival of the Russian might of Peter the Great, whose programme he began to adopt over 100 years before him.

Hoping that my greetings for your anniversary has reached you in time to shake your hand personally in Moscow or London as soon as the United Nations deliver the final smashing blow to Fascism.

> With my best wishes
> Yours sincerely,
>
> S. M. Eisenstein

Although Welles had worked on the script, the uncertainty of the project prevented MGM from generating enthusiasm. When Orson requested a small office and a recording secretary on the MGM lot, he was refused. The prolonged global conflict prevented the Korda-Welles variation of *War and Peace* from ever being started, let alone completed.

Before the Eisenstein endorsement, and just a few weeks before Christmas in 1942, Welles was approached to play the part of the brooding Rochester— a role that once again incredibly suited his temperaments and talents—for the Twentieth Century-Fox production of the romantic melodrama, *Jane Eyre.** David O. Selznick, the packager of *Jane Eyre*, had always wanted Welles to play the part but had lost hope of securing him because of Welles's contract with RKO. When Orson was free from RKO, Selznick made his move and bid. Orson accepted the offer of $100,000 for the role.

Produced by William Goetz, the film called upon the talents of those who already were—or later would be—famous in the literary and drama worlds. Robert Stevenson, who directed, was a member of a professional group known as the Brontë Society and had spent years studying the history and traditions that provide the background for Charlotte Brontë's novel and the film. He collaborated with Aldous Huxley and John Houseman in writing the screenplay. Orson did some writing of the screenplay also and was paid a moderate fee for his work. Bernard Herrmann composed the music, and Orson insisted that his makeup man from *Citizen Kane*, Maurice Seiderman,

---

*Fox also offered Welles the lead in *The Moon Is Down*, but when he became too strenuous and emphatic about his also directing it, they withdrew from further negotiations.

none other, be his cosmetics expert. In addition to Orson, the cast of notables included Joan Fontaine as the fragile Jane.

Welles exercised a control over the production that extended beyond his capacity as actor. He tried to get as many of his own technicians as possible to work with him on the picture. In addition to Maurice Seiderman, other minor helpers were employed as a result of his influence. He also tried to prevail upon the casting.

In a letter to Goetz, Selznick mentioned having lunch with Orson (on the day Orson returned his signed contract) and outlined some of the suggestions made by the future Mr. Rochester:

> I share wholeheartedly Orson's feeling, and have previously expressed my conviction, that you ought to try to get as many new character people in the picture as possible. In proof of this, I interviewed dozens of actors for the various roles in New York, and have many suggestions to make. I would be glad to be present at a casting meeting on the subject, and do hope you will invite me to attend. I should also like to urge that you have Orson there, because I know few people in the history of the business who have shown such a talent for exact casting and for digging up new people.

Despite Orson's and Selznick's pleas, most of the non-starring roles were given to stock character types, many of them transplants from the British stage or motion pictures who had been working in Hollywood for years.

Four earlier adaptations of the novel had been brought to the screen: three silent titles in 1913 and 1915 and one by W. W. Hodkinson in 1921; and in 1934, Monogram made a saccharin version with sound, starring Virginia Bruce and Colin Clive. Perhaps because of Stevenson, no attempt was made to modernize the classic. The treatment was illusory rather than realistic, making every effort that wartime restrictions would allow to keep it faithful to the nineteenth-century setting.

The plot is painfully familiar to most readers but just in case: Orphaned in childhood, Jane is sent by her aunt (Agnes Moorehead) to live in an orphanage run by a cruel and evil minister (Henry Danielle). Upon leaving the school, Jane (Joan Fontaine) is hired as governess to Adele (Margaret O'Brien), French ward of Edward Rochester (Welles). Thornfield, the mansion in which Rochester has installed his ward, is as mysterious and somber as the millionaire who owns it. Nonetheless, Jane stays on through affection for the child and her growing love for Rochester. Rochester proposes marriage, and Jane agrees until Rochester confesses that the inexplicable happenings at Thornfield are caused by his insane wife whom he has hidden away upstairs. Jane leaves, then returns to find the mansion destroyed by the madwoman, who has perished in the fire. Rochester has been blinded in an attempt to rescue the woman from the fire. He and Jane are reconciled, and the two are wed to the accompaniment of crashes of thunder and flashes of lightning.

Fontaine's performance received accolades from most of the critics, who described her Jane as "elfin," "sincere," "projecting an appealing modesty with artistic restraint," and "a perfect childlike foil to Welles." Margaret O'Brien as Adele and Peggy Ann Garner as the child Jane were both unanimously praised in such terms as "astonishing" and "exquisitely effective." A bit player also received industry acclaim and made audiences take notice, the incredibly beautiful ten-year-old Elizabeth Taylor, who played a friend of young Jane. "Remind me to be around when she grows up," quipped Orson half seriously of the violet-eyed beauty.

Critical response to Welles's Rochester, however, was mixed. James Agee objected to his operatic approach, which lacked "symbolic resonance"; Walter Kerr felt he was miscast; others found him "Byronic," "vivid," "darkly foreboding," and too youthful-appearing for the part.

Critic Lowell E. Redelings, of the *Los Angeles Citizen News* perhaps best summed up the critical reaction:

> The disturbing element is Orson Welles. His acting is technically sound enough, at times brilliant. But his facial appearance minus makeup, seems too youthful for his role as the middle-aged Edward Rochester, the anguished hero of the story. Further, his throaty mutterings, at times rasping across the sound track like sandpaper, are too often unintelligible. The final effect is that Welles, dominating the picture throughout, destroys the illusion he strives to create.

Curiously, Welles's makeup, although technically perfect, was what distorted the character's age. Edward Rochester is supposed to be close to forty, almost old enough to be Jane's father. In reality, Joan Fontaine and Orson were in their twenties. Makeup could have added the years, but Stevenson wanted to retain Orson's youthful star appearance for promotional purposes and consequently insisted that Seiderman keep Rochester's wrinkles to a minimum. "Rochester is a man ahead of his time," said Stevenson by way of explanation, after the film was released, "more 1942 than Victorian."

Whatever adverse criticism was offered by the critics toward Orson didn't seem to matter, however; the public loved his role of Rochester.

Joan Fontaine, in her outspoken autobiography, *No Bed of Roses,* clearly admits to not being a fan of Welles, declaring that "everything about him was oversized, including his ego." On the first day at the lot, she recalls the entire cast and crew assembled for rehearsal at one in the afternoon—a time that Welles himself had set. They waited for him for three hours. Then, at four o'clock, the door burst open, and Welles strode in accompanied by his doctor, his manager, his secretary, and his valet. He assumed what he considered to be his place at the lectern and announced to the director and his cast, "Now we'll begin on page four."

With the help of William Pereira, the producer's assistant, Stevenson did manage to regain directorial control. It was rough work, however. Although ten years Welles's senior and having over a dozen films to his credit, Stevenson felt rather intimidated by the giant actor with the colossal reputation.

Welles was a man to be handled as carefully as possible. One reason why he did not succeed in taking over this time, Fontaine posits, was that he was undisciplined, melodramatic, always late. Once, she recalled, she had booked a flight to Mexico City on a day when the cast had been assembled in the gallery for photographs. The photography was scheduled for ten. Welles, after repeated telephone calls were made to him, finally arrived at one. He claimed, she said, that he had spent the morning lying in his bathtub because Fontaine had not trusted him to arrive on time. She made the flight with only seconds to spare.

Welles's costuming, she wrote, was his main concern. One morning as she stood behind him, about to make an entrance, she advised him to stand up straight because his coat hung loosely at the neck. Welles called a halt to the shooting until his jacket was repaired. The jacket was brought to the wardrobe department where it lay, untouched, for an hour. When it was returned, unaltered, Welles allowed the shooting to proceed, satisfied that his demand had been honored.

Not everyone who has thought about *Jane Eyre* has offered so acerbic an appraisal. Joseph McBride, in his program notes to the "Working with Welles" seminar, regretted that Welles had not directed the film. If he had, McBride reflects, "a fully integrated film might have resulted, though the material tends to bring out some of the more purely self-indulgent aspects of his personality and would have required painstaking refinement and styliza-tion to be a complete success." McBride agreed with François Truffaut's opinion that Welles's direction was musical rather than poetic. "*Jane Eyre* suffers," McBride has written, "because it lacks this musical unity."

Despite condemnation from many of those who belong to the ranks of the critical establishment, the public liked *Jane Eyre* as a handsome Halloween study in shadows, a worthy contender for the escapist horror films that were capturing their fancies at that time. And soon after, Welles concretized his image as a man of gloom and foreboding, and received even more offers to play mask and dagger roles on radio.

Jane Eyre turned out to be Robert Stevenson's last feature film for the war period. Instead, he was given a captain's commission in the Army to make training and propaganda films. Orson, still deferred from the service, went on in his own special way to help the war effort, through a remarkable undertak-ing called the Mercury Wonder Show.*

He also fell in love.

---

*For the record, Orson's final 4-F classification was as a result of "chronic myoditis and original syndrome arthritis, bronchial asthma, high fever and inverted flat feet."

CHAPTER 14

"I DISCOVERED AT the age of six," Welles said to a freelance writer in the summer of 1943, "that almost everything in this world was phony, worked with mirrors. Since then, I've always wanted to be a magician."

With more money in his pocket than he had ever had, Welles decided to realize his fondest ambition and invest in the production of his own magic show. He once claimed that he could never get a friend—any friend—to sit still to watch any of his magic tricks, and by producing his own show he gave himself the opportunity of expressing his art. The idea was multifaceted. He would perform in a tent and allow servicemen free admission. If the public wanted to enter, they would have to pay premium prices for seats. All profits, after expenses, would be turned over to charity, specifically the Assistance League, established for the benefit of servicemen who had special financial emergencies. Orson put up $40,000 of his own money to get the show rolling, $30,000 of which was for props alone.

By establishing the Mercury Wonder Show, not only would Orson be getting valuable experience in his first professional attempt at conjuring and legerdemain but he would, magnanimously, be entertaining the troops. His image, as a result, had to improve. He would also be able to use other entertainers (mostly his friends), and if the entire process was a success, it was possible that the government would send the show to army camps all over the country, perhaps the world. Setting up a huge circus tent on Cahuenga Boulevard, smack in the middle of Hollywood, was also, almost by definition, guaranteed to produce substantial amounts of publicity, something that could, again, only help to promote the name and persona of Orson Welles.

To Orson, magic was all romance and mystery. Although he dealt with illusions and fantasy as a filmmaker, the point of the creative film act was to make people believe that something was real and if they accepted it, you succeeded; whereas magic was pure and glorious deceit for those who watched it: mystery for its own sake, the audience willing and gullible victims of their own disbelief.

Welles half seriously saw himself as a conjuring reincarnation from the days of runes and druids, a twentieth-century alchemist delving into the world of charms and witches, a direct descendant of Harry Houdini or Aleister Crowley or Henry Thurston. The Welles magical style, however, was pure

362

vaudeville: cards and rabbits and lighted cigarettes and bouquets of yellow roses suddenly and inexplicably appeared from hat or sleeve or goldfish bowl much to his feigned surprise and the genuine delight of the audience.

Some seventeen weeks—all during *Jane Eyre* and even before—of assiduous rehearsals by Orson and a group of "assistant prestidigitators"* went into the preparation of the Mercury Wonder Show. He purchased with his own money some $26,000 worth of magic equipment and paraphernalia and opened in the first week of August 1943. Seats cost up to $5.50 (except for servicemen), and peanuts went for a dollar a bag. It was a sellout almost every night for weeks.

The carnival spirit that he created, which included red circus wagons, sawdusted floors, a live lion, tiger, and leopard, a group of barnyard types, and an assortment of clowns, acrobats, and other circus-touched performers, was permeated with comedy. Orson fondly and unoriginally called his illusions a series of "mumbo jumbo, hanky-panky and hocus-pocus."

Of all of the magic show personnel, Welles was fortunate, he felt, to secure the services of one of Hollywood's most striking stars, a young lady whose picture was being hung by the millions on barrack walls all over the world and making servicemen's hearts beat faster, Rita Hayworth.

Of Irish and Spanish ancestry, the redheaded Hayworth was splendidly voluptuous and often starred in tempestuous or sirenic roles. She had been in Hollywood since 1935, first, at seventeen years old, under the name of Rita Cansino** as a dancer in *Dante's Inferno* for Twentieth Century-Fox. It wasn't until ten films later, when she was under contract to Columbia Pictures, that her name was changed to Rita Hayworth and the studio began to realize her starring appeal. By the time she had made her twenty-seventh film, *The Lady in Question* with Brian Aherne and Glenn Ford, followed by *Angels Over Broadway* with Douglas Fairbanks, Jr., she was one of the most popular female actresses on the screen.

John Kobal, Rita's biographer, has described how she was perceived at that time, on and off the screen.

> Hayworth's screen persona contained the ingredients of all that wartime taste dictated: she was desirable, yet could be a sex symbol for servicemen without offending the women back home; she possessed an air of romance that made it possible for her to exude those elements of mystery, formerly the stock-in-trade of foreign *femmes fatales,* without reminding the wives and sweethearts of the sort of women their men might find overseas; furthermore, she was an American classic; a heady mixture that enthralled the world.

After costarring with Victor Mature in *My Gal Sal,* the two had a much-publicized love affair, which was helped along by Columbia's publicity

---

*For his "stooges," as he called them, he offered Joseph Cotten, Agnes Moorehead, and fourteen others.
**Her real name was Margarita Carmen Cansino.

department. Press releases and bulletins were issued almost daily about their vicissitudes. Eventually, after he announced his engagement to Rita, Mature went into the Coast Guard.

Welles first saw the twenty-four-year-old Hayworth, at the height of both their careers, during a wartime benefit radio broadcast, when they each made a cameo appearance but were not introduced. A gossip columnist learned through one of Orson's friends that Orson was intrigued by Rita and, a few days after the broadcast, headlined an item about it: "Orson Welles Wants to Meet Rita Hayworth." Rita was incensed and mentioned the item to many of her friends: she was not interested in Orson Welles and had never even met him; only Victor Mature was in her mind and heart. Shortly afterward at the Columbia commissary when Orson was visiting someone, he spied Rita having lunch. She was, however, only superficially polite when Orson approached her table. "The papers say I want to meet you," he said, as she finished her chicken soup. "Guess what? It's true."

A few nights later Welles called her and asked her to dinner. She agreed but only if others were present. More casual dinners, always in the company of two or three of her friends, followed at Orson's insistence and persuasion.

When he began to arrange the Mercury Wonder Show, the idea of working with Rita surfaced. Orson asked and she accepted. It couldn't damage the show's prestige that she had been on the cover of both *Life* and *Time* and literally dozens of movie fan magazines, just a short time previously. Her face and figure had become so popular on magazines that Columbia came up with the idea of a musical called *Cover Girl,* starring Gene Kelly and directed by Charles Vidor. It was to be a showcase especially designed to promote her. Shooting had begun in May of 1943. Orson capitalized on the recognition factor of Rita's name and face with huge four-color banners and flags which he had painted with such slogans as "Only Rita Knows," and displayed in front of the show tents.

Houdini had built his career, his climb to magical fame, in the 1890s, while playing in dime museums and seedy vaudeville theaters, on one trick: metamorphosis, or the trunk substitution. Orson had similar ideas in the opening of his magic show, and Rita would play a crucial part in them. Joseph Cotten would be tied up in a large sack and locked into a trunk. The trunk would be tightly bound with heavy ropes. Orson would draw a curtain in front of the trunk for one second and, presto, after the trunk was untied and then opened, Cotten would be gone and up would pop the most beautiful woman in the world: Rita Hayworth.

The trick was simple but dazzling and captured the imagination of the audience. The bag was basted with strong thread but not sewn tightly and the moment Cotten was put into the trunk, he simply removed the thread; as the curtain was pulled in front, he exited by a secret push-out panel in the trunk and disappeared into the wings. Rita then took his place, entering through the same panel and not disturbing the ropes. Orson pulled away the curtain and, with the trunk in full view, continued his spiel while the enclosed Rita, now in the bag, quickly resealed the bottom so that she was completely enclosed. The substitution was rehearsed and choreographed so that it took only a few seconds.

Gorgeous Rita, in an additional trick, was the Girl with the X-ray Eyes. Another treat for the audience was when, at a dramatic moment in the program, Orson performed the most famous illusion of modern times— sawing a woman (Rita) in half.

If Rita was the attraction, Orson was the show. The Great Orson, or the Great Ham, as he affectionately and privately called himself, bedecked in a fez and a long black-and-white striped silk robe, rose to the magical occasion with all of the nonchalance, self-ridicule, humor, and surprise of a veteran conjurer, beaming gratefully and trembling with gratitude at the conclusion of each trick. "Ladies and gentlemen," he would begin histrionically. "Tonight we are going to reproduce the occult secrets of antiquity, provide original experiments in animal magnetism, and furnish readings on the Magic Crystal *but* because of the unbelievable strain on the practitioner of this incredible feat, the management must reserve the right to change this position of the program without notice."

He swallowed live flames, hypnotized roosters, gave psychic readings, ate needles, and heckled the customers. He worked so hard that dry towels would be periodically thrown to him on the stage so that he could mop up his perspiration. His smash act was what he called the bullet-catching stunt. A rifleman would seemingly fire a bullet directly at Orson and it would appear that he would catch it between his teeth. The trick was simple but sensational: the rifleman always aimed slightly to the side, and the real bullet would end up in a mattress off in the wings. A quick appearance of another bullet hidden in Orson's mouth and the jerk of his head made it look as though he actually caught it.

Rita's career as Orson's star assistant was extremely short-lived. She performed only on opening night. Harry Cohn, the tyrannical president of Columbia Pictures who was grooming Rita Hayworth to be his biggest box office attraction, treating her as a combination daughter, slave, and financial investment, was furious when he read the publicity on the Mercury Wonder Show that filled every Los Angeles newspaper the day after the opening. There was Rita's photograph showing her standing prettily in the trunk at the conclusion of the substitution trick. "Supposing she breaks a leg?" asked Cohn not so rhetorically. He went on, working himself into virtual distemper. "Why am I paying her a huge salary as a star and she's performing for nothing in a tent? It will ruin her image. And she is supposed to be engaged to Victor Mature. Hollywood *wants* that marriage. Who is this Orson Welles nut anyway?" he asked, knowing only too well. Cohn insisted that Hayworth quit the magic show immediately and when she resisted, he reminded her of her contract, which indicated that she was not to perform *anywhere* without the studio's permission. She was forced to relent.

The next night, Orson retaliated. At the point where Rita was supposed to first appear, he stopped the show and addressed the audience:

> And now, ladies and gentlemen, I have come to a very unhappy part in this performance. Rita Hayworth rehearsed for this show for sixteen weeks. No one of us connected with it has been more interested than she in contributing a fine evening for servicemen for whom nothing is too good. But Rita Hayworth also works for motion picture studios, and motion picture studios are very odd. Columbia Pictures in the person of Harry Cohn—and I feel it is only fair to name names—has exercised his prerogative by insisting that Miss Hayworth withdraw from the show. This is terribly unfortunate, and I want to tell you that if any of you feels that the absence of Miss Hayworth in any way spoils your evening, you have only to go to the box office and your money will be refunded, and we hope you will remain, as our guests, for the rest of the evening. We had hoped that reason might prevail, but Mr. Cohn is adamant, a chronic condition with that gentleman. Needless to say, I shall never appear in a Columbia picture. It is, as I say, unfortunate to intrude this one unpleasant note. However, I feel you are entitled to an explanation.

When Cohn heard about the speech he considered suing Welles for slander but learned from his attorneys that he did not have a strong enough case. He then did the only thing he could to make it difficult for Orson and Rita to get together: he barred him from the Columbia lot.

A young, struggling comedian named Johnny Carson stood in as the "victim" to be sawed in half. Thirty years later, he reminded Orson of this on his then famous *Tonight* show.

Orson continued his nightly thaumaturgy for a solid month, playing to almost two thousand people a night, over half of them members of the armed forces. When the sawdust was literally cleared and the show ended, the expenses had been far greater than expected but still, an ample check was donated to the Assistance League.

Despite, and perhaps slightly because of, Cohn's censure of the growing interest of Rita and Orson in each other, the relationship prospered quickly. Orson was overwhelmed by Rita's obvious beauty, her silent mystery, and her stardom; Rita was attracted to Orson's energy and apparent self-confidence, his intellectuality and knowledge. The fact that Rita, who had very little formal schooling or self-education, began the day reading the gossip columnists, appalled and incensed "Orsie," as she called him. He organized a reading curriculum for her: Shakespeare, Plato, Cervantes, Flaubert. Ideas, concepts, theories, and philosophies that she had never considered before spewed forth from him. She enjoyed and was flattered by his concern over her education. He introduced her to some of his more intellectual friends and tried to engage her in conversations of substance; he took her to operas and concerts and plays.

On a one-to-one basis, as his Professor Higgins to her Eliza Doolittle, they seemed to relate. However, the cultural activity was not all without intimidation. At a party of literary types organized by Orson specifically for Rita, she whispered to Joseph Cotten's wife, Lenore: "All these people are staring at me, because they think I'm a dumb woman." Mrs. Cotten admitted that Rita realistically appraised the situation but added: "They're staring all right, darling, but it's not because you're dumb."

Almost in between takes on *Cover Girl*, and only days after the Mercury Wonder Show closed, Orson and Rita decided to get married. The date was September 7, 1943, and Orson was twenty-eight, Rita twenty-four. The wedding was covered by newspaper and magazine reporters and photographers every step of their way: buying the license; Rita's leaving the studio to get dressed; Orson's shaving at home; Orson's stopping by in a car to fetch Maurice Bernstein as his best man; being married by a judge in Santa Monica; attending a wedding dinner party afterward. The fan magazines were busy for weeks on the red-hot story of what they called "the Beauty and the Brain."

Although Orson made no personal income for his summer months' production of the Mercury Wonder Show, the publicity he received was immense. In addition to almost weekly features in Los Angeles newspapers, large picture spreads about the show appeared nationally in *Collier's, Look,* and *Life.* As a result of the fanfare, he was asked to repeat a segment on film.

As a tribute to those of the film community who worked through the Hollywood Victory Committee to entertain the troops, Charles K. Feldman organized a group of stars in what *The New York Times* slurred as a touch-and-go picture called *Follow the Boys,* produced by Universal Pictures and directed by Eddie Sutherland.

In the movie, George Raft plays a vaudeville hoofer who has made good in Hollywood but flunked his army physical. To make it up to the boys overseas, the Raft character organizes a show similar to what its Hollywood Victory Committee and the United Service Organizations (USO) were doing in reality. Raft tours the front lines with his troupe and finally gets torpedoed by the Japanese for his trouble. Among the dozens of entertainers taking part were Jeanette MacDonald, Sophie Tucker, Dinah Shore, Donald O'Connor, a number of dance bands, the Andrews Sisters, W. C. Fields, the Delta Rhythm Boys, Leonard Gautier and his trapeze-swinging trained dog act, and Slapsie Maxie Rosenbloom. Orson was asked to duplicate his trick of sawing a woman in two, but instead of doing it with Rita (locked into her Columbia contract and unavailable for the film) the pretend not-so-willing victim was Marlene Dietrich.

Welles showed up at Universal with his own small army of advisers and aides, including Professor Bill and his Circus Symphony, and a certain "Cactus Mac" who tended the animals in the act, affected ten-gallon hats and spurs, and reportedly had worked with the real Buffalo Bill. There were also a couple of female assistants and Tony Hanlon, professional magician and coach for Welles. And eight chorus girls for background.

In the film, George Raft dances with the film's heroine, Vera Zorina, Orson's real-life old friend from his New York Mercury days. Dinah Shore sings. So does Jeanette MacDonald. W. C. Fields does his classic pool table sequence. The Andrews Sisters belt out a medley of their favorites. Sophie

Tucker, with bawdy innuendo, exhorts women everywhere to give "a lot o'lovin' to the Army and Navy."

Orson's segment lasted only six minutes of screen time but was considered by critics and audiences as having the most energy and being the best of the acts. "Orson, we haven't rehearsed this," says Dietrich as Welles, dressed in white tie and tails, shows two servicemen, picked from the film audience, exactly where to cut and saw. "Gentlemen, I think you ought to know: we lose a girl at every performance," he tells his assistants. "But Orson," Dietrich insists, "how does this trick work?" He looks at her sardonically: "Just wait, Marlene. This'll kill you." When the sawing is completed, the lower half of her body dispatches itself and walks off the stage. The top half of Dietrich ends the sequence by a revengeful reprisal at her predicament. She hypnotizes Orson who topples over and collapses as the segment fades out.

IN THE DECADE leading up to World War II, Hollywood averaged five hundred original productions each year. During the height of the war, 1943-45, that figure dropped by almost 25 percent to some three hundred and fifty or so annual features. Although there were fewer films being made, there were, however, actually more jobs for young male actors since many of the leading men were serving in the armed forces. And there were, despite wartime restrictions on acting and technical talent, some powerful and creative efforts realized: *Shadow of a Doubt, Laura, Double Indemnity, The Mask of Dimitrios, Hail the Conquering Hero, The Picture of Dorian Gray,* and *The Lost Weekend* were all wartime films.

Orson had opportunities, or at least made overtures, to act in some of the above films and others, following his cameo in *Follow the Boys*. His filmic heart, however, seemed to stop beating for a while, at least for most of the war years. There was a world to protect; a U.S. president to be elected; great social and humanitarian issues were at stake. He didn't want to *act* in films, anyway. *Direction* had become his love, but nobody in the industry seemed interested in showing confidence in him any longer. The ignominy of the failure of *It's All True,* and perhaps *Ambersons*, continued to haunt him.

Orson talked of going back to the theater; he also thought of producing more magic shows. But offers for speeches and radio guest appearances arrived almost daily and the momentum pushed him along. When Jack Benny fell victim to pneumonia in Chicago after a debilitating camp tour, Orson hosted his radio show, the most popular in the country, for six straight weeks. It seems that he also traded quips with Charlie McCarthy and Mortimer Snerd on the "Chase and Sanborn Hour" every time the nation tuned in. He was on the Philco "Radio Hall of Fame," acted in a number of segments of "Inner Sanctum," was often a guest on the "Kate Smith Show," talked with Ajax Cassidy and Max Weissbaum in Allen's Alley on "The Fred Allen Show," appeared in a verse play by Norman Corwin, *The Plot to Overthrow Christmas,* and played Edward Rochester in yet another version of *Jane Eyre,* this one representing his first appearance on Cecil B. DeMille's

"Lux Presents Hollywood." He also produced, directed, and starred in Lucille Fletcher's classic radio play, *Hitch-Hiker*.

A few weeks after *Jane Eyre,* DeMille brought Orson and Rita to "Lux" in their first attempt, other than their experience of one night at the magic show, in performing together. The play was *Break of Hearts,* based on the 1935 RKO film, a critical and box-office failure of the same name, which had starred Katharine Hepburn and Charles Boyer. A romantic tale about a world-famous orchestra conductor and a young woman composer, the film had been soundly trounced as stupid pathos with a painfully predictable plot.

Somehow, Orson, despite a thick Viennese accent that made him sound like a more guttural Boyer, and the bright, ingenuousness of Rita, elevated the story into an acceptably heartrending broadcast.

Perhaps the most satisfying radio experience he had at that time was the production of another series that was exclusively his creation, "The Orson Welles Almanac," and in many ways it was the most energetic and entertaining of all the shows he had ever become involved in although, like most of his projects, it developed not without problems. Sponsored by Mobil Gas and Oil, the thirty-minute prime-time show was broadcast every Monday night and consisted of pure Wellesiana. As the title implies, Orson would include "well, anything," as he described it, that he thought would interest his listeners.

Citations of famous anniversaries and dates would be noted: "Today is the feast of St. Christendom; three weeks ago Dick Tracy was kidnapped by Flat Top." General facts would be offered: the average family in the United States consists of 3.5 people; on Sunday, President Roosevelt will be sixty-two years old; there is no soda in soda water.* A fine upbeat orchestra that had a similar sound to Phil Harris's would play at least two popular tunes each show ("I Know That You Know," "Besame Mucho," etc.) and the range of guests was eclectic. In a cigar duel with Orson, Groucho Marx would offer insults:

So this is the new Orson Welles show and you're the new Orson Welles. You don't look so new to me. As a matter of fact, you're the most "used" Orson Welles I've ever seen.

Robert Benchley could be counted on to give one of his famous bumbling lectures (on the *History of Eskimo Love,* for instance), and even Hedda Hopper, "The Hat," as Orson called her, no longer angry over the Hearst affair, would act in a short "skitlet" about Hollywood. ("Orson, I always love

*Poor Orson could not seem to avoid controversy even with a show as pleasant and light as his "Almanac." On the first program, as a part of a list of important dates, he made mention that five years before that week (January 26, 1944), the Loyalists had surrendered Barcelona to Generalissimo Franco. Representatives of Mobil Oil, his sponsors, felt that such a remark on national radio might jeopardize their oil business in Spain. Orson's wrist was slapped, and he had to promise that in the future he would submit his script to the show's agency, Compton Advertising, each week for their approval.

to hear you say 'I am, obediently yours.' Then I know the show is over.") "The Orson Welles Almanac" was free and easy, ad-libs were genuine and plentiful, and Orson gathered some of the greatest names in show business to come frolic with him each week: Monty Woolley, Danny Kaye, Lionel Barrymore, Charles Laughton, and Lana Turner, among many others.

After a few weeks of broadcasting the "Almanac," spokesmen from the sponsor and their agency began to breathe down Orson's neck. They didn't think he was funny enough and pointed to Jack Benny as the quintessential comedian. They wanted more farce. In argument, Welles agreed that Benny was a "character," the clownlike butt of jokes, but Orson offered the personality of a Fred Allen in contrast, who was not funny in himself but a master at timing and hence, quite hilarious.

"Herbert Marshall could do the same show," complained Bob Presnell of the Compton Agency. "Herbert Marshall is available if you want him," Orson snapped back. "I don't mean to either sound huffy or haughty, nor do I protest that I am a more gifted comedian than Herbert Marshall but I think you're exaggerating the importance of projecting me [as Benny] as a comical fellow in myself."

At the end of each show, Orson always gave a reading of serious material, such as a fragment concerning free speech from a tract by Thomas Paine; or the John Donne "For Whom the Bell Tolls" devotion; or a soliloquy from *Hamlet.* The sponsor's representatives were critical of that, too. They wanted the serious material either integrated into the body of the show and dramatized or else deleted. Orson knew it was among the most highly praised parts of the program and to remove it from the ending and place it within the show would confuse the listening audience as to what was comedy and what was drama. Orson's final response: "Go to hell!"

As the "Almanac" progressed, Orson replaced the big-band sound of Lud Gluskin with a patchwork, but highly effective, group of jazz musicians; they had a classic New Orleans sound. Orson was particularly proud of the band because he loved jazz, helped form the group, and seemed to be able to communicate easily with the musicians. It was a particularly fine jazz ensemble. Swingers such as Jimmie Noone, Wingy Manone, Mud Corey, Wade Barkley, Zutti Singleton, and Floyd O'Brien would often rehearse at Orson's house the day before each broadcast; he considered and treated everyone in the band as a personal friend. Noone, a clarinetist, had composed a particularly dark and lovely piece, "The Jimmie Noone Blues," and Orson agreed to have the band play it. The night before the show, Noone died of a heart attack.

Orson was deeply affected. That night the show went on as usual and with about six minutes to sign-off, he slowly approached the microphone and spoke extemporaneously:

One of the things we are most proud of on this show is our New Orleans jazz group. You are going to hear them again tonight. The part of the clarinetist Jimmie Noone is going to be taken by Wade Barkley. Many of you who don't know the history of this music may not realize that in its early beginnings in New

Orleans it was not just played for dances but it was used to express the whole spirit of a people. It was played at festivals, and at weddings, it was played in churches, it was played at funerals. It was only when it moved up the river to St. Louis that it was thought of as dance music for night spots. Yesterday I got a call from Jimmie Noone who told me how proud he was that he was going to be on our program tonight. Jimmie had a particular reason to be proud tonight. The group was going to play one of Jimmie's own compositions. Jimmie died suddenly last night. And now, in his honor, his friends are going to play one of his own works.

What followed was a sweet and saddening lament, a sound as though Noone had written his own jazz eulogy. As one member of the audience poetically recalled: "I've heard blues songs sung in nightclubs by sheathed and sultry ladies who were mourning for a man; in the theater sung against a painted backdrop of some old riverboat, the stage darkened and only a pale spotlighted singer's face; but here, for the first time, I really learned what the blues were all about."

When the piece ended, Orson held his hands up to the audience as a signal not to applaud and then very quietly read the Twenty-third Psalm, "The Lord is my shepherd, I shall not want. . . ." After the show was signed off the air, there was no applause. No one from the audience rose. They sat there stunned. Orson left the microphone and went backstage. A representative of the sponsor, John MacMillan, found him in his dressing room. Orson was tired, somber, moved. "Well, it wasn't show business, was it?" he asked MacMillan. All MacMillan could do was appear supportive. The sponsors never complained about Orson again.

DURING THE YEARS 1942 to 1945, Americans purchased some 49 billion dollars worth of war bonds—10 percent of their salaries—to help buy guns and ammunition, tanks, ships, and planes for the fighting front. Investment in bonds also helped to soak up loose cash that created an inflationary pressure. It seemed to become everybody's patriotic duty to buy war bonds and war stamps, which were eventually turned into bonds. War loan drives, as they were called, were organized many times during the war, and the worlds of industry, academia, small and large business, and entertainment pitched in to spur the public's spirit and resolve. Hollywood stars were used continually to speak at and appear at war bond rallies, to perform on radio shows promoting war bond and stamp investments, and to give their endorsements on posters and advertising.

In May 1944, just weeks before the invasion of Normandy and the capture of Rome, Secretary of the Treasury Henry Morgenthau, Jr., saw that a huge influx of new arms and equipment would be needed to sustain the projected struggle. The Fifth War Loan Drive scheduled to begin on June 12 would, according to Morgenthau, have to be the most successful money-raising campaign of the war. The invasion would be bloody and expensive, the most thunderous clash of armed forces in history. It would not be the end of the war but only the beginning of its most violent phase. In discussions with President Franklin Delano Roosevelt, Morgenthau came up with the idea of an inspiring radio broadcast that would open the drive and serve not only to help sell bonds but to offer to the nation a summation of the deepest causes and highest purposes of the conflict; it would serve as a definition of the democratic ideal and a celebration of the justice of the war.

Who would be responsible for creating such an awesome and important production, the rallying call to 135,000,000 Americans? It was Roosevelt who thought of Orson Welles as the first choice as producer. Welles was one of the most highly regarded and experienced radio personalities in the country; the sound of his voice was known and recognized by just about everybody; he had recently served as master of ceremonies for a highly-successful fundraiser at Ciro's that collected monies to help get Jewish scholars, artists, and scientists out of Nazi Germany; his "Ceiling Unlimited" and "Hello, Americans" shows had proved that he could take sensitive war material and successfully dramatize it; and finally he had long been a supporter and campaign speaker for Roosevelt.

Morgenthau called Welles to Washington, and plans for the show were discussed. Orson accepted the job. He was to be producer and principal narrator, reporting directly to Morgenthau and other officials of the Treasury Department, and on May 15, 1944, just a week after his twenty-ninth birthday, Orson received the official communiqué and orders from Morgenthau elevating him to the status of an official of the U.S. Treasury Department. He was to be paid at the rate of one dollar a year, and the appointment was to last for the duration. The total creative and production responsibility for what was being noised about as probably the most important radio show and crusade in American history would be his.

Welles arranged a one-hour show on all four networks that would preempt regular programming; CBS listeners, for example, would give up their weekly fare of "Screen Guild Players," "Show Time," and "Blondie" to hear the special war loan drive program. Although the show was successful in every sense of the word in the number of listeners who tuned in (something like half the nation) and the fervor it created and ultimately the bonds that it sold, Orson was somewhat restricted as to what he could accomplish as writer, director, producer, and star in such a short time. For example, he wanted Aaron Copland, then in residence at Harvard, to compose an original score for the show but there just wasn't enough time. Other personalities were unavailable for a variety of reasons. Long, important speeches to be broadcast during the hour were planned by Morgenthau and Roosevelt, and so Orson had to work around them. It gave him barely more than thirty minutes of airtime.

The basic format of the show was adroit, if not ingenious. Reconstructing his days at *The March of Time*, Orson brought a number of actors to the show who could imitate a variety of voices—Agnes Moorehead, Edgar Barrier, Alan Napier, Walter Huston, Keenan Wynn. By using "real words by real people," he established antithetical readings of opposing forces: Hitler vs.

Roosevelt, Diogenes vs. Goebbels; Jefferson vs. Goering; Von Papen vs. Churchill, and so on. Unfortunately, some of the statements were difficult to understand, such as Hitler's apoplectic rantings, because of the assumed accents of the actors.

There were other difficulties. When Leopold Stokowski was to conduct Shostakovich's piece on the United Nations, direct from Mexico City, the transmission could not be made. After a second or two of embarrassment the show continued without the planned musical piece.

Orson was the star. He did stirring and substantial readings of Woodrow Wilson and Franklin Delano Roosevelt, of Walt Whitman and Thomas Wolfe; in one of his most bravura radio performances he also created an atypical role—for him—of "Joe," an Everyman character, from Anytown, U.S.A., a soldier who doesn't come back and speaks from the grave to the nation, trying to tell them what it was like "over there" and why the American people should never give up hope until the war is over. "All I can do is die," Joe says, in a weak and slightly disembodied voice. "Its meaning is up to you." Orson truly sounded as though he were crying.

FOR THE REMAINING months of 1944, Orson worked almost full time in campaigning for the Roosevelt-Truman campaign. Roosevelt, who, according to his opponent Thomas E. Dewey, had "grown tired, old and quarrelsome in office," did indeed appear exhausted and in ill health in some photographs. Most of the country's newspapers supported Dewey, and the nation seemed to be wavering. Orson traveled to almost every state of the union and spoke before Democratic clubs, city and statewide conventions, political dinners, and mass rallies. "Wherever the cause of freedom is to be served, a vote for Roosevelt on November seventh will be hailed as a victory," he would boom, fist raised, face red, true conviction in his voice and demeanor. Welles attacked the Republican propaganda line of fear of alien influence and communist plots. "The Red bogey must be strongly rejected by the majority of the people," he observed. "The words 'communism' and 'communist' can no longer be used to smear every liberal and progressive measure."

Roosevelt was grateful for Orson's work and kept *au courant* as to the content of his speeches. And occasionally, Orson and FDR met to discuss important points that needed to be brought to the public's attention. When Orson had a slight bout of jaundice, Roosevelt became sincerely concerned and sent the following wire:

Oct. 23, 1944

To: ORSON WELLES
WALDORF-ASTORIA, NEW YORK, N.Y.

I DEEPLY APPRECIATE EVERYTHING YOU HAVE DONE AND ARE DOING. I HAVE JUST LEARNED THAT YOU ARE ILL AND I HOPE MUCH YOU WILL FOLLOW YOUR DOCTORS ORDERS AND TAKE

CARE OF YOURSELF. THE MOST IMPORTANT THING IS FOR YOU TO GET WELL AND BE AROUND FOR THE LAST DAYS OF THE CAMPAIGN. MY WARM REGARDS.

FRANKLIN D. ROOSEVELT

Orson graciously replied:

Oct. 25, 1944

FRANKLIN DELANO ROOSEVELT
WHITE HOUSE

DEAR MR. PRESIDENT: THIS ILLNESS WAS THE BLACKEST OF MISFORTUNES FOR ME BECAUSE IT STOLE AWAY SO MANY DAYS FROM THE CAMPAIGN. I CANNOT THINK I HAVE ACCOMPLISHED A GREAT DEAL BUT I WILL KNOW THAT THIS IS THE MOST IMPORTANT WORK I COULD EVER ENGAGE IN. YOUR WONDERFULLY THOUGHTFUL AND GENEROUS MESSAGE REACHED ME AT EXACTLY THE MOMENT WHEN THE DOCTORS AND I HAD DECIDED THAT I COULDN'T DO ANYTHING BUT GET WORSE. YOUR WIRE CHANGED MY MIND. I PROMISE TO TAKE YOUR GOOD ADVICE BUT I STILL HOPE TO BE BACK ON THE ROAD BY NEXT WEEK.

SINCERELY,

ORSON WELLES

Welles did recover and was back on the campaign trail shortly afterward. On occasion, he would also send ideas for phrases or sections of a speech to Roosevelt to incorporate into the President's own material. Roosevelt accepted these parts with thanks and did include them into "less important speeches" according to Welles. "Don't ever forget your Bible," Roosevelt once joked with Orson, recognizing the sources of many of his lines. "You'd be lost without it."

At one point, Roosevelt asked Orson to do some special government work for him, the nature of which was so sensitive and classified that the details and purpose of the project were known only to the two of them. Orson had to be out of town on this secret mission for over a week. "But Mr. President, Rita will never believe me if I can't tell her where I am," he complained. Roosevelt understood the dynamics of a relationship as well as any man and suggested that he call Rita personally to explain the matter of Orson's impending absence. Rita was overwhelmed when the call came in from the White House. "The President wants to talk to *me*," she said, "not my husband?"

Roosevelt explained to Rita that Orson would be away for a while and assuaged her jealousy. Not only was the content of the mission to be secret, he explained, but the very fact of the call was not to be publicized. Rita agreed.

Later, when Orson was away on the mission, Hedda Hopper, sensing a possible extramarital affair, kept pressing Rita for details as to her husband's whereabouts. Rita finally relented but only told Hedda about the telephone call from Roosevelt. In her column the next day, Hedda announced to millions of her readers the fact that the President of the United States had called Rita Hayworth about the special work Orson was doing for him.

Orson was intensely gratified at Roosevelt's election to a fourth term and a few days after November 7, he was a luncheon guest, with hundreds of other campaign workers, at the White House, to celebrate the victory. Roosevelt wrote to Orson on November 25 and thanked him for his help. "I may be a prejudiced spectator who had a special interest in the action," his letter said, "but I want to thank you for the splendid role you played in the recent campaign. I cannot recall any campaign in which actors and artists were so effective in the unrehearsed reality of the drama of the American future. It was a great show, in which you played a great part."

WHILE WINDING UP the Roosevelt campaign, Welles in New York had received a cable from William Goetz, the producer of *Jane Eyre,* who wanted him for the lead in a film that was going to be produced by a new motion picture company then just being formed, International Pictures.* The title was *Tomorrow Is Forever,* Claudette Colbert was the female lead, and Orson's acting fee, should he accept, would be $20,000. Although the money was much lower than he thought he was worth, or he felt he could get doing other films, after reading the script he decided to take the part. His tour for Roosevelt, paid out of his own pocket, had cost him close to $10,000 and his coffers were precariously low. In a matter of days, he was back in Hollywood and working before the cameras.

Tomorrow Is Forever was the sort of women's movie that postwar audiences loved. It was released in February of 1946. The supporting cast of George Brent, Lucille Watson, Richard Long, Natalie Wood, Sonny Howe, and John Wengraf played to Welles and Colbert. The film was based on a dramatic and, some thought, stirring novel by Gwen Bristow; the script was written by Lenore Coffee. Goetz appointed David Lewis as producer and Irving Pichel, an actor-director best known for *The Moon Is Down,* directed. The film was cleverly edited by Ernest Nims.

The plot depicts a situation that was by no means rare at the time: a lieutenant who had been reported killed in the war returns to find that his wife has married another man. John McDonald (Welles), a chemist, had been married to Elizabeth (Colbert) for only a few months when he decided to enlist in World War I. Shortly before Christmas, Elizabeth receives a telegram from the War Department informing her that John has been killed in action in France. Afterward, she discovers that she is pregnant. A coworker, Larry Hamilton (Brent), takes Elizabeth to the home of his Aunt Jessie where she

*Later, International Pictures combined with Universal Pictures to form the mammoth Universal International studios.

will receive the attention she needs. During Elizabeth's pregnancy Larry visits her often, falls in love, and soon marries her. Larry comes to love Elizabeth's son as his own; not long afterward another son is born.

The years pass happily for the family until, twenty years later, John's son, Drew, announces that he is concerned about the unrest in Europe and wants to enlist in the Royal Canadian Air Force. Elizabeth is extremely upset by the news, fearing that she may lose another loved one to the war, and forbids Drew to go. Meanwhile, Larry has brought home one of his employees, an expert chemist whom he has placed in charge of his research laboratory. The man has come from Austria, accompanied by a seven-year-old girl who has been orphaned by the war and is now in his charge.

Elizabeth is unaccountably disturbed by the presence of this man, who had plastic surgery and who calls himself Erich Kessler. When, on Kessler's second visit, he encourages Drew's interest in the war, Elizabeth tells him she never wants him to visit their home again. Elizabeth begins to suspect that Kessler is really her first husband, John, and confronts him with her suspicion. Kessler denies it. A few days later, Drew runs away from home to join the RCAF, and Elizabeth calls upon Kessler to help her. Kessler finds Drew and persuades him to return home. Now convinced that Kessler is actually John, Elizabeth once again questions him, showing him old mementos she has kept over the years. Kessler, knowing that she has been very happy with Larry, and unwilling to destroy their marriage, once more emphatically denies the charge. The film ends with Elizabeth recognizing her selfishness and agreeing to Drew's enlistment. Kessler, seemingly weakened by the ordeal of the past few days, dies, leaving the child, Margaret, to be adopted into the home of Larry and Elizabeth.

The film was absorbing and, for the most part, favorably received although at least one critic slammed the plot as "preposterous." Claudette Colbert, in particular, was praised for her acting skills, especially by female critics. Welles as Kessler, dressed in a dark, three-piece suit, graying hair and beard, horn-rimmed glasses, and with his own nose, received adequate critical attention, although most, but not all, objected to what they considered his overblown and rococo style. Actually, of all the characters that Orson would play on the screen, his Erich Kessler was the most moderate and gentle.

At the beginning of the film, Welles in a false nose, appears in a flashback sequence where he bears a strong resemblance to Charles Foster Kane in his earlier years; it is possible that Pichel was trying to capitalize on the success of *Citizen Kane.*

The anonymous review in *Time* was a fairly accurate appraisal of the film:

> Cinemactress Colbert, moving beautifully gowned through a series of handsome sets, manages to convey the idea that she cannot quite pierce the Wellesian disguise of beard, limp and heavy Teutonic accent. Welles himself, posing as an Austrian scientist, does a far more skilled job of characterization than the creaky plot and prevailing platitudes warrant.

Bosley Crowther, in *The New York Times,* wrote that the best way to take the picture was as "a straight piece of Hollywood taffy, slightly saline and gooey clear through."

ON A TRIP to New York to make a radio appearance at that time, Orson met Robert Hall of the *New York Post* who tempted him with the idea of doing a column for the newspaper, with the hope of having it eventually going into syndication. Hall had read some of Orson's guest columns for Leonard Lyons, written in 1943 and 1944, and was impressed with his stories about topics as diverse as Clark Gable and magic and circuses and the Irish stage. The subject matter for this new column would be whatever Orson so chose: politics; arts, entertainment, even philosophy. Orson immediately snapped up the proposal.

A few of the more highly successful syndicated columnists in the United States were known to make high six-figure salaries. The syndicate that handled a column would negotiate with each newspaper individually, based on such factors as exclusivity of area, circulation, and other matters, and whatever fee was agreed upon would be split 50-50 between the syndicate and the columnist. It was possible for some nationally famous columnists to realize a *weekly* income of $20,000 and to be read by over 50 million readers. The idea of making such constant "bread-and-butter" money and the concept of wielding such influence was manna to Orson, and he became as enthusiastic about it as any project he had ever worked on.

He was to be paid $200 a week against the syndication fees that would eventually come in from newspapers around the country. Hall believed that the column would probably net, at its optimum, around $80,000.

As a starting point, Orson gathered the works of as many columnists (such as Dorothy Thompson, Marquis Childs, Walter Lippmann, Mark Hellinger, and Walter Winchell) as he could and attempted to study, not so much their styles, as the kind of information and the depth of the commentary that appeared in their work. Upon some additional investigation, he determined that most of the better columnists subscribed to research services or employed investigators who would furnish most, if not all, the information that eventually made its way into the column. Orson immediately subscribed to several "insider" services. Most of the money that Orson received for the column at first went into the researchers' pockets. He considered it as an investment.

Writing under the title "Orson Welles' Almanac," and with a small photo of himself inserted in the logo, the column began in late January 1945. In addition to the *New York Post,* it was also carried in such fine newspapers as the St. Louis *Post-Dispatch* and the Detroit *News.* In an interview about his new writing career, Orson said: "The column is so important that I plan to devote all my time to it as soon as I can. I've given up all my Hollywood work except to act in one picture each year." At the time, he meant it.

His first columns were a potpourri of political comments (about the impending Cold War, for example); attacks against Hearst's favorite columnist, Westbrook Pegler (who had verbally assaulted Frank Sinatra, a friend of Orson's); excerpts from the *Farmer's Almanac*; astrological asides; a little news, bordering on gossip, about celebrities; and even household and cooking hints. He wrote about people and ideas: film director Sacha Guitry being tried for collaboration with the Nazis; a joint review and analysis of *Ivan the Terrible* and *Wilson* ("Because of the inferiority of Russian film stock, lenses, and other equipment, the camera must assert itself by what it selects, and by the manner of selection. The Hollywood camera has a merchant's eye and spends its time lovingly evaluating texture, the screen being filled as a window is dressed in a swank department store. We have much to learn from each other."). He discussed the acting styles of Henry Irving and John Barrymore; criticized German newspapers; lambasted the "snobbishness" of the National Academy of Arts and Sciences awards as "foolish"; explained the actor's role in society; and championed the painting of Ignacio Zuloaga.

Occasionally, he would use less than ethical journalistic practices, such as describing an event before it happened. One column, written three days before the 1945 presidential inauguration, but published two days after it, told how Franklin Roosevelt "played his part in the ritual like a veteran bridegroom."

As he continued to write, his columns consisted more and more of his personal political theses, indicated by a strong liberalism and a championing of New Deal legislation. When FDR died in April, Orson was devastated and consequently changed the title of the column to "Orson Welles Today" to symbolize the pertinence of his commentary. His political outcries became even louder.

The column was difficult for Orson to complete each week, despite his claim that he would reduce his participation in film projects: he still continued to rummage about for a film or two to do. But the column ate into his time, he fell behind in deadlines, and Robert Hall began to send berating telegrams to get him to deliver.

Although his readership in New York City seemed to be high, the column never really caught on in the more conservative parts of the country. Some other newspapers in the Midwest took it for a short period, but irate letters from their readers forced them to drop Orson's column. Welles's liberalism (he talked of the "phony fear of Communism" for example, and of "America's complacent moral superiority") was just not acceptable to a large portion of their reading public. Hall attempted to get Orson to write more about Hollywood and show business, but Orson insisted on keeping up the political tone of the column.

Six months after it started, Orson's column was dropped by the *Post* and the syndicate, Robert Hall claiming that he had no hope for it and that it was "losing money." Orson made no attempt at selling it to another syndicate and permanently abandoned his career as a columnist.

AFTER COMPLETING HIS six-week acting job in *Tomorrow Is Forever,* Welles arranged to direct a film for International Pictures, *The Stranger,* ironically to be distributed by RKO. In an interview he gave at that time, he confessed: "I wanted to do a film to prove to the industry that I could direct a standard Hollywood picture, on time and on budget, just like anyone else." The rationale was more immediate. William Goetz, at that time a Welles supporter, wanted to establish a long-term working relationship with Orson but like everyone else in Hollywood he had become intimidated by the *It's All True* affair. Goetz promised Orson that if he could bring in *The Stranger* within deadline and on or under the budget, he would sign a four-picture deal with him to produce, direct, and star in films to be exclusively of Orson's choosing. To act in and direct *The Stranger,* Orson was to receive $50,000. The money arrangement for the four other films was open to negotiation. Orson grabbed it.

Sam Spiegel, the Polish-born protégé of Harry Cohn, was to be producer. Traditionally there was no room for argument or discussion with Spiegel on any details concerning a film. There was only one way: the Spiegel way. As strong as Orson often appeared to be, he knew that he would have to defer to Spiegel's directives, and he did.

Edward G. Robinson and Loretta Young were to be Orson's costars. The film would serve to launch Hollywood's postwar spy cycle, a genre that was supposed to indicate what really happened, or could have, during the war, e.g., *Notorious, Cloak and Dagger,* and *Hotel Berlin.*

In *The Stranger,* a Nazi leader, Franz Kindler (Orson Welles), one whose picture never got into the papers, escapes to a small town in Connecticut and sets himself up as a teacher in a prep school. He weds a local beauty, Mary Longstreet (Loretta Young), and starts secretly preparing for the Fourth Reich, which includes murdering anybody who knows his true identity. Pursuing him is a detective of the Allied War Crimes Commission, Inspector Wilson (Edward G. Robinson). Kindler plots the murder of Mary, but she is saved by the astute sleuthing and aggressiveness of Wilson.

The Stranger was a totally atypical Wellesian project. No one who worked on the film can remember any special anecdotes or problems concerning it. Welles wrote to film writer Peter Cowie years later that two reels that covered specific narrative that took place in South America were the best in the film. Spiegel, however, arbitrarily had it edited out of the finished film. Ernest Nims, one of the editors, has since stated that he personally did extensive script editing, cutting out some thirty-two pages before the film began to shoot, albeit with Orson's approval.

During the making of *The Stranger,* Orson was on a severe diet to keep his weight down and would receive Dr. Lee Spiegel every morning in the middle of shooting, drop his pants, accept a hypodermic diet shot into his buttocks, and continue directing. By the end of this film he was his thinnest in years.

He was forced to follow the Anthony Veiller script religiously. Then at the end of the day he would watch the daily rushes and retire to his studio bungalow with as many people from the cast and crew as possible for an extended cocktail hour. It usually consisted, according to those who attended, of his traditional magic tricks and prolonged and purple conversations.

Sometimes he would sleep in the bungalow and not go home to his own house. Although Orson and Rita Hayworth had been married for only three years, their relationship was deteriorating. Orson moved out of his own house and stayed for awhile with friends, such as Georgie Jessel, on a rotation basis. His constant visitor on-and-off the set was sultry singer-actress Lena Horne who was then acting in an MGM film *Ziegfeld Follies*.

Welles has said, since the making of *The Stranger*—which he completed one day *before* schedule and *under* budget—that nothing in the film was his, this despite the fact that the unmistakable Wellesian moods, shadows, acute angles, and depth-of-focus shots are pervasive. Within the film is a second film, another Wellesian touch, consisting of snatches of documentary footage showing Nazi atrocities.

Bosley Crowther's *New York Times* review combined some irony and truth: "At the end, Mr. Welles, puffing wildly and sweating at every pore, is impaled on a sword held by a figure atop a church, a critic, no doubt. We say that because the performance of Mr. Welles in the title role is one of the less convincing features of the film."

Crowther was not the only Welles iconoclast. Others called his acting "boyishly bad," "weak," and suggested that "Director Welles might have hinted to actor Welles once or twice that he was inclined to overdo the glaring eyes and the other bogeyman tricks." Directing others might have also been a problem. Edward G. Robinson wrote of the film in his memoirs, *All My Yesterdays:* "I made a picture called *The Stranger* for RKO, directed by Orson Welles. Orson has genius but in this film it seems to have run out. It was bloodless and so was I."

The apathetic reviews of *The Stranger* quickly eroded Orson's commitment to film once again. He was criticized for copying Hitchcock's *Shadow of a Doubt,* which *The Stranger* does in fact, resemble. It had just recently been released when he gave the following statement to *The New York Times*:

> I do not like being an actor and I don't acknowledge the existence of a job called producer. The only thing I like in films is directing. I think pictures are in a bad way. They need revitalizing. They are in the Fred Waring stage and have no Toscaninis. We should have theaters financed by the Government for private film experimentation and a chain of adult theaters free from Hays Office code censorship. Films dealing with serious and important subjects should be produced, even if the big boys have to be taxed for them.
>
> No matter how bad the Broadway stage gets it will always represent a great art form. If it withers and dies, the movies will die with it. An actor cannot learn anything in a movie studio and should return occasionally to the stage to learn through his public. It might be a big gamble for some of the top players, but haven't they been virtually talking for years through a tube?

Perhaps Orson sensed what was coming and knew he had to leave California and that was why he issued such a pro-legitimate stage comment.

Within a few weeks after the completion of *The Stranger,* Goetz backed out of his promised four-picture deal with Welles. No explanation was offered except the inference that it looked as though *The Stranger* would fail to make money. Goetz, apparently was no longer interested in Welles's vision. Welles was growing less interested in Hollywood's.

ORSON'S FASCINATION WITH the story of *Around the World in 80 Days* by Jules Verne went back as far as the late 1920s when he saw a rough-hewn stage adaptation of it in the Midwest. He elected it as one of the first shows, in 1938, of the "Mercury Theatre on the Air"; and in 1939, he had broadcast another version on "The Campbell Playhouse," in celebration of Howard Hughes's feat of piloting his twin engine monoplane, *World's Fair, 1939,* 15,000 miles around the globe in three days. Six years later in a short-lived series (for Orson) called "This Is My Best," he did still another radio adaptation of it.*

As a stage play, the story had everything that Welles might enjoy in a dramatic production: comedy, elaborate technical pyrotechniques, a circus, dancing girls, and magic. It was fast-paced and if done the way he envisioned, it could be something like a lunatic asylum at the height of an electrical storm, perhaps a perfect expression of Orson's mental and emotional state at that place in time or, as Orson described the tale, "a gaudy old melodrama from our youngest days with equal parts of plot and pluck."

In his early days at RKO, he had tried to interest George Schaefer in doing a film of the novel but had had no success. Casting about in late 1945 and in early 1946 for his next major project, he retrieved his screenplay of *Around the World in 80 Days,* did a fast stage adaptation of it, and began to approach various theatrical producers to see whether he could raise enough capital to put it on in the legitimate theater.

It wasn't necessary to look far. Mike Todd, the flamboyant theatrical producer responsible for such staged extravaganzas as *The Hot Mikado,* a jazz version of the Gilbert and Sullivan operetta, and various hits such as *Something for the Boys* and *Mexican Hayride,* had been interested in working with Orson Welles for years. Without much persuasion needed on Orson's part, both agreed that *Around the World* could and would be a sensation. Todd agreed to back him.

Although both men were attracted to spectacular theater, they also discussed collaboration on more literary projects. Todd had produced *Hamlet* in 1945. Flushed with success, he followed that up with a version of Molière's

---

*"This Is My Best" was a dramatic radio showcase, similar to those Welles had done in the past and in the time he was involved with it, he produced and directed such stories as *The Diamond as Big as the Ritz, The Master of Ballantrae,* and what was to become a standard for him, *Heart of Darkness.* He was peremptorily dismissed from the show without notice or official explanation because of a personality conflict with one of the agency account executives over what was thought of as Orson's conflict of interests. He wanted to do a radio version of *Don't Catch Me,* a property he eventually hoped to sell as a film, and was accused of choosing the story to satisfy his own aims and not because it was "good radio."

The Would-be Gentleman. Welles had long been interested in Bertolt Brecht's brilliant but thus-yet-to-be-produced *The Life of Galileo,* upon which the latter had collaborated with Charles Laughton. Todd now also became intrigued with producing it, and agreement was reached with Brecht and Laughton that, at the conclusion of *Around the World,* production would begin with Laughton playing the title role, Todd producing the play, and Welles serving as director. Both *Around the World* and *Galileo* would be Mercury productions and under Orson's total creative authority. Serious discussions also took place about a Welles-Todd production of *King Lear,* with Orson directing and acting as the mythical tyrant.

Stage versions of *Around the World in 80 Days* were almost as old as the 1873 novel. Two years after its initial publication, Jules Verne himself collaborated on a dramatic version, which opened in London and played in Paris and New York. Every decade or so since then, each generation of producers and playgoers has rediscovered it. Life also imitated the play and story. Thirteen years after publication, a young New York newspaperwoman, Nellie Bly, promptly set off to see if she could equal the time used in the fictional trip and ended up beating par by three days. Twenty-five years later, a Chicago police chief, a friend of Orson's father, made the trek in just over sixty days.

The story line: one day at a gentlemen's club in London, Phileas Fogg, an unemotional and fastidious Englishman, wagers that he can circle the world in eighty days and with clocklike precision report back to the club at a specified time. Accompanied by his valet, Passepartout, and Detective Fix—appointed by the club to verify Fogg's progress and movements—he starts out on his improbable journey. He is confronted with a series of incredible adventures and forbidding escapades, all obstacles that he meets and solves with the stiff upper lip of traditional British aplomb. He travels to Egypt, India, through the American Rockies, Hong Kong, and dozens of other places by boat, train, balloon, bicycle, elephant, and any other conveyance that he can commandeer, and finally ends up back in London. He nonchalantly walks into the club, as the waiting members look at their watches, ten minutes before schedule. "Gentlemen, I am here."

Orson's growing philosophy of entertainment, as displayed by the Mercury Wonder Show and "The Orson Welles Almanac," was that more was better. If a production had many elements, numerous effects of different kinds, then it would be altogether possible, conjectured Orson, that the audience would find *something* of pleasure in the production. It was with this theory of pan art, incorporating music, drama, dance, film, and even a circus, that he began to assemble the elements of his stage version of *Around the World in 80 Days.*

For once, he tried to be sensible as to how much, emotionally, he could put of himself into one project. Although he had played Phileas Fogg on the air three times and had always intended to play him if the story ever reached stage or film, it was too demanding of a role to be confronted while one directed. Fogg was on stage in every scene throughout a projected three hours. A British actor, just from Hollywood *(Random Harvest, Sherlock Holmes Faces Death),* Arthur Margetson, who had recently suffered a flop in the stage play *Little Brown Jug,* was signed on for the lead. Margetson was known to American stage audiences for his roles in *Charley's Aunt* and *Life with Father.*

The idea of the logistics of mounting the show was to open it in Boston, travel to New Haven and Philadelphia, and then make a triumphal entry on Broadway. "A musical extravaganza," Welles called it in all advertising and publicity.

The play would require fifty-five stagehands to maneuver and manipulate the thirty-six scenes that Welles had written. There would be a Hindu temple with a live elephant and burning incense. A complete Japanese circus with real acrobats and a magic act was to be included on stage. Also, a train racing over a bridge in Utah would be somehow constructed; a platoon of marines would march across the stage; a larger-than-life-sized eagle would pluck Fogg from danger and carry him off high into the wings. Orson saw the play as a toy shop at midnight with the toys coming alive, an evening of inspired high jinks, a George M. Cohan and Cecil B. DeMille spectacular all rolled into one.

Todd felt that the play must be considered a high-grade musical comedy. Two seasons previously, he had had a smash success with Cole Porter as composer in his *Something for the Boys,* which starred Ethel Merman. Welles had been warned, however, by friends in the theater, that Porter had been written out, that he really had no songs left in him at that time. When Welles mentioned this to Todd, the latter scoffed and insisted that Porter be hired. Welles was forced to acquiesce.

Rehearsals started in Boston in the spring of 1946. Nelson Barclift did the choreography, Arvin Colt designed the costumes (some two hundred were needed), and Barbette, the famous French female impersonator, was signed on as both director of the circus and trapeze performer.* In addition to Margetson, Welles put some quasi-Mercurians in the cast: Mary Healey, Larry Laurence, Stefan Schnabel, Guy Spaull, Brainerd Duffield, and Julie Warren. Richard Wilson was the stage manager and Welles's loyal valet-chauffeur, Shorty, would serve as general factotum.

Almost from the first rehearsal there were difficulties. The complicated stage business and movements took hours to perfect, with actors, dancers, stagehands, and orchestra all having to master split second timing. Performers and crew were asked to be on hand for ten to twelve hours—sometimes more—each day, and the overtime charges began to mount. As in *Five Kings,* there was hardly a rehearsal that went from the beginning to the end of the play as written: only acts or parts of acts could be managed in a rehearsal in any one session.

At one point during rehearsals, about ten days before opening night, Todd, in the dark at the back of the theater, was watching Orson direct. The scene at

---

*Barbette also took on all the backstage ironing of the cast's shirts and blouses. "If I don't do it, I don't know who will," he bitched.

hand was in an Oklahoma oil field, and Welles was explaining that during the actual play, at the most dramatic moment, one of the oil wells would begin to spout and everyone—and their costumes—would be covered with the black gold. Todd was on his feet in a second, striding down the aisle to the front of the house. "An oil well on stage?" he shouted to Orson. "Are you crazy? How will we clean the costumes after the show? We'll have to have two or three costumes for every performer!"

Orson at first tried to dismiss Todd's irritation as trivial, saying that the cleaning bills would be insignificant, but Todd was adamant. "The whole idea is ridiculous and impractical," he said. And then, as quickly as he invested, Todd announced his abdication as backer and producer. "I'm sorry, Orson, but I've decided I simply can't afford you. The show is yours from this moment on." Welles tried reasoning with him. "You can't quit now," Orson said. "You've already invested $38,000."

Todd hardly smiled: "The way you're operating, by tomorrow, it will be $48,000." Todd left the theater in a huff and consequently relinquished all interests in the show with the exception of the film rights of Cole Porter's musical score.

With a $5,000-a-week payroll to meet, plus all kinds of other expenses, Orson was in desperate financial trouble—about $350,000 worth to be specific—before he even opened *Around the World*.

He managed to sell the screen rights to the play to Alexander Korda for a God-discovered $100,000, but this income could not be advanced until production on the film actually began. Small investments came in from Toots Shor for $5,000, and Shorty, Orson's valet, broke into his life savings and relinquished another $5,000; of course, all of Orson's personal radio and lecture income immediately went into bracing the play.

Somehow, with these amounts, rehearsals continued, but with only days before opening, a major financial crisis had to be confronted and solved. The costumes, hundreds of them, had arrived in Boston by rail and were waiting to be claimed at South Station. In addition to the period costumes of all the nations through which Fogg would travel on stage, there were large supplies of wigs, shoes, stockings, gloves, hats, all accessories, even jewelry for the entire cast. When the notice came to the theater that the material had arrived in Boston, Welles had a truck dispatched to the railway immediately. The cast had been practicing for weeks without costumes and with only a few days to go before curtain time, it was imperative that dress rehearsals begin immediately.

There was one problem: the costume rental bill came to $25,000, and the trunks and trunks of wardrobes, and the other accompanying supplies, would not be given over to the Welles company until payment in full was received. When Orson was called at the theater and informed of the cash-on-delivery dilemma, he could see the play vanishing into extinction. He knew he could conjure up a few thousand dollars on demand but could not envision raising the entire amount even in a matter of days.

A call by Orson from the theater's box office to the manager of the Brookes company in New York was unfruitful: if full payment was not forthcoming, the costumes would be returned to Manhattan right away.

Orson began to place panic-stricken calls all over the country to determine if someone, anyone, would lend or invest the money to bail out the costumes; if not, the play would not open. L. Arnold Weissberger, Orson's attorney, told him he would see if he could find anyone in New York theatrical circles who might be interested; he was not however, hopeful. It was a large amount of money; such a risky investment would have to be considered philanthropy by most people. Financial arrangements of this kind could not be maneuvered with great speed.

Orson started calling most of the Hollywood producers and moneyed movie people he had ever met, even including some with whom he shared a mutual disrespect, to see whether he could raise the costume ransom. Eventually, he called Goetz, Spiegel, Selznick, Goldwyn, and Lasky. Some were impossible to reach, others claimed that they never invested in the theater. Almost ready to give up, he submerged his pride and tried one more call: to Harry Cohn. Even though he and Cohn were barely on speaking terms ever since the Mercury Wonder Show incident—"He looked like a gargoyle off of a spire on Notre Dame," Orson said of Cohn somewhat affectionately— Orson had learned from Rita that she had informally petitioned Cohn to let her star in a Columbia film directed by her estranged husband. She had asked Cohn to hire Orson because she believed it might save her marriage; it would also help Orson's career. She knew he was having financial woes; and she believed that, creatively and opportunistically, Orson might, perhaps, force a performance from her that she was incapable of giving to other directors. Cohn was cautious. On Rita's request, however, he began making inquiries, specifically to Sam Spiegel, to see whether he believed that Orson could bring a movie to completion within budget and on time. (In an interview I conducted with Spiegel in the early 1980s, he claimed that he told Cohn at that time that Orson could be trusted.)

When Orson called Cohn, Cohn was already receptive to the idea of hiring him. The story goes—told by Orson—that as he was dialing from the box office, without knowing exactly what he was going to say, he spied in front of the girl who was selling tickets a paperback copy of a mystery novel, *If I Die Before I Wake* by Sherwood King. The blurb on the jacket showed an illustration of a beautiful woman with a smoking gun in her hand; a young, somewhat rugged and good-looking man is standing nearby. As Cohn's California number began to ring, Orson thumbed through the book. The opening line caught his attention: "'Sure,' I said, 'I would commit murder. If I had to, of course, or if it was worth my while.'"

When Cohn finally answered, Welles told him of his uphill predicament— the need for $25,000 in order to retrieve the costumes. "Harry, I've just read a book," Orson lied. "It's called *If I Die Before I Wake*. It has a marvelous part for Rita and a good one for me. If you buy the rights, I'll direct and write it for free . . . if you can lend me $25,000 right away."

Cohn knew it wasn't really a loan but an investment in Orson's unpredictable future. To get Orson Welles to create a film for $25,000, however, was a bargain in any event. "When do you need it?" Cohn asked. "In two hours," Orson replied.

The money was on its way.*

What Orson couldn't know was that Cohn didn't need to buy the rights of *If I Die Before I Wake*: he already owned them. By pure coincidence, William Castle, the director of *The Whistler* series, had previously bought the rights for $500 shortly after the novel first appeared in 1938 to use as a possible story for his series; he had subsequently sold them to Cohn with the promise that if a film was ever made, he would be the director or else involved in some other way with the project.

WITH THE COSTUMES out of hock, Orson proceeded with the final rehearsals. He believed that after the play opened in Boston and the other try-out cities, and box office income started to accrue, he'd have enough to pay the cast, crew, and orchestra until he reached New York.

In addition to the dozens of spectacular stage effects planned, Orson had one other idea that he was going to incorporate into the play: a film. As with his experience with *Too Much Johnson* and the *Green Goddess,* he felt that adding a motion picture to a live presentation helped to bridge narrative gaps in a stage play that were inherent in the physical limitation of the theater itself. Films within plays also served to show the director's intentions in the setting of mood. Also it was fairly unusual to see a film as a part of a play, and anything that could be considered so singular was to Orson, in itself, a justification for its inclusion.

The weekend before *Around the World* opened, Orson whisked the principal members of the cast to New York, specifically to a small, quiet, and obscure street in the Bronx, where the famed Edison Studios had been in operation since being constructed by the inventor in 1904. Known as New York's oldest active film studio, the Edison workshop was tiny by Hollywood standards but steeped in history. In 1907, D. W. Griffith had stepped out of obscurity and acted in a bloodcurdling one-reeler there, *The Eagle's Nest.* In the decades since then, literally thousands of Westerns, serials, shorts, and features were produced behind the Edison doors. Orson was attracted to the historical ambience of the place even though by the time he arrived in 1946 most of the films being produced there were three-minute musical numbers that could be seen by the public by dropping a dime in a "panorama machine" and known as "soundies," a form of cinema jukebox. "Soundies" were something of an unenthusiastic fad throughout the postwar years.

There were two major scenes that Welles decided to film in the Bronx for the staged *Around the World*: the story at the beginning of the play where a well-dressed gentleman had calmly picked up £55,000 in the Bank of England and absconded with it (Detective Fix believes that Phileas Fogg is the bank

*Ultimately, William Goetz also loaned him $7,500 to help the play.

robber); and Fogg, Passepartout, and Molly aboard the steamer *Rangoon* during the violent hurricane.

Welles had rented the Edison studios for one day only, starting at 8:00 A.M. on a Saturday. The idea was to create the film as a "silent" (as he did with his two previous film-for-stage adventures) and narrate it himself from backstage, his voice to be amplified over the theater's loudspeaker system.

Working hurriedly with a small cluster of carpenters and painters, the interior of the Bank of England was instantly created: it consisted of cages, desks, windows for tellers, and the like, and people going about engaged in bank business.

Then came a more ambitious filming of the storm-tossed *Rangoon*. A tilting platform with a ship's bridge was constructed. It was close to 11:00 P.M. by the time the bank scenes were filmed and the sets disassembled and the *Rangoon* constructed. Welles and his actors had just one hour to film the segment: the ship being tossed and turned by the sea; Molly falling overboard and being saved by Passepartout, and the two men tying her to the mast for safety.

Welles wanted the three actors to walk off balance with storm-produced sea legs, even more than they were doing as a result of the constantly tilting platform. When he couldn't get the uninhibited loss of equilibrium that he sought, he sent one of his assistants to the local liquor store to return with a case of 150-proof Irish whiskey. "Drink," commanded Orson of the actors, before the cameras started. "You're going to be covered by water from the storm and you'll catch cold otherwise."

After each quick rehearsal, Orson ordered yet another drink. "Alcohol! Inside and out," yelled Orson. "Another, dear children, have another!" Eventually, all three actors were truly off balance and walked aboard the ship's deck the way that Orson wanted. Finally, with fans blowing, hoses running, and a corps of assistants armed with buckets of water to drench the set whenever needed, Orson commenced: "Action!" Arthur Margetson had recalled: "What with the water splashing full force *on* us and the whiskey sloshing full force *in* us, it was difficult to hold on to the platform. I really thought I was going to be killed; but at every moment Orson would be yelling, 'Yes, my darlings, that's it, my dears!'"

At the exact stroke of midnight, Cinderella Welles had the footage he wanted, despite the makeshift sets and obvious props: a realistic film of the adventures on the storm-tossed *Rangoon*. With Julie Warren, Arthur Margetson, and Larry Laurence water-and-whiskey soaked, threatening to burst into refrains of "Show Me the Way to Go Home," Orson ordered Shorty to drive them to Manhattan and have them ensconced in a hotel for a night until they were patched up. They were due back in Boston the following day with *Around the World* scheduled to open that night. Other scenes were shot in Boston, a fully orchestrated Keystonian chase, with the actors cavorting among the benches on the Common. Eventually, five full scenes were filmed and used in the play, about thirty minutes of projection time in total.

The span between the calamitous Philadelphia opening of *Five Kings* in 1938 and the Boston debut of *Around the World* was hardly eight years, but Orson had been through a mini-lifetime of showmanship in the interval. It is difficult to know, therefore, why he could not foresee the difficulties that lay ahead with *Around the World*; he would have to face some of the same problems of logistics that plagued him with *Five Kings*.

Opening night was a disaster. The stagehands were as visible during the performance as they were in rehearsal; the painted backdrop of London, which was to be lowered on the cue, "Is this London?" turned out to be a view of the Rocky Mountains. Other cues were confused or missed, lines were forgotten, sets tumbled. The audience howled, but derisively. When the prop eagle was supposed to swoop down to carry Fogg off, it arrived and departed very slowly, pitifully flapping its bogus wings as clumsily as a flying elephant. It added little to the excitement of the moment. It took over three hours to complete the play and then only because Orson did some on-the-spot wholesale excisions of entire scenes.

The reviews were, as expected, terrible. Somehow, Orson was undaunted. "Now that we've read the roasts, we can really get down to some work," he told the cast and crew. He then attempted to hone the play into something worthwhile.

The New Haven opening was reminiscent of the Pittsburgh *Green Goddess* fiasco. The introductory film came on out of focus and then went black altogether. Another try went awry. Orson appeared on the stage in what seemed to be becoming an eternal Wellesian pose and began: "Ladies and gentlemen, I'm so sorry. I will try to explain how this play, or whatever you want to call it, commences..." and thus he followed with a description of the events that were to be seen in the film. "It is obvious," he concluded with cynical humor, "as most of us stage actors have already believed for some time now, that the movies are not here to stay."

Orson could not resist taking some performing part, and at first all he did was a seven-minute skit as the Great Foo San, duplicating almost exactly some of the illusions he had performed in the Mercury Wonder Show and *Follow the Boys* and wearing the same black-and-white silk robe he had retained from the tent show. As the play progressed, however, he took over the role of Dick Fix and also created a new character, not found in the original Verne story, Dynamite Gus, a wild and woolly badman of the West, dressed in a red undershirt, suspenders, and sporting a padded stomach. After that, like Fogg, it seemed that Orson was on stage almost continually. It's possible that if he had stuck to his original intention of remaining only the director, the play might have tied together more cohesively.

With the Mike Todd financial backing withdrawn from Orson's Mercury efforts, Brecht and Laughton were concerned about the fate of *Galileo*. Todd was still interested in producing it; Orson made it disagreeably clear that it would be impossible to work with Todd under any circumstances. He still wanted to direct *Galileo*, however, and perhaps produce it himself should

Around the World realize the profit he hoped it would. Whenever Laughton contacted him, however, Orson would procrastinate in making a decision. Finally, Brecht and Laughton decided on action: they would work with Todd but wanted Orson's talents, also. In a final letter to Orson, Laughton stated:

> You are the best man in the world to put the Church of Rome on the stage, to mention only one aspect of the play. This appears to me to matter. Cannot this important thing between you and Todd be worked out? Todd has never spoken ill of you to either of us. The strongest word he had used is "afraid." That also is nonsense when there is a play to be told.
>
> > Brecht greets you,
> > Charles

Charles Higham, in his biography *Charles Laughton,* explains what happened next: "Welles did not reply to the letter. Annoyed that Charles insisted that Todd be involved in the production, and no longer talking to Todd by late July, he backed out of *Galileo* once and for all. In a sense, Charles was relieved: he could tolerate Welles no longer."*

By the time *Around the World* reached Philadelphia there had been so many mishaps and reverse intentions, so many untoward adventures and major and minor debacles on stage, that Orson was half-seriously claiming that a hex, an evil eye, a double whammy, or a black magic incantation was plaguing the show. On opening night in Philadelphia he approached the footlights *before* the play began and started apologizing for all the things he was *sure* would go wrong. Naturally, that night the play proceeded with the precision of a Swiss watch, the only problem being the lack of a sizable audience owing to the dual train and newspaper strike crippling the city of brotherly love.

Around the World opened to a packed house at the newly air conditioned—although not yet installed on that night—Adelphi Theatre in New York on Memorial Day weekend in 1946. Orson had an amplifier hooked up in his dressing room during rehearsals and also used it later, so that when he was getting dressed and applying makeup for each of his three roles, he could hear what was happening—and the audience's reaction to it—on stage. If the stage business was not to his liking, the offending actor or actors were warned.

Just days after opening, Orson had started a new radio series, the "Mercury Summer Theatre on the Air," sponsored by Pabst Blue Ribbon beer; it consisted of plays and dramas that had already been broadcast in the past by the Mercury. Orson chose an almost exclusively musical version of *Around*

---

*Galileo finally opened in Los Angeles on July 30, 1947, backed by Todd, directed by one of Orson's old detractors, Joseph Losey, and produced—bitter pill for Orson—by two Mercury refugees: Norman Lloyd and John Houseman. To show that there were no hard feelings on his part, however, Orson sent Lloyd, Houseman, Laughton, and Brecht personal telegrams of congratulations on opening night.

the World minus many scenes and much mileage, as his first program: "Tonight is one of the first things we ever put on the radio," he opened. "And by no coincidence, whatsoever, it is the very latest thing we've put on the stage. You can see it now on Broadway at the Adelphi Theatre, Sunday evenings included (here, Orson had to audibly laugh at himself for his blatant self-promotion)—and if you're one of our staunchest friends you'll remember it from among our first Mercury broadcasts."

With the radio plug and a few other major publicity outlets such as a three-page pictorial feature in *Life* magazine, *Around the World* played to filled houses and received, for the most part, enthusiastic reviews. Billy Rose, however, in his syndicated column "Pitching Horseshoes," which appeared in the *New York Herald Tribune* and hundreds of other papers, wrote that he wished he was big enough to punch Orson in the nose, not that he didn't like him, but because *Around the World* was to him a small boy's dream of show business come true: "Isn't it about time that you made up your mind whether you are D. W. Griffith or Joel Kupferman, the Quiz Kid?" he asked Orson rhetorically.

Some additional critique fragments:

"Orson Welles has produced the most overstuffed conglomeration of circus, magic, movies, old-fashioned spectacle and penny peep shows that Broadway has seen since the day of Barnum's Museum."—*Life*

"The most exciting musical in years."—*New York Post*

"It's a damn good show, like nothing you've ever seen before."—*The New Yorker*

"It is wonderful, exciting and funny, and the most thorough and individual example of showmanship of the season, or of any season."—*New York Daily News*

"The State Legislature should pass a bill prohibiting Mr. Welles from leaving the theater. Excitement is needed on Broadway and he is the one who can give it."—*The New York Times*

When Robert Garland at the *World-Telegram* made mention of the fact that the show had "everything but the kitchen sink," Orson, ever eager to please, came to the footlights the next evening accompanied by a stagehand trundling out an enormous porcelain sink.

Despite the favorable balance of critical reaction, in total, *Around the World* barely survived the summer doldrums in mid-August and played to smaller and smaller audiences, trying to maintain itself until the traditionally more active Broadway theatrical season of the late fall.

As box office receipts dwindled, Orson's debts mounted. He was not able to cover all of his weekly expenses out of the income generated, and he continued to borrow, hoping for a miracle that the play would magically transform itself into an unqualified hit. Cole Porter agreed to waive his royalties for each of the musical numbers until the play began to prosper; unfortunately, the predictions about Porter's depleted song reserve proved true, at least for *Around the World*. With the exception of "Should I Tell You

I Love You?" hardly any song proved memorable. "No one walked out of the theater whistling any of the Cole Porter tunes," Welles later lamented.* Despite the musical disappointment, Porter proved a friend and gentleman; at one crucial juncture, he lent $2,500 to Orson so that an emergency bill could be paid.

Cash was so tight and Orson's personal income so intricately involved with the financial base of the show that he hardly ever had any pocket money. Margetson has remembered Orson being surreptitiously given a twenty-dollar bill every night, direct from the box office cash by Hugo Schauff, his theater manager. Richard Wilson, Orson's stage manager, disapproved of such financial circumvention: all box office income was to be deposited into the bank, strict records were to be kept, such "handouts," even to Orson, were prohibited. "What's that I saw?" Wilson once snapped after he spied Schauff slipping the nightly dole to Orson. "Did I see you give some money to Orson?" he asked. Schauff denied it. Orson had secretly passed the bill to Shorty. Everyone refused to recognize its existence. "It was amazing for me to see the expression on Orson's face when he finally outwitted Wilson and kept the twenty dollars," recalled Margetson. "He was like a small boy who believed he had outmaneuvered his arithmetic teacher."

The insinuation of irony in Orson's mendicant ways might not be as powerful as it first appears. *Around the World* was about to sink, and he was several hundreds of thousands of dollars in debt. Twenty dollars was twenty dollars even to an entrepreneur of Orson's stature. The play's overhead was running about $27,000 each week and the best gross income that it had had in any given week was barely $24,000. After seventy-four performances and severely diminishing audiences, Orson closed *Around the World* on August 3, 1946. The only material thing he had to show for it (he lost the sets and props when he couldn't pay the warehouse bill) were five hundred leftover programs. Sadly, he used them for his 1946 Christmas card. "This (the enclosed program) is a souvenir of the expensive reason why the (otherwise deliriously happy) O. Welles family cannot this year wish you Merry Christmas (!) with flowers or anything except this."

IN SPITE OF his latest defeat, and almost through a mass public instinct to keep the Wellesian spirit afloat, Orson began to be flooded with offers as soon as *Around the World* terminated its run. He closed out his New York affairs. To buoy himself—he had only six broadcasts to do before his "Mercury Summer Theatre on the Air" concluded—he elected to amuse his audience, and keep his own mettle high, by playing those roles that he felt would be most enjoyable. Departing from the announced original intention of the series only to use previously broadcast Mercury favorites, he finished his contract by doing plays over the air that were entirely new to him: he acted in Galswor-

---

*As luck would have it with Orson, Cole Porter's next musical was the historic smash hit *Kiss Me, Kate,* which ran for over one thousand performances.

thy's nostalgic romance *The Apple Tree*; played the tragically obsessive Captain Ahab in *Moby Dick*; and for his final show, offered scenes from *King Lear*.

The day after *Around the World* closed he received a telegram from the eminently successful Hollywood director Michael Curtiz, offering him a role in the mystery film *The Unsuspected*. The screenplay had been written with Orson in mind, an improbable story of a writer and producer of a radio crime series who commits what appears to be the perfect murder, then coolly reenacts it on the air. In a follow-up letter, Curtiz outlines his reasons for wanting Orson:

> I believe, too, that you will readily see that this character of Grandy was written with you specifically in mind. The man is an unusual, charming, suave, hypnotic individual with a touch of the genius about him and all of us feel that no one could bring him to the screen with the same finesse and understanding that you could give to the characterization.

Orson politely said he would consider *The Unsuspected*, but he really wanted to act *and* direct or just direct. Eventually, the role went to Claude Rains.

There was also talk, if not serious negotiation, about Orson directing a future Billy Rose stage spectacular, but no formal offer was made.

Serendipitously, Orson received an assignment from Decca, which he accepted, to do a series of recordings of famous speeches and readings. In a matter of days, he intoned such classics as Pericles' dedication of the battleground for soldiers killed in war; Lincoln's "Gettysburg Address"; and Zola's defense of Captain Dreyfus. Louis Untermeyer wrote later that the readings were eloquently interpreted by Orson. Orson was also eloquent in his thanks to the record producers; for his efforts, he earned a relatively speedy and desperately needed $10,000.

The ambivalence that Orson had toward returning to Hollywood—one moment he was avidly attempting to get back into pictures, the next he was making snide comments about his never doing another commercial film again—was reflected, in turn, by the film colony's mutability toward him. The doubters argued that the paradoxes were pure: Orson was a genius but he was unreliable, they said. He was the greatest film director in Hollywood, but he couldn't be trusted, clucked others. As an actor and a personality he ranked with Olivier, Tracy, or Gable but he was also thought of as an unmitigated ham. Nevertheless, it seemed that every time he appeared on national radio, or had a part in a film, offers to appear in other productions materialized as a result of the new publicity. Motion picture producers seemed to be discovering, abandoning, and then rediscovering Orson Welles on a week-to-week basis. The enormous press coverage that he received from *Around the World* and his most frequent radio work was the catalyst to film possibilities in the early fall of 1946. The proposals, too numerous to enumerate, poured in. Here is just a partial menu:

International Pictures wanted him to either act in or direct *Nightmare Alley,* a dark mystery about a magician; he had read the novel upon which it was based (and had reviewed it anonymously for *Variety*) but felt it was not right for him; the role went to Tyrone Power and proved to be among that actor's most memorable roles. He was asked to narrate the King Vidor film *Duel in the Sun,* starring Jennifer Jones, Gregory Peck, and his old friend Joseph Cotten, and he accepted the assignment, working in a Goldwyn sound studio to complete the job in one day (and asking that his name not be used in the credits; Selznick insisted that it appear however, claiming that it added dignity and believability to the film's image). A role in *Roads of Destiny,* an O. Henry story that never did get to the screen, was refused by Orson. He was offered the part of the Chevalier des Grieux in a possible production of *Manon Lescaut*: it seemed too indefinite and so he declined that, also. He also turned down an attempt to get him to produce, direct, and star in an adaptation of Upton Sinclair's *Depression.* Then, Jesse Lasky wanted him to direct and star with Jennifer Jones in a screen version of *The Apple Tree*; Orson's radio broadcast of the story had been widely hailed and Lasky, who had heard the show, could see it as a "beautiful picture." But this, too, was not the appropriate vehicle, the tonic he sought after his heart-stained failure of *Around the World.* The right film for Orson at that time would have to provoke and stimulate him, to inspire and prod him into the creative escape he sought.

Intense discussions about future projects went on for weeks between Sir Alexander Korda and Orson, via telephone, cable, and letter. The idea of *War and Peace* was revived. In addition to the production of *Around the World,* they began serious negotiations or at least conducted long-distance conferences over *The Master of Ballantrae; Salome,* with Welles as Herod (and possibly with Vivien Leigh to play the lead or with a French protégée of Orson's, Barbara Laage); *Carmen* (with Paulette Goddard in the title role); again, *Cyrano de Bergerac*; a remake of *The Bible*; Oscar Wilde's fairy tale, *The Happy Prince*; and dozens of other possibilities including an original screenplay by Jean-Paul Sartre;* adaptations of a short story, *Evidence,* by Isaac Asimov; and a novel, *Mine Own Executioner* by Nigel Balchin.

Good intentions notwithstanding on both their parts, nothing could be cemented. Korda was already becoming involved in two non-Welles projects, *An Ideal Husband* and *Anna Karenina.* He wanted to work with and help Orson—he knew, of course, of his *Around the World* financial disaster—but they could not come to agreement, or generate sufficient impetus to begin work on a specific project. Korda's London Film Productions advanced Orson some $44,000, to be applied toward whatever project they chose and whenever they began to work together. The professional flirtation would continue for years, and it would take that much time for the two men to consummate any kind of deal at all. In the interim, Orson's responsibilities were clear, immediate, and demanding: his debt to Harry Cohn would have to be repaid.

---

*Orson never learned which Sartre play Korda had in mind, but it was probably *No Exit.*

ORSON'S CONTRACT WITH Harry Cohn appeared attractive. He was to pay back the loan of $25,000 as soon as possible, and it was understood that the advanced amount was for his directorial duties only. As an actor in the film, however, he was to receive $2,000 a week for a minimum of twelve weeks; an additional $100,000 was his after Columbia recouped its full negative costs, and Orson was to get 15 percent of all profits made by the film.

According to Joseph McBride, Welles wrote the screenplay of *If I Die Before I Wake* in a seventy-two-hour marathon, dictating it to his secretary while holed up, incognito, in a hotel on Catalina Island. Perhaps more than any other property he had worked with before, Welles transferred the original Sherwood King novel to his personal cinematic vision.

The plot differences between the book and screenplay are so great in detail, although not always in substance, it would take a small catalogue to document them. In essence, however, the story is basically the same in both forms: a culpable, somewhat naive, worker is duped by a higher-classed enchantress, and in the end, innocence triumphs over evil and sophistication. In the basic, highly convoluted plot, Michael O'Hara, an Irish seaman, is hired by Arthur Bannister, a crippled lawyer, to serve on his yacht. O'Hara accepts the job because he is attracted to Bannister's beautiful wife, Elsa. Bannister's partner, George Grisby, convinces O'Hara to accept $5,000 in exchange for helping Grisby to disappear by claiming that he accidentally murdered him. Grisby, as it develops, is really killed and because O'Hara had signed a confession, he is arrested and brought to trial. Before the jury delivers the verdict, O'Hara escapes and discovers that Elsa is the one who killed Grisby. O'Hara, drugged, is then taken to a deserted fun house in an amusement park where Bannister and Elsa shoot it out. Both die and O'Hara walks out free.

Cohn not-so-gingerly informed William Castle about his deal with Welles, and Castle immediately sent Orson a copy of a ten-page treatment he had completed of *If I Die Before I Wake*. Several years previously, Welles had said that he would like to work with Castle: "Let's do a picture, together, Bill. You direct and I'll produce—or I'll direct and you produce." Castle, awed by Orson, admitted to having to "catch his breath" as a result of that offer and "walking on a pink cloud" thereafter.

To guarantee that Cohn and Columbia would consider him as a producer of the film, Castle requested that if Orson had any creative ideas on how the picture should take shape, he submit them directly to Castle. Orson's response:

Dear Bill,

About *If I Should Die*—I love it. It occurs to me that maybe by saying I had ideas for it, you'd think my ideas are creative. Nothing of the sort. What I'm thinking of is a practical use Mercury could use for the property. I have been searching for an idea for a film, but none presented itself until *If I Should Die* and I could play the lead and Rita Hayworth could play the girl. I won't present it to anybody without your O.K. The script should be written immediately. Can you start working on it at nights?

Give Rita a big hug and kiss and say it's from somebody who loves her very much. The same guy is crazy about you and won't ever let you get away from him.

Orson

As it developed, Cohn wanted the full Wellesian treatment on *If I Die Before I Wake*: Orson would write, direct, produce, and star in the film. A tentative budget of $2,300,000 was established. Castle was ultimately named as one of the associate producers, along with Richard Wilson.

Orson changed not only the story line but the title as well—several times, in fact. Though *If I Die Before I Wake* remained the working title, Orson had become convinced that too many people would associate it with the famous child's prayer of this same title. Also it lacked a sinister enough quality. He changed it to *Black Irish,* but the studio didn't care for the nationalistic connotation. *Take This Woman* then remained the official title for some time until someone came up with *The Lady from Shanghai*: there was no question that this film was about a woman, probably a mysterious and diabolical one, and since Rita Hayworth's name would be emblazoned on all of the advertising, the inference was clear. The title seemed to work commercially.

As soon as Orson had a rough first-draft script and basic approval from Cohn, he went to Mexico City, checked into the Hotel Reforma, hired a car and a driver, and began scouting out locations. Although the site of the novel was Long Island in New York, Welles transferred the action in the film to take place in Mexico and Sausalito, California. It's a possibility that in addition to the exotic setting that would keep the appeal of the story, Welles chose Mexico because he wanted to do more shooting on the aborted *It's All True*. This last manipulation never occurred, however.

A great deal of the film was also to occur aboard a ship. Orson knew that Errol Flynn's magnificent yacht, *Zaca,* then docked in Acapulco waters, might be available upon which to shoot. Eventually, Castle worked out the expenses with Flynn: he was to be paid $1,500 a day, including lunches for the crew.

Orson assembled his cast as much from the Mercury ranks as possible or by using actors he had worked with before. In addition to Rita Hayworth, Everett Sloane, Ted de Corsia, Gus Schilling, Erskine Sanford, and Harry Shannon would take either small or substantial parts. Another Mercurian, Brainerd Duffield, served as dialogue director and as an extra.

Glenn Anders, an actor who dates back to the days of D. W. Griffith, and who would play the part of Grisby, told this writer how he was selected by Orson.

I knew Orson pretty well after meeting him at a benefit radio broadcast; Rita Hayworth was there, too, and I remember that they hadn't met, as yet. Late in

1946, I was living at Tallulah Bankhead's and was somewhat depressed because I hadn't acted in anything that could be considered "major" since *Career Angel* in 1944. Tallulah was always attempting to cheer me up, although usually without success, and on one particular weekend we were to be the guests of the du Ponts in Delaware. I was adamant about *not* going; I knew we would meet people who would ask me what I was acting in and I would have to tell them the truth: nothing. Nor did I have anything on the horizon. I fumed. Tallulah insisted. She practically had to drag me to the car. As the chauffeur was loading the baggage, Tallulah's maid yelled from the kitchen window: "Mr. Anders, it's Mr. Orson Welles calling from California." Somehow, in an instant, instinctively, I knew that Orson whom I hadn't heard from in months, was going to offer me a part in some project or the other. Walking the few yards to the house, the "ham" in me began to take over. "ORSON, HOW *ARE* YOU?" I said in a complete personality change. "Glennie, darling," answered Orson: "Get on the next plane to Los Angeles. I want you in a film I'm directing!"

"But what is the picture and what should I wear?"

"Never mind what the picture is. It's a great part. You'll get the Academy Award for it. Just bring spring clothing."

Within days I was in Los Angeles, and brought to the set. Orson, atop a crane, was directing a street scene. "Hi, Glenn," he shouted down. "See that stretcher? Crawl under the sheet and play dead." I did as Orson told me, still knowing nothing about the film. Just before the camera began to film, a representative from Columbia came to the stretcher and handed me a contract to sign. "Your salary starts as of this minute, Mr. Anders," he said. I noticed I was to be paid $1,250 a week.

On October 13, 1946, Orson, his estranged wife, Rita, and thirty-two actors and technicians left for Acapulco to start location shooting. They were greeted in Mexico by a governmental party of welcomers, a group of mariachi players, and a legion of photographers and newsreel cameramen. In a matter of days, amidst a flurry of international wire service stories being published around the world, the company was aboard the *Zaca,* which for the purposes of the film had to be rechristened *Circe.*

Much of the publicity that surrounded the making of *The Lady from Shanghai* concerned the supposed romantic realliance between Rita and Orson. To the public, the couple seemed to be back together again; actually, by the time they arrived in Mexico, there was no chance of rapprochement. Rita had already set her mind on a divorce. She went to Mexico and agreed to appear in the film to help bolster Orson's income so that their daughter, Rebecca,* who had been born on December 17, 1944, might benefit from it when the legal schism occurred.

---

*Perhaps as a symbol of the deterioration of Orson's marriage with the late Rita Hayworth, Rebecca was not one of his favored children. He named her after the character in Sir Walter Scott's *Ivanhoe,* hoping that she, too, would be as generous, gifted, attractive, and unselfish as her namesake.

It was an extremely arduous shooting. Some scenes were filmed near a crocodile-infested river; in a scene where Rita dives into the ocean from Morro Rock, the rock itself had to be scraped of poisonous barnacles, and a Mexican swimming champion, off camera, and armed with a spear, had to continually swim near Rita to ward off the deadly barracudas in the waters. Rita could not take the heat and on several occasions the day's shootings had to be canceled until she could compose herself. At least once she actually collapsed while on camera from the fatigue caused by the soaring temperatures.

William Castle kept a special diary of the filming in Mexico, his own private ship's log. Here are some excerpts:

November 2, 1946:
Hot and sunny. Met with Errol Flynn aboard the *Zaca*. Welles, accompanied by Dick Wilson (his assistant since the origin of the Mercury Theatre), will share credit with me as associate producer. Orson delighted with the yacht. He and Flynn went swimming.

November 3:
Hot and sunny. Dick Wilson and Sam Nelson, the assistant director (who I had worked with on *Penny Serenade*), went to the Mexican union to try to integrate Mexican crews with the Hollywood crew. The language barrier is going to be quite a problem, also everything seems to be "mañana time."

Everett Sloane, cast as the brilliant crippled criminal lawyer, Albert Bannister, tried on his leg braces for the first time. He complained bitterly that they hurt and refused to use them.

November 4:
Cloudy and rainy. Orson, Dick and myself looked for locations. Orson picked several.

November 5:
Hot, sunny. Orson changed his mind. His whims and demands many, he has spent the first week picking locations, then changing his mind and picking others.

November 12:
Orson started rehearsing. Actors, memorizing their lines, arrive on set to find Welles smoking his perennial cigar and doing a complete rewrite.

November 17:
Cloudy and the heat oppressive. First day of shooting on *Lady from Shanghai*. The dark clouds seemed like an evil omen. Orson was rehearsing a scene with Rita Hayworth on the aft deck. We were twenty miles out, in rough waters.

Errol Flynn was at the wheel trying to keep the *Zaca* on a straight course. Charles Lawton, Jr., the cameraman, a filter to his eye, was waiting for a break in the clouds. Orson was ready to make his first take. Sam Nelson yelled for quiet as Orson took his place next to Rita. The sun had now come out. I was standing next to one of the camera assistants. He was working bareheaded, and the sun was beating down with fierce intensity. The mixer yelled, "Speed ... Take One," and waiting a beat, Orson said his first line. The camera assistant started to stagger. Reaching out, I tried to help him.

Horrified, I watched him turn blue, as fighting for breath and clutching his chest, he dropped to the deck. Orson and crew members rushed to his aid but it was too late. The assistant cameraman was dead—a fatal coronary.

Errol Flynn, as captain, took instant command. Pouring himself a stiff drink, he took a hefty swig. "Bring me a duffel bag," he ordered, and swaying against the pitching *Zaca,* announced, "We'll bury him at sea." Opening the duffel bag, he staggered toward the dead camera assistant, "Put him in the bag and sew it up."

Orson ordered me to get ashore as fast as possible and notify the Mexican authorities.

November 20:
Temperature rising; so was the budget. Shooting resumed. Entire day's work ruined because reflections from the water's surface kicked up more intensity than the light meter recorded, causing over-exposure. Insects made shooting a nightmare as thousands of them swarmed over arc lights, blocking them out.

November 22:
Tropical night, a velvet sky, alive with stars. I had been invited to dine aboard the *Zaca.* After a gourmet feast, we lay on deck chairs drinking brandy and appreciating the soft, caressing breeze under the full moon. Nora Eddington, Errol Flynn's wife, pregnant and leaving tomorrow for Los Angeles to have their baby, was seated next to her husband.

Flynn, finished with his brandy, cleared his throat and started to philosophize. "If a wife is no longer able to service her husband because of her pregnancy, the husband should be allowed to bed down with another woman until his wife is able to assume her full responsibility." Pouring another drink, he glanced at his wife. "Don't you agree, darling?" Mrs. Flynn, her eyes blazing, remained silent. Errol Flynn looked toward Orson. "How about you, Orson, don't you agree?"

Orson quickly glanced at Rita and in his booming voice declared, "No comment."

"Rita, don't you agree?" inquired Flynn.

Looking him straight in the eye, Rita spoke softly. "Well, Errol ... I never thought you'd ask me. ... If a male were unable to function ... for various reasons, a female should have the same right. ... Don't you agree, Errol?"

Flynn quickly poured another drink and turning to me, the only bachelor, asked, "What do you think, Bill?"

I thought for a long moment, "Errol ..." All eyes were on me. "May I have a little more brandy?"

November 23:

Hot and muggy. Nora Flynn left for Los Angeles. Errol saw her off and didn't return to the *Zaca*, telling none of us where he was going. A search party was sent, to no avail. He had disappeared. Again, we were forced to stop shooting aboard the *Zaca* until we could find him. The contract clearly stated the *Zaca* would not be used without him.

November 27:

Errol Flynn finally returned. He brought a playmate with him—an Amazonian from the surrounding hills who looks like a Ubangi savage without the plate in her mouth. She has the brawn of several football players and the height of a giraffe. Her skin is the color of the dark amber liquid Flynn gave me to ease my stomach. She understands no English and speaks in a high-pitched voice in a jibberish even the Mexicans can't understand. The romance of the century began when Flynn stowed her aboard the *Zaca*.

November 30:

Cool and beautiful. We have the day off and are lounging on the *Zaca*'s deck. Mexico's president, Valdez Miguel Alemán, accompanied by Nicholas Schenck, president of MGM, and several other Mexican dignitaries, all dressed in immaculate white, pulled alongside the *Zaca* in their motor launch. Errol Flynn welcomed them with great "hero gallantry" and lavishly began the introductions.

"President Alemán, Mr. Schenck, I would like you to meet my guests . . . Rita Hayworth. . . ." The president bowed and kissed Rita's hand. Errol continued introductions. "And this is William Castle. . . ."

Flynn, with great charm, then gestured to the huge Amazonian savage seated next to me, saying, "And this, gentlemen . . . is Mrs. Castle."

The president of Mexico glanced imperceptibly at "Mrs. Castle," then back at me, as Nicholas Schenck did a triple take. Turning scarlet, I decided to jump overboard.

December 5:

2:00 A.M. Temperature down, budget rising. Orson called me from his room. He sounded breathless as he croaked, "Get over here fast." Rushing to his bungalow, I found him stretched out on the bed acting out Hamlet's death scene, as Rita frantic, grabbed my arm and led me to the groaning Orson. One of his eyes was about three times its normal size, red and ugly. He had been bitten by an insect. Moaning, Orson grasped my arm, pulled me closer, and croaked, "My eye, where's my eye?"

I assured him it was still in its socket and that he'd be all right. Pulling me still closer, he whispered, "You'll direct the picnic scene tomorrow, Castle."

"The hell I will, Orson." Getting a doctor in Acapulco quickly was like everything else—"mañana." Shooting suspended again.

December 10:

At a downtown theater in Acapulco, we viewed the film Orson had shot so far. The remarkable footage again proved his brilliance. After the showing, Orson took me aside and told me he had finished filming in Acapulco, and wanted to get the cast and crew back to Hollywood where he would resume shooting. I was delighted, until he informed me I was to remain and shoot additional footage. "Close shots of insects, snakes, iguanas, any reptile you can find in the jungles." I am now a reptile director—teaching snakes and iguanas to act.

After thirty-five days of shooting in Acapulco, just a few days over schedule, the company was back in Hollywood, and with hardly a skipped beat, Orson started filming studio interiors. One observer remembers Orson, perhaps still not recovered from his eye incident, and the strenuous Mexican adventure, as being edgy, complaining about lack of sleep. He harangued the technicians preparing the final camera setup of the day. "There is too much stalling around here. Someone go put pressure on those men." When a benchman yelled, "Hey, let's go," Welles said sharply and cynically: "That's not enough. Go rub up against them the wrong way."

When informed that a horse-drawn cab that was being shipped up from Mexico was stalled at the border by customs men, Orson became furious, since the entire shooting schedule had to be rearranged.

Orson had constructed a virtually operable fun house complete with a mirror labyrinth, sliding doors, and a 125-foot zigzag slide that ran through a thirty-foot-wide dragon's mouth. He painted props himself, often touching them up with a long Chinese paintbrush, with Shorty, his valet, holding a paint can or palette and walking by his side like a medieval apprentice.

At one crucial stage of the production and at the last moment on a Saturday afternoon, Orson asked that the set be entirely repainted and be ready for Monday morning. The tough production chief at the studio, Jack Fier, said it simply couldn't be done. On Sunday, Welles and some of his associates went to the Columbia lot, quietly broke into the paint shop, and surreptitiously entered their studio and repainted their set. When the job was complete, they painted a huge banner over the studio entrance:

THE ONLY THING WE HAVE TO FEAR IS FIER HIMSELF

On Monday morning, when the members of the Motion Picture Set Painters Union, Local 729, arrived at Columbia to find that their work had been completed they protested loudly. Within a few hours they closed the studio with picket lines, demanding that a full crew be paid triple time for the painting done by Welles and friends. Fier was furious but agreed to the pressure since none of the members of the other trade unions would cross the picket line and the entire studio could be inoperative for days. He charged the expense to Orson's personal account, however. By the time everyone was leaving the set, Fier had taken down Orson's banner and replaced it with one of his own:

ALL'S WELL THAT ENDS WELLES

When Orson saw it he laughed heartily, charged into Fier's office, and embraced him. The two men became close friends for the remainder of the film.

In order to give the fun house scene the proper ambience of madness, Orson wanted to model it after the asylum in the classic film *The Cabinet of Dr. Caligari.* A madman's fantasy, *Caligari's* expressionistic sets contained jagged, sharp-pointed ferns and images, and shadows that converted ordinary objects such as walls, ceilings, and furniture into what film theorist Siegfried Kracauer has called "emotional ornaments." Orson's request, however, was difficult to fulfill; almost unbelievably, no print of the film could be found in all of Los Angeles. Finally, the Museum of Modern Art in New York City supplied it. The museum also came to Orson's aid when he was searching for a still print of the *New York Inquirer* columnists group photo that appeared in *Citizen Kane.* It was Orson's belief that a group of columnists looked like a perfect jury, and he wanted to duplicate their appearance as closely as possible, using the same actors in the courtroom scene of *The Lady from Shanghai.* Perhaps still smarting from RKO's rejection, he didn't want to ask them for the photograph.

Cohn and Welles were always at odds, the former constantly charging the latter with extravagances and wastefulness. Rita's contract with Columbia Pictures was about to expire, and *The Lady from Shanghai* was the last opportunity for Cohn to realize a large profit from one of his major stars. *Gilda,* released earlier that year, in which Hayworth did her famous glove striptease while singing "Put the Blame on Mame," was an unqualified smash hit and a huge money-maker for Columbia. Cohn became insanely angry when Orson had Rita's long red hair cut short to a "feather bob" and dyed platinum blonde, more in keeping with the diabolical character she was playing. "Oh, my God, what has that bastard done?" he was supposed to have screamed.

Welles claimed that he liked Cohn *because* he was a monster. He recalled: "He snarled at you as you came in the door ... and you could gradually throw him little goodies and he would quiet down and start lashing his tail." Orson also believed that Cohn was constantly spying on him: "I think he bugged everybody's office but one day I found a microphone behind a picture and discovered that this led up to Harry Cohn's own office so that he could tune in. After that I'd begin every day at the office by saying, 'Well, good morning, everybody. This is Mercury Productions beginning another day's work. We hope you'll enjoy it.'" At the end of the day, Orson would look at the bugged picture and say: "Well, that winds up another day at the Mercury. Tune in tomorrow."

Harry Cohn had assigned Viola Lawrence, his chief editor, to put the film together. When she began to study the rushes, she was appalled to see virtually no close-ups; Cohn consequently ordered Welles to shoot some, especially of Rita. Orson was not permitted to make final editorial decisions: this was done by Lawrence and Cohn himself. Orson, by way of memorandum or conference, outlined his editing strategy, attempted to establish his proclivities, and elaborated on details, but the final choice as to cuts, sound, dissolves, or any editing structure, however small, was not his to make.

When Cohn finally screened a rough cut of the completed film, he was horrified. "I'll give $1,000 to anyone who can *explain* the story to me," Cohn said. All of Cohn's executives seemed to agree: the film was not tied together, they cried; it was almost impossible to follow as it rambled from obscure scenes to an almost covert *mise-en-scène,* where the staging of the action and the way it is photographed become fragmented and murky. Although it might possibly dazzle an audience, it would certainly confuse. Welles tentatively agreed to Cohn's criticism, but he blamed it on the editing. If he could have full creative control of the film, he pleaded, he could make it into a great thriller. Cohn wouldn't hear of it; he feared that the film would never be completed if Orson were given creative *carte blanche.*

Cohn then ordered an entirely new composition for the film in which the trial scene would operate as the main focus and all of the action would appear as flashbacks. This idea proved so complicated that an almost new film would have had to be shot to accommodate the plan. He was talked out of it.

Other details still bothered Cohn, however, and he began dictating further changes. For example, Orson had suggested that when Bannister and his private detective, Broome, are in the canoe, only the inference of collusion be shown and no dialogue used. Cohn had the following line of Broome's inserted into film: "You can stop worryin' about your wife findin' herself a boyfriend. I got somethin' real for you to fret over. This is hot. The way I figure it's worth a little more dough."

Cohn was particularly interested in the music for *The Lady from Shanghai,* hoping that if he could include one song that became popular he might realize additional income from the film as a result of record and sheet music sales; it might also mean that the film would become known because of the song. He selected a tune called "Please Don't Kiss Me" by Alan Roberts and Doris Fisher and ordered Orson to shoot a scene where Rita sings it aboard the *Circe.* The cost of the song and the days of shooting needed added $60,000 to the budget. Not one to overlook the possibilities of any investment on his part, now that he owned the rights to the song, Cohn had orchestrations and fragments from it inserted into almost every scene.

When Orson finally screened the film, with all the music added, orchestrated by Heinz Roemheld it was his turn to be outraged. He felt that the story was so inherently melodramatic in itself, that "utmost reality" was needed in the sound effects and total subtlety was called for in the music, or else the film would be pushed into farce. He complained that Roemheld was guilty of using music in "Disney" fashion, a term then popular in the film industry and meaning an outdated method that makes musical comment with direct reference to physical action. If someone fell down, for instance, Roemheld inserted a few bars of "falling down music." Orson was particularly incensed over the music added to Rita's swimming scene. He wrote to Cohn:

Rita's second dive is overpunctuated. In other words, the score does not comment on the scene, its mood and content, but only refers to a physical action. This is pure "B" picture procedure and without dwelling on the obvious vulgarity of the effect, I think my point is made by simply saying that there is nothing in the fact of Rita's diving to warrant a big orchestral crescendo. The dive itself has no plot importance. What *does* matter is Rita's beauty, the beauty of the scene, the evil overtones suggested by Grisby's character and Michael's bewilderment. Any or all of these items might have inspired the music. Instead, the dive is treated as though it were a major climax or some antic movement in a *Silly Symphony,* a pratfall by Pluto the Pup or a wild jump into space by Donald Duck. If the lab had scratched initials and phone numbers all over the negative, I couldn't be unhappier with the results.

Despite the eloquence and force of Orson's pleas, there was no pliancy of Cohn's will. The music, all of it, remained the way he, Cohn, wanted it.

Orson's ending also displeased Cohn. In the shattered mirror-maze scene, Michael quietly awaits the arrival of the police, guarding Elsa's dead body, and as the film ends, an approaching siren can be heard. Cohn wanted the audience to be clear that Michael has grown or at least learned something from the experience. He also wanted to leave some doubt as to Elsa's fate. A more extenuated, and ambiguous ending was shot. Michael leaves the dying Elsa as she bids him farewell: "Give my love to the sunrise!" and as he walks through the revolving exit gate she screams, "I don't want to die!" Outside, in the glaring sun, Michael muses to himself, and it's possible to read into it a symbolic statement of Orson's future. "Well, everybody is somebody's fool. The only way to stay out of trouble is to grow old. So I guess I'll concentrate on that. Maybe I'll live so long that I'll forget her. Maybe I'll die, trying."

Although *The Lady from Shanghai* was complete and ready to be distributed in the early spring of 1947, Cohn was so disappointed with the result, and so concerned that it would wreck Rita's image, that he held up its release for almost a year, presumably to rush her into one or more conventional roles.* It is also altogether possible that Cohn realized that the story of the film had developed into an unpleasant parallel between Michael-Elsa-Bannister and the real Welles-Hayworth-Cohn and that such an analogy was too painful for him to accept.

Quietly slipping into theaters as the bottom half of a double bill, *The Lady from Shanghai* proved to be a financial disaster. Audiences hardly knew it existed, although the critical reaction was, for the most part, if not favorable, at least not antagonistic. Even though he had lost control of the end product, and the continuity is hopelessly confused, Orson had created a film that continued to show his ability as a master craftsman.

---

*Rita Hayworth had started her own production company, the Beckworth Corporation, for which she ultimately starred in four pictures, all of them distributed by Columbia. The first was *The Loves of Carmen,* which Cohn tried desperately to release before *The Lady from Shanghai;* however, because of contractual commitments it was released several months after *Shanghai.*

Though in later years he would sometimes speak a little disparagingly of the film—saying, for example, of its first ten minutes that "I have the impression it wasn't me that made them"—*The Lady from Shanghai* is very far from being a work of which Orson Welles need be ashamed.

Even before *The Lady from Shanghai* was finished, Cohn, who had deemed himself as "the tightest-fisted bastard in the business," had begun to ridicule Orson's reliability and complain about what he considered his spendthrift ways and his cinematic genius. Cohn could never forgive Welles for tampering with Rita Hayworth's image, just as the American public, as André Bazin has suggested, could not forgive him for killing her off as Elsa Bannister.

CHAPTER 15

WELLES'S HOLLYWOOD DEFEAT, his inability to find both a story and a studio that would meld with him and allow a replication of his artistic triumph of *Citizen Kane,* to say nothing of a commercial success—which he never really had—was overpowering him. A new view was needed to shore up his sinking fortunes. He was certain of one thing—he had to go back to the classics, perhaps to Shakespeare, either on the stage or in films, before he could confront any other project; there could be no more journeys into fear, ladies from Shanghai, no more strangers, or strolls down Amberson Boulevard, until he returned to what he considered to be home.

The Korda possibilities were still extant. Welles did additional work on the screenplay of *Salomé* and also began to work on another: *Enrico IV* by Luigi Pirandello. Orson retitled it *Henry IV.* This difficult and complicated tragedy is about a young man, an American expatriate, who temporarily recovers from the insanity in which he believes himself to be the Plantagenet Emperor Henry IV. A shock proves to be too much to bear, however, and the mania returns. Months later, he begins to recover again but he guards the secret and remains Henry IV to his friends and sweetheart. The lead role is highly subtle, the assumption of a personality that continually is in change. Orson wanted to play it and believed he could with credulity, but the question remained whether the project would be commercially successful. Korda was creatively receptive but financially doubtful. Orson kept searching.

Early in 1947, the Mercury Theatre had received an invitation to participate in that year's Edinburgh Drama Festival with a specific request to consider a Shakespeare offering. Since *Julius Caesar* was already scheduled to be mounted by another group, Orson was instantly seized by the idea of realizing a lifelong ambition: *Othello.* If Korda would back the venture, Orson had in mind a unique idea: rehearse the play in the United States for six to eight weeks; produce it in Edinburgh while simultaneously filming it on stage in color; take another month or so to shoot inserts, work on the sound track and complete the editing all in England. It was a bold plan but one that could work. Of that, he was confident. He and Dick Wilson established a carefully worked-out budget for the project: $740,000. The plan was submitted to Alexander Korda but to Orson's dismay, it was still not the project that captured Korda's visceral or financial fancy. Korda was not convinced that an attractive and meaningful production could be made of any Shakespearean film at the budget Orson was mentioning. While still claiming it could be done, Orson altered his subject and began to operate in another direction.

Now he remembered and decided. It would be *Macbeth,* not *Othello,* for the screen. Back in 1940, he had said he was doubtful about filming Shakespeare for the movies, indicating he felt film improves nearly everything over the stage with the exception of the poetry. *Macbeth,* though, might be different in providing some of the terror found in horror films. He would try to push through a kind of prefabricated movie. First, he would gather together his Mercury troupe rehearsed in the principal roles and take this core of players on the road. They would then put on a limited engagement stage play of *Macbeth* in an out-of-the-way city, picking up local talent for minor roles. The play would serve as a testing ground, a fine-tuning of the direction, a series of rigorous, straight-through rehearsals for the principals, and an occasion for studying the effectiveness and design of special multipurpose lightweight sets. With the experience gained from the stage production, the shooting of a movie could then proceed in record time and with a reduced budget. For the plan to work, however, he would have to adapt the film to a severely limited range of sets and would run the risk of making a static, visually uninteresting filmed play—not his intention at all. But Welles was confident that he could avoid these pitfalls by taking a hand in all phases of the production: unlabored but effective sets and costumes, deft direction, aggressive cinematography, and a sound track making a special appeal to the aural sense. Certainly no one in America at the time could claim greater expertise in the last category, and Orson knew it.

Welles looked for backing from the unlikeliest of places—Republic Pictures, a small, low-budget Western mill. It became a Charles K. Feldman-Orson Welles production. Republic's president, Herbert J. Yates, was satisfied that Welles was not bragging when he said that he could come up with a class picture for less than $700,000 and a quickie, twenty-one-day production schedule. Orson showed Yates his *Othello* budget proposal but scaled toward *Macbeth.* Republic's board of directors were not universally enthusiastic about this venture into the highbrow; they were more comfortable with Vera Hruba Ralston's ice-skating pictures or bread-and-butter Westerns, but the figures did look promising. Welles had made arrangements that would permit the play to be produced as the third offering of the Utah Centennial Festival in Salt Lake City in May 1947.* It was now early April, and he had already cut some corners; the Utah officials had agreed to pay for the play's costumes and props and would allow Welles to use them for the film, too. In addition, Republic could start right away with the construction of the sets, which were simple and relatively cheap. To eliminate delays in the setting up of shots, Welles proposed to use three cameras set up at such angles that different scenes could be shot simultaneously.

*The festival officials suggested to Welles that he do a production of *King Lear,* but he thought it better to start with—because of his experience with it—*Macbeth* as his first Shakespearean film.

Republic also stood to gain from an extra distributional conduit: 16mm prints of *Macbeth* would be sold overseas for educational purposes. Shakespeare on films was then enjoying a certain popularity, especially after the enthusiastic response to Olivier's splendid *Henry V*.

Irritated by the "B" picture image of his studio, Herbert Yates had already begun to entertain more creative projects. Frank Borzage, an Academy Award winning director, was placed on the payroll. Also, Yates had just released two artistic oddities, Gustav Machaty's *Jealousy* (1945) and Ben Hecht's *Spectre of the Rose* (1946), so Orson's project was not quite as antithetical to Republic's urges as has been supposed.

Welles received a provisional go-ahead, but, as *Variety* reported on April 18, recalcitrant members of the Republic board of directors, perhaps thinking of Welles's previous track record with budgets, tried to block progress. Also in the air was the rumor that Feldman Group Productions was having second thoughts and was seeking a takeover of the property.

At Yates's request, Welles gave Republic an unequivocal guarantee that as producer, director, and star, he would deliver a completed negative for no more than $700,000. Included in the budget was a $100,000 fee for Welles as writer, director, producer, and star. *Any* amount over the $700,000, Orson personally guaranteed to pay himself, and he had a contract drawn specifying that detail. In fact, Welles thought it could be made for $600,000. The deal was closed.

In an unusual trans-media adaptation, Orson took one of his *Macbeth* promptbook editions, transposed it into a screenplay, and then adapted the screenplay to a stage version for the Utah festival.

Since it was generally assumed that Lady Macbeth would be the focus of the film, Republic looked for a big-name actress for the role. Tallulah Bankhead was offered the part but turned it down. Mercedes McCambridge, Anne Baxter, and Agnes Moorehead were approached on Orson's request but were unavailable. There is no evidence to suggest that these rejections were much of a blow to Welles, who finally chose a Mercury radio star and colleague from *The March of Time,* Jeanette Nolan. His confidence in her—she had never appeared on the stage or on the screen before—was reciprocated in her long-standing dedication to Welles and his methods; they had done many radio broadcasts together.

Welles then went ahead with the Salt Lake City phase of the plan, taking an early-morning Western Airlines flight from Hollywood with the nine members of his cast, and arriving in Salt Lake on Wednesday, May 21. They began work immediately, and by afternoon Welles had checked out the Kingsbury Hall theater on the University of Utah campus. Director C. Lowell Lees, flattered with the casting of two of his children in minor roles, provided Welles with some amateurs for talking parts and about fifty extras. Orson charmed everyone when he reminisced about Salt Lake City in the days when he had appeared there with the Katharine Cornell troupe.

Welles and company were a hit. Salt Lakers were especially dazzled to get a look at former child star Roddy McDowall, as Malcolm, now a not-so-childish nineteen. McDowall also did a good public relations job, even writing a column for Salt Lake's *Deseret News.*

The cast of the play was basically Mercury with two important exceptions—McDowall and Dan O'Herlihy, fresh from the Dublin Gate Theatre and brought to the United States by Feldman. O'Herlihy was known here at the time for his role as a gunman in *Odd Man Out.* Edgar Barrier was Banquo; Erskine Sanford, Duncan. Stage manager William Alland doubled as Second Murderer. Brainerd Duffield played First Murderer but, more important, was also cast in the role of First Witch. Welles had always liked to make the magic at least partly masculine. He made Hecate and the witches in his voodoo *Macbeth* men and used men, most notably Hiram Sherman, in radio versions. In the most radical departure from Shakespeare's text, Welles compressed a number of minor roles into a new character, "A Holy Father," a sort of Druidian character who serves as an expositional chorus. New, non-Shakespearean lines were also added to the part. John McIntire, Jeanette Nolan's husband, was cast as the added character.

Characteristically, Welles worked against the clock, rehearsing the company by day and formulating physical aspects of the production late into the night—the hot, sticky night, for they had arrived during a heat wave. But within a week they were ready, giving six performances in four days, from May 28 through May 31; one each evening and two matinees, with question sessions afterward for high schoolers.

The stage design was simple: a line of gray-black, cloth-covered stairs extending from extreme upstage right, ending in a circular area at left center. The stage apron was extended over the footlights, with stairs leading into the orchestra pit—a multiple access scheme that was standard procedure for Welles. His players swarmed up and down these stairs and used the aisles as well.*

By all accounts, the production was judged a success, although allowances must be made for reviews a bit too full of provincial awe. Jeanette Nolan, perhaps still getting over the absence of microphones, was weak in the first act of opening night but was said to have been impressive in the famous "Out, damned spot" sleepwalking scene. (This scene would be praised in the film version as well.) The audience was electrified by the spectacle of the drama— Scottish legions passing through the aisles led by bagpipers and most especially the scenes with the witches led by Duffield, who, as one reviewer put it, was an inspired choice for the part. Hovering weirdly over the proceedings, and wearing grotesque phosphorescent masks, the witches made the show. Barrier's Banquo was also singled out for praise. Welles as Macbeth was strong: he was particularly convincing, said a reviewer, because the haunted king looked as if he needed a bath and a couple of nights' sleep. The play was one hour and thirty-four minutes of continuous action, almost perfect timing for a film.

---

*No one seemed to notice that the set looked familiar. In fact, it was the same basic design as the decade-old voodoo *Macbeth* but without palm fronds and other jungle flora.

One important aspect of Welles's interpretation of *Macbeth* received no mention at all: he had decided to have the cast avoid the conventional, hybrid accent usually employed by modern-day Shakespearean actors, and had them adopt instead a Scottish burr. This was a radical departure, but it seemed to be acceptable to the Utah audience. Interestingly enough, some characteristics of the Scots accent are not too far from Shakespeare's Elizabethan pronunciation, but it is far from the manner in which actors, both American and British, are coached. Welles said later that the accent would force everyone to slow down the dialogue and avoid falling into the incomprehensible singsong that is often the bane of modern Shakespearean performance.

With this first phase of the production behind him, Welles returned to Hollywood and made final preparations for the film; he still had some cast changes to make, not the least of which was the problem of assembling new armies large enough to fill the screen rather than the stage. He combed Hollywood for rugged and unusual types, as he described them, and came up with a bizarre crew: giants and dwarfs, men with extravagantly broken noses, hirsute "apemen," snaggle-toothed "village idiot" types. Everything about the movie seemed to be strange and unsettling.

Oddly, too, he had several cast members double up on roles, a practice more commonly found in a small repertory company. Brainerd Duffield again played First Witch and First Murderer, while Peggy Webber ("The Girl with 1,000 Voices" from radio) played Lady Macduff and Third Witch; Lurene Tuttle, also a radio actress, was a Gentlewoman and Second Witch. John McIntire was now replaced by Alan Napier in the Holy Father role. Keene Curtis, in the supporting role of Lennox, was the one University of Utah recruit imported for the film.

Orson also cast his nine-year-old daughter Christopher as the Macduff child—which put him, as Macbeth, in the curious position of engineering the murder of one of his own children on the screen. The role of Seyton, Macbeth's attendant (sometimes misunderstood by reviewers as "Satan") was played by Orson's valet, George ("Shorty") Chirello, all four feet eight inches of him.

Despite the disastrous results he had had with trying to prerecord the sound track of *The Magnificent Ambersons* in advance of filming, he was still convinced not only that it could be done but that with filming Shakespeare, where the word is the thing, it could produce a film of outstanding aural quality. If it was done correctly, the actors in *Macbeth* could lip-sync as the camera rolled while the sound was played from speakers on the set. This method would also help give him additional camera mobility, without his having to worry about hidden or overhead microphones, in the long takes he was planning.

Although many people had grave doubts about the way Welles was going about *Macbeth,* Jeanette Nolan admired his tireless—and for some, exasperating—search for perfection. She and Richard Wilson both agreed years later that, given the time and the cooperation of the cast, Welles's masterful aural sense would have led them to nothing short of a perfect sound track.

That is why she cooperated rather than resented him when he stretched her to her limits, once having her record over and over a sixteen-line speech ("Come you spirits/That tend on mortal thoughts, unsex me here . . .") until she got it right—five-and-a-half hours later.

Orson developed an interesting way of keeping order for all of the different sound-track attempts at reading specific lines. As he would often ask the actor to give dozens and dozens of readings of the same line, he would hand him a deck of cards. The actor, speaking into the microphone would read, for example: "Confusion now hath made his masterpiece," and then take the top card off the deck and name it, "Ten of diamonds."

The actor would then give a second reading, perhaps with a different pacing, emphasis, breathing: "Confusion now hath made his masterpiece," adding, "Three of spades."

This procedure would continue until Orson had as many readings as he believed the actor was capable of rendering. Then taking the deck, kept in the same order, he would ask the sound engineer to replay all of the takes. Placing the cards face up in solitaire fashion, he would wait until he heard those lines that he preferred. If he removed a card and placed it in a separate pile, that meant he wanted to hear the line over again. Perhaps out of twenty to thirty readings, he would be attracted to three. He could then tell John Strunsky, the sound engineer: "Give me the jack of clubs, the ace of diamonds, and the two of hearts," for example. Strunsky would pick these three readings from the track, play them back and save, as a result, hours of time and much confusion in trying to locate them.

Apparently satisfied with the sound track (he would later have to do some live recording anyway, as it turned out), Welles held three days of screen rehearsals. Now in Republic's Stage 11, he and John L. Russell, his cameraman, began the shooting on June 23.

Welles was intent on beating the deadline—twenty-one days with a couple of Sundays off, if not sooner—but he didn't make it any easier on himself when, on the first day of shooting, he ruined the first take of a soliloquy by tripping over a camera track and wrenching his back in the process. However, there were to be no more delays.

Although the hectic shooting schedule prompted Republic to close the sound stage to newsmen, *Los Angeles Times* reporter Philip K. Scheuer managed to get a peek at the frenetic activity going on there:

> Sometimes Welles spoke the lines himself and sometimes mimed them to a playback. Meanwhile, far across the stage, "another" Macbeth—a double—was engaged in a whacking broadsword duel with Macduff atop a parapet. Welles must have been watching it out of the corner of his eye; suddenly calling "Cut!" to his own cameraman he roared to the "second unit"—"What happened with the torches? Why didn't the torches move?"

The sweat we see on Macbeth's face in the film, therefore, can be assumed to be authentic.

The sets, designed by Welles and art director Fred Ritter, were elemental in appearance; eight of them, some movable and interchangeable, were crammed into the studio. The papier-mâché cliffs were as high as twenty-eight feet. Most of the sets appeared to be of rock, or more precisely, recently congealed lava. Even the interiors of Macbeth's castle seemed to be hewn out of stone. "It may be the first abstract film," Welles explained. "That is, the first drama to be shot against abstract backgrounds. These sets could be nearly anywhere—or nowhere." Despite the Stonehenge ambience, Welles seemed more interested in creating the ambiguous quality of a nightmare than in attaining strict verisimilitude: on the one hand there are the richly textured, volcanic rock and pervasive mists and vapors; yet the actors walk on a smooth surface that is unmistakably the floor of a sound stage. These contradictions lend a disorienting quality to the film, as do such queer repeated motifs as the Celtic cross and the two-pronged wands held up by the witches.

Welles's approach, then, is that of an interior view, a stylized representation not of eleventh-century Scotland, nor of possible Elizabethan reconstructions of it, but rather of the sweaty, oozing stone corridors of Macbeth's blasted mind, the visual analogue of a personality overtaken by a monumental despair, a poetic country not of William Shakespeare but of Orson Welles. Lured on by the prophecies of the witches, Macbeth soon discovered that he has lost the battle to a barbarous age. There is no exit but death.

In Welles's created world, magic is a real and potent force; the witches, who owe much to the voodoo *Macbeth,* fashion his image in clay and take possession of him, even placing a tiny crown on his head at the proper time. And the dagger he sees in his mind's eye—and it is imaginary in Shakespeare—is a real dagger placed before the clay image by the weird witches.

The Holy Father, besides being an amalgam of other Scots eliminated from Shakespeare, was designed to counterbalance the evil forces represented by the witches.

The strange tableau of *Macbeth* augmented by costuming dreamed up by Welles—his odd, square crown, his conical, fur-bedecked Tartar hat worn during his first encounter with the witches, and his curiously studded tunic— was vaguely reminiscent of a 1940s idea of a space suit.

Violence was explicit, more so than in Shakespeare. Lady Macbeth is shown jumping from the battlements to her death. Earlier, the luckless Thane of Cawdor has been executed on screen—a graphic reminder that the witches' charms, which will fulfill all the prophecies about Macbeth, including his bloody rise to the throne, work through the direst means.

In a clever move to save time and money, cameramen equipped with light, hand-held Eyemo cameras were sent in to take close-ups during the filming of long shots for battle scenes while wearing reversed doublets and masks on the backs of their heads, to blend in with the crowds. Such innovations, along with simultaneous filming with three main cameras and super-long takes (one actually took up an entire reel) kept the crews right on schedule.

Besides unconventional camera techniques—vertiginous, high-angle shots, floor-level shots, and meticulously detailed deep-focus framings similar to Gregg Toland's work in *Kane*—Welles also employed the voice-over interior soliloquy technique also used eventually in Olivier's *Hamlet*. He included a number of visual surprises, such as a shot of rapidly moving clouds in a dreary sky during Macbeth's "Tomorrow and tomorrow and tomorrow" speech. Blurred images, most memorable in the scene where the ghost of the murdered Banquo appears at the banquet, were achieved by the simple—and becoming traditional—expedient of smearing filters with Vaseline, perhaps the least innovative stunt in Welles's camera case of tricks. More interesting was Orson's overall conception of the banquet scene; he intercut with shots in the subjective camera mode, studying the earthbound Macbeth's reactions through the eyes of the ghost himself.

Many of the filmic techniques were original with the movie, but it is clear that the 1947 *Macbeth* represents a logical step in the progression of Welles through a twentieth-century staging and interpretation of Shakespeare, a progression that finds its origins in the melodrama and spectacle of the voodoo *Macbeth;* the spare, severe *Julius Caesar,* and the multipurpose sets and ambitious sweep of *Five Kings.*

Welles, exhausted but satisfied, wrapped the film in his twenty-one days. He was off to Europe now, to meet Alexander Korda, leaving Wilson and others to do the final cuts and arrange to get a score from Jacques Ibert, composer of some thirty French and Italian films.* The Alexander Korda lottery now seemed to have returned with a rendition of *Cyrano de Bergerac.* As it turned out, Welles needn't have rushed with *Macbeth.* The film was held up in a long and painstaking editing job. Once again, as with *Ambersons,* Welles was called upon to help with the editing while overseas, and long, confusing cables and copies of the prints were exchanged.

Republic now tarried in a general release of *Macbeth*, trying all the while to maximize profits. A commercial embargo on film exports to Britain thwarted their efforts to make quick money from that quarter. They decided to hold off on a full-scale release of the movie, planning instead to launch a test campaign, trying out various promotional approaches in three or four key American cities.

Although the film had, at first, been promised for release by December 1947, it was still not in shape by that time. In fact, it was not until September 1948 that Republic, with many misgivings about the prerecorded sound track and the long-distance editing job, saw the film entered in the Venice Film Festival where, unfortunately, it found itself pitted against Olivier's *Hamlet.* It was soon withdrawn from competition when public sentiment seemed to turn against it, some viewers calling it a sacrilege to the memory of Shakespeare. Welles, however, believed in his film even though it was not exactly the one he had made, this 1948 version having been cut by almost a half hour to 107 minutes at Republic's request.

---

*Orson had originally attempted to secure Marc Blitzstein, who had been responsible for the incidental music in the Mercury production of *Julius Caesar,* but he was unavailable.

Some rumors have grown up around the Italian reviews of *Macbeth* in the wake of the Venice festival, that they basically gave it a universal thumbs-down. That is simply not true. Here is a translation of a review from *Il Tempo,* September 25, 1948:

> *Macbeth* is such an authentic piece of cinematic work that it gets the better of the most adverse public after a few minutes, and grabs the public by the throat with a series of powerful scenes, of such shots as to make the character and his drama leap into relief before the eyes of the audience and holds this audience and does not let go of it until the very end, holding it so forcefully as to make it applaud loudly and spontaneously four times during the showing. . . . (T)his experiment succeeded practically a hundred percent, to the point that Shakespeare acquires . . . a new and magic dimension, abstract and miraculous, potentially coherent from the first to the last shot. . . . If we had more space it would be worthwhile to go further into detail on this *Macbeth,* which is without doubt, the best picture of Orson Welles after *Citizen Kane.* . . .

Welles certainly didn't have to sneak out of Venice in disgrace, as some would have it.

In fact, opinion all over Europe was generally favorable. *Le Figaro* quoted Jean Cocteau as saying that he found it to be a "picture of great power and great mystery, built up from the most unexpected points of view." Another filmmaker, French commentator Marcel Carné, remarked that "speaking professionally, it seems to me that *Macbeth* has greater cinematographic qualities than *Hamlet.*" And a German critic, "L. L." in *Filmstudien* went as far as to say: "One can by good right ask oneself if Orson Welles is not closer to the original idea of Shakespeare than the super-refinement of Laurence Olivier." This last sentiment is echoed in many European commentaries on the film. However, Maurice Bessy, in a rave review in the November 30 *Cinémonde,* made a prediction that turned out to be all too accurate: "*Macbeth* . . . will have a difficult career."

The difficulty really began in the United States when Republic released the film in a handful of cities, including Boston and Salt Lake City, in October 1948. American reviewers, led by the Luce *Time-Life* opinion axis, did indeed savage it, citing, above all, the allegedly poor quality of the sound track and the incomprehensible Scots burr adopted by the actors. Visual and aural inconsistencies were detected—that would be no surprise considering the mélange of prerecording, live recording, overdubbing, and committee editing that made up the film. But Welles's abridgments of Shakespeare's text added to the confusion of reviewers evidently expecting a three-hour traditional Old Vic treatment.

Major modifications of Shakespeare's text included most notably Act I, Scene 1, in which the witches dominate and encircle the scene, appearing at the opening, but contrary to Shakespeare, reappearing at the very end. In fact they, and thus evil in general, encircle the whole film. Welles's intention in this respect was seriously misinterpreted. Here is part (not the worst, to be sure) of the sneering dismissal of the film that appeared in *Life* magazine, October 11, 1948:

> People who are familiar with the original play may have some difficulty in placing the individual lines. Scenes have been ruthlessly juggled, characters interchange their lines freely.... The movie ends with a line from Act I: "Peace, the charm's wound up!" which means, despite what Mr. Welles may think, not "over and done with" but "ready to work."

Welles knew exactly what it meant. The black *Macbeth,* to no one's chagrin, had ended the same way—after Malcolm is elevated to king. Welles's juggling was intended to mean that there is no relief: this is not Shakespeare's hopeful, sunny resolution, but one much darker. Lady Macbeth is a broken heap and her ambitious but fearful husband now merely exists as a severed head skewered on Macduff's lance, yet the evil is still not exorcised. Macbeth's worst suspicions in life are now confirmed after his death: there is no way out ... for anyone.

The stinging, left-handed compliments of *Newsweek* ("If Welles has failed utterly to live up to the standard set by Laurence Olivier's *Hamlet,* he has at least failed honestly") capture the tone of the American critical reception at this time:

> Where the film falls short is not so much in production as in conception. In both acting and direction, Welles' limitations are strongly, sometimes almost offensively, apparent. His Macbeth is a static, two-dimensional creature as capable of evil in the first scene as he is in the final hours of his bloody reign. As Lady Macbeth, Jeanette Nolan . . . shows considerable talent which would have appeared to better advantage under a less bombastic director (*Newsweek,* October 18, 1948).

Republic withdrew the film in the United States and wondered what to do next. They did allow it to play to good reviews in European cities, however. December 1948 reviews from Brussels were filled with praise:

> *Le Peuple:* Far nearer to Shakespeare's spirit than Laurence Olivier's ever was, Orson Welles produced—in 21 days—a masterpiece.... As an actor, Welles is extraordinary....

> *Le Phare:* The other evening several hundred people left the Palais des Beaux Arts stupefied, enthusiastic, shocked—they had attended the special showing of a new picture which will probably make history.

> *Volonté:* It is very likely that, together with Charlie Chaplin, the author-actor of *Citizen Kane* is the only complete man of the cinema on the other side of the Atlantic. He plays with the images as with the voices. His imagination in the

cutting completes and amplifies an astonishing sense of the mimic and acoustic.

It would be hard to ascribe all this enthusiasm to French-speaking reviewers relying on subtitles rather than on the sound track; nevertheless, Republic decided that the Scots accent had to be excised before they would rerelease the picture in the United States. In July of 1949, with Welles in Europe, they called on Wilson to redub in American English. For the next nine months Wilson rerecorded most of the dialogue, having to recall the entire cast for the project. (Welles was not available at first; Wilson eventually received his loopings when Welles found time to do them in London.) It was a valiant attempt on Wilson's part to carry out a virtually impossible assignment: someone likened it to giving a manicure to a flea. The job was additionally time-consuming in that Welles's new dialogue wouldn't always fit the action, so Wilson had to go back to the sound tracks on outtakes and match them up with the new material, which reintroduced the dreaded burr from time to time. The surgery involved sixty-five percent of the sound track.

What was worse, the film was tightened even further, this time down to eighty minutes. This improved version—in which Welles was, according to Wilson, "bitterly disappointed"—was released, after many delays, in September 1950 and finally reached New York in December of that year, *three and a half years* after the twenty-one-day whirlwind shooting.

In order to help the promotion of the film, Republic created a typical Hollywood trailer, which implied all of the action of a medieval swashbuckler. Macduff is seen standing on a parapet of the castle bravely shooting arrows over the heads of soldiers as they raise their torches and spears. A deep, omniscient voice—not Orson's—is heard:

> With all the magnitude
> > ... the grandeur
> > ... the dramatic power
> That only the magic of motion pictures can bring you ...
> > WILLIAM SHAKESPEARE'S
> > *MACBETH*
> Comes brilliantly to the screen!
> > Starring Orson Welles.

Once more—and certainly it should have been expected this time—*Macbeth* took a beating from the critics. What they saw and heard in this hybrid version could not be ascribed to anyone in particular, least of all Welles. (*Cue* magazine: "Mr. Welles, madly in love with Mr. Welles, had chipped, chopped, mangled and murdered a work of art ... a theatrical claptrap.") (*The New Yorker:* "For some reason, Mr. Welles has let his cast decide individually whether or not to follow him in his efforts to fabricate a new kind of Scottish tongue.")

Reaching London in late May of 1951, the film bemused the critics, who were cautious and did not condemn it with quite the abandon of the American press. A May 27 review by major film critic C. A. Lejeune in the *Observer* is fairly typical:

> There are many things monstrously wrong with the Orson Welles *Macbeth,* but the film is not the total loss that the years of delay in showing it might have led us to anticipate. It is uncouth, unscholarly, unmusical, historically unsound, and almost without exception abominably acted; but even at its worst it has a sort of power; it is often horrid, but never negligible.

Perhaps the crowning irony was that Republic discovered, when all the receipts were in, that it had made money on the picture. Orson had been right all along.

MOST BIOGRAPHICAL STUDIES of Orson Welles have him completing *Macbeth* and then, in a final sweep of indignation and disillusionment with the Hollywood system and with continuing tax problems, exiling himself to Europe, establishing a nomadic home there as an authentic expatriate and not returning to the United States for close to a decade. It wasn't quite like that.

Orson's successful confrontation with *Macbeth*—producing it in three weeks, virtually on a *sou*—began being noised about Hollywood in 1947 and helped to dissipate some of Harry Cohn's rancor. The box office results, in any event, were not yet in from *The Lady from Shanghai.* Orson's possibilities in Hollywood were as strong as they had been immediately after the release of *Citizen Kane,* and once again he began to tumble out ideas for films while dozens of interesting projects and offers came his way.

While a dinner guest at that time at the house of Charlie Chaplin, Orson suggested that they collaborate on a documentary, a quintessential "death to women" film as it has been called, about Landru, the notorious French "bluebeard" murderer, the lady-killer incarnate. Chaplin outlined the details of the possible collaboration in *My Autobiography.* Orson's proposition was part of a series he had in mind of films based on characters and stories of real life. He believed Chaplin would make a wonderful and debonair Landru. Welles told Chaplin of his favorite Landru story: on the last day in court during his famous murder trial, as the spectators were filing back after lunch, one woman loudly complained that someone had taken her seat. Landru, forever the gentlemen, stood up in the dock, and asked, politely, "Perhaps the lady would care to take mine?" Welles wanted to call the film *Lady Killer* or simply, *Landru.*

Chaplin asked Welles if he could read the screenplay. "Oh, it isn't written yet," Orson replied, "but all that's necessary is to take the records of the Landru trial and you'll have it. I thought you might like to help with the writing of it."

Chaplin wasn't intrigued by doing a screenplay at that time, at least a documentary, and declined Orson's offer: "If I have to help in writing the script, I'm not interested," he said. A few days later, after thinking about it,

Chaplin changed his mind. The story of Landru could be made into a "wonderful comedy," as he described it. He telephoned Welles and made a counterproposal: "Look, your proposed documentary about Landru has given me an idea for a comedy. It has nothing to do with Landru, but to clear everything I am willing to pay you five thousand dollars, only because your proposition made me think of it."

Orson was not happy with the idea at first; he had wanted to produce and direct the story himself, and he had even begun to develop the screenplay. Chaplin became annoyed: "Listen, Landru is not an original story with you or anyone else. It's in the public domain."

Orson thought a moment and then told Chaplin to get in touch with his agent, (at that time Charles Feldman) to arrange a contract. When Chaplin's representative, attorney Lloyd Wright, drew up the contract, Orson was asked to relinquish credit, which as Wright stated, "Charlie and I will greatly appreciate." Orson refused to sign the contract under those conditions. He would accept the financial terms but only on one condition: that after seeing the film, he could decide to have a screen credit and if so, it would read:

Idea suggested by Orson Welles.

Eventually, Chaplin accepted the conditions and went on to make the film, changing the title to *Monsieur Verdoux*; it was hailed as a masterpiece of acting, perhaps his greatest, according to critic James Agee and others.

When Orson attended a performance of the film in the first few days after its opening, he was shocked. His name appeared nowhere! In a matter of days, after threat of legal suit and injunction, Chaplin inserted Orson's credit line, where it has remained all these years.

After *Macbeth*, Orson lived in the Santa Monica home of Charlie Lederer, the man who had married, and then separated from, Orson's ex-wife Virginia. The two men had become close friends. Lederer had not accomplished much as a screenwriter since his last produced film, *His Girl Friday,* in 1940; he had a fling at directing a 1942 thriller, *Fingers at the Window.*

When Orson moved in with Lederer, they spent hours, sometimes days, discussing various properties, potential film projects that either or both would care to do. They were both enamored of Tennessee Williams's *The Glass Menagerie* and did a partial treatment for the screen but were a bit skeptical as to its commerciality.

Meanwhile, Hedy Lamarr was actively courting Orson to direct a film, any film, for her. Outside of her role as Tondelayo in *White Cargo* in 1942, she had hardly appeared in any picture of which she was proud; vapid roles in films like *Her Highness and the Bellboy* were ruining her image, she felt, and she was anxious to become involved with more prestigious vehicles. She had asked Orson for the part of Lady Macbeth, but he felt her acting wasn't strong enough to sustain the part. "Let me give you a rain check on another role," he told her. When he completed filming *Macbeth,* she contacted him to "cash in the rain check," as she wrote. She started sending him scripts that had been sent to her—through her encouragement—by various screenwriters. Her first submission was *The Return of the Native,* an adaptation of the Thomas Hardy novel, in which she wanted the role of the passionate and exotic Eustacia Vye to play opposite Orson's Clym Yeobright; the role of the "native" was too plebeian for him, however, nor did he believe in the script. An adaptation of Taylor Caldwell's *This Side of Innocence* also proved uninteresting to him as either director or actor; even for Orson, this particular work of the British novelist was too melodramatic for the screen.

Meanwhile, someone came up with a serious idea of Orson doing a film of Shakespeare's sensationalistic tragedy *Titus Andronicus;* with so much blood, mayhem, and horror—over thirty-five people die in the play, and there are ten full-scale murders performed—it was thought to be perfect for a Hollywood project. Orson would play the cold-blooded Titus, it was suggested. Although he was virtually rabid to do another Shakespeare film, *Titus Andronicus* interested him not a whit for the screen. It's Shakespeare's poorest for film, he was supposed to have said in refusing the offer.

Then Leonard Bernstein implored Orson to produce and direct a concert version of Blitzstein's *The Cradle Will Rock,* which Bernstein would conduct, but Orson, still smarting from the tragedy on stage of *Around the World,* and his heart now dedicated to doing a film, graciously declined.

Orson continued to experience the rapture of being pursued. Edward Small, a seasoned independent producer and former agent and actor, responsible for such Hollywood classics as *The Man in the Iron Mask* and *The Corsican Brothers,* wanted to work with Welles, perhaps together with Gregory Ratoff, the Russian-born actor, director, and impresario. Orson suggested: why not *Othello, Cyrano de Bergerac, The Merchant of Venice, Moby Dick, Carmen*? Small responded: "Yes, yes, let me hear more, let me see treatments, give me details and budgets on all."

Since *Cyrano* was still one of his most revered projects, Orson began with that first. The Ben Hecht script had already been sold to Selznick and even if it could be wrested from him it would cost a considerable amount of money; Orson's confidence in his own ability as a screenwriter had continued to grow and so he gave himself the task of writing it. Among scholars, the best English translation of the Rostand play was by Robert Merrill of UCLA, a version, according to many, that was the most accurate ever written and thoroughly equal to the French. Welles secured a copy and began transferring the heroic comedy to the screenplay form, maintaining the dazzling and exquisitely lyrical verse, attempting to retain the theatrical and spontaneous thrust of Rostand's poetry. He also chose his perfect Roxane: Jean Simmons, a British teenager of exceptional beauty and talent, who had caused a stir in Hollywood with her self-possessed roles in *Caesar and Cleopatra* and *Great Expectations.* She was enthusiastic about the role. When Orson discovered that Laurence Olivier had all but signed her for a production of *Hamlet* that he was planning, he sent Simmons a cable stating: "I still find it impossible to think of Cyrano without you as Roxane. . . ." However, Small was unconvinced by Orson's treatment of the *Cyrano* script.

Small was even less dazzled by an oratorio stage version of *Moby Dick* that Orson said could easily be translated to film. In the treatment given to Small for approval, a preamble said in part: "Because of the novel's content, fraught as it is with intangibles, with non-literal sequences and relationships, any ordinary representational form is out of the question."

This was not what Small had in mind. He wanted Welles at his most commercial, not necessarily his most artistic. After also rejecting Orson's version of *Carmen,* Small submitted a screenplay he had purchased from Charles Bennett, who while in England had written Hitchcock's *The Thirty-Nine Steps* and *The Man Who Knew Too Much* and had distinguished himself in Hollywood with the scripts of *King Solomon's Mines* and *Reap the Wild Wind,* among others. Bennett's new screenplay was tentatively titled *Cagliostro,* and it was based on an Alexandre Dumas novel, *The Memoirs of a Physician.*

Welles has said he had been skeptical when he read, as a boy, of the fabulous exploits of Count Cagliostro. "When Edward Small offered me the part I had only vague memories of *The Memoirs of a Physician* as a tale of implausible feats of mental control, villainy, legerdemain and derring-do."

Edward Small himself "was no mean master of suggestion," Welles has recalled. Together with the screenplay, a copy of the novel was given Orson. He became intrigued and has stated that one of Mark Twain's maxims explained his immediate reaction: "When I was twenty I thought my father the most ignorant man I knew; but by the time I was twenty-five, it was astonishing how much the old boy had learned." Dumas had assumed a great deal of knowledge since Welles had last read him. After screening Small's *The Corsican Brothers* and learning that Ratoff would be the director of the Cagliostro tale, Orson accepted the role on the condition that he be paid $100,000 and that he personally direct all of his own scenes himself. Small agreed. It would be a historical costume romance.

Eventually the title, *Cagliostro,* was changed to the more commercial-sounding *Black Magic.* The story centers around the exploits of Cagliostro, a traveling magician who discovers that he has the power both to heal and to hypnotize. Dr. Mesmer, the renowned physician, tries to persuade him to limit his powers to curing and helping the afflicted, but Cagliostro has more ambitious—and diabolical—schemes. Orphaned as a child when Vicomte de Montagne hangs his parents for witchcraft, and afterward tortured by the vicomte, Cagliostro dreams of revenge. The opportunity presents itself when he is summoned by Montagne to cure a young woman, Lorenza, who is seriously ill.

Later, Cagliostro discovers that Montagne has kidnapped the girl because she bears a striking resemblance to Marie Antoinette. The vicomte plans to use her in a plot to discredit the future queen and install Mme. Du Barry in her place. Cagliostro joins Montagne and Du Barry in the plot and hypnotizes the girl, Lorenza, into marrying him. But Lorenza, even though married, remains in love with the captain of Marie Antoinette's guard. The plot succeeds initially, and Cagliostro is presented at the court of Louis XVI. Later, the magician's fortunes decline abruptly when the plot backfires. He is accused of treason; Dr. Mesmer hypnotizes him and forces him to confess his treacheries. His Gypsy friends try to help him escape, but he dies in a duel with his wife's lover, the captain of the guard.

There was an ulterior motive for Orson's accepting the role in *Black Magic*. The film was planned to be shot in Italy to take advantage of the true-to-life setting and the low postwar production costs; and Orson planned to use the time abroad to scout locations and arrange other details for *Othello,* the film he was determined to shoot as his next venture. The fact that he was facing huge income tax problems also served as an impetus to stay out of the country for a while.

The second important American film to be shot in Europe after the war, *Black Magic* was filmed on location at the Villa d'Este at Tivoli, the Castel Sant' Angelo, and the Quirinale. So accommodating was the Italian government in cooperating with the film, in fact, that the newly elected president of Italy waited until certain scenes were completed before he moved into the palace that serves as the Roman equivalent of the White House. Besides Welles, the cast included Nancy Guild, a Hollywood newcomer in her early twenties, playing both Lorenza, Cagliostro's wife, and Marie Antoinette; Frank Latimore as Gilbert, captain of the guards; Akim Tamiroff, Valentina Cortesa, Margot Grahame, and Stephen Bekassy.

Despite Welles's assertion that Gregory Ratoff was a great friend and more fun to work with than anybody he knew ("Perhaps Ratoff is also something of a hypnotist," Orson once quipped), it was Welles and not Ratoff who proved to be the Rasputin behind the scenes. Early in the filming, Welles managed to gain psychological and creative control not only of the production but of the man who had been hired to direct it. Once again, as in *Jane Eyre,* Welles became the director of a film in which he was supposed to be only acting or at least directing only his own scenes. Ratoff would appear, often at dawn, to supervise setups, then would disappear for the rest of the day. Welles would arrive around noon and work at his usual high-energy pace until midnight or after. When the day's work was over, Welles and his cast, still in their stage costumes, would sit down to a Renaissance-like banquet that lasted until far into the night.

Although Ratoff's contribution to the film became increasingly passive and minor, he would appear on the set from time to time when Orson was directing. On those occasions when a dispute arose between the titular director and his usurper, Ratoff would retreat, complaining that he had heart pains. "Grisha, you need some rest," Welles would say sarcastically. A letter from one of Ratoff's associates in Rome to Edward Small in California complained that Ratoff was on the verge of a nervous breakdown. Ratoff's way of responding to being deposed was indirect but effective: he spoke with a Russian accent that became so heavy as the filming continued that eventually no one could understand what he said.

Welles, though, was in fine fettle. Nancy Guild described him as: "The most exciting director I've ever worked with. He had a great sense of timing and intense powers of concentration. Working with him was a classroom experience. He was marvelous; he inspired me to give my best. I really grew as an actress while I worked with him."

Not only did the character of Cagliostro and the psychological implications of his control fascinate Welles, but he also loved the role because it called upon his skills as an accomplished magician. He became so involved in his role that he often refused to step out of character, even at the late-night fetes when he would talk as though he really belonged in the eighteenth century. The whole subject of hypnotism began to fascinate, then grip, him. He studied books on Anton Mesmer, talked to experts, and actually performed hypnosis on willing victims.

His expertise found expression in an article that he wrote in Rome and that appeared in *The New York Times,* titled "Out of a Trance," in which he stated, in part:

> Dumas had an intuitive grasp of the many layers of personality and understood the contradictions of human nature as only genius can. It may be true, as doctors claim, that a truly virtuous lady is impregnable even under hypnosis. But where is this truly virtuous lady? Dr. Freud has pointed out that the more virtuous one seems, the stronger may be the contrary impulses clamoring to burst forth. Is it possible, it has been asked, for a man to love a woman and use her so ill? Of course it is. The final bone of contention lies in Cagliostro's method, which I can only call spontaneous hypnotism. Cagliostro used no whirling lights or glittering watches on swinging chains, nor did he have to croon ten minutes of soothing nonsense to a subject. As one who dabbles a bit in hypnotism himself, I can testify to what all stage hypnotists know, and most doctors acknowledge: it is much easier to get "control" over a person's will in front of an audience than it is in private, and the magician with his air of mystery, however phoney it may be, is more successful in less time than the legitimate man of medicine.

Nancy Guild has recalled her experiences with Orson during the shooting of *Black Magic*: "He liked each scene to be complete in itself, a playlet with a beginning, a middle and an end. I was frightened of him, though," she added. "He was extremely volatile, and everything he said had an air of authority that made it sound true even if it wasn't."

In one scene, Lorenza was to be buried alive so that she would appear to be dead. According to the script, a dummy was to be used. Welles demanded authenticity and insisted that Nancy herself lie in the grave, while dirt was thrown on her. Every once in a while, Welles would yell down to her, "Nancy, are you all right?" When she replied in a muffled voice that she was, afraid to say otherwise, he would yell, "Okay, boys, more dirt!"

During the filming, Welles established a competitiveness toward Frank Latimore, who played the part of Gilbert, the captain of the guard. Although Welles was over six feet two inches tall, Latimore was even taller, and in the high-heeled boots that were part of his costume, he seemed to tower over Welles. Welles could not compensate for the difference in height by wearing high-heeled boots of his own because once again, he had sprained an ankle. Instead, he had a ramp built on which he stood and walked during all his scenes with Latimore, the cinematic artifice creating the illusion that Orson was taller.

In addition to height differences, Latimore aroused Welles's competitive instinct for another reason: in the film he was the successful rival for Lorenza's affections. When Orson remained in character, he was nothing less than insulting to Latimore. Nancy Guild recalls that on those days when she was playing Lorenza, Orson's behavior toward her was very romantic, gentlemanly, sincerely caring. But when she played Marie Antoinette whom Cagliostro/Orson was plotting against, he was openly antagonistic, even refusing to sit next to her at lunch.

An amusing incident occurred during the filming on a night when Orson masterminded a lavish dinner party to celebrate the arrival of Tyrone Power. Both he and Power had been signed on to act together in *Prince of Foxes,* a Twentieth-Century-Fox production to be directed in Italy by Henry King at the conclusion of the shooting of *Black Magic.* Orson invited Power and Nancy Guild, Linda Christian, Gregory Ratoff, and a few others to a magnificent home that was once owned by the Russian bass Feodor Chaliapin. The interior was like a movie set with lavish tapestries and classic sculpture, rare paintings, a grand staircase, and an unsurpassed view of Rome. Candles were lit; the tableau was almost unbearably romantic. The wine flowed and Orson was at his most charming and loquacious, talking of Mesmer, the Renaissance, Barrymore, ancient China, modern theater—all matter and manner of things. Everyone was spellbound by his charisma as he held the center of attention for what seemed like minutes but was actually hours. Linda Christian, seated at Orson's right, appeared especially entranced. At one point after a particularly outrageous and funny story by Welles, Linda and Nancy retired to the ladies' room. As they were freshening up, Linda who had been locked in conversation and admiration with Welles for most of the dinner and seemed to notice no one else, suddenly announced to Nancy: "I'm going to marry him."

"But Orson's already been married twice," Nancy objected.

"Not *Orson,*" Linda replied. "I mean *Ty!*"*

WHEN IT WAS released, *Black Magic* received quite a spate of undistinguished reviews; Orson later claimed that he acted in it "only for fun."

Probably the only outstanding feature about the film was its extremely lavish production both in costuming and settings and in what seemed like thousands of extras. But its pageantry and massive, authentic palace backgrounds were not enough to cover up for an overacted and badly edited melodrama. Orson's acting was both severely criticized for overplaying Cagliostro in a style reminiscent of early silent film acting and highly lauded for giving a lusty portrayal. The *Herald Tribune* stated: "Acted badly in the

*Shortly afterward, Linda Christian and Tyrone Power did marry.

grand manner, it is a postured and heavily costumed romance which misses the dignity and mystery of the original character." *Time* opined that the part "suits him perfectly."

The biggest publicity the film received was not from the traditional critical media. Instead, it came when National Comics included an Orson Welles episode in one of its 1949 *Superman* editions: "Black Magic on Mars" where Orson is blasted out of this world. "This time he found himself fighting frantically to warn the world of a Martian invasion, this time a real one! But the world laughed, for this was the second time that Orson was crying wolf! Only Superman realized the danger. . . ." But Orson saves face when he helps Superman defeat the invading Martians by doing magic tricks! The episode was so apropos and in tune with his personality, one wonders if Welles himself originated the material for the comic book.

Before, during, and after *Black Magic,* Orson attempted to secure backing for the filming of *Othello.* However, neither Small's nor Korda's money could be separated from them as an investment. Yes, it was true that Italian production would be cheaper, but could *any* Shakespeare film really make a profit? And what about all the technical difficulties of waiting to see rushes and other film problems? The answer to the first question, Orson said, was that if it was a well-made film and hung together, if it had spirit and verve—which he had every intention of infusing into it—*Othello* could make money. Faith, he argued, was needed. As to the technical problems, he offered the following solution: he planned to buy an enormous trailer that would serve as a portable production and cutting room, outfitted with moviolas, a small vault for positive film, two cutting tables, and whatever else was needed to keep in daily control of the film. The arguments seemed reasonable but still, no money came forth.

IF ORSON HAD accurately defined his terms without embellishment, he might not have become ensnared in yet another controversy that erupted around him in 1949. During one of his teenage pilgrimages to Europe, he had rented a small arena and tried his hand at bullfighting. Although he once told an interviewer that in the ring he was "no damn good," he continued as a "novillero," fighting under the name of *El Americano* in small rings throughout the south of Spain until such time as he had been buffeted, spiked, and scarred by enough young bulls to come to his senses.

The story of his days as a bullfighter somehow got twisted in an article that appeared in 1947 in which Orson was quoted as saying that he had successfully dispatched some twenty bulls. When Fortunio Bonanova, the excitable opera coach in *Citizen Kane,* read the article he became incensed and offered a public challenge to Orson to perform in a Tijuana bullring. Welles then denied the facts of the original story and said he was really only an amateur enthusiast.

Sometime later, perhaps because of the publicity, Orson was asked if he would appear in a benefit fight to aid an old people's asylum: the *corrida* would be held in a little bullring in Cubas de la Sagra near Madrid. This time he accepted the challenge, not to fight the bulls on foot but as a picador to goad the bull with a lance. He would be well padded and ride upon an equally well armored horse.

Posters, with Orson's name, were printed and displayed throughout Madrid and nearby cities; newspaper advertisements proclaimed that the large American movie star would be the only picador featured that day. The two thousand *aficionados,* sitting patiently in the sun on the Thursday afternoon of the fight were to be disappointed, however. Orson simply didn't show up. His excuse was that film commitments prevented his appearance. "The public in a bullring is no more sadistic than any other audience," Orson once wrote. He may have changed his mind when he heard about the announcement of his absence over the arena's loudspeakers: the entire audience let out with a prolonged boo, followed by angry shouts and cries.

Although clearly not a performer in the spectacle of bullfighting, Orson remained a student or a follower of the bulls and successfully incorporated his theory of the art into his own filmmaking activities. Essentially, his philosophy is best clarified in the following extract from an introduction he wrote for a book called *Memories of a Bullfighter* by Conchita Citrón:

> The vice of the modern corrida is that since the bullfighter has become more important than the bull, playing the bull is now more important than his death. Today he is not so much played, as played with, used rather than dealt with, exploited as a means of pleasing the crowd. The sword thrust has been relegated to a final punctuation, a closing chord or full stop. Essentially, the matador fills the plaza by the quality of his work with the muleta. This is as it should be when work is directed toward the subject of the story, which is the death of its tragic hero. If the central argument is not sustained, and with true reverence, the Fiesta has no moral defense.

Although his idea for a feature film on bullfighting, *Sacred Monsters,* never came to fruition nor did an in-depth profile of his close friend Antonio Ordóñez,* in his prime considered the world's greatest bullfighter, Orson did complete a documentary on the art, which was shown on ITV in London. The project caused a great stir from organizations opposed to blood sports, demanding, to no avail, that it not be shown.

The basis of the film included highly spectacular close-ups of a fight by a young matador, Manolo Basquez, which proved that the great danger to the bullfighter is indeed real. The death of another bullfighter was also shown. At the beginning of the program, Orson added this caution:

> If any of you have very strong prejudices against this contest between man and beast and feel that the spectacle may be unnerving to you, we are giving you this warning. But we hope you will stay with us.

*With a proposed screenplay by Ernest Hemingway.

424

ORSON'S THOUGHTS BEGAN to turn to the prospect of a significant role in *Prince of Foxes,* a striking new film. What character actor could resist the part of the wicked Cesare Borgia? Certainly not Orson. Believed to be the model for Machiavelli's *The Prince,* Borgia, a soldier and politician, was one of the most flamboyantly evil characters in all of history: murderer, plunderer, rival with his father for his sister's incestuous bed, briber, trickster, his legend of terror followed him as a commander-in-chief of the papal army as he seized one town after another throughout Italy. Orson wanted to believe he was perfectly typecast for the part. There was even a physical resemblance: the handsome Borgia was taller than most men of his day, and had broad shoulders. He was also a show-off, dressing himself in insolent magnificence, a study in gaudy conceit.

Starting in November of 1948, *Prince of Foxes* had a 110-day shooting schedule. Scenes were filmed in Rome, in the tiny republic of San Marino on the Adriatic coast of Italy, in San Gimignano with its medieval 175-foot-high towers, on the lovely stone streets of Florence, and in Siena where the film wound up its production. During the several months that Orson lived in Rome, a friend at the United States Embassy arranged a private audience for him with Pope Pius XII, during which the two men discussed the Pope's controversial dictum of excommunicating Italian Catholics for joining the Communist Party. From Florence the cast and crew traveled to Venice and then back to Rome. The work required 7,000 miles of air travel by all members of the cast and an additional 3,500 by Tyrone Power, who also traveled by car.

While in Florence, scenes were shot in the Palazzo Medici, where Lorenzo the Magnificent maintained his brilliant establishment. The Boboli and other Florentine gardens also served as backgrounds for action in the picture. The scenery was spectacular. Three-time Academy Award winning cinematographer Leon Shamroy filmed sights and surroundings along the canals of Venice, in the steamy streets of a Florentine morning, in cool mountain passes, and in the huge splendid halls of ancient palaces. The interiors of these authentic Italian structures are among the most impressive ever filmed, and a credit to art directors Lyle Wheeler and Mark-Lee Kirk, as well as to photographer Shamroy.* Alfred Newman composed the score, and Edward Powell arranged it.

The Borgias were a popular subject for films that year. Paramount had released a film about that Machiavellian family only a few months before, *Bride of Vengeance,* starring Paulette Goddard. The screenplay for *Prince of Foxes,* written by Milton Krims based on the best-selling novel by Samuel Shelabarger, was a fictionalized incident in the life of the despotic Cesare Borgia. As part of his attempt to spread his empire across Italy to Venice,

---

*Henry King, the director, insisted that the film be shot in color, that the opulent nature of the story and the magnificent settings demanded it. Darryl F. Zanuck disagreed, however, and was eager to keep the costs of the film down by shooting black-and-white. Zanuck won.

Cesare murders his brother-in-law so that Lucretia, his notorious sister, will be free to marry the Duke of Ferrara. The marriage arrangements are trusted to an ambitious peasant, Andrea Orsini, who performs his office so well that he is rewarded with another diplomatic assignment. A neighboring duchy, which stands in the way of Borgia's ultimate goal of controlling Rome, is ruled by the aged Duke of Verano. Orsini's mission is to seduce the duke's young and beautiful wife and then to murder the duke, thus bringing the duchy under Cesare's domination. Instead, Orsini falls in love with the young woman, Camilla, and switches his allegiance to the duke, who has treated him with saintly kindness. He joins forces with the old man and helps him to defend the duchy from Borgia's army. But the duke is killed in the struggle, and in order to save his people from starvation, Andrea surrenders and is tortured and sentenced to death. A trusted friend in Borgia's army helps him to escape. When he recovers, Andrea Orsini organizes the soldiers of the duchy and is successful in routing the invaders. He is awarded a lordship and wins Camilla as his bride.

The work on the film began with a flourish that was almost as opulent as the Renaissance itself. When the actors arrived in Florence, delegations and managers from all the city's motion picture houses greeted them. They were joined by delegations of actors and actresses from the *Teatro della Pergola* and *Teatro Verdi,* comedians and opera stars from the *Politeama Nazionale,* players for the *Folies Bergères,* the *Teatro Apollo Politeama Fiorentina* and *Teatro Niccolini.*

Orson enjoyed meeting many Italian actors and actresses of the silent picture days who had played in Henry King's *Romola* and *White Sister,* which were made in and near Florence, and who came to see their old friend.

On the night the company arrived in Florence, bells on public buildings were rung, the hotel where Orson stayed was serenaded by Italian musicians, and, to crown the event, fireworks were launched from a chariot drawn by four white oxen.

The relationship between Welles and Henry King developed and remained on a highly professional level. King, a man in his early sixties at the time of the film, was a no-nonsense director. He was known from his films for a certain intensity of storytelling, and had been responsible for such miniclassics as *Alexander's Ragtime Band, Stanley and Livingstone,* and *Jesse James.* He also had an earlier career as a successful stage director. Feldman had sold King on selecting Orson for the part of Cesare Borgia, but King had accepted him with some reservations. The late film writer Hector Arce, in his biography of Tyrone Power, has related the following conversation between Feldman and King:

> "I understand from Gregory Ratoff," said King, "when they were doing *Black Magic,* that Orson doesn't start working until two o'clock in the afternoon, but then he'll work all night. I want him to know that I start at eight o'clock in the morning and I quit at six, whether there are actors or not."

"He'll do anything you want," Feldman replied.

"Well, you better impress upon him that if he wants the part he is due to be on the set when I call him," insisted King.

"I'll guarantee that because he wants to do it more than anything in the world," said Feldman. "Furthermore, he needs the money. I'll tell you what I'm doing. I'm not charging any commission, so you're getting him wholesale."

"Very good," King answered. "Then we can have that understood."

On the first day of filming, Orson was scheduled to appear at noon. At 8:00 A.M. King arrived on the set and found Orson, already in makeup and costume, mulling about the reception hall where the filming was to take place that day.

"What are you doing here?" King inquired.

Orson explained that he was trying to inculcate the atmosphere of the setting, to make sure the clothes felt right on him and also to watch King work. From that day forward, Orson appeared on the set at eight o'clock every morning, even if he had no scenes to play that day, to watch the proceedings.

"He was the most cooperative actor I've ever worked with," King said at the film's end.

Tyrone Power seemed totally awed at being in the same film with the great Orson. Their relationship seemed to develop as if life were imitating art, because of the characterizations both were creating in the film. Power, who played Andrea Orsini, seemed more of a disciple than an equal, and unlike Orsini, he never rebelled. Orson would invariably comment on Power's takes and without King's knowledge would suggest subtle changes and nuances that Power could usually add to his portrayal of Orsini.

It was a happy set for Orson. His trusted colleague Everett Sloane also had a major part in the film; Orson then became friendly with Katina Paxinou, the Greek actress who had won an Academy Award for her earthy portrayal Pilar in *For Whom the Bell Tolls*.

The only problem that occurred between Welles and King proved to be an absurd but all-too-typical encounter. In a scene that took place in the Boboli gardens, Borgia is being entertained, and all of the Florentine nobility is supposed to bid him welcome. Everyone is called to bow to Borgia as he approaches. King envisioned this as a slight bow from the waist; Orson thought the Florentine protocol in this situation called for a deep, fawning, and flourishing obeisance. Orson became upset: "I can't do anything unless these people bow to me and give me the respect that I desire," boomed Orson off-camera. "You're getting a damned sight more respect *than* you deserve," King responded. "You just play the part. The people will do what I tell them."

Despite King's obvious control of the film, it is possible that Orson's suggestions about camera placement and other filmic matters of a technical and creative nature were heeded by the older man. The film does contain a richness and depth of image that surpasses King's *The Black Swan,* which it most closely resembles. James Naremore thinks: "*Prince of Foxes* (1949)

... is ostensibly directed by Henry King, but parts of it bear the marks of Welles's style as vividly as the Robert Stevenson *Jane Eyre* had done in the early forties."

Orson used virtually every spare minute away from the set trying to come to terms with how he would film *Othello*. And of course, he continued to tour Italy, with and without the company, looking for sites, actors, technicians, ideas, points of reference. "A man who has not been in Italy," proclaimed Samuel Johnson, "is always conscious of an inferiority." Orson agreed. His travels, north and south, were a combination of opportunistic professionalism and cultural self-education. The lure of the country was overwhelming to him, and Rome, with its classical ambience, captured his heart. He continued to immerse himself in the culture of the Renaissance in his own self-styled Grand Tour.

Prince of Foxes received somewhat better than mediocre reviews. Orson's acting, as the villainous Borgia, was given a nod of approval by most critics, but the film itself, despite its swashbuckling spectacle and pictorial excellence, was regarded as slow-paced and seeming to lack any kind of narrative flair. *Variety* deemed that Orson "tastefully etched his finest screen portrait to date." Even old enemy Louella Parsons broke down and gave him a left-handed compliment: "Although Orson Welles is never my favorite actor, I must admit he doesn't overact too much as Borgia. This is the awesome Orson at his best." And Hedda Hopper quoted Henry King as saying he believed Orson would win the Academy Award for Best Supporting Actor.*

When the film was shown in New York, it played to fairly full houses for several weeks. In London, where it was released during the height of a film crisis that threatened to reduce the country's motion picture quotas or even force the closing of many theaters, audiences packed one of the big theaters of the J. Arthur Rank chain night after night. In order to ensure their dominance in the English market, Twentieth Century-Fox refused to allow a British-made film to appear on a double bill with *Prince of Foxes* lest any release that might be of inferior quality should benefit from the box office success of its American competitor.

Finally, just when things seemed to be going smoothly for Orson Welles, his insatiable appetite for publicity and controversy pushed him into trouble. He had written a series of articles, which were ultimately published in a Paris newspaper, that were sharply critical of postwar Germany, implying that Nazism was still very much alive. "I don't find many anti-Nazis in Germany today," he wrote. As a result, movie houses in many major German cities boycotted the film. The German press demanded a retraction of Welles's statement. Welles remained obdurate and Twentieth Century-Fox was forced

---

*Orson wasn't nominated. Dean Jagger won it that year for his performance in *Twelve O'Clock High*. *Prince of Foxes* did receive one nomination, however, for Leon Shamroy's black-and-white cinematography.

to withdraw the film from Germany. The loss to Fox was estimated at $250,000.

THE BLACK ROSE, the third film that Orson acted in that was made in Europe at that time, was, if not a thematic sequel, then at least a spiritual one to *Prince of Foxes*. Shooting began on March 20, 1949. It was the first Technicolor film that he had ever been in. Once again, Welles starred with Tyrone Power and once again Orson played the dominant and evil figure with Power as his incorruptible protégé. Adapted from a popular historical romance by Thomas B. Costain, the film is set in North Africa, China, and thirteenth-century England shortly after the successful Norman invasion.

Power was cast in the role of Walter of Gurnie, the Oxford-educated bastard son of a Saxon nobleman who, willing to serve the Norman king, leaves England for the Far East in the company of his friend Tristram, brilliantly played by Jack Hawkins. En route, they meet with Bayan, a ruthlessly brilliant Mongolian warlord played by none other than Orson Welles. Bayan and his troops are traveling to Mongolia with gifts for Kublai Khan. One of these gifts is a caravan of eighty-one slave girls, among them a blonde beauty known as the Black Rose who is played by the diminutive— barely five feet tall—French actress Cécile Aubry. The two Saxons join Bayan's caravan, where Tristram becomes disgusted by Bayan's savageries and Gurnie falls in love with the Black Rose. Gurnie helps Tristram and the girl escape to China where he later encounters them at the palace of the empress. After a struggle in which Tristram is killed, the Black Rose disappears and Gurnie returns to England with the secrets for making paper, explosives, and compasses. In appreciation for these important inventions, the Norman king honors Gurnie and restores his estates. Later, the tyrant Bayan sends the Black Rose to England where she is reunited with her lover and the two presumably live happily ever after.

The two-hour spectacular, which was filmed on location in North Africa and England, was produced by Louis B. Lighton for Twentieth Century-Fox. Henry Hathaway, perhaps best known for his galloping *Lives of a Bengal Lancer,* directed the Talbot Jennings screenplay. The supporting cast consisted of Michael Rennie, Finlay Currie, Herbert Lom, Mary Clare, and Laurence Harvey.

Within the first few days of shooting, Orson began to make news, although more of a press agent's manufactured dream than legitimate information or controversy. Welles was being touted as the first male star to wear a mink coat in a film. The garment, made of brown Russian leather and lined with natural mink, was so heavy it required two wardrobe men to help him into it. To crown this uniform of barbaric splendor, Orson wore a spiked Saracen helmet made of steel, inlaid with a brass design. A high-standing brim of mink encircled the headpiece and a veil of chain mail fell from the edges. The design was calculated to convey that its wearer was not only a soldier but also a lover of luxury and opulence. Again, Orson felt he was perfectly typecast. The majesty of his costume, designed by Michael Whittaker, was a mixed blessing to Welles, who staggered under the weight. "Imagine," he said, "wearing it with the temperature of 120 degrees!" Nevertheless, weighted down so that he could hardly walk, he still preened in it during each wearing, allowing the still photographers to shoot publicity shots of him in all his glory.

The intense heat of North Africa not only was a trial for the other actors but also proved to be a disaster for some of their costuming. Five hundred helmets and breastplates, which were made of plastic, started melting just as a battle scene was being filmed. The "war" had to be called off until a shipment of metal replacements arrived from England.

The armor was only a small part of the million dollars' worth of equipment. Cecil B. DeMille would have been impressed: there were also 150 tents, 12,000 arrows, 1,000 bows, 500 shields, 200 lances, 300 swords, 26 carts, and 72 Chinese dragons. Some 5,000 Arabs, 1,000 horses, and 500 camels were rounded up for the battle scenes.

At least one of the off-camera adventures was nearly as exciting as any that were recorded on film. En route to Casablanca from Meknes, 120 miles to the east, Welles, Tyrone Power, and Linda Christian were cut off by flash floods, a rare occurrence in the desert. The Foreign Legion searched for them, but they were taken in by a Russian innkeeper and remained safe. The torrential rains washed out half the production compound at Quaouizert, 110 miles southeast of Casablanca, and held up production for weeks.

Cécile Aubry's flood experience was even more hair-raising. Traveling between locations with her mother and a driver, she was caught up in the torrents and stranded high in the Atlas Mountains without food. The rain turned into snow and sleet, and even after they were located, it was another twenty-four hours before they were rescued by native mounted police who had to swim a raging river in order to get to them.

Although an attractive film to look at, in some ways a triumph of polished craftsmanship in visually capturing its sweeping and epic story, *The Black Rose* was damaged by bathetic dialogue, pretentious acting, and a convoluted, confusing plot. Orson's performance, although condemned by *The New Yorker* as "nothing more formidable than a Kewpie doll," was actually impressive and one of the better parts of the production, his enjoyment as the leering, fat visionary Bayan, swaggering across desert backgrounds and plotting the conquest of the world, quite evident. "His attack of the material at hand is certainly more enlivening than that of his colleagues," said Howard Barnes in the *Herald Tribune.* "Actor Welles proves surprisingly convincing as the tough Mongol general," reported *Time.* And Philip K. Scheuer in the *Los Angeles Times,* although criticizing *The Black Rose* for its emphasis on purple dialogue, haggard pace, and episodic structure, had this sinistral compliment to offer: "As Bayan, Orson Welles exploits a juicy role to excellent advantage. That his acting was better than it usually is may be due to the fact that he is heavily made up. Years ago, I saw Welles on Broadway as the profusely bearded Captain Shotover in 'Heartbreak House.' The beard, I recall, helped to obscure his hamming."

HENRY HATHAWAY HAS been quoted as saying that he was disappointed at Orson's lack of interest in the role of General Bayan (although such disinterestedness is not discernible in Orson's performance) and found it difficult to persuade him away from constantly discussing and worrying about *Othello.* The Twentieth Century-Fox publicity department, however, seemed delighted with Orson's multidimensional pursuits, issuing a press release that said in part, "At the same time he was playing the Mongolian, he was rehearsing actors and going over scripts for two pictures of his own which he planned to make in North Africa."*

It was true that Orson was preoccupied with production matters concerning *Othello* while acting in the three costume dramas. The story of his involvement with *Othello,* its final shooting, editing, and distribution, is prolonged, intricate, and bewildering.** Pieced together from Orson's own account, MacLiammoir's observations, and the remembrances of some of the cast and crew, the basic story of how the film was formed and made is herewith briefly related.

Of all of the possible Welles-Korda projects discussed in the late 1940s, *Cyrano de Bergerac* kept recurring as the most compelling idea that had emerged between the two men. A cash-flow problem began to develop with Korda, however, when he wanted to produce *The Third Man.* The film would be based on the Graham Greene novel and directed by the distinguished filmmaker Sir Carol Reed, of *Odd Man Out* and *The Fallen Idol* fame. As Alexander Korda began to gather production money for *The Third Man,* he surveyed his existing properties to determine what he could sell in order to bolster his coffers. Writer, producer, director Carl Foreman had in the past evinced interest in the film rights to Rostand's *Cyrano,* owned by Korda. Foreman agreed to pay Korda a goodly sum, which would be instrumental in beginning production on *The Third Man,* and the film rights to *Cyrano* were sold to him. "I need the *dollars,* dear fellow," Korda said on the phone from

---

*In addition to *Othello,* the other project was to be a film of Homer's *Ulysses,* the scenario for which was being written by Canadian anthropologist-turned-screenwriter Ernest Borneman, in collaboration with Orson. The screenplay was never finished, mainly because Orson failed to fulfill a promised salary of $250 a week and all expenses to Borneman. After Borneman had desperately wired him and asked what he was going to do to support himself and his family if he were not paid, he received a cabled response: DEAR ERNEST. LIVE SIMPLY. AFFECTIONATE REGARDS. ORSON WELLES. Ultimately, although it took years, Borneman was paid all the money that Orson owed him.

**The many details and stories of Orson's saga in launching *Othello* are beyond the scope of a *part* of any work. It actually has become the subject of a 100,000-word book itself—the delightful diary account, *Pul Money in Thy Purse,* by Micheál MacLiammoir, written during the time he played Iago to Orson's Moor. It is an account of the film's gestation, the hunt for a constantly changing cast, and the misadventures of Orson and cast and crew on location in North Africa and Italy. "I would have preferred to be the only reader," Orson has written of his friend's diary. "Indeed, my portrait emerges from the MacLiammoir journal as a rather unpalatable cocktail of Caliban, Pistol, and Bottom, with an acrid whiff here and there of Coriolanus." Decades later, in 1978, in a confrontation with his own and the film's mythos, Welles offered his account of *Othello,* by directing and producing a documentary film of tribulations and intrigues.

his Piccadilly office in London, to the complaining, heart-stricken Orson. Korda was somewhat considerate of Orson's concern, however: although it was the end of Orson's ten-year flirtation with *Cyrano* and he was openly depressed at losing the project, he was appeased by Korda's promise of a major role in *The Third Man.*

Now once again a director without a film, Orson pushed, "out of regret" as he said, more aggressively toward *Othello* and traveled between Rome, Paris, and Venice and several cities in North Africa to coordinate both business and filmmaking tasks. He met his perfect Desdemona. Lea Padovani, a statuesque and enchanting Italian actress in her late twenties with sparkling black eyes and hair to match, who had just completed a British-made film, *Give Us This Day,* came into Orson's life. Given the impetus to proceed with *Othello* after the forfeit of *Cyrano,* Orson was even more resolved to do so after meeting her. Her willingness to play the role was combined with a near-miraculous offer from an Italian producer, Montatori Scalera, to back the film. "*Dobbiamo fare Otello*" ("We *have* to make Othello"), Scalera suddenly announced gravely to Welles who was still doing scenes for *Black Magic* in a Roman film studio. "I didn't see any reason to disagree with him," Welles said, struck as he was by what he considered nothing less than a miracle delivered through the mysterious effects of divine omnipotence. It wasn't until shooting had begun with Padovani and an Italian actor who played Iago (whose name everyone seems to have since forgotten), however, that it became clear that Scalera's idea of *Othello* was not Shakespeare's but Verdi's. He wanted to make a film of the opera, not the play, and although production money was given at first, it eventually ran out.

Welles shot most of *Othello* in Italy and Morocco only through the momentum of circumstance—the Scalera money, Orson's acting jobs in North Africa, and the availability of inexpensive technical and creative talent. He originally had planned to shoot the film in the south of France, working out of an old studio near Carcassonne, a site chosen by Alexander Trauner, his art director, who knew the area intimately from his work on *Les Visiteurs du Soir* and *Les Enfants du Paradis.* Welles and Trauner were going to "build" the island of Cyprus on the Côte d'Azur.

Orson had begun language lessons for Lea Padovani. Children's books in English, purchased at a store in Rome that specialized in American works, were used as her texts and she began to improve. He even imported his friend Hortense Hill to give Padovani English lessons. The undertaking was not entirely successful, since Hortense's mid-Western accent was so marked that Lea had trouble understanding her. "I do not ever know what she say," Padovani complained. "She has funny voice. I do not hear anything." Orson never expected the actress to learn English well enough to retain her voice in the film. He intended to have Lea's part dubbed. But he reasoned that as long as her lip movements were close to the correct English, the dubbing would serve to eliminate the Italian accent. To cast her more closely to the flaxen-haired Desdemona, Orson had her hair bleached blond.

Financing for *Othello* came from many sources. All of Orson's own money, "every penny" as he once noted, from his film acting and any other residual income, went into it; various angels, investors, altruists, and almsgivers were approached by Orson and occasionally could be counted upon to come up with *some* money, seemingly from scene to scene, to keep the cameras rolling. Often, however, the investments would vanish as quickly as they were promised, and Orson would be forced to temporarily forsake filming.

One of the biggest investors was Michel Olian, a mysterious Russian millionaire, known for his ownership of hundreds of thousands of acres of timberland in the Cameroons, dozens of factories in Argentina, a utility company in Switzerland, and a substantial film studio in Rome.

Welles had been in Rome for a relatively short time when he met Olian. A garrulous extrovert, and one of the city's lustiest prodigals, Olian immediately welcomed Orson into his inner circle of friends, which included at that time Mike Frankovitch and his wife, Binnie Barnes. In the years after the war, Olian first became involved in the motion picture business as a backer of an American production, *The Dark Road,* filmed in Italy and released by Republic Pictures. He then became a key figure in the financing of American films as a result of earnings made in Italy that were blocked and tied up in Italian banks. It became common practice for major American studios to pay as high as a 30-percent premium on international money exchanges to obtain release of their funds, which otherwise could be freed only if the money was used for film production on Italian soil. It worked this way: Olian would have a contract drawn up with the studio, calling for the production of a film to be made in Italy with the blocked Italian lire. As a guarantee of completion of the production, he would issue a check to the studio for approximately 30 percent less than the stipulated budget figure in the contract. As soon as the funds changed hands, both sides would tear up their respective contracts. The studio would have the total amount of money it sought from the blocked funds, less the 30-percent premium, and Olian would have his initial investment returned plus a profit of 30 percent that he would, in turn, invest in the film. It was a remarkably simple manipulation, and Orson was overwhelmed at the subtlety of Olian's financial genius.

Welles and Olian made an extravagant and eccentric pair in Roman society. Olian's calculated, but seemingly unrestrained, spending was matched only by Orson's flamboyance as they dined at such fine restaurants as *Il Pasetto* and *Cancello d'Oro.* One of their favorite amusements was late-night visits to the Florida Club, where Olian was known to occasionally buy a drink or two for the entire crowd, some $500 per round, depending on the number of imbibers. Their activities, especially after hours with virtual chorus lines of Florida Club lovelies, were often reported in the daily newspapers such as *Momento-Sera* or, occasionally, the English-language *Rome Daily American.* Olian accumulated enormous tabs; he also entertained lavishly at his rented home, the Villa Madama, a sixteenth-century palace designed by Raphael, one of the showplaces of Rome, owned by the Countess Dorothy Di Frasso. Orson became so enamored of the intrinsic loyalty and impeccable ministrations of the servants of the Villa Madama that he became

Olian's guest there and used it as his base of operations for *Othello* for almost a year.

The financial arrangement that Welles had with Olian seemed typically advantageous for the latter, fortuitous for the former. In what appeared to be the final stages of filming, Orson asked Olian for a loan of a mere $35,000 for which the latter would receive recoup rights in England and the United States plus a 50-percent general ownership in the film. An agreement was instantly reached, but it turned out that filming was still over a year away from completion and Olian would end up investing close to $200,000 in the project before the matter was closed. The final expenses came to a shade over $500,000, most of it Orson's.

Another principal investor was Darryl F. Zanuck. Mel Gussow, Zanuck's biographer, has told of at least one amusing incident concerning that investment. Living in Europe, Zanuck often dined with Welles, and the fast-talking, cigar-wielding tycoon enjoyed Orson's company immensely. During a stay at the Hotel du Cap on the Riviera, Zanuck called for room service one morning and was told by the hotel's manager: "Orson Welles is sleeping in the lobby. He arrived at four in the morning and said he had to see you on a desperate matter." Afraid to call Zanuck at that hour, the manager had convinced Welles to wait until morning to see him. Welles had also asked the manager to take care of his taxicab and to charge it to Zanuck's bill. Zanuck recalled: "The fare was more than $420. He had taken a cab from Italy."

When Zanuck finally came down, he found Welles at his cabana at the poolside. Welles was effusive and threw his arms around Zanuck.

"What the hell are you doing here?" Zanuck asked. "I thought you were shooting a film in Italy."

Orson explained his financial straits: "Unless you help, I'm dead. I need $75,000 to finish the picture. We're two-thirds through. The actors are not being paid."

Zanuck claimed he didn't have that kind of money to invest in such a speculative venture, but eventually his heart ruled his head and Zanuck's Hollywood office, after an exchange of telegrams, consented to forward the money. In a day or two, a representative of the local bank arrived at the hotel with a mail sack with locks on it. The equivalent of $75,000 was contained within, with the largest note being 100 francs, a pile that took over three hours to count. Welles gave Zanuck a 60-percent interest in the film, thanked him for the money, returned to Venice, and continued where he had left off.*

Orson grew to become impatient with the acting of his Iago; he was not as evil or as cunning as the role, as Orson interpreted it, called for. He knew the man he wanted, the actor whom he had vainly hoped would play Iago to his Othello almost twenty years before on the Irish stage: Micheál MacLiammoir. After discussing the possibility with Hilton Edwards by phone, Orson sent

---

*It seems that Welles sold more than 100 percent of the film to sundry investors, but the financial machinations are so complicated that it is difficult to ascertain exactly how much was sold to whom. It is altogether possible that Welles lost track, himself, over the years.

MacLiammoir the following telegram: DEAREST MICHEAL. ENTHUSI-ASTICALLY REPEAT OFFER MADE BY ME TO HILTON YOU PLAY IAGO WITH ME IN OTHELLO FILM STOP CAN YOU COME TO PARIS TO ARRANGE THINGS STOP WHEN CAN YOU COME TO DUBLIN IF YOU CAN'T COME TO PARIS STOP LOVE TO YOU BOTH, ORSON."

Although MacLiammoir was a distinguished actor of the stage, he had never been in a film. He gave this as an excuse to politely refuse (although he said he wanted to perform) Orson's offer and added that his age (he was close to fifty) and his weight (he had begun a respectable middle-aged spread) precluded any possibility of his accepting the role. If those exemptions did not prove substantial enough, MacLiammoir offered another: he was just recovering from a nervous breakdown.

"For all sad words of tongue and pen, the saddest are these: It might have been," quoted Orson. *Nothing,* absolutely *nothing,* would stay his desire in having MacLiammoir.

In a matter of days, MacLiammoir was in Paris and Welles continued other casting adjustments. His relationship with Lea Padovani had begun to deteriorate for reasons that are not particularly clear, although Orson's friend Maurice Bessy, the editor of *Cinémonde* and the director of the Cannes Film Festival, had these cryptic remarks to offer (which might lose some of their clarity through a translation from the French): "He avowed that she revealed to him the true depth and keenness of love and that after having made love since he was eleven, he had known nothing about it except gymnastics. And yet, in the end, he felt that Lea had destroyed him, minimized him, that with her he was no longer himself, and that he accepted everything at her hands. She had said to him: 'You're nothing more than a Machiavelli ... no, not even that, for Machiavelli left something in the world when he departed.' And then his old rancor came to the fore: 'During the nine months that I spent with her, I paid for everything that I had ever done to women for twenty years, but in two days I made her pay for what she did to me during those nine months.'" In an interview given to the London *Daily Mail* at that time, Lea said of Orson: "I must have a strong, real man. I am very strong. Orson is a strong man but he play all the time on the surface. On the top." Within a short time, Padovani was on the London stage, talking almost continuously in English for three hours in Tennessee Williams's *The Rose Tattoo.*

Whether Orson's meted "punishment" might have been the act of excising Padovani from his film or some other form of rejection is not known, but shortly after Padovani quit Orson's heart and the set of *Othello,* he was auditioning other possible Desdemonas.

First he persuaded his young friend from *The Black Rose,* Cécile Aubry, to do the part; she began filming but after two days she failed to show up at the set, eventually sending word through her agent that she had signed to do another film, *Bluebeard.* Betsy Blair (who had played a small but distinguished part in *The Snake Pit* and was recommended to Orson by her director Anatole Litvak) came and went, not by her own caprice but from Orson's realization that her look was too modern for the Moor's bride. MacLiammoir helped to fan Orson's rejection: "She has a face like a golf ball," he told him. The fourth Desdemona proved to be the final one—at least for most scenes. Suzanne Cloutier, a French Canadian actress in her early twenties, who had appeared in several films made in Quebec (*Au Royaume des Cieux, Juliette ou la Clef des Songes*), proved to be exactly the actress that Orson sought and needed.

Peter Noble has described Cloutier's impact on Orson and the rest of the *Othello* company: "With her wide-eyed innocence, coupled with a will of iron and a determination to get her own way at all costs, she constituted a strange mixture. Orson, who found her a fascinating psychological study and who spent hours trying to get the performance he wanted from her, nicknamed her 'The Iron Butterfly,' and the name stuck until the film was finished." Mlle. Cloutier's intransigence was not entirely confined to her professional life. Orson, filled with puissance and at his most charming, spent months attempting to seduce her, but she was inflexible: although they dined occasionally, usually in the company of others, her interest in him was merely, and most emphatically, centered about her dedication to the characterization of Desdemona. Because of her rejection of him, he could be brutal toward her. Once, at dinner, surrounded by the rest of the cast, he snapped: "You contribute nothing to the conversation unless you talk about yourself."

The other parts eventually fell into place. British actor Robert Coote, one of the swordsmen in the 1948 MGM version of *The Three Musketeers,* was cast as Roderigo, and Fay Compton, known mainly for her work on the London stage but who made occasional films (*Odd Man Out, Laughter in Paradise*), took the role of Emilia. Orson's old mentor, Hilton Edwards, would play Brabantio.

It took nearly four grueling years from the first day of shooting to complete *Othello.* Money continually ran out; actors, sometimes unpaid by Orson, would go off to other films before finishing their parts in *Othello*; assembling the principals in one city at the same time, became almost impossible; and Orson was contracted for, acted in, and dubbed *The Third Man* during the time of his extended shooting of *Othello.* Almost like a group of medieval players traveling from town to town, the *Othello* troupe would gather wherever and whenever Orson needed them. In order to save money and time, natural rather than studio sets were employed. Nothing could be built; everything had to be found or invented. It was a study in pure improvisation; filming continued only in spurts—on the installment plan—whenever money was available and wherever Orson could gather some of his cast, commandeer a crew, and find a few makeshift weeks to continue. As a vagabond, Orson lived and filmed off the land, so to speak, employing the wares of local craftsmen if at all possible. Because of the constant permutations nothing was shot in continuity or sequence. "There was no way for the jigsaw puzzle to be put together except in my mind. Over a span, sometimes of months, I had to hold each detail in my memory," Welles has recalled.

The making of any film is usually an exercise in creative subterfuge; with

Othello, Welles elevated the deception to highly contrived art. "I had no company," Orson has lamented about his problems with *Othello.* Each time he stopped shooting, his crew members sought work that paid better—some of the crew actually worked for nothing—and when he was ready to continue, a new staff had to be assembled. This meant he often had to have a new cameraman substitute in the middle of a scene, sometimes in the middle of a sentence, and as a result, the problems of maintaining consistency were enormous. "Everytime you see someone with his back turned," Orson said, "or with a hood over his head, you can be sure it's a stand-in. I had to do everything by cross-cutting because I was never able to get Iago, Desdemona, and Roderigo, etc., together at once in front of the camera."

Orson and his band traveled back and forth to Morocco, where they shot in Mogodor. Filming was also done in Venice, Rome, Paris, London, and Perugia; then it was back to the towering battlements of an eighteenth-century citadel at Mogodor, which proved to be the perfect setting for the scenes supposedly set in Cyprus.

Originally, he had conceived of the film with a small number of camera setups; whole scenes, and sometimes several scenes, would be played without a single cut. But this kind of continuous long-take shooting would have required the resources of a large movie studio, unfortunately not at his command. Instead, the pilgrimages from city to city, with the change of crews, forced him to shoot snippets of film, short filmic statements that would be combined together later on. *Othello* has far more individual shots than any other Welles film. Although any particular scene might *appear* to have been filmed all at one time, in one place, it was only through the patching together through the editorial process that it appeared to be an uninterrupted take.

For instance, when Iago steps from the portico of a church shot in Torcello, an island in the Venetian lagoon, the next image was actually filmed in a Portuguese cistern off the coast of Africa. A Tuscan stairway and a Moorish battlement are in the film, both appearing as parts of a single room. Roderigo kicks Cassio in Massaga and gets punched back in Orgete, a thousand miles away. The fight between Cassio and Roderigo is shot in a cistern in Mazagan with the water dyed black. Desdemona is murdered by Othello in an abandoned chapel in Viterbo. Emilia's death takes place in a studio in Rome.

The story behind the scene where Iago instructs Roderigo about the murder of Cassio has become a part of cinematic legend. While in Mogodor awaiting the Carpaggio-inspired costumes that were to be shipped from Rome, Welles received word that the backer who was to supply the clothing had run out of money. With cast and crew assembled, a complicated feat of logistics and outlay of money that had taken Orson several tortured weeks to accomplish, he had to work quickly or else the film's cast and crew would begin to vanish to other projects. Three assistants were dispatched to London, Paris, and Rome, respectively, to attempt to sell percentages of the film rights to potential backers for just a few thousand advance dollars. With this money, Orson hoped to have new costumes made. Meanwhile, after showing them pictures of Carpaggio dress, he commissioned many of the Jewish tailors in

Mogodor to begin constructing the needed costumes (it was during Ramadan and by religious custom no work could be done and the local Arabic tailors couldn't seem to understand what was needed in sewing Renaissance doublets in any event). But this process would take at least ten days, and Welles and his company could not hold out that long before the commencement of shooting.

Orson's solution to the problem displayed a force of imagination that has touched many of his works: since he couldn't quickly provide makeshift medieval costumes, he decided to shoot the scene with the actors wearing no clothes at all.

"*Without* clothes?" asked Robert Coote, who had one of the major parts in the scene.

"Yes," Orson answered. "I am setting the scene in a Turkish bath."

Towels and sheets then became the costumes of the day. Roderigo, after his bath, is seen resting. Iago talks to him of the murder of Cassio. Black masseurs carry great vats of boiling water. There is steam, water, and swirling vapor everywhere. The scene ends when Roderigo, having failed at murdering Cassio, is killed himself by Iago through the slatted floor of the bath.

Orson's Turkish bath scene, which developed into one of the most effective in the film, was crafted out of a fish market, filled with steam and incense; it is a monumental testament to his ingenuity.

It's not to be thought that all of the filming of *Othello* was insecurity and drudgery, however. Part of Orson's style was to work during the day—usually starting after lunch—and entertain the cast and crew at night. If actors or cameramen were being paid a pittance, they could at least be assured of banquets and lavish (or at least wholesome) dinners even in the sparseness of the Moroccan desert, somehow conjured up by Orson. There was much talk, much wine; Orson, with his friends, remembered the *Othello* years with great fondness, despite the pervasive financial difficulties that continually plagued the venture.

If filming *Othello* proved difficult, and it did, the editing was even more burdensome. Attempting to smoothly connect pieces of film of different stocks, developed and processed in laboratories of several countries, incorporating newly dubbed or added dialogue into the sound track, was a nightmare that lasted some two years.

Orson went through editors with immense velocity and abandon: Jean Sacha in Paris; Renzo Ludici in Rome; a lady named Olga somewhere else; John Shepridge in London. Because the meaning of the multitudinous details, the inserts and brief shots, the occasional close-up or the elaboration of an object, were all encompassed in Welles's mind and imagination, it was difficult for him to explain what he meant or wanted.

He grew impatient too quickly, demanded knowledge of minor points and specifics that could not possibly be grasped; frustrated from the years of filming and anxious to possess the completed film, he treated his editors despotically, refusing to allow them the *quid pro quo* with the director that usually accompanies the editorial function, indeed is insisted upon in its definition. Shepridge, a gentle man, never seemed to be able to contest

Orson's remarks or editing direction, even when he knew they were wrong. Pushed to the point of nervous exhaustion, he finally left England with the dramatic announcement that he was never coming back. He soon immigrated to the United States and found his way to Hollywood where he wrote, ironically, the screenplay *Rapture,* among others.

The man who ultimately managed to put the film together by clearly and loudly voicing his own editorial prerogatives—and hence withstanding Orson's sometimes preposterous verbal onslaughts—was a young free-lancer by the name of Bill Morton, who had gained some experience working on British films. Why he elected to remain uncredited in the titles of the finished film is a mystery, but in addition to *Othello,* he went on to edit or coedit many of Orson's other projects, as well.

Orson once explained his editing techniques to André Bazin:

> The one place where I exercise absolute control is in the editing room; it is only then the director has the power of a true artist. . . . I search for the precise rhythm between one shot and the next. It's a question of the ear: editing is the moment when the film involves a sense of hearing. . . . I work very slowly at the editing table. . . . I don't know why it takes me so long; I could work forever on the editing of a film.

Although this slavish attention to the fine points of his film helps to create a certain unity or consistency of vision, it can also serve as a detriment to the final look or as an impediment to the logic of the story. Orson's editors have indicated that he spent *too* much time reiterating the scenes of his film on the editing machine. His initial response to an episode was reasonable, syllogistic, luxuriant, but after the one hundredth or one thousandth viewing, he forgot that a member of the audience will see that same scene only once and could not be equipped with Orson's knowledge or programmed prescience of what is to come later or the memory of certain minuscule details that came before. Editing for himself, therefore, a privileged and informed viewer of his own material, produced a film that sometimes went beyond the comprehension of the average person. The more Orson continued to view the film, again and again, the more he distrusted or even forgot his initial reactions.

Nonetheless, he insisted that his dictums be followed. Once, he became impatient with Morton. "Your job as a film editor is not merely to get from one shot to another. There is a living part to this film and a dead part. Please eliminate the dead."

Orson's determined arrogance of editing seemed to know no bounds in *Othello.* Instead of reshooting the long or medium shots taken with Lea Padovani, he simply included them, hoping that the audience would not notice a body shape, even a face, different from the "real" Desdemona, Suzanne Cloutier or any of the Moroccan stand-ins. If that artifice wasn't enough, he began to believe that Cloutier's voice was not quite to his liking; certainly some of her lines had to be redubbed because of sound problems. Unfortunately, she was unavailable to do her own dubbing because she was making a British film called *Derby Day* and also preparing for her wedding to Peter Ustinov. Orson hired a Scottish actress, Gudrun Ure, to do her redubbing and privately remarked that he thought her voice far superior to that of Cloutier.

"Wouldn't it be fun to dub her completely?" Welles asked Morton mischievously. Morton couldn't believe what he was hearing. "But Orson, there's no need to do more than just a few tracks," he replied. "Nonsense," boomed Orson with a Bacchic laugh. "We'll have Ure dub the entire Desdemona. I can't wait to see what Cloutier's reaction will be when she attends the premiere and finds out it's not really her, at least not her voice, and in many shots not her body—on the screen."

And so it went. Orson also personally dubbed all of Roderigo because he didn't like the sound of Robert Coote's voice. "His voice doesn't sound like it's coming from his body," he complained. Other voices of both principal and minor characters were also dubbed into the track: all by Orson.

The pressure Welles was experiencing in completing *Othello* was not all self-imposed. Some of his backers, with both large and small investments, were beginning to complain of broken promises, unfulfilled dates, demanding return of their money. Over everything hung the shadow of defeat.

Michael Stern, a writer based in Rome, recounts an incident that he witnessed between Welles and Olian in the lobby of the Excelsior Hotel. While the exchange was not quite audible to the passersby in the Via Veneto, everyone in the lobby could clearly hear Olian demanding his money, according to Stern, "calling Welles a fool, dwelling on the reasons, while the embarrassed actor-director tried desperately to mollify him." *"Tu as raison, Michel,"* was all the humiliated Orson could offer. "You are right, Michel."

NEVER ACKNOWLEDGING THAT his heart was ruling his head, relentless in his resolve to some how, someway, finish *Othello,* no matter what the emotional price, Orson magically emerged with a completed film in the spring of 1951 and entered it in the Venice Film Festival of that year. The film, in its totality, still wasn't exactly what he wanted, but there simply were no more investors in Europe or anywhere else in the world, as far as Orson could see, and he went on to paraphrase the scientist Agassiz: he simply could not afford to waste his time trying to accumulate money. Indeed, he had put his heart and soul, his body, and his psyche into the making of *Othello,* but there were other countries to visit, other films to make.

"We didn't run out of food or wine, or certainly out of talk," Welles has remembered with a gentle nostalgia. "We simply ran out of film." The surcease of filming *Othello* had been reached.

At Venice, some thirty films were competing for the Lion of St. Mark award, and there was much speculation about *Othello,* the mysterious film that Orson Welles had been working on for years. All details for the screening of *Othello* were arranged, and the 1,200 seats of the Festival Palais were entirely booked. A final print of the film was being processed and the sound mixed in a laboratory in Rome; it arrived on the morning of the scheduled premiere. Orson privately screened it that afternoon and was aghast at what he saw and heard: the sound effects and dialogue were not synchronized, the images were overly dark and murky, the print entirely inadequate. Overlapping dialogue was one thing, but when the Duke opened his mouth to say, "If you please, be't at her father's," it was Brabantio who spoke; and Brabantio's line, "I will not have it so," was spoken by Othello; Othello's line, in turn was uttered by Desdemona.

He simply could not show *Othello* as it was and risk the poor critical reaction the film was bound to engender. It was too late to make another print; seeing it in total for the first time also convinced him that he had to correct some additional errors, redub some more lines, continue with the editing procedure. Just hours before the film was to be shown, Orson called a press conference—which close to one hundred critics and journalists attended—and announced in both English and Italian that he was withdrawing *Othello* from competition, the first time in the history of the oldest film festival that a scheduled entry was canceled. Dressed in a white smoking jacket and blood-red shirt, he looked larger and older than his thirty-six years. His voice was fatigued as he explained that he could not jeopardize his reputation on a print that was in such a deplorable state.

"Why don't you just show the print to the working journalists in a special screening?" one of the reporters asked. Orson declined. A fair amount of complaining was heard. Someone suggested that a vote be taken by all assembled to see whether they would want to privately see the rough cut. The group began to grow surly. Orson raised his hand and exclaimed: "We must for the moment forget the democratic principle of the majority vote. In this case I am a small fortress and I will hold out!" Despite repeated grumblings, the conference was over, ticket holders were refunded their money, and Welles left Venice. The Best Film award that year went to Akira Kurosawa for *Rashomon.*

Eventually putting the film back together the way he wanted it, Welles entered *Othello* in the Cannes Film Festival, the largest and most prestigious of film competitions, in May of 1952. It was now almost close to what he was seeking, a film that *lived,* with scenes in constant movement played against menacing walls, mysterious arches, imposing columns, gray skies: a poem of somber images and exquisitely subtle acting.

Now, MacLiammoir's Iago was near perfect: asexual, brutally psychotic with reptilian intensity and bursts of sharp-tongued assaults. Even the laboratory creation of the Cloutier/Padovani/Ure character of Desdemona seemed to work as a compassionate and bewildered victim. His own portrayal of the Moor was of a sensitive and intelligent man, terribly ravaged by the sickness of the jealousy spread to him by Iago; Welles played it tirelessly with vitality and verisimilitude.

He was particularly pleased with the opening scene. As the bodies of Othello and Desdemona are carried in a procession that is silhouetted against a heavily clouded and heroic sky, a grave mourning chorus is accompanied in the background by bells and drums. Except for the one close-up shot of the dead Othello, Orson did all the camera work for the opening procession scene, using a double for distant shots of the Moor.

The unofficial experts at Cannes that year were predicting that one of two American films might win the festival's highest award—the Golden Palm— either *Viva Zapata!* or *Detective Story.* Although Orson believed *Othello* was relatively better, he was more hopeful of gaining a distributor than winning a prize.

Several hours before the awards ceremony, with the winners still unannounced, Welles was in his room at the Carlton Hotel when he received a visit from the festival's director. Orson had entered *Othello* as a Moroccan nomination because it was really a film without a country, financed by backers from many nations and shot on two continents. There was no official Moroccan delegation at the festival, just Orson and his cans of film. When the director asked whether he knew the Moroccan national anthem, Orson surmised all at once that as the winner's name is announced and he walks to the podium to receive the prize, the orchestra plays his national anthem. Later that evening, as Orson strode to the stage to collect the Golden Palm, the orchestra played, in Welles's words, "something vaguely Oriental from one of the French operettas and the audience stood solemnly to attention."*

Winning the top award among some of the finest films from countries all over the world (as many as six hundred films were screened during festival week) was immensely gratifying to Orson and virtually vindicated his years of frustration with *Othello.* When he also gained a worldwide distributor for the film, United Artists, he felt, finally, that his troubles were over.

"My film did not do justice to the play," Orson has said publicly, but he has also been quick to point out that he made no attempt to imitate Shakespeare. He said:

> In *Othello* I felt I had to choose between filming the play or continuing my own line of experimentation in adapting Shakespeare quite freely to the cinema form. Without presuming to compare myself to Verdi, I think he gives me my best justification. The opera *Otello* is certainly not *Othello* the play. It certainly could not have been written without Shakespeare, but it is first and foremost an opera. *Othello* the movie, I hope, is first and foremost a motion picture.

In the United States, *Othello* opened in September 1955 and was appraised as Orson hoped it would be: as a faithful cinematic adaptation of a play by William Shakespeare. Paul V. Beckley in the *Herald Tribune* wrote: "Orson Welles has made an impressionistic and gloomy *Othello,* as larded with melodrama as a ninteenth-century German romance, but nonetheless an intriguing and often exciting film." The anonymous reviewer in *Newsweek* called it a "powerful, darkly beautiful movie." *Time* proclaimed that everything in the film was done "with great bravura style," and in the deadly serious

---

*Actually, *Othello* shared first prize (a fairly common occurrence at Cannes) with an Italian entry, *Due Soldi di Speranza,* directed by Renato Castellani.

Films in Review, Robert Downing wrote that Welles's *Othello* "was a worthy attempt to bring Shakespeare to the screen." However, not all of the American reaction to *Othello* was positive. Bosley Crowther in *The New York Times* wrote: "This extraordinary picture, which took more than three years to make and equally as long—or longer—to redub and prepare for showing here, is strictly an un-literate, inarticulate and hotly impressionistic film, full of pictorial pyrotechnics and sinister shadowy moods." In the *New Republic,* Eric Bentley savaged both Welles and the film: "*Othello,* a film bad from every point of view and for every public. It is, technically, gauche, the dialogue being all too obviously dubbed. It lacks popular appeal, as the story is neither simply nor skillfully told. To connoisseurs of Shakespeare it can only be torture."

If Orson reacted badly, and he did, to the spotty, sometimes adverse criticism of *Othello* in the United States, one wonders how he coped with the British comments. The film opened at the London Pavilion on February 24, 1956, and the next day's reviews were virtually a consensus that Welles simply did not know his "place" in interpreting Shakespeare.

The headlines bear out the reaction: "The Crime of Orson Welles," or "Mr. Welles Murders Shakespeare in the Dark," or "The Boor of Venice—Wicked Welles." Here is a potpourri of British press reaction:

> Garbled, as well as gabbled, Shakespeare.

> This film of *Othello* will remain as a classic—of the silent screen. It will be enjoyed to the full only by those who are slightly deaf and have exceptional eyesight.

> His *Othello* is a showman's piece, a wonderful display of cinematic connotations. But the plain glorious tale of the Moorish commander, the gentle wife and the scheming ensign has somehow been lost along the way.

> The Shakespearean text is not so much cut as slashed to the bone.

George Bernard Shaw once wrote of a performance of *Othello*:

> The actor cannot help himself by studying the part acutely, for there is nothing to study in it. Tested by the brain, it is ridiculous, tested by the ear, it is sublime. He must have the orchestral quality in him. . . . Let him be as crafty as he likes without that, he can no more get the effect than he can sound the bottom C on violoncello, the note is not there, that is all; and he had better be content to play Iago, which is within the compass of any clever actor of normal endowments.

The English, in general, felt that the note was not there in Welles's performance, that his interpretation of the Moor was musically empty. Almost every review in London also criticized his excision and changes of Shakespeare's text, taking particular offense at his alteration of the famous line, "It is the cause, it is the cause, my soul," to run, "It is the cause, it is the cause, O my soul." Orson had added that one syllable in the dubbing at Morton's editorial insistence, because the line without the "O" interfered with the rhythm of the matching image. It greatly offended English ears. What would it be like, some argued, if Hamlet's key line had been changed to "To be or not to be . . . Ah! . . . that is the question"? It might scan better but it just wasn't Shakespeare, they complained.

There were other problems with the film that British audiences, not the critics, complained about. People who were somewhat unfamiliar with the tale had difficulties sorting out who was doing what to whom. Was Emilia the wife, mistress, or mother of Iago? Who killed Roderigo? How did he become involved? When and why did the action shift from Venice to Cyprus?

Strangely, it was only Dilys Powell, doyen of British film critics, who stood up for Welles's *Othello*, pronouncing it in the *Sunday Times* as superb: "large, noble and tragic." She said:

> I find this a moving *Othello*, one of the few to reconcile the man's moral size with his weakness. Mr. Welles's stature, gesture, tones, make the crumbling of reason, the blind, deaf rage believable. When I think of the Moor now, this is the Moor I imagine.

Despite Powell's plea, the general echo of protest and offense over the film in London was enormous. It ran only four days at the Pavilion.

DURING THE TIME that Welles was making *Othello* and living in Rome, Errol Flynn was also there acting in *The Adventures of Don Juan*. Both men caroused together; Welles had already severed his relationship with Lea Padovani and was filled with a sense of depression that seemed to be abated only by wild excessiveness into the intemperance of Roman nightlife. One evening, a small party was given at one of the nightclubs for the cast of *Don Juan*. Orson was invited, and it was there he was introduced to Paola Mori, a starlet in the film.

Orson was immediately attracted to the regally beautiful Mori but other than an exchange of some pleasant Italian conversation, nothing more romantic occurred, although he made attempts to manipulate the first meeting into a more fanciful direction.

A few weeks later, Luchino Visconti, who was then directing *La Terra Trema*, had a private dinner party for Flynn and a few other guests. Orson and Paola were also, separately, invited and during a conversation between them, Orson discovered that she was not merely an aspiring actress but a genuine countess, descended from the di Girfalcos, a noble Italian family. The count di Girfalco and his line represented a noted family of princes connected to the famous Aragona Pignatelli Cortes of Naples.

Paola's father had been a colonial administrator for the Italian government in Tripoli; she was born in 1934 in a little desert oasis called Tajourah, where she lived until she was seven. During the war, the Italians accused her father of antifascist sentiments, ordered him back to Rome, and imprisoned him. The British, when they overran Libya, briefly imprisoned Paola along with her mother and a younger sister but eventually repatriated them aboard the mercy ship *Giulio Cesare*. The family lived on the outskirts of Rome until Mussolini was overthrown and her father freed. Immediately, they reestablished residence in the center of the city in an impressive villa.

The count di Girfalco was appalled at Paola's ambitions to be an actress, but her mother approved. Postwar film production in Italy was booming, second only to that of the United States in total number of features made; the opportunities were enormous. Eventually, her father gave his permission.

After hearing the story of her life and spending the remainder of the evening talking only with her, Orson was totally enamored. As the party was breaking up, Orson walked slowly over to Paola and "in a voice that made his words sound like an accusation," as one eyewitness has recalled, growled, "I love you."

Orson became an ardent suitor, besieging Paola and her family with gifts, flowers, telephone calls, invitations to dinners and parties. Eventually, she began to appear at various *Othello* locations; soon they were living together at a large and quite luxurious house, the Casa Pilozzo, a villa in Frascati on the outskirts of Rome.

CHAPTER 16

ASIDE FROM THE three swashbucklers in which Orson Welles acted primarily to keep himself and the production of *Othello* afloat, he also starred in *The Third Man,* a film that, according to André Bazin, would for the first and perhaps only time offer a part to Welles that would identify him in the public consciousness.

Alexander Korda's call to play the promised role of Harry Lime produced a medley of emotions in Orson. He desperately wanted to finish *Othello* and equally needed the money he would earn from *The Third Man.* He could not spare the time away from *Othello,* yet he could not forgo the acting fee from Korda. Not knowing how to handle the decision he was forced to make, he simply postponed making one.

Korda and Carol Reed, the director, began calling Welles in various cities throughout Italy in an attempt to discuss details. Each time they tracked him to a hotel, he usually had just departed or had given instructions not to be disturbed. Korda believed that Welles was holding out for a larger amount of money than had been originally discussed. If he had only realized how financially destitute Orson was, he probably would have remained more detached. Finally, Korda dispatched his brother Vincent, the art director, to Italy in order to meet Welles and ferry him back to London for negotiations. "Find him. Bring him back somehow. Try not to let him know how much we need him, but get him back here and I'll persuade him to sign a contract."

Vincent Korda and his young son Michael began sleuthing Orson through Rome, Florence, Venice, Naples, Capri. As Michael described it thirty years later in his family's romance, *Charmed Lives*:

> My father was not upset. He liked a sea voyage, and we set off on the steamer for Capri, like a pair of pilgrims on some obscure religious quest. As we pulled into the dock at Capri, we looked over the side to see a motorboat heading out toward the mainland at top speed. In the back, waving grandly to us, sat Orson, surrounded by a mound of luggage, on his way, as we soon discovered, from Naples to Nice. At a day's interval we followed after him, now followed by a storm of cables from Alex, urging Vincent on. It is impossible to say whether these increased Vincent's zeal or Orson simply ran out of money or credit, but

we finally tracked him to the Bonne Auberge, in Cognes-sur-Mer, where Madame Boudoin, always my father's friend, champion and advisor, had informed us he could be found, eating the small raw artichokes of Provence, which were served with an anchovy sauce, before plunging into a steaming bouillabaisse and a roast chicken.

Somehow Vincent commandeered Orson back to London, and within a matter of days Orson and Sir Alex were locked in friendly discussion in the former's penthouse suite atop the Claridge Hotel. When agreement was reached, Orson went back to Italy to continue *Othello,* and production planning for *The Third Man* continued in London.

Korda had a particular fascination for and personal love of *The Third Man* because the story idea was originally his. One evening over dinner, the Austrian correspondent of the *The Times* of London had given Korda a graphic description of Vienna as the once-proud and exalted Hapsburg capital, which since the war had been divided by four occupying nations. It was now a city permeated with a substratum of spies and black marketeers, and Korda wanted to weave a story of intrigue and mystery around it. He suggested to Sir Carol that his collaboration with Graham Greene, which started with *The Fallen Idol,* be revived. Both men wanted to continue working together. Greene was called in and the idea for a script was discussed. He went to Vienna to begin working and, as a point of commencement, used an opening paragraph for a story that he had abandoned nearly twenty years before: "I had paid my last farewell to Harry a week ago, when his coffin was lowered into the frozen February ground, so that it was with incredulity that I saw him pass by, without a sign of recognition, among the host of strangers in the Strand." Eventually, he produced *The Third Man* in prose form and this was, with Sir Carol's assistance, adapted to a screenplay.

The story concerns the bizarre experiences of Holly Martins, an American author of cheap, Wild West novelettes, who comes to Vienna to visit his lifelong friend Harry Lime, only to learn that he had been killed in a street accident. Martins's curiosity is piqued after he hears conflicting stories on how Lime died. He becomes increasingly upset and confused after Major Calloway, head of the British police, tells him that Lime is a penicillin black marketeer whose activities had either killed or maimed innocent children. Martins refuses to believe that Lime is guilty of corruption, let alone murder, and starts an investigation of his own, thinking that Lime may have been murdered. He cultivates a friendship with Anna Schmidt, an actress who was in love with Lime; through her he learns that when Lime was struck down, three men carried his body to the curb. For some reason, two of the men, whom he eventually meets, are unwilling to identify or acknowledge the third man. After a series of experiences during which his life is in jeopardy, Martins learns that Lime is alive, allowing another man to be buried under the name of Harry Lime. They meet and Martins's fears are confirmed: Lime was the monster of evil that Major Calloway has been describing. Despite Anna's pleas, Martins agrees to help in the capture of Lime, to lead him into a trap. Lime is finally killed, betrayed by his friend, after a hectic chase through Vienna's labyrinthine sewer system.

As the story was internationally intertwined, so would be the mounting of the production. Korda efficiently coproduced with David O. Selznick; after Cary Grant turned down the role, Joseph Cotten of the United States would play Holly Martins; Trevor Howard of England would play Major Calloway, Alida Valli of Italy would play Anna Schmidt; and Orson Welles, the man who seemed to be without a country, would play Harry Lime.

Even though Orson had signed a contract to play Lime, getting him to Vienna to begin filming proved to be no journeyman's task. Carol Reed was already in the city. Shooting had begun, and he was awaiting his star, the elusive Orson, to arrive. From Italy, Welles had informed Reed that because of *Othello* and his other commitments, he could not appear in Vienna on the scheduled date and he could only be there for a few weeks within a specified time limit. When Korda heard of Orson's vacillations, he became angry and suggested that Reed consider replacing him; as much as he liked Orson and thought of him as so ideal for the part, he believed they could not jeopardize the production because of Orson. Reed, however, insisted that Welles remain in the film. As the two men discussed the situation by telephone—Reed in Vienna, Korda in London—and Korda was beginning to *order* Reed to replace Welles, Reed's other phone rang; his secretary informed him that it was Orson calling from Rome. In the middle of Korda's sentence, Reed thumbed the button on the receiver, as if the line was inexplicably disconnected, and took Orson's call. Their conversation became heated.

"Can you be here by October 16?" Reed asked. "If you say 'no,' Alex wants you replaced."

Since there was no alternative, Orson immediately agreed. When Reed called Korda back, he pretended that the connection had been broken; now, however, he had good and substantial news: Orson promised to be in Vienna on the scheduled date and would give the film whatever time was needed. Reed guaranteed it and Korda relented.

When Orson arrived in Vienna, Reed was preparing the famous chase scene in the eerie sewers. On the first morning of shooting, when Orson went down under the Vienna streets, he was horrified. The smell was overwhelming; the sewers were cold, damp, and oozing with filth. Since he had just recovered from a bout of mild influenza, he was concerned that spending days in the cold and wet tunnels would plunge him into pneumonia. "Why can't this be done at Shepperton?" demanded Orson of Sir Carol, mentioning the comfort of a sound studio and the danger of the narrow and winding stairs, among other difficulties. Since many of the interior scenes *were* going to be shot at the English studio, Orson did not accept the reasons why his parts in the sewer chase scenes couldn't be duplicated there also. Reed explained that he sought an authentic setting; the scene, as he had arranged it, took weeks of preparation. It was one of the first postwar British films to be made on location. The Austrian sewer brigade, a unit of sixteen specially selected policemen, whose job it was to patrol the sewers day and night, looking for would-be suicides and thieves thinking up new ways to engage in burglary, were called in to assist and were to be used as actors in the film. Lighting the pitch-black tunnels became an enormous problem. Sound recording, with unpredictable echoes, was difficult to manage; however, Reed seemed to have everything under control. Everything . . . except Orson.

No, Orson said, there was no way that he was going to act in those sewers; in fact, he announced quite pompously, he was withdrawing from the film altogether. "As I had the cameras and crew all waiting to go," remembered Sir Carol, "I begged Orson to change his mind. I entreated him, in any case, just to play the scene we had prepared. I told him that if, afterwards, he was adamant in not playing in the picture, we could still use the shot, as it would only show his back."

Welles reluctantly agreed. Reed was totally satisfied with the first take but Orson was not. It was not quite dramatic enough. He talked with the cameramen, discussed it further with Reed, and soon he was completely immersed not only in the acting of the part of Harry Lime but in the making of the film. After some ten more takes, both Reed *and* Welles had what they wanted, both practically and psychologically. Orson remained.

The rest of the filming went well as far as Orson was concerned, and eventually certain scenes with him in his role of the erstwhile phantom of the sewer were shot at Shepperton as he had originally wanted.

There were other problems. The scene where the police are about to trap Harry—a huge shadow is seen on the wall that looks as though it is Harry but turns out to be a balloon man—caused some aesthetic consternation among the crew. The shadow is obviously of Lime/Welles and the audience would be duped by the cheap cinematic trick, the crew believed, when it is discovered that it is someone else. The cameramen protested to Reed and even threatened to quit or go on strike if forced to film it, but Sir Carol insisted, his resolve prevailed, and the scene remained. The desire for authenticity was always present in Reed's approach, however. He made an effort to capture the neglected and hopeless ambience of fear-ridden, downtrodden Vienna, rendering an impression of it as a city of obstacles, while at the same time trying to show some of its historical parts, from the towering Stephen's Dome to the deserted Prater and its giant Riesenrad.

One of the strongest elements in the film was the zither music. Used as a melodic aphorism, "The Third Man" theme complemented virtually every scene and held the story together. Its origins are interesting: one night Sir Carol, Joseph Cotten, Alida Valli, and Orson, after a tiring day of shooting and an evening of a long dinner and some touristic roaming of the capital, repaired to a Viennese wine cellar, similar in atmosphere to the ones that were so popular in prewar days: a smoky, cavelike bistro with a feeling of international intrigue permeating the personality of the customers and waiters. There they found Anton Karas, a forty-year-old musician, plucking a zither for hours on end just for tips. Almost from the instant that he heard the zither music, Reed believed that it epitomized both Vienna and a sense of mystery.

He wanted it for his film. Orson was equally captivated. The fact that a single instrument was rarely used to provide the music for a modern film didn't disturb Sir Carol. It was the exact sound for which he had been searching.

Since Karas spoke only German, and no one in Reed's group had a particular command of the language, it was difficult to communicate with him. Eventually, through the help of several bilingual customers, Reed informed Karas that he would like him to compose and play the music for *The Third Man*. At first Karas was skeptical and unenthusiastic, especially when he heard that the job entailed traveling to England to record the track. Reed persuaded him to change his mind.*

There has been much discussion about whether *The Third Man* was partially directed by Welles or at least influenced by him. The first-person singular style of many vintage Wellesian projects, which does not appear in the original Graham Greene screenplay, is integral to the finished film. Martins opens *The Third Man* with a line that sounds as though it came from a 1939 Mercury broadcast: "I never knew the old Vienna before the war, with its Strauss music, its glamour and easy charm. Constantinople suited me better." The baroque construction, through careful cinematic manipulation, evoking "a spirit of place far beyond any usual preoccupation of setting," as noted by British film scholar John Russell Taylor, as well as distorted camera angles, variegated shadows, and overlapping dialogue does make the film appear to be stylistically close to a project that Welles might have created. From interviews that have appeared of both Reed and Welles, however, it is fairly certain that Orson had only a peripheral effect, as any actor might, on the final look or heart of the film.

There is also a myth that Welles completely wrote his entire part of Harry Lime, the origin of the story probably arising from the knowledge that he did create the famous cuckoo clock speech. Martins arranged to meet Lime (the only time in the film that they have any extended communication) in an amusement park; so that they can be alone and talk in private, they take a ride on a huge ferris wheel.** Martins is unable to touch Lime's sense of humanity. Lime wants Martins to work for him. As they part, Lime says: "When you make up your mind, send me a message—I'll meet you any place, any time, and when we do meet, old man, it's you I want to see, not the police.... And don't be so gloomy.... After all, it's not that awful—you know what the fellow said: In Italy for thirty years under the Borgias they had warfare, terror,

---

*Although there is only forty minutes of music in the film, it took Karas several hours a day for six weeks to compose and play it, since the entire story had to be translated for him as he sat in a Shepperton Studio screening room. His work was well rewarded. In addition to the money he made for composing and playing the music, within weeks after the release of the film, "The Third Man" theme record sold over 500,000 copies; subsequent sales, additional albums, and public appearances supposedly made Karas wealthy.

**It is here that Lime professes the nihilistic, almost Nietzschean, rationale for murder, pointing to the people in the crowd below as a series of dots: "If I said you can have £20,000 for every dot that stops, would you really, old man, tell me to keep my money—or would you calculate how many dots you could afford to spare?"

murder, bloodshed; and they produced Michelangelo, Leonardo da Vinci, and the Renaissance. In Switzerland they had brotherly love, five hundred years of democracy and peace, and what did they produce? The cuckoo clock. So long, Holly."

Of that speech, Carol Reed has remarked: "The popular line of dialogue concerning Swiss cuckoo clocks was written into the script by Mr. Orson Welles." Welles has claimed that the line was not entirely original on his part but stolen from, or based on, a fragment of an old Hungarian play.

The fact that Welles did not write his own part in entirety in no way detracts from the unrivaled manner in which he plays the despicable Harry Lime. From the moment he makes his electrically startling ingress into the film, a full fifty-nine minutes from the beginning, to his ignominious denouement in the slime of the sewers, Welles plays the somewhat foppish Lime with dynamic believability. Oddly, it is one of the few films of his career that he played without makeup, false nose, or other physical changes, and yet it is the one film, as critic Manny Farber has observed, in which Welles succeeds in certain wonderful moments, in creating the illusion of being someone other than Orson Welles.

Aside from the cuckoo clock dialogue, the two other most gripping Lime scenes, or images, are ones in which he doesn't speak at all. The first is his entrance, when the cat is seen nestling up against someone's highly polished shoes in a darkened doorway; when light from Anna's apartment illumines the image, punctuated with the dramatic and urgent zither music, Lime is shown for an instant with a sardonic smile, makes eye contact with Martins and then disappears. It is an unforgettable bow for a character, one of the most stunning in all of film history. The other scene is the final one in which the wounded Lime pulls himself up the iron stairway in the sewer but is too weak to dislodge the manhole cover. His fingers reach through the sewer grating like a lost soul from Dante's *Inferno,* vainly and feebly searching for salvation, a portrait of the agony of the impossible-to-reach freedom.

Although Lime appears in the film only for a few scenes, Welles created such an indelible characterization that for years later, whenever he walked into a restaurant or a nightclub, "The Third Man" theme would invariably be played in his honor by the resident orchestra. That Welles did not identify with Lime personally, however, he once made clear: "I hate Harry Lime: he has no passion; he is cold; he is Lucifer, the fallen angel."

The Third Man broke at least one of the popular film traditions: Lime *was* killed in the end and Holly Martins did *not* go off happily with Anna Schmidt. As Holly waits for her after Harry's definitive funeral, she comes toward the camera down a road that looks not unlike a reproduction of Van Gogh's early *Avenue of Poplars.** Will she accept Holly and forgive him for trapping

---

*Since the film was shot in late winter, the trees were bare. Sir Carol wanted falling leaves, however, to indicate that time was passing and the story was ending. As a consequence, baskets of leaves had to be transported from another part of Austria and crew members were stationed in the trees and on ladders, off camera, to drop them, one by one, on the exiting Valli.

Harry? No. She walks past him as though he were invisible. Holly lights a cigarette. The zither agonizes. Fadeout.

The critical reaction upon release of *The Third Man* was universally positive, and Orson's efforts particularly, with such restrained compliments as a "nice job of shaping a dark and treacherous shadow" (Bosley Crowther in *The New York Times*). Orson was serious when he said that he'd rather play Lime than Hamlet. He felt that the abbreviated part *was* the whole film, in miniature. *The Third Man* was awarded the Golden Palm as the best film at the 1949 Cannes Festival.

AS IF STARRING in a major motion picture and the continuous nightmare of the epic *Othello* were not enough to plague him, Orson took time in the early 1950s to write a curious little novel entitled *V.I.P.* Never published in English, the book appeared in 1953 in a French edition under the title *Une Grosse Légume,* which loosely and idiomatically means "A Big Shot" or "Big Wheel." The Gallimard edition was translated from English to French by .Maurice Bessy, who also wrote the preface.

Bessy introduces Welles to his French readers in glowing terms; he writes in the French tradition, perhaps begun by the poet Baudelaire's adulation of Edgar Allan Poe, of an attempt at understanding the misunderstood, or allegedly misunderstood, American genius. The Bessy introduction says that Welles in the early 1950s was an undervalued artist, a lonely titan always on the move, going here and there to satisfy his cravings and do his work: he is the prototypical American solitary in the process of becoming a citizen of the world. The droll *Une Grosse Légume* was, according to Bessy, a tiny but brilliant spark thrown off by his scintillant genius.

Regardless of what one may think of French enthusiasms, it can be said that *Une Grosse Légume* is a slapstick comedy of errors employing the standard farcical devices of mistaken identity and broadly sketched character types. It is the story of the naive Joe Boone-Cutler, an American soft drink salesman, and his misadventures on an island run dictatorily by the improbably stupid, Mussolini-inspired Admiral Cuccibamba. The setting is Mediterranean, but the trappings are those of any banana republic where not even the dictator takes himself seriously.

Boone-Cutler, who has come to the island of Malinha to sell a franchise for the drink Fresco (read Coca-Cola), is mistaken for a dispenser of U.S. overseas aid. In the ensuing complications, he is given the red-carpet treatment, all the while believing that the cheers, marching bands, and testimonial dinners are the government's expressions of gratitude for bringing the world-famous Fresco to Malinha.

In brief, the book is a light satire poking fun at American simplicity, international profiteering, and cold-war politics. Malinha, like the kingdom of Grand Fenwick in *The Mouse That Roared,* is a tiny country that will do anything for American dollars. In this case, the admiral's advisers hatch a plan to simulate a threatened communist takeover in the hope that the U.S. government will counter with a liberal application of foreign aid. The plan backfires when the stooge candidate actually wins and throws everybody out, including the "Fresco Wall Street lackey," Joe Boone-Cutler. The victory is of no moment, however, because the true communists, getting wind of the disturbances, cannot even find Malinha on the map.

Those few who ultimately brought copies of the little yellow paperback from Paris would probably agree with Bessy that it is less a novel than a sketched-in treatment for a comedy film—one Welles never got around to making. He did, however, make a few pennies from authoring the work, which was undoubtedly his intent all along.

As soon as the book began making appearances in the Paris bookshops, reviews, respectful but hardly rave for the most part, began to appear. One of the most interesting, in *Les Nouvelles Littéraires,* also contained a short interview of Orson holding forth on the arts: "The essential is to excite the spectators. If that means playing *Hamlet* on a flying trapeze or in an aquarium, you do it. I rather think the cinema will die. Look at the energy being exerted to revive it—yesterday it was color, today three dimensions. I don't give it forty years more. Witness the decline of conversation. Only the Irish have remained incomparable conversationalists, maybe because technical progress has passed them by."

ANOTHER ATTEMPT AT making money, while editing the interminable *Othello* in Paris, involved Orson's entrepreneurial return to the theater, his first such incursion since the *Around the World* debacle. Working with Micheal MacLiammoir and Hilton Edwards, he mounted an evening of theater—a two-play offering—under the title, *The Blessed and the Damned.* The first part of the bill was a sketch called *The Unthinking Lobster,* an original Welles drama, a comedy of manners about Hollywood producers, which included by inference portraits of some of his past and close cinematic associates. The second portion of the performance, called *Time Runs,* was based on the legend of Dr. Faustus, sprinkled with quotations of Milton, Marlowe, even Dante, but without a hint of Goethe. It was a one-acter that attempted to modernize the well-known Faustian theme and showed its implications for the twentieth century and the evils of hell and the atomic bomb, perhaps even of heaven itself. The stage was shrouded in black velvet and complemented with a suggestion of high prison gates and a small strip of sky.

During the time he worked on mounting the show, he often toured the Parisian nightspots in the evening, a pursuit that MacLiammoir felt was too tiring if one wanted to accomplish any work the next day. It was during one of Orson's all-night elixirous evenings at a club called Carroll's, on rue de Panthéon, a block off the Champs Elysées, that he first saw a seductive American singer belt out jazz, improvisational, and blues songs all night long. She was tiny, bitter in tone, ironic, defiant, fantastically, almost wickedly sexy. The French called her voice "the most haunting in the world." Her name was Eartha Kitt.

Welles wanted the then-unknown Eartha for the part of Helen of Troy in *Time Runs* before he was even introduced to her. Duke Ellington was going to write some original music for the play (with lyrics supplied by Orson), and Orson was certain that her vocal interpretations of the songs would offer tremendous dramatic impact of melodic quality.

Before he had time to discuss the matter with her, however, Eartha had mysteriously left Paris; the people at the club said they thought she had gone to some country in Scandinavia. Actually, she briefly returned to the United States to attend the funeral of her aunt. Upon her return to Paris, she heard that Welles was eager to cast her in a part in his forthcoming play. She described her audition for Orson and Hilton Edwards, in her autobiography, *Alone with Me*:

> Orson kept his back to me, seated at first, then pacing the floor all during the reading. When I began, Mr. Edwards started to direct me. "Leave her alone!" Orson said. I read: "I couldn't think that God would create a man such as you." I kept reading, and reading, and reading, for what seemed like hours, progressing from youth to old age. Finally, Orson said, "All right, I don't know what we'll do about the other girl. As far as I'm concerned, you've got the part. Be here tomorrow at one for rehearsals. I'll have a script for you then."

When she began her rehearsals the next day, Orson peremptorily informed her that there would only be four sessions. The play opened on Saturday. It was then Tuesday. The diminutive Eartha, more than a foot shorter and two hundred pounds lighter than Orson, was nevertheless just as forceful as he during the rehearsals.

"The word is *world*!" Orson shouted at her.

"I *said* world!" she shouted back.

"Speak as though you came from New York," he told her.

"I *did* come from New York. How does one from New York speak?"

"Not the way *you* speak!"

"Why should I talk like someone special?"

"Because you are."

"Yes, but I don't want you to be conscious of it."

The other half of the bill, *The Unthinking Lobster,* had an unusual name but a familiar theme: Hollywood's penchant for big-budget schlock movies on biblical themes. A spate of these epics in the late 1940s and early 1950s sparked Orson's reaction in the form of an irreverent spoof, taking on the received ideas about heaven, saints, miracles, and angels, as well as movies like *David and Bathsheba* and *Samson and Delilah.* One slight miscalculation, however, seems to have been the title—nobody could remember it accurately. Newspapers garbled it until it became *The Thinking Lobster* or, with greater originality, *The Brainless Lobster.*

Welles probably knew that he was taking a chance in spoofing Hollywood, so he decided to slur everybody and strive for laughs at all costs. His satire became a comedy of manners, specifically those of the ruthless producers who had entered his life over the years. Ranging even further afield, he took some swipes at communists and, not content with that, evened the score with a few affronts at gossip columnists, Joe McCarthy, Vassar College, and Romanoff-type restaurants. Propriety was an issue.

Basically, the story of *The Unthinking Lobster* concerns a movie starlet who, while playing the role of a saint, Ann de Beaumont, discovers to her amazement that her "miracles" really are working. As an homage to Orson's idea of a movie within a play, he included a short burlesque on film, *La Miracle de Sainte Anne,* in which a group of cripples—extras in the film—are cured. Soon the set turns into a Lourdes-like shrine; producers get into the act and go to devotions instead of board meetings. Heaven is not pleased, and an emissary is sent to earth, finally extracting an agreement: heaven will stop the disruptive miracles that are keeping the backers from making money if Hollywood will refrain from making any more religious movies. Orson played an oppressive movie producer. The satire was unsubtle.

Welles had problems with French technicians and stagehands who could not understand his directions. "They just don't get our methods," he told a Paris correspondent. "Although I have made films in six different countries I can assure you that I never encountered the language problem that we have here." The play's opening was delayed four times for a series of trivial, although real, obstacles. An ornamental curtain that was to be pink returned to the theater colored mauve, and Orson refused to accept it. Arguments over the cost of the rental of the piano took days to resolve. One night the scenery was put out in the alley by the backstage personnel while another performance took place. A cloudburst diminished it to a soggy, paint-streaked mess, and new scenery had to be built. "Heartbreaking," cried Orson. Then, first-night patrons, who had been requested to wear black tie and formal gowns, showed up only to be turned away. The play was just not ready to open.

Time Runs finally opened on June 19, 1950, at the Théâtre Edouard VII, to mixed reviews, although mentions of Orson's acting, Ellington's music, and Eartha's singing were all hailed as if not significant then at least competent. Within days, photographs of Orson and Eartha at Paris bistros, such as Bricktop's, were being published all over Europe with the implication that the enticing Miss Kitt was not only his Trilby but also the new love of his life.

As attendance waned, Orson sought other presentations to use in *The Blessed and the Damned.* He changed his mind and definitions almost every day as to what comprised the perfect theatrical evening: MacLiammoir and he would do jealousy scenes from *Othello.* No, Orson didn't want that after all: they were a shade too long, too difficult to pare, and why spoil it, he felt, for those who had yet to see the film. The Antony and Brutus tent-scene quarrel might do. No, somehow that was not quite right either. Finally, an abbreviated forty-five-minute version of the perennially popular *The Importance of Being Earnest,* which had just then slipped into the public domain (and hence no royalties need be paid), was mounted, with Orson as Algernon Moncrieff and MacLiammoir as Jack Worthing. (Orson deftly inserted Lady Bracknell's best lines into his own dialogue.)

An additional skit was added to the potpourri, the very last scene from

Henry VI where Richard III kills Henry in prison, Orson, with an enormous hunchback, playing the new king, MacLiammoir serving as Henry. Should any of these playlets or scenes prove to be unsuccessful in bringing people to the theater, Orson threw in some magic tricks in between acts, and even a lecture, mostly about the responsibilities of the theater, the precise details and contents of which changed every night.

A clash between Eartha and Orson almost ended their theatrical relationship. In the scene that called for him to envelop her in his arms and say, "Helen, make me immortal with a kiss," on one night, for some unexplained reason, the irrepressible Orson grabbed her and sunk his teeth into her lower lip, almost bringing her to tears on stage. "Either he was feeling his oats a little more than usual or he resented something I had done unwittingly," she has recalled. Blood began to appear and her lip swelled to twice its size. Backstage she lunged at him and began hitting him with her fists, without effect, demanding to know why he had bitten her. "I was just in the mood," he said nonchalantly, without ever giving any further explanation.

She forgave him, however. Normally, she considered Orson a delight on stage, especially when his back was turned to the audience and he would try to make her laugh by making funny or grotesque faces.

After a six-week run in Paris, *The Blessed and the Damned* was rechristened *An Evening with Orson Welles,* and the company toured Germany for a month: Frankfurt, Berlin, Munich, Düsseldorf, Hamburg, and other cities. Orson was not particularly charmed by or caught up with the German people or their life-styles. Also, the hot weather, poorly attended performances, and absence of those brilliantly blue Italian skies, to which he had started to become accustomed, depressed him.* He gave a few surly press conferences to German journalists and theater and film critics, and the savage press coverage that resulted indicated that the effort was hardly worth it. "I didn't rewrite *Faust* any more than Goethe did nor Marlowe," Orson hurrumphed. "*Faust* is a legend about which anyone can write a play or opera if he feels like it." And then in *non sequitur:* "What is wrong with this country? They haven't produced a decent film since the war."

Within weeks he was so bored with what he was doing on stage, so filled with vexation, despite the fact that he knew the German tour was about to end, that he searched for something, anything, to fill his hours. An idea, hinting of recklessnesses, but fired by his feeling of isolation and ennui, seized him: he would make a film! Two films!

His idea was to do an even more reduced version of *The Importance of Being Earnest* on film and then also perform the sketch of Henry and Richard, before the cameras. Just how these fragments were to be used commercially, Orson failed to announce, but all of those involved believed that he had ideas

---

*The only successful performance he had, in his own opinion, was when the show played in a U.S. Army camp where his comedy of *Importance* could be understood by the audience without hesitation, and hence Orson concurred, they laughed from the stomach, not from the head.

of eventually projecting them on stage, alternating them with the other acts of his roaming repertory.

Without script or plans, not knowing of the extent of the equipment available, Orson rented a small studio in Geisengige, a suburb of Munich, and gathering up his meager and tired cast after a performance, Orson told them that the films would be made by working through the whole evening. Filming little more than the plays as they were performed on stage and complaining about the lighting and the cameras all the while, Orson had his two films completed by the time dawn began to break over the small Bavarian town. Two weeks later, reviewing the rushes in a Berlin hotel, he was totally disenchanted by the results and said *Auf Wiedersehen* to the films and to Germany.

ORSON'S ONE OTHER effort in the theater, before entering other realms, was to direct himself in a 1951 production of *Othello* for his first appearance on the London stage. Invited to come to England by Sir Laurence Olivier, who had never actually seen Orson in a legitimate performance, he accepted to play in Olivier's rented theater, the St. James, in the hope of continuing to promote his film version of *Othello* and also for the sheer and intrinsic challenge of mounting a full-scale Shakespearean production in its birthplace.* With characteristic daring, Orson arranged to open the play at virtually the same time that the venerable Old Vic, England's national theater, would present its own version of *Othello*.

So that he could mold and influence his actors in the way he believed their parts should be played, he made it clear before casting that only those who had never played Shakespeare on the stage would be considered for roles. Peter Finch, principally a film actor and protégé of Laurence Olivier and Vivien Leigh, and who had played Professor Winke in *Captain Corvallo* the previous season at the St. James, was signed on as Iago. Gudrun Ure, the owner of the voice Orson used to dub Suzanne Cloutier's in his film, would play Desdemona.

If Orson was confident about mounting the play, that feeling may have been temporarily weakened by the incredulity as expressed by Sir John Gielgud's now oft-quoted, gulping inquiry of him: "You're going to do *Othello*? [pause] On the *stage*? [longer pause] In *London*?" [total speechlessness].

Stories about Orson's rehearsals quickly became London legends: wielding an enormously long stick from his seat in the front rows to direct and guide his actors where he wanted them to move; disappearing for days before opening night; forgetting his own lines; changing his own entrances from stage left, then stage right, from the back curtains, down stairways, without telling his cast in advance where he would appear, so as to keep them alert; having an enormous picnic hamper prepared by a restaurant called The Ivy delivered to

---

*Orson had originally suggested playing *Faustus,* but Sir Laurence believed that *Othello* would be more acceptable to British audiences.

the theater each day packed with his individual lunch, which consisted of large sherried oysters, paté de foie gras, a wheel of Runesten cheese, and other delicacies and always accompanied by a bucket of chilled Pouilly-Fumé or a Musigny Blanc. And although he was inches taller than virtually everyone in the cast, he wore four-inch lifts on his shoes to appear even more enormous, dwarfing everyone on stage, a device that his English actors felt was highly unnecessary and pretentious.

The play opened in Newcastle, had a trial run in some of the other provinces, and finally invaded the St. James stage in London on October 18, 1951. The theater was overflowing with a standing-room-only audience eager to see the great Orson make his debut. And it was memorable. Shortly after the curtain rises, Orson—looking ten feet tall and appearing to weigh some three or four hundred pounds—dressed in a black velvet djellaba, is seen at the top of a flight of stairs. He glances down, walks a few steps and then has a brutal realization. "Fuck!" he blurts out loudly enough for those in the front rows to hear. Orson, in the press of directing and acting, had confused his own entrance cue and had come on too early. "Did he really say what I thought he said?" went the whispers.

When he finally made his proper entrance, his deep voice, his commanding presence and untypical restraint, which climaxed into a release of his pent-up power in a spectacular bed chamber scene, enthralled and captured the audience. "I came away genuinely impressed by his intellectual as well as his vocal and physical power," wrote critic Cecil Wilson in one of the London dailies. Gudrun Ure's Desdemona was lauded for a dramatically colorful effort, and Peter Finch's sinister, analytical approach to Iago was cheered. The only controversy that temporarily marred the play's run once it commenced (and this made international headlines) was when Orson banged Gudrun Ure's head against the bed so violently in the murder scene that members of the audience protested. After the performance, Welles apologized and said he guessed he just was caught up too realistically in the spirit of the play.

Early on in the run, Winston Churchill attended one of the performances and Orson heard some low murmuring from the vicinity where Churchill was sitting, somewhere in the first few rows. Orson thought the old man was either sleeping or talking to himself; he was unaware that Churchill often attended the theater and would mouth the words of the principal parts, sometimes complete soliloquies, that he had set to memory.

Later, Churchill went backstage to Orson's dressing room and began their visit with: "Most potent, grave and reverent signiors, my most approved good masters . . ." and then went on with a great deal of extra emphasis to give a number of Othello's speeches, always including the cuts that Orson had made.

The British critical reaction to *Othello* was, if not ecstatic, certainly respectful, for the most part. John Griffin, the London correspondent for the *Herald Tribune,* referred to the Welles production as a "star vehicle for a star actor" and noted that Orson's interpretation, "his slow heavy movement and upright stance reflect the methodical, ingenious mind of the Moorish general." T. C. Worsley, in the *New Statesman,* wrote: "The great lumbering dazed bull which Mr. Welles gives us for Othello may have its shortcomings in detail; but the fact remains that it imposes itself on us so powerfully and terrifyingly that we hardly notice them. This huge, goaded figure rolls on to the stage with a dreadful fog of menace and horror, thickening, wave after wave, with each successive entrance. The very deliberation of his movements, of his great lifted head and rolling bloodshot eyes, and the deep slow notes rumbled from his massive chest, pile up the sense of inevitability almost to the point of the unbearable. In the end we long (and isn't this the point of tragedy?) for the tension to be burst."

Only the late Kenneth Tynan, the caustic and stuttering young drama critic of the *Evening Standard,* seemed displeased with what he considered the play's complete artistic collapse: "No doubt about it," he slurred, "Orson Welles has the courage of his restrictions."

After its six-week run, *Othello* closed at the St. James without making any money, but also without losing any. Olivier was delighted with his experience with Welles, and both men agreed that they wanted to continue to work together on additional theatrical projects.

Olivier later summed up his opinion of Welles's Othello. Believing that no actor in history had ever achieved complete success with the role, neverthe-less, he felt that Welles had come closest: "He had everything for Othello, everything except the breath. He didn't go into training, and after 'Like to the Pontic sea,' he had to pause. When all is said and done, for Othello you need the breath, the lungs. You need the self discipline and the rhythm."

AFTER CAREFULLY STUDYING Orson's methods of filmmaking with *Othello* and his short flights into *The Importance of Being Earnest* and the Henry and Richard film, Hilton Edwards decided to make his own first film with Orson's help. Shot in Dublin and called *Return to Glenascaul,* the film was a twenty-two-minute short that mixes humor with mystery. Orson narrates a ghost story told to him by a man to whom he had given a lift in the Irish countryside in the dark of a foggy and eerie night. The man explains that his engine is not operating properly. "I've had trouble with my distributor, too," remarks Orson in a not-so-inside joke that could be a comment on his past problems with *Kane* and his then-current ones with the film of *Othello.*

Peter Cowie, among others, believed that *Return to Glenascaul* sprang primarily from Orson's creative sway: "One has the feeling that the hand of the master may have chosen a camera angle here, or set an extra shadow there." It won an Academy Award nomination for Best Short Picture in 1952.

CHAPTER 17

SINCE FLIGHT BACK into the theater could not earn him enough money to fulfill his own creative ambitions, Orson resumed where he had left off some five years before—he returned to radio. He became involved with three on-the-air series, all made in London by a young and dynamic producer, Harry Alan Towers: "The Black Museum," "Sherlock Holmes," and "The Adventures of Harry Lime."*

Although the title *The Third Man* belonged to Alexander Korda, the literary and dramatic rights of the character of Harry Lime were the property of Graham Greene. After negotiations with Greene and an agreement to pay Korda a token fee, Towers flew to Rome to meet with Welles. Orson was skeptical about how a series could be built around a character who was already dead. Towers explained how it could be done.**

> We start off with Anton Karas on the zither playing *The Third Man* theme, which everybody knows, and then we interrupt it with a shot. And you say, "That was the shot that killed Harry Lime. He died in the sewers beneath Vienna, but before he died he lived many lives. How do I know? I know because my name is Harry Lime." And then we lash into anything we can cook up.

Some fifty-two episodes of the Harry Lime broadcasts were eventually recorded, mostly in London but also in Paris and Rome, wherever Orson could be found by Towers and herded into a studio to do another taping. Orson wrote approximately a dozen of the shows himself; Ernest Borneman, his erstwhile *Ulysses* screenwriter, did many of them; and there were other writers who did anywhere from one to several each. Graham Greene retained veto power over the scripts but he rarely exercised it.

In concert with the weekly broadcasts, which started on the Light Programme on BBC in August of 1951, the *Empire News* took a number of the scripts, converted them into prose-form short stories and published them

---

*Towers wrote and produced radio programs for BBC during World War II, and in 1947, at the age of twenty-six, he was responsible for signing the world-famous Noel Coward—who had snubbed radio for some two decades—to his first radio series.
**From an unpublished interview with Towers by Dr. Frank Tavares.

every Sunday for several months. Welles not only narrated the radio programs, and starred in them as Harry Lime, but also produced and directed them.

This series was a technical improvement over earlier Welles broadcasts. Previous radio programs were created on records, which made editing impossible. By 1950, acetate-base recording tape had been perfected, which allowed greater freedom in planning and timing a program because it could be easily edited. Welles used this new technique in producing the Lime shows much the way he directed a film. Rather than record a program in one unit, he would build it scene by scene, just as he would construct a sequence of individual takes in one of his films.

Agent Mary Harris did most of the casting for the production, which included in its regular cast: Irene Prador, Agnes Bernelle, Dana Wynter, Betty McDowell, Ferdy Mayne, Dino Galvani, Sebastian Cabot, Robert Rietti, and Robert Arden. Anton Karas, who had originally performed the background music for the film, also provided the zither music for the series.

As memorable as the character of Harry Lime had been on film, the characterization had to be revised to make him appealing to a somewhat less sophisticated radio audience. The character Greene had depicted and Welles played in the film was cold, amoral, ruthless, a man who took no responsibility for his actions, nor how they might affect the lives of his victims. At the same time, he possessed the characteristics that have made most of his Satanic ancestors so much more appealing than the representatives of Good—he was witty, courageous, and immensely attractive.

But while the Harry Lime of the film had been despicable, Harry Lime of the radio series became a lovable rogue with whom his listeners could identify. True, he was a confidence man, a soldier of fortune who is sought after to help with schemes of blackmail, espionage, smuggling, and thievery because of his extensive knowledge of the underworld, political machinations, art, jewelry, and languages. But he was also shrewd and romantic, often an easy mark for women, who, he philosophizes, are "like appearances—deceiving." Some elements of Lime's character were modeled on those of Orson, written into the scripts by Welles and the other writers. The radio Lime was cosmopolitan, a connoisseur of food and drink, both of which he partook quite liberally. Not infrequently, his adventures began in a bar or restaurant where he was enjoying his newspaper and a glass of brandy, one of Welles's passions. He seemed always to move from one hotel or restaurant to another, from one country to another.

Both the character and the themes of the series reflect the concerns and morality that were characteristic of the fifties, a world still recovering from World War II, while at the same time coping with the growing threat of communism. But the fifties was also the age of conformity, and with Harry Lime, the listener could live out unrealized fantasies of escape, romantic dalliances, and the flaunting of the law. In most cases, the people Harry assists are more corrupt than he is and frequently are defeated in their attempts to doublecross him, not unlike the character of the hard-boiled private eye so popular in Hollywood films. But he is urbane and wily, more often than not preferring to depend on his wits rather than his fists to get him out of a tight spot.

The quality of the scripts varied, ranging from predictable detective story dialogue to flashes of elegance that suggest the hand of Welles even in those scripts for which others received credit, as when a girl would be described as having hair "the color of red clover honey" and "eyes that might have been too big, except on her, they were a threat."*

One of the more intriguing shows was based on a character called Gregory Arkadian.** Arkadian, one of the richest men in the world, tells Lime that he is undergoing an intelligence check by the United States Army. On the basis of whatever information they gather, Arkadian may be awarded a contract to build an army air force base in Portugal. He claims that he has amnesia, cannot recall his life previous to twenty years before when he found himself in Zurich, Switzerland, with one suit of clothes to his name and his pockets full of money. He wants to hire Lime to trace his past. Lime discovers that Arkadian was once a member of a gang of Polish criminals. Three members of the gang disappeared—one of them being the ringleader, Sophie, another Arkadian himself, who has absconded with their loot. Later, Lime is informed that Sophie and another member of the gang have been found together, strangled. Lime tells Arkadian's daughter the entire story, then tells Arkadian that his daughter knows all. Fearing to confront his daughter, Arkadian commits suicide in an unusual way, by jumping from his plane.

The Arkadian broadcast was taped in Paris, the major part of Arkadian being played by Frederick O'Brady, a puppeteer and actor who had a small part in *The Unthinking Lobster*. One morning in Paris, Welles invited O'Brady to his hotel—the Lancaster—at ten o'clock, and as they were sipping champagne, Orson asked him to hire an entire English-speaking cast and have them assembled by three o'clock that afternoon in order to do a taping for the Lime series. "Don't worry about their accents," he told O'Brady. Too numb to refuse such a preposterous task, and needing the money, O'Brady somehow accomplished the demanded miracle. After the recording, Welles told him, "I'll do a film with this story one day."

"Won't that be wonderful, Orson!" O'Brady exclaimed, thinking of the potential fame and fortune from his screen debut.

But Welles replied dryly: "However, *I'll* play Arkadian then."

The Third Man-based radio series and the character of Lime captured the British as much as, if not more than, the film had. The program spread to

---

*Orson wrote, among others, *A Ticket to Tangier, Operation Music Box, Two Is Company, The Dead Candidate, Too Many Crooks,* and *The Golden Fleece.* Also, never one to waste any previous work, he adapted the script of *The Unthinking Lobster* into a highly satirical Lime episode, changing the name of the banana republic to "Malina," and the soft drink to "Buzzo," but retaining the basic theme of the play.

**Later, in *Confidential Report,* a film based on the same character, Welles changed the spelling of his name to the less Armenian-sounding "Arkadin."

Canada, Australia, South Africa, and Hong Kong, and (with someone else doing the voice of Lime) it was translated into Spanish, French, Hebrew, Dutch, German, and Italian.

Only the United States, already involved in what would be its Golden Age of television, seemed to ignore, or at least deprecate, the series. Jack Gould, writing in *The New York Times,* described "The Adventures of Harry Lime" as, "a hackneyed trifle that primarily serves as a means for Orson to brush up on his guttural flourishes."

Orson began to recognize the show's immense popularity in England when he had a backstage visitor one night after a Northumberland performance of *Othello.* He asked his guest what he thought of the play. His guest replied: "Mister Welles, for us, you'll never be nothing but 'Arry Lime."

Almost as popular as "The Adventures of Harry Lime" was Welles's "The Black Museum," which followed soon after with thirty-nine episodes. The series was based on accounts of real-life murder cases, and the theme of the show revolved around Orson's ostensible walk through Scotland Yard's grim fortress on the Thames, rummaging through its warehouse of icons of homicide and unearthing objects that played an important role in criminal history. To the background of the tolling Big Ben and clanging, jail-like doors, his footsteps resounding on stone floors, Orson would take everyday items from the Yard's glass cases—a piece of carbon paper, a broken teacup, a powder puff stained with blood—and begin to weave the evening's story around that object. The dramas were tightly crafted, well acted, and fast paced, and Orson sometimes played roles and at other times served as host and narrator.

At the conclusion of "The Black Museum" episodes, Towers offered Orson the possibility of yet another series, the lead in "Sherlock Holmes." Welles accepted a part on just one show, the last, entitled *The Final Problem,* but not that of the super-sleuth. He played Professor Moriarty, the super-villain and Napoleon of crime, who corrupts all of London with his evil influence. John Gielgud was the imperious Holmes, pacing to and fro, bowing the violin in his study on Baker Street, and Ralph Richardson played Dr. Watson.

Welles, as Moriarty, interpreted the part with subtlety but with a very British accent. In this last adventure, the brilliant but evil mathematician Moriarty meets Holmes in the Alps for a final struggle and death-clash atop the abyss of Reichenbach Falls. Locked in each other's arms they fight above the rocks below. Later, two sets of footprints are found at the edge of the precipice. The bodies are never found.

AS HAPPENED TO him in the past in the United States, Orson's radio fame in England not only helped to keep his name in front of the public but also served as a reminder of his talent to those in the film industry. In the mid-1950s, Orson received and accepted offers to act in three British films, *Trent's Last Case, Three Cases of Murder,* and *Trouble in the Glen.*

Trent's Last Case was a classic detective novel. E. C. Bentley, the author, wrote it in 1913 as the result of a wager between himself and his old friend

G. K. Chesterton, actually as a response to Chesterton's *The Man Who Was Thursday.* Bentley was sick to death of the "infallible sleuth" who had become so popular in detective fiction published before World War I. He wanted to create a somewhat unreliable, and therefore believable, character who would proceed along less dogmatic lines than his boring predecessors. The result was a new genre in detective fiction that was strong on style and character development—and ultimately, enormously appealing to filmmakers. Agatha Christie called it "one of the three best detective stories ever written."

It was 1952, however, before the tale finally made its way to the screen. The cast starred Michael Wilding, Margaret Lockwood, and Welles in the leading roles. John McCallum, Miles Malleson, Hugh McDermott, John McNaughton, and Sam Kydd made up the supporting cast. Pamela Bower wrote the script, and Herbert Wilcox both produced and directed it on a very tight budget.

Sigsbee Manderson, a wealthy industrialist, played by Welles, is found dead on his country estate in Hampshire. To all appearances, he has committed suicide, a theory that is later confirmed by a jury. Philip Trent, a painter, crime reporter, and amateur sleuth, is not so sure, and sets about investigating what he suspects may be a murder. During his investigations he meets the dead man's secretary, whom he suspects of the murder, and the dead man's self-possessed and beautiful widow with whom he falls in love. The denouement is an unexpected plot twist of the sort that had made British films so popular in the United States.

Since the film starts with the death of Manderson, like Kane, Orson appears only in flashbacks as each character describes what happened on the night of the shooting. Audiences responded well to *Trent's Last Case,* despite fairly slow pacing, and when it was ultimately distributed in the United States, Orson's acting was commended:

"Orson Welles is every bit the villainous and almost insane millionaire."—*Variety*

"Orson Welles makes the best of his belated appearance. In new makeup— aquiline nose, black homburg, graying hair—he is a tough broody schemer, a composite of Machiavelli and a Wall Street tycoon."—*The New York Times*

UNDOUBTEDLY INSPIRED BY the success of *Trio* and *Quartet, Three Cases of Murder* consisted of a trio of thrillers contained in one film and produced in Britain for Associated Artists by Ian Dalrymple. Curiously enough, the film was released in Britain only after it was first shown in America to such an enthusiastic response that Warner Brothers cabled their London office: "Why can't we show this film over there?" Two major British circuits had initially turned down the film because they did not consider it a big enough box office draw. Warner Brothers finally released the £150,000 film in Leicester Square in the West End.

American film critics, for the most part, viewed two of the stories with a ho-hum attitude. One of these is a straight whodunit about two friends who fall in love with the same woman and later accuse each other of being her murderer. The other is a supernatural tale about the spirit of a dead painter who tempts a museum guide to step into a room in one of his paintings and then, yes, murders him.

Somerset Maugham wrote the story that inspired the third segment, and Orson starred in it—two factors that account for its critical and popular success. Orson's story, "Lord Mountdrago," was directed by George More O'Farrell and included Helen Cherry, Alan Badel, André Morell, and Peter Burton in the cast. Orson plays a pompous British foreign secretary given to demolishing his opponents with sarcastic wit. One of these opponents is a young MP from a Welsh mining town who threatens revenge. Maugham's description of Mountdrago was used as a casting guide for the film, and Orson seemed perfectly typed for the part: "He was a brilliant debater and his gift of repartee was celebrated. He had a fine presence: he was a tall, handsome man, rather bald and somewhat too stout, but this gave him solidity and an air of maturity that were of service to him."

Mountdrago begins to have bizarre dreams in which he is humiliated by the young MP. On the day after each dream, the MP mocks him in Parliament in such a way that it is clear that he knows exactly what Mountdrago has dreamed. Is Mountdrago going mad, or is it his own conscience that is torturing him? These questions give a psychological depth to the story that elevates it above the two others in quality. Mountdrago, believing that his tormentor is driving him insane, resolves to murder him.

Although complaining all the while about the demanding shooting schedule, pointing out that the filming took twenty times as long as Maugham needed to write the story, Orson gave a performance that was a study in caustic urbanity.

IN 1954, WELLES again teamed up with actress Margaret Lockwood and producer-director Herbert Wilcox for another British-made film, *Trouble in the Glen*. It was filmed in color in the Scottish Highlands. Frank Nugent wrote the screenplay from a book by Maurice Walsh. The two writers had also scripted a previous classic, *The Quiet Man*. Forrest Tucker, Victor McLaglen, John McCallum, Eddie Byren, Archie Duncan, and Ann Gudrun* were also featured in the cast. Orson had little faith in, or hope for, the script but the offer of £10,000 to play in the film convinced him not to quibble.

The rather flimsy comedic plot had some appeal to family audiences, although critics tended to be patronizing. The story concerns a rough-and-ready South American millionaire (Welles) who returns to the Scottish Highlands of his grandfather and takes up residence in the ancestral castle with his high-spirited daughter (Lockwood). One of the initial blunders of the new Scottish laird is firing one of his servants because the man has insulted him on a fishing trip. This sets up a feud with the townspeople that the laird exacerbates by closing off the main road that runs through his land. In the

---

*Previously known as Gudrun Ure, of Orson's *Othello* companies, who supposedly changed her name because of Orson's mispronunciation: "Uh-er."

middle of all this furor comes Forrest Tucker, who plays an American ex-paratrooper, in Scotland visiting his eleven-year-old daughter, a polio victim who has been adopted by a local couple. He goes to visit the laird to see what can be done about the road and is ordered off the premises by the laird's feisty daughter. The two fall in love, of course, and the millionaire tyrant is persuaded to change his ways. The movie ends with a party celebrating the engagement of Tucker and Lockwood. The child, on the road to recovery, looks forward to a happy future with her father and new stepmother.

Not even Orson, despite a ludicrously tartaned appearance—smoking a cigar, dressed in a pleated kilt, with a white fur sporran dangling in front of his crotch, his elephantine legs swathed in plaid stockings—could engender any critical hilarity, although his performance was thought to be "eloquent" (*Los Angeles Examiner*); "effective" (*New York Herald Tribune*); and "one of the best things in the picture" *(Variety).*

IN AN ATTEMPT to get back into his own filmmaking, in 1951 Welles had taken two of the Harry Lime radio episodes and begun forming them into a screenplay: the story of Mr. Arkadin, as previously noted, and another broadcast of an incident that takes place in Marseilles. Lime helps out a dying gangster, who in turn gives him a name that he says is worth money. It is a tale that involves blackmail and a man of mystery who commits suicide. Certain narrative elements from the former were combined into *Confidential Report*. Its working title was X (the unknown name and identity of Arkadin). The film was then known as *Masquerade* (later known as *Mr. Arkadin* in the United States).

It was during this time that Orson flew to Venice to see if he could find a producer—any producer—at the film festival, to finance *Mr. Arkadin*. He entertained, one after another, bright and lesser lights of the film world, until he found "a hustling, semi-Armenian Russian," as Orson described him, who seemed interested but unconvinced of Orson's reliability. Orson strategically planned a series of lunches, dinners and prolonged afternoon drinks with the man in order to charm and convince him of the film's and his own worth. At the first lunch, at the renowned Danieli Royale Excelsior, Orson felt his negotiations had to be consummately persuasive and seductive. As the two men entered the dining room, Orson spied Winston Churchill with his wife, Clementine. As they passed the great man's table, Churchill smiled and nodded. Orson's potential backer was deeply impressed. "He went wild," remembered Orson.

The next morning, while swimming at the Lido beach, Orson noticed that Churchill was also in the water and he paddled over to him. "Mr. Churchill, I think you ought to know what you did for me," said the buoyant Orson. "I almost have the money for my next film." Churchill acknowledged Orson's gratitude and swam on.

That evening, at another restaurant, Orson was back with his likely benefactor and Churchill was seated at a prominent table. As Orson and the businessman passed by Churchill's table this time, the grand man knew what

Orson was up to, and he ceremoniously rose and gave Orson a deep bow! Despite this consummate act of bonhomie by one of the greatest statesmen on earth, the investment was still not forthcoming.

By 1954, Orson had finally convinced a group of Swiss and Spanish backers to finance the film. It was completed in eight months of location shooting, mostly in Spain, Germany, and France. Although Welles could passably speak several languages, he hired Ivan Desny, a practiced linguist fluent in five languages, to act as his assistant from country to country.

Welles made Gregory Arkadin into a virtual caricature of Charles Foster Kane, a fabulously wealthy tycoon with a castle in Spain rather than a Xanadu in Florida. But Arkadin's origins are mysterious, and there is an aura of evil about him.* Claiming amnesia, Arkadin hires Guy Van Stratten, an American drifter, to investigate him and prepare a confidential report about his past. The trail leads Van Stratten throughout Europe, to Mexico and back at last to Germany at Christmastime. Whenever he interviews a witness, or finds someone who knew Arkadin when he was a member of an international dope and prostitution ring, that person winds up dead. Ultimately, Van Stratten realizes that Arkadin is behind the murders and that he himself is marked for death, because Arkadin is terrified that his beloved daughter, Raina, will find out about her father's unsavory past. When the last witness is murdered, Van Stratten rushes desperately back to Spain to tell Raina the truth and so save his own life. Arkadin rents a private plane and tries to get to Raina first, but Van Stratten locates her in an airport just as Arkadin's plane flies overhead. As Arkadin's voice booms out of the radio, beseeching Raina not to believe the terrible story, Van Stratten tells her the truth about her father. She picks up the microphone and tells Arkadin that she knows all about him, then waits for a reply. There is none. Arkadin, in despair, has jumped to his death, leaving the empty plane circling in the sky.

Welles assembled a paradoxically uneven cast for the film, and the performances range from the superb to the hopelessly banal. The supporting actors in cameo performances, however, are often magnificent. Michael Redgrave plays a Polish pawnbroker, sinister, dirty, somewhat effeminate. Patricia Medina (in real life Mrs. Joseph Cotten) plays Van Stratten's betrayed girlfriend. Akim Tamiroff, Mischa Auer, and Katina Paxinou create memorable characters in brief, scintillating gems of brilliant acting.

Orson had offered Marlene Dietrich the role of the exiled countess. She was ready to accept, always wanting to work with him since *Follow the Boys*; she had to decline, however, because of her postproduction commitments to *The Monte Carlo Story*. Auer plays a sardonic flea trainer; Tamiroff gives a memorable screen interpretation as a decrepit tailor who knows his onetime association with Arkadin will cost him his life. Welles managed to get one of the best performances out of Akim Tamiroff since his role in *For Whom the Bell Tolls*. Looking not unlike a character that stepped out of a tortured,

---

*Years later, Welles likened Arkadin to Harry Lime, rather than Kane: "because he is a profiteer, an opportunist, a man who lives on the decay of the world."

expressionist drawing by George Grosz, Tamiroff was also spurred on by his wife, actress Tamara Shane (who had a small part in the film), although not always with the most cordial rapport. Their fights on and off the set, half in Russian and half in English, were tempestuous but funny: "Don't teach me act!" Tamiroff would often sputter loudly after hearing Tamara's critique of a scene; invariably, however, he would follow her advice and do exactly what she had suggested in the next take.

Paxinou, cigarette dangling from her heavily rouged lips, her voice an echo of jaded huskiness, excels as Arkadin's ex-mistress who had headed the most infamous white slave ring in Europe. It was from a member of this notorious group that the young Arkadin had amassed the beginnings of his fortune.

But the principal characters are totally inept. Robert Arden, a little-known actor who had performed in the "Harry Lime" series, was playing in *Guys and Dolls* when Welles began casting *Confidential Report.* Welles bought him out of that role and cast Arden as the second lead, in the part of Guy Van Stratten. The role of Raina, Arkadin's not-so-innocent daughter, was played by Paola Mori, an incarnation, one might think, of Susan Alexander Kane; Welles, like Kane, was insistent that the love of his life be thought of as a star. As Kane created an opera house for Susan, Welles created a movie for Paola.

As he had promised years before, Welles reserved the title role for himself. *Confidential Report* became the latest of Welles's intensely personal films, related thematically to *Citizen Kane* and *The Lady from Shanghai.* The echoes of *Kane* are obvious and were picked up by almost every critic: the uncommonly wealthy, powerful man, whose life story is revealed in bits and pieces ferreted out by a resourceful stranger. But where the reporter seeks to learn the truth about the very much alive Gregory Arkadin, and where, in *Kane,* Welles seemed to be saying that a man is far more complex than the sum of his parts, in *Arkadin* Welles has become more disillusioned. Here, truth becomes the instrument of destruction, first for all who know Arkadin's sordid background, and finally for Arkadin himself, leaving alive the daughter who had long lost the innocence Arkadin hoped to protect, and the jackal-like Van Stratten, whose self-serving interests make him even less sympathetic than the evil Arkadin.

Here, too, is a wealthy, powerful person whose relationship with a young man is filled with duplicity. Van Stratten is victimized, just as is the young sailor Welles plays in *Lady from Shanghai.* Welles continued his concern with revealing the degrees of power held by the very rich and with exposing the machinations they engage in to retain that wealth and power.

But *Confidential Report* fairly hurls its message at the audience. Where Welles had probed the depths of character to play Charles Foster Kane, the Gregory Arkadin he created was a sinister shell, a baroque caricaturization of evil. And where he had developed a range of subtle makeup to enable Kane to appear to age realistically, as Arkadin he wore makeup so obvious, and in some scenes so ostentatious, that it appeared to be for the stage. This time, the ubiquitous false nose was sharp and aquiline, clearly the product of another makeup man. Prior to this film, Orson had obtained his false noses from his "nose man," John O'Gorman, who would ship dozens of noses—made of mortician's wax—to any part of the world. This time, however, he failed to get his realistic noses to Orson to use as Mr. Arkadin, a fact Orson complained about for years afterward.

The rest of the Arkadin makeup was no more realistic. The angular, arched eyebrows were overtly Mephistophelian, as were the pointed beard and the squared-off hair that appeared to come to two horn-like points.* The heavy makeup used to emphasize his cheekbones and conceal the seams of the false nose was, in some scenes, applied so crudely that it matted along his hairline, and sometimes the backings of his wig, beard, and mustache were left exposed. This can be no accident, for Welles had far too much experience and expertise with greasepaint to overlook such glaring omissions. Instead, he had begun to move toward surrealism. The character of Arkadin appears to be wearing a sinister mask—for the man was, in fact, concealing a ghastly past and a dishonest motive. The audience was deliberately given two levels of information; not only that Arkadin was evil and fearsome, but that viewers were *supposed* to think him evil and fearsome. There is no pretext of naturalism here. *Confidential Report* is a highly stylized, melodramatic production, a continuation of the direction in which Welles was moving.

Completed in 1955, it was first released in Great Britain in August that year. French director Eric Rohmer, reviewing the film in *Les Cahiers du Cinéma,* called it:

> . . . an absolutely brilliant illustration of a genre which has become more and more debased. It creates something which is nearly impossible today, a romantic fiction that involves neither the future nor any removal from one's usual surroundings. This unrealistic tale rings even more true than many narratives where care has been taken to ensure verisimilitude. Most of the time, Welles made a point of taking his crew to the very location where the action is supposed to take place, and this paid off. The actors, who are all excellent, create "characters" but also play on their own physical and even ethnic qualities. The power of money is depicted with a precision that only Balzac would have envied. All these real elements make up an exceptional world, which we believe in all the more because it is presented as exceptional.

The following year, a court battle tied the film up in litigation, preventing its distribution to the United States. There were charges and countercharges. According to the *New York Herald Tribune,* Welles was furious that his releasing company had cut fourteen minutes from the finished film. For their

---

*It has been noted that the character Arkadin has some resemblance to the real-life munitions king Basil Zaharoff and in the film, one of Arkadin's aides refers to him as looking exactly like the Roman god of sea, Neptune.

part, the international distributors charged that Welles had been drinking heavily during the shooting of the film, wreaking havoc with the production schedule and causing distress to the cast and crew.

"We will make us a picture," he would say to one of his assistants in advance of any scene and then piece together the rhythm and setting, occasionally but not always, following the script. While directing himself, he seemed to know instinctively what was working. Often, he would simply say: "Cut. That was terrible," talking of his own performance, and then do more and more takes. He seemed obsessed with reshooting and usually could explain why a shot was lacking, and if he couldn't explain, he would ask for help: "Won't *anybody* give me a rationale for doing another take?" he would ask of his cast and crew.

Welles's method of working was, as usual, erratic. Actor Frederick O'Brady was summoned to a movie studio in the suburbs of Paris early one morning. He arrived to find the building deserted and only an old watchman about. The man had been expecting O'Brady; he led him to his dressing room and informed him that Welles would arrive shortly. O'Brady wasn't feeling well. His left arm ached, an indication of his ailing heart. There was a bed in the dressing room, and as there seemed nothing better to do—Orson had not even bothered to provide him with a script to study—he lay down to take a short nap.

A makeup man woke him at four that afternoon, to tell him that Welles had just arrived and was waiting for him downstairs. O'Brady rushed down to the studio, reminding himself not to let Welles know about the pain in his arm. Orson was standing in the middle of a huge, mostly empty studio. He beamed when O'Brady entered, embraced him, and suggested that they go to a nearby bistro to have a drink before beginning. It was not to be a long shooting; they had only O'Brady's scene to do.

The brandy was poured and O'Brady lifted his glass. Orson looked quizzical. "What is wrong with your left arm?"

"Why?" asked O'Brady, trying to be nonchalant.

"You are left-handed," Orson answered, "and I've always seen you lift a glass with your left. Why the right this time?"

O'Brady brushed off the question, knowing that they had never discussed his left-handness in the past. Welles was, by nature, highly observant, and he usually remembered whatever he perceived.

Welles then explained the scene to be shot. O'Brady was to play a character named Oscar, a drug addict who knew Arkadin when they were both young men in Russia. Van Stratten, tracking down Arkadin's past, kidnaps Oscar, takes away his drugs, and locks him up in the cabin of a boat. Oscar can have his dope again only if he reveals what he knows about Arkadin. Oscar refuses to talk, and the scene ends with him muttering something in Russian and collapsing.

Orson and O'Brady improvised the dialogue, and scribbled it down on paper. The setting was a wooden box mounted on a dais, to represent the cabin. Welles, again working with low-angled shots, put the camera on the right, focusing on O'Brady, who was lying on his belly, elbows up, playing a concertina.* To simulate the effect of water and waves, a few pieces of broken mirror were thrown into a basin of water. When a spotlight was pointed at the basin, it made the water shine and cast a flickering reflection onto the ceiling of the makeshift cabin.

They began shooting the scene, Welles, O'Brady, and the most minimal crew. O'Brady recalled afterward: "He works quietly like a man who is sure of what he's doing. As far as I know, his only outbursts are laughs, and they are big, loud, healthy laughs. Now they echoed in that cobwebby old studio which looked like a bombed-out factory."

They shot the scene, and they shot the scene. Welles was continually complimentary, but he kept insisting that they reshoot it yet again. Finally, after the seventeenth take, Welles embraced O'Brady and told him that his performance had been absolutely perfect. "Matchless, my dear boy. Wonderful."

But he wanted it done again. Just one more time, he implored, and this time with "genius." So O'Brady did it one more time. "Cut," Orson said. "Print with enthusiasm," and they finally broke for the day. Sometime later, speaking with the technicians, O'Brady found out that it was indeed, the eighteenth take that appeared in the film.

When *Mr. Arkadin* was being prepared for French release, O'Brady was asked to dub his part in French. Welles was by then working on another project in another part of the world. The sound engineer played the original version for O'Brady, then asked him if it sounded normal. O'Brady didn't understand. The engineer asked him if he recognized his own voice, speaking Oscar's lines. "Why, of course," he told the man, wondering what he was getting at.

"But it isn't your voice," the engineer told him with a smile.

"Whose is it?" O'Brady asked.

"Orson's," the engineer said.

It seemed that there had been a flaw in the recording. Welles, sensing O'Brady's illness or just not wanting to call him back to the studio to rerecord the sequence, had said it wasn't necessary to bother O'Brady, and Welles himself had recorded the Oscar sequence, imitating O'Brady's voice. Many of the male voices in the film were eventually dubbed by Orson, including the man who dies on the dock at the beginning of the film, and Mischa Auer's flea trainer.

The film was plagued by what Orson called "international bureaucracy." When he was in Paris developing the rushes of the footage that he had shot in Spain, he had to have special authorization from French authorities to print it. The film had to be examined by the customs officials, who stamped a clearance seal at the beginning and end of each roll of film, a process that took

---

*Almost every scene in the film is shot at an oblique angle to emphasize the labyrinthian dimensions of the story. "Build the set up," Welles would order; even in the scene with the dead body lying on the dock at the beginning of the film, the camera is lower.

two whole days, even if the footage was a short fragment. Because of this interference, precious time was lost and Orson was unable to enter the film in that year's Venice Film Festival, a crucial business deadline for its future at the box office. "The challenge of time is one that I can accept," he wrote in outrage in a film journal at the time. "I am perfectly willing to fight that duel. But there is another, the futile and insidious struggle against the thousand and one formalities by which cinema finds itself chained down."

After a seven-year delay, the retitled *Mr. Arkadin* finally opened in the United States on October 11, 1962. Daniel Talbot, owner of the New Yorker Theater, had spent two years trying to arrange to bring it to the United States as one of a series of films by major directors that had been ignored by American distributors. *The New York Times*'s Eugene Archer reviewed the long-delayed premiere, and said of *Arkadin*:

> To less specialized observers, the film seems more like *Citizen Kane* revisited. It is, in turn, baffling, exciting, infuriating, original and obscure. It is also, from start to finish, the work of a man with an unmistakable genius for the film medium. In other words, it is typically Orson Welles.

The film isn't easy on the audience, however. Marshall McLuhan notwithstanding, the viewer of *Mr. Arkadin* cannot relax and expect to (in which the means of communications has a greater influence on people than the content itself) be spoon-fed an entertaining story. Herman G. Weinberg, writing in *Film Culture,* praised this very theory, with which some reviewers found fault. He called the film "A relief from the literalness of most pictures with their a-b-c progressions from word to word and scene to scene, because it is not pre-chewed and pre-digested and because the spectator cannot 'sit back and relax' but must meet the film at least half-way to try to figure out what the hell is going on practically every second or he's lost. [Welles] disdains telling a story chronologically, he must 'back-track' on himself, past and present are like a great fugue, intermingling."

Such a film cannot be easily edited or cut; rather, its editing must be carefully orchestrated. Bill Morton, who was editing the film at first, finally quit over disagreements with Orson; Renzo Lucidi, who worked on *Othello,* was then called in to complete *Arkadin.* Welles's dispute with his European distributors arose because they cut several minutes from his finished film, and in so doing, he claimed, they butchered the delicate balance of its complexity. Ironically, this same shortened version seems to have been the one selected when the film was televised in this country. Though it is only seven minutes shorter than the ninety-nine-minute complete film, it is confusing, technically sloppy, and jumbled, with dangling bits of plot that are never satisfactorily cleared up. The complete version opens with Robert Arden talking with Akim Tamiroff in a dirty little garret in Germany. Then it cuts back and forth, from flashback to the present. Each time it returns to the two men, the audience is given important information that explains what's going on. The film thus requires careful attention but is not at all obscure.

The cut version, which Welles did not quite disown, but nevertheless disputed, butts all the flashbacks together in a string, omits much of the explanatory bridges, and trims some of the internal scenes. One suspects that it is possible to tell which version of the film a particular reviewer saw just by judging the gist of the review. Welles was not interested in creating an easy film. *Arkadin* is filled with sardonic humor, with the fearfulness and legend that a wealthy, powerful man can draw about himself, with the death of innocence and the helplessness of morality in the face of determined, aggressive, amoral passion.

In an early scene, Gregory Arkadin holds a party in his castle. When his masked, costumed guests are assembled around him, he tells them a fable that in effect is a key to understanding both Arkadin and the film:

> A scorpion, who could not swim, begged a frog to carry him to the other side. The frog complained that the scorpion would sting him. This was impossible, said the scorpion, because he would then drown with the frog. So the pair set forth. Halfway over, the scorpion stung the frog. "Is that logical?" asked the frog. "No, it's not," answered the scorpion, as they both sunk to the bottom, "but I can't help it, it's my nature."

The immutability of nature, the consistency of character that even allows it to supersede logic, is what Welles was dealing with in *Mr. Arkadin,* in *The Lady from Shanghai,* in *Citizen Kane,* and even in *Macbeth* and *Othello.* It is a theme that fascinated him; that, and another, again expressed in a line by Gregory Arkadin: "There are two kinds of people in the world; those who give and those who ask, those who don't care to give and those who don't care to ask. . . ." Whichever type of person Welles felt himself to be, he chose to portray on film the interactions of both types of men and the inevitable destruction the former brings to the latter.

Also timed with the release of *Mr. Arkadin* was a novel of the same name, supposedly written by Orson (his name appears as author), and the blurb reads "The outstanding thriller by the movie master of suspense." It was published by W. H. Allen in England and later issued by Panther Books as a mass-market paperback, with a lone and deadly dagger emblazoned on the cover. Decades later, Welles denied that he ever wrote the book; apparently it was written by a ghostwriter and Orson's name used for promotional purposes. He wanted no credit when he discovered the book was advertised as "A skillful, bizarre novel of white slavery, corruption and contraband spanning the underworlds of two continents. . . . In the fast-moving suspense thriller, the Harry Lime-ish atmosphere of turbulent post-war Europe is captured as only a master knows how—peopled with extraordinary, almost larger-than-life characters as unforgettable as their creator."

Although no literary masterpiece, the book was not indifferently written and served to deepen the mystery of Mr. Arkadin.

The film *Mr. Arkadin,* despite its difficulties and problems of audience comprehension, quickly generated something of a cult following. Was it the worst film ever made by Orson Welles, or was it the best? People's opinions seemed to vacillate with each subsequent viewing. A group of French critics in a poll published in *Les Cahiers du Cinéma* a few years after the film release proclaimed *Mr. Arkadin* one of the twelve best films ever made.

In retrospect, Orson dubbed it a "flawed masterpiece . . . a disaster."

CHAPTER 18

BY THE FALL of 1953, the distinguished British stage director, and Orson's good friend, Peter Brook, was enjoying a two-year run of his play *The Little Hut* in London and was invited to mount a production of it in New York. While making arrangements to open it in the United States, Brook was also contracted to direct something of his own choosing on the prestigious CBS weekly television series, "Omnibus," funded by the Television-Radio Workshop of the Ford Foundation. Brook approached Orson to see whether he would consider returning to the United States after his absence of over five years. Orson had never acted on television, and the whole explosion of American video drama had occurred after he had left the country. Such series as "Omnibus," "Studio One," and the "Actors' Studio," all dramatizations of famous works and stories, were beyond his personal viewing experience. The small amount of television he had seen on the Continent had been, in his opinion, terrible. The BBC productions he had viewed, however, were interesting enough to act as a catalyst.

The BBC dramatic productions had problems, although Orson felt that their fidelity to the actual length of the plays as written, two- and three-hour versions of sometimes difficult-to-understand words, "grew tiresome" after a while. The viewer was forced to squint at a brightly lit "Punch and Judy box," as he called it, for too prolonged a time.

He wanted to do something, anything, on television, as long as it was classical in nature and promised an attempt at quality; any project connected with Peter Brook suggested those requirements. A television adaptation of *Othello* was discussed, but the competitive factor with Orson's own film might have depleted the potential American audience who, after seeing it on television, would possibly avoid another version of it in the movie theaters.

One of the great heroic roles in Shakespeare that Orson had always wanted to play was *King Lear*. Previously, his only experience with *Lear* was on radio for "The Mercury Theatre on the Air," but he had long considered it probably the most substantial tragic part in English literature. "Omnibus" was a ninety-minute show, minus some sixteen minutes of commercials. Orson felt that the remaining seventy-four minutes were all that was needed to do an abbreviated version, without the subplots, of *King Lear*. He said at the time to a television critic: "The central story would still be there. That's all people remember anyhow." Brook was greatly attracted to the idea, and eventually the Ford Foundation directors also agreed to the project. A production budget of $150,000 was established.

Brook discarded almost all of the sub-machinations involving the Duke of Gloucester and did a remarkable joining of the characters of Edmund and Oswald. Brook's wife, Natasha Parry, would play Cordelia and Micheál MacLiammoir was cast as Edgar in a highly abridged version of that role. To avoid further fragmentation, the commercial sponsors agreed that their announcements would appear only before and after the play itself, an unusual innovation at that time. Virgil Thomson was secured to compose the music and direct the orchestra.

Orson shrewdly negotiated his acting fee in order to avoid unnecessary taxes: part of the payment would be by check, another part in cash, and there would be, even for Orson, an enormous daily expense account, which included a lavish suite at the Plaza Hotel. On October 5, 1953, he returned to the United States for his television debut.

Every night, after rehearsal, he stationed himself in front of the television set in his suite and, with the help of a few drinks, began an instant introduction to American television drama: "Fireside Theater," "Ford Theater," "Four Star Playhouse," "The Hallmark Hall of Fame."* Outside of dramatic presentations, he watched variety and talk shows and situation comedies such as "The Life of Riley," becoming familiar with those performers who had been created by television during his absence in Europe. "Who's he?" he asked a guest in his suite when Perry Como came on the screen to sing; Dave Garroway was also totally unknown to him.

Orson was appalled by the quality of the images that appeared on his television screen: "As bad as a picture of a Chinese play, in which someone brings on a chair and tells you it is a mountain," he said. "Snow" seemed to fall constantly; characters appeared in triplicate; halos and shadows accompanied objects; the heads of performers were often cut off at the ears. "Good God, is this what *Lear* is going to look like?" he asked one of the television producers visiting him at his hotel. A new television set was ordered for his suite, but the reception was equally bad. Finally, the hotel suggested that he move from the Fifth Avenue side of the building to the Central Park side, where, they claimed, reception would be better. Orson chose to suffer with the ghostly images, however, rather than go through the difficulties of packing and unpacking again.

Rehearsals went fairly well. "It's been terribly exciting working with Peter Brook," he was reported as saying in the *The New Yorker*. "I think he's the best Shakespearean director." The only minor mishap occurred when Mac-

---

*Unfortunately, Orson returned one month too late to see "First Person Singular," a reverberation of the technique he had used so successfully on radio some fifteen years previously. The television version had the camera function as the eyes of the characters and starred such actors as Wally Cox, Kim Stanley, and James Dunn who performed regularly until the last show, September 1953.

Liammoir grabbed Orson's jacket and accidentally smashed a cigar in its pocket. "There goes sixty-five cents," quipped Orson. "I'm in no position to afford that." Orson had his lines tape-recorded, and in the evenings in the privacy of his room, he would go over them again and again, sometimes mouthing them as he sat in his nightly bath.

He felt good about being back in New York. He briefly visited with his daughter Rebecca, whose mother, Rita Hayworth, had since married singer Dick Haymes. He attended a performance of *The Little Hut* along with Marlene Dietrich, conferred with his attorney about his tax problem, dined at "21," had drinks in the Oak Room. "New York doesn't seem a bit changed," he observed. "Europe has changed; it's become sad after the war. The thing that hits you when you come back to New York is that incredible combination of friendliness and impersonality."

The producers and technicians at the television studio were expecting temperamental outbursts during the two weeks of rehearsals, but they never really came, though Orson did quietly insist on a few indulgences: the velvet in his costume had to be *silk* velvet; his gloves were to be handmade; for his mad scene with the Earl, there must be real, ocean-wet seaweed to adorn his wig and a real starfish as a prop. "I'm scared stiff I'll be no good," he told a friend, consuming large quantities of brandy as fortification.

By the time *King Lear* was broadcast on October 18, 1953, Orson had become a convert to television. He was impressed with the mobility of the cameras, the lightness and ease of set movement, the immediacy of the image, and the relative lack of expense compared to film. "Technologically, television is a hundred years ahead of film," he observed. But there was a hint of cynicism behind his enthusiasm, as witness his remark to columnist Art Buchwald: "Everything you do now in television is considered original. In ten years the critics will kick you in the teeth for doing the same things, and call you arty."

Surprisingly, given the talents of Orson Welles and Peter Brook plus a fine supporting cast, the broadcast did not go altogether well. Many of the scenes were disconnected and much of the action appeared unmotivated and sometimes almost inexplicable. In the complicated storm scene (where the actors did not seem to get wet), Orson, perhaps concerned lest he overplay his lines, ended up underplaying them. This was doubly strange since the scene ("Howl, howl, howl, howl! O you are men of stone") is traditionally a feast of histrionics.

Somehow, Orson could not master the intricacies of the sound in television, and his voice came over as either too soft or too rumbling. Peter Hamburger, reviewing the play in *The New Yorker,* explained it this way: "Part of Mr. Welles's difficulty with his diction unquestionably arose from the hairy encumbrances he was hidden behind; Jove himself could not thunder forth clearly were he so burdened. But Mr. Welles's difficulty also had another source—one entirely distinct from his grotesque makeup. He apparently has the notion that if he starts a sentence far enough down in his stomach and sends it rumbling up through his system in ever-increasing volume until it reaches his larynx and heads for the open road, it will take on a tragic ring."

But the broadcast received some high praise, too. *Newsweek* referred to Orson's "fine effect" as he roared his way through the part, and Jack Gould, in the *Herald Tribune,* thought Orson's interpretation of Lear "caught the human qualities of the King." In other regions of the United States, Orson's Lear was enjoyed, if not hailed. Said the *Philadelphia Bulletin,* "Welles emerged as a fierce, ranting thunderous-voiced ruffian getting his just desserts," and the *Cincinnati Enquirer* said of his lines that they were "reasonably well mouthed." With *King Lear,* "Omnibus" had one of its most positive mail pulls of any broadcast it had ever aired; if some of the critics disliked the play, evidently the public did not. Some fifteen million persons saw *King Lear,* more than all the people put together who had seen the play since it was written in the early 1600s.

Despite the drams of adverse criticism, Orson was satisfied with his performance and let it be known that he would be available for future television roles. Bob Saudek, the producer of "Omnibus," in turn, agreed that they should do more shows together, specifically some adaptations of stories by Steinbeck and Hemingway. Other producers from CBS-TV conferred with Orson about producing and directing a story of his own choice as a special dramatic presentation, perhaps *Don Quixote.* There was talk of a contract. Perhaps Orson would agree to do a series of specials—the number six was mentioned. He could head all-star casts in productions based on contemporary and classical plays or novels. The budget? Three million dollars.

Hubbell Robinson, Jr., a CBS-TV vice-president, initiated talks with Welles and his attorney, Arnold Weissberger. Orson said he would like to do *Trilby* as one of his six shows and then quickly changed his mind when NBC broadcast a poorly received musical version, *Svengali and the Blonde.* As talks went on, representatives of the other two networks, ABC and NBC, began vying with CBS for his services. It was like a two-decade-old dream come true, a reincarnation of the days before *Citizen Kane*: producers were lining up to give *him* money.

But as negotiations and seemingly endless talks continued in and out of the corporate offices, nothing seemed to coalesce. None of the properties Welles suggested really seemed to excite the television people. *King Lear* was a novelty, they argued, but how much Shakespeare could the American public take? Instead, they suggested all manner of slapdash stories to Orson, not one of which he found even remotely acceptable. Talks went on, and on, and on, and slowly Orson's relationship to television network production slipped into an ever-deepening haze of confusion. At last, disillusioned, he returned to England.

ORSON AND PAOLA had now been living and traveling together for several years. When, eventually, they married, it came about in a typically informal and Wellesian way. At the conclusion of a trip to Madrid, he was to go to Paris and she to Frascati; as they were saying good-bye at the station, he turned to her and asked if she would marry him. She accepted, and a year later, a week before his fortieth birthday, they were wed in London, with director Peter Brook and Natasha Parry acting as best man and matron of honor.

IN ADDITION TO the British films in which he starred, Welles also acted in three other movies during the mid-1950s, all made on the Continent. Two of them were produced and directed by the controversial Sacha Guitry, the French writer-director who had been accused of collaboration with the Nazis during World War II. The first film that Welles did for Guitry (and Orson's first French film), *Royal Affairs in Versailles,* was a story written by Guitry about the famous French palace from its construction in 1661 to modern times. The film was budgeted at almost one million dollars, more than ten times what other French movies were being produced for at that time.*

Guitry virtually hypnotized his backers into believing that a lavish historical spectacle with well-known stars (in addition to Orson, he secured Claudette Colbert, Jean-Pierre Aumont, and Edith Piaf, among others) would make an enormous profit and perhaps even bolster the French self-image. "It is my earnest hope that *Royal Affairs in Versailles* will be regarded as more than a motion picture," Guitry pontificated to the press, "for it is, to me, my crowning achievement in more than a half-century of activity in the world of arts."

The first French film to be shot entirely in the new and expensive Eastman Kodak color process, *Royal Affairs in Versailles* was splendidly photographed in the actual Château of Versailles, the French Ministry of Beaux Arts reluctantly giving its permission to Guitry to use the building as his studio. Unusual precautions were demanded. The art treasures were insured for millions of dollars; the legs of the cameras were wrapped in felt so as not to mar the elegant marble and parquet floors; some of the particularly fragile and rare furniture, tapestries, and paintings were removed for safety; sound engineers had to improvise ingenious devices to reduce reverberations so as not to harm the chandeliers; cameramen were forced to find odd angles to avoid the reflections from the many mirrors in such gilded rooms as the Galerie des Glaces. The result was a two-and-a-half-hour pageant that was long on pomp and elegance but unfortunately lacking in dramatic appeal.

Orson played a fat and gouty Benjamin Franklin who, speaking in English, seeks financial aid for the United States from the shrewd and scandalous Louis XIV, played with a certain tired wisdom by Guitry himself. Orson's role was briefly episodic and received mixed reviews, everything from "conspicuous,"

---

*Owing to a sagging economy and poor attendance at French movie theaters during the mid-1950s, any film costing as much as 40,000,000 francs (slightly over $100,000) was considered a risky investment.

as noted by Bosley Crowther in *The New York Times,* to *The New Yorker's* "Benjamin Franklin, played by Orson Welles, looks like a botched embalming job, and his mortuary croaking contributes nothing in the way of wisdom to the affair."

Although *Royal Affairs in Versailles* had an enthusiastic international distribution, soon after its release it quickly disappeared from theaters around the world.

GUITRY'S NEXT FILM, *Napoleon,* in which Orson had a part, was even more lavish than his previous effort. No studio was large enough to accommodate the elaborate sets, and the Parc des Expositions had to be commandeered to create the palaces and streets of Napoleonic France, peopled with a cast of five thousand, one day acting as the army of Henry IV and later as the revolutionary insurgents. Orson played Napoleon's jailer, Sir Hudson Lowe, in all of his glowering glory and was backed by a cast consisting of Guitry in the role of the wily Talleyrand, Michele Morgan, Danielle Darrieux, and Maria Schell. Erich von Stroheim, draped with an unruly wig, was an unforgettable apparition of Ludwig von Beethoven as he played his *Eroica* Symphony in a piano arrangement. Welles predicted immediate triumph for the film as soon as it was released. During the shooting, he told biographer André Maurois, "There are very few sure-fire subjects. Napoleon is one of them. You can always write a *Life of Napoleon* and a *Life of Jesus* and find a hundred thousand readers."

The opening night of the film in Paris was a luxuriant and celebrity-studded affair with no less than French President Coty attending with his entourage. What they saw was a three-hour extravaganza. Austerlitz, Napoleon's self-coronation, the burning of Moscow, the battle of Waterloo, and the exile to St. Helena were all depicted faithfully and with verve, and the opening night audience cheered the film to a rollicking applause at its end. Although publications such as *Variety* were, like Orson, predicting immense popularity for *Napoleon* ("The 70-year-old Guitry, who with Cocteau, is France's most versatile theatrical genius has turned the trick again."), this film also quickly faded into oblivion after a few weeks of international release.

THE OTHER FILM Orson acted in during that time was *Man, Beast, and Virtue,* based on a love story by Luigi Pirandello. It was a complicated tale of husband-wife-lover triangle that involves the efforts of the lover to reconcile the wife to her sea captain husband in order to evade the legal paternity of the child she is bearing. The film was an international production written and directed by a young man with the pseudonym of Steno (Stevano Vanziano) and was shot on the busy Neapolitan coastline and in nearby Cetora. Orson, bedecked in a huge Neptunian beard, played the sea captain (the "beast") who, because of the lover's success, finds himself together with his wife by the film's end. French actress Vivienne Romance played the female lead, and Italian comic Toto was the lover.

Although distributed by Paramount Pictures in the United States, the film was rarely shown in this country and is hardly known, even in Italy.

ORSON'S EUROPEAN FILMMAKING activity had ended for a while with *Mr. Arkadin,* but he continued with bursts of activity in other areas of the arts and entertainment.

He was enormously successful with a reading on BBC Radio of Walt Whitman's "Song of Myself." Not yet as bearded as his American forbear, but having a psychic relationship to him—he was roughly the same age as Whitman when the poem was written—Orson seemed to perfectly capture the lament over "the sickness and desperate revolt at the close of a life without elevation or naiveté," as Whitman described his work.

Trying to maintain a dialectless and somewhat wearied intonation, Orson gave a splendid reading and ultimately developed an interpretation with an astonishing variation of pace, tone, and inflection that captured his English audience. "Probably no other known voice could have so satisfyingly brought out the vigor, weight and sweep of Whitman's lines," wrote the radio critic of the *Times Educational Supplement.* And Morris Wiggins in the *Sunday Times* said of the reading that it was "A virtuoso performance which added up to perfect radio. . . . It is not easy to believe that any listener even mildly susceptible to fine acting could fail to feel a communicated surge of life and hope and optimism while Mr. Welles was speaking."

An offer was made to him at that time, by his friend Sam Spiegel from *The Stranger* days, to direct *The Bridge on the River Kwai,* based on Pierre Boulle's novel. Orson, believing that an agreement had been reached, canceled all his other projects and waited for the screenplay (being written by Carl Foreman and Michael Wilson). After four months, Orson was dumbfounded when he read in one of the London newspapers that the directorship had been awarded to David Lean, that Alec Guinness and Sessue Hayakawa had been signed to the lead roles, and that the company was already filming in Ceylon. He was never told why he had been passed over.

Orson then did two television series for BBC, as director and narrator, with Sir Huw Wheldon as producer, both incarnations of his "Orson Welles's Almanac" from his radio days: "Around the World with Orson Welles" and "The Orson Welles Sketchbook." The former consisted of film essays on everything from bullfighting to Viennese coffee, and from the joys of the Left Bank of Paris to old-age pensioners in London; the latter was made up of a series of stories told by Orson with the aid of an actual artist's sketchbook, in which he would always start with a self-portrait. Then while doodling on camera, he would talk on such subjects as John Barrymore, his boyhood meeting with Harry Houdini, his own experience with the *War of the Worlds* broadcast, or his life at the Gate Theatre in Dublin. He used a camera technique that was unusual for him and consisted of medium to extreme close-ups of himself talking; it was a device that many viewers found tiring and many critics pretentious. Peter Black in the *Daily Mail* talked of Orson's remarkable face: "The heavy jowl and alert mouth; the oddly slanting eyes; the pudgy nose and the comedian's eyebrows; all as striking a melange as you could find outside the decline and fall of the Roman Empire."

British viewers appreciated the "Around the World" shows, however, lauding Orson's powerful personality and enjoying his remarkable gift for drawing the most out of people during interviews. In one show, the old almshouse widows of Hackney almost danced for him in their garden. He loved doing the show, as proved by the fact that he accepted only £75 per program as his fee.

In addition to performances, Orson's other activities at this period consisted largely in giving lectures (mostly about film) and writing for esoteric cinema journals. An article in *Film Culture* gave suggestions on saving the cinema (*force* the distributors to release films internationally, he commanded); articles in subsequent years (1957 and 1958) in the *International Film Annual,* respectively, talked of how important it was for man to use his leisure time productively and how the wide-screen is a form of madness. It was the latter article that contained the two quotes brilliantly summing up his cinematic philosophy that would be connected with him for years to come: "A film is never really good unless the camera is an eye in the head of a poet"; and "A film is a ribbon of dreams."

IN THE SUMMER of 1955, Welles gave observers even more reason to cast him as the incurably overreaching showman. This latest of impossible or unplayable theatrical projects was an adaptation of Herman Melville's epic American novel, *Moby Dick.* Even before an adapter faced the staging problem presented by the whale, he would have to grapple with the challenges of the Melville text. Long and complex, extraordinarily varied in approach and rich in detail, *Moby Dick* seems possible only on paper.

This is not to say that adaptations had not been attempted before. One of the first stage versions had been a French one: a 1949 Parisian production translated by the popular French novelist Jean Giono and adapted by Paul Oettly. Barely antedating the Welles play was Howard Robman's American version of April 1955 at the Phoenix Theater. There had also been the 1930 Warner's film with John Barrymore.

And Welles had already had a run-through of sorts with a film production of *Moby Dick.* By the spring of 1955, he had completed acting his part of Father Mapple, the fiery, whaling-town preacher, in the John Huston movie that starred Gregory Peck as Ahab. Welles's performance in the film, which was released in 1956, was electrifying; he and the U.S. Navy surplus rubber "whale" got at least as much press attention as did Peck.

The story of the white whale had intrigued Welles for some time; he had been working on and off on a playable script for the previous eight years; and he was actually crestfallen when Huston announced his film production. Clearly he wanted to direct it himself. As it turned out, the stage adaptation was sensible in that it was, for him surprisingly, brief; Orson did not fall into his usual error of trying for too much on the boards. He stripped the novel to its core—the story of Captain Ahab in his mad, headlong pursuit of the white whale, culminating in the chase scene and final confrontation in which the *Pequod* and all her hands go down with only Ishmael, the "orphan," left to tell the story.

On the other hand, Welles, with his streamlined script in draft, decided to add something. *Moby Dick* became a play within a play and concerned a traveling New England theatrical company at the turn of the century. The troupe commences by trying to iron out a few wrinkles in its production of *King Lear,* and then at the behest of the Governor, the manager-director-actor, begins rehearsal of a "new piece," *Moby Dick.* The play-within-a-play device—an acting company's rehearsal in street clothes—allowed Welles to go without elaborate scenery, and, of course, obviated the necessity of anything to represent water, ships, or even the leviathan whale.

Choosing a nineteenth-century interpretation of Melville gave Orson other kinds of leeway as well. Somewhat inflated oratorical styles of acting called for by the high-flown rhetoric of *Moby Dick*'s text would not seem out of place. He was primarily interested in getting Melville's words on stage, words that at one time or another touch all the important names of life, echoing the language of the familiar heroes of English literature such as Shakespeare and Milton, as well as the more esoteric prose stylists like Sir Thomas Browne.

As Welles developed it, the script is strongly Shakespearean in character. It is written for the most part in blank verse, the words derived to a great extent from Melville's own. For example, the book's introductory chapter, Ishmael's introduction of himself to the reader, becomes the first speech of the Young Actor in Welles's play. Several pages in the book are condensed to a speech of slightly over two dozen lines. Orson did not compromise with the original: the set speeches—for example, the harangues of Ahab—are rhetorically extravagant, the lines swelling and sonorous. And, as in a Shakespeare play, the heightened language is complemented by the ordinary, colloquial language of commoners and clowns—in the case of *Moby Dick,* the shouts and slangy interchanges of the seamen. The texture of life aboard ship is evoked through the use of sea chanteys with text from Melville, performed by the actors, and the music of a harmonium.

As might be expected, Welles cast himself as the manager-director Governor who plays Ahab in the "rehearsal." In the play, this same character takes on the juicy role of fire-and-brimstone preacher Father Mapple, who, naturally enough, delivers a sermon based on the story of Jonah and the whale. (This, of course, was the same role Welles played in the Huston film, unreleased at the time.) Patrick McGoohan was chosen to play the Serious Actor who performs Starbuck, the role of reason and common sense that is contrasted with Ahab.

The opening date of the play was set for June 16, 1955, at the Duke of York's Theatre in London. One experimental casting decision proved especially interesting. In the script, a young girl of the troupe (the only female part, in fact) is pressed into service to play Pip, the little black cabin boy who has gone mad. The boy actor doesn't show up, and the Governor has her run through the part for this rehearsal. Welles sorted through hundreds of British girls before coming up with the twenty-six-year-old, virtually unknown actress Joan Plowright.* She had played only once in a top-line London theater before landing this role, a part that turned out to be particularly taxing in that she was forced to play it on her knees.

As befitted a "rehearsal," the sets were rudimentary. The bare stage was relieved only by a few packing crates and baskets, and the shipboard scenes were suggested by a tangle of dangling fly ropes that could sway to suggest heavy weather and a rolling ship. Recorded sea sounds were also employed. In the climactic pursuit scene, Ahab's longboat was represented by a table placed down in the front row.

The play begins with the Young Actor trying to perform his Ishmael soliloquy through the interruptions of the stage manager. ("Call me Ishmael. . . . Whenever I grow grim about the mouth; whenever/it's a damp November in my soul;/I count it time to go to sea . . ."). The members of the troupe are then introduced in turn, as the Serious Actor asks the Governor about the proper way to play the role of Starbuck—and in fact, the relationship between the two is similar to that between Starbuck and Ahab in the piece they are about to engage in. Then the young girl is introduced. The obvious problem of the whale is brought up by a Cynical Actor. The Young Actor replies, "The white whale is like the storm in *Lear*—it's real, but it's more than real; it's an idea in the mind." The whale controversy subsides. *Lear* is on their minds since it is apparently the current offering of the troupe. The Governor takes the young actress through her paces in a few key interchanges in *Lear* and then, above objections of the cast who would like to continue with the tried and true, the Governor orders a rehearsal of *Moby Dick*.

The Serious Actor, still concerned about his role as Starbuck, asks the Governor, "What exactly do you want me to do?" Welles's reply is, "Do? Stand six feet away and do your damnedest!" And *Moby Dick* is under way.

Dressed in a black greatcoat and dramatic cape, and sporting his traditional aquiline putty nose, Welles seemed to enjoy himself immensely in the role of Ahab, comporting himself in an expansive and oratorical way while hobbling around with a cane as a stand-in for the peg leg. In the dim light, most of the other actors were reduced to silhouette. Welles was in the spotlight and carried on with characteristic gusto, although he admitted to reviewer Richard Watts, Jr., during the run that he had spent so much time on the production that he felt he was still working out the role while playing it.

His exuberance, in fact, led to a unique kind of performance on opening night. At the very last, as Ahab is about to cast the harpoon that seals everyone's fate, Welles's booming lines (and they are Melville's) read, "For hate's sake I spit my breath at thee! From hell's heart I stab at thee!" London *Daily Mirror* critic Fergus Cashin was never to forget those lines, for Welles's

---

*Later to become the wife of Sir Laurence Olivier.

animation and delivery were such that he made good on his promise, spitting in Cashin's eye, seven rows back!

Cashin forgave him, saying that Welles's liquid punctuation was only a minor inconvenience for the pleasure of seeing "a magnificent effort, tremendously exciting and effective."

Other critics had some reservations based on subtler concerns. Some felt that the audience had some difficulty following the words, although the text actually offers fewer difficulties than the clearest passage in Melville. Critics were also perplexed about the casting of a girl in the Pip role.

Having the opportunity of placing an attractive young woman in a cast that would otherwise be all male had some obvious appeal, but Welles may have had more in mind than that. It seems clear that he was attempting to create parallels between *Moby Dick* and *Lear*: there *is* something of Lear in Ahab, and something of Cordelia in Pip. The troupe performs both plays, and the parallels are sometimes explicit, as in the remark that Moby Dick is like *Lear's* storm. Welles may have believed that a more convincing relationship could be established between Ahab and a female Pip, that on the stage Ahab's rapport with an eight-year-old boy would appear artificial or strained. In any event, Orson never considered it a miscalculation, for the play, which enjoyed a brief revival in New York in 1962, was to continue to use a young woman in the role.*

The Welles *Moby Dick* completed a four-week limited engagement in London. A 1961 Dublin appearance of the play, with Jack Aronson as Ahab, is also on record.

AFTER THE CLOSE of *Moby Dick,* Orson again began toying with a battery of those interesting-sounding projects that, in the volatile world of the theater, so seldom seem to gel. At first, he was to do a sixteen-week production of *Othello* (with Jennifer Jones as Desdemona) in a repertory that would also include either *The Merchant of Venice* or *Much Ado About Nothing,* at the City Center in New York; but the potential producers, James Russo and Michael Ellis, backed out because of scheduling conflicts. There was also talk of a contemporary drama written by Orson, *Fair Warning,* that would open in New York. And perennial entrepreneur Billy Rose and Orson had long and extravagant transatlantic telephone calls between New York and London about a repertory project consisting of *Macbeth, Othello*, and a new version of Fernand Crommelynck's *The Magnificent Cuckold.* For whatever reason, perhaps the difficulties of long-distance negotiation, no agreement could be reached.

Orson also announced that he was considering a version of *Fiesta,* based on Hemingway's *The Sun Also Rises*; however, it never got beyond this first stage.

He thought he could improve on Peter Brook's direction of *King Lear* and

---

*Rod Steiger and Frances Hyland were the pairing in the later version, directed by the British-Canadian actor Douglas Campbell.

his own television performance of the play. The glimmers of human love and compassion, and the action enfolded by darkness, madness, and disillusionment, constituted a compelling challenge.

On October 7, 1955, the news in New York was that, along with *Lear,* Ben Jonson's comedy *Volpone* was to be adapted by Welles and none other than television star Jackie Gleason was to play the parasitic Mosca; the two fat men would in character outwit and outpaunch the other on the stage. It was at that time that Orson dubbed Gleason with a nickname that would remain with him for the rest of his life: the Great One. Orson arrived in New York on October 26 aboard the *Andrea Doria.*

Welles planned to have alternate performances of the two plays. *Lear* was to begin rehearsals in the second week of November, the cast fleshed out with English actors Edgar Reyford, Patrick McGoohan, Sheilah Burrell, and Donald Pleasence, and would open three weeks later. By November 22, plans had changed. The play was now slated for a mid-January opening at the City Center on West Fifty-fifth Street.

Complications followed almost immediately. Orson was not to have his English actors after all. A week after the City Center opening was announced, it was reported that the Immigration Service, in collaboration with an irate Actors' Equity, was denying entry permits for the Britishers. Permits were refused for Reyford, Burrell, Pleasence, Hazel Penward, and Jack May. Equity claimed that actors with comparable ability were readily available in the States, and furthermore, they suggested strongly, as they had done in the past, that importation of actors was simply a ploy to get people willing to work for less wages.

None of this was good news for Orson. Along with labor difficulties, he was attempting to solve his problems with the Internal Revenue Service, and reporters waited with anticipation for the first signs of a misstep. Walter Kerr, in a general reflection on Orson, described him as a grand old *enfant turning terrible.*

Welles's visit to the United States was sponsored by Henry M. Margolis and his old Mercury colleague Martin Gabel. By early December, they had worked out an agreement with Jean Dalrymple, director of the City Center Company. Geraldine Fitzgerald and Viveca Lindfors were signed on to play two of Lear's daughters. Welles would have full creative control and was working on the budget. *Lear* was to play six weeks, to February 12.

Days later *Volpone* was dropped because of difficulties with money. The plan now called for a six-day stint of previews of *Lear* with a premiere on January 12, 1956, with a two-and-a-half-week run to Sunday January 29. Tallulah Bankhead and *A Streetcar Named Desire* were to move in on February 15.

Money became a point of contention. On December 8, the press reported that Welles's original plan was far too expensive. With such a short run the City Center would never have a chance of climbing out of the red. Welles agreed to emerge with an economy version of *King Lear* but continued to put pressure on Dalrymple for greater freedom. They went ahead with rehearsals anyway. (By now the plan was for Lindfors to play Cordelia and Fitzgerald to play Goneril. Sylvia Short was cast as Regan.) Two weeks later a compromise on budget was reached, and Welles was back to his original conception of the play. It was going to be the most expensive production ever for the City Center, $60,000 more than ever before, to be exact.

Welles wanted to explain himself to a wider audience, and so he wrote an article that appeared in *The New York Times* on the first page of the second section on Sunday, January 8, 1956. He justified his attempt at *Lear*:

> We of the theater may never manage the beginning of any sort of justice to this towering and tremendous work, but it is clearly up to us to make a brave try at it just as often as we may.

He pointed out that the British had had six productions of the play since World War II, while the United States had had fewer than that in this century. He claimed that, paradoxically, the old man's role must be played by a young man with enough energy to do the part justice. And he regretted the loss of *Volpone* for budgetary reasons:

> It should be easy to see why I would have been more at ease if it had been possible for me to present my credentials as a classical theater man to a new generation of New York playgoers with two productions instead of one. I can only hope that, if this new "Lear" should be considered redundant after all, such an opinion will not extend to, or discourage, our hopes for the founding, as soon as may be, of a solid theater establishment.

Welles believed, perhaps unrealistically, that *Lear* was to be the first step toward the birth of a classical repertory theater on Broadway.

Every aspect of *Lear* was touched by Welles. He edited, cast, and staged it, even going so far as to submit sketches for the costumes by Robert Fletcher and the scenery by Theodore Cooper. He knew the risks; he had said, "*Lear* gets as close to the Greeks as anything else in Shakespeare. When it does this it's either terribly exciting or terribly boring."*

Marc Blitzstein generated the basic musical score (he also played harpsichord) and, for music to accompany the progressive madness of Lear, Welles had tapes of bizarre electronic bleatings by Vladimir Ussachevsky. The playbill credit simply read, "The production by Mr. Welles."

Before the premiere, something happened that would utterly change the complexion of the play. During an early performance, Welles fell from a ramp backstage and broke two bones in his left foot; it was perhaps the tenth time in his life that he had had an accident with the same foot. He decided to go on, nevertheless, with the premiere on the scheduled date, January 12.

---

*Of course he made excisions in the original. Supposedly when Orson told Bertolt Brecht he was preparing another Shakespeare play for the stage, Brecht asked: "When are you going to write the script for it, Orson?"

So on opening night, Welles performed *Lear* with cast and cane. It seemed eminently reasonable: certainly the aged Lear could use a cane. Welles's startling performance was not affected too much. He was able to stick to his idea of bursting through the gigantic map with which Lear divides his kingdom. But Walter Kerr was not entirely pleased, calling the show a simple assemblage of "rich visual diagrams" concocted by "a much too conniving mind." Kerr had no way of knowing what was to happen to Lear next.

At the conclusion of the premiere, Welles, who later admitted to completely losing himself in the part during the latter portion of the play, tripped over a prop at his final exit and sprained his right ankle. Completely hobbled now, he found himself faced with an extremely expensive, short-running show, a physically demanding part of his own invention, and acidulous reviews of the premiere by the likes of the major critic of the *Herald Tribune*, Walter Kerr.

He showed up to a packed house on the second night confined to a wheelchair. Roughly 2,800 people saw Welles roll on stage and begin to explain what had happened. His first responsibility, he said, was "to keep the audience in its seats, at least until the box office closes and the chance for refunds is past." Few left. He vowed that he would play out the run of *Lear,* "if they have to swing me over the stage with wire." Then he heard and saw someone using a camera in the first row center: "Please don't take pictures," he said with a smile. "That clicking noise sounds like the breaking of bones." This second night, then, was an impromptu performance, "An evening with Orson Welles," in which he read selections from the play and gave his commentary on them. He also had some words about the first night critics, wishing the journalistic establishment no particular ill but concluding, "I do wish to remind them that today is Friday the thirteenth."

He apologized for looking more like "the man who came to dinner" than like Lear. The newspapers, cynically, weren't sure if he had slimmed down to 280 or 260 pounds for the role, but mobility was no longer an issue; Orson was in a wheelchair and that was it. He felt he had little choice, under the circumstances, but to continue with *Lear.* The third day's matinee would be canceled, but the show would go on that night. Lear's fool would conduct him around in his chair.* Actually, he began to enjoy being wheeled about.

Before the curtain went up on the night's performance, Welles was frank with his performers: "Don't change a thing," he said, "unless something idiotic happens. Then stop being idiotic and do what's intelligent." Then he rolled over to the microphone and addressed the audience, telling them that Lear was an old man full of troubles, and added ruefully, "Tonight he's collected a few more."

---

*As it turned out, there was another similar accident affecting the New York stage at the time. Shelley Winters, playing in *A Hatful of Rain* at the Lyceum, hurt her foot teaching her daughter how to roller skate in Central Park. She opted for an understudy at first but finally did show up in the play with her cast.

Lear did indeed continue, playing out its run to veteran playgoers and curiosity seekers—certainly Welles didn't try to turn anyone away. He was counting on grossing $150,000 in order to put the City Center firmly in the black. And under these almost inconceivable conditions, he did manage to get them over $90,000 on his short run.

Kerr did see fit to write again about *Lear* on January 22, toning down his criticism and praising Welles, who was, he felt, "still a mental magician."

In an article in *Commonweal,* March 2, 1956, Richard Hayes, though not entirely satisfied with *Lear,* concluded with this rational observation of what had come to pass:

> . . . (W)as there not something punishing and harsh in the meager critical and popular response to Mr. Welles's elaborate production? How we do make the prodigy pay for his early audacities, long after he has sloughed them off! Mr. Welles illustrated that he was not the absolute Lear of this generation (if there is, indeed, such a thing) but he came out of the attempt with a brighter honor than so many of his contemporaries who have settled for such mild victories. Quite possibly, he does lack "a sense of direction," as we so consistently remind him, yet at least his confusion is the distress of plenty, not poverty.

IT SEEMED AT the close of *King Lear* that the only constancy in Orson's world was that of change itself. From the depths of Shakespeare and the culture of New York, he flew to Las Vegas to appear as an entertainer at the Hotel Riviera, doing magic tricks, reading popular classics, and even cracking some obsolete jokes. For his three-week stint there, he was paid the kingly sum of $45,000. He never had the opportunity to spend it all, though. Rita Hayworth sued him for $22,450 which he allegedly owed her in child support for their daughter, Rebecca, then twelve. Orson again left the country.

Once Orson was back in England, as in the past, offers to act in films continually came his way. Although hardly past forty, because of his enormous bulk and presence, he was then usually invited to play older roles, character types that would take advantage of his mammoth size and bearing. Joseph McBride has observed: "It didn't matter that Welles was actually not much older than a Jeff Chandler or a Charlton Heston: he *seemed* much older. He was certainly bulkier and more mature, and he could no longer pass for the dashing young romantic figures he had played in *Jane Eyre* or *The Lady from Shanghai.*"

Not all directors, however, felt that Orson was ready to be relegated to the background in support of a young and virile looking star. He was signed to play the highly romantic role of the dueling and dashing Alexandre Dumas in *King of Paris,* based on the best-selling biographical novel by Guy Endore and to be directed by the author. Endore's first line in the book seemed to describe both Dumas and Welles: "He was one of those men who live ten lives while the rest of us are struggling through one." In convincing Welles to play the role (which Orson had wanted to do ever since he had gone to Hollywood in 1939) Endore read a contemporary description of Dumas from a joint diary of the Goncourt brothers. How could anyone else but Orson, he argued, play the part?

> Dumas is a kind of a giant with the hair of a Negro, the salt beginning to mix with the pepper, and with little blue eyes buried in his flesh like those of a hippopotamus, clear and mischievous; and an enormous moon face, exactly the way the cartoonists love to draw him. No doubt about it; there's a magnetism that radiates from him. A kind of mesmerism. You sense at once the showman of freaks and prodigies; the vendor of wonders; the traveling salesman for the Arabian Nights. He talks volubly and, it must be admitted, engagingly; but what holds you is not brilliance, nor mordance, nor color; it is an endless array of facts, facts that he keeps dredging up in a pleasantly hoarse voice from a memory that is like a bottomless ocean.

Yes, yes, Orson said. He *would* play it. He *must* play it. Unfortunately, Endore's screenplay proved too difficult and controversial, backing was impossible to secure, and eventually the project was abandoned.

Olympic Films of Rome announced that they had signed Orson to write, direct, and costar in two films, done in Italian and English, one to be a version of *The Autobiography of Benvenuto Cellini,* possibly to use the score of Berlioz, and the other a comedy consisting of well-known comics from Italian vaudeville. Those films also never materialized owing to undercapitalization. An official Russian invitation to film the Bolshoi Ballet in a performance of *The Nutcracker Suite* curiously did not interest him aesthetically or financially.

Portrait of a Murderer, another film project in which Welles was to direct and play a circus performer, to be produced by twenty-six-year-old Jacques Gauthier, with a screenplay by Charles Lederer, didn't get off the ground because of a personality clash, never publicly delineated nor explained, between Orson and Gauthier. Then Twentieth Century-Fox also tried tempting Orson back to Hollywood, in vain, to play the part of a murderer in *The Killer Is Loose,* with former archrival Victor Mature, as his costar. MGM was another studio that also had no luck in enticing Orson to the United States, for reasons perhaps even obscure to him, even though he was immensely interested in directing Robert Taylor in Irwin Shaw's crime story, *Tip on a Dead Jockey.*

A film about French-Canadian life and lore was also seriously discussed ("I am tremendously interested," Orson said to the potential producers) but never consummated. Later, a French-Italian production company proposed to do a film based on the purpled life of ex-King Farouk, with Orson playing the renowned reprobate, costarring French actress Micheline Presle and film heavy Erich von Stroheim. Orson asked for script approval but never received it, and the project went no further. However, it seems likely that his heart was in none of these projects but was instead taken by an old love: a TV film version of *Don Quixote.*

CERVANTES HAD BEGUN *Don Quixote de la Mancha* as a simple satire on the chivalric romances of the sixteenth century, but once he began to write, his penetrating and humorous insights into the follies and hopes of man prevailed. Orson was deeply interested in the personality of the errant knight, the similarities of his tilting at windmills and Orson's attack on the ordered structure of filmmaking quite obvious. Cervantes was forced to write a second part to his novel after another writer published a spurious *Further Adventures of Don Quixote*; the original author gave Don Quixote and Sancho Panza an added dimension that transcended their own fictive lives. (In the second volume, characters refer to the fact of having read about Quixote and Panza in the first volume.)

Orson changed the story to include, in spirit, Cervantes's manipulation of the fictional aspects of his characters, by propelling them with deliberate anachronism into modern times with twentieth-century settings. "My Don Quixote and Sancho Panza are exactly and traditionally drawn from Cervantes but are nonetheless contemporary," he told Bazin. But as much interest as he felt for Quixote, his film showed more rapport with Panza: "I think Cervantes showed Panza first making fun of Quixote and then admiring him and loving him," Orson said.

With initial funds from CBS-TV to create a thirty-minute television drama, Orson began shooting *Don Quixote* in Spain and Mexico in the mid-1950s. The noble-looking Mexican actor Francisco Reiguera would play Quixote and Akim Tamiroff his page. What is striking is the physical correctness of these two. Reiguera's Quixote seems to have stepped out of the famous illustrations of the book. Indeed, there are framed Quixote engravings in doorways the Don rides by during the film, and the similarity, in every detail, is striking. It is almost as if Welles is saying, "Look how clever I am, to have found the perfect image for my purposes." When a representative of CBS screened a small portion of the unedited film and was dissatisfied, Orson was refused any further monies to complete it. Actually, he was delighted with the rejection. This was no mere half-hour television drama he was creating: it was becoming a full-blown feature film, perhaps the magnum opus of his career. He then transposed the focus of the idea into a longer film, framed by scenes of himself as narrator. As the film opens, he is seen reading Cervantes's novel in a Mexican hotel. Child actress Patty McCormack, who plays a young American tourist visiting Mexico with her parents, asks Welles what he is reading: Orson has her sit on his lap and he begins to weave the tale, and the film progresses, his voice coming in from time to time to link the narrative flow with explanatory commentary.

Not all of the film was directly related to the Cervantes tale; it emerged as a quasi-documentary concerning Spanish folklore or history. At one point, Welles is seen with Patty McCormack at the gate of a huge bullring. "Was Mr. Quixote a bullfighter?" she asks. "Not exactly," Orson answers. "It's a profession, not a vocation. A bullfighter works for money. Don Quixote was an aficionado."

Orson shot the film with only script fragments and sometimes without any written screenplay at all, going out into the streets as silent filmmakers used to do and working improvisationally. When he didn't have sophisticated 35mm equipment, cameramen with hand-held 16mm cameras would be employed from time to time. He worked on *Don Quixote* in roughly the same way he did on *Othello*: wherever a minimal cast and crew could be assembled and wherever Orson, equipped with a few personal dollars, could wrench himself away from his other commitments he would resume shooting. The sight of a sunset in Ibiza, the carnival parade of a saint in Pamplona, or an ancient cobbled street in Seville would be enough to get Orson reinterested in the attenuated film and to instantly reorganize his crew. Peter Cowie, an astute British writer on film, has observed: "He would meet his actors and technical crew in front of his Spanish hotel each morning and then would set about improvising the film in the streets in the style of Mack Sennett."

Orson updated Cervantes so that Don Quixote pits himself against the monsters of the electronic age. In one of the episodes in the film, Don Quixote goes into a movie theater, observes the heroine on the screen who is shackled and about to be abused, perhaps slain, and with his legendary gallantry comes to her rescue, leaping upon the stage and plunging his lance into the screen.

In one scene, as Quixote and Panza ride into a modern city, complete with automobiles, buses, neon lights, and other artifacts of the twentieth century, they are cheered by crowds of bystanders who urge them on. In an aside of trenchant wit and satire, a large poster of Don Quixote Beer can be seen in the background as the two men pass resolutely by.

Other modern parallels to the novel are created: the windmills becoming power shovels, for instance. Quixote and Panza rocket to the moon. For a while, as a working title, he called the film *Don Quixote Goes to the Moon*. The penultimate scene of the film, also a commentary on contemporary life, which Orson could not seem to complete, was to be an episode that showed an atomic explosion where everything is destroyed and everyone in the world is killed, except Don Quixote and Sancho Panza.

But Orson kept putting off this cataclysmic scene because of the huge expense and logistic difficulties. And after a period of shooting, getting Reiguera and Tamiroff together became almost impossible—the former returned to Mexico and the latter went off to act in other films; insert shots and other reshooting *had* to be included. Without such additions, Orson really had no film. And then each time he viewed the rushes, he felt that some of the shooting was inadequate. It would have to be scrapped. Years went by without *Don Quixote* being completed.

Despite the haphazard schedule of the film, Orson was meticulous about its editing. Establishing a small cutting room in the basement of a house in which he lived in Madrid, Orson had a crack editor, Peter Parasheles, slice and cut the film at his behest. Orson would run the film himself through the moviola and usually mark where the cut was to take place. Occasionally, he would give Parasheles complicated instructions ("Move the tree sequence, to *follow* the house; pause for not quite two seconds, then take the second insert from can three and work it in afterwards") and expect that each detail would be carried out faithfully. It usually was. The country scenes, cinematically, were among Orson's finest: long, silhouetted images of the pair riding across lonely landscapes; shots of Quixote talking to the absent Dulcinea.

In the "documentary" sequences of *Don Quixote* he wanted the static look of a newsreel and, as he had done before in films, he ordered that every other frame be excised. If he had been working under a normal budget, this process would have been done optically, in a laboratory, but in order to save money, he had a young editing apprentice, Ira Wohl, razor-out each frame by hand.*

Eventually the seventy-year-old Reiguera contacted Welles and gently reminded him that if the shooting was not completed in short order, owing to his growing ill health, he might not ever be able to complete it. Shortly after that Reiguera died and, as predicted, the continuity of the film could not be maintained. The film, uncompleted, still sits in its cans today, probably never to be commercially released.**

DURING THE MID-1950'S, while living in a fashionable apartment in London with Paola Mori and their newly and New York born daughter Beatrice (named after Orson's mother), Orson came to be thought of as even more of a theatrical character than he had been in the past. In an uncredited 1956 article in the *New Statesman,* Orson was described as becoming "a European society lion, a celebrated diner-out, a voyager in that jostling caravan, led by Aly Khan and Porfirio Rubirosa, which trails its way from the Carlton to Eden Roc and back again." The story further reported on his "endless chases around Europe to raise money, the constant casting sessions for plays which are never produced, the gigantic schemes, planned only to be abandoned, the gargantuan, irresistible bursts of wit with which Welles dissolves his troubles." He switched his editing chores for *Don Quixote* from Madrid to London and continued working on the film there. He made deals with various companies, such as Star Sound Studios in Hampstead, and soon had huge cans of footage sitting in several locations, consisting of bits and pieces, outtakes, rushes, and almost-finished stock. Derek Faraday, the producer of

---

*Years later, Wohl went on to win an Academy Award for his documentary *Best Boy*.

**In May of 1986, at the Cannes Film Festival, a forty-five-minute compilation of some outtakes, rushes, and other shots of *Don Quixote* compiled by archivists of the *Cinématèque Français* was shown. Although hailed as "visually splendid," the compilation was so rough as to be almost impossible to follow. Welles had dubbed the voices of Quixote and Panza with his own, changing accents and timbre.

The visuals include beautiful, low-angle shots with sweeping clouds, and many moving camera shots of the two traveling. At one point, a stationary camera catches them riding across a hilltop, silhouetted against a brilliant sun.

Welles wanted to end the film with the two riding into the twenty-first century, against a background of old, burnt-out cars, and deserted landscapes, riding through towns populated with peasants. Welles captures both their moral strength and their physical fragility. The theme of a headstrong man struggling with his own lonely existence and illusions against a harsh reality is a dominant Welles motif.

As with so many projects associated with Welles, these fragments, or treasure, in the truest sense of the word, from many periods of his fascinating career, remain tantalizing signposts to the oft and deservedly lamented land of what might have been.

Star, was a friend of Orson's and allowed him full use of all editing equipment at cost.

ALTHOUGH WELLES HAS denied that financial problems forced him to return with Paola and Beatrice to Hollywood in 1956, he probably did so in order to pay off his various tax debts. In a two-year period he acted in two films, *The Long Hot Summer* and *Man in the Shadow,* and later starred in and directed what some critics have thought to be one of his finest films, *Touch of Evil.*

Orson's return to California, ten years after he felt he had been all but forced to leave after the *It's All True* affair, was met with the customary Welles publicity: a picture spread in *Life,* stories in *Variety* of new deals to be consummated at any moment, and wire service bulletins telling of his every move while on location in Louisiana.

The Long Hot Summer, from *The Hamlet* by William Faulkner, spins out a steamy interlude in a Mississippi delta town. Welles played a blustery plantation owner, the cigar-chomping widower Will Varner, who believes he can dodge marriage to Minnie Littlejohn, played by Angela Lansbury. Eager for grandchildren to inherit his various estates, Varner taunts his son (played by Anthony Franciosa) for failing to produce an heir by his baby-doll wife (Lee Remick). Varner's daughter is played by Joanne Woodward. When a young drifter (Paul Newman) comes to town it is a meeting of the minds. "You're no better than a crook," Welles says. "You're no better than a con man," Newman answers.

Producer Jerry Wald, of *Peyton Place* fame, hired Welles for $150,000 to play Varner and then appointed the highly volatile and opinionated Martin Ritt to direct the film. Almost immediately there was friction between the two men. "Two weeks after we started, you could bet we wouldn't finish the film," Ritt has recalled. Orson observed: "There was a note of suspicion. I did not know what kind of monkeyshines I would have to put up with and the cast did not know what kind of caprices they would have to put up with with me." Battles over camera angles, costume details, interpretation of lines, and body movement raged, but somehow the two men managed to get through the film. Orson's performance was shrewd and roisterous and, aside from the occasionally difficult-to-understand and greatly thickened Southern accent, impressive.

ALBERT ZUGSMITH, PRODUCER of the forthcoming film *Man in the Shadow,* received a call in the fall of 1956 from a representative of the William Morris Agency stating that he knew that a leading part for his film had not yet been cast and that Orson Welles would like to play it. The story goes, according to Zugsmith, that Welles was desperately looking for work because of his continuing tax debts and was willing to play in virtually any film as long as he received $60,000 for it. Welles was ultimately contracted for the part.

For the whole summer of 1956, Orson acted before the cameras as a cattle baron (opposite Jeff Chandler as the sheriff) in the Universal film, first called *Pay the Devil* and released as *Man in the Shadow.*

Perhaps somewhat ashamed that he was lowering himself in playing in a Western, Orson totally rewrote his part to shape his character more completely and was quick to point out that there wasn't a horse in the film; the two characters ride over the countryside in jeeps. The new personality of the character also interested him in that the despotic rancher was transformed into a man who doesn't want to do evil things but is forced into them by circumstances. Although quickly overlooked by critics and forgotten by audiences, *Man in the Shadow* was a tight and fast-paced little film, well photographed and containing a believable and powerful role by Orson.

CHAPTER 19

THE STORY OF how Orson came to direct his first Hollywood film in a decade, *Touch of Evil,* is as oblique as the narrative of the film itself; how the film was conceived and directed is an excellent example of a typical Welles project, filled with flair and imagination and produced with great difficulties while he was at odds, once again, with studio hierarchy.

Universal International bought the film rights to the mystery novel *Badge of Evil* by Whit Masterson. Published in March of 1956 by Dodd, Mead, the book received generally favorable reviews ("Savage melodrama, wild, exciting and persuasive," claimed the *New York Herald Tribune*), and its sales were brisk, with two printings in the hardcover edition.

Edward Muhl, head of Universal at that time, believed that the novel had film possibilities and arranged for its purchase through Curtis Brown, literary agent for the book's author. Muhl then assigned the property to Albert Zugsmith, among the studio's most active staff producers. The so-called King of the B's, Zugsmith was, in his own words, "one of the studio's script doctors." He had dozens of film projects that he was working on at the time that he received the novel. The scripts of these films were scattered about his office: some were being cast, others were about to be filmed, still others were being adapted from stories and plays or were in various forms of negotiation. He was just finishing up the release arrangements on *Written on the Wind* and *The Incredible Shrinking Man.* It was the summer of 1956.

Zugsmith assigned the novel, for adaptation to a screenplay, to a young writer, Paul Monash, who for a flat fee completed the task in four speedy weeks' time. Zugsmith read the script but did not care for it and temporarily shelved the project until a future date when either he or someone else could work on it.*

In December of 1956, Zugsmith received a memo from Mel Tucker, a Universal executive and an assistant to Edward Muhl, inquiring about the status of *Badge of Evil* and suggesting the possibility of using Charlton Heston as the leading man. Heston was well liked at the studio ever since he had made *The Private War of Major Benson,* a successful comedy, for Universal the

---

*Monash subsequently sold two other screenplays to other studios, which were ultimately made into films: *The Safecracker* and *Bailout at 43,000,* and later did a stirring and memorable television adaptation of *All Quiet on the Western Front.*

previous year, and he was already a star by virtue of his role as Moses in *The Ten Commandments*. Zugsmith sent the screenplay to Heston, who read it over the holidays. "It's a good enough script," Heston recalls telling Zugsmith, "but police stories, like Westerns and war stories, have been so overdone that it really depends on who's going to direct it."

Heston claims that Zugsmith told him that he didn't know at that time who would direct it, but that they had already secured Orson Welles to play the part of the heavy. Heston further states that he then suggested that Welles be considered as the director. "At that time, Orson had not directed a picture [in Hollywood] since *Macbeth*," Heston said. "They were a bit nonplussed, but they got back to me in a couple of days and said, 'Yeah, well, that's a very good idea. A startling idea.'"

Zugsmith, however, remembers it differently. According to his account, he and Welles had become friends during the shooting of *Man in the Shadow*. After the last day of filming, they shared a bottle of vodka in Zugsmith's bungalow on the studio's grounds. "I'd like to direct a picture for you," Welles suggested. Zugsmith pointed to the scripts that were in his care (which he claimed were all properties with which Universal was having difficulties) and rather flippantly stated, "You can have any one you want." Welles asked, "Which one is the worst?" Zugsmith handed him *Badge of Evil*. "Can I have two weeks to write it?" Welles asked. Zugsmith agreed and Welles delivered the rewrite in seventeen days. Zugsmith claims that he went through the script with Welles, excising parts—cuts that Welles agreed to—wherever he felt that "this is where the kids would go out for popcorn."

Welles himself offers yet a totally different, third version of how he became involved in the film: "I wasn't attracted to the theme of *Touch of Evil*. I was offered the job of acting in it. It was a book that had already been dramatized, already the screenplay had been made. I said no. They called up Charlton Heston and asked him if he wanted to be in it and they lied and said they had me. And he said, 'Any picture that Orson Welles is directing, I'll be glad to be in.' He didn't understand them on the phone. So they quickly got back (to me) on the phone and said, do you want to direct it? And I said, yes, *if* I can write the script and pay no attention to the book it comes from. I had two and a half weeks before it started. And I invented a whole new story that was *Touch of Evil*."

It's difficult to determine exactly *how* Welles became the director of the film. It's possible that all three men are telling the truth as they remember it: that Heston *had* suggested Welles as director *before* Zugsmith and Welles had their evening of drinks together and that a tentative, informal agreement *had* been reached that night only to be consummated afterward, via the phone, by the studio, as Welles described it. Since a Hollywood film directed by Orson Welles was considered a "cinematic event," a filmic happening electric to motion picture history, all three men appear to want to take credit for Welles's participation.

But did Orson Welles create a whole new story for the film? "I made up the theme to fit the material that roughly seemed to be indicated there in (in the original screenplay)," he said on the BBC a few years later.

The similarities between the Masterson novel, the original screenplay by Paul Monash, and Welles's final efforts on the screen are quite marked and prove that at least thematically, and in some cases structurally (to the point of using dialogue and action as it appears exactly in the novel or in the Monash script), Welles, despite his denials, used both forms freely.

For example, in both the novel and the film (in a scene written and directed by Welles) but nowhere in the Monash screenplay, is the following dialogue by the shoe clerk, which virtually proves that Welles read at least portions of the novel:

> *In the novel:*
> I care about the money. I wouldn't have given her a tumble in the first place. I told her that right in the beginning. But she still wanted . . . why bother? You wouldn't believe it anyway.

> *In Welles's screenplay:*
> If it weren't for the money I wouldn't have given her a tumble. But I told her that right at the beginning . . . but she still wanted . . . why bother? You wouldn't believe it.

There is also a scene (at the conclusion of the arrest of the shoe clerk) where the Vargas character accuses Quinlan of framing the man, and Quinlan, enraged, raises his cane as if to strike Vargas and then lowers it. This scene does not exist in the Monash screenplay but *is* in the novel, with the exact action precisely as it appears on the screen.

Since Welles had already tampered with Shakespeare and Cervantes, writers such as Whit Masterson and Paul Monash might have appeared to be fair game for his scalpel. Nonetheless, if the Welles efforts and the Monash screenplay were submitted to the Writers' Guild of America for arbitration, on a line-to-line basis there is enough word and detail changed that Welles might possibly be judged the actual screenwriter. The theme and substance of the story, however, one of corruption and betrayal, is most assuredly taken directly from Masterson's novel. Welles's contribution is mainly clever dialogue—"An old lady on Main Street last night picked up a shoe. The shoe had a foot in it. We're going to make you pay for that"—and some changes of emphasis or action, such as not having Quinlan actually take a shot at Vargas (before the last scene as in both novel and Monash script) or having Menzies realize by himself that he must trap his partner, whereas in the novel and the Monash script he is pressured into it by Vargas. Also, Welles gives the Mexican-American tension much more emphasis than does the novel or the Monash screenplay, and he changes certain characters: Vargas's *wife*, not Vargas, is Mexican, for example, in the novel and screenplay, and Uncle Joe Grandi is given a more important role in the film.*

*The introduction of Tanya and the night clerk are pure Welles inventions and although marvelous additions to the film, as characters, really have nothing to do with the movement of

When Welles was hired to direct the picture, he moved into one of Zugsmith's offices on the Universal lot. The two men worked together on the revision of the screenplay and eventually began to assemble both the crew and the cast. A budget of $895,000 was established for the film. Welles's director of cinematography, Russell Metty, had worked with him before on parts of *The Magnificent Ambersons* (1942) and on *The Stranger* (1946), and Metty's camera operator Phil Lathrop (Metty and Lathrop had worked together for some ten years) was also hired. Metty had also worked with Zugsmith on several pictures, and Zugsmith claims that it was he, not Welles, who had opted to have Metty on *Touch of Evil.* Though it is not clear which of them decided to use Metty, Welles certainly had no objections to the idea. Metty had a reputation as a superb technician, capable of producing any kind of shot requested by a director. Welles and Metty had had a strong rapport before and they reestablished it on this film, recreating the use of deep focus, the long takes, the low lighting, and the sharp-angled shots for which Welles was already famous.

The actual ideas, such as doing the opening scene and the Sanchez interrogation all in one take, each; the avoidance of artificial light during the daytime scenes, the constantly moving camera through the flying litter, the use of a wide-angle lens in an extreme close-up of the Grandi gang's faces, or the masterful use of shadows in the hotel room where Quinlan strangles Grandi, were all Welles's. Metty followed Welles's instructions or fulfilled his wishes as a technician but added little to the conception of the shots.

The costumers and set designers were all Universal staffers. Robert Clatworthy and Alexander Golitzen, the art directors, who had worked with Zugsmith on previous films but never before with Welles, were excited by the assignment and recall feeling fortunate to be able to work on a film directed by him. Welles also helped to design the sets. The use of a bed sheet as the ceiling for the bar, for example, was Welles's idea, mainly because he wanted to solidify a sleazy feeling but also because he wanted variation in his renowned upward ceiling shots.

Zugsmith had already cast Charlton Heston and Janet Leigh into the film, but all other members of the cast, with hardly an exception, were auditioned and cast by Welles himself. Heston claims that the casting of Janet Leigh was imposed on Welles because the studio was convinced she was good box office. Akim Tamiroff had worked with Welles in *Mr. Arkadin* (1955) and in the unreleased and unfinished *Don Quixote.* The two men were friends and Tamiroff was given a principal role here.

So eager were they to be in a film directed by Orson Welles that Joseph Cotten, Marlene Dietrich, Mercedes McCambridge, and Keenan Wynn agreed to work for union scale wages and without credit, simply to be included. Perhaps out of jealousy over the fact that Welles was hiring so many friends, Zugsmith insisted that *his* friend, Zsa Zsa Gabor, be given a cameo

---

the story. In the film Marlene Dietrich played Tanya, Janet Leigh was Susan, and Charlton Heston was Vargas.

role. Ultimately, Cotten, Dietrich, and Gabor were granted slight salary increases over the union scale. They were also given credit in the titles. Keenan Wynn served simply as an extra, a member of the *Lumpenproletariat,* as Welles once described him, and he appears only in the crowd scenes at the opening of the film.

The role of the mad-hatter night clerk, played by Dennis Weaver, who had had minor roles in a half-dozen other films, was conceived by Welles after seeing Weaver as Chester on the television program *Gunsmoke.* Weaver was asked to come to the studio for a brief audition, given a screenplay that had no dialogue, just an indication of a highly eccentric, possibly mad character, and told to improvise. Welles fell in love with Weaver's act and Dennis was given the role.

Welles worked very closely with all his actors and actresses in developing their parts and as a result secured some extraordinary performances. He began working with Janet Leigh not only before the picture began but even before she signed her contract. She has related that experience:

> Mr. Welles gives absolutely free rein to the actor because he himself is so creative ... We may do a scene forty different ways, you really are free. Yet he, too, is a Svengali, though his Trilby is the picture, not necessarily the person, and he will not be harnessed by any kind of conformity—even in the story, which sometimes makes it difficult. But for me as an actress, he gave me the freedom.

Leigh did the film with a broken arm (the left) in a cast. In most of her scenes that arm is either covered by a coat, or disguised—or not shown—in some other way.

Marlene Dietrich said of herself, because of working with Welles, that she had been "terrific" in *Touch of Evil* and elaborated: "I think I never said a line as well as the last line in that movie—'What does it *matter* what you say about people?'" And through close work with Welles, Joseph Calleia gave one of the best performances of his career.

Dennis Weaver explained to this writer how Welles worked with him in developing his role: Orson told him that he wanted Weaver to expand the part of the night clerk, that he saw possibilities of high drama in the part. They rehearsed for one day before they began shooting the part. After the shooting, they discussed the role and what had been done. As Welles saw the rushes, he began to write more and more for the character of the night clerk. Finally, Welles told Weaver that he wanted him to improvise totally, to give more of what he had been giving but without using the script at all. Weaver felt insecure and asked if he could see the rushes of what he had already completed. Welles complied (on the spur of the moment, disregarding the shooting schedule and closing down the set that day so that the two men could go back to the studio), and they both studied the rushes and discussed the character. Welles wanted Weaver to depart from the Chester role and asked Weaver about Chester's principal characteristic. Weaver believed it to be the habit of following people, to be literally behind them all the time, deferring to them, in effect as he limped behind. "In this role," Welles told him, "you will always try to walk in front of people and if you have to talk to them, you'll turn around." Welles explained to Weaver that because the character was half-insane, he always wanted to be noticed and was *afraid* of being "behind." This kind of characterization analysis went on until Weaver had completely conceptualized the night clerk and could portray him extemporaneously. When the shooting began again, Dennis Weaver gave one of the most memorable performances of his career, perhaps the most stylized and effective in the film.

Heston has explained: "Welles had the capacity as a director to somehow persuade you that each time is *indeed* the most important day in the picture and that's kind of marvelous. . . ."

Because one of the most important themes involves the corruption of the police, Welles wanted to shoot the film in a town that looked physically as though it, too, was decaying and touched with evil. (The novel describes it as a town that was "rotting.") He opted to shoot most of the film in a border town, either Tijuana or Juarez, to make it look real. He also thought that the constant shifting back and forth between borders would increase tension and disorientation, and he was particularly anxious that the location have a dark, corrupt feeling to it, the landscape of a nightmare, a labyrinth, in which not only the characters but the audience would feel trapped. The script was sent to the Mexican government for location approval, but the film was questioned for censorship reasons (the drug scenes, the rape in the motel, the depiction of Grandi and other Mexican types). But Welles was not willing to make any revisions in the script to please the Mexican censors, so for a period of weeks the location of where the film would be shot was undetermined. The executives at Universal were also concerned about high location fees and attempted, unsuccessfully, to convince Welles to shoot the entire film on the Universal lot.

It was Aldous Huxley who convinced Welles that Venice, California, originally intended as a romantic imitation of the Italian city and featuring a Grand Canal and even a Bridge of Sighs, was magnificently decayed and that the town might make a superbly decadent site for his film.*

Welles drove out to Venice with Metty and his art directors and inspected the entire town by foot. It was exactly what he had been looking for. When he saw the bridge over the slimy, stinking canal, backed by the oil derricks, he announced that he would rewrite the end of the film. The betrayal of Hank Quinlan (Welles) by Menzies (Joseph Calleia) and their ultimate denouement would now take place on and around the bridge. The location of the Mirador Motel was a setting that was actually as remote as it looked, on a lonely stretch of road outside of Los Angeles, en route to Las Vegas. Even though Welles was two hundred and seventy pounds, he wanted his own character to appear even more obese and consequently added another sixty

---

*At the turn of the century, Venice-by-the-Sea, as it was called then, was a fashionable resort and had miles of canals laced with gondolas.

pounds to his bulk with a false stomach and a hump on his back. His nose and his jowls were built up to look fatter and more grotesque, and he walked with a limp, leaning on a cane, because the character had "stopped a bullet" meant for his sidekick, Menzies. Welles actually fell into the canal during a shooting and again hurt his ankle so badly that he *really* needed a cane to walk for the rest of the film.

Charlton Heston was brought to a Mexican tailor, and two suits, exactly the kind worn by most Mexican businessmen, were made for him. His hair was dyed black, his skin was darkened, and a mustache was painted on his lip.

Orson gave Marlene Dietrich the temporary use of a limousine, and she went from studio to studio, assembling her own costume from her old pictures. Her black wig came from Paramount, where she had done *Golden Earrings*, her spangled shoes came from her role in *Rancho Notorious* at RKO, and from Warner Brothers she took a blouse that she had worn in *Stage Fright.*

Dennis Weaver was given his clothing by the costume department after he and Welles had discussed it thoroughly. The night clerk, they felt, was a deeply religious man, in the orthodox sense, and hence would always wear a hat, no tie, and always have a shirt that was buttoned at the collar.

Henry Mancini, then a young Universal staff composer, was assigned by Joseph Gershenson, the film's music director, to do the music. Mancini had done the first rock musical, *Rock Pretty Baby,* and, as the youngest composer on the lot, usually received the nonclassical assignments. Orson wanted the music to come from a real, practical source, without underscoring (music played in the background without a discernible outlet). Mancini has related: "When Welles told me what he wanted, I thought it was marvelous because that's exactly what I thought the music should be." To make sure that his intentions would be carried out exactly as he wanted them, Welles issued an extensive memo about the music:

> It is very important that the usual "rancheros" and "mariachi" numbers should be avoided and the emphasis should go on Afro-Cuban rhythm numbers. Those few places where traditional Mexican music is wanted will be indicated by special notes. Also, a great deal of rock 'n' roll is called for. Because these numbers invariably back dialogue scenes, there should never be any time for vocals. This rock 'n' roll comes from radio loudspeakers, juke boxes and, in particular, the radio in the motel.

Welles felt that the music from the player piano—an old-fashioned Mexican waltz and a blues piece—was very important to the film since it expressed both a loss of innocence (in reminding Quinlan of his brothel days) and a sentimentality for the past on Quinlan's part, both important elements in understanding the character. It is also, of course, Tanya's theme, a nostalgic tone to which the film and Quinlan keep returning more than to any other. Mancini composed a special piece for the piano and it was then cut on an actual player piano roll and finally recorded for dubbing. Whenever under-scoring was performed—as in the Quinlan death scene—Welles insisted that it be used sparingly. "What we want," he wrote, "is musical color, rather than movement—sustained washes of sound rather than tempestuous melodra-matic or operatic scoring."

For the most part, Welles's directives were followed by Mancini and the Universal music department, with the exception of the opening scene where the theme has no source. What Welles thought of this opening music—which is actually indicated in the Monash script—is not known, but its power and rhythm serve greatly to heighten the melodrama of the beginning scene.

Principal shooting of the film began in the early months of 1957 and was completed by April 1 of that year. Although Zugsmith claims to have given Welles a free hand as director, he did become worried when Welles drifted off schedule or else began shooting scenes totally out of the agreed-upon sequence.

Welles worked on the editing of the film first with Virgil Vogel, who "froze up" according to Welles, and then with Edward Curtiss, with whom Welles had a personality conflict (according to Zugsmith). Finally, Aaron Stell was appointed as editor, and the two men established a good working relationship.

Stell edited with Welles for several months, while Welles simultaneously completed the postproduction photography. It's important to note how Welles operated in the actual editing of the film; he would have it projected on a regular screen in a studio screening room and make notes. Then by way of memo, or by discussion, he would inform Stell what he wanted changed. Although Stell still considers Welles's editing overview to be highly devel-oped, and considered it a great experience to work with him, he also said that in all the months they worked together Welles never once entered the cutting room. In light of Welles's later complaints about the film not looking the way he had envisioned, it was probably because he was absent during the actual time of cutting, splicing, and so on.

On July 18, Welles was informed that Eddie Muhl wanted to see the edited picture. Welles at first objected. He complained that it was like a writer about to complete the last page of a novel, and just as he was touching it up and revising it to send to the publisher, the page was yanked out of the typewriter. Muhl insisted, however—Welles had already gone way beyond schedule—and on July 22, Eddie Muhl, Mel Tucker, Albert Zugsmith (who had already left Universal but came back to comment on the film as a courtesy), and other studio officials viewed it.

Welles was informed of the studio's discontent with the logic of the narrative, and he claimed that he agreed with them: the film *wasn't* ready to be released. He needed more time. In order to speed up the process and to be certain that Welles would complete the project with all due haste, Muhl appointed Ernest Nims, a Universal executive with an editing background, to work on the film with Welles. Nims's assignment was to see how he could improve and change the film by editing, and without incurring further shooting costs. Welles respected Nims—they had worked together on *The Stranger,* which Nims had edited, and even though Welles was dissatisfied with the end result of *The Stranger* he still had admiration for Nims's technical expertise. But at the moment that Nims began to reedit the film, Welles left Hollywood and went to Mexico. The explanation of why he went varies. In memos to the studio, he claimed that he was ill and needed time to recuperate. To Zugsmith, he mentioned that he needed a vacation. Aaron Stell wrote to me that although Welles had said he was ill, Stell did see him shortly after that on the MGM lot, looking fit. Zugsmith told me that it was his opinion that Welles was so crushed by the adverse studio criticism and the fact that the control of the film had been virtually taken away from him that he went on what might be considered a month-long psychological bender—not quite a nervous breakdown but a serious withdrawal from the concerns of the world and all personal responsibilities.

Welles made no effort to do any further work at the studio for about five weeks while Nims edited the film. Then on August 28, Welles returned to Hollywood, and Nims ran the recut version for him. Welles expressed general satisfaction with the recutting but stated that he had a few minor suggestions to make, which he would put in writing and send to Nims immediately. A week or so later Muhl also screened the recut version, and although still not entirely happy with it (constantly muttering about its twisted narrative) he elected to see what changes Welles would suggest.

After Nims waited patiently for three weeks without any word from Welles, his secretary contacted Welles's secretary, who claimed that a memo *had* been sent to Muhl, Tucker, and Nims, and that since it had apparently been lost in the mail, another copy would be sent out immediately. After a few days, when the copy failed to appear, Muhl, Tucker, and Nims discussed the film and came to the conclusion that it did, indeed, need a few additional scenes shot for heightened clarity and exposition. Since Welles was incommunicado and had not personally spoken to anyone at the studio for over a month, arrangements were begun for the shooting of additional footage.

In the meantime, before the reshooting began, Welles contacted the studio and was told about the additional scenes that were going to be added. He offered to reshoot them, but Muhl had already become disillusioned. Orson's request to direct the scenes was refused. Welles also wanted to shoot some inserts, original takes that he had been dissatisfied with, and this request was also denied on the grounds that insert shooting was normally the job of assistant directors. The staffers could easily handle the inserts at a much lower cost and, what was more important, more *quickly* than Welles. Welles grudgingly accepted the fact that he was not going to be allowed to direct the new scenes, but he was insistent that the studio follow his suggestion on the editing. The studio agreed in principle to consider Welles's editing direction but warned him that unless they received either written or oral instructions from him within a reasonable amount of time, the film would have to be released unapproved by Welles.

Finally, on November 4, almost ten weeks after Welles had promised to submit the suggestions, the studio received a nine-page memo from Welles outlining the changes that he wanted.

Some of the changes Nims had already made on his own, such as the omission of a line at the beginning of the film when Quinlan is referred to as "bloodhound of the border." Even though Welles had written the line, it didn't come across effectively as spoken, and both Nims and Welles wanted it out. Of the approximately forty unanticipated additions, changes, and deletions suggested by Welles, about half were followed by Nims.

It's important to understand Nims's position at this stage of the film. Although he had great respect for Welles's ability, his commitment was to follow the studio's instructions to make the film more understandable. If Welles suggested a change that *did* add clarity, that change was made immediately. Or, if Welles suggested a change for stylistic reasons—even though it might not have necessarily clarified anything—that change was also made immediately. But when Welles suggested a change that, in the opinion of Nims and other studio people, muddied the waters of an already obscure film, Nims held firm.*

The result was not always ideal. For example, when Grandi is trying to intimidate Susan in his shop, loudly referring to his brother's arrest by Vargas, Grandi mentions Mexico City. In the original footage, Pancho, standing nearby off-camera, quickly interrupts him with a loud "Shh!" This warning hiss was accidentally cut from the work print, and Welles wanted Nims to dub it in. Perhaps because the request seemed too minor, the sound was not restored. But an alert viewer can easily detect its omission: in the midst of his harangue, Grandi now turns toward Pancho for no discernible reason. In the long shot that follows, we see Pancho leaning toward Grandi, his hand unaccountably raised conspiratorially to his mouth as he looks at Susan. Obviously Pancho has just said "Shh!" even though we don't hear the sound.

Following is an example of a major editing change that Welles insisted upon, referring to this same scene between Grandi and Susan at the beginning of the film:

> The inter-cut with a return back to the scene of the explosion keeps the two stories alive at a time when this is most important. Furthermore, the Grandi scene plays infinitely better in two sections, cutting away from Susan and Grandi and leaving her at the mercy of this odd-ball for good suspense editing and creates a stronger situation by far than staying with her the whole time. After all,

---

*To complicate the editing history of *Touch of Evil,* some ten years later in an interview broadcast on the BBC, Orson complained of a series of sequences that had been cut out of the film against his will: "There was a whole section of the film which was rather surrealistic, a mad, sort of dark, black comedy and this struck the heads of the studio as being irrelevant and irreverent and they took all of it out." Unfortunately, no mention of these scenes appears anywhere in the studio's archives. It is possible that Orson shot them without the studio's knowledge.

the whole point of the Grandi scene is a sort of anti-climax which is, in the writing, deliberately intended to create a certain bewilderment. By staying off this scene and not breaking it up with a short inter-cut of the doings at the scene of the explosion, we only undermine the effect of the anti-climax and the result is that the scene falls rather flat. Above all, the patching together of the two scenes seems to have been done in considerable haste so that the effect is brusk and rough. I very much hope to prevail upon you to return to the inter-cut, but in case you should win this argument, let me urge that the marrying of the two sections of this scene can be accomplished with more care.

It's obvious from this passage that Welles *did* see the film in terms of a nightmare, and he attempted to create "a certain bewilderment" through the splintering of certain scenes, keeping the audience off balance and disjointed. His logic seems irrefutable. But viewing this scene in the final released film, we also note a certain rationality in maintaining it as is. Staying with the scene affords the opportunity of being caught up with what we began to sense—without the dilution of the suspense through back-and-forth cutting—is a genuine predicament that is growing into a frightening dilemma: will Susan actually escape from the menacing company of Grandi and his nephew?

In a later memo Welles also contended that if the scene were broken down into two distinct parts—and although he shot it as one scene, he claims that he always intended to edit it so that it would be reduced to two, or even several—it would keep Vargas alive in the audience's mind and maintain a tension, admittedly a distant one, between Vargas and Grandi. Nims and the rest of the studio people disagreed, and the scene remained as they, not Welles, wanted it to appear.

However, whether Welles was creatively "right" or "wrong" in wanting it his way, the scope of this specific editorial change goes beyond its structural authenticity. It appears that Welles had already willingly relinquished control of the film or else he would not have given up the fight so easily. Outside of the memos he sent, he did nothing else to prevail, offering no further evidence or rationale to support his claim, despite his later public statement that he was "forbidden to participate" in the "wholesale reediting of the film." Since certain changes *were* made (about half as I discern), it is not unlikely that others, such as the Susan-Grandi scene, could have been made also if Welles had taken the time to explore each problem with Nims or if he had *insisted,* as the director, that his intentions be followed.

The question that emerges from all of this is whether the studio executives felt that Welles's version was simply too uncommercial for release. It is possible that no matter how much finesse or diplomacy Welles might have used, he would still have gotten nowhere with those scenes that the studio insisted were unclear.*

---

*Unlike the reshooting, which involved a severe alteration of the budget, the editing costs at the stage when Welles asked for changes were relatively slight.

The rest of the changes requested by Welles in his first memo concerned additional trimming, some deletion of dialogue, occasional reshifting of emphasis, all as indicated above. He made no suggestions that involved reshooting any scenes, to be directed either by him or by anyone else.

After Nims incorporated what was agreed upon, the new scenes wanted by the studio were shot, edited, and added. Peter Bogdanovich, in his 1961 Museum of Modern Art monograph, *The Cinema of Orson Welles,* described the studio's schema:

> The additions: four scenes between Vargas and his wife, particularly in the hotel lobby, but they only last about a minute of screen time. The cuts are more serious: a humorous scene between Quinlan and Vargas at the beginning in which their characters are defined and they become enemies; a scene in which Menzies drives Susan Vargas to the hotel and explains to her how Quinlan saved his life years ago by stopping a bullet for him, thus crippling himself and necessitating the cane which explains Quinlan's line: "That's the second bullet I've stopped for you, partner"; a scene in which Tanya and Quinlan spend the night together and he sees Vargas passing by the window but doesn't identify him with certitude, motivating his later line to Menzies: "I thought you were Vargas"; dialogue between Menzies and Vargas in which Vargas studies the recording machine used at the end and states his distaste for that part of the job. As Welles said: "They kept all the scenes of violence but cut out the moral ones." Also, the credits were to have appeared at the end instead of the beginning, where they distract from the brilliant flow of the opening sequence.

Bogdanovich's comments pertain to the originally released version of the film. A longer version, by about fifteen minutes, was found about twenty years later by Professor Robert Epstein, a UCLA film studies teacher, when he ordered a print for screening in his class and discovered it contained the missing footage as described by Bogdanovich. This longer version was then released by Universal as the official version, although as of 1981, the shorter version was still being shown commercially in most theaters.

What Bogdanovich apparently did not know about the film was that most of the footage he describes was shot not by Welles but by Harry Keller, a staff television director for Universal who was assigned to shoot what his studio wanted. (Keller had just finished directing a Universal feature film, *Voice in the Mirror.*) The four scenes between Vargas and his wife, the love scene in the car, the scene where Quinlan's car meets Vargas's en route to the motel,* the scene where Menzies explains about Quinlan's leg, were all shot by Keller with Cliff Stein as his cameraman, not Metty, the characters speaking dia-

---

*Welles is not really in this scene, though it is made to appear that he is. A double, dressed as Quinlan, sits in the patrol car while Schwartz and Menzies (carrying Quinlan's cane) get out to speak to Vargas. We hear Welles's voice-over remark, so it seems that the seated Quinlan is speaking from the car, but the voice was dubbed in. Welles actually did not appear in any of the scenes that Keller directed, and never met him personally.

logue written not by Welles but by Franklin Coen, a staff scriptwriter for Universal.

Keller told me that he was given strict instructions by the studio heads to "duplicate the style of Orson Welles" and that he made every attempt to do so. He said that he attempted to be as "unobtrusive, as gentle and as unstartling as I could." Keller shot for a week and also worked with "Heston, Leigh, and Tamiroff in dubbing sessions," Keller said. "And Welles *had* to agree with that. The death scene between Quinlan and Menzies, for instance, could not be reshot since Joseph Calleia was out of the country already, working on another film. The location shooting of that scene was the most difficult in the film and the line, 'That's the second bullet I took for you, partner' made no sense, unless it could be explained in an earlier scene, which is why I included a new scene of Menzies telling Susan that en route to the motel." Welles, however, has since implied that this was cut out of something that he had filmed. In an interview in *Les Cahiers du Cinéma* with Bazin, Bitsch, and Comarchi in September 1968, Welles was asked: "There was one thing we didn't understand; when Quinlan is dying, by the recording machine, he says that this is the second bullet which he got because of Menzies." Welles replied: "That's why he limps. He saved Menzies's life once in the past, and in the process got a bullet in the leg. Menzies tells Vargas's wife about it when he takes her away in the car." "Perhaps they cut it?" Answer: "Yes, they cut it."

It could be that Welles misremembers and thinks he directed that scene, which seems unlikely, or it could be that the Welles-directed scene was unusable and was scrapped and Keller started anew.

Keller went on: "And in the scene in Sanchez's apartment, Menzies returns Quinlan's cane. Where did it come from? Because we couldn't reshoot the scene again because of technical difficulties, we had to have a scene that explained that Menzies accidentally kept the cane after Quinlan drove off to the construction site."

As it developed, one of the Keller scenes is patently not in the Wellesian style and was filmed in front of a process screen as Susan and Vargas are driving to the motel.*

It shouldn't be assumed that *all* of the longer Welles scenes are necessarily better than the shorter versions and that all of Welles's work was cut or changed by Keller or Nims to the detriment of the film. Again, unknown to Bogdanovich, Welles himself felt that the shorter version of the first Vargas-Quinlan confrontation was more effective. He wrote to Nims: "I cannot agree that the new and considerably lengthened scene between Quinlan and Mike is an improvement." The longer confrontation is what appears in both short and long versions of the film. Additionally, it should not be concluded that Welles was entirely unhappy with the reediting of his own work. At some points he felt Nims improved upon what he had done. For example, he wrote:

---

*Stein was the foremost process-screen cameraman in Hollywood at that time, which could possibly account for its use.

I'd like to congratulate whoever edited the street scene in which Vargas drives into the traffic jam, fails to hear Susan, and continues across the international boundary. The cutting here is not only superior to what it was at the stage when I left it, but actually better than the effort I'd been hoping for.

It is curious to note that although the shorter version contained none of the additional footage shot by Harry Keller, it was this version that was in circulation by the studio for some twelve or thirteen years before it was recalled and replaced by the longer. Why did Universal go to the great expense of shooting additional scenes, scenes that were used to clarify the meaning of the film, and then not use them? Here are three possible answers, none of them definitive: first, the film was distributed directly to the neighborhood theaters as the bottom half of a double Universal release, and it is possible that the studio wanted to keep the film's length down, so instead of reediting the longer version to the desired length, to save money they simply released the shorter; secondly, it is possible that even after the expense of shooting the new scenes, the studio wanted to give the film a chance on its own terms, as Welles directed it; and thirdly, when the prints for distribution were made in the laboratory, it is possible that the wrong version—the shorter—was printed, purely through error, and the studio decided to release it rather than go to the expense of manufacturing an entirely new set of release prints. When one considers that Universal was in financial trouble at the time of the film's release and that there was so much confusion about the editing and the reshooting, the last explanation rings most true.

After the Harry Keller scenes were added, the film was screened again by Welles, and this time he did respond immediately with a series of memos, totaling some seventy-odd pages, reemphasizing those points or suggestions he had made in his previous memos that had been disregarded, and making some new suggestions. Here are a few of the new suggestions made by Welles at that time:

In the version I was shown yesterday, it's not clear where you decided to put the credits. . . .

Welles wanted them at the end of the film, when Tanya is walking away. The idea of having the credits at the beginning was Zugsmith's. They stayed at the beginning.

The moment when Vargas says to Susan, "Don't be morbid . . ." is an unpleasant one and creates a harmful impression.

This was changed.

"He must be driving up from that turkey ranch of his" is unclear and must be redubbed.

This was done.

Welles went on to comment about some of the new Keller-directed scenes—he wanted line changes, better or other editing, and the like—and he also greatly expanded his arguments about intercutting the Susan and Grandi scene as outlined in his first memo. "No point concerning anything in this picture is made with such urgency and with such confidence as this." As indicated, the studio was intransigent and the scene remained as one piece.

Welles considered the scene with Vargas and the night clerk, when Vargas comes back to the motel to find his wife missing, to be one of the finest in the film because of its power of futility and madness. Nims had cut this scene drastically, and Welles practically begged him to reinstate it as originally shot. Nims complied, and all the original footage in the longer version of the film was restored exactly as Welles wanted.

In the rape scene, he wanted more syncopation, more cutting from the bedroom to the front office, more sounds of gasps and screams coming from the room. This was not done.

He insisted that at the end of the film—and he was accommodated—that the playback on the tape recorder, which had been deleted in the editing, reinstate Quinlan's ominous words, "Guilty, guilty, guilty." About half of his *new* suggestions were followed and the other half declined.

In a film so marked by director-studio controversy, it seems only fitting that the title itself was a subject of dispute. Sometime during the early months of shooting, the name of the film was changed by Zugsmith from *Badge of Evil* to *Touch of Evil*. When the film was finally released in the spring of 1958, Welles wrote a letter to the *New Statesman* wherein he claimed, among other things, that he had never heard the title before and thought it was "silly." Pauline Kael has also proclaimed the title *Touch of Evil* as "idiotic" and Howard Thompson in his *New York Times* review of the film (May 22, 1958) deprecated it. In France, the film opened with the title *Vengeance d'un Flic (A Cop's Revenge)*.

It is probable, however, that Welles really did know about the title change before the film release but felt slighted that he had not been consulted about the change. Universal studio correspondence refers to it as *Touch of Evil* as early as fall 1957, and the mass-market paperback edition of the book, published in February 1958 by Bantam and distributed all over the country with Welles's picture on the cover, is called *Touch of Evil*. Actually, the title *Touch of Evil* is more subtle than *Badge of Evil*, which would have made the film sound simply like a "bad cop" movie, rather than a film that concerned itself with how being *touched* by evil—Quinlan plants false evidence, but only to convict the truly guilty—can grow until a man becomes totally corrupt.

When the film was finally released in the spring of 1958, Universal was still not satisfied with the film and virtually no press screenings were given, nor was there a national advertising or publicity budget established for it, although there was a studio screening in Hollywood for the motion picture trade journals. The conflict between Welles and Universal was so intense that he wasn't even invited to the preview. As indicated, it was slipped into the neighborhood theaters as the lower half of a double bill, without fanfare. It is possible that since Universal was a half-million dollars in the red during the first half of 1958, it decided, in the midst of an austerity drive, not to spend additional dollars in promoting a film about which most of the corporate executives felt unsure. (There were even rumors at that time that Universal was going to close down its film division altogether in order to save and bolster Decca Records, its profit-making arm.)

American critical reaction was mixed. National media such as *Time* and *Newsweek* did not even review the film. Here's a sampling of those reviews that did appear:

"*Touch of Evil* is not a good movie, but it is good bad movie, which is more fun to see than the mediocre or even the adequate."—Gerald Weales in *The Reporter*

"Smacked of brilliance and ultimately flounders in it."—*Variety*

"Sums up all the negative characteristics which appeal to Welles. . . . He must return to the moral values of America if he is ever to be the artist he could be."—*Films in Review*

"A Goya-like vision of an infected universe."—Peter Bogdanovich in *MOMA* monograph on Welles

"A personal tour-de-force—Rembrandtesque."—Paul Beckley in the *New York Herald Tribune*

Europe's reaction was more enthusiastic. Although the film was scheduled to have run only two weeks in Paris, it played for the whole winter. It won two prizes at the Brussels Film Festival that year: The Critics' Prize for Best Film and the First Prize for Best Performance by an Actor, which was awarded to Welles.

Can we assume that *Touch of Evil* is a Welles film? Perhaps if he were another kind of director, another kind of personality, this question need not be asked. However, since he is a director who has always been recognized as an *auteur,* an evaluation of the responsibility of the authorship of *Touch of Evil* becomes necessary.

As indicated earlier, despite his protestations to the contrary, Welles did not invent the theme and the plot of *Touch of Evil,* nor did he create most of the characterizations; this is fairly conclusively proven by the comparison of the Masterson novel, the Monash script, and the film.

On the other hand, despite the loss of control of the final editing through what appears to be entirely his own fault, and the shooting of a few moments of expository scenes by another director, the film itself is unmistakably, brilliantly, even grandly Welles's intention and invention. *All* the members of the cast and crew, *without exception,* have stated that the finished film was extraordinarily close to Welles's design, and Heston and Leigh have corroborated that in published books and interviews.

Zugsmith told me: "Of course it is Welles's film. The film expresses his ideas, his creativity and it was his talent that made it what it was. You should look at the tampering the studio did simply as copy-editing of a manuscript. In effect, all that Universal did to the film beyond what Welles might have wanted, was to sharpen his grammar, dot his 'i's' and cross his 't's.'"

This, of course, is very much open to question. In editing a film the director does the final shaping, the ultimate polishing of his vision. A director such as Bergman has been known to spend six months in editing a film and Welles has made it clear that editing is the key to cinema. Welles never was able to put the final finish on *Touch of Evil,* this last, unmistakable flourish on his signature.

Welles's mistake was not being able to work with the studio executives; after a few clashes, as well as his going off on tangents, and his disappearance during the editing, the studio began to erode his control in order to protect its investment.

Although the studio did not carry out all of his directives, they followed many, perhaps most, of them. It is quite possible that had they permitted Welles, himself, to do his own final editing, he might have realized that some of his ideas, particularly the desire to intercut the Susan-Grandi scene, were not completely successful, and he might have finished with a version not too unlike that done by the studio. But the control Welles exercised over the acting, costumes, lighting, music, sound, mixing, photography, and even on the *basic* editing of the film, make it indisputably his.

There is reason to believe that *Touch of Evil* is one of Welles's most advanced films; just a cursory look at it reveals his distinctive style: low-angle shots that magnify and dramatize a character's importance; shots that indicate the reality of space by including ceilings; imaginative application of sound through the use of radios, sirens, and the intercutting back and forth of dialogue; constant use of shadows; baroque dissolves and cuts maintaining the logic of a nightmare. The opening shot, all in one take, is filled with tension; it not only encompasses some of the leading characters but also establishes the mood and location of the film; the long take during the interrogation of Sanchez is a masterpiece of fluidity; the murder of Grandi, with rapid cutting, intense angles, and expressionistic lighting, fills the screen with terror.

Welles's filmic syntax in *Touch of Evil* has its roots in all of his previous films, and although it is clear that not every last word, inflection, splice, or effect was personally engineered by him, and despite his occasional public disavowals, the end result is a manifestly authentic Welles creation, a totally acceptable film classic.

Andrew Sarris summed up the now-prevailing opinion of the film in a review twenty years later in the *Village Voice: "Touch of Evil* is a movie which makes you rethink what a movie should be."

AROUND THE TIME that he became involved with *Touch of Evil,* Orson was given his second opportunity to become seduced by American television—his first as director—and in effect, re-inaugurate and adapt his two-decade-old

512

Mercury Theatre to a new medium. The then-burgeoning Desilu Productions, which, ironically, had taken over the old RKO studios, contracted Orson to produce, direct, and act in a series of television films; it was agreed upon that he would use some of the first-person storytelling techniques that he had employed so successfully on radio and combine them with the inherent intimacy of television.

A thirty-minute pilot, *The Fountain of Youth* based remotely on a John Collier short story, "Youth From Vienna," was Orson's first project. It was given a single showing on ABC-TV's "Colgate Theater" on September 16, 1958.

"How would you like to stay just as young as you are, not to grow a day older . . . for the next two hundred years?" questioned Orson as narrator at the start of the program. He then went on to tell the story of a typical romantic triangle, but this one complicated by a scientist who claims to have discovered the secret of eternal youth.

The story is set in the 1920s: honky-tonk and banjo variations of such old-time favorites as "Oh, You Beautiful Girl," are heard as the background theme. Orson's voice intoned under, over, and in place of his characters in long stretches, combined with rapid cutting to stills (or "slides," to better capture the feel of the time) showing some of the action of the story in a "freeze-frame" state. Instead of using the regular method of cutting from scene to scene, however, as in most films or television productions when a situation changed, Orson isolated his character in darkness and then increased the light to show a new set or character or situation. It was a technique similar to the one used in the theatrical productions of *Our Town* or Orson's own *Doctor Faustus* and gave the production an eerie and disquieting ambience.

The story was not particularly profound but Orson handled it engagingly: Humphrey, the scientist (Dan Tobin) falls in love with a "dumb" hussy (Joi Lansing*). She was "beautiful, but Humphrey found her amazingly ignorant of recent advances in science," Welles notes sarcastically; she reciprocates the scientist's affection, but then he goes off to Vienna to study endocrinology. When Humphrey returns, he finds his love about to be married to a champion tennis player (Rick Jason). His wedding gift to the couple is a phial of elixir that guarantees its taker youth for two hundred years. There is only one dose, however. It cannot be divided or diluted. At first, the newlyweds attempt, nobly, to dispense the elixir to each other. Eventually, they each quaff the extract in secret and refill it with a bogus substitute. And then, over the next few years, they begin to see the awful signs of aging, not in themselves but in the other. After parting, she returns to the scientist. The narrator confides to the audience: Humphrey knew she would be back because the elixir contained nothing but salt water all along.

In many ways, *The Fountain of Youth* was a remarkable production quite

---

*Welles had used Joi Lansing as an actress just before in his previous cinematic outing: she was the blond stripper who is killed in the explosion at the beginning of *Touch of Evil.*

unlike anything that had been seen on television before: it seemed to combine the qualities of both film and stage, while utilizing the fluidity of the new medium of television. The show was highly praised ("It was clever and funny and fresh as spring water," said Harriet Van Horne in the *World-Telegram and Sun,* for example).

Despite the fact that it won a Peabody Award for creative achievement, Orson was not invited to continue directing any further episode. Critic Charles Higham has suggested that Welles's erratic and costly methods—he had taken over a month to do *The Fountain of Youth*—were impossible in a tightly organized and structured studio like Desilu and that was why the series was scrapped. That is a possible explanation but the fact that no sponsor could be found to back the series was the major obstacle. Being back on the RKO lot, Orson must have felt at that time a wave of unpleasant nostalgia for his *Citizen Kane* days, when Schaefer was demanding something more "commercial" from him after he had just completed what some people were claiming to be one of the great artistic accomplishments in cinema history.

WELLES'S RESILIENCE, IN moving from television to film and back again was beginning to erode, and once again, his inability to successfully operate within the entertainment structure in this country served to overwhelm and discourage him. However, before heading where he knew he would make less money but at least enjoy the comforts and possibilities of a freer life-style, he acted in one Hollywood film. A generous $100,000 acting fee encouraged him to accept. It would be his last for a number of years—and ironically it would be considered by many to be one of his finest roles.

Compulsion, based on Meyer Levin's long, meandering, and fascinating book about the notorious Leopold-Loeb thrill-murder of Bobby Franks in 1924, was produced as a film by Richard D. Zanuck in 1958 (released by Twentieth Century-Fox the following year) and directed by Richard Fleischer. Welles played the character of Jonathan Wilk, a thinly veiled version of Clarence Darrow, who defends the murderers, using the same kind of theatricality and rhetoric that Darrow employed in the actual trial when he defended the two men. E. G. Marshall was the prosecuting attorney. Bradford Dillman and Dean Stockwell played the killers.

Zanuck used the film as a plea against capital punishment. This is why he, or Fleischer on his behalf, did not include any scenes representing the actual kidnapping or murder, and although propagandistic to that extent, *Compulsion* developed into a tightly scripted and eloquent film.

Orson believed in the film's statement and immersed himself in his role. In his concluding speech to the judge, which was done in a sweltering courthouse, with his collar wilted, his hair disheveled, his shirt sleeves in garters, and his pants carelessly hoisted by wide suspenders, Orson offered a masterpiece of dramatic persuasion, a study in classic oration. Dozens of takes were made in his attempt to produce a near-perfect scene. At one point, Orson asked for the camera to be stopped and then gently approached E. G.

Marshall. "Do you mind not looking at me when I talk to you when the camera is on me?" Orson asked. "Of course not, Orson, but why?" replied the genial actor. "Because I don't want to fight your look," Welles answered.

Apparently Orson felt that E. G. Marshall's thoughts, as reflected in his eyes, would interfere with his delivery; if Marshall went out of character, or at least didn't project the contempt he was supposed to be feeling during Orson's close-ups, Orson believed he could play the scene more effectively. So when over-the-shoulder shots were made (over Marshall's shoulder, the camera directed at Orson) Marshall would keep his eyes closed, pretending, however, that he was looking at Orson. When other shots were done that showed only Orson, Marshall would leave the set. Orson's concluding speech was filmed all in one take to preserve the continuity of his force.

Whatever the chemistry, or psychic manipulation, Welles took over and dominated the film from the moment he entered it (as in *The Third Man,* about an hour of film time elapses before he appears) and with the summation plea—twelve minutes, one of the longest monologues ever filmed—he persuades the courtroom audience and perhaps most of the filmgoers watching *Compulsion* to consider a compassionate solution. Wilk dared not plead his clients "not guilty by reason of insanity" because that would invariably place their fate in the hands of a jury and an almost-certain death penalty would have resulted. He therefore entered a plea of guilty and attempted to prove that they were insane, allowing the mercy to rest upon the court.

In a voice just above a whisper, restrained but showing a deep and compassionate energy, Orson concluded:

> It's taken the world a long, long time to get even where it is today. Your honor, if you hang these boys, you turn back to the past. I'm pleading for the future. Not merely for these boys but for all boys, for all the young. I'm pleading not for these two lives but for . . . life itself, for a time when we can learn to overcome hatred with love, when we can learn that all life is worth living and that mercy is the highest attribute of men. Yes, I'm pleading for the future in this court of law—I'm pleading for love.

With this one scene Welles did more than achieve a sentence of life imprisonment for his two screen clients. He proved, convincingly, perhaps for the first time in his career as some critics believed, that he could play a totally believable, highly dramatic scene completely without corn or ham.

The reviews for *Compulsion* were universally positive and virtually all mentioned Welles's performance as a *tour de force* of motion picture acting. The *Saturday Review* said: "To Orson Welles's thinly veiled Darrow goes the lion's share of the credit for its [the story's] dramatic persuasiveness." *Harrison's Reports* said that the performance "was outstanding. . . . [It] will long be remembered." Of the monologue, *Variety* noted that, "The lines he speaks become a part of the man himself, and an almost classic oration against capital punishment."

As usual, more offers to act in films came Orson's way. He was set on Europe, however, and he would return as a polarized prodigal son, of sorts. Shortly after his return to Europe, he attended the Cannes Film Festival, where *Compulsion* was entered, and he walked off with the prize as Best Actor.*

The previewing audience gave Orson a standing ovation as he left the theater at the film's end and a crowd of some three hundred journalists, photographers, and fans followed him to his hotel.

LAURENCE OLIVIER RESUMED talks about doing more stage productions with Orson, and Hilton Edwards kept suggesting some kind of Irish tour. Orson was also trying to do (without success, as it turned out), a television documentary on "the heart and soul of Dublin" as he described it; and there was talk of his doing another show, with his old friend Marlene Dietrich, on Paris. Neither came about. However, before Orson could work on any plans or details, he had a debt to pay. Darryl Zanuck still had not received parity for his loan on the making of *Othello*; therefore, Orson agreed to act in a film for him without being paid.

Filmed mainly in French Equatorial Africa, *Roots of Heaven* was a rugged adventure of a man infused with the mission of stamping out the ruthless killing of elephants. John Huston directed a cast that included Errol Flynn, Trevor Howard, Paul Lukas, Juliette Greco, and Eddie Albert. Orson's cameo role was that of a self-important television commentator, Sy Sedgewick, full of bluff and sputter, who eventually comes to endorse the conservationist's cause but not before his enormous rear end, looking as large as one of the elephant's, in a brilliant exercise in typecasting, is riddled full of buckshot.

Orson did his work (worth about $15,000 toward his debt) for *The Roots of Heaven* in two days time, acting in the Boulogne Studios outside Paris and enjoying the dining companionship of Zanuck and Huston at night. Although the film's message, or sermon, is noble and clear enough and the photography of the steaming jungles and sprawling plains of the Dark Continent is handsome, sometimes majestic, the story never quite becomes gripping enough to sustain interest. *The Roots of Heaven,* with Orson's massive behind spread across the Cinemascope screen, must have been an embarrassment to him but the payment toward his debt to Zanuck relieved his mind and served to temporarily deliver him from further demeaning temptations in order to pay it back.

WHENEVER HE COULD, Orson would take Paola and Beatrice with him on movie locations and, after the few days or few weeks of work, would usually extend the trip as a vacation in whatever part of the world he found himself. Buoyed by the income that he had just received from his acting, Orson would

---

*The prize was shared equally with his costars Dean Stockwell and Bradford Dillman. 1959 was a watershed year at Cannes not only for Orson: *Black Orpheus* won for Best Film, François Truffaut was named Best Director for *The 400 Blows,* and Simone Signoret was awarded the Best Actress prize for *Room at the Top.*

play the *grand seigneur* as he toured the island of Madagascar, stayed at a snow-covered inn in Basel, Switzerland, or strolled across the Ponte Vecchio in Florence; and always there were fresh flowers in his hotel suites and long, leisurely lunches at one of the best restaurants.

Orson would hold forth, sometimes only with Paola and Beatrice as audience, but often with a group of actors or theater people that he might have met during another time and who had, by chance, just reconnected with him. Wherever he went in the world, Orson met people he had known. He was hard to overlook.

During one of his trips, Orson arranged what turned out to be a somewhat intense dinner party in Biarritz, consisting of himself, his old bullfighting friend Antonio Ordonez, and Ernest Hemingway. The idea for the dinner was more than social: Orson wanted to make a documentary based on *Death in the Afternoon,* with Hemingway contributing the screen play, Orson narrating and directing it and Ordonez serving as star and technical consultant. Orson had flown into Rome especially to meet Hemingway, and after the dinner the three men drove across the Pyrenees to San Sebastian and back again to Bayonne to catch the last fights of the season. That no agreement was reached to commence the project can be surmised by the fact that neither Welles nor Hemingway ever mentioned the meeting again.

His traveling habits were unusual, going from place to place with a group of highly disparate and inexpensive cardboard suitcases, each held together by whatever was at hand: rope, cord, even old ties and bathrobe belts. As the Welleses entered some of the finest hotels in Europe, Paola and Beatrice were invariably embarrassed over the state and condition of their luggage. But Orson was resolute in keeping the bruised and tattered bags. It wasn't that he couldn't afford better, or that he didn't appreciate a matching set of Louis Vuitton; rather, he believed that if his luggage appeared gypsylike and inexpensive, there would be little chance of its being stolen. He was virtually paranoid about his baggage, as it contained his custom-made clothing (which, owing to its huge size, would have been almost impossible to replace quickly), his makeup box, and perhaps most important, his scripts.

WITHIN A FEW days of arriving back in London after *The Roots of Heaven,* Orson began making arrangements for his next project: once again into the breach with Shakespeare. Hilton Edwards flew over from Dublin equipped with an offer to produce any stage production of Shakespeare that Orson would agree to direct and to star in as long as he would initiate it in Ireland. The Gate Theatre company was ailing in audience attendance—the building that normally housed the theater was closed—and Edwards believed that with Orson's presence and innate sense of publicity, the company could have a meaningful revival.

Orson needed no convincing: to be working with his friends again, doing classical theater, and to be back in Ireland after an absence of almost thirty years, was close to his definition of happiness. A possible production of *The Merchant of Venice* was discussed, with Orson as Shylock, Paola Mori as his daughter, Jessica, and Dame Peggy Ashcroft as Portia, but the political climate in Europe inhibited him. Although it was a lifelong ambition for him to perform as Shylock, there was at that time a widespread outbreak of anti-Semitic smearings of swastikas on synagogues throughout the Continent. Orson penned, for the *London Express,* an exegesis of his abandonment of the project which said, in part: "No, until all the church walls are clean—and safely clean, too—I think Shylock, with his Jewish gabardine, his golden ducats and his pound of flesh, should be best left on the bookshelves until a safer period."

As a promotional device, Orson filmed a few scenes of himself as the vengeful moneylender. Years later, in a seminar on Welles, these fragments were shown. The brief scenes, shot in vivid color, suggest that the film would have been an admirable addition to Welles's eclectic Shakespearean canon.

Welles's makeup appears heavily theatrical. Sporting an ostentatious beard and what is surely the obligatory fake nose, he combines physical elements of Father Mapple and Mr. Arkadin to create another uniquely Wellesian character.

There are sequences of Shylock walking through the streets, with figures in black garb and white masks as background. Many of these were simply that—figures—supported and maneuvered by real people next to them.

One viewing was not enough to provide an intimate critique, but the vivid angles, literate tone, beautifully spoken language, and chiaroscuro are pure Orson.

The plan also dovetailed with a future project Welles had in mind: not Shylock but the idea of eventually doing a film largely based on the character of Sir John Falstaff. If he could use the stage version of such a play as an informal rehearsal for the film, as he did with *Macbeth* in 1948, he would be engaged in a multipurpose pursuit within a single project, a theatrical state of affairs that he always found immensely attractive.

He had little work to do on the script, simply taking the first part of his long-dormant *Five Kings,* which included segments from the two parts of *Henry IV* and much from *Henry V* and with bits of *The Merry Wives of Windsor* and *Richard II,* shortening and simplifying it and then excising the complicated staging directions. There would be no revolving stage this time; no near-assassination of the audience with the misfiring archers; no interminable production destined to go awry because of its complexity.

"This will be Shakespeare without tears," he glibly told a member of the British press in his first interview about the play. "It's designed, really, for people who know nothing about Shakespeare." He called it *Chimes at Midnight* ("We have heard the chimes at midnight," Falstaff says to Shallow in *Henry IV, Part II*). Edwards arranged a provincial tryout of five performances at the once-elegant Grand Opera House in Belfast; the production was then scheduled to move to Dublin's Gaiety Theatre, remain there for a season, and then move on, it was hoped, to London's West End. Orson also talked dreamily of an intercontinental tour: Paris, Athens, Brussels, and Cairo.

Casting and initial rehearsals were begun in the least-expensive rooms that

Welles and Edwards could find, the YMCA on Great Russell Street in Bloomsbury, across from the British Museum. Orson would play Falstaff, of course; but he began worrying immediately about who could adequately fill the role of Prince Hal. A rising young British actor, Julian Glover, read for Hal, but Orson was not quite sure he would be able to work with him, to mold him into the part he envisioned. Then another young man appeared: Keith Baxter. An ex-army sergeant from Wales who had served with the British troops in Korea, Baxter had only limited stage experience, but he was a graduate of the Royal Academy of Dramatic Art, and he had the Shakespearean look Orson was searching for. As his audition, Baxter offered a spirited ten-minute reading from Emlyn Williams's *The Wind of Heaven,* a play about a traveling salesman who believes he has found the true Christ. Orson was charmed by the effort. It made one's mouth water, Orson observed of the piece chosen by Baxter. "That was a remarkable experience," he said to the young man. "Will you read Prince Hal for me?" he asked with extreme politeness.

Without waiting for an answer, he gave a copy of the script to Baxter and asked him to read Hal's famous renunciation speech. Baxter recalls that he read it "hopelessly" but it mattered not: Orson had found his man and had already decided to give him the part. The other casting, as far as Orson was concerned, was uninspired, the exception being Thelma Ruby as Mistress Quickly. February in London was a peak time for actors and the announced, somewhat abbreviated wages and Orson's reputation of unpredictability kept the leading West Enders away from auditions. Edwards embraced the task of directing preliminary rehearsals, still at the YMCA; a week before opening in Belfast, Orson conducted them himself.

Tyrone Guthrie once described playing to the traditionally dispirited Belfast audiences as a "death trap." Welles may have felt that he was entering the same joyless snare when he arrived in the city with his company of twenty-one, to discover that advance bookings for seats were less than enthusiastic and very little advertising or press coverage had appeared.

In a familiar pattern on the night before the play opened, February 24, 1960, Orson conducted his first all-the-way-through dress rehearsal, starting at 7:30 P.M. and finishing twelve hours later, 7:30 the next morning, with an exhausted and complaining cast. The rehearsed performances were not at all what he wanted; he hoped for improvement by the time the play reached Dublin. Opening night reviews in Belfast were better than he expected. They were hardly raves but still gently approving, his dramatic team, despite their tiredness, praised for their coherence and believability.

Orson's own unlabored role of Falstaff was close to estimable as, night after night, he confronted and defined the importance of the character and intensified his interpretation of the lecherous knight. His Falstaff was breezy, licentious, comic, gentlemanly; a man to share a joke with rather than to be laughed at. Welles told Maurice Bessy that, to him, Falstaff represented

an affirmative spirit, courageous in many ways, even when he makes sport of his own cowardice. He is a man who represents a virtue that is disappearing, he is waging a battle lost in advance. I don't believe that he is looking for anything. He represents a value, he is goodness. He is the character in which I most believe, the most entirely good man of all dramatic literature. His faults are minimal, and he derives the most enormous pleasure from them. His goodness is like bread, like wine.

Although Orson's passion and respect for his role was great, and the rest of the company's efforts adequate, no audience for *Chimes at Midnight* could be found. Even before the company left Belfast at the week's end, it looked as though no international, or even London, production would materialize.

But at first the Dubliners, at least, took to the play almost as a novelty, eager to see the awesome Orson do his thing. He was ebullient on opening night and approached the footlights at the play's end: "Thirty years is a nice round figure—as I am tonight—but it is one year less than thirty since I first appeared with the Dublin Gate."

He proclaimed himself an "honorary Irishman." As such, a self-proclaimed member of the family, he expressed some criticism toward the Dublin theatergoers. "Why does the Gate have no theater of its own?" he demanded. Whether out of guilt or out of irritation, the public's dander was raised, and Orson's plea for support of the Gate was at first roundly booed and then, as an afterthought and counterpoint, randomly applauded. Nothing was solved, of course, but the whole "bloody do" made headlines in the Dublin papers the next day. Eventually the Gate did get its theater back, whether through Orson's efforts or not, is not precisely known.

As the performances of *Chimes at Midnight* continued, the Dublin audiences grew smaller and smaller and Orson grew more irritable and discontented. With the exception of Keith Baxter, he began to actually despise his cast and this made for spitefully careless rather than inspired performances from them. Orson had also put on so much weight and had grown so large that, together with extra padding to make his Falstaff appear gargantuan, it was difficult for him to maneuver on stage; in fact, after one piece of action in which he was forced to fall down each night, he elected to remain prostrate, speaking his lines from the stage floor for the rest of the scene, simply because it was too difficult to get up.

In addition to the difficulties Orson was experiencing with his cast, he didn't like the house he rented, the mansion-sized Dargle Cottage owned by Sir Basil Goulding. He complained that it was too cold, and hence was forced to move to the much more expensive Hotel Shelbourne.

As temporarily well-received as *Chimes at Midnight* was in Dublin, the highlight of Orson's stay was not any single performance of that play, but instead a typical cornucopia of Wellesiana, called *An Evening with Orson Welles,* which was held at the Gaiety and simultaneously filmed for later showing in England by the BBC. The show consisted of two parts, the first being a bare stage reading of his *Moby Dick*: he played Ahab unshaven and with little makeup and offered several other voices, in character, when the script called for them. During the second half of the program he answered questions of the audience. Asked about theater critics, he offered his opinion about the differences between the British and American variety, stating that the former group's perception "was not that great," while the latter had the power to "make or break a play." His opinion of Dublin? "There's too much ersatz Americanism creeping in." On the speech of Dubliners: "In my youth, the best English in the world was spoken in Dublin and I still subscribe to that view. It is not impeccable speech but I would rather hear poetry spoken by Irish people than by any other speakers in the world." The greatest actresses he had ever seen? There were two: "Greta Garbo and Sarah Bernhardt."

When Orson began to pontificate just a shade more than the democratic Irish sensibility seemed capable of tolerating, he was hit with the following: "Who do you think is God, Mr. Welles? You?"

"I don't know," quipped Orson. "I never met the man."

JUST AT THE time when it appeared that *Chimes at Midnight* would not be able to sustain a London opening, Orson asked Laurence Olivier to fly to Ireland to discuss a possible joint production of a project to be decided upon. Olivier arrived, sat through a performance of *Chimes at Midnight,* and then went backstage afterward. Before they had a chance to discuss anything, however, Orson insisted that Olivier meet his protégé, Keith Baxter. "Keith, oh, Keith!" Orson bellowed to the actor's upstairs dressing room. "Come down here. I want you to meet someone."

Baxter has related that while Orson's pride in him was appreciated, being treated or coveted as a piece of personal property, being shown off to Laurence Olivier made him feel somewhat uncomfortable, almost feminine. Orson beamed as he introduced the two Britishers, *en grand seigneur,* displaying his merchandise. "Don't worry about the closing," Baxter remembers Welles telling him at about that time. "The play was only a rehearsal for the movie and you'll be Hal, I promise you that, when I film it."

Orson suggested that he and Olivier do a play of his called *Brittle Honor,* a rough draft of which he had with him that evening. It was not exactly a *roman à clef* of the tribulations of the Duke and Duchess of Windsor but it did examine the idea of monarchy through royalty in exile. Olivier really didn't have to remind Orson that there were still bitter feelings and smolderings by the British toward the abdication of King Edward VIII. Since *Brittle Honor* was incomplete and rough-hewn in any event, Orson vetoed the idea himself.

Olivier's suggestion of a possible play to be produced in London was a bold one; the two men tentatively discussed it and then Orson enthusiastically championed the idea. It would be Eugene Ionesco's masterpiece, *Rhinoceros.*

Rhinoceros is one of the prime examples of the Theater of the Absurd, the characters caught up in an epidemic of people changing into rhinoceroses. Those who do turn also seem to welcome their transmogrification. As more and more animals appear, the play moves from farce to allegory; it soon becomes clear that the horned beasts are symbolic of the fascist or totalitarian elements of any society. Only one character, Stanley Berenger, holds out against the herd: therein lies the dramatic and human element.

Orson was attracted to *Rhinoceros* on several levels: the political message of a cry for freedom, which was obvious to some, obscure to others, and the belief in absurdity as a way of life. Typecasting notwithstanding, Orson would *not* play one of the horned pachyderms, and in fact, he wouldn't act at all but would serve as director; Olivier would take the part of Stanley Berenger. Peter Sellers also wanted a role in the production but instead was eventually convinced by others to play the part of the scoundrel in the film *Only Two Can Play,* opposite Mai Zetterling.

Rhinoceros in all of its modernity, would be a startling departure not only for Orson but also for Laurence Olivier. Olivier's recognition as one of the legendary interpreters of Shakespeare had just been clarified once again in *Coriolanus* at Stratford-on-Avon; he could continue matching himself against the great actors of history in classical roles or he could experiment. *Rhinoceros* could be a turning point in his career should it be a hit. He was also happy to turn over the directorial reins and duties to someone he trusted; *his* last directorial effort, *The Tumblers,* had closed in New York after poor reviews and only five nights of performances. *Rhinoceros* was scheduled for a five-week run, more if it could be arranged and if the public demanded it.

Eventually, in late March, *Chimes at Midnight* closed at the Gaiety Theatre, and Orson returned to London to begin the Ionesco production. The project was carefully kept under wraps, perhaps to take advantage of any advance publicity that might be generated by photographers and members of the press, who were ostentatiously and pointedly barred from rehearsals. In order to maintain the secrecy, rehearsals were held not at the Royal Court nor in any of the other theaters in the West End but in a small church hall in Maida Vale with a miniature stage and a patchwork curtain.

Olivier and Welles worked together famously until just before opening night when a clash of temperaments brought on by the nervousness of both men caused Orson, his feelings hurt, to skulk off and disappear for a few days.

Despite, or perhaps because of the press blockade, opening night was attended by a goodly amount of hoopla and publicity. The fact that Joan Plowright was also starring in the play added to the coverage; it was no secret that she and Olivier were engaged in a romantic liaison and that he was attempting to secure a divorce from Vivien Leigh.* Orson was more than just there that night: he was ubiquitous. Only minutes before the curtain went up, his job as director was still not over. There were complex changes in lighting and sound effects and the coordination of actors-to-stage business had not been totally solved in the rehearsals. The experience of theater is never complete, complained Orson halfheartedly, as he had a microphone rigged up in the right-hand aisle of the dress circle and proceeded to give, during the

---

*During the run of *Rhinoceros,* Vivien Leigh made an announcement from New York, covered by all the media and given international play, that she was prepared to give Olivier his freedom in order to wed the woman he wanted. Eventually, Olivier and Plowright were married.

performance, instantaneous lighting directions to the stage electricians and general advice and instruction to his actors.

"Louder, louder," he whispered over the sound system. "Take down the music." "Now lift the curtain. Now, *now*. Faster!" "More rhino roars! More . . . That's it."

Some of the members of the audience began to wonder whether the real performance was not on stage but being offered by Orson as he spoke through the microphone.

Orson had indulged himself with the production and had crammed as many gimmicks onto the stage as he could get away with. A Paris street (in Ionesco's original) was changed into a London pub and there were constant rushings, to and fro, through swinging glass doors. Major stampedes—as if by hundreds of animals—produced by a combination of the voices of the live actors and sounds from recordings, could be heard offstage. A television monitor shows only pictures of rhinoceroses running through the streets. There were trapdoors, trick lighting, and general Wellesian chaos. And although the somewhat stiff audience failed to laugh during a few of the truly funny scenes, the play emerged as entirely strange and new and delightful; and with the names of Welles, Olivier, and Ionesco sprawled over the marquee, *Rhinoceros* assumed virtual hit status.

Joan Plowright, as the prosaic office girl that Berenger (Olivier) loves, his last human support in a world of trumpeting beasts, gave an exceptionally fine performance. But when she too, succumbs to rhinohood and Stanley is really isolated, Olivier rose to one of the most moving performances of his career, a note of sudden and terrifying pathos. All alone on stage, white-faced in a dying spotlight, with the sound of the moaning and trumpeting beasts in the background, Stanley goes through an existential confrontation. He no longer wants to be literally a breed apart. He's become ashamed of his body; he would prefer, desperately, to change and become a rhinoceros like everyone else, but he knows he can't. He realizes the price he must pay. He bellows: "I'm the last man left. The last man! And I'm staying that way until the end. I'll never capitulate! I'll never give in!"

The reviews of *Rhinoceros* were excellent, although Kenneth Passingham in London's Sunday *Observer* obtusely wrote that the spectacle of two aging gentlemen, one of whom had been often described as the world's greatest actor, playing hide and seek with a rhinoceros was "somewhat pathetic." The play had its run and made some small money, but attendance began trailing off just as the play neared its scheduled end. "A hit show in London doesn't change anybody's attitude toward you," Welles offered to an American columnist passing through town. "In New York, it's different. Suddenly a bright light flashes down from the sky when you have a hit."

FOR ORSON, EVERY new adjustment in his career and life-style seemed to be a crisis in self-esteem. This is not to say that change was unwelcome; on the contrary, it was always difficult for him to stay committed to one project until its completion. But as the run of each play ended, the sets for each film were dismantled, and the costumes for each show returned to their owners, Orson would invariably begin to panic in his belief that his next theatrical adventure, whether entrepreneurial or not, simply had to fail to materialize. He was a man with a family to support; children from his present and former marriages had financial claims on him, his life of exaggerated appetites had to be satisfied, debts were still unsettled. He had no investments, no residuals to speak of, no substantial savings, no quick or constant source of income on demand. Just as the rent was due or the next loan payment was to be made, he was forced to accept whatever theatrical work was offered in order to meet his obligations. He wasn't poor but he was bitter about his insecurity. "When you're down and out," he said sarcastically at that time to a reporter for *The New York Times,* "something always turns up—and it is usually the noses of your friends." He was insolvent in the spring of 1960 and a group of British creditors filed a bankruptcy petition against him as: "An actor of South Eaton Street, formerly of Brown's Hotel, Dover Street." He promised to repay everything.

In the early and mid-1960s Orson took acting jobs in films, many of them atrocious, because he desperately needed the money, and also, although he might have hated to admit it, because he believed that some of the films had long-term financial or artistic possibilities.

An actor is usually remembered for just one or two roles during his lifetime and so the right selection of a part is of extreme importance; that Orson felt he was forced to accept eminently forgettable parts, although understandable, did very little to advance his career. It actually set it in reverse motion, temporarily, as he became known as an actor who would slum into virtually any part, however demeaning to his image. Film writer Joseph McBride had noted that Orson's appearances in some films throughout the 1960s took him to new lows in buffoonery. This is true for most of his roles, but in a few others his performance emerged as the only redeeming aspect of the film. In retrospect, it is simple to criticize his decision to become involved in the potboilers that he did at that time, but the fact remains that they produced enough income so that he could survive until the next, perhaps meaningful, project.

As briefly as possible, then, here is a survey of some of those films from the period that could be described as the nadir of Orson's acting career.

In *Austerlitz* (1960), the late director Abel Gance brought the most modern techniques of sound, color, and wide screen cinematography to the same subject that he had approached over three decades before.* This time Gance concentrated on the events leading up to the battle. Orson played the inventor Robert Fulton, who sputters an offer to Napoleon to give France the first opportunity to use the steamboat. He is turned down.

Despite the technological advances, *Austerlitz* was a feeble imitation of

---

Napoleon (1926), the split-screen silent masterpiece that enjoyed a revival in Paris in the mid-1950s for over a year, and then again in this country as a spectacle at Radio City Music Hall in 1981.

Gance's previous efforts and contained historical inaccuracies matched only by past productions of Cecil B. DeMille. In one scene, for example, a conversation takes place in the Houses of Parliament between Nelson and Pitt, and a shot of Big Ben, not due to be built for another fifty years, can be seen through the window.

In *Crack in the Mirror* (1960), a film about a crime of passion, Darryl Zanuck, Richard Fleischer, and Orson teamed together again, hoping to repeat their *Compulsion* success; Juliette Greco and Bradford Dillman co-starred. The film is a story based on a French novel by Marcel Haedrick and practically its only distinguishing aspect was that all three principals play dual roles in two adulterous triangles, Zanuck ingeniously securing six characters for the price of three. Orson played a drunken sadist, a foreman of a steam shovel crew, who is married to an attractive wife (Greco), and who is murdered by his mistress with the help of her young lover; and he also assumed the part of Lamorcière, Paris's most noted lawyer who, although he is in failing health, is still enamored of his mistress, the fashionable Florence (Greco again).

"You have never seen the things you will see in *Crack in the Mirror*," proclaimed the advertisements, and as a publicity gimmick, an "Important Request!" was inserted in the newspapers and posted in front of all theaters that were showing the film, stating: "Because it is a requirement of the story itself and an essential part of your viewing pleasure, we urge you to see it from the beginning. [signed] Darryl F. Zanuck." Despite the advice, one of the difficulties with the film was the confusion of two story lines having the same characters. The doubling of the actors was provided, it seems, to offer a message to the effect that everyone faces the same moral dilemmas, whether rich or poor.

Orson seemed to dominate all the sequences in which he appears and because his final sequence in *Compulsion* had been successful under Fleischer's direction, another lawyer's soliloquy was inserted into the ending of *Crack in the Mirror*. It was splendidly done.

The making of that final scene was acutely captured on paper by Cynthia Grenier, a free-lance writer in Paris at the time *Crack in the Mirror* was being filmed. She offered an unforgettable portrait of Orson as actor, in a feature story that appeared in *The New York Times*:

> The mood on the set of *Crack in the Mirror* was strangely austere, formal and tense the day of the big courtroom scene, destined to be the high moment of the finished film. Welles, now an obviously adult *enfant terrible,* strode imperiously onto the set of the big empty courtroom with its pale green satin walls and golden woodwork. He poked cautiously at his Roman plastic nose, stared sourly up at the technicians and extras chatting softly about him. "Can't we have it a little quieter?" he asked director Richard Fleischer with a plaintive majesty.
>
> Welles lumbered into his position, breathed deeply and spoke: "Do you want a rehearsal first, Dick? It's quite a long scene, after all." Fleischer agreed that it would be a good idea and Orson went through the scene almost without mistake

or incident. But the noise of the extras on the sidelines bothered him: "Can't these people ever learn to keep quiet when we are talking?" he demanded.

Orson gave his "last plea" on camera. The courtroom was dead silent, and as he came to the line, "and as for this unfortunate young man," turning to Bradford Dillman, he suddenly stopped acting and stepped out of character, becoming Orson the director, speaking in his normal voice: "I guess you'll want to have a cut here, won't you Dick?"

Whether Fleischer wanted such a cut at exactly that second had suddenly become beside the point: the camera was stopped and Fleischer congratulated him: "That was fine, Orson, just fine. I'm going to print that."

But Orson wasn't satisfied: "God, can't we do something about all this noise? I heard an airplane on my last lines." He called to the sound man: "Is that on the track?" When told that it was not, he continued his grievances: "And then all that pounding! What in the name of heaven *is* it? I heard pounding all through my speech," and, in demonstration, he began to beat on the railing that separates the judge's bench from the spectators' section. When told that the noise was from the building of a house next door to the studio, over which there was no control, all Orson could do was snarl, pout and whimper.

Crack in the Mirror was comprehensively panned: "Artificiality hobbles it" *(Saturday Review)*; "A disappointment" *(Herald Tribune)*; "Peculiarly bloodless" *(The New York Times)*. But Orson's part, especially his courtroom elocution, was lauded: "Welles plays it with skill and effect" *(Films in Review)*; "Welles is fine as the drunken old slob and close to superb as the elderly lawyer" *(Variety)*.

WELLES PLAYS A hog-like skipper of a ferry boat in *Ferry to Hong Kong* (1959) ("A caricatured combination of Jackie Gleason and Winston Churchill," observed Bob Salmaggi in the *New York Herald Tribune*). He wrote his own dialogue; had a much-publicized feud with costar Curt Jurgens, who objected to having *his* lines edited by Orson (to which Orson replied: "I hate all actors, stupid empty-headed creatures"); and refused not only to attend the world premiere but also to see the finished picture at all, perhaps not realizing what a favor he did himself.

The only benefit that Orson received from acting in *Ferry to Hong Kong*, aside from a small fee, was that he was given the opportunity to visit Hong Kong and Macao—it was filmed on location—and this stimulated an idea for ultimately directing his own film about Macao, based on a story by Isak Dinesen (pseudonym of Danish writer Karen Blixen).

Ensconced in the Repulse Bay Hotel in Hong Kong with Paola and the three-year-old Beatrice, Orson began to assemble the props that he thought he would ultimately need for his Dinesen film: colored lanterns, reproductions of Ming dynasty vases, various jade ornaments, and Oriental lamps. He also had a portable camera and sound equipment and a compact but efficient lighting system, some $10,000 worth in all, shipped to Hong Kong from a Hollywood supplier. During lulls in the filming of *Ferry to Hong Kong*, Orson would haul out his equipment and assemble a makeshift crew to shoot atmosphere shots for the Dinesen film: an armada of fishing junks, twisted streets, dilapidated buildings, a Chinese funeral. Some of the footage would eventually find itself in Orson's own film. In the meantime, he continued to act.

He had roles in two Italian films, *David and Goliath* (1961) and *The Tartars* (1962); Orson, together with the films themselves, began to deteriorate even further. In the former he played the unscrupulous and brooding King Saul with sonorous but ostentatious "thee's" and "thou's," and shuffled behind huge palace pillars; and in the latter, with his old rival Victor Mature, he was a Tartar chief and "looking like a walking house" (as critic Howard Thompson described him), in a thoroughly dull and overstuffed production.

In more than twenty years of acting on the screen, Orson never repeated a role until *Lafayette* (1963) where he played a pasty-looking Benjamin Franklin with a gossamer and balding wig. (He played Franklin in *Royal Affair at Versailles* in 1955.) The film was disastrously overlong, pedantic, gaudy, and artificial. Despite the fact that it took him over five hours a day to be made up, Orson's role was a cameo and in later prints was excised altogether, perhaps to his lasting advantage. His role in *The VIP'S* (1963), that of tax-plagued film director Max Buda, was not particularly distinguished but seemed to be a parody of a cross between himself and Alexander Korda. David Frost, in a cameo role, plays a reporter who meets Max at Heathrow Airport. "Aren't you rather overweight?" he asks Buda. "Overweight, *Me?*" snaps Buda and then realizes that the reporter was talking about his luggage.

Later, Buda, hardly recognizable as Welles, costumed in a fur-collar coat, porkpie hat and toothbrush mustache, philosophizes about filmmaking: "It is not the purpose of the modern cinema to entertain. Never. No, we use our cameras to search. To use as a scalpel."

Then, in *Marco the Magnificent* (1964), he played a character-narrator, Ackerman, a Venetian tutor who inspires Marco Polo. *Marco* offered an all-star cast: together with Orson, there was Anthony Quinn, Omar Sharif, Elsa Martinelli and Akim Tamiroff, but the script was complicated and improbable, the editing inconsistent, and the unintended tongue-in-cheek performances, by virtually everyone, shoddy. As in *Lafayette*, Welles's performance was so fleeting and possibly poor that it was eventually edited out of television and later release prints.

ORSON ENJOYED AT least one serendipitous experience during the time he was mucking his way through junk films during the early and mid-1960s. The producer of *Austerlitz*, Alexander Salkind, became intrigued with him, first as an actor and then as a possible director. Although nothing happened at first, two years later, Salkind and his father, Michael (who had produced Greta Garbo's first film outside Sweden), approached Orson with a list of classics, (including those of Dostoyevski, Tolstoy, and Dickens), any one of which they wanted him to direct in a screen adaptation if the money could be raised. They believed that with Orson's name and their production reputations, such backing would be forthcoming.

Salkind the elder was also impressed with the results of the poll conducted by the British Film Institute in January 1962 of seventy international film critics who had chosen *Citizen Kane* as the best film in motion picture history. (The Italian drama *L'Avventura,* directed by Michelangelo Antonioni, placed second; and Jean Renoir's 1939 social satire, *The Rules of the Game,* was third.) He felt that this rediscovery of Orson Welles would add a great deal to a film's promotional possibilities.*

Orson studied the proposed list of fifteen possibilities given to him by Salkind and selected *The Trial* by Franz Kafka, written in 1923 but totally apropos for the anxiety-ridden 1960s. It is a strange novel that no one can seriously read without being disturbed. The story is of a petty bureaucrat in a mythical state, who is accused, tried, and executed for a crime, of which he may or may not be guilty. The exact nature of the offense is never identified by the prosecutor or revealed to the reader. It is all at once a prophetic vision of the totalitarian state, a labyrinthine nightmare, a parable of the law, a study of paranoia, and a paradigm of the inability of man to communicate. Talking of novels that still had not been made into films, Orson had once said in an interview that he believed a good film could be made of *The Trial,* but until the Salkind offer, he never seriously considered directing it himself.

Financing was not so easily secured as Salkind had originally projected. While he scoured Europe for possible backers, Orson worked on the screenplay. Many of the same people who had financially ventured into the ill-fated *Don Quixote* were approached but were generally outraged even at the mere suggestion that they were to be asked for money; they had not recouped their original investments and it was beginning to appear that *Don Quixote* might never make it to the theaters. Orson was just too great a financial risk, they argued, to pour money into another of his projects. But the script for *The Trial* began to look impressive as Orson continued to labor over it, and responses to financial inquiries started to improve. Eventually a budget of 650 million francs, about $1,300,000, was established and secured with German, French, and Italian capital. To sweeten the international participation, a multinational cast was developed; the idea was that if stars from many countries appeared, it would encourage, if not guarantee, a lively worldwide distribution. Anthony Perkins, Jeanne Moreau, Romy Schneider, Katina Paxinou, Elsa Martinelli, and Akim Tamiroff were signed on, with most of them accepting a fraction of their regular salaries simply because they wanted to work with Welles.

At first Orson was only going to direct the film, but he could find no one suitable (who would work for less-than-majestic wages) to play the part of the tormenting Advocate. Claimed Orson: "I absolutely did not want to perform, and, if I did it, it is because of not having found an actor who could take the part. All those we asked refused." By the time filming began, Orson just naturally slipped into the role; he introduces himself swathed in a steaming

---

*The story of Salkind's initial confrontation with Orson has become legend. When offered a walk-on part in *Taras Bulba,* although he needed the money, Orson was indignant: "Are you crazy," he said to Salkind. "I *am* Taras Bulba!"

towel looking not unlike a modern-day Buddha surrounded by clouds of incense. And much to his own delight he played almost the entire role of the Advocate while in bed.

He took about six months to work on the script, paring it down to a workable approximation of the novel, changing some of the chapter orders and making a series of powerful sketches for the settings. He also took this time to scout locations in various parts of Europe, finally settling on Yugoslavia for its natural settings, which most audiences would find difficult to place and, as he described his reasoning, because "the faces in the crowds had a Kafka-look to them, and the hideous blockhouse, soul-destroying buildings, were somehow typical of modern Iron Curtain architecture."

The younger Salkind surprisingly deferred to Orson's own devices, trusting him and leaving him alone to put the film together. In return, Orson offered Salkind the kind of gentle respect that he had not shown for a producer since the days he worked for George Schaefer at RKO.

In many ways his direction of *The Trial* would be similar to his making of *Citizen Kane,* the first time in over twenty years that Orson had as much control to complete a film on his own terms from its screenplay to its final editing, and with an adequate budget. Through his determination to erase his public image of a profligate and procrastinator, and to repay Salkind's belief in him, Orson "adhered to his limited budget with scrupulous precision," as one of his associates described it. "I have never been so happy as when I was making that film," Orson told an interviewer for *Les Cahiers du Cinéma.*

The company spent three weeks in Yugoslavia. In a mammoth exhibition hall outside of Zagreb, Orson created one of the most indelible sets in motion picture history: 850 desks, 850 typewriters upon them, and 850 secretaries to clatter mindlessly away at the machines, all in the huge office where Joseph K, Kafka's protagonist, lives out his daily death of insignificance, inhabiting it, as it were, as the real world of a faceless nightmare.

Other locations in cities across the face of Europe were used: Dubrovnik, Rome, Milan, and Paris. In France it was planned to use the French studios of the Bois de Boulogne, but the Salkinds had problems collecting some of the promised investments and could not afford it, so the interiors were shot at an abandoned railway station, the Gare d'Orsay, close to the Place de la Concorde.

Orson was worried and under pressure about where to film the interiors when he stumbled onto the idea of the railway station. William Chappel, who plays the part of the mad painter, Titorelli, in *The Trial,* described how Orson came to use the building:

Welles is a poor sleeper, and standing sleepless at five in the morning at the window of his hotel in Paris he became half-hypnotized by the twin moons of the two great clocks that decorate the deserted and crumbling Gare d'Orsay, that triumphantly florid example of the Belle Epoque that looms so splendidly across the trees of the Tuileries gardens. He remembered that he had once been offered an empty station . . . as a location, and his curiosity was aroused.

By 7:30 he had explored the lunatic edifice, vast as a cathedral: the great vulgar corpse of a building in a shroud of dust and damp, surrounded and held together by a maze of ruined rooms, stairways and corridors. He had discovered Kafka's world, and the genuine texture of pity and terror of its damp and scabrous walls, real claustrophobia in its mournful rooms; and also intricacies of shape and perspective on a scale that would have taken months and cost fortunes to build.

The ghostliness and baroque massiveness of the station seemed an inspired choice for the filming of *The Trial*; it was symbolic of the phenomenon that dominated the nineteenth century and was responsible, in Kafka's terms, for many of the ills of the twentieth: the Industrial Revolution. In its dark, sordid, and intertwined rooms and halls, the film would undergo a symbiosis. Everything connected with everything else: the bank with the courtroom, with the Advocate's apartment. The structure looked as though it could have been designed by Kafka himself; in any event, he would undoubtedly have been pleased by its selection as the setting.

Although Orson was delighted to be able to secure the Gare d'Orsay, the location was not how he originally planned the film. During the *Cahiers du Cinéma* interview, he explained how he wanted to ease the film into a slow, scenic starvation:

Everything was improvised at the last moment, because the whole physical concept of my film was quite different. It was based on the absence of sets. And the gigantic nature of the sets, which people have objected to, is partly due to the fact that the only setting I had was that old abandoned station. An empty railroad station is vast. In the production as I originally envisaged it, the sets were to gradually diminish, and to be seen to diminish by the spectators, until only open space remained, as if everything had been dissolved away.

Film critic Elliot Stein has suggested that Welles's sets and locations for *The Trial* emerge as the first important fruition of Kuleshov's pioneering 1923 montage experiments in creating arbitrary filmic space. For instance, as Joseph K. walks out of the Gare d'Orsay in Paris, the next scene cuts to him walking down the steps of the Palazzo di Giustizia, filmed in Rome, to meet his cousin who has been waiting for him. They then stroll together to the entrance of a factory that was shot in Milan. Finally, he bids her good-bye and returns home to the council house in which he lives: this last part was filmed in Zagreb.

Although only the most astute film scholar, or highly observant filmgoer, would be aware of the fact that to shoot those few minutes of film time it took weeks of traveling to four different cities, a certain simultaneous disorientation and connection, as if in a dream, is established and the setting of *The Trial* becomes as important as Xanadu in *Citizen Kane,* in a sense the very essence of the film itself.

True to his word, Orson stayed either on or ahead of the shooting schedule of *The Trial* although he often drifted into overtime with his cast and crew. Floating in a sea of convenience, with his hotel room right across the street from the Gare d'Orsay, Orson was more inclined to spend extra time on the set preparing, rehearsing, and shooting than he might normally do, since he could stroll back to his room when tired or bored. But the station, with its white cell-like rooms and elaborate chambers stuffed with old timetables and railway ledgers of countless journeys crisscrossing the continent, became more than just a set for Orson. He moved in splicing machines, moviolas, and other equipment to work on the finishing of the film as he went along shooting it. Editors and film cutters were set up in abandoned ticket offices, and like the railway station it once was, the Gare d'Orsay hummed with activity and light around the clock. The Advocate's gilt bed sometimes provided real sleep when Orson wanted it; the hundreds of dripping candles gave actual, not just atmospheric, light; from time to time the decaying tables and chairs were used for genuine, not film, dining. And it was like a dream come true, this sweeping integration of his work and life in one basic, physical site, consisting, as it did, of stage, laboratory, publicity office, bedroom, and home.

In an official statement regarding the meaning of the film, Orson released the following: "*The Trial* is a contemporary nightmare, a film about police bureaucracy, the totalitarian power of the Apparatus, and the oppression of the individual in modern society. I've told the story of a particular individual. If you find a universal parable behind this story, so much the better."

As usual, the editing of the film took longer, by some five months, than anyone except Orson expected. François Truffaut indicated that the strong point of *The Trial* was in its editing. Welles was able to put together seemingly disparate elements that he had shot out of sequence, and sometimes without apparent logic or sense, only to splice and cut them into a coherent statement: "When he films, he works by instinct, full of élan and impetuosity; afterward, as though taking severe stock of his flights, he criticizes himself pitilessly on the editing table . . . the films of Orson Welles are shot by an exhibitionist and cut by a censor."

The Trial developed into one of Orson's most thematically abstract films; he made every attempt to create the feeling that Joseph K. was encapsulated in a nightmare and the image of the world as a madhouse, of a time or world once remembered. Most of the characters have no names; K.'s crime is never specified; there is constant spatial dislocation and synthetic geography; an attempt is made to break out of the fiction of the film with the use of a narrator, as one might try to revive oneself out of a deep sleep or dream. To visually sustain the illusiveness and false light of his filmic incubus, Welles used all the techniques and strategies available in his lexicon: deep shadows, flat, overbright lighting, disproportion between sight and sound, ceilings so vast as to be cavernous and awe-inspiring or so low as to be claustrophobic, a constantly moving camera, startling, extreme fish-eyed and angled close-ups, a mixture and careful selection of classical music with jazz, single takes that last as long as six minutes each, the use of a dizzying number of shots overall —more than seven hundred in total.

When specific scenes or patches of dialogue made the story and its meaning *too* clear, Welles would delete or excise the clarification in order to maintain its murkiness. For instance, a statement of the Narrator originally in the script but not part of the finished film explains much:

> This is a story inside history. Opinions differ on this point, but the error lies in believing that the problem can be resolved merely through special knowledge or perspicacity—that it is a mystery to be solved. A true mystery is unfathomable and nothing is hidden inside it. There is nothing to explain. It has been said that the logic of this story is the logic of a dream. Do you feel lost in a labyrinth? Do not look for a way out. You will not be able to find it. There is no way out.

Also, as usual, there are many Wellesian touches, including novelties with occasional references to his past films and to his personal life that add to the film's atmosphere and aura: a print of a painting by Van Gogh on K.'s bedroom wall, a symbol of the madness in society; a slight mustache, but clearly visible, an unmistakable feeling of androgyny, on Romy Schneider; an inspector who looks exactly like Jack Moss, the killer in *Journey into Fear*, and coincidentally, Orson's former manager; Orson's wife, Paola Mori, playing the bespectacled librarian in the records room ("I'm not use to fresh air") but not mentioned in the credits; Orson whispering the word "guilty" in almost exactly the same voice and inflection as does his Hank Quinlan in *Touch of Evil*; enormous doors opening and closing like a trap; Akim Tamiroff's rear end sticking high in the air pointing at the camera, as he kisses Orson's hand.

And to add to his thumbprint of *The Trial* as his own personal vision, as in *Othello*, he personally dubbed the voices of almost a dozen characters himself: K.'s office manager; the judge; the ominous man with the whip; the night operator of the computer; Titorelli, the painter; the priest; Uncle Max; the *two* inspectors in the closet; the accused old man; Hilda's husband. He is, of course, his own voice, that of the Advocate and the Narrator.

To some critics, one of the disturbing qualities of Kafka's novel is that most of its surrealistic happenings occur against an ordinary, everyday, realistic background, while Welles in *The Trial* has been criticized for establishing a world that is in itself surreal, baroque, and bizarre. But Welles's re-creation of Kafka was an interpretation of his own nightmare, not meant to be slavishly derivative, nor anti-Kafkaesque, but simply an expression of one man's inner landscape of hallucination.

Whether the outer world of Kafka differed markedly from Orson's vision of it really matters little; he captured the essence of Kafka's fantasy of obsession, guilt, and resignation to one's fate and couched it in a blackly comic atmosphere. But the criticism that he did not faithfully adapt Kafka's novel found itself creeping into most of the reviews of the film when it finally appeared. For example, the pundits did not like the fact that Titorelli had become an action painter; or that Miss Burstner was no longer K.'s typist but a cabaret entertainer; or that the line, "That's just my pornograph," when

K. means "phonograph," does not appear in the original novel.

Nevertheless, despite some sarcastic or vicious reviews ("Fortunately, for art house exhibitors, there is enough pretentiousness, ineptness, meaningless symbolism and pseudo-symbolism to make it the most talked-about film of the year . . ."—*Film Daily*), there were some critics who believed it to be one of Orson's finest films since *Citizen Kane*. Ernest Callenbach, editor of *Film Quarterly* (Summer 1963), wrote, in part:

> The film is an attempt to create a nightmare world, rather like that of *1984*. It is vaguely European in decor, with a mélange of nineteenth-century monumentalism, now decayed, and some twentieth-century counterparts which at first seem to give the film an unfortunate dislocation; gradually one realizes that this is the landscape of a totalitarian nightmare. . . . It is, we soon learn, a world of sudden violence, avid sexuality, and inexplicable happenings generally.
>
> In this world lives a young man, named K, a vaguely disconnected and gangly person. K is himself a petty bureaucrat, assistant chief of his division—the work of the division is, of course, never specified—who gleefully boasts that on some occasions he had made petitioners wait weeks to see him. (Yet he is in his own mind innocent of any crimes.) When the police appear in his ill-furnished room he insists on knowing the charge against him; his private-individuality rationalism is intact, he is still the same person confronted with puzzling or outrageous acts by others. . . . The dialog is mostly quite successful in conveying a sense of sinister schizophrenia—making sounds which sound reasonable, yet also steadily dissolving the distinctions between what is reality and what is individual or collective fantasy. Little by little, as K is drawn into an obsession with his possible guilt, he and we learn more about the weirdly hierarchical world of the film. . . . The film has the close texture of madness: if *Marienbad* is a fantasy of obsession, *The Trial* is a fantasy of an infinite asylum.

David R. Slavitt discussed Welles's artistic experiment in an article in the *Yale Review*:

> Orson Welles came through with a picture that showed clearly the mark of an individual style and bore evidence of what Eisenstein called the film sense. . . . Welles' camera angles, his selection of sets, his cutting, and his casting are exhilarating. Welles takes risks, is confident enough to risk, and that confidence seems to have deserted the other masters. . . . Welles was right in putting Perkins into the role (of K), for Perkins combines a studied ordinariness with a twitchy energy that suggests the verge of madness. . . . The appearance of Perkins, like the appearance of the bleak housing development in Zagreb, or the exuberant dilapidation of the Gare d'Orsay in Paris, is truly Kafka-esque, sinister and whimsical, and all the more sinister for being whimsical. The proof, I think, is in Welles' ability to slide into scenes which are directly from the novel without any rupture of tone or style. Indeed, K's flight from the studio of Titorelli down a long corridor of horizontal laths, with a crew of debauched little girls in pursuit, is Welles at his best, and pure Kafka.

A prescreening of *The Trial* in Paris was attended mostly by members of the film community; directors Anatole Litvak and Jules Dassin both said they were privileged to be witness to the birth of a classic. As for Orson, with the film completed, he insisted on a mammoth party complete with a group of Gypsy musicians and singers, and with his cast, crew, and half of Paris society invited.

Orson was at his most elated the night of the fete. He sat crosslegged on the floor, told stories, kissed all the ladies, cigarred all the men. "Mousseux!" "Sparkling!" said some of the Parisians of his hospitality, his laughter. He drank endless jiggers of vodka according to one account. At three in the morning, when a few people decided to leave, Orson, stepping into the role of clichéd host from a Grade B movie, would not hear of it: "You're not leaving already, my friends. The night is still young. Play, Gypsies! Play, play, play!"

CHAPTER 20

ONE OF THE most difficult problems of being a success in the world of art or entertainment is the necessity to follow one triumph with another, and then another in rapid succession, to capitalize on the public's interest. Orson understood this thoroughly; he knew that offers to act in films would come again—as they always did—after his artistic victory with *The Trial,* and perhaps even directorial overtures would be made. It was not the time to rest.

Old projects were disinterred, re-waxed, and made presentable for the inevitable impresarios who would be making their respective obeisances to him. Flush with some of his own money from acting in and directing *The Trial,* Orson was nothing but cavalier when he announced to the press that it now looked as though he would finally be able to finish *Don Quixote.* Although neither Francisco Reiguera nor Akim Tamiroff was available to act, shooting started; only crowd and bull-run scenes at Pamplona were attempted. Once again, however, the precise planets of money, actors, sets, locations, and Orson's enthusiasm for *Don Quixote* were not in conjunction, and, eventually, the project was temporarily adjourned.

Film and stage ideas were discussed with possible backers, often argued over, tentatively planned, semi-arranged, and then abruptly discarded when money failed to materialize. Many of Orson's concepts knew their only identities over a somewhat dreary dinner discussion, or a round or two of double brandies, never to be raised again, perhaps even totally forgotten by him forever. Others went through the formalities of proposals, some the conceit of contracts. A few came tantalizingly close to being realized.

There was a Salkind follow-up classic, in effect, to *The Trial,* with Dostoyevski's *Crime and Punishment,* to feature Maximilian Schell as the new Raskolnikov*; a revival of *The King of Paris* with Orson as Dumas; a Wellesian version of *King Lear* to be filmed in Romania; Orson's long-awaited, semi-autobiographical bullfight film, *Sacred Monsters,* with Jeanne Moreau in one of the lead roles; a post-Civil War Western, *The Survivors,*

---

*The idea was eventually blue-penciled partially because everyone realized, with the possible exception of Orson, that it might have been difficult to have improved on Josef von Sternberg's 1936 classic adaptation of the story (with Peter Lorre as Raskolnikov). The poor reception to an American version produced about that time, *Crime and Punishment, U.S.A.,* also dimmed hopes for a Welles attempt.

costarring Deborah Kerr and with a screenplay by Irwin Shaw; a film adaptation of Orson's modern-dress *Julius Caesar,* initially to be produced for Italian television, starring Charlton Heston, Robert Morley, Richard Burton, and Trevor Howard*; and what would probably be the most ambitious undertaking in the history of the theater, a multimillion-dollar musical version for the stage of *Gone with the Wind.***

It was with one of his old pets, however, *Treasure Island,* a project that seemed to have real commercial possibilities, that he caught the attention of a young Spanish producer, Emiliano de la Piedras, and his partner-attorney Angel Escalano, who were willing to part with a sizable portion—about $1 million—of their bankroll. Harry Saltzman, the Canadian producer of the James Bond films, secured world distribution rights for another $1,500,000.

Orson was vague on the details of his production of *Treasure Island* other than to name himself as screenwriter, director, and star—to play the scheming but lovable peg-legged pirate chief Long John Silver; and to reveal that he had already signed two other principals: a Scots youngster, Fergus McIntosh, to appear in the central role of Jim Hawkins, the cabin boy who discovers the treasure maps; and Academy Award winner Hugh Griffith, who would play, "one of the leading characters" the specificity of which role Orson was reluctant to share.†

There was only one difficulty to be solved before contracts were to be signed: Orson wanted to direct *two* films, virtually for the price of one. His idea was to do a film based on his *Chimes at Midnight* stage production, in effect a screen version of the life of Falstaff, *and* simultaneously work on *Treasure Island,* using the same locations, extras, and crew where possible. Although Piedras was skeptical, Orson was reassuring. What the producer did not know was that Orson had attempted, but failed, to secure Italian and Yugoslavian money to make *Chimes at Midnight,* and it was the film in which he was most interested. *Treasure Island,* therefore, was offered as a gambit; Orson would make it for the producers if they, in turn, would let him make *Chimes at Midnight.* But why not do *Chimes* first? It would be the simpler and less-costly film, Orson contended, and as soon as it was completed, if shooting on *Treasure Island* was maintained apace, the two films would be ready almost simultaneously. Somehow, Piedras agreed.

---

*The producers for *Julius Caesar* complained that Orson's budget for costumes—some $5,000—was too great. "The television executives were spending some $17,500 for their own hotel expenses during the production and they were complaining about *my* budget," Orson complained. "This is how rumors have been spread over the years about how I squander money."

**A Wellesian dream if there ever was one (although conceived by British designer Sean Kenny). Initial plans consisted of sixty horses; dozens of wagons; hundreds of extras; rear-screen Cinemascope projection from the stage and all sides of the theater. The Battle of Gettysburg! The burning of Atlanta!

†Somehow Orson convinced his producers that he could deliver a better film than the splendid 1934 version of *Treasure Island,* which starred Wallace Beery as Long John Silver and Jackie Cooper as Jim Hawkins.

In a sense, Orson had planned to direct and star in a film version of *Falstaff* for almost a quarter of a century, ever since he first became enamored with the possibilities of the role with his 1930s *Five Kings*.*

Orson felt that there was more than just a touch of Falstaff in his own personality, primarily the knight's rogue wit and insatiable appetite. The fact that Falstaff was physically huge, often gross, always lusty, and usually well-meaning also added to Orson's empathetic identification. Although Falstaff was never intended to be a central figure by Shakespeare, Orson, in the screenplay, would concentrate on the relationship between Prince Hal and his older friend and on the covetous triangle with King Henry. *Chimes at Midnight* would, therefore, be less a struggle for power at court (where Falstaff serves as psychological motivation and dramatic relief) but more a fatherly love story as the two elder men engage in an all-too-human psychological battle over the younger. In essence, Orson's plot would be as follows:

Lord Bolingbroke, with the support of the Duke of Northumberland, is chosen King Henry IV of England. Rumors spread, however, that Henry IV had a hand in the elimination of Richard II, and the country becomes divided. A growing number of rebels rally behind Hotspur, son of the Duke of Northumberland, while Prince Hal, the Prince of Wales, passes his time in taverns in the company of his inseparable friend, crony, drinking companion, and adviser in debauchery, Falstaff.

The valiant Hotspur leads the rebels in battle against King Henry at Shrewsbury, only to die at the hands of Prince Hal. But Falstaff attributes this exploit to himself, and King Henry, deceived by Falstaff's bragging, thinks his oldest son and heir a coward. While Prince Hal continues his carousing with Falstaff, the rebels led by the Duke of Northumberland regroup and march against the Crown. But the rebels are defeated once and for all by Henry IV's army, led by his other son.

King Henry, told the good news on his deathbed, extracts from Prince Hal a promise to change his ways and reform. And on being crowned Henry V, the latter breaks completely with his tumultuous past, much to the despair of Falstaff, who had hoped to receive a noble title from his friend.

In seeing Prince Hal thus change, from a wastrel prince to a responsible king, Falstaff dies of a broken heart.

WORKING OUT OF AN APARTMENT in Madrid, Orson began making costume designs and sketches for a massive open-plan set of the Boar's Head Tavern. Since English audiences and critics were the most difficult to please in presenting any kind of Shakespearean production, as insurance, Orson set about to assemble a distinguished cast that was mainly British and schooled in Shakespeare productions on the stage or film: Sir John Gielgud would play the King; Keith Baxter, as promised, Prince Hal; Norman Rodway took the

---

*His attraction to Falstaff actually went back as far as his school days when he once played the rotund knight at the Todd School.

part of Hotspur; Dame Margaret Rutherford was Mistress Quickly; Sir Ralph Richardson would narrate the film, tying all the pieces together, mainly with text from Holinshed's *Chronicles*.

In order to keep his producers happy, Orson had others concerned with the production comprise an international crew. The executive producer, Alessandro Tasco, was a Sicilian prince; the assistant director, Tony Fuentes, was an ex-bullfighter from Mexico; the director of photography, Edmond Richard, and all of his cameramen were French; and Jesús Franco, a young Spaniard, served as the second unit director.

Chimes at Midnight was shot not in Merrie Olde England but entirely in Spain, often in semi-exotic locations throughout the country: on a hilltop in the Pyrenees; in a quiet plain of the Sierra de Guadaramma; near the twelfth-century Cordova Castle in the Catalan north country; in the city park, Cosa del Campo, in the center of Madrid; and in a huge, 2,500-square-yard warehouse, serving as a sound stage, located in the suburbs of the capital city.

Filmed during the winter and spring of 1964-65, *Chimes at Midnight* had its share of typical Wellesian difficulties. After announcing a ten-month shooting and post-production schedule, Orson faltered in his timing and was forced to postpone the planned release date. As a result, Saltzman immediately backed out of his commitment to distribute the film, making Piedras's financial position untenable. The film went into hiatus. Only when another backer, Alfredo Matas, was found to underwrite the distribution, could shooting resume.

Then in early January of 1965, with just a few weeks left to complete the shooting, Orson fell ill with a serious gall bladder infection, and filming was held up again. After treatment and convalescence, Orson, now over several months behind schedule, resumed shooting. But then Piedras insisted that the making of *Treasure Island* also continue. Whenever the protests and complaints became too great about the pirate film, Orson would dispatch Jesús Franco to one part of Spain or the other for more location shooting. Orson was not averse, on rare occasions, to do some shooting himself, but such opportunities were scarce and were always done without a formal cast. He went to places like Alicante to film an eighteenth-century vessel (used also in the film *Billy Budd*) sailing off in the sunset, and manned by a rough crew of real sailors and actors that Orson hired for a day's wages; or to Casteldelfels just to shoot the ocean waves breaking upon the beach. Eventually, Orson's conflict of interest between the two films became too great and John Hough, the British director, was brought in to complete the *Treasure Island* project.

One other thing that stifled Orson's creativity at that time was the report of Maurice Bernstein's death. His old mentor—then seventy-nine—had been pruning a tree in the yard of his home in Beverly Hills and had plunged from the ladder to his death. Despite a feeling of ambivalence toward the old man (and they hadn't seen each other in years), Orson fell into a deep depression and could only mope about his Madrid house for weeks after hearing the news.

As with almost all of Orson's films, with the possible exception of *Citizen*

Kane, there were major weaknesses combined with some heartrending and powerful cinematic moments in *Chimes at Midnight.* The sound track was particularly lamentable during long stretches; Orson and Margaret Rutherford were almost impossible to understand. The dubbing was not synchronized, so that when highly stylized details were used—such as being able to see the breath from an actor's mouth on a frosty morning in the great cathedral—the puffs came out at the wrong time in relationship to speech, and the whole process looked sloppy and unprofessional.* Orson could sometimes direct other voices better than his own, however, and Gielgud's melancholy tremolo and authoritative performance were not only perfectly understandable but also archly masterful. And in typical Wellesian fashion, Orson dubbed the voices of Worcester (played by Fernando Rey) and several of the messengers on horseback; a number of the grunts, groans, and wails heard on the battlefield are also the dubbed Orson.

The film suffered from a clash of acting styles. As counterpoint to Gielgud's classical interpretation of Shakespeare, there was a more modern, casual approach affected by Keith Baxter (who bore a certain resemblance to his screen father); and a realistic earthy manner was projected by Margaret Rutherford. Jeanne Moreau although brilliant, was often unbelievable as an Elizabethan, sometimes acting as though she had just wandered onto the set of *Chimes at Midnight* in the middle of making a French New Wave film by Jean-Luc Godard.

But aside from the temporary difficulties of understanding some of his lines, there was the sheer presence of the hippopotamic Orson looking like a figure from a Rubens painting or an early-Victorian Christmas card picture of Santa Claus, playing the role of his life. Orson duels, dances, drinks and revels through the night. A greatly articulated Falstaff, he was filled with relish and tenderness, first as the self-destructive roisterer and anti-king and then, with expert balance, as the self-pitying exile, poisoned by unendurable melancholy for the loss of his friend. In a beautifully choreographed finale, when Prince Hal, assuming the formal and Machiavellian personality of his father, is expressing himself by way of a cold and chilling sobriety in his famous rejection speech and he banishes Falstaff ("I know thee not, old man"), Welles speaks not a single word, but through a wonderful use of his eyes and expression manifests a sorrow of grandeur, a tortuous smile of realization of what he is to remain and Hal is to become. There is a silent and devastating communication between them as the twinkle goes out of Orson's eyes and an understanding that the rejection of Falstaff is not only a betrayal of friendship but a rejection of the Merry Old England for a new kind of empire. So perfectly does Orson capture the meaning of the confrontation, as has been pointed out by many critics, that it is difficult to tell where Falstaff begins and Welles ends. It is probably Orson's finest moment on the screen.

The film has other superb, even stunning, moments, particularly the battle

---

*Years later, Orson claimed that the sound had been acceptable in the original print but, through some fault of the laboratory, became unsynchronized in the release copies.

scene at Shrewsbury, so filled as it is with visual energy and poetry. Before the conflict begins, a view of the troops, shot through a line of raised lances, is brilliantly conceived; in long shot, the soldiers can be seen in a perfectly choreographed, geometric pattern. The editing of this one scene was meticulous and took Orson, working from eight-thirty in the morning until seven in the evening, nearly three weeks to complete. And, as in actual warfare, great clouds of debris and fog obscure the details of precisely which side has the advantage. As the camera closes in and reveals more, the mud-covered, desperate, and confused foot soldiers of both armies can be seen clubbing and stabbing whatever is physically proximate to them, whether it be man, horse, or carcass, and the result is an antithesis of the chivalric battle. And all during the melee, Falstaff, weighted down by his great armor and perennial cowardice, stands and wanders about as an irrelevant bystander, symbolic of the time to come when he will be rejected. Even Welles's detractors have been forced to acknowledge the bravura accomplishment of that six-minute sequence in *Chimes at Midnight*; Pauline Kael, for one, compared it to a painting by Uccello and ranked it with the work of Griffith, John Ford, Eisenstein, and Kurosawa as among the best battle scenes ever accomplished on the screen.*

In the early spring of 1965, with the shooting of *Chimes at Midnight* completed, Orson left Spain for Paris to cut and mix the film and to rerecord some of the exterior dialogue and sound effects. It was hoped by the producers that the film would be finished and ready for showing by the time of the Cannes Film Festival that May. Instead, Orson went off to act in *Is Paris Burning?*, playing the role of the Swedish consul, Raul Nordling, and spending precious weeks away from the chore of editing his own film. As it developed, *Chimes* was subsequently submitted to Cannes as an official Spanish entry for the 1966 competition.

Orson celebrated his fiftieth birthday in Cannes, and the night afterward *Chimes at Midnight* was shown to the festival judges and assembled critics, journalists, and members of the motion picture business. Too nervous to attend the premiere, he roamed the streets of Cannes and had a drink on the terrace of the Carlton Hotel while awaiting the audience's reaction. Although ultimately not winning any awards, the film was roundly hailed by almost everyone that night—a standing ovation was given and judges and audience alike clapped with their hands over their heads—and was eventually accepted by the European critical establishment.**

Much of what was written in Europe about *Chimes at Midnight* negatively compared Falstaff's life to Welles's own career: a prodigy who was hardly

---

*Typically, Orson was criticized in some quarters for taking liberties with Shakespeare, although his parings were much less drastic than Zeffirelli's *Taming of the Shrew,* as a point of comparison. Orson's rationale: Shakespeare's language was particularly dense because he was filling in the scenery. With films, that imagery is supplied and so condensation is virtually obligatory.

**Orson received a special award that year at Cannes, although not for *Chimes at Midnight*: the festival's Twentieth Anniversary tribute to a distinguished filmmaker: "To Monsieur Orson Welles, for his contribution to world cinema."

ever accepted as a serious interpreter of Shakespeare, the man who was never a king but always a clown. But if Orson rebelled at that criticism, he was undoubtedly ecstatic at some of the other comments that pointed to the film's verisimilitude, its fine interpretive sense of the period, the lyricism and rhythm of its images, the realization of the character of Falstaff as perhaps no actor had played him in history. "I think Falstaff is like a Christmas tree decorated with vices," he told the late Kenneth Tynan. "The tree itself is total innocence and love." David Ansen, film critic of *Newsweek,* said of *Chimes at Midnight* that it "might be the greatest Shakespearean film ever made." Not everyone agreed.

When *Chimes at Midnight* was released in the United States, a year after its debut at Cannes, it was roundly trounced. Bosley Crowther thought that the camerawork was "patchwork" and that in general, it was an "uneven" film despite the fact that the depth of settings, especially in the Old House, are not dissimilar to the Xanadu of *Citizen Kane,* and the chiaroscuro lighting, expressionistic beams and shafts of light, and acute camera angles make the film a handsome set-piece. The review in *Variety* mentioned that the film was "repetitive, slow and mannered," when, indeed, it was lusty, funny, feral and totally Breughelian. Other reviews were more savage. Only a few art houses in the major cities exhibited it as a limited run. All Orson could do was cry. In early 1967, a story actually made its way to the international press—true in spirit if not accurate in fact—that he was seriously considering becoming a French citizen because he was so disappointed by the poor reception of the film in his own country and so elated by the praise it was receiving in Paris.

The crowning insult came a few years after the appearance of *Chimes at Midnight,* when a producer contacted him to appear in a film that he was planning to produce—based on the character of none other than Falstaff—and wanted Orson, yes, to act in the lead role; it was the one part that the man said he had always wanted to see Welles play. McBride reports Orson's reaction: "Welles shook his head in amazement as he told me about the telegram; I could see that he wanted to laugh, but the laughter stuck in his throat. What can a man do after making the greatest film of his life—and hardly anyone goes to see it in his own country?"

TO ORSON, THROUGHOUT most of his post-Hollywood years, the art of living became the art of knowing how to survive between making films. After completing his Falstaffian adventure, he continued in the style to which he was becoming begrudgingly accustomed: acting, over a period of every two or three years, in some six to eight films, many of them poor, to raise enough money and to give himself enough time to direct a single project of his own, an always difficult, often frustrating, and rarely successful process. Until his death in 1985, and since *Chimes at Midnight* in 1966, he was able to complete only two feature films, *The Immortal Story* and *F for Fake,* and one documentary, *The Making of Othello.*

Orson made headlines in the fall of 1966 when he was sentenced, *in absentia,* by a Roman court to two months' imprisonment and fined

1,060,000 lire for importing a car into Italy without paying customs duties. Orson eventually pleaded ignorance, paid the fine (about $1,700) and served no time in jail.

Orson's bulky figure could be seen all over Europe during the late 1960s. In England, he was signed as the lead in the film version of James Munro's spy drama *The Innocent Bystander*, but was replaced by Donald Pleasence because of the conflicting work he had to complete on *F for Fake*. In Italy, he discussed a possible part with Pier Paolo Pasolini in *The Canterbury Tales* but again, because of a conflicting schedule, was unable to take the role. He peremptorily turned down a part—after he had first accepted it—in *Black Stockings for Chelsea*, a British film about Mary Jane Moore, a twenty-one-year-old prostitute. Although the producers flew to Nice where Orson was vacationing to ask him to change his mind, he was adamant. He was attracted to Alvin Toffler's *Future Shock* and ended up narrating a documentary based on it:

> If the book shocked Americans, the film will shock the world. We are creating every day our own horrid future. We shall have to do something about our own environmental conditions. They are stifling us. Soon they will strangle us all.

For years, Orson had been saying that he wanted to direct a film of an Isak Dinesen story; any would do, really, because he was so gripped and overwhelmed by her ability to weave a masterful and imaginative narrative and by the cinematic possibilities that her plots promised.* He was particularly taken by the melodramatic "Le Raz de Marée de Nordenay," from the author's *Seven Gothic Tales*, in which a false and disreputable cardinal (the character Orson wanted to play himself), during the course of a flood, attempts to get the people in a farmhouse surrounded by water to come to terms with God. The technical difficulties and budget, however, were too great for Orson to assume on his own and no co-backer could be seduced. But Parisian executives from *Organisation Radio-Télévision Française* (known as ORTF) were interested in working with Welles, creatively and financially, on another more modestly structured Dinesen tale, "The Immortal Story," from a collection of hers titled *Anecdotes of Destiny*. The idea was to create an hour-long, limited-budget version of the film in French, for television, and then to release it commercially to the motion picture theaters, with a special English-language print for distribution in Great Britain and the United States. Then ORTF would gain the rights to a single telecast on its Second Program, and Welles would retain all other distribution income.

He became involved in negotiations on the assignment and was simultaneously exhilarated and disappointed when he discovered that the producers

---

*Said Welles of his adoration of Dinesen in an interview published in *Sight and Sound* (Autumn 1971): "I spent four years writing a love letter to her and she died before I finished the letter. And I went to Denmark to see her, and I stayed three days, and I didn't have the nerve to go and see her."

wanted the story shot in color. Outside of acting, all of his experience with film, for almost thirty years, was in black-and-white. The investors and producers of *Chimes at Midnight* had also wanted him to shoot in color but he had held out against it then, claiming with a certain sense of sarcasm, that he wanted to direct the last picture ever to be made in black and white in the West. Just shortly before being asked to make *The Immortal Story*, he had elaborated in an interview in a film journal on why he preferred black-and-white: "Color enhances the set, the scenery, the costumes, but mysteriously enough it only detracts from the actors; today it is impossible to name one outstanding performance by an actor in a color film. Color is fatal to the film actor." Only the Japanese knew how to make films in color, he believed. "They are a race apart, the only people who leaped from the Middle Ages into modern times in one generation."*

For whatever reason he denied the possibilities of color—insecurity, unfamiliarity, or true aesthetic repugnance—Orson eventually had to overcome his objections to it when ORTF forced the issue, and he began shooting *The Immortal Story* in Paris and Madrid during the fall of 1966. Working with his own script, he kept meticulously close to the Dinesen text; although episodically shorter, the film has hardly a word of dialogue altered or added other than what appears in the story. At first he used the working title *The Hour of Truth* but ultimately returned to the author's title.

The Immortal Story is a discourse on the power of stories, a modern parable that confronts the nature of narration. A sad, lonely, and gout-ridden American millionaire, Mr. Clay (played by Orson), living in merchant splendor in the city of Macao, tells his bookkeeper, Levinsky (played by Roger Coggio), a true erotic story that he once heard from a sailor on a voyage from China.

The sailor told him that one night while in port, a rich and powerful old man, who was impotent, offered him five guineas to sleep with his beautiful young wife so that he could finally have an heir. Levinsky brashly lets Mr. Clay know that this is a story that could be told by any sailor, that it is mere legend and has been related for decades by sailors in every port. Clay, however, believes only in facts and figures; fiction plays no part in his life. He decides, therefore, to show how fiction can become fact by hiring a young sailor (Norman Ashley) to make love to a beautiful girl (Jeanne Moreau) whom Clay also hires, thereby making the tale come true. After the liaison, Clay believes that the young man will be the only sailor in the whole world who can tell the story without lying because it really happened to him and that as he tells it on ships and ports around the world he will be offering a true tale. But the sailor rejects Clay's bidding and states that he has no desire now to tell the story—because he has fallen in love with the girl—and even if he did tell it,

---

*Perhaps it was Orson's abortive proceedings with the legendary *It's All True* that left him with such disdain for color. There were some obviously fine performances in color films made prior to 1966, which he ignored when making the above statement: Terence Stamp in *The Collector*; Rita Moreno in *West Side Story*; Peter O'Toole in *Lawrence of Arabia* and *Beckett*; Omar Sharif in *Dr. Zhivago*; Paul Scofield in a *A Man for All Seasons* (in which Orson also played a strong, although abbreviated, part).

no one would believe him. With his attempt to tamper with the laws of nature foiled, Clay dies.

Orson created a splendid miniature with *The Immortal Story,* and Clay emerges as a quintessential Wellesian character, similar to Kane or Arkadin, living as he does in a Xanadu-like mansion. Like Kane, Clay wants to prove his omnipotence and use his power to manipulate the puppet-people around him. Both characters ultimately fail, of course, because they discover that people are not, in fact, marionettes and cannot be arbitrarily controlled.

As it developed, Orson's concern about using color film for *The Immortal Story* proved to be unwarranted; he amplified the entire film as a virtual paean to color, an exquisite set piece of what really can be done—and rarely is—with color film in motion pictures. When he saw the first rushes, all at once his resistance to color was demolished. The whole tone and look of the film is something suggestive of an impressionistic exercise by Renoir or Degas. Violent reds, somber browns, lofty blues, deep shadows, seem to have special tints and pastels of their own and permeate every scene. The look of the film is poignantly, uniquely Wellesian. And, as usual, with everything that Orson has ever done on the screen, the critical reaction was sharply divided. "A little piece of cinematic art," claimed the reviewer for *Variety*; Steven M. L. Aronson of the *Chicago Sun Times* elevated it to the status of high art. But Renata Adler in *The New York Times* thought it "ineffective in a surprisingly feeble way" and complained, as did many others, about the film's dubbing.*

AFTER MAKING *The Immortal Story* (which was distributed in France in the spring of 1968 and premiered at the New York Film Festival later that fall for U.S. release) and acting in nine mostly undistinguished films,** over the next several years, Orson started a new film project early in 1970, in the United States. Unearthing his old screenplay *Sacred Monsters,* he changed the title to *The Other Side of the Wind,* made some major revisions such as excising the bullfight sequences (the original rationale for the film), and expanded upon the part of the film director, a role he had no intention of playing himself, however autobiographical the story seemed. As he shot, then scrapped, then altered scenes and changed dialogue and action in the script, *The Other Side of the Wind* became a thinly disguised psychodrama of his own tattered and tangled knot of a career, a dramatic discourse on what Hollywood is and what it can do to people. It is filled with sardonic Wellesian references, personal asides, and nostalgic connections to Orson's rococo pursuits, all at once humorous, ironic and entertaining. For whatever reason, he subsequently denied the character's similarity to his own life. "It's not a cute thing, not Felliniesque, where you have to guess who it is," he told a film class at the University of Southern California in 1971. "It really is about a fictional movie director, and not a parody of himself."

---

*Variety responded to the criticism of the dubbing of *The Immortal Story* and insisted on a clarification: "There still abounds in the U.S. the misapplication of the word 'dubbing' to what is really post-synchronization. When actors record in a sound studio the very same words, in

The financing of the film was at first provided by Orson's own money and then through further investment by Astrophore Films, a Parisian-based Iranian company whose president was Medhi Mouscheri, brother-in-law of the late Shah of Iran. Some money from a Spanish firm was also used, and Andres Vincente Gomez acted as his studio's representative and the film's producer for a while. Over the years, Mouscheri gave Welles over $1 million in amounts of a few hundred thousand dollars at a time.

As Welles defined and clarified the narrative of *The Other Side of the Wind* for himself, it developed as follows: a lavish seventy-fifth birthday party is given for an aging Hollywood film director, Jake Hannaford, something of a psychological composite of Ernest Hemingway and John Ford.† Hannaford is a macho figure, noted for his sexual excesses and political radicalism; additionally he seems to be a closet homosexual. Emerging from years of European exile, Hannaford sets out to direct his one last Hollywood film, an avant garde, low budget feature filled with sex, nudity, obscure symbolism, and shot partially as *cinéma vérité*.

The hostess of the party, Zarah Valeska (patterned after Orson's old friend Marlene Dietrich), is a Hollywood legend in her own right; she invites many young filmmakers, cinema historians, film dilettantes, critics, journalists, and camera crews from all over the world. Documentary footage of the master is constantly shot throughout the party. Hannaford becomes somewhat sickened and yet secretly pleased at all of the adulation heaped upon him.

Hannaford's film, which is also titled *The Other Side of the Wind* (the meaning of which is never explained), is only partially completed when the party takes place. One of his assistants arranges for a screening of the available footage—recently shot, silent, raw footage—for a studio chief who consequently becomes totally bewildered by what he sees. These scenes watched by the two men in a screening room, were designed by Welles to be obscure, drawn out, and not very good. As the evening presses on, the complexity of Hannaford is revealed. He has an intense rivalry with, but sincere attachment

---

the same language, that they have spoken or 'mouthed'; on set, this is not dubbing. It is, moreover, a perfectly common method, one used for almost all Italian, Spanish and East European films—and by the greatest directors.... All such films have a 'post-sync feel' which a professional reviewer must accustom himself to; experienced sound directors said this week that the soundtrack of the Welles film was not significantly lower in quality than those for most foreign pictures."

**Not all of the films that Orson acted in during this period were bad, the exceptions being *Catch-22,* directed by Mike Nichols (a story Welles had longed to direct himself, claiming that it was the greatest book of modern times and that it would make "the movie of the century," but was forced to settle for a small part, that of the muddled General Dreedle); and *A Safe Place,* directed by Henry Jaglom, in which he plays a thoroughly lovable, Jewish, chess-playing magician who offers such mystical lines as: "Last night in my sleep I dreamed that I was sleeping, and dreaming in that sleep that I had awakened, I fell asleep."

†The name is an amalgam. Also, "Jake" was Orson's pet name given to him by his friend Frank Sinatra; "Hannaford," aside from the syllabic similarity to Hemingway and its relationship to "Ford," was one of Orson's cameramen on the miscarried *It's All True.*

to, a young film director, Brooks Ottlerlake (modeled after Peter Bogdano-vich, a close friend in reality of Welles and played by him); he is also immensely attracted both to the lead actor in his uncompleted film and to a beautiful and scantily dressed actress at the party. There is also a scene in which Hannaford rather cruelly interviews a professor, not so gently impugning his sexual integrity.

Amidst the sexual under- and overtones, Hannaford's attitudes are analyzed by a film critic (based on Pauline Kael) and debated by his biographer (based on Joseph McBride). The party becomes more boisterous, permeated with jealousies, conflicting emotions, and drunken outbursts. Filled with liquor and suffering from his own confrontation with himself, Hannaford quits the party and drives away in the sports car he was to give as a gift to the young actor. He is subsequently killed in a highway accident.

Those who have seen excerpts from *The Other Side of the Wind* proclaim it to be vintage Welles, one of the most visually energetic and eloquent films in his repertoire. It is a complex work, utilizing a variety of viewpoints, styles, and visual mediums (color, black-and-white, super 8, 16mm, etc.). Charles Champlin, film critic of the *Los Angeles Times* and one of the few who were permitted a peek, wrote: "The scenes are blizzards of very fast cuts, dramatically and even luridly lighted and full of extreme close-ups."

The acting of the late John Huston is supposedly of Academy Award quality and Susan Strasberg, Mercedes McCambridge, and the late Lilli Palmer also give wonderful performances.*

With *The Other Side of the Wind* about 96 percent finished, as Welles described it, its distribution became hopelessly entangled in a series of financial misadventures. He had been hoping to secure a "no tampering" agreement with any U.S. distributor but instead received just the opposite. Certain monies given to him by Astrophore for direct production costs were used for his legitimate expenses, but not of the type that his producers had agreed upon. As a settlement was being worked out between Welles and Astrophore, one of the non-Iranian investors embezzled some $250,000 from the project. Then when the Shah of Iran fled his country, the entire financial future of the film became even more obscure. Since Astrophore was the principal investor, and hence owner of the film, its representatives blocked all further work on it until all the legal problems could be unraveled. At this writing, the negative and most of the workprints of the almost-completed film are under lock and key in a laboratory in Paris. It is altogether possible that it will never be released and may by now be under the legal jurisdiction of the Ayatollah Khomeini.

BEFORE THE ENTANGLEMENTS of *The Other Side of the Wind* had reached

---

*Lilli Palmer said that working with Welles was one of the most rewarding professional experiences of her life. "He makes love to you with the camera," she explained. "'Give me less, yes less, less, even more less,' he whispers, until you have created with him something very special in the part." And John Huston, after directing Orson in three films, *The Roots of Heaven, Moby Dick,* and *The Kremlin Letter,* found it somewhat aberrant, but rewarding, to face him on the other side of the camera.

their most embarrassingly anarchic state, Orson and Astrophore had come to terms on another film, one of extremely low budget, which he was able to complete with untypical ease. (Others investing in the project were SACI Films of Teheran and Janus Films of Munich.) Originally called *Vérités et Mensonges (Truth and Lies),* it also had an alternate European title, *Question Mark,* or simply the symbol *?,* while the film was being made; and for a while he used the working title *Hoax.* Eventually, it was released as *F for Fake.* Its theme of artistic charlatanism is by far the most personal film, even more than *Othello,* that Welles has ever made.

Curiously, a large part of *F for Fake* was not shot or directed by Welles at all, but by the noted French documentarist François Reichenbach. In the early 1970s Reichenbach had shot an extended interview with the late art forger Elmyr de Hory and his biographer, Clifford Irving, whose book about de Hory was called *Fake.* Filming for the de Hory interviews had been done on the island of Ibiza about one year before Irving wrote his infamous unauthorized biography based on counterfeit interviews with Howard Hughes. After using the footage for a conventional documentary that enjoyed international distribution on television, Reichenbach allowed Welles the use of it and all other unused footage; when the Clifford Irving hoax erupted, Welles was overwhelmed by the preposterous magnitude of the caper. He originally had set off to make a film about the mischievously bizarre life of Elmyr de Hory but became equally intrigued with the Hughes affair and shifted some of its focus toward Clifford Irving.

Welles appears as himself, the perennial narrator, and as the filmmaking magician he is, amusing children with sleight-of-hand tricks and levitating willing victims. And, as though he had become a living reincarnation of his own Charles Foster Kane, Orson introduces into the film footage of one of his protégées, the beautiful and unknown Yugoslavian actress Olga Palinkas (whom he renamed Oja Kodar), her seductive wiggle relentlessly filmed from every possible angle, much to the delight of the male audience and onlookers in and outside of the film. Orson promises that for the next hour he will tell only the truth, and then introduces, by way of the Reichenbach footage, the colorful team of de Hory and Irving.

De Hory relates the story of his life and explains how he could not make a living as an artist until he began to copy the styles of such masters as Picasso and Matisse, selling them as authentic paintings. (It is pointed out that a major museum that has what it thinks are twenty-two impressionist masterpieces has, in fact, the largest collection of de Horys in the world—all are fakes). Irving corroborates the greatness of de Hory by saying: "I had Elmyr paint me a Picasso and a Braque and I took them to the Museum of Modern Art to be authenticated. After two hours, the museum experts assured me they were absolutely genuine."

Orson then takes the film on an autobiographical diegesis during which he discusses his own reputation as a mountebank, from the days of the Gate Theatre when he presented himself as an accomplished actor, to the infamous *War of the Worlds* radio incident. Colleagues of Orson's are introduced, people such as Joseph Cotten and Richard Wilson, who discuss his history as artistic impostor and creative manipulator and who introduce the fact that *Citizen Kane* was initially to be based on the life of Howard Hughes, rather than William Randolph Hearst. After a newsreel biography of Hughes's life, similar in feeling to the *News on the March* segment that opened *Citizen Kane,* Orson wonders how much an artist's name really matters in appraising a work of art: wasn't the Cathedral of Chartres built by thousands of people, all of them anonymous?

Then the film switches to a story about Oja. According to Orson, Pablo Picasso devoted an entire summer to painting a series of portraits of her; in return for posing, Picasso allowed Oja to keep the paintings as long as she promised not to sell them. Later, the paintings *were* displayed at a gallery; Picasso, however, claimed they were fakes. Upon confronting her, the story goes, Picasso is taken by Oja to the hidden studio of her grandfather, the world's greatest art forger, who confesses to having burned the original paintings that Picasso made of Oja and to having, in turn, created a whole new Picasso period. The anecdote completed, Welles then admits the story is pure fiction. He reminds the audience that he had promised to tell the truth for an hour but that for the past seventeen minutes, after the hour was up, he had been lying his head off.

F for Fake is a film about lies, says Welles:

> Every true artist must, in his own way, be a magician, a charlatan. Picasso once said he could paint fake Picassos as well as anybody, and someone like Picasso could say something like that and get away with it. But an Elmyr de Hory? Elmyr is a profound embarrassment to the art world. He is a man of talent making monkeys out of those who have disappointed him. This film doesn't exalt the forger. It denounces the art market, because it is elementary, isn't it, that if you don't have the market, then fakers couldn't exist.
>
> And Clifford Irving? He couldn't make it with his fiction, but making a fake made him the best-known writer in the world. Who are the experts? Elmyr de Hory had dramatized the question of whether or not art exists. It has always existed, but today I believe that man cannot escape his destiny to create whatever it is we make—jazz, a wooden spoon, or graffiti on the wall. All of these are expressions of man's creativity, proof that man has not yet been destroyed by technology. But are we making things for the people of our epoch or repeating what has been done before? And finally, is the question itself important? We must ask ourselves that. The most important thing is always to doubt the importance of the question.

The critical reaction to *F for Fake* was typically characteristic of Orson's work. Andrew Sarris wrote in the *Village Voice* that he toyed for a long time about naming the film as one of the "ten best" of 1978 (he didn't ultimately); *Variety's* French correspondent praised Orson's shrewd addition to and manipulations of footage; *New Republic's* Stanley Kauffman indignantly huffed that *F for Fake* was, "a piece of gimcrack japery, an *ad hoc* pastiche that Welles is trying to pass off as a planned work of charlatanry." Writing of Welles's incessant trick editing, Kauffman continued: "Welles could doubtless rationalize this method as being the cinematic equivalent of sleight of hand. It simply tries the eyes and suggests very early that we're getting all this editing glitter because there's so little film underneath."

ALL DURING THE 1970s as Welles worked on *The Other Side of the Wind,* he appeared constantly on television. It became his principal source of income. He played the insufferable Sheridan Whiteside, spinning about in a uniquely made wheelchair to accommodate his bulk, opposite Lee Remick, in an NBC special of *The Man Who Came to Dinner*; hosted a British-made series called "Orson Welles, Great Mysteries"; narrated any number of documentaries; showed up almost every week in cameo spots on comedy shows such as those of Dean Martin and Dinah Shore; and became a perennial guest on the talk shows of Dick Cavett, David Frost, Merv Griffin, Tom Snyder, and Johnny Carson, being just, not-so-plain, Orson Welles.

At one point, in the late 1970s, there were serious talks by executives at ABC to launch Orson on his own talkfest at 11:30 each evening in an attempt to compete in ratings and revenue against Johnny Carson's *Tonight* show. The potential producers, however, opted for a Variety called *The Henrietta and Lorenzo Music Show,* which, although high in spirit and entertainment lasted barely a few weeks against the firmly entrenched Carson.

It was Greg Garrison who persuaded Orson to appear on the "Dean Martin Show" back in the United States. Garrison had been a young stagehand for Welles during the *Around the World* run and had looked up to the older man as a mentor and father figure; he was now a television producer, and although years had passed without much close contact between them, Welles was open to Garrison's surprising suggestion.

In 1969, Garrison had originally attempted to produce for NBC a highly ambitious special called *Around the World with Orson Welles,* similar in spirit to Orson's old BBC series but not studio-bound, with Orson as the lone star. Garrison had plans to shoot Orson in such obscure lands as Manchuria, and having such stellar guests as Charlie Chaplin and Laurence Olivier. Although never launched, it was an instructive failure in its attempt to surpass the normally bland television fare at that time. Now Garrison convinced Welles not only that regular appearances on the highly rated "Dean Martin Show" would be lucrative but also that the exposure might reactivate interest in him by American directors and producers. Orson agreed to appear.

At that time, Dean Martin was enjoying spectacular success not only on television but in motion pictures as well and was, if not a box office idol, at least a financial guarantee to those who produced the films and shows in which he appeared.

Orson began a multi-year experience with Dean Martin, making biannual appearances on the show. He would play in skits and trade quips that would invariably have both men criticizing themselves and making fools of each other, much to the hilarity of the television audience, but to the consternation of certain Welles purists. These Wellesian fans and cinematics would rather have seen him beset by every imaginable misfortune, while remaining true to a classicist's stance in directing fine films, rather than humiliating himself in front of millions.

The income from his various television guest spots also enabled him to pay off some of the enormous tax bills that he still owed to the Internal Revenue Service.

Just as Greg Garrison had predicted, people from Hollywood started talking to Orson about directing, producing, or perhaps starring in several feature films. One of those projects particularly interested him, a film in which Welles very much wanted to gain a principal role.

He had read *The Godfather,* Mario Puzo's novel, and knew that the film rights had been sold and that it was going to be made into a motion picture. He'd heard that a young screenwriter, Francis Ford Coppola, whom he had met when he acted in *Is Paris Burning?* in the early sixties, when Coppola was a co-writer on the project, was scheduled to direct it.

Orson coveted the role of Don Corleone. He believed he was physically perfect for the part: his immense size and the depth of his voice, alone, assured it. He saw himself whispering slowly as his minions and those who sought his favors came to kiss his hand; he envisioned them listening as he dispensed grave advice and wisdom to the "children" of his family.

Word went out to the producers that Orson was available for *The Godfather,* but Coppola could not imagine Welles playing the lead role. Not even an audition could be arranged. "I would have sold my soul to have been in *The Godfather,*" he said a few years after the film eventually came out with Marlon Brando in the title role.

Another film project was initiated at that time by Mick Jagger to be shot in Marrakesh starring himself and Orson and with Norman Mailer as screenwriter. It never materialized. And then when Franco Zeffirelli made his twelve-million-dollar television epic *Jesus of Nazareth,* there was at first to be a part for Orson, playing one of the non-principal biblical characters, but the offer was never officially made.

AS HE RECEIVED more contracts to do voice-overs for radio and television commercials, the idea seized Orson to return to the United States on a more permanent basis. Clearly there was work to be had there; every time he spent a few weeks in the United States, offers to do commercials came almost daily. The work may not have given him creative satisfaction, but it provided necessary income. Orson felt that if he established a known and permanent base somewhere in his own country, a place where people would know invariably how to reach him, more and more work would be forthcoming and eventually he might be able to gather enough money to produce and finance his own films.

At his height as an actor in television commercials, Welles could, and did, earn several hundred thousand dollars a year.

Los Angeles seemed the most obvious place for Orson to make his home.

Paola Mori, Orson's wife, was not eager to live in Los Angeles, however. Her mother was living with them in Europe, and the old woman's health was not good. Smog-laden Los Angeles might have endangered her life. And, since Orson himself still had the asthma problems that had plagued him for decades, it seemed to Paola that a dryer, cleaner climate would be more healthful.

Paola also knew that if Orson lived in Los Angeles, with its ready accessibility to the members of the press, film scholars, and budding producers, there would be a constant round of visitors and telephone calls, parties and speeches, requests for dinners and interviews. Their residence was bound to become more studio and office than house and home. None of this, in Paola's view, would have been good for Orson. She was also concerned about their teenage daughter, Beatrice. Paola wanted her to be brought up more normally than would have been possible if the girl had been constantly exposed to what Paola thought of as the glitz and glitter of many show-business people.

Arizona was a logical solution. The climate was perfect for both Orson and his mother-in-law, and the Welleses bought a modest but lovely house in Sidona. It is one of the most beautiful areas in America, combining the quiet of the mountains and the desert. The sky is a clear, crisp blue almost every day; evening usually brings a blazing twilight. The schools were excellent, no strangers or business contacts could or would drop in unannounced, yet if commerce called, Orson could fly to Los Angeles in just about an hour.

Orson was happy in Sidona. He seemed proud when he told me, in the late 1970s, with a touch of awe in his voice, "I live in *Arizona!*" It was almost as if he was saying, "No, sir, I don't live in one of those polluted, overcrowded war zones that people call cities. I live in the land of the gods!"

SHORTLY AFTER WELLES returned to the United States and established his home in Arizona, and with his continued and increasing exposure on television, it seemed that certain members of the film establishment began to recognize the contributions of Welles to cinema.

During the 1970 Academy Awards ceremony, he was presented with a special award for his lifetime achievement in motion pictures. Welles accepted the honor but did not appear in person to receive it. Instead, he sent a short videotaped acceptance speech and informed the Academy that he would be out of the country during the time of the Awards. Actually, he was staying in a house in Laurel Canyon, not far from the Chandler Pavillion where the festivities were being conducted. He said on the tape that in order to make good films one must love his work, that you're crazy if you do but without such dedication there would be no art in motion pictures. Still somewhat alienated from the Hollywood establishment, he just couldn't bring himself to appear that night. But he watched the entire ceremony on television.

As the Hollywood of the 1970s began to acknowledge its prodigal son, the academic community also seemed to become more aware of him. University courses in the oeuvre of Welles films began to proliferate; masters' theses on such films as *Citizen Kane, Touch of Evil* and *The Lady from Shanghai* were written in colleges throughout the country. There were doctoral dissertations analyzing Welles or his films and comparing them to other directors or genres, and film societies on college campuses constantly ran Orson Welles film festivals. George Washington University devoted an entire course to *Citizen Kane* that analyzed not only the film itself but also the social, political, and artistic tendencies in America in the 1930s that led to *Kane*'s production in the 1940s.

Andrew Sarris, professor of film at Columbia University, made discreet inquiries in the early 1970s as to whether Welles would accept an honorary doctorate at one of the school's summer commencements. Orson was nothing but courteous in his rejection of the offer but let it be known that he considered that such awards should be given to someone at the *end* of his career. Orson was only fifty-five at the time and was still working, not yet ready for deification, or as he would put it, mummification.

He did agree though, at that time, to give a lecture and to answer questions before an assembled body of film (and other) students at the University of Southern California. It was a lively affair, with Orson offering comments on everything from the Vietnam War to the origin of *Ambersons* to the state of the motion picture business in this country. One of the most touching incidents occurred when he arrived at the university and saw a glass-enclosed exhibition of stills and memorabilia from many of his old films. There in the case was *Rosebud*—there had been several of the sleds made for *Citizen Kane* in addition to the one that is burned at the end—in all of its symbolic prominence. It was the first time that Orson had seen the actual sled since the filming; almost thirty years and what seemed like many lifetimes had transpired since then. His wry response had more meaning than those assembled might have thought:

"It's smaller than I remembered."

Articles about Welles and his films in scholarly journals and film publications also seemed to appear almost weekly during this period. There was hardly an annual volume of *Film Comment, Sight and Sound, Films and Filming, Film Quarterly,* or *Les Cahiers du Cinéma,* that didn't contain an appraisal or an interview, an analysis or a recollection of Welles.

Orson usually cooperated with the writers and editors of the publications that treated him and his work with respect. He was known for promptly answering, by telephone or mail, most inquiries or questions about his work, past, present, or future. He even kept up a small correspondence with some of the writers who had done major pieces or minor mentions of him over the years.

A former neighbor and friend of mine, the late Herman Weinberg, author of *Saint Cinema* and other works on film, often included something on Welles in his columns. Consequently, he heard from Welles fairly frequently, and he would always show me his latest note, postcard, letter, or Christmas card from Orson as they arrived. Some were cordial and friendly, others quite personal. Many contained little sketches Orson had done of himself or other subjects.

One such card was from Madrid, where Orson said he was playing a role in Gonzalo Suarez's *Aoom,* as "an actor tired of himself."

An assortment, what one might call a sampler, of disparate books about Orson and his films also emerged in the early 1970s. One of the most informative was a 192-page work, published by Viking and called simply, *Orson Welles,* by Joseph McBride, a young journalist and former television cameraman, who had written about films for such publications as *Variety, Sight and Sound,* and *Film Quarterly.*

In the four years that it took McBride to write the book, he never had the opportunity to meet Welles until it was nearly completed. Not only did Orson agree, then, to a series of interviews, which were held in a house he had just rented in Los Angeles (to use on his frequent trips away from Sidona), but he secured McBride to play a character based on himself in *The Other Side of the Wind,* as well.

McBride's book was filled with little tidbits of Wellesiana never before known: *Shoeshine* was Orson's favorite film; the character of Eugene Morgan in *Ambersons* was patterned after Orson's father, and so on. His research into Orson's film work before *Citizen Kane* led McBride to unearth Orson's first film, *Hearts of Age.* Perhaps the most important part of the book, together with his astute analysis of the body of Orson's films, is his description of this initial film and Welles's other early works.

McBride also came to Orson's defense in his book and in an article he wrote for *Film Heritage,* "Rough Sledding with Pauline Kael," over Kael's controversial article in *The New Yorker* called "Raising Kane." In essence, Kael stated that Herman J. Mankiewicz was virtually the sole author of the screenplay for *Citizen Kane* and that he had written it without the assistance of Orson Welles.

Welles had been deeply hurt by *The New Yorker* article and even more so by Kael's subsequent essay in *The Citizen Kane Book,* which was issued by Little, Brown & Co. and then by Bantam Books shortly afterward. The book contained that offending essay, as well as the entire script of *Kane.* Kael had admitted to McBride that she had deliberately avoided talking to Welles and his colleagues when she was researching the essay. By failing to even consider Welles's side of the authorship controversy, she was unable to confront the problem fully, unable to refute the untrue claim, and unable to provide or even attempt a logical analysis of the issue. It appeared that Kael was determined to make her case against Welles as *auteur* of *Kane,* and didn't even wish to listen to any argument by Welles or anybody else that might dissuade her from that point of view. "She never sought me out," said Orson. "She knew it would spoil her copy. 'Orson Welles, on the other hand, insists that . . . Welles maintains however . . .' It would have been boring for her rhetoric." She did talk to John Houseman, who after a lifetime of feuding with Orson was not particularly prone to be fair or friendly. William Friedkin, director of *The French Connection,* also dashed to Orson's support. In *Movie Mailbag,* a column in *The New York Times,* he wrote: "I'm one of many of my generation who was inspired to become a filmmaker as a direct result of having experienced *Citizen Kane.*" Sometime later, Friedkin told me that he owned a print of *Citizen Kane* and had viewed and studied it over one hundred times.

Because Kael had sullied his most distinguished achievement, Welles wanted somehow to retaliate, to tell *his* story about how he *had* been responsible for the script of *Citizen Kane.* He wrote a letter to the London *Times* after that paper had reviewed the Kael book, defending the contributions he had made to the script of Kane, and he also worked with Peter Bogdanovich on an interview the latter did for *Esquire* magazine, "The Kane Mutiny," in which Bogdanovich quite convincingly proves that Welles *did* contribute a great deal to the script. For example, Bogdanovich quotes Charles Lederer, the screenwriter who married Virginia Nicholson after her divorce from Orson: "Manky was always complaining and sighing about Orson's changes. And I heard from Benny [Hecht] too, that Manky was terribly upset. But, you see, Manky was a great *paragrapher*—he wasn't really a picture writer. I read *his* script of the film—the long one called *American*—before Orson really got to changing it and making his version of it—and I thought it was pretty dull."

Orson had lengthy telephone consultations with his attorney, Arnold Weissberger, about whether a legal suit could be instigated against Pauline Kael, Little, Brown, Bantam Books, and *The Citizen Kane Book* for libel (written defamation of character). "Wasn't she calling me a liar?" Welles asked. "Wasn't she saying that I lied about the credit on the work? Wasn't she saying, in fact, that I didn't create *Citizen Kane?*"

Weissberger studied the book and the law and concluded that because Orson was a public figure, and because there probably could not be *proof* of any malice on Kael's part, and because her ideas were theories and *matters of opinion,* a libel suit would not hold up in court. But Weissberger offered additional advice. He pointed out that even if a successful lawsuit could somehow be constructed, the ensuing publicity that would invariably arise from such a case would perhaps leave permanent doubts in many people's minds. There was another problem, too, that weakened Orson's potential suit. In order to publish the book with the *Citizen Kane* script in it, Bantam Books had had to secure Orson's permission and agree to pay him a percentage of the royalties. It would have been difficult to sue the publisher of a book from whom one was receiving money. As Orson's very good friend, as well as his attorney, Weissberger suggested that Orson try to forget about the slur.

But to Orson, the book was more than just an insult to his integrity, it was a brutal attack upon his stature as an artist. He believed Kael was taking away one of the most important parts of his life—his reputation as the creator of *Citizen Kane,* perhaps the greatest motion picture ever produced.

In his more composed moments, Orson chided the book not so much for its ostensible fire but more for leaking out a "greasy smoke." He hoped that the public would find it unreadable. As it turned out, much to his sorrow, the book sold extremely well and has been reprinted many times over for the past fifteen years.

In 1970, even before *The Citizen Kane Book* was released, the University of California Press published Charles Higham's *The Films of Orson Welles,* in which Higham contended that *all* the problems Orson had in Hollywood with *It's All True, The Magnificent Ambersons,* and *Touch of Evil* were because of an unconscious wish to avoid the agony of editing. He chided Welles for forgetting his audience and described the only time he had ever seen Welles on stage, when he "sensed the face of a man at once anguished by all that had been lost and afraid that beyond the gargantuan meals and wine-bibbing, the anecdotes and the backslapping, the raucous laughter and the assembly of famous friends, there would only be silence and loneliness and invalid rugs: the cold truth of dissolution."

Orson was furious at Higham's description, and from that point on, his confidants knew better than to ever mention the name of Charles Higham in his presence. Of course, Orson was partially to blame for his own failures, but Higham's brutal criticisms added to Orson's overall resentment of his treatment by the press and by critics and scholars. It is possible that after this initial souring, he was even more sensitive toward the Kael essay. Bogdanovich once again came to Orson's aid by writing an article about Higham's "destructive misrepresentation." Entitled "Is It True What They Say About Orson?" and published in *The New York Times*, Bogdanovich's discourse stirred up an exchange of letters between himself and Higham that were also published.

Two more books about Welles published at that time were more kindly disposed toward the man. One, also called *Orson Welles,* was a tiny volume written in French by his friend Maurice Bessy; the other, *A Ribbon of Dreams,* was a study of Welles by a former Cambridge professor, Peter Cowie.

Bessy's book was translated into English and released in the United States by Crown Publishers. He presented an essay that analyzes the films and philosophy of Orson Welles through interview fragments, sections of Welles's own writings, and even extracts from yet-to-be-produced scripts, such as *Salome.* Although the small book delighted Welles, it received virtually no critical attention, poor distribution, and hardly any sales.

Cowie's book, published by A. S. Barnes and Co., was larger, profusely illustrated, and contained almost forty pages of appendices of highly valuable reference material for all of Welles's work in film, television, theater, and radio, and the most extensive bibliography about Welles and his work that had ever been published. "Ambition, jealousy, egotism and retributions," Cowie wrote, "are the recurring tokens of his universe. Like the Elizabethan stage that he adores so much, his own screen is filled to abundance with a rich selection of characters, clowns mingling with kings and villains with innocent men." Welles was said to have beamed when he finished reading the book.

Charles Champlin, film critic of the *Los Angeles Times,* met with Welles for lunch at a restaurant in Century City shortly after the Kael brouhaha, and conducted a feisty interview. Welles showed up at the restaurant with a box of cigars under his arm, and during the course of the afternoon, he smoked his way through a large portion of the contents. Orson was less interested in discussing Kael's or Higham's brickbats than he was in trying to find backers for *The Other Side of the Wind,* as well as talking about his idea of making a sequel to *The Magnificent Ambersons,* to be set twenty years later, with Agnes Moorehead, Joseph Cotten, and Tim Holt recreating their original characters.*

He told Champlin that he believed that the balance of the evidence, if one did a total appraisal, was against his working in Hollywood, not for it. Had he stayed in Los Angeles and not moved to Europe, he said, attempting to work within the system, he probably would not have made all bad movies. "But of course," he said with a glint in his eye, as if he could see his triumphs aborning, "one doesn't know."

FOR YEARS, THROUGHOUT the 1970s, Welles jockeyed back and forth between his home in Sidona (via Phoenix) and Los Angeles, in a scene that was right out of *The Captain's Paradise*: two cities, each with a different woman, each to suit a different part of his personality. Sidona represented home, where Orson could work and think and literally breathe; there he had his wife, Paola, and Beatrice, the youngest of his three daughters and the one with whom he had the closest relationship. In Sidona he rarely discussed the particulars of his business. He operated as an extremely private citizen; as husband, father, son-in-law, and one of the gentlefolk of Arizona.

Los Angeles meant Oja Kodar (who had followed him to the United States), and was where Orson wrote, gave interviews, looked for money, voiced commercials, had long, elaborate business lunches, collaborated with Oja on everything, and attempted to advance his career in any way he could.

Orson had been able to balance these two parts of his personal life for a number of years, keeping both women happy, even though each knew about the other. Both loved him deeply, and he loved each of them. "My mother and father were true friends," Beatrice has recalled fondly. Paola often said, certainly in the early years, that she and Orson had a sophisticated marriage. "If we meet, it is at weekends."

Although Orson did feel love for his two elder daughters, Christopher and Rebecca, neither of them had grown up with him. After his first two marriages ended, he spent little more than holidays with either girl. Sadly, Rebecca wrote to me in the late 1970s from the state of Washington, to see if I could supply her with certain information about her parents, Orson Welles and Rita Hayworth; it seemed to me at that time that she knew little about her father. And after becoming friends with Christopher, a poet and writer of educational materials who lives in New York, I found that although she had a deep love for her father, there were major gaps in the information that she had about him. "You probably *do* know more about my father than I do," she told me.

Orson had provided for his daughters financially—both divorces cost him heavy alimony and child support payments. But Beatrice, his child by Paola

*Tim Holt died in 1973 and Agnes Moorehead died the following year, denying Welles the opportunity to direct the sequel.

Mori, had been with him since birth. With her he truly acted as a father. As nature would have it, Beatrice inherited the beauty of her namesake, Orson's mother, as well as some of the handsomeness that had been Orson's in his youth. She also had Paola's beautiful eyes. Statuesque, and with the female equivalent of her father's powerful voice, Beatrice was an excellent student, did some modeling, and when she worked for the local Sidona radio station, Orson prompted and encouraged her. Eventually she managed a restaurant in Phoenix.

ORSON GREATLY VALUED the exposure that television gave him. He especially enjoyed appearing on the widely syndicated talk shows. There were no rehearsals, they usually were taped in the late afternoons or early evenings—a favored time for working for him—and he was paid to do exactly what he liked doing anyway: talk.

He often would appear dramatically dressed completely in black, his shirt open at the neck or with a wide frock tie, carrying a cane and wielding a huge rapier-like cigar, and could be counted on usually to contribute a lively conversation: trading quips with Gloria Steinem (*"vive la différence!"*); telling Merv Griffin that he thought television was building jealousy in our society; occasionally talking about *The War of the Worlds* or *Citizen Kane,* but valiantly attempting to avoid details about his professional past.

An integral part of Orson's talking act on television was his sheer physical bulk. The sight of his three-hundred-and-excess pounds waddling out on stage (not without a certain grace sometimes characteristic of people who are excessively overweight) became as much a part of his performance as what he had to say. Orson long knew that since his clothes no longer fit, it was *he* who needed the alterations. He once pointed out that although he thought that all vices were bad, gluttony was the worst because it could not be kept secret: it showed. And then in a reverse rationalization, he told Kenneth Tynan: "But I feel that gluttony must be a good deal less deadly than some of the other sins. Because it's affirmative, isn't it? At least it celebrates some of the good things in life. Gluttony may be a sin, but an awful lot of fun goes into committing it." Fat jokes about Orson Welles on television became almost commonplace:

> Orson Welles's recipe for how to make a casserole:
> "First you kill a herd of animals. . . ."

> "Have you heard that Orson Welles overdosed on Twinkies?"

> Question: "Name three things that President Carter can't carry."
> Answer: "Connecticut, New York, and Orson Welles."

If he was less than enthusiastic about the ribbing, he received it with good nature and occasionally expounded: "I was born to be fat but people shouldn't *be* fat."

Perhaps the best rationale, however, for his enormous weight was offered by Orson in a line from his radio play *His Honor, the Mayor,* broadcast over forty years ago: "Take my word for it, when responsibilities get to be almost unendurable, a man on a diet takes to his sugars and starches as an addict retreats to his opium pipe, or a drunkard to his bottle."

As the public became more and more familiar with Orson through his appearances on television talk shows, advertisers believed that he might prove to be an excellent image in promoting their products. He was a man of the world, outspoken, somewhat controversial, and he had the ability to sound almost religiously honest when he wanted to.

Actually, Orson had been doing endorsements for European television commercials for almost two decades before American advertising agencies discovered him. He was the voice for a highly successful Shredded Wheat commercial that ran for years in England; he related the virtues of Texaco as *the* petrol for Britishers to use; and when Pedro Domecq Sherry began its assault on Harvey's Bristol Cream, a great part of their annual $2 million promotion budget was spent on producing commercials with Orson as their chief spokesman. Their business increased so markedly that they flew Orson to London (in *two* first-class seats with the armrest removed to accommodate his bulk) from wherever he was in the world, whenever they wanted to do a new series of thirty-second and sixty-second commercials.

When criticized about lowering his standards or demeaning his talent by doing commercials, Orson was indignantly outspoken. "I'd rather do an honest commercial than act in a dishonest film," he countered. The pay was reasonable, residual royalties came often, and although he probably would have preferred to be directing, his commercial work helped pay his standard expenses. Sometimes even this relatively simple work went awry, however. Once, while doing a voice-over for a variety of products in a London agency, Orson became more and more irritated over the copy and the direction he was receiving. A pirated tape of that session quickly circulated around the world. I first heard it in an engineering booth in Toronto, just moments before I went on national television. Orson began to grow testy when *two* directors gave him instructions on how to read a line. He complained that he directed actors less in Shakespearean productions than they were doing with him. When more corrections and requests for additional takes were made, Orson finally blew up. "You're such pests!" he fumed. Eventually, he tossed the script into the air and as the pages fluttered to the floor, he walked out. "No money is worth going through all this," he complained.

Continuing through the 1970s and into the 1980s, Orson attached himself to a variety of endorsements and commercials in this country: Vivitar Cameras, Jim Beam Bourbon, a local Los Angeles big and tall man clothing store. However, it was with a commercial for Paul Masson Wines, which inundated the nation, that he probably became most closely identified in the public's mind.

Touting a Cabernet Sauvignon, for example, Orson, seated at a restaurant table, would talk of the maturity and complexity of the vintage and then, with what many people felt was unmitigated ham, would deliver the following cryptic line: "Paul Masson will sell no wine before its time."

Within a short while Orson's message began jokingly to be applied to other subjects in the vernacular. Libya, it was said, will sell no oil before its time, to the United States. Steinbrenner, it was reported, will sell or trade no Reggie Jackson before his time. Perhaps it was the editorial cartoons that appeared around the country showing Orson, dressed as an Arab sheik, refusing to sell one thing or other "before its time" that began to annoy Welles. Late in 1981, over a dispute about the copy he was to read for another Masson commercial, he was fired. The wine company was also starting a campaign to sell its white, light wines and felt that Orson's image was exactly the opposite of what it wanted for a diet-conscious nation. (The company eventually hired the lean-as-a-rake John Gielgud to sell its products.)

His income tax problems haunted him still. In early 1973, he was audited again and hit with a tax bill for $30,681, which included fines and interest, from the state of California, based on income he had earned during 1956 and 1957 when he was acting in *Man in the Shadow, The Long Hot Summer, Touch of Evil,* and *Compulsion.* Orson eventually paid out all he owed to the state over an extended schedule.

IN THE MID-1970s, Orson regretfully decided to leave Sidona. A flood there had nearly wrecked the Welles home, and even if that misfortune had not occurred, Orson was finding the trip to Phoenix, the first lap of his flight to Los Angeles, to be too laborious. By then he also acknowledged the difficulties other people—producers, journalists, financiers—had in trying to get to him in Sidona. It was Merv Griffin who suggested to Orson that he move to Las Vegas, where Griffin produced his nightly show. Air transportation in and out of the city was much more facile and, should Merv Griffin want him to guest-host his talk show in an emergency, Orson could be at the studio within minutes.

Orson bought a charming, Oriental-style house in Las Vegas. Though not a mansion, it was very comfortable, with five bedrooms, four bathrooms, a spacious lawn, and a large swimming pool, and it was located in a prestigious community that was gated, guarded, and secluded. So understated and unpublic was his life in Las Vegas that in all the years that he lived there, most of his neighbors had no idea that the great Orson Welles and his wife lived across the street. The only incident that marred this privacy was when his neighbor, singer Jerry Vale, in an attempt to sell his own home, placed an ad in a local newspaper, promising, "Have Orson Welles as your next door neighbor." Orson was furious.

Merv Griffin was true to his word: Orson was a constant guest or guest-host on the show, and he seemed to truly enjoy his appearances, spelling out his adventures in Europe, spinning arcane tales, criticizing or commenting on the films of the day, talking politics.

Perhaps as a result of his television exposure, in 1975 Orson received an offer of acclamation that he could not refuse: the Life Achievement Award of the American Film Institute. Only two others had been so honored by the AFI in previous years: John Ford and James Cagney. The fact that Orson had been chosen to be given the third annual award, above many other actors and directors in the Hollywood pantheon, touched and inspired him. With Paola and Beatrice, he appeared at a celebrity-studded dinner of 1,200 people at the Century Plaza Hotel in Los Angeles. The stage was decorated with huge blowups of Orson as he appeared in some of his more interesting screen identities: the feisty and young Charles Foster Kane; the bloated and evil cop, Hank Quinlan, from *Touch of Evil*; the tubby Falstaff of *Chimes at Midnight*; and the virile Michael O'Hara of *Lady from Shanghai*. The orchestra played *The Third Man* theme when Orson entered, obviously unaware that he had grown bored and annoyed with the tune because no matter what the occasion, it had become a clichéd way to introduce him.

Thirty minutes of clips from some of Welles's films were shown and disciple Peter Bogdanovich contributed a running commentary. Then Orson was witness to an evening of tribute. Joseph Cotten, Natalie Wood, and Ingrid Bergman all told of how Orson either had influenced them personally or had influenced Hollywood itself. Though such ceremonies tend to be filled with generalized statements of praise, many of that night's speakers went out of their way to personalize their tributes to Orson. Here, in part, are some of their remarks:

Robert Wise: "I do know, as one who worked closely with Orson on *Kane*, that there is no doubt in my mind, and I'm sure in most others who worked on the picture, whose film it is. *It is Orson Welles's film.* As the filmmaker, he was the creative and driving force behind every frame and in many frames with his fine portrayal of Charles Foster Kane. Orson Welles's stamp is indelibly on every aspect of that classic film and this should never be forgotten."

Charlton Heston: "His phenomenal talent, unquenchable energies, and unflagging enthusiasm have served him well on both sides of the camera."

François Truffaut: "He is a moralistic director, always showing the angel within the beast, the heart in the monster, the secret of the tyrant. This has led him to invent an acting style revealing the fragility behind power, the sensitivity behind strength. . . . We have become so accustomed over the last thirty-five years to consider Orson Welles's powerful personality that we have simply forgotten that Orson Welles is also a prodigious actor."

Jeanne Moreau: "When he owns the screen he owns us. Flowing sequences, close-ups, words, camera movements; the eye of Orson Welles's camera, looking, staring, gazing, glaring, creates the magic spell that breaks the bad one. We watch. We know we won't be misled."

When Welles was called to the stage, he turned first to kiss Paola on the cheek, smiled at Beatrice, made eye-contact and exchanged a secret word or two with his old friend and colleague Joseph Cotten, and then lumbered to the microphone.

The irony of the moment rested in the fact that Orson was being feted by people in the industry who, for years had refused to work with him, to give him acting roles, or to finance his films; yet they still claimed to have recognized his greatness as a cinematic genius.

Although Orson was at his most charming when he spoke to the assembled leaders of the movie community, there was a hint of bitterness in his acceptance, more sad than sarcastic, more melancholy than cynical. Here was an opportunity, he felt, to humbly ask, hat in hand, without actually asking, for support for his uncompleted *The Other Side of the Wind.*

He believed that perhaps even one of the millions of television viewers, who were watching the proceedings from their homes throughout the country, might also become interested in the project. Reining in his voice, he spoke softly of his feelings:

> My father once told me that the art of receiving a compliment is of all things the sign of a civilized man. And he died soon afterwards leaving my education in this important matter sadly incomplete. I'm only glad that on this, the occasion of the rarest compliment he ever could have dreamed of, that he isn't here to see his son so publicly at a loss.
>
> In receiving a compliment—or trying to—the words are all worn out by now. They're polluted by ham and corn and when you try to scratch around for some new ones, it's just an exercise in empty cleverness. What I feel this evening is not very clever. It's the very opposite of emptiness. The corny old phrase is the only one I know to say it.
>
> My heart is full. With a full heart—with all of it—I thank you.
>
> This is Samuel Johnson on the subject of what he calls "Contrarieties."
>
> "There are goods so opposed that we cannot seize both and in trying fail to seize either. Flatter not yourself," he says, "with contrarieties. Of the blessings set before you, make your choice. No man can at the same time fill his cup from the source and from the mouth of the Nile."
>
> Well, this business of contrarieties has to do with us. With you who are paying me this compliment and with me who have strayed so far from this hometown of ours. Not that I'm alone in this or unique. I am never that. But there are a few of us left in this conglomerated world of ours who still trudge stubbornly along the lonely, rocky road and this is, in fact, our contrariety.
>
> We don't move nearly as fast as our cousins on the freeway. We don't even get as much accomplished, just as the family-sized farm can't possibly raise as many crops or get as much profit as the agricultural factory of today.
>
> What we do come up with has no special right to call itself better. It's just different. No, if there's any excuse for us at all it's that we're simply following the old American tradition of the maverick. And we are a vanishing breed. This honor I can only accept in the name of all the mavericks. And also as a tribute to the generosity of all the rest of you—to the givers—to the ones with fixed addresses.
>
> A maverick may go his own way but he doesn't think that it's the only way or ever claim that it's the best one—except maybe for himself. And don't imagine this raggle-taggle gypsy is claiming to be free. It's just that some of the necessities to which I am a slave are different from yours.
>
> As a director, for instance, I pay myself out of my acting jobs. I use my own work to subsidize my work. In other words, I'm crazy. But not crazy enough to

pretend to be free. But it's a fact that many of the films you've seen tonight could never have been made otherwise. Or if otherwise—well, they might have been better. But certainly they wouldn't have been mine. The truth is I don't believe that this great evening would ever have brightened my life if it weren't for this—my own particular contrariety.

Let us—let us raise our cups then standing, as some of us do, on opposite ends of the river and drink together to what really matters to us all—to our crazy and beloved profession. To the movies—to good movies—to every possible kind.

I leave you now in default of the eloquence this high occasion deserves with another very short scene from the same film—a piece of which you saw earlier with John Huston and Peter Bogdanovich—just by way of saying good night from one who will remember tonight—not as a sort of gala visit but as a very happy homecoming. And who remains not only your obedient servant, but also in this age of supermarkets, your friendly neighborhood grocery store. Good night. Thank you.

The evening was not all fete or nostalgia. Tom Nolan, a journalist for the *Village Voice,* who was covering the event, reported that one misanthrope said to him: "I mean, what has he done for Hollywood? I thought the purpose of this award was to honor people who had made contributions to their industry. Except for one great film 30 years ago, what has Welles contributed? There are so many others who are so much more deserving . . . Frank Capra . . . Bette Davis would have been marvelous."

And the magazine *Millimeter* ran an editorial which angrily asked film-goers and producers to forget Welles as an *enfant terrible,* and think of him as simply America's greatest and most complete film artist. The editorial went on to say: "What do the honors of the AFI and praise from *cinéastes* like Frank Sinatra, Dennis Weaver, Edgar Bergen and George Stevens exactly mean when that very same week a genius has to beg for the right to complete his work? We wish simply that all those capable of smiling graciously into the camera to deliver some more or less relevant homily would rather retire to the seclusion of their gold-plated studios and write a check and send it to Orson Welles so that Welles can get to what really matters, and what alone concerns him: Doing his films."

Orson was somewhat felicitous about receiving his AFI award. Local Los Angeles television stations had begun to dust off some of the old Welles vehicles—*The Magnificent Ambersons* and *Lady from Shanghai,* for example, in the days preceding the ceremony, and on the day that one station aired *Citizen Kane,* the Hearst-owned *Los Angeles Herald-Examiner* broke its thirty-four-year-old rebuff of ever mentioning either the movie or Welles's name, and actually reviewed the film on its movie page. Then, on the day after the AFI event, on page two, the *Herald-Examiner* ran a two-column story by Roy Loynds, headlined: "Hollywood Tribute to Orson Welles." Loynds wrote: "Welles's greatest film contribution is *Citizen Kane* (1941), which stunned the film world with its memorable cinematic control and invention, and did for post-World War II cinema what D. W. Griffith's *The Birth of a Nation* had done for cinema before the 40s."

Orson was surprised and somewhat pleased at what he thought was a relaxation of the vindictiveness that the Hearst corporation had displayed toward him for so many decades. Even though William Randolph Hearst had died in 1951, Orson had still been *persona non grata* in all Hearst publications. However, this surcease was extremely short-lived. The ghost of Hearst walked again almost immediately after the paper's first printing, and by order of the managing editor, the article was entirely deleted in later editions. Roy Loynds's wrists were slapped for "extreme editorializing," and the clanking of the Hearstian chains were still. Orson quoted Shakespeare in describing his stoical reaction as "like Patience on a monument smiling at grief."

Nonetheless, the award and its concomitant publicity were having some positive effects on casting directors, if not on newspaper editors. Orson continued doing commercials, sought acting work, and found himself appraising offers and scripts. Throughout all of it, though, he continued to search for money to launch his directorial efforts.

He was offered the starring role in *Caligula,* but when he read the Gore Vidal script and found it to be a mixture of hard-core pornography and violence, he peremptorily turned it down on moral grounds, despite a reported offer of a salary of more than $1 million. It would have been the largest amount of money he had ever received for acting in a motion picture.

Peter Bogdanovich did not cast Orson as Sam the Lion in *The Last Picture Show,* despite the fact that his friend desperately wanted the role and was the one who suggested to Bogdanovich that he shoot the film in black-and-white to sustain a look of the past. "I didn't want a movie star in the role," Bogdanovich explained and cast Ben Johnson, a character actor used in many of John Ford's films. McBride has revealed that all Orson could do was laugh when he heard of Bogdanovich's decision. He wasn't bitter, though; in fact, it was Orson who suggested to Bogdanovich that he use a particular makeup solvent to tint Johnson's hair gray. (Johnson later won an Academy Award as Best Supporting Actor for his performance in the film.)

Orson turned down respectable roles in *The Serpent's Egg, Murder by Death, Innocent Bystander,* and *Nickelodeon* because he was trying to complete *The Other Side of the Wind.* He also refused literally dozens of other roles in lesser films that he felt would add nothing to his career. Since his income had continued to rise from all of his television and radio commercials, he could be somewhat more selective as to what he would and would not do for money. He kept hoping for a starring role, with all that that would imply, but the offers never materialized. Occasionally, just wanting to feel the connection with film, the glare of the key light, the whirr of the camera, he yielded and took a role that was beneath him. Talking of those less-than-profound films that he sometimes narrated or appeared in at that time, often in cameo roles, he said: "They hire me when they have a bad film and they want a little class. I chip off a little of myself each time."

As a result of his connections with Yugoslavian filmmaking, he landed a respectable role as J. P. Morgan, with Oja Kodar as Catherine Johnson, in an unimpressive film, *The Secret of Nikola Tesla,* which was released in 1980.

There seemed to be no specific pattern as to how much time Orson spent in Las Vegas with his family, as opposed to the time he spent with Oja Kodar in Los Angeles. He flew to Los Angeles when the work called for it, such as a guest host spot for the *Tonight* show, or when he thought that a genuine backer might be convinced to invest in one of his projects. And he flew back to Las Vegas when he wanted to rest up from these demands.

In order to make ends meet, Orson made a closed-circuit television tape for Caesar's Palace (available for guests twenty-four hours a day) that explained the intricacies of dice, baccarat, roulette, and blackjack. It is not known whether he wrote any of the Olympian narrative:

> The biggest dice game in history was for some very high stakes indeed. Zeus, Poseidon, and Hades rolled for the universe. Poseidon won the oceans, Hades the underworld, and Zeus the heavens. It is thought that Zeus owned the dice.

Often Orson also popped up as moderator of various television specials. He was host of *Highlights of the Russian Dance Festival,* for example, or *Tut, the Boy King.*

BY THE LATE 1970s, Welles began lunching regularly at Ma Maison, a small but pricey French restaurant with an outside patio and an unlisted telephone number. From the moment it opened, on Melrose Avenue in Los Angeles, it attracted a trendy Hollywood clientele, with an occasional tourist or two who went there primarily to gape at the famous faces. Eventually Orson was given his own table, near the *maitre d's* station, where he sat almost daily with his vicious French poodle, Kiki. Ma Maison was one of the few good restaurants in Los Angeles that would allow Orson to dine with his dog. Invariably Kiki would sit next to him, her nose resting on his great thigh for the duration of the meal. It was at Ma Maison that Orson began the years of performing what he would describe as his Dancing Bear act. It went something like this: a young producer or director, sometimes an actor, who wanted to "work with Welles," would contact him, by telephone or mail, with the astounding news that a possible financial backer had been found for one of Orson's projects. Often, it was explained to Orson, this backer had not been connected with Hollywood before, but he was a "legitimate businessman" from Boston or Beirut or Atlanta, who was simply interested in becoming involved in speculative projects that could make money. After a few preliminary questions as to authenticity, Orson would arrange a lunch at Ma Maison and said backer would be mailed one of Orson's potential scripts.

Orson always arrived early for these business lunches and attempted to be as effervescent as possible. Often, what resulted was not so much a business meeting as an Orson Welles performance. Orson's lunchtime repertoire consisted of stories of his exploits in films and filming; of his days with RKO and *Citizen Kane,* of his experiences in South America or Paris, London, or

New York, of Hollywood gossip and political pronouncements, and even an occasional recitation from *Lear* or *Macbeth,* altogether an engaging interlude calculated to impress, overwhelm, and seduce his companions of the hour into recognizing that they *must,* above all, invest in his project at hand. He acted respectfully toward his guests, often saying "Yes, sir," or "No, sir," to clearly delineate a certain subservience on his part. Occasionally he would lapse into Spanish, graciously translating his words, if necessary, for his table guests.

Often, these recollections were command performances, and Orson acted on cue. If the potential backer happened to mention that he had heard *The War of the Worlds* when he was a child, for example, Orson would insist on telling a perhaps heretofore unknown anecdote or two about the infamous event.

When the discussion got down to money, usually only when Orson broached it, he would invariably try to assure the financier that, unlike many of today's Hollywood directors, he had never gone over budget on any of his films. As semiotician, Orson tried to "read" his listener, altering his presentation or commentary according to the signs the person was projecting. If he sensed that the listener needed further assurances about his dependability, Orson would trot out a story such as his finishing *The Stranger* under budget and within schedule. If he thought that his new companion was more interested in becoming attached to the social Orson, he would emerge with tales of parties and stars, of the on-the-set adventures and off-the-set revels of Chaplin, Dietrich, Olivier. The result seemed always to be successful. At the conclusion of the meal, the potential backer would often smile, nod his head, and indicate that, *yes,* money would be forthcoming; and that *yes,* he would produce *The Other Side of the Wind* or whatever film Orson was in the process of promoting, and *yes,* he would be back to Orson within a week with a final and formal commitment.

Invariably, though, the week stretched on, the waiting would continue, the response and the money would never come. It became obvious that most of these backers really wanted only to bask in Orson's presence so that they would be able to say that they had lunched with or met the great man. Orson sensed this, yet as he was still forced to try to secure his necessary monies, he felt he had to continue with the process. He knew no other way of doing it. "If you only knew how many 'next weeks' there were in the past fifteen years," Orson once sighed to his friend Henry Jaglom.

When he wasn't trying to impress or secure a financier, Orson often lunched at Ma Maison anyway. Sometimes he was alone, for unlike many people he was comfortable eating by himself. At other times he dined with such friends as Jaglom or Peter Bogdanovich, or with a magazine writer doing a profile, or, later, with Barbara Leaming, who became his official biographer.

Patrick Terrail, the owner of Ma Maison, became a deep admirer and friend of Orson's, and Orson reciprocated by showing loyalty to Terrail and the restaurant. Once, when a building had been razed across the street from Ma Maison, the restaurant suffered from a brief infestation of rats. One of the rodents made its way into the dining room and jumped onto the chair at the table next to Orson's. A few of the customers sitting nearby became under-standably disconcerted, pointing at the rat and calling for the waiter to do something. Orson continued to sit quietly, then finally, with great aplomb and kindness, as Terrail later recollected, he said loud enough for the disturbed patrons to hear, "This would not be a true French restaurant, ladies and gentlemen, *unless* there was a rat here."

Perhaps Orson instinctively knew that virtually all of his Dancing Bear lunches would lead to nil and therefore felt that the investment of his time should be limited. Before the lunch began, usually at 12:30, Orson would privately make arrangements to have the check brought no later than 2:00 P.M. "Should I be bored," he told Terrail, "I can then always leave." If the afternoon seemed to be promising, however, Orson would stay at the table, sometimes for more than three hours, and he and his party would be the last to leave, stepping out into the late afternoon Los Angeles sunshine, and down the green Astro-turf carpeting toward his car. After the lunch, Orson sometimes stopped off at a secondhand bookstore on Pico Boulevard or went elsewhere in Los Angeles to do some serious browsing, searching for reading material for pleasure and continuing to look for books and stories that might suggest films, or others that might prove to be worthy of direct adaptation. Occasionally he went to an afternoon movie, but stayed only for a few minutes, leaving if the film was bad—or if it promised to be good, noting it for future reference and another longer visit.

In the spring of 1979, I was in Hollywood doing some writing on the thirteen-part radio adaptation of *Star Wars,* and I suggested to the producers that Orson be approached as narrator for the series. Everyone connected with the show greeted the idea with enthusiasm—especially Mark Hamill, who was recreating his role of Luke Skywalker—but Orson was in Paris just then, trying to straighten out financial problems with *The Other Side of the Wind,* and could not return in time to make the scheduled production dates.

It was then that his friend, director Henry Jaglom, was attempting to help Orson to try to raise money to back a film version of *The Dreamers,* an adaptation of two stories by Isak Dinesen from her first major book, the 1934 *Seven Gothic Tales.* Jaglom thought it would be a fairly simple proposition to raise money for production (perhaps only a few million dollars) but was shocked when he discovered that all the Dancing Bear lunches, the registered letters of request, and the long-distance phone calls of inquiry led to nothing.

The other potential backers that Jaglom met with either were critical of the fact that Welles had never produced a financial blockbuster or thought that the screenplay lacked commercial potential. Northstar Productions, under the helm of Hal Ashby (the director of the Academy Award winning *Coming Home* and other great films) did offer some seed money, just so that Orson could complete the script (at first called *Da Capo*), but Northstar decided not to exercise its option to produce the film after they read the script.

Orson had cowritten the screenplay with Oja Kodar, and it had the elements of a haunting, poetic film: a storyteller's story told in hazily delin-eated scenes, filled with psychological and romantic excursions into inner fantasies. The story is about an opera singer in the nineteenth century named Pellegrina Leoni (to be played by Oja Kodar) who is blessed with a remarkably clear, bell-like voice and is known as the greatest singer in the world. Her voice is the basis of her life, and when she loses it she abruptly leaves home to seek new experiences, to live different lives. She has many adventures; in one, she finds a young boy in a remote mountain village whose voice is uncannily similar to the golden soprano tones that she once had. Ultimately, she is denounced as a witch.

Welles shot a small segment of *The Dreamers* at his Los Angeles home on Stanley Avenue, thinking that this scene might even be of use in helping to raise some financial interest. In the scene, Pellegrina says good-bye to her oldest and closest friend, Marcus (played by Welles), and tells him that she is about to leave immediately.

"Is it true, then?" Marcus asks.

"Yes," Pellegrina replies.

"Alone like this and in the dead of night?"

He calls her his "little lioness" and offers money and continued friendship, wherever she is, whenever she needs it.

Film historian Jonathan Rosenblum saw the brief segment and described it in an article in *Sight and Sound*:

> Admittedly, the scene is no more than an unfinished fragment: Welles never got round to shooting his own close-ups (in the part of Marcus Kleek, the elderly Dutch Jewish merchant who is Pellegrina's only friend), and the dialogue—a lonely duet of two melodious accented voices, accompanied by the whir of crickets and even the faint hum of passing traffic—is recorded in direct sound. But the delicate lighting, lyrical camera movement and rich deployments of blue, black and yellow, combined with the lilt of the two voices, create an astonishing glimpse into the overripe dream world that Welles envisioned for the film.

Rosenbaum's description captures the flavor of this simple but elegant fragment from Welles's in-progress adaptation of the Isaak Dinesen story. Kodar recently screened this footage at a New York University-sponsored conference on Welles, and confirmed that it was shot at night in the backyard of Welles's home. The sound of crickets is intended not only to heighten atmosphere, but also to mask the sound of nearby Los Angeles traffic.

True, it is impossible to judge an entire film, especially an unfinished one, on the basis of a short segment, but in this scene Welles attained a subdued, pastoral quality that one can imagine would pervade the entire work. The dialogue is soft, somber, with the camera, and our attention, focused on Kodar. The camera angles and movements are straightforward, in keeping with the hushed quality of the drama. We do not see Welles's face, but view much of the conversation from directly behind him, almost looking over his shoulder. He remains, however, a magisterial presence and voice.

Welles budgeted the film at $6,000,000. No backing could be found, even though he insisted that it would be his most important film.

Jaglom then convinced, almost coerced, Orson into writing an original screenplay, *The Big Brass Ring,* cajoling him, page by page, scene by scene, to deliver the script. The idea was for Orson to write something that was eminently commercial and to have it produced (to ostensibly make money), thereby enabling him to make the films he really wanted to make—such as *The Dreamers.* At first Orson seemed to lack confidence in producing a totally original screenplay, one not based on an adaptation. That was the method with which he was the most familiar. Most of his screenplays, including *Ambersons, Touch of Evil, The Trial,* and his three Shakespeare films had been derived from another source. The exception, of course, was *Citizen Kane.*

Each time Orson had a few more pages he would give them to Jaglom, who would then comment on them and have them neatly typed. As Jaglom waxed enthusiastic over each page, every line, all the scenes, Orson's confidence grew. After about eight months, a poignant screenplay was completed.

The story, which was to be shot in black-and-white, had a homosexual theme in which a Texas senator, Blake Pellarin, who has just lost a presidential election, goes on a sailing trip with his wife. Eventually, the politician temporarily leaves his wife to have a rendezvous with his former Harvard professor, mentor, and lover, Kimball Menaker, who was to be played by Welles. A woman journalist discovers the secret love affair of the two men and helps to destroy Pellarin's political career. Orson began to believe that *The Big Brass Ring* would be the bookend to *Citizen Kane,* a film that looked at the political and social fabric of the last part of this century.

Although the theme of homosexuality was never an enormous box office draw in Hollywood, several people in the film community thought that *The Big Brass Ring* was a brilliant script, and that if a big star could be contracted to play the part of Pellarin, the film could realize both financial and critical success.

Eventually, Arnon Milchan, an Israeli industrialist and producer who was not afraid of working with directors who had commercially difficult projects (he went on to finance Martin Scorsese's *The King of Comedy,* Sergio Leone's *Once Upon a Time in America,* and Terry Gilliam's *Brazil*), agreed to back Orson's new film with an $8 million budget, on the condition that a leading star could be signed for the major role.

Milchan was not among the financiers to whom Orson had to give his Dancing Bear act. "I thought it was a wonderful story," the producer has said. "To me, he was just one of the greatest filmmakers. I wanted to work with him." Orson had a party at Ma Maison and ordered several magnums of Cristal champagne to celebrate the occasion of going into business with Milchan.

The producer guaranteed large-scale distribution and decent promotion money. Orson was also promised certain controls that would enable him to create the film he envisioned. And Milchan further promised to bankroll *The Dreamers,* if *The Big Brass Ring* proved profitable.

Jaglom acted as the intermediary in trying to secure a star. He first went to

Jack Nicholson, who said he had always wanted to be directed by Welles ever since he acted with Orson in Jaglom's *A Safe Place*. The budget called for a $2 million fee for the starring role, a figure that both Welles and Jaglom thought absurd but necessary. It may have been absurd, but it was also an underestimate. Nicholson claimed that he could not possibly work for less than $4 million, his going fee, lest people in the industry think he had reduced his price.

Jaglom also approached several other actors, including Warren Beatty, Clint Eastwood, Robert Redford, and Burt Reynolds, to see if they were available to star in the film. Although Jaglom will not reveal who said what, he did provide a chronicle of their extraordinary reactions and requests upon being offered the role. One of the actors contacted turned down the role because he thought that the homosexual context of the story and the character might tarnish his image. Another said that he didn't really understand the story but would take the part if he were made producer of the film, given the right to rewrite his role, and given the right of final cut approval. "That's preposterous!" boomed Orson when he heard of the demands; nothing further could be negotiated with that thespian.

A third starring actor claimed that after reading the script, it was apparent to him that the role of Pellarin was subordinate to Menaker. He would not sign until a complete rewrite was crafted wherein he, not Welles, would be the true star of the film. Naturally, Orson refused.

Yet another of the leading actors, a man with decidedly conservative beliefs, revealed that he had political ambitions, and that the liberal views of Pellarin might be associated with him, thereby damaging his future career in politics.

Finally, an agent for one of the seven stars who were approached wrote back with what may have been the cruelest response: "[The star] is sorry but he's busy for the next four years doing real movies."

Orson was crushed. How could these men, who claimed they had deep respect for him and who had told him personally over the years that they wanted to work with him, turn him down now in his one chance in years to prove that he could make a commercial film.

"They hurt him very badly," said Jaglom, reporting Welles's feelings. "In the fifteen years I knew him, that hurt him more than anything."

Although disheartened and sickened at not being able to realize the production of either *The Big Brass Ring* or *The Dreamers,* to say nothing of some of his other properties that he had put aside because of lack of financing, Orson still plunged himself into work, doing his ubiquitous voice-overs for television commercials and engaging in other journeyman tasks.

He recorded two narratives, to musical accompaniments; neither one proved to be either financially or critically successful. The first was a recording entitled "I Know What It Is to Be Young (But You Don't Know What It Is to Be Old)," with Orson at his most histrionic, voicing, not singing, the lyrics while the Ray Charles Singers and the Nick Perito Orchestra accompanied him musically for all of his five minutes and five seconds. The words and the music were so syrupy, so patently Lawrence Welkian that it is remarkable that Orson even consented to allow his name to be associated with the project at all. The album and cassette contained a large photograph of Orson, dressed in black hat and clothing, with the name "Orson Welles" dropped out in white letters. It is possible that a certain number of Orson Welles fans mistakenly purchased the album thinking that it was a Welles creation. There was even a suggestion that Orson should make his first music video of the recording. He was interested but nothing came of the production.

Although it seemed incongruous to many, a new heavy-metal band called Manowar also attracted Orson when he happened to hear a tape, played by his daughter Beatrice, of their combative rock music. He was surprised and impressed with Manowar's deep clashing and slashing sounds and approached them about doing the narrative of one of their singles. "Dark Avenger" is a song about a Viking warrior who returns to his land bent on revenge, a tale of brutality and violence with resonances of the heroism of the ancient Norse sagas. Orson spent an afternoon in a Los Angeles sound studio with the four long-haired members of Manowar and produced a stirring and booming narration of the tale for their album *Battle Hymns*. His name, however, appears in nearly microscopic print on the cover.

Beatrice had more than just an accidental influence on Orson's musical tastes. She had always been interested in music, and when the Welleses lived in Europe, she toured with groups as diverse as the Rolling Stones and the Osmonds and wrote reviews and feature articles for the London *Times*. Sometimes the albums that she played or the music that she listened to on the radio would pique Orson's curiosity. He would sit, listen, and try to be convinced. When he was, and sometimes when he wasn't, he and Beatrice would discuss the particular piece. Although Welles had learned to love classical music from his pianist mother, he grew to accept and enjoy certain hard and soft rock music more than many adults of his generation. It was a way of sharing with his daughter.

Although Beatrice felt that Orson was a real father to her, she found it difficult to relate to his status as a famous personality. Most of the time Orson acted as other fathers might, discussing such routine family business as the purchase of a new car, weekly household chores, personal goals and problems, or the menu for the evening's dinner. On occasion, however, she would be sharply reminded about who Orson was to the general public. Once, while walking with him through the lobby of the MGM Grand Hotel, a tourist pointed at Beatrice's father and blurted excitedly: "Look, that's Orson Welles!" A crowd quickly gathered around the pair and people began to touch Orson, to shake his hand, and to talk about him almost as if he weren't an actual person—as if he were just a statue or a hologram of the real Orson Welles. "I wanted to tell them to stop that," Beatrice said later. "I wanted to say that he's a real person and you just don't rudely point at people as if they weren't there." Although Beatrice had accompanied Orson to all kinds of celebrity events, and she knew her father was a famous film director and a movie star, she felt that that one incident was able, more than anything else, to illustrate the agony she sometimes experienced because of her father's fame.

IN 1979, ORSON traveled to Toronto to star in a light thriller—with comedic touches—called *The Great Madison County Robbery*, based on a true story about a $2 million scam that took place in upstate New York. Welles played the "good" Sheriff Paisley, complete with badged Stetson and aviator glasses, and with Michael Murphy as his deputy assistant, Jason. The film went through title changes, *Never Trust an Honest Thief, Going for Broke,* and finally *Hot Money,* and bounced around from distributor to distributor but never was released. Orson said he was attracted to the role because only a small portion was shot in Canada and most of the film was shot on Nevada locations that were only minutes from his house in Las Vegas. There was also a personal thematic or philosophical rationale: In the film, as Welles stated it, "The villains are the tax-gatherers." One of the film's screenwriters told me: "It was made so poorly that I walked out of the screening of my own film after twenty minutes." Orson rarely ever mentioned that he had made the film, embarrassed as he was not so much of his performance but of the material and how it was handled creatively.

In the spring of 1979, Orson came to a noncontractual agreement to write the screenplay of a film called *Ice People,* to be produced by the co-producer of *Superman,* Pierre Spengler. Perhaps because of the savage reactions to Robert Altman's arctic drama *Quintet,* no money was forthcoming for *Ice People,* and Orson was once again without a firm project.

That disappointment was followed by an even greater loss. The great film producer Darryl F. Zanuck died a few days before Christmas, at the age of seventy-seven. Orson delivered the eulogy for his old friend and financial backer, describing the late producer as the last of his breed. Then, on a more personal note, Orson continued: "If I were guilty of an unspeakable crime and the police of the world were hunting me and I fled to Zanuck's door, he would have taken me in and not made any speeches about 'the good of the industry.' He would have merely said, 'Get under the bed!'"

ORSON'S NOTORIETY CONTINUED through the early 1980s. At the inauguration of a new national film theater in the Hague, the *Haagsfilmhaus,* a retrospective of his films was chosen to launch the opening. Orson declined an invitation to attend but sent his respects and good wishes. In addition to ten films in which he had acted, all of his directorial efforts were shown, as well as fragments from uncompleted or never-released films. A panel of filmmakers and Welles colleagues, such as Henry Jaglom and Joseph McBride, were on hand after each screening to discuss Orson's contributions to the art of the cinema.

In the fall of 1981, some thirty international film directors, including Bernardo Bertolucci of Italy and Roger Vadim of France, and 350 other guests, honored Orson at a Hollywood Foreign Press Association tribute dinner given at the Beverly Hilton.

Bertolucci, speaking English but seeming somewhat uncomfortable, said, in part: "What I need from a film director is like food—eating movies and I'm starving. I just heard that Orson Welles is preparing a new movie, and this is very good news."*

Henry Jaglom paraphrased Bernstein's much-quoted remark from *Citizen Kane*: "I'll bet there isn't a month that goes by that all of us don't think of Orson."

And when Peter O'Toole dedicated to Welles a reading of Hamlet's speech to the Players, Orson's eyes filled with tears:

> ... for the play, I remember, pleased not the million; 'twas caviare to the general; but it was an excellent play, well digested in the scenes, set down with as much modesty as cunning.

When Orson spoke, he reminded the audience that in a few months he would reach the fifty-year mark in show business and that receiving the tribute that evening "is an occasion for the mortal sin of pride."

Regaling the crowd with humor and personal insights, he was also serious:

> All of us are suffering from an incurable vice, that we can't stay out of the movie theaters, and we ought to. Going to movies too much is a kind of narcissism. It infects you too much with the visual imagination of other directors. Joking aside, if there is going to be another kind of picture making—and there had better be—we had better spend more time looking at life.

IT WAS SHORTLY after the Hollywood tribute that Orson began feeling ill—all the time. His doctor told him that he would have to lose considerable weight. A lifetime habit of excessive eating and drinking had begun to affect major parts of his body. His heart was weak, his liver was in trouble, and his blood pressure was astronomically high.

A strict diet was prescribed. According to the physician, Orson had the choice of militantly following the regimen, or else he would die—quite quickly. Orson chose to live.

But how does a gourmand, a man who would think nothing of starting off a meal with a bottle of Moët et Chandon just for himself, followed by a Boudin Noir aux Pommes (blood sausage with apples), then a bottle of Beaujolais Nouveau to help wash down a Terrine de Canard and a huge porterhouse steak, and finally a Mousse à l'Armagnac, followed by four or five glasses of Calvados, and several cups of very black coffee, stop a lifetime custom of grossly overeating? It was not easy. He said that he felt lonely.

Orson went "cold turkey." His habit of snacking on four or five large portions of caviar every day of his adult life was regretfully abandoned. He gave up a twenty-cups-a-day habit of coffee, cut out all alcohol including his tumblerfuls of 100-proof vodka, and took up Perrier with a twist of lime and

*He was referring to *The Big Brass Ring*.

no ice. He eliminated all the delicious, rich desserts; grapefruit, which he hated, became one of his staples.

All of this abstinence, however, did not prevent Orson from *thinking* about food and drink. It had been his muse for so many years, and he was overjoyed when others had exotic foods brought to the table; he encouraged them to order daring desserts simply so that he could be near the luscious confections, almost as long-lost friends. Often he would demand a detailed description, an inventory of taste, of those white-chocolate mousses, those hot fruit tarts, those icy raspberry sherbets garnished with mint leaves. "Tell me," he would whisper conspiratorially, precisely when his dinner companion had his or her mouth full: "What are you experiencing at this very moment? Describe it to me."

His goal was to lose 125 pounds and he began shedding tens of pounds each week. As he slimmed he joked "thinly," as he liked to say: "I can no longer do a remake of *The Girth of the Nation.*"

And it seemed that his public, too, became involved in his new eating habits. One day he received a fairly bulky package postmarked from Philadelphia but bearing no return address. As Orson lifted the package, he heard a small noise coming from within it. The noise frightened him. Could it be a bomb? Who would send him something from Philadelphia, anyway; he didn't know anyone from Philadelphia. Orson dialed his local precinct of the Los Angeles Police Department, and the bomb squad carried the package off in a padded security van to an open field. There, with long cutting rods, they gingerly opened the package.

Inside, no bomb was found. There were, however, six sirloin steaks packed in dry ice, with a note that said: "From an admirer." The noise that had emanated from the package was caused by the scraping of the pieces of ice as they rubbed against each other. The police politely returned the steaks to Orson, but he elected not to partake—partly because of his diet and partly because of continued fear. "Who knows," he said. "They might be poisoned."

Since he no longer drank alcohol and never became involved in the use of cocaine that was then infecting Hollywood, he considered himself something of a dampener of spirits at any given party. The invitations from film people still came, and at first Orson just sat at these parties like a wet blanket, never joining in. Within a short time after his abstinence started, the invitations dwindled, and he stopped making the regular rounds of Hollywood cocktail frolics and shindigs and—by his own description—took up the life of a hermit.

If he became a recluse, it was more in principle than in fact. The year 1982 marked an active journey for Orson, if not a conclusive destination.

In the first days of January, he appeared on national television as cohost of what NBC described as its First Annual *Magic with the Stars* program, where such television luminaries as Erik Estrada performed the "Table of Death" trick, and Linda Evans and Cindy Williams participated in the "Psycho Illusion," performed by David Copperfield. Orson was an eminent presenter of the feats of legerdemain, but it seemed as though he would have preferred to have been performing the tricks himself rather than just merely talking about them.

He did have an opportunity at that time to become a bit more involved in the actual process of magic, when he acted as a "Magical Consultant" for cameraman Gary Graver's low-budget horror film *Trick or Treats*.

Shortly after that, he was hit with a sizable lawsuit. An agency that placed actors in television and radio commercials and voice-overs had had some success in getting Orson various spots. The agency fee was 10 percent of all income realized by the placement. Orson claimed that all of his fees had been paid to that agency before he had moved on to another organization. The agency counterstated that Orson had earned in excess of $2,500,000 on residual income generated by the commercials that they had originally arranged while Orson was under their wing, and that he owed them in excess of a quarter of a million dollars. Orson disputed the substance and details of the contract, and an out-of-court settlement was finally arranged.

Orson then traveled to New York with Oja Kodar to make a guest appearance as one of the hosts for Alex Cohen's *Night of the 100 Stars* at Radio City Music Hall. It was a money-raising event designed to aid the Actors' Fund retirement home. Stars such as George Burns, Liza Minnelli, Placido Domingo, Grace Kelly, Elizabeth Taylor, Jane Fonda, Paul Newman, and dozens of other celestials participated. Millions of dollars were raised. However, Orson's weight, his general ill health along with a persistent cold that he could not shake, his recent legal troubles, and an interminable wait to go on, all combined to make him irascible.

The long aisles in the theater and the cavernous corridors backstage made it difficult for him to negotiate, and he insisted on either a wheelchair or some other conveyance to propel him about. Someone suggested that he might not be able to fit into a wheelchair and came up with the idea of using a golf cart. With nose running, eyes red, and a continuous hacking cough, Orson sat in the cart during rehearsals, wrapped in a hat, coat, muffler, and blanket. He looked quite ill. When it came time to go over the names he was to introduce—new-wave rock musicians called the Doobie Brothers—he was annoyed. "Who the hell are these people anyway?" he asked from the stage. "I never heard of them."

Despite his anger, the *Night of the 100 Stars* attracted a large rating at its subsequent television airing, and Orson's participation was well received.

He was then directly off to Paris, again with Oja, to accept what he considered to be the greatest and most prestigious award of his career, the French Legion of Honor. Because he wasn't French, a special act of Parliament had to be passed in order to present the award to a foreigner. At a gala affair at the Elysée Palace, the formally garbed Orson was decorated by President François Mitterrand in the Order of the Commander. "You have expressed through film what is deepest in the human soul and reached a universal audience," said Mitterrand as he hung the emblem around Orson's neck and kissed him on both cheeks. In an aside, Mitterrand mentioned that he had seen all of Welles's films and pointed out that one of the first books ever written about Welles was by a Frenchman, André Bazin (in 1950). One of the officials of the *Cinémathèque Française,* who was present, virtually claimed the sixty-seven-year-old Orson as a French citizen: "He is certainly more popular in France than the U.S."

Orson spent time in Paris attending the César Awards, the French Oscars, where he was made president of the event, giving interviews and talking to television, motion picture, and government people about doing a film in France. He informed everyone of wanting to do *King Lear* and indicated that he had new ideas for handling the sometimes-criticized obscurity of plot and the arbitrary motivation of some of the characters. He had felt in the past that *Lear* might be too difficult to film. As far back as 1949, in an interview in the *International Herald Tribune,* he said: "Lear's plot is too hard to clarify. I hope Laurence Olivier does it. Then I can always say that I wanted to, but . . ." Lear's blindness and the terrifying action and force of the play's tragedy, however, were so great as to almost overcome Orson. He felt that somehow he could solve the dramatic obstacles of *Lear.* The French found his remarks riveting.

Ideas were exchanged and although no promises were made, Orson was led to believe that should he construct an acceptable screenplay, launch money, perhaps government-initiated, could be forthcoming. "I have special links with France," quipped Orson in a quote that found its way into *Time* magazine. "I'm one of those Americans who thinks that when I die I'll go to Paris."

Back in the United States, Orson saw two films that he had been involved with released in March. The first was *Butterfly,* a slight effort, based on a James M. Cain novel, with Pia Zadora and Stacy Keach, in which Orson, white-haired and bearded and with steel-rimmed glasses, credibly plays a judge and is the only actor who distinguishes himself in this forgettable movie. Although he gave a few interviews about *Butterfly* at that time, he just wished it would go away. It did.

The other film, *Genocide* had much more depth. Orson and Elizabeth Taylor narrated a ninety-minute documentary that restated, through film clips, interviews, letters, and other materials, the atrocities committed by the Nazis against the Jews. Orson's voice was authoritative, believable, beautifully forthright. The result was a visual and audio document that was powerful, sad, and unforgettable.

Also that month, wearing the same formal clothing that he had in Paris, Orson stood in for Warren Beatty and accepted the latter's Best Director Award, at the Los Angeles Critics' Circle, for his monumental and sprawling film *Reds.* Orson enjoyed the attention he received. This time there was an oversized wheelchair to move him about. It seemed to have become his favorite form of personal transportation.

He also felt somewhat better when it was pointed out to him shortly after that in her review of *Diva* in *The New Yorker,* Pauline Kael had likened the dazzling film to a "romanticized and gift wrapped" version of a Welles production, in effect a 123-minute interpretation of one of Orson's dream films.

In April, this was followed by an especially candid interview with Orson by Merv Griffin during which Griffin asked Orson about his religious beliefs. "I try to be a Christian," Orson answered. He went on: "I don't pray really, because I don't want to bore God."

Then he was contacted by the British Broadcasting Corporation to see if he could come to London for an extended and in-depth interview to be shown just prior to a season of his films that were going to be aired in a retrospective in England. No, he wouldn't go to London, he replied—his health prevented it—but if the BBC wanted to send a small crew to Las Vegas, he would grant the interview.

Producers Alan Yentof and Leslie Megahey flew to Las Vegas, rented a top floor suite at the Riviera Hotel, and proceeded to interview Orson from 9:30 in the morning until dusk. That day Orson was in fine and cooperative fettle. Dressed in a black suit and enormous dotted frock tie, he told the British broadcasters the story of his life in an open and animated manner. Before the interview, they had digested what they described as a mountain of books and biographies, and their questions were knowledgeable, incisive, and sensitive.

Orson related the story of how he thought of running for the Senate, based on Roosevelt's suggestion. "He was very anxious to have me run." Although still only in his late twenties at that time, Welles felt he might be able to carry California because of his celebrity presence, his ability as an orator, and the possible overt backing of F.D.R. It was Alan Cranston who dissuaded him from running, Orson stated. "He told me I couldn't carry southern California, because the Beverly Hills Communist Party was against me—I was a dangerous revisionist, they thought. I only had northern California." Later, Cranston became a senator himself, leading Welles to believe that the former's advice was not all that disinterested.

A study was then made by the Democratic Party to see what Orson's chances would be to run in 1947 in his home state of Wisconsin. The powerful dairy interests in that state supported a Republican candidate, former circuit court judge Joseph McCarthy, and it was believed that the only way that Orson could defeat him was if Orson could develop into one of the great campaigners of all time. Orson decided not to take the challenge, but mused: "Supposing I did become such a great campaigner and I did defeat him? There would not have been a McCarthy era. I have that on my conscience."

The cogent reason that he did not run for the Senate, however, Orson explained, was that he believed that he really wanted it only as a stepping stone to the presidency. "I didn't think anybody could get elected president who had been divorced and was an actor," he said. Thinking of Ronald Reagan, he declared "I made a helluva mistake!"

He also revealed that Jean Renoir was, in his opinion, the best motion picture director "ever." He lamented the plight of most people who want to make movies not being able to make any money from their endeavors, and he complained that producers simply did not want to finance the kinds of movies *he* (Orson) really was interested in making.

After the interview had been completed, Orson excused himself to hurry home to watch the Academy Awards on television that night. He saw *Gandhi* receive the Best Picture award; Ben Kingsley was presented the Oscar for Best Actor; and Meryl Streep was awarded the prize for Best Actress.

IN JUNE, A CURIOUS little controversy erupted in which Orson became peripherally involved. "Rosebud" had come back to haunt him. Supposedly, three Rosebud sleds had been made for *Citizen Kane*: one was burned at the film's end; another still extant, the one that the young Kane played with in the scene in the snow drifts of Colorado, belonged, ironically to Tom Mankiewicz, the son of Herman J. Mankiewicz; and the third was owned by John Hall, RKO's archivist. Perhaps this last sled was the one that had made an appearance in *Native Son* and then made its way back to Hollywood after the run of the play. Hall had bought the sled from a studio watchman who had found it, discarded, outside the old RKO studios. Hall decided to put the sled up for auction at the Sotheby Parke-Bernet Gallery in New York, and publicity about the sacred icon of one of the most famous movies of all time immediately captured international media attention.

Rosebud was thirty-four inches long, was made of balsa wood painted red, and had varnished runners and a white blossom with green leaves stenciled on its surface. The sled, together with the Maltese falcon, Chaplin's derby, and the slippers in *The Wizard of Oz,* is clearly one of the most famous props in motion picture history. It was believed that the Rosebud auction would bring about $20,000 as the top bid.

After the sled was authenticated and word began to spread that it was to be auctioned, directors George Lucas and Steven Spielberg became interested in buying it, but as colleagues and friends they didn't want to bid against each other. It was eventually decided between them that Spielberg would be the one to be the bidder, and if he won, to take possession of it.

Why was Steven Spielberg, the most financially successful director in motion picture history, so interested in owning Rosebud? He explained his reasons clearly: "This [sled] is a symbolic medallion of quality in movies. When you look at Rosebud, you don't think of fast dollars, fast sequels, and remakes. This to me says that movies of my generation had better be good."

Sotheby Parke-Bernet had listed the sled in its catalog at a floor price of between $15,000 and $20,000, and on June 9, 1982, offered it at auction.

Spielberg bid for the sled over the phone from California; a Texas tycoon, Lucian Flourney, seated in the auction gallery in New York, was his major competition. The bids continued to rise until Flourney reached $50,000. Spielberg topped it with $5,000 more. Flourney lowered his bidding paddle, the spectators burst into applause, and Spielberg was the owner of Rosebud.

But a new Rosebud puzzle began to develop. After the announcement that Spielberg was the victorious bidder had been made on radio and television and in newspapers and magazines, a man by the name of Art Bower, of Port

Jefferson, Long Island, claimed that he was the owner of the original Rosebud. Bower said that he had received the sled as a prize in 1941, when he correctly predicted the year's top ten films chosen by the New York Film Critics' Circle. The auction gallery denied that Bower's sled was one of the originals.

Spielberg began to wonder whether he had bought one of the authentic sleds. He was also criticized for spending so much money on what some people thought was a "trivial" object. Why didn't he give the money to the poor? they asked.

At that time I asked Spielberg why he had bought the sled, expecting him to confirm its importance as an authentic motion picture artifact and the influence that Welles had had upon his own picture making.* He was angry. "Wouldn't you have bought it if you had an extra $55,000?" was his only comment.

But it was Orson's comment during a phone interview with a Washington, D.C., newspaper that really annoyed Spielberg: "I say the sled he bought was a fake."

---

*The last shot of *Raiders of the Lost Ark,* which showed a warehouse filled with crates, was a confirmed tribute to the penultimate scene of *Citizen Kane.*

CHAPTER 21

IN THE FALL of 1982, Orson was approached by the high-powered literary agent Irving Lazar to see if he would be willing to write his autobiography. He had been a guest at some of Lazar's parties and they knew each other quite well. The prestigious publishing firm Alfred A. Knopf had long been interested in tempting Orson to pen his life story but could not convince him to do so, nor could his attorney, Arnold Weissberger, change his mind. Lazar, however, spurred on by a new crop of Hollywood biographies of people such as Cary Grant, Bette Davis, Laurence Olivier, and Richard Burton, was successful in getting Orson to contract, and a high six-figure advance was secured from Knopf by its then editor-in-chief, Robert Gottlieb.

Orson had originally signed a contract, in 1977, with a small San Francisco publishing house, to write *The Memoirs of Orson Welles,* despite the fact that he thought that "memoir" was an awfully pompous word. He planned to write a book about subjects and people who had interested him, rather than the disasters and pleasures that he had had. He told Dick Cavett, "It will not be a 1-2-3, A-B-C, you know, 'One sunny morning in Kenosha, a chubby little one . . .'"

Orson believed that modern biographies and autobiographies were expected to reveal a great deal of personal material of the sort that he wouldn't tell *anybody,* much less whoever had the price of a book.

In any event, the publishers seemed happy to get anything that Orson cared to write, and he collected a $195,000 advance against royalties. But he never delivered a word to them, so the company sued and won for breach of contract. Orson returned all the money.

However, with Knopf he was determined to get something on paper. "I'm afraid the time has come when I just have to lock myself up and tell a lot of lies," Orson was supposed to have said. Whether lies, truth, or a bit of both, Orson wrote the first section of his book for Knopf, a portion of which was ultimately published in the French-language edition of *Vogue*. Although this initial effort was no literary masterpiece, it did assume a certain provocativeness and interest in the promise that it held in telling the story of the once and future Orson. "I was in no condition to interfere," he wrote mysteriously of his father's funeral, "being convinced—as I am now—that I had killed my father. (I'll try to write about this later.)"

The British rights to the proposed book were immediately sold to publisher Lord George Weidenfeld for his house, Weidenfeld and Nicholson. And although there were promises made of a certain number of pages each month to be delivered from Orson to the publisher that were to contain all manner of personal matter, such as the explanation of his enigmatic statement about killing his father and his difficulties in radio and his relationship with Rita Hayworth, none was forthcoming. When, eventually, Viking Press contracted Barbara Leaming to do a biography of Orson, and he agreed to cooperate with her, all ideas about writing his anecdotal *auto*biography were abandoned.

As the year's end approached, Orson did more voice-overs, a number of them for *Newsweek,* and one that advertised a spooky children's board game just in time for Christmas. About this last work, columnist James Brady commented upon what he thought was the pathos of Orson, "arguably the most talented man this country's movie business ever had" being reduced to doing work that any hack could do while "Hollywood shells out millions to . 'B' actors in 'C' movies made by 'D' directors."

Echoes of Orson's *War of the Worlds* scandal of 1938 were also heard during the last days of 1982. A TV spoof in Germany of an extraterrestrial landing sent thousands of viewers to their telephones to determine what to do. A show had been interrupted with the news that a flying saucer had landed in Duisburg. And in England, on Radio Sheffield, a news reader interrupted a music program to announce, in a promotion of another show, that Russian missiles and bombers were heading for London. Before there was a chance to explain that the announcement was not a genuine warning, thousands of listeners began calling the police and attempting to contact relatives in London.

Although Orson had no comment on either of the incidents, the two episodes were likened by the media to his *War of the Worlds* episode.

AT THE BEGINNING of 1983, Orson was emotionally ambivalent. It seemed that virtually everybody he had known in Hollywood, and in the theater, and in his personal life, was dying: Arnold Weissberger, Hortense Hill, Hans Conreid, Glenn Anders, and George Schaefer, to name but a few, had all died within a relatively short span of time.* But in a Jungian sense he seemed to feel their deaths—and his, possibly—were somehow responsible for the birth of the ideas he was then expressing. He was full of vigor while finishing the crafting of his screenplay of *King Lear.* He would soon celebrate his sixty-eighth birthday, and he believed that he was at a perfect age, finally, to play the part. Oja Kodar would play his Cordelia, a remembrance of movies past when Paola Mori played his daughter in *Mr. Arkadin,* and he was going to try to cast Mickey Rooney as the Fool.

---

*At the time of his death, Weissberger had been working on his memoir, which came to be called *Double Exposure.* It consisted of stories about the lawyer's famous clients, such as Rex

Money for *King Lear* seemed more than remotely possible. Alexander Salkind, who had produced Orson's *The Trial* and had gone on to make tens of millions of dollars launching *Superman I* and *II,* wanted Orson to act in his extravaganza *Where Is Parsifal?* Orson, not so reluctantly, took the acting job in Europe in the hope that he might interest Salkind in backing his *King Lear.* Salkind did show initial interest, only to have his enthusiasm diminish when he experienced a rude financial dampener with *Superman III.*

Orson then went, with Henry Jaglom, to the Cannes Film Festival, specifically to see if any money could be generated for *The Dreamers, The Big Brass Ring,* or *King Lear.* "I can't spend my whole life at festivals or in restaurants begging for money," he said to Jaglom in despair-shaped tones. But beg he did, and several French producers showed interest in *King Lear* and contended, again, that money would be forthcoming from the Mitterrand government. Several other European producers said that they thought television money might be raised.

Upon his return to the United States, Orson, buoyed by Cannes, not only continued to work on the screenplay for *King Lear* but also created a complete budget for the film, somewhat less than $2 million, a sum almost unbelievably low for a film of the caliber that he was going to make. He would shoot it in black-and-white; it would even be darker, visually and thematically, than his *Touch of Evil.* There would be many close-ups, and the cinematography in general would be abstractly expressionistic.

He went back and forth to Paris that year, sometimes sitting in the Hotel Lancaster for weeks on end, waiting for production meetings or financial discussions.

In order to sell *King Lear* more forcefully, he did costume designs, constructed small models for the sets, penciled in camera movements, distances, and special pieces of action on the screenplay, and even had a number of still photographs taken of himself, complete with makeup and ragged robes, as the mad, flower-bedecked Lear.

He then shot a six-minute videotape that would act as his proposal-at-arms, something that he could and did send all over the world, a sort of ambassadorial presentation that would speak in his and *King Lear's* behalf. Some of his set-ups for the abbreviated *King Lear* were supposedly borrowed from other directors, a practice that Orson would occasionally engage in over the years. In his indefatigable pursuit of money and his attempt to cut costs wherever possible, he would ask working directors if he could employ their lights and sets during their down times, thereby saving Orson equipment rental and location fees. As soon as the director and his cast and crew quit the set for the day, Orson—on constant standby—would dash in with his cast and crew and, if things went right, get a few minutes of footage. All of this presumed, of course, that the set was applicable to whatever Orson was shooting at the

---

Harrison and Helen Hayes. Orson was advising Weissberger and contributing certain recollections of their past experiences.

time. He was, however, nothing if not adaptable: "I was looking for a pre-Roman castle but if you have an art deco American bedroom, perhaps . . ."

Jonathan Rosenbaum explained that in the taped proposal for *Lear,* Welles elaborated some of the details of the film: "It will be . . . free from the cinematic rhetoric, my own as well as others, which have already accumulated in the history of these translations of Shakespeare into film."

He promised to offer a new kind of Shakespeare, not the usual costume drama, but one that would be modern, intimate, simple, and ferociously earthy. "In a word," he said, "not only a new kind of Shakespeare, but a new kind of film."

It was now the summer of 1984, and as Orson waited, for what seemed an interminably long time, for the go-ahead from the French to do *King Lear,* and for any other monies for his other projects, he was approached, although indirectly at first, about another film.

MICHAEL FITZGERALD, THE producer, with his wife, Kathy, of such films as *Wise Blood* and *Under the Volcano,* had heard a rare recording of *The Cradle Will Rock* on which Marc Blitzstein explained the difficult and controversial circumstances surrounding the 1937 staging of the opera because of the Federal Theatre Project's decision to withdraw the play, and Orson's direction and participation. Fitzgerald became obsessed with the idea of turning the story into a screenplay and, after several years of waiting, finally convinced the screenwriter Ring Lardner, Jr., to construct a scenario based not just on the opera itself but on the whole incredible theatrical happening that was its first historic and defiant performance.

Lardner produced what Fitzgerald thought was a remarkable first draft, and the latter took it to Welles for a reading. "I want your blessing," he said. Orson talked of the WPA days and nights and so enthralled the young producer that he quickly realized that he should try to secure Welles as the director of the film. Although Orson at first was reticent, after Fitzgerald paid court, he soon became quite interested in the project. Eventually, Fitzgerald would name Orson director, coscreenwriter, and one of the executive producers. In effect, it instantly became Orson's film.

The idea of the film was to create the ambience that led up to the theatrical sensation of 1937, *The Cradle Will Rock,* and have actors portraying the young Orson Welles, his wife Virginia Nicholson, John Houseman, Marc Blitzstein, and others, set in the backstage drama of putting on the play in defiance of the government. Orson would actually narrate the film himself and be seen at the beginning as the sixty-nine-year-old he then was. Then his adventures in radio—as the Shadow, on the "Mercury Theatre of the Air"—how he and Houseman collaborated, and finally how they arrived at *The Cradle Will Rock* incident would be portrayed.

The concept of Orson doing a film about himself was overwhelming: the old Welles choreographing a re-creation of himself of almost half a century ago: the director directing the director; Orson the filmmaker and the man, attempting to reincarnate the memory of himself during his most vital days. "I really don't know this man," Orson said to Barbara Leaming, talking about his twenty-two-year-old self. It was obvious that in order to creatively solve the personal conundrum that the film was going to produce, Orson had to go back to his youth, examine and analyze it, put it into perspective, and emerge with a self-portrait.

The shooting, as far as location or studio, would not be too demanding. Most of the action would take place indoors, except for the celebrated march up Broadway, and Fitzgerald immediately secured two theaters, one in Los Angeles for principal shooting and one in New York. To save money, some interior work would also be done in Rome's Cinecittà. A three-month shooting schedule was established, and a budget of five and a half million dollars was set. Universal Studios talked of handling the distribution.

Casting proved not to be as difficult as Orson had imagined. He had seen Rupert Everett in the absorbing film *Another Country,* which was just then playing, and Orson and Fitzgerald both agreed that, despite Everett's British accent, he would offer a strong portrayal of the young Orson.

Since the character of Virginia Nicholson would play a major part in the film, Orson thought that the actress who played her should be special; if she happened to be a star, it would greatly add to the film's ultimate acceptance by the public. He had an inspired idea: Amy Irving.

Orson had seen Amy Irving in *Yentl* and was impressed with her charm, beauty, and inner resources, all qualities that he believed Virginia Nicholson possessed. He had also been pleasantly affected by some of Amy Irving's television work.

But his wanting to cast her had other, more expedient motivations. Amy Irving was married to director Steven Spielberg, the man who had said, when he bought the Rosebud sled, that he would "jump through the air" just to meet Orson Welles, the man who claimed that *Citizen Kane* was a film of such audacity, daring, and foresight that it probably never could be matched. Spielberg was also the most successful director-producer in Hollywood; the man who had the number-one top-grossing film in the history of motion pictures (*E.T. The Extra-Terrestrial* has grossed over $680 million in theatrical release, not counting earnings from videotape) and many others—*Jaws, Raiders of the Lost Ark, Indiana Jones and the Temple of Doom, Close Encounters of the Third Kind*—were among the most profitable films of all time.

Even as *The Cradle Will Rock* project began, Fitzgerald warned Orson that there might be some financial difficulties. Bringing Spielberg into the picture, through casting his wife, Orson argued, might help the film. All of Hollywood seemed to revolve around Spielberg: casting directors, bankers, actors and actresses, and agents and directors were all eager to be associated with him. Perhaps Spielberg could be convinced to invest. Just at that time, Spielberg's *Indiana Jones and the Temple of Doom* took in close to $10 million in box office receipts *in one day!* Only half of that was needed for *The Cradle*'s entire production budget.

Orson arranged a lunch at Ma Maison to talk to Amy Irving about her part—yes, she was extremely interested in the film after reading the script—and, by the way, could she bring her husband, Steven Spielberg, with her?

The lunch was lively. The threesome had much to talk about and Orson was winsome and engaging. Spielberg even forgot that Orson had said his Rosebud was a fake.

Amy Irving would make the *perfect* Virginia Nicholson, Orson was convinced. But when Orson began to broach the question of needing investment capital for the project, Spielberg didn't budge. It was almost as if he knew in advance at least one reason why his wife had been cast in the film and why he had been invited to the lunch. Orson quickly saw that there would be no money forthcoming from Spielberg for *The Cradle Will Rock*. He was saddened, disappointed, and a bit surprised.

When the lunch check finally arrived, Orson assumed that Hollywood's most financially successful director, and one of the richest men in America, would pick it up. Orson waited, and after an embarrassingly long time, paid the check himself.

He flew back to Las Vegas that night and told Beatrice about the lunch and the discussion, something he rarely did, just because he needed to exorcise the afternoon. He managed a wistful laugh about not getting the money. "And I had to pay for the lunch," he said to her, shaking his head ruefully.

Perhaps he had a premonition that day. Shortly afterward, Fitzgerald announced that his financial difficulties were real enough and that he had to temporarily abandon the *Cradle* project.

THE ONLY QUASI-BRIGHT spot in Orson's career at that time was being named as host for a new television series, "Scene of the Crime," which was broadcast on NBC. Orson introduced the suspects, summarized the clues, and then asked the audience if they could solve who the murderer was, before the solution was revealed at the end of the show. Orson liked the arrangement he made with the producers; he was permitted to film his introductions and denouements wherever he was in the world, and, also, since many of the scripts were done far in advance, he could do several shows in a single day.

Right after that, he also did a thoughtful narration of Jacques Cousteau's series on the Amazon River for WTBS in Atlanta.

In early 1985, Orson then narrated a film called *Almonds and Raisins*. It was a documentary history of the Yiddish cinema that flourished during the Depression, and it gave millions of Jews the opportunity of reliving and understanding their immigrant experience in their own language. Most of the footage came from the archives of Brandeis University's National Center for Jewish Film.

Orson loved working with director Russ Kavel and especially enjoyed learning about an area of cinema that he knew little about, one filled with music, humor, folklore, romance, and tears. (For example, he noted with pleasure that in a Yiddish remake of *The Jazz Singer,* when the cantor's son returns from a triumphant singing tour—as in the original—in this version he marries the *shtetl* girl who lives next door.)

Almonds and Raisins was eventually released nationally in August of that year and received almost unanimous critical praise, but like most documentaries quickly disappeared from the screen. Shortly afterward, it was broadcast on PBS television.

ORSON SPENT PART of spring 1985 in Paris, again attempting to work out the details and financing for his *King Lear*. He had extended meetings with television producers and with representatives of the French Ministry of Culture. There were disputes about money, with the government amending his budget, actually raising it and then saying that they could not afford to start the production based on the very figures that they had inflated. They also wanted editorial and final cut approval. Orson protested the bureaucracy. Minister of Culture Jack Lang seemed to be of no help in solving the problem, and Orson eventually returned to the United States with a heavy heart.

A FEW DAYS before Orson's seventieth birthday on May 5, 1985, William Scobie of the London *Observer* flew to Los Angeles especially to interview him for an in-depth profile for the newspaper.

Orson met Scobie at Ma Maison and although cooperative, he seemed a bit labored in his movements, a bit cynical in his comments. "I've always pretended to love Hollywood," he said. "Sour grapes are not my dish. But when the day of judgment comes and the executives and moguls are placed in the balance against the writers and directors, they will be found wanting."

On May 6, 1985, in celebration of his birthday, the BBC repeated its renowned 1982 interview and showed a few of his more distinguished directorial efforts. Then London's National Film Theatre screened a program of Welles films over several months. England seemed to be saying that even if the United States was too blind to recognize one of its own greatest filmmakers, they were not. When he heard about the commemoration, he was pleased but his spirits were low. His health was poor: he had been diagnosed as a diabetic, and his heart ailment was still bothering him.

John Gielgud burst through Orson's depression. Gielgud thought he could raise enough British money for a film of *The Tempest*, with himself playing Prospero to his menial servant Caliban, to be played by Orson. Ever since he was a boy and had seen a silent version by Sir Herbert Beerbohm Tree, Gielgud had always been attracted to the idea of filming *The Tempest*.

Orson was touched by Gielgud's offer, but felt he was too old for Caliban, and physically unable to play such a strenuous role. He sent the aging British actor, who was then seventy-nine, an appreciative, warmhearted note declining the offer.

A newspaper account at the end of June stated that Orson had decided to film *King Lear* in Utah and that it would "stand people on their ear in much the same way that *Citizen Kane* did." Welles might have *planned* to take the film away from the French at that time, but nothing came of it.

Joseph Cotten was in touch that summer and asked if Orson would read his forthcoming autobiography. Since so much of it revolved around Orson, he wanted him to go over the book and approve it, especially those specific parts that concerned Orson.

Orson not only agreed to read the book, he offered to rewrite it and to help have it published. There were sections that were, he believed, not quite right. Some of the chronology was skewed, some of the recollections tarnished. Cotten readily agreed to the editorial and sequencing suggestions, and Orson began working on it.

Shortly after that, Cotten was to celebrate his eightieth birthday and invited Orson to dine at his house that evening, but Orson was ill with what he described as a virus and courteously declined. As a gift, he sent Cotten an audiotape of recollections, good cheer, and witty remarks, ending it with a reading of Shakespeare, the last two lines of which really touched his old colleague:

> But if the while I think on thee,
> dear friend,
> All losses are restored and
> sorrows end.

IF MOST OF Orson's own film projects were in limbo, Orson Welles as a personal industry seemed to be flourishing. Retrospectives and showings of his films continued in many parts of the world, and three major Orsonological works appeared, almost simultaneously, early that fall. "Everyone needs ten biographies," Welles pointed out, and it seemed that his prophecy was near to being fulfilled. Barbara Leaming's book, *Orson Welles: A Biography* (Viking Press), was the work that received the most attention, written as it was with cooperation from the master himself. It was an intimate work.

Leaming had done substantial research, tried to talk to as many people as possible who knew Orson, and dined with him at Ma Maison as many times as he allowed. He genuinely liked and admired her. The first indication of what her book was going to be like was when an extract that she had sold to *Playboy* appeared, "The Genius Takes on Tinseltown," mainly about the financial and legal difficulties Orson had with *The Other Side of the Wind* and his dining ritual at Ma Maison. It was lively and showed a personal side of Orson that had rarely been revealed. When the book was published, the reviews were mixed. Although the book was well written, one of its problems was that almost everything Orson had said at his restaurant lunches with the author, including superficial and scatological gossip, made its way into print. It is a work written by a friend for a friend. Although Orson was pleased by the book, even he criticized Leaming's portrait of him as Hollywood's Don Juan during his early days there.

Henry Jaglom had been videotaping and audiotaping Orson for several years in loosely structured but regularly scheduled autobiographical sessions, with Orson talking directly to the camera or the microphone and giving the story of his life. When Leaming's book appeared, Jaglom suggested that they give up the project. "No," Orson said. "I haven't read the book yet. Let's keep taping. When I get too old to make movies, I'd still like to write *my* book."

There was also another biography written about Orson with his cooperation, a work by Peter Bogdanovich started in the early 1970s, which had never been published for reasons that are unclear. Orson's only wish was that Bogdanovich would have the book published before Orson's death.

Charles Higham's book, *Orson Welles: The Rise and Fall of an American Genius,* published by St. Martin's Press, was painstakingly researched, but whereas Leaming seemed to accept, perhaps too lovingly and indiscriminately, all the tenets and the victories of Orson's life, Higham rejected them and concentrated on the negative aspects of his life. Some of Higham's social and critical observations seemed to be naive. He also spent pages tracing Welles's genealogy back to the Mayflower and virtually ignored the last three decades of his life. Orson never commented on the book.

Robert L. Carringer's study, *The Making of Citizen Kane,* published by the University of California Press, was a comprehensive and scholarly behind-the-scenes look at Welles and his most famous film, in which he takes the reader, step by step, through every department concerned with *Citizen Kane*: cinematography, sound, props, costumes, makeup, distribution, and release. The book is accurate, and entertaining with the possible exception of the author's attempt to prove that Orson *did* try to take solo credit for writing the screenplay of the film. Writing about Welles's and Mankiewicz's receipt of the Oscar for the screenplay of *Citizen Kane* in 1942, Carringer unearthed this exchange: Orson wired Mankiewicz: "You can kiss my half." Mankiewicz replied: "You wouldn't know your half from a hole in the ground." Orson, it was reported, thanked Carringer for the book.

Not the books, but illness along with melancholia—what Orson called his "acidie"—over his inability to realize any of his film projects caused him to stay away from Los Angeles and spend more of his time at his home in Las Vegas.

He continued to work on the screenplays of *King Lear, The Cradle Will Rock,* and *The Dreamers* but seemed to lose heart over *The Other Side of the Wind* and *The Big Brass Ring.* Of course, *Don Quixote,* which he now called *When Are You Going to Finish Don Quixote?* because everyone asked him that all of the time, was still lying in the wings. He did tell an interviewer at that time that he had every intention of finishing it but he did not explain how or when. Orson never lost his talent but occasionally his inspirations would wilt.

Orson read, swam twenty laps a day in his swimming pool, and carried on an extensive correspondence with the French concerning *King Lear.* He was sad but he would not give up.

Occasionally he would watch television but stayed away from films that he either starred in or directed, finding it too painful to see the excruciatingly young Welles in acting parts and to analyze some of the directorial mistakes that he had made in his films. Incredibly, he had not seen *Citizen Kane,* either on television or in a theater, since it had been released in 1942. He did watch *The Magnificent Ambersons* one night.

While doing some brief location shots for *The Other Side of the Wind,* Oja Kodar has recalled, Orson was in his motel room watching *Ambersons* late one evening. The door was ajar, and as she neared the room she could hear the voices and see the reflection of the film in the window. She was about to enter but stopped. Orson, sitting in the darkness, in front of the television set, was weeping. She quietly closed the door and went out.

That Orson was still disturbed and saddened, forty years later, about the creative tampering on *The Magnificent Ambersons* is not surprising. He had only made 12 films in his lifetime as compared to the 54 in Hitchcock's or John Ford's 74 or the 38 that Ingmar Bergman made, and he was frustrated. He still had ideas to express, images to make, messages to send, films to shoot.

The French backing for *King Lear* seemed to be evaporating. Nothing saddened Orson more than the cruelty of this apparent indifference. He had spent years working with the government producers, and the only way that the film was ever going to be made was for Orson to relinquish all creative and financial control of the project, to become a hired hand on his own film, his beloved *Lear,* and shoot it in a way that was antithetical to his heart and to his head, opposed to everything he knew and wanted to say about filmmaking. Orson had already agreed to pare off $300,000 of his own salary as star, director, and screenwriter, in effect donating his talent to the screen. And whatever money he was to receive, it was to be paid to him *after* the film's completion, the French insisted. But the negotiation still could not be consummated. They wanted more financial cuts and more control. The studios that they offered him for shooting were totally unacceptable. An executive producer, Philipe Dusart, long associated with Alain Resnais, was named as creative guide on the forthcoming film; Orson sadly considered the appointment as an even further diminishment of his jurisdiction.

Orson began to suspect that the French television people never really intended to back the film. Perhaps it was all politics. The minister of culture, Jack Lang, who had committed an international *faux pas* and insult by showing his open disdain for American culture, claiming it nonexistent, now needed to offer an apology of sorts, a token of rapprochement, for speaking so inopportunely. Backing a film made by one of the greatest American film directors could lessen the tension between the United States and France, at least provisionally, and Welles could have been the olive branch.

Finally, in an angry and heartrending statement, Orson cabled:

> In 55 years of my professional career, I have never, not even in the worst days of the old Hollywood, encountered such a humiliating inflexibility. Need I say that this is a bitter disappointment to one who has, until now, received so much heartwarming and generous cooperation in France. To my profound regret, therefore, I must accept that your own last is the last word about *Lear* and that there is no longer any hope that in this affair a constructive relationship is possible.

HE SWITCHED HIS creative allegiances and put *King Lear* out of his thoughts for a few weeks. Orson had been sporadically working on *The Magic Show* for over fifteen years. He now focused on the film with more resolve than ever before, envisioning it first being aired on television and then going into theatrical release.

When I met Welles's cameraman, Gary Graver, in the late 1970s, he told me that he had filmed Orson and a magician named Ab Dickson doing a series of the greatest magic tricks of all time and that there were also interviews (unrelated to magic) of Burt Reynolds, Skipper and Hortense Hill, and others. This was all to become *The Magic Show.*

To this potpourri, Orson intended to add a section with the working title of "Orson Welles Solo," in which he would do a recitation of Isak Dinesen's "The Old Chevalier," plus selected readings from *Julius Caesar* and other works. Scripting and shooting still had to be completed on this last section and Orson began working on it and stayed on it every day.

He also acted, for minimum-scale wages, in a film of Henry Jaglom's initially called *Is It You?,* and then changed to *Someone to Love,* a story of how a film director (Jaglom) invites all of his old friends to a theater on Valentine's Day to give their definition of loneliness. Orson (as a character) played the director's mentor, which was, of course, the case with their roles in real life. Orson scripted his own definition: "We're born alone, we live alone, we die alone. Only through our love and friendship can we create the illusion for the moment that we're not alone."

For "Moonlighting," the television show starring Bruce Willis and Cybill Shepherd, Orson, in a voice-over, introduced a black-and-white dream sequence in which the two actors travel back to the 1940s to investigate a murder.

On October 6, 1985, Orson had lunch with Jaglom at Ma Maison, mainly to celebrate the release of Jaglom's film *Always.* He had a copy of a Los Angeles paper with him that contained a glowing review of the film and he showed it, triumphantly, to Jaglom. "Orson, don't you realize I've read all of the reviews?" Jaglom asked. "Yes," Welles answered, "but you haven't heard *me* read them." He then went on to pull out some of the most laudatory phrases and read them aloud to Jaglom, stressing, pausing, whispering: "Once in a great while there's a movie that you not only recommend, critique, etc. but that you *have* to take your *friends* to see—I mean take them *yourself,* practically by the *hand,* because you want not only to hear but to *feel* their reactions, sitting in the next seat, watching them as much as the movie."

"Did you hear that?" Orson said, and he continued reading: "Very funny, embarrassing, scary, challenging, silly, profound, and above all, *alive.*"

That weekend Orson worked on *The Magic Show* script, toyed with Joseph Cotten's autobiography, and again dreamed about doing *King Lear.* A few weeks earlier, a professor of broadcasting at the University of Cincinnati, E. Bruce Weiss, had contacted him about possibly producing one of his projects. Weiss represented an anonymous backer from New York who, he said, might be interested in investing some $10 million in one of Welles's then-unrealized films. Weiss flew to Los Angeles and had dinner and a lengthy discussion with Orson. It all seemed legitimate and possible. The problem was, which project to select.

Orson gave Weiss a copy of the screenplay of which he was most proud, that of *The Dreamers,* to take back home to Ohio to read. However, it was Weiss's unvoiced opinion (his expertise was in promotion and marketing), that *The Dreamers* had little commercial potential and would not interest the backer. To avoid hurting Welles, he then asked to see *King Lear* as a second choice, should the backer request one, he said. Orson complied, thinking that *The Dreamers* was still a possibility. When Weiss read the script for *King Lear* he was overwhelmed. He was certain that his backer would indeed finance such a literate, enlightened, and provocative film. Once again, Orson began to believe in the possibility of *King Lear.*

Orson lunched with Burt Reynolds at Ma Maison, on Tuesday, October 8, at the latter's insistence. They talked of the edited interview that Orson had done of him for *The Magic Show* and whether it could still be used, since several years had gone by and Reynolds had lost considerable weight and no longer looked like the same person. Perhaps another interview could be shot quickly, Orson suggested. Reynolds was doubtful; he was, however, eager to work with Orson, and they discussed other possibilities. Reynolds told him that he would be happy to act in virtually any vehicle that Orson might direct and that Orson could use Burt's name in trying to gain backing for films.

Orson picked at his food; Reynolds noted that he looked quite drawn and tired. Orson acknowledged that he wasn't looking well. He had just seen the series of photographs taken of him by Michael O'Neill for a story that *People* magazine was doing on him, and he was appalled at his appearance. "I look like I'm about to be laid out in a coffin," he told Reynolds. In the photos, he was wearing too much makeup (meant to hide his pallor), his eyes seemed rather bulgy and baggy, his skin was heavily wrinkled, and he looked almost cadaverous. As a result of his diet, he had taken some twelve inches off his waist.

When he and Reynolds left the restaurant, they shook hands and both promised to see if some kind of project could be worked out for the near future.

On Wednesday, October 9, Orson was chauffeured to the "Merv Griffin Show" for an appearance. He wasn't feeling well and asked his chauffeur to drive as close to the studio entrance door as possible. The security guard, however, insisted that the car not go beyond a certain point. Orson alighted and labored into the studio, cursing under his breath.

Griffin was expecting a lively show. He had invited not only Welles but his biographer, Barbara Leaming. The idea was to see if there might be some controversy, perhaps with Orson disputing the authenticity of some of the book's material. Nothing of the sort happened. Both Welles and Leaming talked of Welles's life and the segment was a nostalgic interlude. Orson talked about Rita Hayworth and Marlene Dietrich and quoted Charles de Gaulle: "Old age is like a shipwreck." And when Griffin then asked, "But you feel wonderful, don't you?" Orson sarcastically replied: "Oh, sure. All those old people that walk along saying that they feel just the way they did when they were kids . . . liars, every one of them."

That night at Ma Maison, Orson had dinner with Barbara Leaming and Alessandro Tasco, his production manager and close friend. It was a pleasant evening, but Leaming noticed that Orson seemed to be in great pain when he rose from the table, even though he gallantly blew a kiss to her with both of his hands.

At home that night in Los Angeles, Orson, dressed in his bathrobe, worked on the script for *The Magic Show*, typing in stage directions and camera movements, among the last to be shot to complete the film. He planned to do the shooting the next morning and then to have lunch by himself at Ma Maison.

Sometime very late that night, October 9, 1985, Orson Welles died. He was alone and had been sitting at his typewriter when he was overcome by a massive heart attack. His chauffeur found him late the next morning when he was to pick him up. His doctor, Thomas Dailey, indicated that he had been treating Orson for diabetes and a heart ailment and that he had died of natural causes.

The news of Orson's death skyrocketed around the world. Most large metropolitan newspapers ran front-page headlines and, ironically, the Hearst-owned *San Francisco Examiner* ran a six-column head, "ORSON WELLES DIES," in large type.

When informed of Welles's death, *Examiner* publisher William Hearst said, "Goddamn it. It makes me mad because I wanted to meet that man. I really wanted to talk about that movie."

Despite the fact that Orson was in poor health, and people continually said that if he didn't slim down his heart wouldn't be able to carry his weight, his death still came as a shock. But shock is only a small segment of grief. The *loss* of someone close is the major factor. As Gary Graver said, lamenting the loss of his friend: "I wish I could talk to Orson. There are so many things I want to tell him just now."

In Paris, Orson's death was treated almost as if it were that of a head of state. In a matter of days, the daily newspaper *Libération* was out with a special Orson Welles issue, all the other newspapers carried lengthy, profusely illustrated articles, and for at least ten days afterward, Welles's films were constantly shown on French television.

In this country, film people invariably eulogized him: "We all wish we could have made more use of Orson's genius," Janet Leigh said. John Huston saw an element of sadness in Welles's life: "What a shame, and I mean that literally, that one of the finest talents motion pictures has ever had was rejected out-of-hand." Charlton Heston proclaimed: "We have lost the most talented man I ever knew."

Vincent Canby's "Appreciation," along with the official obituary in *The New York Times,* seemed a strange eulogy. Although he admitted that *Citizen Kane* forever changed the way that he—and millions of others—saw movies and that Orson had to be considered the premier American film director of his generation, Canby also blamed his troubles with the Hollywood establishment on Orson's own personality. Talking of Orson's acting career, Canby erroneously claimed that the large fees that he collected as an actor enabled Orson to live well and that that was the reason he never finished making the films he intended.

"It was once said of him," Canby went on, "that he left bits and pieces of unfinished films around Europe the way traveling salesmen leave laundry in hotel rooms," and called him "something of a con-artist."

Patrick Terrail, the owner of Ma Maison, paid tribute to his patron and late friend. No one was permitted to sit at Orson's favorite table. In memory of Orson, the table was "closed" for one week.

Orson was cremated, by previous agreement with the executor of his estate, Greg Garrison. There was a short, formal funeral service for the members of his family and a few other close friends.

Orson had wanted his ashes shipped back to Spain, the country he grew to love so much; however, it took two years to complete these arrangements. Beatrice wanted to escort the ashes to Orson's designated spot, the tranquil country house of retired bullfighter Antonio Ordonez in Ronda, Spain, where Orson had often spent holidays.

On what would have been Orson's seventy-second birthday, in May of 1987, Beatrice traveled to Ronda and placed a blue urn containing his ashes into a small brick well, which was then sealed. No marks or designation of any kind marked the burial spot.

Ironically, the farm was one that William Randolph Hearst had wanted to buy in the 1930s for his personal use, but Ordonez refused to sell it . . . at any price.

AS HIS LIFE was controversial, so was his death. Orson's will, signed by him on January 15, 1982, just at the time when his doctor was warning him that he might die if he didn't lose weight and start taking care of himself, caused some problems with his family. The sum of $10,000 each was left to his three daughters, Christopher, Rebecca, and Beatrice. His wife, Paola, was to receive the house in Las Vegas and the remainder of his estate, with the exception of the house in Los Angeles and all of its contents, which was to go to Oja Kodar. This last entry in the will was contested by Paola Mori for both financial and symbolic reasons. As Orson did not admit Oja into his life with Paola, so did she refuse to allow Oja to share in his death.

Another aspect of the will disturbed Paola; should she die, Orson bequeathed the remainder of his estate to Oja, not to his children. Should Oja not survive him, then his children were to receive it. If there were no surviving heirs, Orson left his estate to the Motion Picture and Television Home in Woodland Hills, California.

Paola immediately contacted an attorney to establish her rights.*

WITHIN A FEW days after Orson's death, a group of his friends and colleagues (Richard Wilson, Gary Graver, David Shephard, and Chuck Warne) met to discuss some sort of memorial service for Orson. A date was set—November 4—and the auditorium of the Directors Guild of America in Los Angeles was secured. Telegrams and letters were sent all over the world to the people in Orson's life whom he most respected, asking them to either attend or send a statement to be read.

Then, curiously, Joseph Cotten's manuscript of his autobiography could not be found among Orson's effects. This turned out to be a substantial problem since Cotten had not kept a copy for himself. Eventually, with the help of writer Sidney Sheldon, the manuscript was recreated and a publisher secured.

Early in the morning of the memorial, people began lining up outside the DGA. The auditorium could hold only five hundred, and soon it was filled beyond capacity, with many others remaining outside. Someone pointed out that Orson would have been happy to see all the people who wanted to get in . . . as if they were standing in a line for a hit movie. Strangely, there was no formal introduction, just the disembodied voice of Orson, a tape from the speech that he had given at the Hollywood Foreign Press Association in 1981. At first people were still talking when Orson began to speak, but in a matter of moments everyone quieted down. It was dynamic and beautiful and eerie, hearing Orson talk about what he—and most of the audience—seemed to love more than anything: movies. "The director is simply the audience," he said convincingly in typical Wellesian style. "So the terrible burden of the director is to take the place of that yawning vacuum, to *be* the audience and to select from what happens during the day which movement shall be a disaster and which a gala night. His job is to preside over accidents, and that's an important one."

After a few moments of pure Welles, in which he ended by saying that film is the most expensive mistress any man can have and he had spent his whole life "trying to support her," the recording was turned off.

After a few seconds of embarrassed silence—people just didn't know what to do—everyone burst into enthusiastic applause, just as if Orson had been present.

Peter Bogdanovich, who introduced most of the speakers, then told how the memorial came about and asked everyone who was about to speak to try to stay within three minutes. Virtually no one did. The ninety-six-year-old Skipper Hill was the first speaker; he was introduced by . . . Orson Welles by

---

*On the morning of August 12, 1986, Paola Mori was killed in an automobile accident just a short distance from her Las Vegas home. That afternoon she was to have viewed a 1961 Italian documentary, *In the Land of Don Quixote,* about Orson's Cervantes epic, in which she and Beatrice had appeared, and which she had never seen. It was going to be updated and she was going to give another interview. On August 14, 1986, she and Oja Kodar were scheduled to meet to sign an agreement indicating an amicable settlement for both sides.

means of a recording of Orson introducing Skipper at the "Working with Welles" seminar in 1978.

When Skipper finally did get to speak, he was engaging and showed a keen understanding and love for his former student. He said he promised himself that he wouldn't weep—but he did anyway—and this produced a sadness among many of the people in the audience.

Others—Greg Garrison, Gary Graver, Patrick Terrail, Barbara Leaming, and Charlton Heston—spoke of their love and respect for Orson. This was interspersed with film clips from the breakfast scene of *Citizen Kane,* the opening of *The Magnificent Ambersons,* the scene when Harry Lime is first seen in *The Third Man,* the first encounter between Welles and Dietrich in *A Touch of Evil.* Watching these pieces of visual poetry and realizing that the man who had made them was now dead was almost unbearably depressing.

There were reminiscences by friends and associates. Peter Bogdanovich, Dan O'Herlihy, Arthur Knight, Charles Champlin, Richard Wilson, Geraldine Fitzgerald, and others told stories about Orson, anecdotes that seemed precious crystallizations of the man. Messages that had come from people throughout the United States and around the world were read. Interspersed between the eulogies were movie clips of some of his unrealized, uncompleted projects. That, in itself, was cause for mourning.

Stanley Cortez was introduced. He bowed and waved, but did not speak. Dennis Weaver sent a message about how, as a young actor in *Touch of Evil,* he had learned so much from Orson. Joseph Cotten sent a note that said, in part: "No one had ever engaged in a *dull* conversation with Orson Welles. Exasperating, yes; sometimes eruptive, unreasonable, ferocious, and convulsive . . . yet eloquent, penetrating, exciting, and always, never *failingly* always—even at the sacrifice of accuracy and his own vanity—witty and never, never, *never,* dull."

The eminent French film publication *Les Cahiers du Cinéma* sent a message stating that they felt they had lost a dear friend.

One of the most touching moments occurred when Henry Jaglom spoke, telling about how he and Orson met when Jaglom cast him in *A Safe Place.* He ended by showing a clip of Orson's last performance, in *Is It You?* Jaglom spoke of his best friend brightly, with humor, but sometimes apparently on the verge of tears. At one such moment he paused. "Orson would have hated this," he sighed, referring to the fanfare of the memorial service, but also knowing that Orson would have appreciated the respect that he was receiving from the hundreds of fans, friends, and colleagues present.

Oja Kodar, dressed in black, surprised the gathering when she stepped to the podium. Her voice was outraged and bitter, her face streaked with tears. It was clear that she was disturbed over the presence in the audience of some of the very people, uninvited guests now mourning Orson, who wouldn't even lift a telephone receiver to help him when he was alive.

She talked of the "dreary little selves whose fingers are still sticky from plucking at his wings." Lowering her voice for a moment, she told them that Orson, being generous, would have forgiven those who plucked a feather or two in their attempts to stop *him* from defying the force of gravity. Despite all the defamation against Orson, and the lack of cooperation he received from the film community, she continued, her voice rising now, almost strident—"I promise you it didn't make him bitter."

Oja claimed that Welles, at the time of his death, was on the verge of receiving all the money that he needed for all of his films. Then she read, first in French and then in English, a message from the French president:

> With the death of Orson Welles, a genius of cinema has gone forever. We have followed his itinerary from film to film and we have seen this actor transform himself while maintaining all the strength and power of his youth. His last film, *King Lear,* was to be made in France. He may not have been able or have not wanted to follow an end to this film, a testimonial to power and solitude. He leaves us with sorrow of a great project unachieved. Orson Welles had many friends and admirers in our country. I address to his family and those near him all my sympathy.
>
> François Mitterrand.

Oja Kodar seemed to be fairly reeling by the time she finished reading the message. Then, unexpectedly, she launched into a scathing attack on Mitterrand for playing politics and "defending his establishment even at this sad hour." Bitterly criticizing the French government and the minister of culture, Jack Lang, for their hypocrisy in using Welles to punish the United States for Lang's disdain of "the existing imperialism of nonexistent American culture," she concluded with sadness and anger that Orson "had never encountered such bitter humiliation, not even in Hollywood—he was forced, with a broken heart, to end the whole project."

The audience gave her a thundering ovation. Virtually everyone in the auditorium, especially those who worked in motion pictures, was feeling outraged and depressed and at least somewhat guilty. Some commented, afterward, that they wondered at the time why they hadn't helped Orson more.

When Robert Wise, the president of the Academy of Motion Picture Arts and Sciences, who had also been Orson's editor on *Citizen Kane* and *The Magnificent Ambersons,* spoke, he recalled the time more than forty-five years before when Orson, in his attempts to get *Citizen Kane* released, had talked to a roomful of attorneys, distributors, and stockholders to get them to approve it, using all the charm, energy, erudition, and logic he could muster. "It was Orson's greatest performance," Wise recalled. "I'll never forget it."

In closing, Wise talked specifically of the circumstances surrounding Orson's death, alone in his bedroom, perhaps feeling alone in the world. "We don't know what his last word or words could have been. It's unfortunate there wasn't a microphone there to catch his last words—if he realized what was happening to him. I wonder if it might have been . . . 'Rosebud.'"

Peter Bogdanovich ended the memorial by thanking everyone for coming, and people began to file out onto Sunset Boulevard.

EPILOGUE

NOBODY WAS EVER quite like Orson Welles. Even he had difficulty, at times, assuming the role. It's almost as if his *persona* had been constructed from diverse fictive elements, and then one day a young, very large actor came along to embody and embellish the myth of the man we came to know as Orson Welles: bearded, rotund, and possessed of a uniquely powerful and melodious voice.

Micheál MacLiammoir often said of Orson, not unkindly, that his courage, like everything else about him—his imagination, egotism, generosity, ruthlessness, forbearance, impatience, sensitivity, grossness, and vision—was magnificently out of proportion. And Hilton Edwards often compared Orson to America: because of their immensity, everything you can say about them—negative or positive—*had* to be true. It is for this reason that an analysis or even a summation of the life and career of Orson Welles is, almost by definition, a painfully futile construct.

There can be little contention that he has placed, indelibly, his creative stamp on the theater and on film. In this country, and perhaps internationally, there can be no history of the cinema, no archive of broadcasting, no chronicle of the stage, that can fail to include among its pages the name of Orson Welles as one of its most illustrious talents.

If he had accomplished nothing other than the astonishing poetry of dialogue and movement, the thematic unity, impact, and the visual poignancy of the chiaroscuro lighting of *Citizen Kane,* his stature among the great film directors of the world would be secure. It gave American film, all at once, its own vocabulary, and it is our motion picture legacy. In retrospect, even though it was essentially his first film, *Citizen Kane* with its Gothic echoes already had the *look* of a Welles film.

Citizen Kane revolutionized Hollywood. Refusing to pander to the tastes of the public, it signaled the death of the classical film. With narrative and technical means surprisingly advanced for that time, the film operated on several levels, enabling the viewer to receive meanings and ideas that he or she had not yet perceived on a conscious level.

Welles's elliptical style was that of disorientation, and a departure from the linear way of telling a story in which time proceeds in a synchronous cause-and-effect fashion. Viewers had to find their own way through the

597

incredible algebra of his films. Most of the time he offered no easy road maps, no clearly marked blueprints to the meaning of his images. Sometimes these labyrinths, these comedies of menace and operas of darkness, were difficult to fathom, and audiences became, in a Brechtian sense, distanced, uncomfortable, confused. Everything in his films was infused with tension. In effect, Welles was one of the originators of the *film noir* genre of Hollywood motion pictures, those films that were visually and thematically darker and more abstract, and which were more cynical in their presentation of contemporary society than any of the films that had been made before. In it, he invented his own unmistakable and controversial style, the mark of a true original. Motion picture history is relatively young, and many of the Welles films had such a purposefully rough-hewn and wolfish quality, that five hundred or one thousand years from now Orson Welles might conceivably be considered the Homer or Chaucer of the screen.

Because he was so ahead of his time, Welles had no popular following, and the industry, in an absence of shared values, never forgave him for this lack of sentimentality and commercialism—or what they would call melodrama—in his films. Perhaps they also sensed a certain brutality and pessimism in his narratives.

Film historian Richard Roud has talked about first seeing *Citizen Kane* in postwar Paris of the 1940s, with an audience of professional filmmakers, and how unsettled and electrified they became as they watched a film that disturbed all their preconceptions of what America was capable of producing and what cinema was all about.

Like a great novelist, Welles didn't *show* everything in his films but often allowed the viewer's imagination to create the exotic landscapes that the narrative demanded. His subtexts were as powerful as some of his most dramatically eloquent shots. He turned American movies into an art form. As did Proust, who recreated an epoch in *Remembrance of Things Past,* Welles used the technique of involuntary memory, through which stimuli connected with past experiences set in motion a virtual stream of consciousness. Proust's Marcel becomes Welles's camera in *Citizen Kane.* Both must record the accounts of characters while they can still remember things past.

Before Welles, Hollywood seemed only interested in telling the story as neatly organized as possible. With the advent of Welles, the process of how the story was told became almost equally as important.

Citizen Kane was also perhaps the first American film to present the subject of alienation in a realistic manner. This produced a certain alienation toward Welles. Previously, all Hollywood films had addressed themselves to the concept that man is the measure of all things; but in *Citizen Kane,* man is shown to inhabit a world of loneliness and futility. There are vast spaces and depths of field, but the characters never really occupy that space. They can't connect to their world. Kane becomes an object, not a human being, in that region, and is eventually disintegrated, trapped by the very space that he attempts to dominate. Welles's use of long takes also stressed the helplessness of life. Without visual progression, he seemed to be saying, there cannot be a progression in life.

By unearthing and ingeniously using many of the most effective stylistic methods of the past, such as the panning and tracking shots of F. W. Murnau and Max Ophuls, reinforced with the improved Hollywood technology, *Citizen Kane* made discerning audiences unhappy with the status quo, and in effect they demanded that other films use these innovations, too. To show the baroque and lonely world of Charles Foster Kane, Welles pushed his methods of portraying reality further; the result was a film that was a magnificent statement of estrangement. Hence, the comment by some critics that *Citizen Kane* ruined Hollywood. Certainly, it assaulted.

Welles's departure in *Citizen Kane* was not that he invented new techniques, but that he employed so many effects in such a personal and imaginative way, pushing them to their furthest limits. He integrated and absorbed many styles, and managed to tell a story in a way that both surprised and fascinated the modern audience.

He was interested in avoiding a conformism to certain stencils of thought, as he once so eloquently expressed it. Such was the range of his perceptions.

For years before there were serious film schools in this country, Orson had educational ideas about learning to make good motion pictures, and how that could be united with the film industry. One such program was to establish a cinema laboratory of sorts, financed by the studios and the more successful producers and directors, where filmmakers could experiment with the sole intention of raising the standard of cinematic entertainment. The labs could allow and encourage directors, young or experienced, to test new approaches to directing, acting, cinematography, music, and special effects with themes and plots that were in the vanguard of social, political, and aesthetic expression. Always there would be an attempt to create finer pictures. He thought a second motion picture circuit could be established, or another means of distribution, where these pioneer efforts could be shown at higher prices and perhaps someday, if an audience could be built, a profit could be realized by the studios. "Hollywood is the only industry, even taking in soup companies, which does not have laboratories for the purpose of experimentation," he complained.

The influence of *Citizen Kane* is still being felt. After touching such films as *Sunset Boulevard, Double Indemnity,* and *Mildred Pierce,* to name just a few examples, it was then seen in the works of more modern films, like Hitchcock's *Psycho* (especially in the use of the Bernard Herrmann music to heighten tension), in Godard's *Les Carabiniers* with its abrupt transitions, and even more recently in Scorsese's *Taxi Driver* with its expressionistic lighting and camera distances.*

---

*Manny Farber, the galvanic and perceptive critic of *Commentary,* once indicated that Welles's cinematic innovations could also be seen in such films as *The Lost Weekend, The Best Years of Our Lives, The Treasure of The Sierra Madre,* and *Champion.*

Taken individually, the specifics of *Citizen Kane* could have been achieved—and were—by many other directors; but Welles breathed life into his film, synthesizing the entire knowledge of the cinema in a way so powerful that it is still responsible, in its influence upon virtually all modern-day motion pictures, for the heart of film beating today.

But some of his other films, such as *The Magnificent Ambersons, Touch of Evil, The Trial, The Lady from Shanghai,* and his unusual encounter with and contribution to three Shakespearean efforts represent such stylistic accomplishment and contain such highly special organized unity that they, too, have influenced the very syntax and semantics of motion pictures.

Echoes of Welles's films in style and substance, in the selection of subject matter, and in the very manner of the development of narrative can be found in the works of many later directors, a debt they are usually eager to publicly acknowledge.

François Truffaut's sense of nostalgia and his preoccupation with death could be derivative of Welles (who dies in *Citizen Kane, Mr. Arkadin, Touch of Evil, Othello,* many others of his films). Roman Polanski's absurdist black comedy *Cul-de-Sac* seems to quote, in parts, *Touch of Evil.* In Peter Bogdanovich's *The Last Picture Show* he creates, in effect, a replication, although different in content and theme, of *The Magnificent Ambersons,* an exploration of an authentic American milieu. Francis Ford Coppola, like Robert Bresson, employs innovative uses of sound and overlapping dialogue, as in *The Conversation,* which appears to be a direct Wellesian influence. Michelangelo Antonioni's depth-of-focus, in *The Passenger,* for example, comes from the head of *Citizen Kane.* Andrzej Wajda's harsh and irresolute look to his films is reminiscent of *The Trial.* Stanley Kubrick's ironic use of music in many of his films is similar to the same ironies in Welles's pictures. The abstract and rhetorical strategies used by Jean-Luc Godard can be seen in *Mr. Arkadin.* Akira Kurosawa's handling of an alternative to modern narrative, as in Welles's *Citizen Kane,* is what *Rashomon* is all about. The baroque and overblown look to the films of Joseph Losey and Luchino Visconti appear to be mimetic replicas of intent from the *mise-en-scène* of Welles. Ingmar Bergman's deep concern with the storyteller's art shares the same attraction that Welles has always felt toward story, as in *Citizen Kane* and *The Trial,* and infused in his films, right to the end of his life.

The potency of Welles's influence went beyond film and into literature, as well. Experimental novelist Carlos Fuentes has readily acknowledged that *The Death of Artemio Cruz* was his structurally direct version of *Citizen Kane* in its attempt to unearth the truth of a character already dead. And Nobel laureate Gabriel Garcia Marquez has indicated that the breaks and interconnections of the chronological narrative in Orson's films, influenced his own retrospective approach to fiction.

The era of the Mercury Theatre, both over the air and in front of theater audiences, a time of experimentation that was rewarded by increasing critical success, brought the young Welles not only into his own but also into national prominence. Then, for over a half century, he participated in an ideational flirtation with the consciousness of film and theater audiences everywhere. He often succeeded in engaging them and sometimes failed to grip them, but despite his reputation (admittedly self-induced) as artistic manipulator or magician, he was never guilty of any kind of fraudulence. Indeed, he occasionally cheated himself by giving more than was needed of his heart, his time, and his money to sustain an acceptable production. In all of Welles's efforts, film or theater, he attempted to get his audience to join as his accomplice; not to judge the work, but to *become* it.

Although film has been the insignia of Welles's contemporary achievement, it was in the legitimate theater that he wielded his greatest influence and found a most profound romance. The world of the stage, the continuous familial and communal experience, perhaps prompted him to establish the family he lost at an early age. The theater, a mirror of life, became *actual* life for Orson, a highly ingenious, elegant, and amusing universe, and a refuge. To solidify his community, Welles established a group that was similar in intent to the literary factory of Dumas or the fabulous studio of Rubens. And as a result of his experience with the theater, he brought new life to film. As Truffaut has pointed out, Welles's frequent use of upward angles might very well be an echo from the legitimate stage, where most of the audience looks *up* at the actors. Film, though, became and remained his muse. "The trees of the cinema comprise the forest of life," he once said as an existential explanation of himself and his career. Jean Renoir once put it this way: "Orson Welles is an animal made for the screen and the stage. When he steps before a camera, it is as if the rest of the world ceases to exist. He is a citizen of the screen."

Orson had a rare kind of prescience about the aesthetic possibilities and limitations of a medium, whether it be film, radio, or theater—witness *Citizen Kane, The War of the Worlds,* and his modern-dress *Julius Caesar*—but he often lacked the practical insight that might steel him against such obvious blunders as *Five Kings, Around the World in 80 Days,* or *Don Quixote.* Even so, many of Orson's magnificent failures were so bold and noble in concept that they served to enhance his reputation even though they may have blunted his spirit. Sometimes, he was undeservedly thought of as being arrogant because of his demand to get everything executed properly. He had the persistence of a bulldog and the tunnel vision of a mud-turtle, as he continually described himself. "I can see ahead only to the next thing," he would often say to technicians. "Let's solve that next thing first. Then we can go on to other things."

Immersed in a world of prejudices and clichés typical of the reportage about entertainment personalities, Orson had to suffer the paradox of great success at an early age and was, in effect, taunted because of this youthful fame. "What has he done since *Citizen Kane?*" was the usual query, which later would be tossed out as a flat statement meant to sum up the man. Both audience and establishment maintained a love-hate relationship with him. Despite their admiration, their criticism was lifelong: rejection of his *Julius Caesar* for being too streamlined; jibes about his Martian hoax; disdain because he was not able to launch *Heart of Darkness* or *The Smiler with the*

Knife; ridicule when he could not finish *It's All True*; and later, the almost scornful attitude of the motion picture community toward his inability, after almost twenty years of trying, to attract the financial backing that would enable him to produce a Hollywood film.

"What a waste of talent," people would cluck when they saw him on television in one of his ubiquitous commercials, not realizing that he made the commercials to earn enough money to live. Certainly he would have preferred directing films.

"What happened to Orson Welles?" I've been asked, literally hundreds of times. "Other than making the best motion picture ever to come out of Hollywood, nothing happened to him," is my usual answer.

Continuous lamentations over Orson's unfulfilled projects—and his weight and flamboyance—became the clichéd appraisals, and were more wasteful than the subject criticized. Welles's life could hardly be called tragic in the dramatic sense, as much as it was, at times, unfortunate and unprosperous.

Since he seemed to start at the top, or at least arrive there with early and startling speed, Orson's problem was that whenever he accomplished anything later in his career that was less than overwhelmingly magnificent, he was said to be slipping. The perfectly acceptable idea that some artists do their best work as young men, and then continue to amplify, expand, and repeat on a central theme for the rest of their lives seemed to be quite unacceptable and unforgivable in appraising Orson's work.

He was accused of taking on too many projects, on a scale too grand for sure success, so that if he failed at one project he could blame it on the demands of the others. People pointed to what they said was his great sloth, claiming that the only reason he liked to play kings in Shakespeare and other classical drama was because they are usually the only characters who get to sit down. And another observer once cynically claimed that the *real* reason he preferred to direct rather than act was because, in the former role, he didn't need to shave every day, a chore he sorely hated. Perhaps there was some truth in the spirit of all these accusations.

Acting did not come easily to him. "I must call upon an entire complicated mental process, to do what Gary Cooper did as easily as breathing," he revealed. It is for this reason that he always considered himself more of an actor for the stage than on film. Somehow, with body language and eye contact, he felt he could reach and sometimes touch a live audience, while the camera was not that kind or considerate to him. He believed that his very physical bulk was more suited for the stage than for the screen. Very few actors have managed to become virtuosos in both areas, and yet the criticism that Orson was not all things to all arts was still heaped upon him. ("I can show you, frame by frame," he once complained, "that my eyebrows move less than Ray Milland's in *The Lost Weekend*. If I permitted myself one-tenth of his expressions in that excellent performance, I would be howled out of the theater.") He was never really a star, but more of a character actor; at times he attempted the chameleon change required to play a part believably, to become the character, as some actors are able to do; but always, insistently, he was Orson Welles, trapped inside his indelible body and *persona*. I doubt that he acted only with his voice, and not his heart, as some have claimed.

Despite his problems with acting, he began experimenting with a film called *The One Man Band* in which he would play *all* the roles in the film, from a British bobby to an old lady selling violets on the street.

Welles's self-exile to Europe was always exaggerated or misinterpreted. It was not a political or legal exile; he was no Charlie Chaplin or Ezra Pound. His break with America came more from his desperate need to find work—or opportunities to freely do the kind of work he wanted to do—than from a disenchantment with his own country although his tax problems did keep him abroad when he wanted to be in America. "In show business you're a fruit picker," he said without rancor. "You go where the work is." The fact that he moved back to the United States and was living here for well over a decade, acting in films, appearing on television, and at least attempting to direct his own projects, proved that the so-called artistic break with the Hollywood establishment was not as great as touted by the press.

He was disheartened by his failure to find backing but not thoroughly disillusioned, even though it seemed at times that the industry had rejected him and the public had discarded him. "Antagonism in the United States would disappear," he said, "if I had a roaring financial success. I've had healthy box office but no blockbuster. It really isn't antagonism. They're really friendly. . . . They just don't want to put in the dough."

At a seminar called "Working with Welles," held in Hollywood at the Directors' Guild in the late 1970s, Orson was genuinely surprised to discover that one entire evening had been set aside to discuss his future. "My *future*?" he asked the audience incredulously, as if he really knew that he didn't have one. The audience laughed. Sadness can be funny.

Did he really believe that he had no professional future, that the promise to someday produce a film even greater than *Citizen Kane* was a spiritual contract that both he and the audience knew never would, or could, be fulfilled?

Before his death, Orson was often propelled about in a wheelchair, sometimes creating a figure eerily reminiscent of the elderly Charles Foster Kane. But he was far from ever behaving or thinking like an old man, and there was no sign whatever that his creative vigor had diminished. Nor should Orson's chronic lack of opportunity be confused with his lack of potential. More than twenty years ago, André Bazin pointed out that, like the careers of D. W. Griffith, Erich von Stroheim, Abel Gance, and Sergei Eisenstein, the life of Orson Welles could be seen as a prime example of an artist faced with intractable social or commercial obstacles in the attempt to exercise his art, and like Robert Flaherty and Mack Sennett, he just could not figure out how to work in the Hollywood system. When thinking of Orson's career in retrospect, one is reminded of Norma Desmond's line in *Sunset Boulevard*: "I'm still big. It's the pictures that got small."

No doubt it was ungenerous of the public to be forever harping on Welles's unfulfilled promise when, in fact, he lavished upon film audiences everywhere visual gifts of the greatest value and spent almost 70 percent of everything he ever made as an actor to finance his films. He pursued his endless quest to find the means to make his future films, to spin out, in his words, his "ribbon of dreams." An Orson Welles happens only once in several lifetimes. Unfortunately, with his death we can no longer savor the prospect of more and even higher achievements to come, although the knowledge of his unfinished films is tantalizing, and the thoughts of the projects that were only Orson's dreams will haunt our imaginations always.

Even during his lifetime, Welles was in the process of being transformed into a legend. Now that he is dead, he has been elevated almost to cinematic mythology, and we are left the task of scrutinizing what is left of his art, a ritual of trying to understand and appreciate the small body of work that he has left us, great flickering artifacts that will undoubtedly continue to be studied and enjoyed as long as motion pictures are shown.

THE CAREER
OF ORSON WELLES

Please note that this is a selected list of works and does not mention every movie, radio, or television credit of Orson Welles.

I. AS DIRECTOR

ON STAGE

1925   **Camp Indianola**
Dr. Jekyll and Mr. Hyde, adapted, produced, directed, and performed entirely by Welles.

1926-31   **Todd School, Woodstock, Illinois**
Approximately thirty plays, either directed and/or performed by Welles.

1931   **Dublin Gate Studio Theatre, Dublin**
The Lady From the Sea, by Henrik Ibsen; *The Three Sisters,* by Anton Chekhov; *Alice in Wonderland USA.*

1934   **Todd School, Woodstock, Illinois**
Trilby, by Gerald du Maurier; *The Drunkard,* by Mr. Smith of Boston; *Hamlet,* by William Shakespeare; *Czar Paul,* by Dimitri Merejewski.

1936   **Negro People's Theatre for the Federal Theatre, Lafayette Theatre, Harlem, New York**
Macbeth, by William Shakespeare, adapted by Welles. Music by Virgil Thomson. With Jack Carter as Macbeth and Canada Lee as Banquo.
Turpentine, by A. Smith and P. Morell.

Federal Theatre, Maxine Elliott Theatre, New York

Horse Eats Hat, by Welles and Edwin Denby, based on Eugene Labiche and Marc Michel's *An Italian Straw Hat.* Music by Paul Bowles, arranged by Virgil Thomson. With Joseph Cotten as Freddy, Arlene Francis as Tillie, Virginia Nicholson Welles as Myrtle Mugglethorpe, and Edgerton Paul and Welles alternating as Mugglethorpe.

1937   Federal Theatre, Maxine Elliott Theatre, New York

Doctor Faustus, by Christopher Marlowe. Music by Paul Bowles; costumes by Welles and Nat Karson; puppets by Bil Baird. With Jack Carter as Mephistopheles, and Welles as Dr. Faustus.

Mercury Theatre at Comedy Theatre, New York (later at National Theatre)

Julius Caesar, by William Shakespeare, adapted by Welles. Music by Marc Blitzstein. With Joseph Cotten as Publicus, George Coulouris as Marc Antony, Joseph Holland as Caesar, Martin Gabel as Cassius, and Welles as Brutus.

The Music School of the Henry Street Settlement, Henry Street Playhouse, New York (three performances only)

The Second Hurricane, music by Aaron Copland, libretto by Edwin Denby.

Mercury Theatre, Venice Theatre, New York

The Cradle Will Rock, by Marc Blitzstein. With Olive Stanton as Moll, Will Geer as Mr. Mister, and Howard da Silva as Larry.

1938   Mercury Theatre, Comedy Theatre, New York

The Shoemaker's Holiday, by Thomas Dekker, adapted by Welles. With George Coulouris as the King, Joseph Cotten as Rowland Lacy, and Vincent Price as Master Hammon.

Heartbreak House, by George Bernard Shaw. With Geraldine Fitzgerald as Ellie Dunn, Mady Christians as Hesione Hushabye, Vincent Price as Hector Hushabye, George Coulouris as Boss Mangan, and Welles as Captain Shotover.

Danton's Death, by George Büchner. English text by Geoffrey Dunlop, adapted by Welles. Songs by Marc Blitzstein. With Martin Gabel as Danton, Arlene Francis as Marion, Vladimir Sokoloff as Robespierre, Joseph Cotten as Barrère, and Welles as Fouquier.

Stony Creek Summer Theatre, Stony Creek, Connecticut

Too Much Johnson, by William Gillette, adapted by Welles. With Joseph Cotten as Augustus Billings, Ruth Ford as Mrs.

Billings, Edgar Barrier as Dathis, Howard Smith as Johnson, Virginia Welles as Lenore Faddish, Eustace Wyatt as Mr. Faddish, Guy Kingsley as Henry MacIntosh, and, in the film sequence, Arlene Francis, John Houseman, and Marc Blitzstein.

Cape Playhouse, Dennis, Massachusetts
The Importance of Being Earnest, by Oscar Wilde. (Credits not available.)

1939   **Theatre Guild, Colonial Theater, Boston**
Five Kings, adapted from Shakespeare's history plays by Welles. Music by Aaron Copland. With Morris Ankrum as Henry IV, Burgess Meredith as Henry V, John Emery as Hotspur, and Welles as Bracy.

RKO Vaudeville Circuit
The Green Goddess, adapted by Welles from the work by William Archer.

1941   **Mercury Theatre, St. James Theater, New York**
Native Son, by Paul Green and Richard Wright.

1942   **A circus tent on Cahuenga Boulevard, Los Angeles**
The Mercury Wonder Show (a performance for American soldiers).

1946   **Adelphi Theatre, New York**
Around the World, adapted by Cole Porter and Welles from *Around the World in 80 Days,* by Jules Verne.

1947   **Utah Centennial Festival, Salt Lake City, Utah**
Macbeth, by William Shakespeare.

1950   **Théâtre Edouard VII, Paris**
Time Runs, adapted by Welles from *Faust*: played on a bill with scenes from *The Importance of Being Earnest* and *Henry VI, Part I.*
Une Grosse Légume/The Unthinking Lobster/Miracle à Hollywood, adapted by Welles from his novel.

1951   **St. James's Theatre, London**
Othello, by William Shakespeare.

1953   **Ballet de Paris, Stoll Theatre, London**
The Lady in Ice, a ballet written and designed by Welles.

1955   **Duke of York's Theatre, London**

Moby Dick—Rehearsed, adapted by Welles from Melville's *Moby Dick.*

1956 **City Center, New York**
King Lear, by William Shakespeare.

1960 **Grand Opera House, Belfast, Dublin**
Chimes at Midnight, adapted by Welles from Shakespeare's Falstaff plays.

Royal Court Theatre, London
Rhinoceros, by Eugène Ionesco.

ON FILM
(Date in margin is year of release; films without date were never released for distribution.)

— *The Hearts of Age* (a ten-minute, 16mm film made at the Todd School in Woodstock, Illinois, summer 1934). Produced by William Vance; directed by Welles and Vance. With Virginia Nicholson, Vance, Welles, and students of the Todd School.

— *Too Much Johnson* (a forty-minute, 16mm film made in and near New York City, spring 1938, for the Mercury Theatre stage production, *Too Much Johnson, q.v.*). Produced by Welles and John Houseman for Mercury Productions; written by Welles, based on the play by William Gillette; assistant director, John Berry; director of photography, Paul Dunbar. With Joseph Cotten as Johnson and Virginia Nicholson, Edgar Barrier, Arlene Francis, Ruth Ford, Mary Wickes, Eustace Wyatt, Guy Kingsley, George Duthie, John Berry, Herbert Drake, Marc Blitzstein, and Howard Smith. (No prints remain of this film, the last-known copy having been burned in 1970 in a fire in Welles's villa in Madrid.)

1941 *Citizen Kane* (RKO, 119 minutes). Produced by Welles for Mercury Productions; executive producer, George J. Schaefer; associate producer, Richard Barr; assistant director, Richard Wilson; written by Welles and Herman J. Mankiewicz; director of photography, Gregg Toland; music by Bernard Herrmann; camera operator, Bert Shipman; editors, Mark Robson, Robert Wise; art director, Van Nest Polglase; associate art director, Perry Ferguson; set decorator, Darrell Silvera; special effects, Vernon L. Walker; costumes, Edward Stevenson; sound recordists, Bailey Fesler, James G. Stewart. With Welles as Charles Foster Kane; Joseph Cotten as Jedediah Leland and the newsreel reporter; Everett

Sloane as Mr. Bernstein; Dorothy Comingore as Susan Alexander Kane; Agnes Moorehead as Mary Kane; George Coulouris as Walter Parks Thatcher; and Ray Collins, William Alland, Erskine Sanford, Harry Shannon, Philip Van Zandt, Paul Stewart, Fortunio Bonanova, Georgia Backus, Buddy Swann, Sonny Bupp, Gus Schilling, Richard Barr, Joan Blair, Al Eben, Charles Bennett, Milt Kibber, Tom Curran, Irving Mitchell, Edith Evanson, Arthur Kay, Tudor Williams, Herbert Corthell, Benny Rubin, Edmund Cobb, Frances Neal, Robert Dudley, Ellen Lowe, Gino Corrado, Alan Ladd, Louise Currie, Eddie Coke, Walter Sande, Arthur O'Connell, Katherine Trosper, and Richard Wilson.

1942   *The Magnificent Ambersons* (RKO, 131 minutes). Produced by Welles for Mercury Productions; executive producer, George J. Schaefer; assistant director, Freddie Fleck; additional scenes directed by Freddie Fleck and Robert Wise; written by Welles, based on the novel by Booth Tarkington; director of photography, Stanley Cortez; additional photography, Russell Metty, Harry J. Wild; editors, Robert Wise, Jack Moss, Mark Robson; art director, Mark-Lee Kirk; set decorator, Al Fields; special effects, Vernon L. Walker; music, Bernard Herrmann; additional music, Roy Webb; costumes, Edward Stevenson; sound recordists, Bailey Fesler, James G. Stewart. With Welles as Narrator, Tim Holt as George Amberson Minafer, Joseph Cotten as Eugene Morgan, Dolores Costello as Isabel Amberson Minafer, Agnes Moorehead as Fanny Minafer, Anne Baxter as Lucy Morgan, Ray Collins as Jack Amberson, and Richard Bennett, Don Dillaway, Erskine Sanford, Louis Johnson, Gus Schilling, Charles Phipps, Dorothy Vaughan, Elmer Jerome, Olive Ball, Nina Guilbert, John Elliott, Anne O'Neal, Kathryn Sheldon, Georgia Backus, Henry Roquemore, Hilda Plowright, Mel Ford, Bob Pittard, Lillian Nicholson, Billy Elmer, Maynard Holmes, Lew Kelly, Bobby Cooper, Drew Roddy, Jack Baxley, Heenan Elliott, Nancy Gates, John Maguire, Ed Howard, William Blees, James Westerfield, Philip Morris, Jack Santoro, and Louis Hayward.

It's All True (an uncompleted semidocumentary in three parts, filmed in Mexico and Brazil in 1941-1942). Produced by Welles for Mercury Productions for the Office of the Coordinator of Inter-American Affairs and RKO Radio. Executive producers, Nelson Rockefeller and George J. Schaefer; associate producer, Richard Wilson; codirector, *Bonito* episode, Norman Foster; written by Welles, Norman Foster, and John Fante; director of photography, W. Howard Greene; second cameraman, Harry J. Wild; editor, Joe Noriega. With Jesús Vasquez as Chico and Domingo Solera as Don Luis ("My Friend Bonito"); Grande Otelo and the people of Rio ("The Story of Samba"); and José Olimpio "Jacaré" Meira, Tata, Mané, and Jeronimo as the fishermen ("Janga-deiros").

1943   *Journey Into Fear* (RKO, 71 minutes). Produced by Welles for Mercury Productions; executive producer, George J. Schaefer; directed by Welles (uncredited) and Norman Foster; written by Welles and Joseph Cotten from the novel by Eric Ambler; director of photography, Karl Struss; art directors, Albert S. D'Agostino and Mark-Lee Kirk; set decorators, Darrell Silvera and Ross Dowd; special effects, Vernon L. Walker; music, Roy Webb; costumes, Edward Stevenson. With Welles as Colonel Haki, Joseph Cotten as Howard Graham, Dolores Del Rio as Josette Martel, Ruth Warrick as Stephanie Graham, Agnes Moorehead as Mrs. Mathews, and Everett Sloane, Jack Moss, Jack Durant, Eustace Wyatt, Frank Readick, Edgar Barrier, Stefan Schnabel, Hans Conreid, Robert Meltzer, Richard Bennett, Shifra Haran, Herbert Drake, and Bill Roberts.

1946   *The Stranger* (RKO, 95 minutes). Produced by S. P. Eagle (Sam Spiegel) for International Pictures; assistant director, Jack Voglin; written by Anthony Veiller and, uncredited, John Huston and Welles; story by Victor Trivas and Decia Dunning; director of photography, Russell Metty; editor, Ernest Nims; art director, Perry Ferguson; music, Bronislaw Kaper; orchestrations, Harold Byrns, Sidney Cutner; costumes, Michael Woulfe; sound, Carson F. Jowett, Arthur Johns. With Welles as Franz Kindler (alias Charles Rankin), Loretta Young as Mary Youngstreet, and Edward G. Robinson as Inspector Wilson, and Philip Merivale, Richard Long, Byron Keith, Billy House, Martha Wentworth, Konstantin Shayne, Theodore Gottlieb, Pietro Sosso, and Isabel O'Madigan.

1948   *The Lady from Shanghai* (Columbia, 86 minutes). Produced by Harry Cohn, executive producer, with Richard Wilson and William Castle, associate producers, for Columbia Pictures. Assistant director, Sam Nelson; written by Welles from Sherwood King's novel *If I Die Before I Wake*; director of photography, Charles Lawton, Jr.; camera operator, Irving Klein; editor, Viola Lawrence; art directors, Stephen Goosson, Sturges Crane; set decorators, Wilbur Menefee, Herman Schoenbrun; special effects, Lawrence Butler; music, Heinz Roemheld; musical director, M. W. Stoloff; orchestrations, Herschel Burke Gilbert; songs, Allan Roberts, Doris Fisher; gowns, Jean Louis; sound, Lodge Cunningham. With Welles as Michael O'Hara, Rita Hayworth as Elsa Bannister, Everett Sloane as Arthur Bannister, and Glenn Anders,

Ted de Corsia, Gus Schilling, Louis Merrill, Erskine Sanford, Carl Frank, Evelyn Ellis, Wong Show Choong, Harry Shannon, Sam Nelson, Richard Wilson, and players of the Mandarin Theatre of San Francisco.

1948   *Macbeth* (Republic, 107 minutes, later cut to 86 minutes). Produced by Welles for Mercury Productions for Republic Pictures. Executive producer, Charles K. Feldman; associate producer, Richard Wilson; assistant director, Jack Lacey; written by Welles from the play by William Shakespeare; dialogue director, William Alland; director of photography, John L. Russell; second unit photographer, William Bradford; editor, Louis Lindsay; art director, Fred Ritter; set decorators, John McCarthy, Jr., James Redd; special effects, Howard and Theodore Lydecker; music, Jacques Ibert; musical director, Efrem Kurtz; men's costumes, Welles, Fred Ritter; women's costumes, Adele Palmer; makeup, Bob Mark; sound, John Stransky, Jr., Garry Harris. With Welles as Macbeth, Jeanette Nolan as Lady Macbeth, Dan O'Herlihy as Macduff, Edgar Barrier as Banquo, Roddy McDowall as Malcolm, and Erskine Sanford, Alan Napier, John Dierkes, Keene Curtis, Peggy Webber, Lionel Brahan, Archie Heugly, Christopher Welles, Brainerd Duffield, William Alland, George Chirello, Gus Schilling, Jerry Farber, Lurene Tuttle, Charles Lederer, Robert Alan, and Morgan Farley.

1952   *Othello* (United Artists, 91 minutes). Produced by Welles for Mercury Productions; associate producers, Giorgio Patti, Julien Deorde, with Walter Bedone, Patrice Dali, Rocco Facchini; assistant director, Michael Washinsky; written by Welles, based on the play by William Shakespeare; directors of photography, Anchise Brizzi, G. R. Aldo, George Fanto, with Obadan Troiani, Alberto Fusi; editors, Jean Sacha, John Shepridge, Renzo Lucidi, William Morton; art director, Alexander Trauner; music, Fernando Lavagnino, Alberto Barberis; musical director, Willy Ferrero; costumes, Maria de Matteis; sound recordist, Piscitrelli. With Welles as Othello and the Narrator; Micheál MacLiammoir as Iago; and Suzanne Cloutier as Desdemona; and Robert Coote, Michael Lawrence, Hilton Edwards, Fay Compton, Nicholas Bruce, Jean Davis, Doris Dowling, Joan Fontaine, and Joseph Cotten as a Senator.

Don Quixote (uncompleted, filmed in Mexico and Paris in 1955). Produced by Welles and Oscar Dancigers; assistant director, Paola Mori; written by Welles from the novel by Miguel de Cervantes; director of photography, Jack Draper; assistant cameraman, Welles. With Welles as himself and the Narrator, Francisco

Reiguera as Don Quixote, Akim Tamiroff as Sancho Panza, and Patty McCormack as Dulcinea.

1962   *Mr. Arkadin* (British title *Confidential Report*) (100 minutes). Executive producer Louis Dolivet for the Cervantes Film Organisation, Sevilla Studios (Spain)/Film Organisation (France). Production manager, Michel J. Boisrond; assistant directors, José Maria Ochos, José Luis de la Serna, Isidoro Martínez Ferri; written by Welles from his own novel; director of photography, Jean Bougoin; editor, Renzo Lucidi; music, Paul Misraki; sound, Jacques Lebreton; sound recordist, Jacques Carrère; art direction and costumes, Welles. With Welles as Mr. Arkadin and the Narrator, Paola Mori as Raina Arkadin, and Robert Arden, Akim Tamiroff, Michael Redgrave, Patricia Medina, Mischa Auer, Katina Paxinou, Jack Watling, Grégoire Aslan, Peter van Eyck, Suzanne Flon, Tamara Shane, and Frederick O'Brady.

1958   *Touch of Evil* (Universal, 93 minutes). Produced for Universal Pictures by Alfred Zugsmith. Production manager, F. D. Thompson; additional scenes directed by Harry Keller; assistant directors, Phil Bowles, Terry Nelson; written by Welles, from the novel *Badge of Courage,* by Whit Masterson; director of photography, Russell Metty; editors, Virgil W. Vogel, Aaron Stell; art directors, Alexander Golitzen, Robert Clatworthy; set decorators, Russell A. Gausman, John P. Austin; music, Henry Mancini; musical supervisor, Joseph Gershenson; costumes, Bill Thomas; sound, Leslie I. Carey, Frank Wilkinson. With Welles as Hank Quinlan, Charlton Heston as Mike Vargas, Janet Leigh as Susan Vargas, Akim Tamiroff as Uncle Joe Grandi, Marlene Dietrich as Tanya, and Joseph Calleia, Valentin de Vargas, Ray Collins, Dennis Weaver, Joanna Moore, Mort Mills, Victor Millan, Lalo Rios, Michael Sargent, Mercedes McCambridge, Joseph Cotten, Zsa Zsa Gabor, Phil Harvey, Joi Lansing, Harry Shannon, Rusty Westcott, Wayne Taylor, Ken Miller, Raymond Rodriguez, Arlene McQuade, Domenick Delgarde, Joe Bassulto, Jennie Dias, Yolanda Bojorquez, and Eleanor Dorado.

1963   *The Trial* (Paris Europa Productions/FI-C-IT/Hisa-Films, 118 minutes). Produced by Alexander and Michael Salkind; production manager, Robert Florst; assistant directors, Marc Maurette, Paul Seban, Sophie Becker; written by Welles from the novel by Franz Kafka; director of photography, Edmond Richard; camera operator, Adolphe Charlet; editors, Yvonne Martin, Denise Baby, Fritz Mueller; art director, Jean Mandaroux; music, Jean Ledrut and Tomaso Albinoni; costumes, Hélène Thibault; sound, Jacques Lebreton; sound recordists, Julien Coutelier, Guy Villette; pin-screen prologue, Alexandre Alexieff, Claire Parker. With Welles as Hastler and the Narrator, Anthony Perkins as Joseph K., and Jeanne Moreau, Romy Schneider, Elsa Martinelli, Suzanne Flon, Madeleine Robinson, Akim Tamiroff, Arnoldo Foa, Fernand Ledoux, Maurice Teynac, Billy Kearns, Jess Hahn, William Chappell, Raoul Delfosse, Karl Studer, Jean-Claude Remoleux, Wolfgang Reichmann, Thomas Holtzmann, Maydra Shore, Max Haffler, Michel Lonsdale, Max Buchsbaum, Van Doude, and Katina Paxinou.

1967   *Chimes at Midnight* (Internacional Films Española/Alpine, 119 minutes). Produced by Emiliano Piedra, Angel Escolano; executive producer, Alessandro Tasco; production manager, Gustavo Quintana; second unit director, Jesús Franco; assistant directors, Tony Fuentes, Juan Cobos; written by Welles from Shakespeare's history plays and Holinshed's *Chronicles*; director of photography, Edmond Richard; camera operator, Adolphe Charlet; second unit photographer, Alejandro Ullos; editor, Fritz Mueller; art directors, José Antonio de la Guerra, Maraino Erdorza; music, Angelo Francesco Lavagnino; musical director, Carlo Franci; sound recordist, Peter Parasheles; costumes, Welles. With Welles as Falstaff, Ralph Richardson as the Narrator, John Gielgud as Henry IV, Jeanne Moreau as Doll Tearsheet, Margaret Rutherford as Mistress Quickly, and Keith Baxter, Norman Rodway, Marina Vlady, Alan Webb, Walter Chiari, Michael Aldridge, Tony Beckley, Fernando Rey, Andrew Fauldá, José Nieto, Jeremy Rowe, Beatrice Welles, Paddy Bedford, Julio Peña, Fernando Hilbert, Andres Mejuto, Keith Pyott, and Charles Farrell.

1968   *The Immortal Story* (ORTF/Albina Films, 58 minutes). Produced by Micheline Rozan; production manager, Marc Maurette; assistant directors, Olivier Gerard, Tony Fuentes, Patrice Torok; written by Welles, from the novella by Isak Dinesen; director of photography, Willy Kurant; color by Eastman; assistant cameramen, Jean Orjollet, Jacques Assuerds; editors, Yolande Maurette, Marcelle Pluer, Françoise Garnault, Claude Farny; art director, Andre Piltant; music by Eric Satie, played by Aldo Ciccolini and Jean-Joel Barbier; Mme. Moreau's costumes by Pierre Cardin; sound, Jean Neny. With Welles as Mr. Clay and the Narrator, Jeanne Moreau as Virginie Ducrot, and Roger Coggio, Norman Eshley, and Fernando Rey.

The Deep (Dead Reckoning) (filmed in Yugoslavia, 1967-69). Written by Welles, from Charles Williams's novel *Dead Calm*; photography, Willy Kurant; color by Eastman. With Welles as Russ Brewer, Jeanne Moreau as Ruth Warriner, Laurence Harvey as Hughie Warriner, and Olga Palinkas and Michael Ingram.

The Other Side of the Wind (filmed in Los Angeles and Arizona, 1970). Written by Welles and Oja Kodar; photography, Gary Graver, color by Eastman, production design, Polly Pratt. With John Huston as Jake Hannaford, Peter Bogdanovich as Brooks Otterlake, Lilli Palmer as Zarah Valeska, and Bob Ransom, Howard Grossman, Joseph McBride, Tonio Selwart, Cathy Lucas, Norman Foster, Edmond O'Brien, Cameron Mitchell, Mercedes McCambridge, Benny Rubin, Richard Wilson, John Carroll, Paul Mazursky, Curtis Harrington, Dennis Hopper, Henry Jaglom, Claude Chabrol, Stéphane Audran, and Gary Graver.

1973   *F for Fake* (Les Films de l'Astrophore/Saci/Janus Film, 85 minutes). Produced by Dominique Antoine and François Reichenbach; associate producer, Richard Drewett; written by Welles; photography by Gary Graver and Christian Odasso; music, Michel Legrand; editors, Welles and Marie Sophie Dubus and Dominique Engerer; titles by Lax; sound recording, Paul Bertault. With Welles, Oja Kodar, Elmyr de Hory, Clifford Irving, Edith Irving, François Reichenbach, Joseph Cotten, Laurence Harvey, Richard Wilson, Paul Stewart, Howard Hughes, Sasa Devcić, Gary Graver, Andres Vincent Gomez, Julio Palinkas, Christian Odasso, François Widoff, Peter Bogdanovich, and William Alland.

—   *Filming Othello* (a ninety-minute documentary made for German television, 1978). Produced by Klaus and Juergen Hellwig; director of photography, Gary Graver; music by Francesco Lavagnino and Alberto Barbaris; editor, Marty Roth.

ON RADIO

1938   "First Person Singular" (CBS), July 11-September 5). Adaptations by Howard Koch, Richard Brooks, Abraham Polonsky, and Herman J. Mankiewicz; casts were drawn primarily from the Mercury Theatre.

July 11: Bram Stoker's *Dracula*; July 18: Stevenson's *Treasure Island*; July 25: Dickens's *A Tale of Two Cities*; August 1: *The Thirty-Nine Steps*; August 8: an anthology of three short stories, including Lardner's "I'm a Fool" and Saki's "The Open Window"; August 15: Shakespeare's *Hamlet*; August 22: *The Affairs of Anatole*; August 28: Dumas's *The Count of Monte Cristo*; September 5: Chesterton's *The Man Who Was Thursday*.

"Mercury Theatre on the Air" (CBS, September 11-December 4). September 11: Shakespeare's *Julius Caesar*; September 18:

Brontë's *Jane Eyre*; September 25: Doyle's *Sherlock Holmes*; October 2: Dickens's *Oliver Twist*; October 9: *Hell on Ice*; October 16: Tarkington's *Seventeen*; October 23: Verne's *Around the World in Eighty Days*; October 30: H. G. Wells's *The War of the Worlds*; November 6: Conrad's *Heart of Darkness* and Clarence Day's *Life with Father*; November 13: (not available); December 4: Thornton Wilder's *The Bridge of San Luis Rey*.

1938-40 "Campbell Playhouse" (CBS, December 9, 1938-June 2, 1939, and September 10, 1939-March 31, 1940). When Campbell took over sponsorship of the program, guest appearances by Hollywood stars were added to the format.

1938 December 9: Daphne du Maurier's *Rebecca*, with Margaret Sullavan; December 16: *Call It a Day,* with Bea Lillie and Jane Wyatt; December 23: Dickens's *A Christmas Carol*; December 30: Hemingway's *A Farewell to Arms,* with Katharine Hepburn.

1939 January 6: *Counselor at Law,* with Gertrude Berg; January 13: *Mutiny on the Bounty*; January 20: *The Chicken Wagon Family,* with Burgess Meredith; January 27: *I Lost My Girlish Laughter,* with Ilka Chase; February 3; Sinclair Lewis's *Arrowsmith,* with Helen Hayes; February 10: *The Green Goddess,* with Madeleine Carroll; February 17: *Burlesque,* with Sam Levene; February 24: *State Fair,* March 3: *The Royal Regiment,* with Mary Astor; March 10: Dashiell Hammett's *The Glass Key*; March 17: *Beau Geste*; March 24: *Twentieth Century*; March 31: Edna Ferber's *Showboat,* with Edna Ferber, Helen Morgan, and Margaret Sullavan; April 7: Hugo's *Les Misérables,* with Walter Huston; April 14: *The Patriot,* with Anna May Wong; April 21: Noel Coward's *Private Lives,* with Gertrude Lawrence; April 28: *Black Daniel,* with Joan Bennett; May 5: *Wickford Point*; May 12: Wilder's *Our Town*; May 19: *The Bad Man,* with Ida Lupino; May 26: *American Cavalcade,* with Cornelia Otis Skinner; June 2: *Victoria Regina,* with Helen Hayes; September 10: Gerald du Maurier's *Peter Ibbetsen,* with Helen Hayes; September 17: *Ah, Wilderness*; September 24: Barrie's *What Every Woman Knows*; October 1: Dumas's *The Count of Monte Cristo*; October 8: *Algiers,* with Paulette Goddard; October 15: *Escape,* with Wendy Barrie; October 22: *Liliom,* with Helen Hayes; October 29: *The Magnificent Ambersons,* with Walter Huston; November 5: *The Hurricane,* with Mary Astor; November 12: Christie's *The Murder of Roger Ackroyd,* with Edna May Oliver; November 19: *The Garden of Allah,* with Claudette Colbert; November 26: Sinclair Lewis's *Dodsworth,* with Fay Bainter; December 3: James Hilton's *Lost Horizon,* with Sigrid Gurie; December 10: *Vanessa*; December 17:

There's Always a Woman, with Marie Wilson; December 24: Dickens's *A Christmas Carol,* with Lionel Barrymore; December 31: *Come and Get It.*

1940   January 7: *Becky Sharp,* with Helen Hayes; January 14: *This Lonely Heart,* with Bette Davis; January 21: *The Citadel,* with Miriam Hopkins; February 4: *Broome Stages,* with Helen Hayes; February 11: *Mr. Deeds Goes to Town,* with Gertrude Lawrence; February 18: *Dinner at Eight,* with Lucille Ball and Hedda Hopper; February 25: *Only Angels Have Wings,* with Joan Blondell; March 3: *Rabble in Arms,* with Frances Dee; March 10: *Craig's Wife,* with Fay Bainter; March 17: Mark Twain's *Huckleberry Finn,* with Jackie Cooper; March 24: *June Moon,* with Jack Benny; March 31: Brontë's *Jane Eyre,* with Madeleine Carroll.

II. AS ACTOR*

ON STAGE

1918   **Opera House, Ravinia, Illinois**
Butterfly's child in *Madame Butterfly.*

?   **Chicago Opera House, Chicago, Illinois**
Various juvenile roles.

1925   **Washington Grade School, Madison, Wisconsin**
Scrooge in *A Christmas Carol;* other roles.

1926-31   **Todd School, Woodstock, Illinois**
Appearances in *Julius Caesar, Richard III, Androcles and the Lion,* and others—about thirty plays in all (many of which he also directed).

1931   **Dublin Gate Theatre, Dublin**
Duke Alexander in Feuchtwanger's *Jew Süss*; Ralph Bentley in Sears's *The Dead Ride Fast*; General Bazaine in Robinson's *The Archduke*; The Grand Vizier in O'Conaire's *Mogu of the Desert*; additional minor roles.

1932   **Dublin Gate Theatre, Dublin**
Duke Lamberto in Casella's *Death Takes a Holiday;* the Ghost and Fortinbras in Shakespeare's *Hamlet;* various minor roles.

Abbey Theatre, Dublin
Lord Porteus in Maugham's *The Circle;* minor roles.

*Includes only roles in productions that Welles did not also direct.

1933-34 **Katharine Cornell Touring Company, USA**
Octavius Barrett in Rudolph Besier's *The Barretts of Wimpole Street*; Mercutio in *Romeo and Juliet*; Marchbanks in Shaw's *Candida.*

1934 **Katharine Cornell Company, Martin Beck Theater, New York**
(Followed another season at the Todd School, in which he produced and directed a number of plays.) The Chorus and Tybalt in *Romeo and Juliet.*

1935 **Phoenix Theater Group, Imperial Theater, New York**
McGafferty in Archibald MacLeish's *Panic.*

1936 **St. James Theater, New York**
André Pequot in Sidney Kingsley's *Ten Million Ghosts.*

ON FILM
1937 Narrator, *The Spanish Earth* (additional release narrated by Ernest Hemingway), directed by Ivors Jornes.

1940 Narrator, *The Swiss Family Robinson,* directed by Edward Ludwig.

1943 Colonel Haki, *Journey Into Fear,* directed by Orson Welles (uncredited) and Norman Foster.

1943 Rochester, *Jane Eyre,* directed by Robert Stevenson.

1944 Himself, *Follow the Boys,* directed by Edward Sutherland.

1945 John MacDonald, *Tomorrow Is Forever,* directed by Irving Pichel.

1946 Narrator, *Duel in the Sun,* directed by King Vidor.

1947 Cagliostro, *Black Magic,* directed by Gregory Ratoff.

1948 Cesare Borgia, *Prince of Foxes,* directed by Henry King.

1949 Harry Lime, *The Third Man,* directed by Carol Reed.

1950 General Bayan, *The Black Rose,* directed by Henry Hathaway.

1953 Sigsbee Manderson, *Trent's Last Case,* directed by Herbert Wilcox; Benjamin Franklin, *Versailles,* directed by Sacha Guitry; The Beast, *L'Uomo, la Bestia e la Virtù,* directed by Stefano Vanzina; Himself, *Return to Glenascaul,* directed by Hilton Edwards.

1954 Hudson Lowe, *Napoleon,* directed by Sacha Guitry; Lord

Mountdrago, *Three Cases of Murder,* episode directed by George More O'Ferrall.

1955   Sanin Cejador y Mengues, *Trouble in the Glen,* directed by Herbert Wilcox.

1956   Father Mapple, *Moby Dick,* directed by John Huston; Narrator, *Lords of the Forest,* directed by Henry Brandt and Heinz Sielman. Released in the United States as *Masters of the Congo.*

1957   Virgil Renckler, *Man in the Shadow/Pay the Devil,* directed by Jack Arnold; Varner, *The Long Hot Summer,* directed by Martin Ritt.

1958   Cy Sedgwick, *The Roots of Heaven,* directed by John Huston; Narrator, *The Vikings,* directed by Richard Fleischer.

1959   Jonathan Wilk, *Compulsion,* directed by Richard Fleischer; Saul, *David and Goliath,* directed by Richard Pottier and Ferdinando Baldi; Captin Hart, *Ferry to Hong Kong,* directed by Lewis Gilbert; Narrator, *High Journey,* directed by Peter Baylis; Narrator, *South Seas Adventure,* directed by Carl Dudley.

1960   Fulton, *Austerlitz,* directed by Abel Gance; Hagolin and Lamorcière, *Crack in the Mirror,* directed by Richard Fleischer; Burundai, *The Tartars,* directed by Richard Thorpe.

1961   Narrator, *King of Kings,* directed by Nicholas Ray; Benjamin Franklin, *Lafayette,* directed by Jean Dreville.

1962   The Director, *La Ricotta* episode, *RoGoPaG,* directed by Pier Paolo Pasolini; Narrator, *River of the Ocean,* directed by Peter Baylis.

1963   Narrator, *The Finest Hours,* directed by Peter Baylis.

1964   Ackermann, *Marco the Magnificent,* directed by Denys de la Patellière and Noel Howard.

1965   Raoul Nordling, *Is Paris Burning?* directed by René Clément; Long John Silver, *Treasure Island,* directed by Jesús Franco (unfinished).

1966   Louis from Mozambique, *The Sailor from Gibraltar,* directed by Tony Richardson; Cardinal Wolsey, *A Man for All Seasons,* directed by Fred Zinnemann.

1967   Le Chiffre, *Casino Royale,* episode directed by Joseph McGrath; Jonathan Lute, *I'll Never Forget What's'isname,* directed by Michael Winner; Tiresias, *Oedipus the King,* directed by Philip Saville.

1968   Charles Leschenhaut, *House of Cards,* directed by John Guillermin; Plankett, *The Southern Star,* directed by Sidney Hayers.

1969   Senator, *The Battle of the River Neretva,* directed by Veljko Bulajic; *Michael the Brave,* directed by Sergiu Nicholaescu; Col. Cascorro, *Tepepa,* directed by Giulio Petroni; Markau, *Twelve Plus One,* directed by Nicolas Gessner; Bresnavitch, *The Kremlin Letter,* directed by John Huston; Himself, Narrator, *Start the Revolution Without Me,* directed by Bud Yorkin.

1970   General Dreedle, *Catch-22,* directed by Mike Nichols; Louis XVIII, *Waterloo,* directed by Sergei Bondarchuk; Michelangelo, *Upon This Rock,* directed by Harry Rasky; Narrator, *To Build a Fire,* directed by David Cobham; Magician, *A Safe Place,* directed by Henry Jaglom.

1971   Long John Silver, *Treasure Island,* directed by John Hough; Cassavius, *Malpertuis,* directed by Harry Kumel.

1972   Theo Van Horn, *La Décade Prodigieuse (Ten Days' Wonder),* directed by Claude Chabrol; An Unnamed Mgician, *Get to Know Your Rabbit,* directed by Brian De Palma; Mr. Cato, *Necromancy,* directed by Bert I. Gordon.

1976   Narrator, *The Late Great Planet Earth,* directed by Robert Amram.

1977   José Estedes, *Voyage of the Damned,* directed by Stuart Rosenberg.

1979   Lew Lord, *The Muppet Movie,* directed by James Frawley.

1980   J. P. Morgan, *Tajna Nikole Tesle (The Secret of Nikola Tesla),* directed by Krsto Papic.

1981   Judge Rauch, *Butterfly,* directed by Matt Cimber.

1983   Klingsor, *Where Is Parsifal?,* directed by Henri Helman.

1985   Himself, *Someone to Love,* directed by Henry Jaglom.

BIBLIOGRAPHY

WRITINGS BY WELLES

BOOKS

Citizen Kane. New York: Simon & Shuster, 1969.

Everybody's Shakespeare. New York: Harper and Brothers, 1933.

Mercury Shakespeare. Woodstock, Illinois: Todd Press, 1934.

Miracle à Hollywood suivi de À Bon Entendeur. Translated by Serge Greffet. Paris: Editions de la Table Ronde, 1953.

Mr. Arkadin. London: W. H. Allen, 1956. Paris: Gallimard, 1954.

The Trial. New York: Simon & Shuster, 1970.

Une Grosse Légume. Translated by Maurice Bessy. Paris: Gallimard, 1953.

ARTICLES

"But Where Are We Going?" *Look* (November 3, 1970).

"Je combats comme un géant dans un monde de nains pour le cinéma universel." *Arts* (Paris) August 25, 1954).

"Un ruban de rêves." *L'Express* (Paris) June 5, 1958). Reprinted in English in *International Film Annual* (London), No. 2 (1958).

"The Scenario Crisis." *International Film Annual* (London), No. 1 (1957).

"The Third Audience." *Sight and Sound* (London) (January–March 1954).

LETTERS

Letter to the *New Statesman* (London) (May 24, 1958) concerning *Touch of Evil.*

Letter to *The Times* (London) (November 17, 1971) concerning the script of *Citizen Kane.*

PREFACES

Preface to *He That Plays the King,* by Kenneth Tynan. London: Longmans, 1950.

Preface to *Précis de Prestidigitation,* by Bruce Elliot. Switzerland: Editions Payot, 1953.

Preface to *Put Money in Thy Purse,* by Micheál MacLiammoir. London: Methuen, 1952.

Preface to *Les Truquages au Cinéma,* by Maurice Bessy. Paris: Editions Prisma, 1951.

SERIES

Series of articles in *Free Worlds,* the *New York Post,* and the *Old Farmer's Almanac* (1942–45).

Series of reflections in *La Démocratie Combattante* (Paris) (April–May 1952).

BOOKS AND MONOGRAPHS ON WELLES

Allais, Jean-Claude. "Orson Welles." In *Premier Plan,* No. 16. Lyon: SERDOC, 1961.

BIBLIOGRAPHY

Bazin, André. *Orson Welles,* with a preface by Jean Cocteau. Paris: Editions Chavane, 1950. English edition, translated by Jonathan Rosenblum with a foreword by François Truffaut. New York: Harper & Row, 1972.

Bessy, Maurice. *Orson Welles, Cinéma d'Aujourdhui Series,* No. 6. Paris: Editions Seghers, 1963 and 1970. English edition, New York: Crown Publishers, 1971.

Orson Welles. Paris: Editions Pygmalean, 1982.

Bogdanovich, Peter. *The Cinema of Orson Welles.* New York: Film Library of the Museum of Modern Art, 1961.

Carringer, Robert L. *The Making of Citizen Kane.* Berkeley, CA: University of California Press, 1985.

Cowie, Peter. *A Ribbon of Dreams.* South Brunswick, NJ: A. S. Barnes & Co., 1973.

Fowler, Roy Alexander. *Orson Welles, A First Biography.* London: Pendulum Publications, 1946.

France, Richard. *The Theater of Orson Welles.* Cranberry, NJ: Associated University Presses, 1977.

Gottesman, Ronald, ed. *Focus on Orson Welles.* Englewood Cliffs, NJ: Prentice Hall, 1976.
_____, ed. *Focus on Citizen Kane.* Englewood Cliffs, NJ: Prentice Hall, 1976.

Higham, Charles. *The Films of Orson Welles.* Berkeley, CA: University of California Press, 1970.
_____. *Orson Welles: The Rise and Fall of an American Genius.* New York: St. Martin's Press, 1985.

Kael, Pauline, Mankiewicz, Herman and Welles, Orson. *The Citizen Kane Book.* Boston: Little, Brown, 1971. (Contains essay, "Raising Kane," first published in *The New Yorker* in 1971.)

Leaming, Barbara. *Orson Welles.* New York: Viking Press, 1983, 1985.

MacLiammoir, Micheál. *Put Money in Thy Purse,* with a preface by Orson Welles. London: Methuen, 1972.

McBride, Joseph. *Orson Welles.* New York: Viking Press, 1972.
_____. *Orson Welles.* New York: Jove Publications, 1977.

Naremore, James. *The Magic World of Orson Welles.* New York: Oxford University Press, 1978.

Noble, Peter. *The Fabulous Orson Welles.* London: Hutchinson, 1956.

Tavares, Frank. A Critical Analysis of Selected Dramatic Elements in the Radio Series, "The Lives of Harry Lime." Ph.D. dissertation, University of Texas, Austin, 1976.

Taylor, John Russell. *Orson Welles: A Celebration.* Boston: Little, Brown & Co., 1986.

Various Authors. *Orson Welles. l'éthique et l'esthétique.* Paris: Etudes Cinématographiques, Nos. 24/25, 1963.

GENERAL WORKS

BOOKS

Ambler, Eric. *Journey into Fear.* New York: Ballantine Books, 1977.

Arce, Hector. *The Secret Life of Tyrone Power.* New York: William Morrow, 1979.

Baxter, Anne. *Intermission.* New York: Ballantine Books, 1978.

Bawden, Liz-Anne, ed. *The Oxford Companion to Film.* New York: Oxford University Press, 1976.

Blake, Nicholas [C. Day Lewis]. *The Smiler with a Knife.* London: Collins, 1939.

Bogdanovich, Peter. *Pieces of Time.* New York: Dell Publishing Co., 1973.

Calder-Marshall, Alexander. *The Way to Santiago.* London: Jonathan Cape, 1940.

Cantril, Hadley. *Invasion from Mars.* New York: Harper & Row, 1966.

Castle, William. *Step Right Up!* New York: G. P. Putnam's, 1976.

Chaplin, Charles. *My Autobiography.* New York: Simon & Schuster, 1964.

Comito, Terry. ed. *Touch of Evil.* New Brunswick, NJ: Rutgers University Press, 1985.

Conrad, Joseph. *Heart of Darkness.* Edited by Robert Kimbrough. New York: W. W. Norton, 1963.

Cotten, Joseph. *Vanity Will Get You Somewhere.* San Francisco: Mercury House, 1987.

Davies, Marion. *The Times We Had: Life with William Randolph Hearst.* Foreword by Orson Welles. New York: Bobbs-Merrill Co., 1975.

Eckert, Charles W., ed. *Focus on Shakespearean Films.* Englewood Cliffs, NJ: Prentice Hall, 1972.

Eels, George. *Hedda and Louella.* New York: Warner Books, 1973.

Engel, Lehman. *This Bright Day.* New York: Macmillan Publishing Co., 1974.

Fielding, Raymond. *The March of Time: 1935-1951.* New York: Oxford University Press, 1978.

Flanagan, Hallie. *Arena.* New York: Duell, Sloan & Pearce, 1940.

Fontaine, Joan. *No Bed of Roses.* New York: William Morrow & Co., 1978.

Gottesman, Ronald, ed. *Focus on Citizen Kane.* Englewood Cliffs, NJ: Prentice Hall, 1971.

Guiles, Fred Laurence. *Marion Davies.* New York: McGraw-Hill, 1972.

Heston, Charlton. *The Actor's Life.* New York: E. P. Dutton, 1978.

Hill, Roger. *One Man's Time and Chance.* Privately printed, 1977.

Houseman, John. *Front and Center.* New York: Simon & Schuster, 1979.

———. *Run-through.* New York: Simon & Schuster, 1972.

Huston, John. *An Open Book.* New York: Ballantine Books, 1980.

Huxley, Aldous. *After Many a Summer Dies the Swan.* London: Watts and Windus, 1939.

Jewell, Richard B. and Vernon Harbin. *The RKO Story.* New York: Arlington House, 1982.

Kaminsky, Stuart. *John Huston, Maker of Magic.* New York: Houghton Mifflin & Co., 1978.

Kauffmann, Stanley. *American Film Criticism.* New York: Liveright, 1972.

Kawin, Bruce F. *Mindscreen.* Princeton, NJ: Princeton University Press, 1978.

Kennedy, Harold J. *No Pickle, No Performance.* New York: Doubleday, 1977.

Kitt, Eartha. *Alone with Me.* Chicago: Henry Regnery Co., 1976.

Knight, Arthur. *The Liveliest Art.* New York: Macmillan, 1957.

Koch, Howard. *The Panic Broadcast.* New York: Avon Books, 1970.

Korda, Michael J. *Charmed Lives.* New York: Random House, 1979.

Kreuger, Miles, ed. *Souvenir Programs of Twelve Classic Movies, 1929-1941.* New York: Dover, 1977.

Lesley, Cole. *The Life of Noel Coward.* London: Jonathan Cape, 1976.

Lloyd, Ronald. *American Film Directors.* New York: New Viewpoints, 1976.

Lundberg, Ferdinand. *Imperial Hearst.* New York: Modern Library, 1937.

MacLeish, Archibald. *Six Plays.* Boston: Houghton Mifflin, 1980.

MacLiammoir, Micheál. *All for Hecuba.* London: Methuen & Co., 1946.

———. *Each Actor on His Ass.* London: Routledge and Kegan Paul, 1961.

———. *Enter a Goldfish.* London: Thomas & Hudson, 1977.

Madsen, Axel. *John Huston.* New York: Doubleday, 1978.

McCambridge, Mercedes. *The Quality of Mercy.* New York: Times Books, 1981.

McClintic, Guthrie. *Me and Kit.* Boston: Atlantic, Little, Brown, 1955.

Meryman, Richard. *Mank.* New York: William Morrow & Co., 1978.

Mosel, Tad. *Leading Lady.* Boston: Atlantic, Little, Brown, 1978.

Older, Freemont. *William Randolph Hearst, American.* New York: Appleton-Century, 1936.

Sarris, Andrew. *Interviews with Film Directors.* New York: Avon Books, 1967.

Swanberg, W. A. *Citizen Hearst.* New York: Scribner's, 1967.

Tarkington, Booth. *The Magnificent Ambersons.* Garden City, NY: Doubleday, 1918.

Thomas, Bob. *King Cohn.* New York: Bantam Books, 1967.

BIBLIOGRAPHY

Truffaut, François. *The Films in My Life.* New York: Simon & Schuster, 1975.

Warrick, Ruth. *The Confessions of Phoebe Tyler.* Englewood Cliffs, NJ: Prentice Hall, 1980.

Zorina, Vera. *Zorina.* New York: Farrar, Straus and Giroux, 1986.

Zugsmith, Albert. *Kings of the Bs.* New York: E. P. Dutton, 1975.

ARTICLES

Andreas, Cyrus. "I'm a Lurid Character!" A Note on Orson Welles. *Film Miscellany* (Winter 1946/47).

Bazin, André. "L'Apport d'Orson Welles." *Ciné-Club,* No. 7 (May 1948).

———. "Orson Welles chez les Jivaros." *Les Cahiers du Cinéma* (Paris), No. 88 (October 1958).

———. "Orson Welles, la télévision et le magnétophone." *France-Observateur* (Paris) (June 12, 1958).

Bazin, André, and Charles Bitsch. "Entretien avec Orson Welles" *Les Cahiers du Cinéma* (Paris), No. 84 (June 1958).

Bazin, André, Charles Bitsch, and Jean Domarchi. "Nouvel Entretien avec Orson Welles." *Les Cahiers du Cinéma* (Paris), No. 87 (September 1958).

Bazin, André, and Jean-Charles Tacchella. Interview in *L'Ecran Français* (Paris), No. 169 (September 21, 1948).

Bentley, Eric. "Othello on Film." *New Republic* (October 3, 1955).

Bessy, Maurice. "Les vertes statues d'Orson Welles." *Les Cahiers du Cinéma* (Paris) (May 1952).

Billard, Pierre. "Chimes at Midnight." *Sight and Sound* (London) (Spring 1965).

Bitsch, Charles. "Orson Welles consacre Shakespeare au Cinéma au Festival mondial du film à Bruxelles." *Arts* (Paris) (June 18, 1958).

Björkman, Stig. "My Name Is Orson Welles." *Chaplin* (Stockholm), No. 33 (1962).

Borde, Raymond, and Etienne Chaumeton. "Panorama du film noir Americain." *Editions de Minuit* (Paris) (1955).

Bordwell, David. "Citizen Kane." *Film Comment* (Summer 1971).

Brady, Frank. "The Lost Film of Orson Welles." *American Film,* 4, 2 (Nov. 1978) 63-69.

Bucher, Felix, and Peter Cowie. "Welles and Chabrol." *Sight and Sound* (London) (Autumn 1971). (Other parts of this interview, not published in *Sight and Sound,* are quoted in the present book.)

Carringer, Robert L. "*Citizen Kane* Remembered." *Action!* Vol. 4, No. 3 (May–June 1969).

———. "Orson Welles and Gregg Toland: Their Collaboration on *Citizen Kane.*" *Critical Inquiry,* Vol. 8, No. 4 (Summer 1982).

———. "Rosebud, Dead or Alive: Narrative and Symbolic Structure in *Citizen Kane.*" *PMLA,* Vol. 91, No. 2 (March 1976).

———. "The Scripts of *Citizen Kane.*" *Critical Inquiry,* Vol. 5, No. 2 (Winter 1978).

Castello, G. C. "The Magnificent Orson W." *Bianco e nero* (Rome) (January 1949).

Chappell, William. "Orson Welles Films Kafka." *The Sunday Times* (London) (May 27, 1962).

Clay, Jean. Interview in *Réalités* (Paris), No. 201 (1962).

Cobos, Juan, and Miguel Rubio. "Welles and Falstaff." *Sight and Sound* (London) (Autumn 1966).

Cobos, Juan, Miguel Rubio, and Jose Antonio Pruneda. "Voyage au pays de Don Quixote." *Les Cahiers du Cinéma* (Paris), No. 165 (April 1965). English translation (by Rose Kaplin) printed in *Cahiers du Cinéma in English,* No. 5 (1966), and in *Interviews with Film Directors,* ed. by Andrew Sarris (New York: Bobbs-Merrill, 1967) and *Hollywood Voices* (London: Secker and Warburg, 1971).

BIBLIOGRAPHY

Cocteau, Jean. Profile of Welles in *Cinémonde* (Paris) (March 6, 1950).

Cowie, Peter. "Orson Welles." *Films and Filming* (London) (April 1961).

Cutts, John. "Citizen Kane." *Films and Filming* (London) (December 1963).

Gambill, Norman. "Making Up Kane." *Film Comment,* Vol. 14, No. 6 (November–December 1978).

Gerasimov, Sergei. "All Is Not Welles." *The Observer* (London) (November 17, 1963).

Gilliatt, Penelope. Review of *The Trial* in *The Observer* (London) (November 17, 1963).

Grigs, Derrick. "Conversation at Oxford." *Sight and Sound* (London) (Spring 1960).

Johnson, Alva, and Fred Smith. "How to Raise a Child." *The Saturday Evening Post* (January 20, 27, February 3, 1940).

Johnson, William. "Orson Welles: Of Time and Loss." *Film Quarterly* (Fall 1967).

Kerr, Walter. "Wonder Boy Welles." *Theatre Arts* (September 1951).

Koval, Francis. "Interview with Welles." *Sight and Sound* (London) (December 1950).

Labarthe, André S. "My Name Is Orson Welles." *Les Cahiers du Cinéma* (Paris), No. 117 (March 1961).

Leigh, Janet (in conversation with Rui Noguiera). "Psycho, Rosie and a Touch of Orson." *Sight and Sound* (London) (Spring 1970).

Leonard, Harold. "Notes on *Macbeth.*" *Sight and Sound* (London) (March 1950).

Levin, Eric. "At His Final Exit, Orson Welles Leaves a Legend and a Debate as Large as the Man Himself." *People* (October 25, 1985).

Lightman, Herb A. "*The Lady from Shanghai,* Field Day for the Camera." *The American Cinematographer* (June 1947).

MacLiammoir, Micheal. "Orson Welles." *Sight and Sound* (London) (JulyÇSeptember 1954).

Magnan, Henry. "Orson Welles s'explique." *Les Lettres Françaises* (Paris) (June 19, 1958).

Maloney, Russell. "Orson Welles." *The New Yorker* (October 9, 1938).

Martinez, Enrique. "The Trial of Orson Welles." *Films and Filming* (London) (October 1962).

McBride, Joseph. "Citizen Kane." *Film Heritage* (Fall 1968).

———. "First Person Singular." *Sight and Sound* (London) (Winter 1971/72).

———. "The Magnificent Ambersons." In *Persistence of Vision* Madison, WI: Wisconsin Film Society Press, 1968.

———. "Welles before *Kane.*" *Film Quarterly* (Spring 1970).

———. "Welles' *Immortal Story.*" *Sight and Sound* (London) (Autumn 1970).

Nowák, Petr. "Kafka's Prague." *The Observer* (London) (November 17, 1963).

Pecher, William S. "Trials." *Sight and Sound* (London) (Winter 1963/64).

Powell, Dilys. "The Life and Opinions of Orson Welles." *The Sunday Times* (London) (February 3, 1963).

Prokosch, Mike. "Orson Welles." *Film Comment* (Summer 1971).

Raynor, Henry. "Shakespeare Filmed." *Sight and Sound* (London) (July–September 1952).

Robson, Mark, quoted in *The Celluloid Muse,* ed. by Higham and Greenberg. London: Angus and Robertson, 1969.

Rosenbaum, Jonathan. *"Heart of Darkness."* *Film Comment* (November–December 1972).

Sarris, Andrew. "Citizen Kane: the American Baroque." *Film Culture,* Vol. 2, No. 3 (1956).

———. "Orson Welles." In *The American Cinema: Directors and Directions 1929-1968.* New York: E. P. Dutton, 1968.

Sartre, Jean-Paul. "Quand Hollywood veut faire penser" and "Citizen Kane." *L'Ecran Français* (Paris) (August 1, 1945).

Shivas, Mark. "The Trial." *Movie* (London) (February–March 1963).

Silver, Charles. *"The Immortal Story."* *Film Comment* (Summer 1971).

Silverman, Doré. "Odd Orson." *You* (London) (July–August 1951).

BIBLIOGRAPHY

Slavitt, David R. "New Films in Review." *The Yale Review,* Vol. 52, No. 4 (Summer 1963).

Sloane, Everett. Interview in *Film* (London), No. 37 (1963).

Stanbrook, Alan. "The Heroes of Welles." *Film* (London), No. 28 (1961).

Stein, Elliot. Article on *The Trial. The Financial Times* (London) (February 18, 1963).

Toland, Gregg. "How I Broke the Rules in *Citizen Kane.*" *Popular Photoplay Magazine,* No. 8 (February 1941).

_____. Article on *Kane's* camerawork. *The American Cinematographer* (February 1941).

Tynan, Kenneth. "Orson Welles." *Show* (October and November 1961).

_____. "Playboy Interview: Orson Welles." *Playboy* (March 1967).

Weinberg, Herman G. "Confidential Report/Mr. Arkadin." *Film Culture,* Vol. 2, No. 3 (1956).

_____. "The Legion of Lost Films." *Sight and Sound* (London) (Autumn 1962).

_____. "Touch of Evil." *Film Culture,* No. 20 (1959).

Wilson, Richard. "It's Not *Quite* All True." *Sight and Sound* (London) (Autumn 1970).

UNSIGNED ARTICLES

"Checklist 10—Orson Welles." Monthly Film Bulletin (London) (January and February 1964).

"Orson Welles." *The Observer* (London) (November 20, 1955).

Reprint of the 1938 broadcast version of H. G. Wells's "The War of the Worlds." *Film Culture,* No. 27 (1962/63).

"Winged Gorilla." *New Statesman and Nation* (London) (January 21, 1956).

INDEX

INDEX

INDEX

INDEX

INDEX

The author gratefully acknowledges permission to reprint material from the following sources:

Selection from Orson Welles's speech accepting The American Film Institute Life Achievement Award, copyright © 1975, reprinted by permission.

Selection from *Fortune* magazine review of *Macbeth* reprinted by permission.

Selections from the actors' notes by Welles for *Macbeth* reprinted by permission of the Special Collections and Archives, George Mason University Library, Fairfax, Virginia.

Selection from *Voices Offstage* (1968) by Marc Connelly, reprinted by permission of Henry Holt and Company.

Selections from *The Fall of the City* and *Air Raid* in *Six Plays* by Archibald MacLeish, copyright © 1980 by Archibald MacLeish, reprinted by permission of Houghton Mifflin Company.

Selection from *Leading Lady* by Tad Mosel reprinted by permission of Little, Brown and Company.

Selection from *All for Hecuba* by Micheál MacLiammoir, copyright © 1946, published by Methuen & Co., reprinted by permission.

Selection from letter by Arthur Miller to Welles regarding "Ceiling Unlimited" reprinted by permission.

Selection from the review of *Citizen Kane* by John O'Hara in *Newsweek*, reprinted by permission.

Selection from the review of *Macbeth* by Bosley Crowther, April 5, 1936, copyright © 1936 by The New York Times Company, reprinted by permission.

Selection from *Step Right Up . . . I'm Gonna Scare the Pants Off America* by William Castle, copyright © 1976 by William Castle, reprinted by permission of The Putnam Publishing Group.

Photographs and selections from RKO Archival Material, copyright © 1989 by RKO Pictures, Inc., all rights reserved, reprinted courtesy of RKO Pictures, Inc.

Selections from *Run-Through* by John Houseman, copyright © 1972 by John Houseman, reprinted by permission of Simon & Schuster, Inc.

Selection from *The Sunday Times* (London) review of *The Trial*, reprinted by permission.

Selection from the review of *F for Fake* by David R. Slavitt in *The Yale Review*, reprinted by permission.

MORE BIOGRAPHIES AVAILABLE FROM
HODDER AND STOUGHTON PAPERBACKS

All these books are available at your local bookshop or newsagent, or can be ordered direct from the publisher. Just tick the titles you want and fill in the form below.

Prices and availability subject to change without notice.

Hodder & Stoughton Paperbacks, P.O. Box 11, Falmouth, Cornwall.

Please send cheque or postal order, and allow the following for postage and packing:

U.K. – 80p for one book and 20p for each additional book ordered up to a £2.00 maximum.

B.F.P.O. – 80p for the first book, plus 20p for each additional book

OVERSEAS INCLUDING EIRE – £1.50 for the first book, plus £1.00 for the second book, and 30p for each additional book ordered.

OR Please debit this amount from my Access/Visa Card (delete as appropriate).

Card Number | | | | | | | | | | | | | | | | | | |

Name...

Address...

....